MEASURES
OF SOCIAL
PSYCHOLOGICAL
ATTITUDES

John P. Robinson

Phillip R. Shaver

SURVEY RESEARCH CENTER

INSTITUTE FOR SOCIAL RESEARCH

Revised Edition 1973

ISR Code No. 2928

Library of Congress Catalog Card No. 79-627967
ISBN 0-87944-130-5 paperbound
ISBN 0-87944-069-4 clothbound

Published by the Institute for Social Research
The University of Michigan, Ann Arbor, Michigan 48106

Revised Edition 1973
Sixth Printing 1980

Manufactured in the United States of America

TABLE OF CONTENTS

Preface

The attitude measurement series published by the Institute for Social Research has reached a wide audience, indicating the professional need for such a research sourcebook. The series was intended more as an illustration of the type of source that was needed than as a definitive guide to the attitude measurement literature. This being the case, suggestions for continual improvement of this series are being encouraged.

In no respect is improvement more crucial than in the matter of updating. Our books, in a sense, became dated the day they were printed. Nor could we claim that the measures reviewed comprised an exhaustive list in all the attitude areas. Thus, we looked forward to the time when specialists in a particular attitude area might take it upon themselves to produce a more updated and complete review of measures in that area.

The present compilation represents a realization of that hope, although for only two of the many areas covered in our series. Rick Crandall, a graduate student at The University of Michigan and a staff member of the Institute for Social Research, is mainly responsible for the current revisions. Crandall has produced a chapter on self-esteem measures that expands the scope of self-esteem measurement examined in the initial edition of Measures of Social Psychological Attitudes. Crandall was also instrumental in the new chapter of internal-external control measures prepared by A. P. MacDonald, Jr. of the Frank Porter Graham Child Development Center of the Child Development Research Institute of The University of North Carolina. Both Crandall's and MacDonald's chapters introduce useful innovations to the format of our series, particularly in their fuller theoretical and methodological treatment of the literature in each area.

Our volumes are intended as basic empirical reference works in the social sciences. We expect them to be of use to three different audiences:

1) Researchers actively involved in social research, especially those carrying out survey work in psychology, sociology, and political science.

2) Students taking course work in research methods who may be interested in gaining familiarity with the tools of social scientists.

3) Non-researchers in relevant content areas, such as social commentators, political analysts, and journalists.

The aim of these volumes has been to provide a comprehensive listing and evaluation of empirical measures for a number of important social attitude variables. It is our hope that the form of presentation adopted in this work (which includes actual scale items and scoring instructions) will help the reader to make his own judgments about the current "state of the art" in social attitude research. The advanced scholar will perhaps share our concern that we have not completely achieved our various goals and that we may inadvertantly contribute to the spread of ill-conceived attitude research. However, to us it seems worth the risk to make attitude measures more accessible to interested people and to enhance one's ability to choose among alternative measures more systematically than has been the case in the past. This book should encourage, rather than eliminate, careful examination of available instruments. It is not intended as a substitute either for reading original articles or for conducting further item analyses and validation studies.

The bulk of this work was supported by grant MH 10809-02 from the United States Public Health Service. However, the volumes would not have been completed had it not been for generous supplemental support from the Survey Research Center, which agreed to underwrite the cost of this revision and publication, and from the Inter-university Consortium for Political Research.

We also wish to express our appreciation to Dr. Jeanne Knutson of the Stanford University Institute of Political Studies, who provided us with invaluable leads to attitude scales we had overlooked. We are especially indebted to Eileen Marchak, Virginia Nye, Susan Hudson, Karin Klue, and Carolyn Crandall, for their patient typing and retyping of unreadable manuscripts. We are also grateful to Robert Krull, Barbara Surovell, Douglas Truax, William Haney, Christine Linder, and Betsy Carroll for their contributions and editing skills.

Finally, we would like to thank the authors of the scales included in this monograph. They have kindly given permission to reprint their scale items, and many have offered useful supplementary information and references.

September, 1973

John P. Robinson
Phillip R. Shaver

CHAPTER 1 - INTRODUCTION

Background

The inspiration for these handbooks came from the pioneer efforts of Professor Robert Lane, the noted Yale University political scientist. Professor Lane was disturbed at the proliferation of empirical instruments in fields related to his area of interest. In the summer of 1958, he attempted to pull together those scales that would be of value to researchers in the field of political behavior, whose interests range from personality characteristics (e.g., neuroticism, authoritarianism) to occupational background (e.g., job satisfaction or status) to political attitudes (e.g., internationalism, conservatism). While Professor Lane was able initially to interest the National Institute of Mental Health in supporting this research, previous commitments on his time prevented him from pursuing it further. Subsequently, the availability of personnel at the Survey Research Center ensured that this valuable work would be continued under the general supervision of Professor Philip Converse.

There exist, of course, many cogent reasons for such an undertaking. Empirical instruments are likely to appear under surprising book titles, in any one of 15 social science journals (and may appear in 20 others), in seldom circulated dissertations, or from commercial publishers, as well as in the long-undisturbed piles of manuscripts in the offices of social scientists. Surely this grapevine of information is inefficient for the interested researcher. One must stay in the same area of interest on a continuing basis for several years (and not enough social scientists can) to become aware of the empirical literature and instruments available. Often, inter-disciplinary investigators are interested in the relation of some variable, of which they have only casually heard, to their favorite area of inquiry. Their job of combing the literature to pick a proper instrument needlessly consumes long hours that often end in a frustrating decision to forego measuring the variables. Worse still, they may resort to devising their own measures rapidly, adding to the already burdensome number of inadequately conceived instruments. Our search through the literature revealed considerable repetition of previous discoveries as well as an unawareness of related, and often better, research done in the same area.

Our searching procedure took us back through the earliest issues of Psychological Abstracts as well as through the printed histories (through 1966) of the most likely periodical sources of psychological instruments (Journal of Abnormal and Social Psychology, Journal of Social Psychology, and the Journal of Applied Psychology) and sociological or political measures (Sociometry, American Sociological Review, Public Opinion Quarterly, and the American Political Science Review). Doctoral dissertations were combed by examining back issues of Dissertation Abstracts and we are grateful to University Microfilms of Ann Arbor for providing us with pertinent dissertations. Still, not all universities belong to this service; Harvard, notably, is not a member. Dissertation Abstracts is also relatively recent. Contact with the large variety of empirical research being done at The University of Michigan opened new leads and widened our search, as did conversations with researchers contacted at the 1965 and 1966 annual meetings of the American Sociological Association and the American Psychological Association; several papers at these meetings contained empirical instruments. We also benefited greatly from the compendia assembled by our predecessors: Miller (1964),

Shaw and Wright (1967), and Bonjean, McLemore, and Hill (1967). Finally, Dr. Jeanne Knutson of Stanford University directed us to a number of instruments that had eluded our search.

The emphasis in our project has been on compiling attitude _scales_ (that is, series of items that are homogeneous in content) which are especially useful in survey research rather than in laboratory settings, although of course many will also be useful for laboratory research. We have not attempted the gigantic and perhaps hopeless task of compiling single attitude items, which often tap important variables for purposes of analysis. We have made two major (and occasional minor) exceptions to this rule: questions that have been used in the Survey Research Center election studies (in Chapter 13 of _Measures of Political Attitudes_), and measures of life satisfaction and happiness (in Chapter 2 of this volume).

A further attitude literature that we largely chose to ignore centered around the application of Osgood's semantic differential technique. An exhaustive bibliography of research applications of this approach to attitude measurement, in a variety of attitude areas, can be found in Snider and Osgood (1968).

Despite our desire to be as thorough as possible in our searching procedure, no claim is advanced that this volume contains every scale pertaining to our chapter headings. We feel confident however that we have brought attention to the vast majority of higher-quality instruments available. The list will have to be revised as oversights and new scales come to light.

Contents of This Volume

A brief outline of the contents of the 11 chapters of this handbook may prove helpful to the reader. The remainder of this introductory chapter[1] lays out in brief detail the contents of each chapter and concludes with a review of some important research areas that we unfortunately could not cover in this volume.

In Chapter 2, John Robinson reviews survey evidence on the correlates of (single questions about) life satisfaction and happiness in the general public.[2] He finds a number of consistent findings in this attitude area—the percentages of the population reporting themselves as dissatisfied, the high stability of such reports among individuals, and the consistent correlations obtained with background variables (particularly marital status and income). Especially important is the consistency with which persons expressing satisfaction with their way of life also manifest attitudes related to other topics covered in this volume, namely high self-esteem, low alienation, and high trust in people. Finally, he stresses the need for more attention to how such questions relate to the behavior of suicide and to how the black and other low income sectors of the public respond to them.

----

1. In the introductory chapter of our companion volume we have outlined the major criteria for scale construction which we used in evaluating the 126 scales reviewed in this volume. These evaluative criteria fall into three groups:

1) Item construction criteria (sampling of relevant content, wording of items, and performing item analyses).

2) Response set criteria (controlling the spurious effects of acquiescence and social desirability on responses to items).

3) Psychometric criteria (representative sampling, presentation of proper normative data, test-retest reliability, item homogeneity, discrimination of known groups, cross-validation, and further statistical procedures).

2. An updated review of empirical work in the area is planned for a monograph tentatively titled Measures of the Quality of Life now under preparation at the Institute for Social Research.

Rick Crandall surveys a large number of measures related to self-esteem and the self-concept in Chapter 3. The terms embrace a disturbing variety of definitions and operationalizations. Crandall notes several basic psychometric deficiencies in the available literature, particularly with regard to validity. Nevertheless, he does recommend eight scales to researchers.

In our original volume, scales to measure the degree of internal-external control were included in the self-esteem chapter. Since then interest in the concept has grown to the point that we can devote a single chapter to it alone. A. P. MacDonald has provided a comprehensive literature review and bibliographic guide to this literature and has highlighted several unresolved methodological problems. He has also included detailed reviews of eight major measures of the internal-external variable.

Fourteen measures relating to the often abused term "alienation" are reviewed in Chapter 5. One of the main problems with the most widely-used instruments in this area is their failure to provide for any control over agreement response set. Nevertheless, the general correlates of alienation, or alternatively anomia, seem well-established: low social status, minority race, and general lack of social participation. While a number of sociologists have suggested that specific components of alienation (e.g., powerlessness, isolation) need to be distinguished, the empirical fruitfulness of such a division has not been amply demonstrated. In one of the most thorough investigations of attitude states in the literature, McClosky and Schaar find their Anomy Scale to be significantly related to an awesome array of psychological variables--life satisfaction, low self-esteem, inflexibility, pessimism, misanthropy, acquiescence, extreme political beliefs, and aggression. These findings tie in with the pattern of intercorrelations noted in Chapter 2, and further suggest a common syndrome potentially encompassing many of the constructs in this volume.

The vast literature on authoritarian and dogmatic personality characteristics is represented by 27 scales in Chapter 6, including the major instruments from the well-known California Study, scales related to Rokeach's
conception of closed-mindedness, Eysenck's T scale for measuring "toughmindedness," and several measures of components of the authoritarian syndrome,
such as "intolerance of ambiguity." In the introductory portion of Chapter 6,
Shaver indicates the major theoretical issues on which research in this area
has focused and discusses the complex relationship (still a matter of
considerable controversy) between acquiescence response bias and "true"
authoritarianism as factors contributing to high scores on measures of
authoritarianism and dogmatism.

In Chapter 7 we review seven promising instruments that deal with political content (e.g., nationalism, social responsibility); these came to our
attention too late for inclusion in Measures of Political Attitudes.

Chapter 8 is devoted to measures of values, to which many psychologists
refer as something like "meta-attitudes," i.e., constructs that are more
general and pervasive than attitudes. In other words, an individual's attitudes across many areas (e.g., nationalism, conformity) can be explained as
emerging from one common value (e.g., loyalty). Teresa Levitin examines a
total of 12 scales of values in this chapter, including two (by Bales and
Couch, and by Scott) that provide extensive multidimensional analyses of
this domain.

The scales in Chapter 9 may be seen as tapping one basic value, that
of favorableness toward people in general. Considering the range of
behaviors and attitudes that have been found to relate successfully to the
five scales in this chapter, it is surprising that one does not find more
application of them in the social science literature. Of particular interest

in this chapter is Christie's intriguing scale developed successfully from the writings of the 16th century writer, Niccolo Machiavelli.

Religious values are among the topics reviewed in Chapter 10 by Shaver. Here again we find an attitude area in which some promising multidimensional spadework has been undertaken, especially in the case of the research of Glock and Stark.

Finally, in Chapter 11 we examine four sets of scales that are mainly of methodological interest--primarily for the measurement of social desirability response set. The social desirability scale of Crowne and Marlowe is particularly noteworthy for its rigorous tests of validity (although some questions remain about the scale's internal consistency and usefulness as a control for social desirability in attitude measurement).

What Could Not Be Included

There exist a number of other attitude areas that properly belong in a monograph with a title such as ours but which could not be included because of time and financial constraints. Areas that immediately come to mind are: achievement (and other motives such as power and affiliation), aggression, conformity (although scales of inner- vs. other-directedness are included in a volume we've prepared of occupational measures), marital and family attitudes, and personality characteristics. Important compilations in the latter two areas are now available--marriage and family attitudes having been reviewed by Straus (1969) and personality measures (with main emphasis on variables with mental health implications) by Chun et al. (in press).

The arrival of Lake et al. (1973) provides a systematic review of 84 different instruments related to "social functioning"--defined as "the properties of the individual as he or she takes part in social interaction,

and to properties of the immediate social system involved." Almost half of
the instruments reviewed by Lake et al. are personal in orientation, about a
quarter are interpersonal, and the remainder have the group or organization
as their focus.

It is our hope that by making available a wide range of attitude scales
from the growing social science literature this monograph can contribute to
a reduction of the vast number of construct names and measures to their most
basic dimensions. It should then be quite feasible to develop standardized
instruments to measure these dimensions as accurately and efficiently as
possible.

Although we could not hope to provide exhaustive coverage of attitude
scales in these volumes, important omissions can be incorporated into subsequent volumes or revisions with little difficulty. Ideally, our efforts will
provoke a larger scale undertaking (perhaps on an annual review basis) in
which each attitude area could be reviewed by a specialist familiar enough
with each area to unearth all relevant instruments and to assess the construct
validity of each measure (along the lines of the more clinically- and
educationally-oriented Mental Measurements Yearbook). In this way social
scientists can be provided with a truly definitive dictionary of attitude
measures.

REFERENCES

Bonjean, C., McLemore, D., and Hill, R. Sociological measurement. San
   Francisco: Chandler, 1967.

Chun, K., Cobb, S., and French, J. Measures for psychological assessment:
   A guide to 3,000 original sources and their application. Ann Arbor,
   Michigan: Institute for Social Research (in press).

Lake, D., Miles, M., and Earle, R. Measuring human behavior. New York:
   Teachers College Press, 1973.

Miller, D. Handbook of research design and social measurement. New York:
   David McKay, 1964.

Shaw, M. and Wright, J. Scales for the measurement of attitudes. New
   York: McGraw-Hill, 1967.

Snider, J. and Osgood, C. The semantic differential: a sourcebook. Chicago:
   Aldine Press, 1968.

Straus, M. Family measurement techniques. Minneapolis, Minn.: University
   of Minnesota Press, 1969.

CHAPTER 2 - LIFE SATISFACTION AND HAPPINESS

The types of questionnaire responses examined in this chapter focus
primarily on feelings of contentment with one's style of life. Our main
attention is devoted to overall assessments of such global feelings as
how satisfied or happy respondents in social surveys claim they are.
While the use of such global measures obscures known complexities in these
assessments, we shall see that they do produce predictable findings with
uncommon regularity.

Data on life satisfaction serve important functions in various fields
of inquiry. The sociologist may consider replies of unhappiness as one
component of alienation from the social system, and indeed we do find that
measures of the two constructs intercorrelate to a moderate degree. The
clinical psychologist may view them as an indicator of an individual's
"social adjustment," or use them to chart swings in the moods and emotions
of individuals over a period of time (for some interesting developments
along this line, see Maisel,1969). The political scientist might use such
data to find ways in which the political system can maximize satisfaction
in a society. Finally, the practical politician should be aware of the
sources of discontent in society to instigate programs of adjustment before
such discontent reaches crisis proportions. Presumably, all of the efforts
in the "war on poverty" in this country have been motivated by the assumption that the life of poverty is one that needs correction to assure a better life for poor people. Unfortunately, no data have been collected
during the last few crucial years to see whether poor people whose incomes
have increased with the advent of the war on poverty have indeed attained
higher levels of personal satisfaction or happiness with their lives.

For the most part this review will attempt to duplicate as little as
possible of the material covered in Wilson's (1967) comprehensive survey
of the literature. Rather it will be mainly concerned much more deeply
with documenting the variations in the statistical distributions of these
global assessments. For purposes of simplicity, we shall ignore data obtained from countries other than the United States.[1]

The review is divided into five sections: 1) description of the
studies in which global assessments of satisfaction have been obtained,

_____

[1]Wessman (1956) has found levels of reported unhappiness to be slightly
higher in the United States than in England or Holland, but lower than
in Canada or, especially, France. Cantril (1965) found ratings on self-
anchoring scales to be higher in the United States than in any of the
other countries included in his study.

2) stability and reliability of these global assessments, 3) variations
in reported satisfaction according to background factors (e.g., sex, marital status, socioeconomic status), 4) relation between reported satisfaction and other attitudes, and 5) relation between satisfaction and behavior.

Social Surveys into Life Satisfaction

Wilson (1967) includes studies of reported happiness that extend back
into the 1930's. Since few surveys conducted prior to the 1950's employed
sophisticated sampling methods, their value is too limited to report here.
Wilson does describe a nationwide study by Wessman (1956) in which 46% of
the population was characterized as "very" happy, 45% as "fairly" happy,
7% "not very" happy, and 1% "not at all" happy.

Probably the first extensive survey into happiness with a nationwide
probability sample was that of Gurin, Veroff, and Feld (1960). The authors
asked a single three-alternative question (see Table 1) on happiness as
part of an interview schedule that lasted well over an hour, dealing in
depth with reported psychological adjustment and problems with work, family,
and social relations. The sample consisted of a national cross-section of
2,460 respondents chosen by probability methods to represent the entire
adult (over 21 years of age) population of the United States. The study
was conducted in the spring of 1957.

Bradburn and Caplovitz (1965) employed the Gurin et al. happiness question in a study of four towns in Illinois with between three and ten thousand population. Two of the towns were classified as economically depressed,
the other two as relatively well-off economically. Approximately one hundred interviews were taken with a cross-section of men between the ages of
25 and 49 in each community. These were supplemented with short questionnaires distributed to other adult members of the same household, bringing
the total number of responses up to over 2,000. Interviews were conducted
in the spring of 1962, with a special reinterview with 547 respondents being
completed in the fall of 1962 to gauge the effects of the Cuban missile
crisis on reported happiness. (It had practically no discernible effect.)

A single question on satisfaction with life[2] was included in the 1965
nationwide study of Americans' use of time by Converse and Robinson (in
press). The intent of the question was to relate life satisfaction to the
ways in which different individuals allocated their time. One particular
expectation was that lower satisfaction would be reported by individuals
spending the most time viewing television. The sample consisted of 1,244
adults living in homes where at least one member of the household held a
regular job in a non-farm occupation and was under age 65. The survey was

---

[2]In the first survey, the alternative "not at all" satisfied was used.
Less than 1% of the sample chose this alternative and so it is merged
with the "not very satisfied" alternatives in Table 1. The alternative
was not used at all in the 1968 survey.

Table 1: Basic Satisfaction Items and Distribution of Responses
in Sample Populations

HAPPINESS: Taking all things together, how would you say things are these
days--would you say you're very happy, pretty happy or not too
happy these days?

	Very	Pretty	Not Too	
1958 (Gurin et al.)	35	54	11	= 100%
1962 (Bradburn and Caplovitz)	24	59	17	= 100%

LIFE SATIS- In general, how satisfying do you find the way you're spending
FACTION: your life these days? Would you call it completely satisfying,
pretty satisfying, or not very satisfying?

	Completely	Pretty	Not Very	
1965 (Converse and Robinson)	24	65	11	= 100%
1968 (Survey Research Center)	24	66	10	= 100%

SELF AN- All of us want certain things out of life. When you think about
CHORING what really matters in your own life, what are your wishes and
SCALE: hopes for the future? In other words, if you imagine your future
in the best possible light, what would your life look like then,
if you are to be happy? Take your time in answering; such things
aren't easy to put into words.

Now taking the other side of the picture, what are your fears and
worries about the future? In other words, if you imagine your
future in the worst possible light, what would your life look like
then? Again take your time in answering.

Here is a picture of a ladder. Suppose we say that at the top of
the ladder (pointing to Value 10) represents the best possible life
for you and the bottom (pointing to Value 0) represents the worst
possible life for you.

Ladder Value	10	9	8	7	6	5	4	3	2	1	0	
Percent	14	8	16	14	10	25	6	3	2	1	1	= 100%

High (7, 8, 9, 10)	Middle (4, 5, 6)	Low (0, 1, 2, 3)	
52	41	7	= 100%

restricted to people living in or near cities of 50,000 population or
more--which eliminated individuals in "rural" areas containing about one-
third of the United States population. Respondents were interviewed in
late fall, 1965 and early spring, 1966.

The question was repeated in the 1968 Survey Research Center post-
election study of political behavior. This sample of 1,315 respondents
provided full representation of the entire population and was, moreover,
supplemented with a special sample of Negro citizens to allow more detailed
analyses of this important segment of the population. Table 1 shows that
the distribution of replies remained amazingly constant over the three-
year time period between 1965 and 1968.

The final measure included in this section is the standard self-anchoring
scale devised by Cantril (1965) and employed by him in a thirteen-nation study,
in which nearly 20,000 people were interviewed. In the United States survey,
1,549 people were interviewed in the summer of 1959 using a modified probability sample. The self-anchoring device employs an eleven-point ladder, the
lowest end (point 0) referring to the respondent's own description of the
"worst possible life" and the highest end (point 10) to his description of
the "best possible life."

Measurement difficulties arise in trying to compare the self-anchoring
scale data with the other measures in Table 1. Cantril gives descriptions
of his data in terms of average scores along this eleven-point scale (the
average score for the entire sample being 6.6).[3] The arithmetic midpoint
of 5 does provide a logical division between the satisfied and dissatisfied,
and some 13% of the Cantril sample chose response options below this value.
This percentage ends up being very close to those giving the responses "not
too happy" or "not very satisfied" to the two previous questions in Table 1.

---

[3]This value is lower than the 7.6 value obtained with a scale that Cantril
(1965, p. 265) employed to more directly inquire into people's present
satisfaction.

"Some people seem to be quite happy and satisfied with their
lives, while others seem quite unhappy and dissatisfied. Now,
look at the ladder again. Suppose that a person who is entirely
satisfied with his life would be at the top of the ladder, and
a person who is extremely dissatisfied with his life would be
at the bottom of the ladder.

Where would you put yourself on the ladder at the present stage
of your life in terms of how satisfied or dissatisfied you are
with your own personal life?"

Unfortunately, Cantril does not present the rich body of correlates for
this question that are available for the question in Table 1. While the
correlation between replies to this question and that of Table 1 is only
.36, the pattern of relations with background variables (especially race
and socioeconomic status) is quite similar. The pattern of relation to
questions on the components of satisfaction--such as self-respect and
religion (for the complete list, see Appendix A)--is also similar, although
the correlations are lower for the question in Table 1 (as can be seen in
Appendix A).

Cantril's technique both controls for and obscures variations due to individual differences in aspiration levels. However, open-ended material dealing with choice of standards for "best" and "worst" possible life conditions provides rich ancillary information on the types of factors that people consider responsible for satisfaction or dissatisfaction. In Table 2, we have summarized those factors in Cantril's study that were prominently mentioned in this regard.

It can be seen that almost two-thirds of Cantril's sample mentioned economic factors in describing their best possible life, with just under half mentioning good health or family contentment. In terms of the worst possible life, however, poor health was mentioned more often than undesirable economic circumstances, with unhappy occurrences to family an even less important consideration in this connection. Only a quarter of the population noted family concerns in connection with the worst possible life, the same proportion as mentioned the international situation[4] in this regard. Thus one's family is far more likely to be thought of as a source of hopes rather than fears, the international situation having the opposite function.[5]

In the left side of Table 2, we have taken the liberty of comparing these replies to those obtained by Gurin et al. in response to open-ended questions on sources of happiness and unhappiness. Percentages are lower in these tables because less probing was employed by SRC interviewers with these questions than in the Cantril study. Again, however, the finding emerged that the family is more often a source of happiness and occurrences in the larger community a source of unhappiness. In the Gurin study, however, economic factors were relatively more prevalent as sources of unhappiness than of happiness.

This last difference, probably resulting from the serious incompatibilities that exist in the connotations of the two sets of questions,[6]

---

[4] About 90% of these responses refer to fear of war.

[5] Cantril did uncover one major source of perceived discontent that does not appear in Table 1 when he asked about "things...you feel may be keeping you from having a more satisfying life than you are having now?" Over 40% chose "lack of training and education" from a list of eight factors. No other factor was chosen by more than 20% of the sample. Furthermore, over half of the sample listed education as an item that "you really feel would make a big difference in your own happiness." The only item to exceed this one was income. Of course, many respondents value education only to the extent that it will assure them a larger income or a more prestigious job (Chase, 1962).

[6] One interesting figure is the 11% in Cantril's study who give "status quo" replies to the questions. This may be compared to the 8% in the Gurin et al. study who have replies coded as "independence or absence of burdens or restraints." In both studies, no respondents mentioned such factors in a negative context.

Table 2: Types of factors mentioned as leading to personal satisfaction and dissatisfaction

	Cantril (1965)[a] Factors in[c]		Gurin et al. (1960)[b]	Sources of	
	Best Possible Life	Worst Possible Life		Happiness	Unhappiness
Economic	65	46	Economic and material	29	27
Health	48	56	Respondent's health	9 } 17	7 } 12
			Family's health	8	5
Family	47	25	Children	29 } 46	7 } 12
			Marriage	17	5
Personal values	20	3	Independence	8 } 10	-- } 13
			Personal characteristics	2	13
Status quo	11	--		--	--
Job or work situation	10	5	Job	14	11
International situation	10	24	Community/world problems	--	13
Social values	5	3	Other interpersonal	16	3
Political	2	5			
			Miscellaneous	12	4
Nothing mentioned	<5%	12%	Nothing	5%	18%

[a] Questions asked in the Cantril study are given in Table 1.

[b] Questions asked in Gurin et al. were: For sources of happiness, "What are some of the things that you feel pretty happy about these days?" For unhappiness, "Everybody has things about their life they are not completely happy about. What are some of the things that you're not too happy about these days?"

[c] Totals add up to more than 100% because of multiple responses.

makes precise comparisons untenable. Nevertheless, it can be seen that in both studies over three times as many people can think of no negative factors as can think of no positive factors.

Reliability of Satisfaction Measures

One of the most impressive features of the questions in Table 1 is the stable test-retest reliabilities they exhibit. It could well be expected that measures of satisfaction would comprise the example par excellance of a measure subject to the ups and downs of daily life. In a small random sample of 90 residents in Jackson, Michigan, however, Converse and Robinson (in press) found a correlation (Kendall's tau) of .59 between reported satisfaction at one time and satisfaction reported in an interview four to six months earlier. The happiness question was added to this follow-up survey and it correlated .46 with the satisfaction question (and .43 with the satisfaction reply in the first interview). Bradburn and Caplovitz reported a test-retest table with the happiness question recorded over an eight month period which, when reduced to a value of Kendall's tau, equals .43; less than 2% of respondents chose the opposite extremes (i.e., "not too happy" at time 1 and "very happy" at time 2 or the reverse) across the time interval. Wilson (1960) reports two studies with test-retest correlations, one with a value .70 (a one-month interval) and the other a value of .67 (a two-year interval).

We shall comment on the internal consistency aspect of reliability (correlations with such variables as depression, adjustment, alienation, and self-esteem) in a later section.

Correlates of Reported Satisfaction

In this section we shall review briefly and document quantitatively the extent to which differences in satisfaction are related to standard background factors. The factors are considered under the following headings: sex and marital status, age, socioeconomic status, status incongruence, race, and other background factors.

Sex and Marital Status. Only insignificant differences in satisfaction are reported between men and women. Some interesting differences have emerged, however, when sex is examined by what seems to be the most powerful single predictor of satisfaction--marital status. Differences in contentment, outlined in Table 3, give little support to the stereotypes of the frustrated spinster and the carefree bachelor. The Bradburn and Caplovitz study in fact shows markedly higher unhappiness among single men than single women.

All studies indicate married people to be significantly happier than unmarried people. Among the unmarried (where small sample sizes could

Table 3: Differences in reported satisfaction
by marital status and sex, and by age

	Men				Women			
	Married	Single	Divorced	Widowed	Married	Single	Divorced	Widowed
% Not Too Happy								
Gurin et al. (1966)	8%	13%	20%	40%	7%	11%	27%	24%
Bradburn and Caplovitz (1965)	14	31	38	43	11	15	36	39
% Not Very Satisfied								
Converse and Robinson (in press)	10	12	46	25	9	17	28	14
Robinson (1969)	6	11	32	26	7	10	23	22

account for considerably more instability than appears in Table 3), the widowed and divorced[7] generally emerge as the least satisfied, with single people (excepting single males in the Bradburn and Caplovitz study) significantly more satisfied than either the divorced or widowed. If it is "better to have loved and lost," it seems better to have done so before entering the state of matrimony. One final note of interest is that all of these results were also found in Wessman's (1956) national survey.

Age. Differences by age generally show decreased satisfaction for older people, as can be seen in Table 4. The differences are larger and more monotonic for the happiness question than for the satisfaction item or the self-anchoring scale. Methodological procedures may account for the reversals in the Converse-Robinson and Cantril studies: the lack of many unemployed, elderly, and retired people (who were largely excluded) in the Converse-Robinson study and the reduced aspirations (which form the top of the "ladder") of elderly people in the Cantril study. Moreover, in the latest Survey Research Center study, it can be seen that differences by age largely disappear when unmarried people are excluded. In other words, the consistent finding of increase of unhappiness with age may well hinge upon the higher incidence of divorce and death of marital partners for this group.

The present author has also had the opportunity to ask the standard satisfaction and happiness questions of several samples of students at various high schools and colleges in Michigan over a two-year period. No possibility for probability sampling has presented itself, but these students consistently evidence higher levels of personal dissatisfaction than the adult samples we have been examining. Upwards of 25% of the high school students and students in the social sciences at the University of Michigan chose the alternatives "not very satisfied" or "not too happy" in response to the questions. The rate of choice was more nearly normal (11%) for a small sample of students at Adrian college,[8] which indicates that the University of Michigan results should not be generalized to all college students. Nevertheless, the higher personal discontent among students compared to other individuals under age 30 in cross-section samples (Table 3) may indicate that the student role is not a particularly satisfying one.

Social Status. Persons of higher social status invariably report higher levels of satisfaction than persons of lower status. Inkeles (1960) noted the finding in a number of different countries and Cantril (1965) subsequently found it to be true in each of the countries for which he had socioeconomic data available. The same has constantly been found in the area of job satisfaction (Robinson, 1969) and, although the assumption

---

[7] Gurin et al. found that 17% of respondents whose parents were divorced or separated rated themselves as currently unhappy vs. 11% of those from intact homes.

[8] The rate is also relatively low (5%) for 18 individuals classifying themselves as students in the 1968 election study. All of these students were over 21 and most were probably graduate students.

Table 4: Differences in satisfaction by age

Gurin et al. (1960)

Age	21-34	35-44	45-54	55 and over
% Not Too Happy	5	10	13	18

Bradburn and Caplovitz (1965)

Age	Under 30	30-39	40-49	50-59	60-69	70 and over
% Not Too Happy	11	10	13	18	24	30

Converse and Robinson (in press)

Age	Under 30	30-39	40-49	50-59	60-66
% Not Very Satisfied	13	10	11	11	12

Survey Research Center (1968)

Age	21-29	30-39	40-49	50-59	60-69	70 and over
% Not Very Satisfied	9	7	9	13	11	15
(Married only)	(8)	(6)	(5)	(7)	(6)	(8)

Cantril (1965)

Age	Under 29	30-49	Over 50
% Low Personal Present Ratings	6	9	6

that grades are a criterion of social status in the college community may be open to question, the author has found that college students with high grades report higher levels of personal satisfaction.

We shall defer detailing the exact differences in satisfaction by status until the next section which deals with the interaction of the two main indicators of status:[9] income and education. With few exceptions satisfaction has been associated monotonically with increasing levels on these two variables. However, interesting patterns of response have occurred when the two variables are examined simultaneously and these have interesting theoretical implications, as we shall see.

Status Incongruence. The literature on the effects of status incongruence--referring to the inequities of individuals as to their position on separate dimensions of status (especially for education and income)--generally has yet to show clear and consistent results necessary to justify the attention this phenomenon has received (Kasl, 1969; Jackson and Curtis, 1968). One of the puzzling aspects of much of this research, especially as it affects psychological states such as happiness or frustration, has been the failure of researchers to separate "desirable" incongruence (e.g., income level higher than expectations based on educational level) from "undesirable" incongruence (e.g., income level lower than corresponding educational level). We devote attention to this aspect in Table 5, with our interest directed toward the likelihood of very high satisfaction for "overachievers" (low education but high income) and very low satisfaction for "underachievers" (high education but low income).

The interaction of education and income in the four studies in Table 5 produces mixed results regarding the significance of incongruence. Stronger support for the unusually low unhappiness associated with desirable incongruence appears most notably in the Bradburn and Caplovitz data (i.e., the low 3% figure for persons with grade school education earning the relatively high income of over $7,000 per year). It also holds true in the latest Survey Research Center data, but significantly only for those with extremely high incomes (i.e., for those with less than a high school education earning over $15,000 per year, of whom not one reported himself as not very satisfied). It fails to hold in either the Converse-Robinson study or for the Gurin et al. data (although the range of income and education categories for this study is too restricted to fully test the incongruence hypothesis).

----

[9]Since the Cantril study does not include such a breakdown, the reader may find the univariate differences of interest.

		Low	Middle	High
% Low personal rating (0, 1, 2, 3)	Education	5	7	9
	Socioeconomic status	5	7	10

Table 5: Differences in satisfaction by education
and income

Gurin et al. (1960) -- % Not Too Happy

	Grade School	High School	Some College or more	Total
Under $5,000	22	9	10	16
Over $5,000	11	6	3	6
	24	8	5	11

Bradburn and Caplovitz (1965) -- % Not Too Happy

	Grade School	High School	Some College or more	Total
Under $3,000	33	27	21	31
$3,000-6,999	13	13	8	12
$7,000 and over	3	7	10	8
	25	14	10	17

Converse and Robinson (in press) -- % Not Very Satisfied

	Grade School	Some High School	High School Grad	Some College or More	Total
Under $4,000	6	24	33	27	21
$4,000-5,999	12	14	18	19	16
$6,000-9,999	4	14	14	5	10
$10,000 or more	21	6	9	7	8
	11	14	15	9	11

Survey Research Center (1968) -- % Not Very Satisfied

	Less Than High School Grad	High School Grad	Some College or More	Total
Under $6,000	18	18	9	16
$6,000-9,999	9	7	6	7
$10,000-14,999	12	4	6	7
$15,000 and over	0	9	4	5
	14	10	6	11
Under $4,000	21	18	21	20
$4,000-7,999	10	12	3	10
$8,000 and over	4	6	5	5

Support for the negative consequences of undesirable incongruence is not strong in Table 5. In fact in three of the five sets of data, the opposite effect holds true--the college-educated low income group turns out to be even less dissatisfied than other low income individuals. The Converse-Robinson study does show the predicted effect of undesirable congruence. The effect also appears in the latest Survey Research Center study if one lowers the income range to under $4,000 annual income, as we have done at the bottom of Table 5. The results show that the effects of incongruence are extremely sensitive to the income boundaries that the analyst decides to employ.

In these analyses, the small sample sizes and the inconsistent results preclude definitive conclusions about the effects of status incongruence. Moreover, no matter how important or interesting incongruence is theoretically in predicting discontent, in terms of explaining variance in discontent among all members of American society, incongruence certainly cannot be considered as important a factor as the singular effects of either marital status, income, or education.

Race. With Negroes comprising only a tenth of our population, sample sizes again pose a major limitation in the data of Table 6.[10] Nevertheless, only one study in which race has been included as a variable shows less discontent among Negroes than whites: the 1965-66 Converse-Robinson study. This reversal again may be attributable to the sampling restrictions on individuals who were unemployed or who resided in rural areas in the 1965-66 study. In the 1968 data, Negro-white differences are considerably reduced if one looks only at married respondents. Households in which such unmarried persons were unemployed would have been excluded in the 1965-66 study. Outside of this study, however, roughly twice as high a proportion of Negroes as whites report themselves as not too happy or not very satisfied.

Differences in satisfaction by race are examined in Table 6 as a function of income and region of the country,[11] since these are important factors that come to mind in connection with the relation between race and satisfaction and that have not been examined previously in the literature. It can be seen in Table 6 that regional differences are generally insignificant, but that the effects of income are strong in both regions for whites.

---

[10] As noted earlier, the 1968 data do have the advantage of including a special supplementary sample of Negroes which essentially doubles the size of the Negro sample in Table 6.

[11] Cantril (1965) found some of the largest differences in ratings on his self-anchoring scale were due to race, Negroes scoring an average of 1.4 ladder steps below whites; moreover, this difference was maintained when the question was repeated with a national sample in 1963. Cantril, however, does not examine differences in the Negro population either by income or region so that his data cannot be included in the Table 6 format.

Table 6: Differences in Satisfaction by Race
as a Function of Region and Income
(Sample sizes for Negroes in parentheses)

Gurin et al. data -- % Not Too Happy

	Negroes		Whites	
	South	non-South	South	non-South
Under $2,000	21 (71)	40* (5)	29	20
$2,000-3,999	36 (22)	19 (43)	10	15
$4,000-5,999	0* (5)	27 (26)	6	10
$6,000 and over	-- --	33* (9)	6	5
TOTAL	23%	24% = 23%	12	10% = 10%

Converse and Robinson (in press) -- % Not Very Satisfied

	Negroes		Whites	
	South	non-South	South	non-South
Under $4,000	11 (19)	17 (12)	20	26
$4,000-5,999	10 (10)	8 (13)	15	19
$6,000 and over	13 (16)	5 (22)	7	10
TOTAL	11%	9% = 10%	10	12 = 12%

Survey Research Center (1968) -- % Not Very Satisfied

	Negroes		Whites	
	South	non-South	South	non-South
Under $4,000	16 (74)	27 (34)	17	21
$4,000-7,999	10 (31)	29 (24)	8	10
$8,000 and over	6 (17)	12 (33)	7	4
TOTAL	14%	22% = 18%	8	9 = 9%

* Sample size under 10.

Reexamination of the Gurin et al. data, however, fails to uncover a monotonic relation between income and satisfaction for Negroes--in either the South or the non-South. Actually, the large differences in income levels between these regions may be partially to blame. If we used revised categories so that income distribution is more equitable within each region, we have for the Negro population:

	South			non-South	
Under $1,000	26%		Under $3,000	27%	
$1,000-2,999	24%		$3,000-4,999	21%	
$3,000 and over	9%		$5,000 and over	26%	

This arrangement indicates no relation between income and satisfaction for Negroes outside the South and not much relation in the South (except for the handful of Negroes who had earned over $3,000).

These results differ somewhat from those found in the Survey Research Center studies using the life satisfaction question. The Converse-Robinson data if anything show the opposite effect: little relation with income in the South and the expected decreased satisfaction with lower income outside the South. The most recent Survey Research Center data, on the other hand, tend to show the expected decreases with lower income in both the South and non-South. Of particular interest is the shift towards higher dissatisfaction in the non-South, particularly among middle income Negroes.

One would be sorely tempted to speculate on the findings from any one of these studies seen separately, but when they are arranged comparatively as in Table 6, the inconsistencies seriously dampen any enthusiasm about the validity of such speculations. It would be truly fascinating to find that increased income does not result in greater happiness for Negroes in the non-South (as in the Gurin et al. data) or that the patterns of relation between income and satisfaction are reversed in the South and the non-South (as in the Converse-Robinson data) or that Negroes in the South are more satisfied than those in the non-South at all income levels. However, the lack of any clear thread of meaning in the trends of relations across the time period preclude any fruitful speculation about intriguing historical changes in Negro attitudes about their lot in life.

What is obviously needed are questions about happiness and satisfaction to be asked of a large sample of Negro respondents so that adequate benchmark data can be established.[12] The question should then be repeated with similar samples on a regular basis, or even incorporated into panel studies. With such data, we would be on surer ground in learning about

_____

[12]If such samples are taken, special care needs to be exercised to control for the effects of one factor that has not been measured in connection with questions of personal contentment--the race of the person doing the interviewing. Previous studies have shown interviewer's race to influence the replies of Negroes generally, and questions of this nature would seem to be highly subject to such influence.

important questions such as whether Negroes migrating from the South will find life more rewarding than those who stay behind. Unfortunately the ambiguities from past studies in Table 6 render answers to such questions totally inconclusive.

Other Factors. A further prime predictor of unhappiness appears to be employment status. Bradburn and Caplovitz (1965) found high rates of unhappiness among the unemployed (31%) and retired (27%). In a more recent study (Noll and Bradburn, 1968) these rates were again abnormally high-- 39% for the unemployed[13] and 30% for the retired. In the recent Survey Research Center data, 37% of the unemployed rated themselves as "not very satisfied."

Differences by religious affiliation have not generally proved to be very significant. Catholics reported slightly more unhappiness in the Gurin et al. data, but report less dissatisfaction in the most recent Survey Research Center study. In this latter study, people of the Jewish faith report somewhat higher dissatisfaction (17% say they're not very satisfied), but Cantril found that Jews rated themselves somewhat higher on his self-anchoring scale. Again the small proportion of Jews in the population may well be responsible for these inconsistencies.

Gurin et al. located higher rates of unhappiness (18%) in metropolitan areas, and slightly lower than average unhappiness in the suburbs compared to residents of small cities and rural areas. The same pattern of results held true in the 1968 Survey Research Center data, even when controlled for the factors of income and race. Finally Cantril found a slightly higher preponderance of low self-anchoring scale ratings for urban dwellers (8%) than residents of rural areas (5%).

Relation with Other Attitudes

One of the more interesting features of measures of satisfaction and happiness is the wide range of other psychological attitudes with which they correlate. Yet for many of these attitudes one is not sure whether these correlations should not actually be higher than those which are obtained. This is especially true for variables tapping general psychological adjustment, which include measures of concepts like depression, self-esteem, and alienation. It can easily be expected that expressed happiness would be a prime indicator of a person's general adjustment and that one would be alarmed at low rather than high correlations between the two sets of variables.

---

[13]In this study, the unhappiness rate was twice as high for wives of the unemployed vs. wives of the employed. This phenomenon held true in the 1968 SRC data with 28% of wives of the unemployed reporting dissatisfaction vs. 6% of wives of the employed.

Perhaps the most impressive evidence of the essential congruity of satisfaction and self-esteem is provided in the Survey Research Center data for 1965-66 and 1968. The correlation of the satisfaction item with each of the items in the Survey Research Center personal efficacy scale is given at the top of Table 7. The average inter-item correlation of .23 for the 1968 data and .18 for the Converse-Robinson study[14] is relatively high considering that average inter-item correlation for each of the personal efficacy items themselves is .30. Furthermore, these results held true when controlled for sex and education.

More direct measures of self-esteem were included in Bachman et al.'s (1967) national study of 2,500 tenth-grade boys.[15] Unfortunately, the life satisfaction questions employed did not include the one in Table 1, but the correlation between the three-item life satisfaction scale and a ten-item self-esteem scale was .53 for the entire sample. Some of the inter-item correlations for selected items from these scales are noted at the bottom of Table 7. It can be seen that again items measuring happiness and satisfaction correlate almost as well with self-esteem items as the self-esteem items do with each other. (A complete list of the actual items in the satisfaction and self-esteem scales, along with the distribution of replies of the sample of boys to these items, are outlined in Appendix B to this chapter; items from other scales which correlate with the satisfaction scale are also included in Appendix B.)

Further evidence for the close interconnection of self-esteem and satisfaction is provided at many points in Wilson's (1967) review. Wilson notes, for example, studies which have demonstrated drops in self-esteem accompanying periods of unhappiness and depression and studies which report correlations in the .40's between unhappiness and discrepancies between real self and ideal self (see Chapter 3) and between need for achievement and actual achievement.

Wilson concludes that the most impressive single finding in research on happiness is the correlation of happiness and successful involvement with people. Subsequent corroboration of this conclusion is evidenced by correlations of .50 and .40 between the negative end of the satisfaction scale of Bachman et al. and their measures (reproduced in Appendix B) of lack of social support and personal anomie respectively. Again the anomie scale items correlate almost as highly with satisfaction items as they do with each other.

Also in line with Wilson's conclusion are the positive, but not high (average being .15), inter-item correlations with items measuring trust

---

[14] The present author has found correlations in the .30's and .40's between satisfaction measures and efficacy in samples of undergraduates at the University of Michigan and correlations in the .20's and .30's between satisfaction and more direct measures of self-esteem.

[15] We are grateful to Dr. Bachman for making these correlational data available to us before they are formally published.

Table 7: Correlations between satisfaction and items
tapping self-esteem (Survey Research Center data,
1965-66 and 1968)

	Correlation with Satisfaction	
	1965-66	1968
1. Have you usually felt pretty sure your life would work out the way you want it to*, or have there been times when you haven't been sure about it?	.22	.26
2. When you do make plans ahead, do you usually get to carry out things the way you expected*, or do things usually come up to make you change your plans?	.14	.20
3. Do you think it is better to plan your life a good way ahead*, or would you say life is too much a matter of luck to plan very far?	Not Asked	.18
4. Some people feel they can run their lives pretty much the way they want to*; others feel the problems of life are sometimes too big for them. Which one are you most like?	Not Asked	.28

* Indicates response reflecting personal competence)

_____

Bachman et al., 1967

		Life Satis.	Happi-ness	Not Proud	Nothing Right	Do Job Well
Life Satisfaction	1. I am very satisfied with life	X				
	2. I find a good deal of happiness in life	.47	X			
Self-esteem	3. I feel I do not have much to be proud of	-.12	-.16	X		
	4. I feel I can't do anything right	-.18	-.24	.26	X	
	5. When I do a job I do it well	.24	.28	-.07	-.11	X

in people in the 1968 election study. Possibly the conclusion may also be extended to encompass the repeated finding that satisfaction is strongly related to reported marital and job satisfaction.

Among some of the research findings employing other psychological variables that have been or could be related to reported satisfaction and happiness are:

--a .41 correlation with social adjustment and -.44 with anxiety (Wilson, 1960)

--a correlation of -.19 with worry and -.20 with a psychosomatic symptom score (Gurin et al., 1960)

--a -.41 correlation with anomie and the implication that life satisfaction is only one of numerous psychological variables (e.g., guilt, bewilderment, misanthropy) that are encompassed by the same syndrome (McClosky and Schaar, 1965)

--correlations of .53 with depression, .59 with sadness, .42 with irritability, .41 with anxiety, and .34 with resentment noted in the Bachman et al. data

--the fact that the social correlates of reported satisfaction (especially marital status and income) lead to the largest differences in Srole's et al. (1962) estimate of psychological impairment.

With all these positive correlations,[16] one might rightly inquire as to what it is that we really are measuring (or not measuring) with satisfaction and happiness questions. More specifically the problem of psychological response sets is one factor that immediately springs to mind, especially the response set of social desirability. Yet items from Crowne and Marlowe's (Chapter 10) social approval scale fail to correlate consistently (average .06) with any of the satisfaction items, or for that matter with the items from the myriad of scales that we have found to correlate with satisfaction in the Bachman et al. study.

Finally, we should mention the attempt of Bradburn and Caplovitz to isolate the various component feelings related to happiness and unhappiness. The authors constructed twelve items describing pleasurable and unpleasurable ways people feel and asked each respondent to indicate how often he had felt that way during the past week. Five items describing positive feelings and four items describing negative feelings were formed

---

[16] The reader should not interpret the preceding discussion to mean that there are no instances in the literature which show opposite patterns. Wilson (1967) notes several instances of correlates of this type that have failed to stand the test of replication. However, the present author is encouraged by the fact that he has found that these patterns of correlation hold up consistently in data he has collected for classroom use from students at the University of Michigan. Simmons (1966) reports much the same pattern of results, adding a new variable--attitude uncertainty--to the list of basic correlates of dissatisfaction.

into separate indices (three of the original negative feeling items failed
to correlate substantially with the other negative items and were dropped
from further analysis). They found that a statistically insignificant
positive correlation existed between the two indices, contrary to expectations that there would be a strong negative correlation. This can be seen
at the inter-item level in Appendix C, where we have reproduced the items
and the inter-item correlation matrix.

This implies that individuals with strong positive feelings are just
as likely to have strong negative feelings as they are to have no negative
feelings. In other words, a person can have strong negative feelings and
yet describe himself as very happy, because he has strong compensatory
sources of positive feelings. The advantages of considering the two
indices separately (a procedure we have recommended on page 19 of Robinson
et al., 1968) can be seen in Table 8. Only 12% of those having high

Table 8: Relation of unhappiness to positive and negative feelings
(from Bradburn and Caplovitz, 1965)

	% Feeling Not Too Happy	Positive Feelings		
		High	Medium	Low
	Low	1%	5%	13%
Negative Feelings	Medium	5%	8%	17%
	High	12%	26%	40%

positive feelings to compensate for high negative feelings describe themselves as not too happy--in comparison to 40% of those with high negative
feelings but few sources of positive feelings. Similarly among those with
low negative feelings, only 1% of those with high positive feelings described
themselves as not too happy vs. 13% of those with low positive feelings.
In the same way that Gurin et al. found better-educated people describing
more positive and more negative aspects of their self-concept, Bradburn and
Caplovitz find further evidence of this heightened self-awareness. They show
individuals who had been to college to be far more likely than those
with grade school education to give responses that combined high positive
feelings and high negative feelings.

Wilson has suggested that the reason Bradburn and Caplovitz find no
relation between positive and negative items was their failure to construct
items that were polar opposites. For example, he points out that whereas
"pleasure over accomplishments" is included as a positive feeling, "disappointment over failure" is a logical counterpart that should have been
included as a negative feeling. He claims that his own research has shown
that such polar opposites do correlate negatively as expected. He further

notes that the Bradburn-Caplovitz negative items refer to negative emotional feelings of a general nature, while the positive items refer to success and energy.

It may also be argued that the regular increases in unhappiness across rows and columns in the Table 8 data do not argue well for the need to separate positive and negative feelings. The real value of separating dimensions is provided when they produce complex interaction patterns (as in the Table 5 status incongruence data). Nevertheless, the practice of separating the two dimensions does become fruitful when we find the systematic differences by educational level noted by Bradburn and Caplovitz.

Relation of Life Satisfaction to Behavior

Neither Gurin et al. (1960) nor Cantril (1965) devote attention to the relation between professed contentment and any actual behavior. Although Wilson (1960) implies at many points that satisfaction is associated with increased social interaction, he reports on only one study (Fellows, 1956) that examines actual behavior. Fellows did find that people who spent more time in leisure time activities expressed more happiness.

Bradburn and Caplovitz also found that among males aged 25-49 (the only segment of the population for which they had data available), higher scores on their positive feelings index (Appendix C) were attained by people active in a wide variety of activities. Although the differences were in many cases neither startling nor monotonic with the amount of activity, increased participation in the following activities (in the previous month or shorter periods) was associated with higher positive feelings: contact with relatives, get-togethers with friends, telephone contact with friends, meeting new people, organizational membership, taking a trip in a car, eating out in a restaurant, participating in sports, and attending sports events.[17] Moreover, these differences generally held up when controlled for socioeconomic status. When seven of these items were formed into a participation index, 44% of the high scorers on this index scored highly on the positive feelings index vs. 23% of those scoring low in participation. Controls for status reduced this gap to about 16% (instead of 21%). Unfortunately, the authors related the Table 1 happiness question only to the activity of organizational membership, and it seemed to make a difference only for those of low status. Presumably, the direct correlation between happiness and other activities produced similarly unexciting results.

As noted earlier, the inclusion of the life satisfaction question in the Converse-Robinson study was intended to permit observation of whether a certain patterning of activities was associated with more satisfaction

----

[17]Higher positive feelings were not reported by those taking longest trips in the previous week, those participating in religious services, or those viewing most television.

than other patterns. The correlations between satisfaction and participation in 18 types of activities are presented in Table 9, separately for men and women. It can be seen that the relation between participation in activities and satisfaction is much more pronounced for women than men. As was the case with the Bradburn and Caplovitz data, none of the correlations is outstanding. However, 12 of the 18 coefficients are significant and in the expected direction for women[18] (although only 3 of 18 are for men). The two activities which did correlate for both men and women were activities that did not work well for Bradburn and Caplovitz: attendance at organizational functions and church attendance.[19] This correlation with frequency of church attendance was replicated in the 1968 election study, and held true separately for Protestants, Catholics, and Jews.

With such an unpromising pattern of correlations across studies (although the weight of the evidence does point to greater satisfaction among the more active), it may be well to conclude on a more consistent note concerning the relation between expression of satisfaction and behavior. Specifically, if one is looking for the ultimate behavioral manifestation of unhappiness, it would be the act of suicide. Fortunately, statistics on suicide have been collected for well over a hundred years (e.g., Maris, 1969). Moreover, most of the variables which we have seen relate to unhappiness--the unmarried state, the student role, low economic status, and low education--turn out to be prime associates of suicide. Furthermore, for some variables the differences in suicide rates for these groups are of roughly the same magnitude as those observed for unhappiness; e.g., three-to-one ratios for the widowed or divorced to those who are married.

Again all is not perfect, the higher suicide rates for males and whites are not reflected in their expressed unhappiness. However, it is known that attempted suicides are higher for women, which Maris feels might completely offset the large disparity in male-female completed suicide rates. Moreover, Maris speculates that the peculiar life circumstances of Negroes in America leads them to direct their aggression to external targets.

Therefore, the relation between unhappiness and suicide may prove to be one of the most dramatic examples of the basic congruity of attitudes and behavior. This is not to say that there is a one-to-one correspondence between unhappiness and suicide. Rather, in the spirit of Campbell's (1963) application of the Guttman scale model to the relation of attitudes and behavior, dissatisfaction with life is a necessary but not a sufficient

---

[18]All but three of these correlations for men and women hold when controlled for education and income.

[19]The expectation that the less satisfied would spend more time watching television also held true for women but not for men. On an average day, women who said they were "not very satisfied" watched 136 minutes of television vs. 105 minutes for those saying they were completely satisfied or pretty satisfied. The figure for all groups of men was about 135 minutes per day.

Table 9: Correlation between participation in various
types of activities and life satisfaction
(Converse and Robinson, in press)

We're also interested in things people do in their spare time, when they
aren't working.

I have a list of free-time activities, and I would like to have you tell
me about how often you have been doing these things during the past year
(HAND CARD). For example, "Going to the movies." Would you say that you've
generally been going to the movies once a week or more, every two or three
weeks, half-dozen to a dozen times all year, one to five times a year, or
not at all this year?

	Correlation with Life Satisfaction	
	Men (N = 490)	Women (N = 640)
a. Going to the movies.....................	- .04	.03
b. Going to club meetings, activities (PTA, union, etc.).......................	.15	.14
c. Going to church (or religious activities).	.12	.14
d. Going to classes or lectures.............	- .03	.05
e. Going to watch sports events.............	.03	.08
f. Fishing, hunting, camping, hiking........	- .02	.06
g. Boating, swimming, picnics, pleasure-drives...................................	- .02	.14
h. Playing active sports (bowling, softball, etc.).............................	- .05	.10
i. Going to nightclubs, bars, etc...........	.00	- .03
j. Going to concerts, plays, etc............	.04	.04
k. Going to fairs, museums, exhibits, etc...	.04	.10
l. Gardening and working around yard........	.09	.07
m. Making and fixing things around house....	.05	.10
n. Shopping, except for groceries...........	- .01	.11
o. Helping relatives, neighbors, friends....	.04	.11
p. Visits with relatives, neighbors, friends	- .02	.10
q. Playing cards, other indoor games........	.01	.10
r. Working on hobbies, painting or music....	.04	.12

condition for suicide. That is, only unhappy people commit suicide, <u>but</u> not all unhappy people commit suicide. In terms of a two-by-two table, there are no people falling in the upper right hand cell:

	No Suicide	Suicide
Satisfied		0
Dissatisfied		

One main implication of this model is that fewer people will commit suicide than express dissatisfaction, which is borne out by the statistical discrepancy between the roughly 10% of the population who express dissatisfaction compared to the .01 to .04% who commit suicide in any one year.

Such speculation is now based solely on the striking parallels between the demographic correlates of the two behaviors. Although the sample sizes for a panel study to directly test the hypothesis would be prohibitive for a cross-national study, it would seem to be a most fruitful area for more intensive study.

SUMMARY AND CONCLUSIONS

In this review we have found a number of constant relationships when respondents in social surveys are asked to report on their general satisfaction with life. First of all, it was found that there has been relatively little change in the percentage of the population expressing discontent--Gurin <u>et al</u>. found 11% of a nationwide sample saying they were "not too happy" in 1958; Converse and Robinson found 11% professing their life to be not very satisfying in 1965, and when the Survey Research Center asked the question three years later 10% chose this alternative. The overall figure for the Bradburn and Caplovitz study was 17%, but dropped to 13% if the economically depressed communities were excluded. Cantril found the same 13% figure falling on the negative side of his self-anchoring scale. As is the case with job satisfaction (Robinson, 1969), the vast majority of the population seem content with the way they are spending their lives.

A second constancy was that people who express satisfaction at one time period are quite likely to express satisfaction if interviewed some months later. Expressions of satisfaction then are much more stable at the individual level than one might at first imagine.

A third constancy centered around the relations with standard demographic variables. Widowed and divorced people consistently show the highest rates of dissatisfaction and unhappiness. Unemployed people and other extremely low income individuals also show very high rates of dissatisfaction with life. The present author has also noted a persistent trend of students to rate themselves as not very satisfied. Older people and Negroes express more dissatisfaction, but the latest available data indicate that these differences are considerably reduced or disappear when controlled for marital status.

While almost all studies show a consistent trend for satisfaction to increase with both income and education, some irregularities do appear when the two variables are examined simultaneously. Specifically, highly educated individuals in extremely low paying jobs express higher life dissatisfaction than other individuals in low paying jobs. On the other hand, individuals in high paying jobs but with relatively little education have been found to profess more satisfaction than other individuals at comparable salary levels. Such interesting patterns have not appeared in every study that has been conducted and, furthermore, explain relatively little variance in life satisfaction across the whole population. Differences by sex, religious affiliation, size of city, and region of the country are even less significant.

The pattern of correlations with other psychological attitudes is another area where consistent results have been located. Particularly significant is the finding that persons of high self-esteem or personal competence express more satisfaction with life. Satisfaction has also been found to be greater among people who are better socially adjusted, who demonstrate more trust in people, who feel less alienated, and who suffer less from anxiety, worry, and psychosomatic symptoms. Even stronger attitudinal correlates of satisfaction, as might be implied from the findings mentioned above, are marital and job satisfaction.

Finally, we found that a number of studies point to greater satisfaction among people who are actively involved in a number of leisure-time activities, such as membership in organizations and church attendance. Again, not all studies show that participation in the same activities leads to greater satisfaction nor that differences between those at different levels of activity are particularly large.

Suicide is one behavior with which dissatisfaction with life would most likely be correlated. Although no studies of suicide have included attitudinal questions administered some time beforehand, there are striking similarities in the pattern of correlation that the two behaviors have with background variables (e.g., marital status, age).

The above summary has glossed over many inconsistencies and unreplicated findings that do exist in this literature. What would be particularly useful at this stage of research would be some attempt to collect all of the above types of information (personal attitudes, behavior patterns, and background variables) on the same individuals in a panel design study. We may then come to more fully understand the ways in which satisfaction changes in representative populations. With such information, perhaps we could begin to address ourselves to the more important problem of methods of decreasing the ranks of the dissatisfied in this country.

If such studies do become feasible in the near future, they should attempt to go beyond the single questions to which we have devoted most attention here and delve into sources and components of satisfaction. Such a strategy proved fruitful in the Bradburn and Caplovitz study, as well as in the studies by Gurin et al., Cantril, and Converse-Robinson. For this purpose, researchers might well find detailed instruments developed in research on non-representative populations to be of considerable benefit. The scales of Green (1965), Clyde (1963), Wessman and Ricks (1966), and Wilson (1960) are some of the most recent efforts that would deserve consideration in this connection.

There are two further methodological side-issues to which future research in this area should address itself. One, the effects of interviewer characteristics on these responses (especially racial differentials), we have already mentioned in an earlier footnote. The second was also brought up in previous discussion--the effects of the response set of social desirability. While the available research evidence from Bachman et al. generally indicates that measures of social desirability show relatively little relation to measures of life satisfaction, their specific relation to the measures of Table 1 has yet to be investigated. No matter how strong such correlations turn out to be, the effects of this response set need to be assessed and controlled before measures of life satisfaction can achieve maximum applicability.

REFERENCES

Arscott, A. Univariate statistics describing a nationwide sample of tenth-grade boys. Interim Report, Working Paper 2, Ann Arbor, Michigan: Institute for Social Research, July, 1968.

Bachman, J.; Kahn, R.; Davidson, T.; and Johnston, L. Youth in transition - volume 1. Ann Arbor, Michigan: Institute for Social Research, 1967.

Bradburn, N. and Caplovitz, D. Reports on happiness. Chicago: Aldine, 1965.

Campbell, D. Social attitudes and other acquired behavioral dispositions, in S. Koch (ed.), Psychology: a study of a science. New York: McGraw-Hill, 1963, pp. 94-172.

Cantril, H. The pattern of human concerns. New Brunswick, N.J.: Rutgers University Press, 1965.

Chase, S. American credos. New York: Harper, 1962.

Clyde, D. Clyde mood scale manual. Coral Gables: University of Miami Biometrics Laboratories, 1963.

Converse, P. and Robinson, J. The use of time in American society. (in press)

Fellows, E. A study of factors related to happiness, Journal of Educational Research. 1956, 50, 231-234.

Green, R. On the measurement of mood. Technical Report No. 10, 1965, University of Rochester. Research Project NR 171-342.

Gurin, G.; Veroff, J.; and Feld, S. Americans view their mental health. New York: Basic Books, 1960.

Inkeles, A. Industrial man: The relation of status to experience, perception, and value, American Journal of Sociology, 1960, 66, 1-31.

Jackson, E. and Curtis R. Conceptualization and measurement in the study of social stratification, in Blalock and Blalock (eds.), Methodology in social research. New York: McGraw-Hill, 1968.

Kasl, S. Status inconsistency: Some conceptual and methodological considerations, in Robinson, J. et al., Measures of occupational attitudes and occupational characteristics. Ann Arbor, Mich.: Survey Research Center, 1969.

McClosky, H. and Schaar, J.   Psychological dimensions of anomy, American Sociological Review, 1965, 30, 14-40.

Maisel, R.   CAPEC: Case studies on evaluating public mood and ideology. Paper presented at the annual meetings of the American Association of Public Opinion Research, Boltons Landing, New York, 1969.

Maris, R. Social forces in urban suicide.   Homewood, Ill.: Dorsey Press, 1969.

Noll, E. and Bradburn, N.   Work and happiness.   Paper presented at the 63rd annual meeting of the American Sociological Association in Boston, September, 1968.

Robinson, J.   Occupational norms and differences in job satisfaction, in Robinson, J.; Athanasiou, R.; and Head, K., Measures of occupational attitudes and occupational characteristics, Ann Arbor: Survey Research Center, Institute for Social Research, 1969.

Simmons, J.   Some intercorrelations among 'alienation' measures, Social Forces, 1966, 44, 370-372.

Srole, L., Langer, T., Michael, S., Opler, M. and Rennie, T. Mental health in the metropolis. New York: McGraw-Hill, 1962.

Wessman, E. and Ricks, D. Mood and personality. New York: Holt, Rinehart and Winston, 1966.

Wessman, D.   A psychological inquiry into satisfaction and happiness. Unpublished doctoral dissertation, Princeton University, 1956.

Wilson, W.   An attempt to determine some correlates and dimensions of hedonic tone. Unpublished doctoral dissertation, Northwestern University, 1960.

Wilson, W.   Correlates of avowed happiness, Psychological Bulletin, 1967, 67, 294-306.

APPENDIX A

Questions on components of satisfaction (Cantril 1965)

Now I am going to ask you some questions which you can easily answer by looking at the ladder I showed you before.

After I ask you each question, just point to the place on the ladder you think is appropriate for you now. Don't be hesitant or embarrassed in putting yourself near the top or near the bottom of the ladder if that is the way you happen to feel. Just give your first reaction without thinking too much about it.

	Mean Rating	Correlation with Personal[a] Present	Life[b] Satisfaction
How important would you say religion is in your life. If religion is extremely important, use the top of the ladder; if it is not at all important, use the bottom.	8.5	.11	.18
Now, how about the respect you have for yourself as a person --that is, your feelings of being a worthwhile and worthy person, as contrasted to feeling that you are a failure and don't amount to much. Think of worthwhileness as the top, sense of failure as the bottom.	8.1	.21	.39
To what extent do you feel there is a good deal you can do yourself to make your life happier and more satisfying than it is, as contrasted to the feeling that there isn't very much you can do about it yourself. Let the top of the ladder stand for being able to do a good deal for yourself, the bottom stand for a feeling of rather complete helplessness.	7.6	.29	.35
How about your confidence in yourself in general--that is, how sure you feel of yourself. Think of the top of the ladder as complete confidence in yourself, the bottom as not being at all sure of yourself.	7.4	.28	.31
Would you say that, by and large, you enjoyed yourself yesterday? Let's see, yesterday was: _____. Think of the top as having enjoyed yourself a lot, the bottom as not at all.	7.3	.25	.38
Now, how about the extent to which you feel you have an opportunity to do what you would like to do, as contrasted to the feeling that you are doing only what you have "got" to do. Think of the top of the ladder as being completely free to do what you want to do, the bottom as doing only what you have to do.	7.0	.32	.46
How would you rate yourself as to how successful or unsuccessful you have been in terms of achieving your own goals and aims in life? Think of the top of the ladder as being completely successful, the bottom as being entirely unsuccessful.	6.7	.39	.45
To what extent do you feel your life is full of troubles or obstacles? This time think of the top of the ladder as indicating a person whose life is mainly a whole series of problems and obstacles he is facing and the bottom as a person without troubles or obstacles.	4.3	-.25	-.35
To what extent are you worried or afraid that things might get worse for you and your family; that is, to what extent are you anxious that such things as your financial situation, your security, your health, your social position, your opportunities, etc., might become worse than they are now? This time think of the top of the ladder as indicating you are extremely worried; the bottom indicating you are not at all worried.	4.1	-.27	-.24

[a] See Table 1.

[b] See footnote 3.

APPENDIX B

Measures used in the Bachman et al. (1967) study and the distribution of responses to these questions by a cross-section of 2,500 tenth-grade boys. Reproduced from Arscott (1968).

(R - reversed item)

		Almost always true	Often true	Sometimes true	Seldom true	Never true	Missing data
		(1)	(2)	(3)	(4)	(5)	

SATISFACTION WITH LIFE

		(1)	(2)	(3)	(4)	(5)	
A28	I generally feel in good spirits	23%	48%	22%	5%	1%	1%=100%
A51	I am very satisfied with life	23	33	29	11	4	1
A65	I find a good deal of happiness in life	30	39	23	5	2	2

SELF-ESTEEM (Rosenberg)

		(1)	(2)	(3)	(4)	(5)	
A5	I feel that I'm a person of worth, at least on an equal plane with others	29%	38%	26%	5%	1%	2%=100%
A9	I feel that I have a number of good qualities	18	42	33	5	1	2
A19	I am able to do things as well as most other people	17	47	31	5	-	1
A24	I feel I do not have much to be proud of (R)	5	9	17	30	37	2
A29	I take a positive attitude toward myself.	18	38	34	8	1	1
A39	Sometimes I think I am no good at all (R)	5	12	30	35	18	1

SELF-ESTEEM (Cobb)

		(1)	(2)	(3)	(4)	(5)	
A1	I am a useful guy to have around.	17	41	39	2	-	-
A13	I feel that I can't do anything right (R)	4	8	22	37	29	1
A48	When I do a job, I do it well	17	41	36	4	1	1
A63	I feel that my life is not very useful (R).	4	6	20	34	34	2

		Almost always true (1)	Often true (2)	Sometimes true (3)	Seldom true (4)	Never true (5)	Missing data

LACK OF SOCIAL SUPPORT

		(1)	(2)	(3)	(4)	(5)	
A73	I feel that nobody wants me	4	6	22	36	31	2
A82	I feel lonesome	6	11	28	34	20	1
A90	These days my parents really help out; they don't let me down (R)	25	30	30	11	7	1
A101	I feel loved (R).	20	29	35	12	3	1

ANOMIE

A23	No one cares what happens, when you get right down to it	6	11	25	32	24	1
A31	The life of the average man is getting worse, not better	13	19	26	26	15	1
A36	People don't really care what happens to the next fellow	7	23	36	27	7	1
A41	I get the feeling that life is not very useful	4	7	19	35	34	2
A45	These days I get the feeling that I'm just not a part of things	5	14	35	32	12	1
A53	These days I don't know who I can depend on	7	19	33	28	12	1
A98	It is hardly fair to bring a child into the world the way things look now	7	12	25	31	25	1
A107	I feel no one really cares much about what happens to me	4	9	25	36	25	1

APPENDIX B (cont.)

		Almost always true (1)	Often true (2)	Sometimes true (3)	Seldom true (4)	Never true (5)	Missing data

DEPRESSION

A70	I feel the future looks bright (R)	23	36	30	8	2	1
A88	Things seem hopeless	3	6	22	39	30	1
A89	I feel bored	5	12	33	35	14	1
A93	I feel down in the dumps	4	8	29	40	18	2
A96	I feel depressed	3	9	31	40	17	1
A111	**I am bothered by noise**	5	13	33	34	14	1

SADNESS

A20	I feel like smiling (R).	21	41	29	6	1	1
A35	I feel happy (R)	25	47	24	4	1	1
A110	I feel sad	3	8	33	41	15	1

RESENTMENT

A56	Although I don't show it, I am very jealous	9	13	24	34	18	2
A72	I am likely to hold a grudge	5	10	25	43	17	1
A75	When I look back on what's happened to me, I feel cheated	1	10	30	37	18	1
A76	I don't seem to get what is coming to me	4	10	33	37	15	1
A78	I feel I get a raw deal out of life	4	7	23	41	25	1
A83	If I let people see the way I really feel, they would think I was hard to get along with	9	12	28	34	15	1
A85	Other people always seem to get the breaks	10	21	43	21	4	1

APPENDIX C

Product-Moment Correlations of Items on Feelings Scale
(Males, age 25-49 only)

Bradburn and Caplovitz, 1965

Items from Feelings Check-List	Proud	Excited	Top of World	Uneasy	Restless	Bored	Lonely	Depressed
Positive cluster								
Pleased about having accomplished something	.47	.38	.31	.03	-.09	-.11	-.14	-.13
Proud because someone complimented you on something you had done	--	.28	.26	.11	.01	-.10	-.08	-.02
Particularly excited or interested in something		--	.31	.08	.03	-.02	-.08	.04
On top of the world			--	-.09	-.14	-.12	-.16	-.19
Negative cluster								
Vaguely uneasy about something without knowing why				--	.34	.31	.31	.38
So restless you couldn't sit long in a chair					--	.38	.31	.38
Bored						--	.40	.45
Very lonely or remote from other people							--	.54
Depressed or very unhappy								--
Rejected negative items								
Angry at something that usually wouldn't bother you								
That you had more things to do than you could get done								
That you couldn't do something because you just couldn't get going								

CHAPTER 3 - THE MEASUREMENT OF SELF-ESTEEM AND RELATED CONSTRUCTS*

The construct of self-esteem has been used by many people in diverse ways. Gordon and Gergen (1968), Shaver (1969), Wylie (1961, 1968) and others have amply reviewed the use of the construct since William James (1890). While most people acknowledge having a sense of self, research in the area of self-esteem has been plagued with ambiguities. Reviews of the literature (e.g., Wylie, 1961) suggest that self-esteem has been related to almost every variable at one time or another. Despite the popularity of self-esteem, no standard theoretical or operational definition exists. Careful work is needed to put self-esteem research on a sound footing.

Definition

Self-esteem is defined here simply as liking and respect for oneself which has some realistic basis. Self-acceptance means accepting oneself. Self-acceptance and self-esteem are empirically and conceptually related. In general, self-acceptance might be considered a necessary but not suffi-cient basis for high self-esteem. Researchers may often attempt to distin-guish conceptually between self-esteem and self-acceptance. However, em-pirically the two are usually highly related (e.g., the Bills scale). One of the few instruments which offers empirical support for a distinction is the POI self-actualization measure (a construct related to self-esteem as discussed later). In this instance, the correlation between the self-regard (another synonym for self-esteem) and self-acceptance sub-scales is only .21. One probable explanation is that the self-regard sub-scale in-

The author would like to thank the many people who communicated information to him. Interested readers are invited to point out mistakes, omissions, and new information; he can be reached through the doctoral program in Social Psychology at The University of Michigan, Ann Arbor, Mi.

volves affirmation of one's good points while the self-acceptance scale involves the admission and acceptance of negative characteristics. The relevant point, however, is that various measurement approaches can lead to different relations between self-acceptance and self-esteem, or between esteem
and the behaviors in which we are interested.

The ways in which self-concept has been operationalized are even more
diverse than the related labels which have been used. Conceptually, different labels often have different meanings. Empirically, however, such distinctions can often be ignored, as in the extreme case of Upshaw and Yates'
(1968) use of a measure of social desirability as a measure of self-esteem
with perfect empirical justification.

Measurement Approaches

The approach one decides to use to measure self-esteem reflects assumptions which are in themselves testable. For instance, a general assumption
is that self-reports are valuable. The extent to which they are should be
tested by correlating self-reports with behavior and other criteria. Self-
reports involve certain givens no matter what format is used; forced-choice
scales, Likert scales, and Guttman scales all have a direct self-report
factor in common. In addition each scaling method involves different procedures which can be tested for their effect on self-reports. Unfortunately,
little research has been done on the relative values of self-report methods.[1]
Each measure reviewed here tends to use a different format. Because of the
lack of evidence on the general values of different formats, they are not

---

[1]Little guidance is available even on the basic question of how many response categories to use. Using content variables other than self-esteem,
some research finds no difference in validity or reliability between 2, 3,
4, or even 19 response levels (Matell and Jacoby, 1971), while other research
suggests that 7 is indeed a magic number (e.g., Finn, 1972).

discussed in detail here.

Most important, but still ignored for all types of measurement, are the specific items (whether adjectives, phrases, etc.) which make up the scales. Most factor analyses or conceptual breakdowns of self-esteem scales reveal several dimensions (e.g., Bailey, 1970; Berger, 1968; Smith 1960, 1962). Theoretically, self-esteem is directly tapped only by asking people how much they like themselves. However, dimensions of self-esteem emerge when people are asked about their responses to different aspects of themselves: physical, mental, moral, in school, with people, at work, etc. Two basic theoretical points arise with regard to these various dimensions. First, some important dimensions for each unique individual may not be included (e.g., Snygg and Combs, 1949); that is, different people may derive esteem from widely differing sources. By letting people define their own dimensions, these important but perhaps unique sources of esteem can be tapped. Second, perhaps a gain in our precision of measuring overall self-esteem can be accomplished by weighting sub-areas according to importance rather than by just combining them additively; this also takes into account individual differences in sources of esteem.

Both these points seem worth considering, but so far neither has been empirically validated. Although two scales presented here--one by Miskimins, the other by Sherwood--allow individuals to define some rating scales for themselves, neither author has reported any gain in validity from these personal items. Weighting items by importance to self-concept is also theoretically appealing. Here again, however, there is no convincing evidence that added validity is gained by this sophistication. The Sherwood Scale also includes this possibility, but the only real support for weighting has come from three studies with the Secord and Jourard physical esteem scale. Watkins and Park (1972) obtained especially good results.

The fact that specific operationalizations of these two theoretical refinements of simple additive scales have not proved useful does not mean that they will not prove so in the future. In our current state of research, development of basic items is probably most important; however, eventually the frontier of improvements in measurement will probably involve added sophistication in techniques such as these and Miskimins' double-centering technique.

When we turn to approaches for measuring self-esteem, beyond the measurement of esteem in various areas, added theoretical and empirical dimensions suggest themselves. Super et al. (1963) defined seven self-concept dimensions[2] and six self-concept systems[3] which they felt were useful in understanding self-concept. In one test of this formulation, twelve of these aspects reduced to five factors which suggests that not all thirteen aspects of esteem need be considered for comprehensive measurement (Bailey, 1970).

In addition to work from the conceptual side which can suggest areas to be measured reflecting self-esteem, empirical analyses of self-esteem inventories generally suggest that more than just liking for self is being measured in practice. For instance, in many of the reviews which follow, anxiety is found to relate strongly to self-esteem (i.e.-.60). Since anxiety can also be conceptually related to self-esteem, it seems reasonable to include anxiety-type items in self-esteem measures, as many scales do.

One can also suggest behaviors such as assertiveness or risk-taking which might be related to self-esteem. In areas of esteem which are largely

---

[2]Self-esteem, clarity, abstraction, refinement, certainty, stability, and realism.

[3]Structure, scope, harmony, flexibility, idiosyncrasy, and regnancy.

objective (e.g., social behaviors) self-reporting biases may be reduced and validation may be possible through direct behavioral observations, peer ratings, etc. While any one behavioral criterion of self-esteem may be quite imperfectly related to "true self-esteem," by using several such imperfect criteria considerable accuracy can be gained (assuming that error variance tends to be random). When a multidimensional measure is used, the pattern or profile of an individual's self-esteem can give us additional information. By discovering what facets of self-esteem relate to particular criteria, our overall understanding of self-esteem is also increased. Eventually, the use of behavior to measure esteem is bound to improve measurement in this area.

The self-ideal discrepancy has been proposed as one criterion of self-esteem, although it is only questionnaire "behavior." This approach assumes that people with high self-esteem are living up to their ideals. People are asked to rate both their ideal and actual responses to each item; the relationship between ideal and actual responses is computed so that a low discrepancy or high correlation between the two sets of ratings indicates high esteem. This idea was first introduced with the Q-sort procedure in which clinical patients sorted statements into normal distributions as true or false to varying degrees of their ideal and actual selves. At the time it was introduced, this method was novel and exciting. The idea of measuring self-esteem as a discrepancy between each individual's ideal and real selves was a significant theoretical breakthrough. In many ways, however, the theoretical potential of this technique has not been reflected in empirical results. What little evidence exists suggests that ideal ratings control very little variance (e.g., Wylie, 1961) and simple self-ratings are generally at least as valuable (e.g., see the Worchel and Bills measures in this chapter).

At their worst, discrepancy measures generate results as unsatisfactory as Hamilton's (1971) data in which ideal-self discrepancies on the Leary Interpersonal checklist were only related at the .20 to .25 level to the CPI and Janis-Field measures and were totally unrelated to peer ratings (-.02). Another discrepancy measure (Weinberger, 1951) which was widely used in one research area (e.g., Stotland and Dunn, 1962) was found to be unrelated to several apparently similar scales (Taylor and Reitz, 1968). In a case like this, the instrument may have caused poor results in the research. When discrepancy scores are created from rating statements that are not in themselves salient, the discrepancy measure may be better (e.g., the Miskimins Scale), but this advantage is probably offset by the possible increase in error variance.

The point is that the discrepancy approach does not directly measure self-esteem, but that it is a theoretical derivation. Such scores are often highly correlated with direct measures of self-esteem (e.g., the Bills and the Worchel measures), but they are derivations. As a measure of one aspect of self-esteem used with others, the discrepancy approach may yet prove useful. However, as a sole measure of self-esteem there are many drawbacks to most discrepancy measures, a few of which can be listed here:

1) Adjustment and self-ideal discrepancy may be curvilinearly related, making it difficult to select high- and low-esteem people who also differ in adjustment (e.g., Block and Thomas, 1955).

2) People may differ in the tendency to see discrepancies between anything in its actual and ideal state in ways unrelated to self-esteem (e.g., Levy, 1956; Wilcox and Fretz, 1971).

3) Self-ideal discrepancies may increase as a function of age

or cognitive complexity, without suggesting that older or more intelligent people have lower esteem (e.g., Katz and Zigler, 1967).

4) There is little evidence that discrepancy scores are better than simple self-report scores on the same scale, and some evidence exists to the contrary (see the reviews of the various discrepancy measures such as the Bills and Worchel scales.)

Measurement Validity

The central problem in self-esteem research is validity. Because validity has been ignored in the past it will be repeatedly emphasized here. The general lack of psychometric work in this area makes it easy to criticise all existing measures. However, the emphasis here is on organizing what little psychometric work has been done so that future directions for validation become clearer. Research must deal with careful operationalization to make self-esteem research valuable. Subsequent findings can then improve our knowledge. When findings are negative, the construct suffers even if it is the measures that are at fault. In a very real sense, such as in the case of IQ, the concept is literally that which is measured.

Unfortunately, such validation data are largely missing in the self-concept area. What is needed to realize the potential of the self-concept is painstaking hard work. We must have individual item and format analyses against detailed criteria before real progress in measurement can be made. And the ability to measure self-esteem is the prerequisite sine qua non for useful research in this area.

In her first book, Wylie reviewed over a hundred measures of self concept (1961). In her forthcoming revision (Wylie, in press) she will probably face at least twice that number, despite her earlier pleas for more attention to measurement problems and less to measurement generation.

Two forces seem to contribute to the number of measures in the field. First, it is tempting to create one's own measure and, in many cases, interesting results are obtained with such measures. Second, since no clearly superior measures exist it is difficult to decide what measure to use even if we want to build on previous work.

There are two ways in which measurement will improve in this area. First, if new scales are introduced which are supported by massive validation data, and second, if usage is concentrated on a few scales causing the gradual accumulation of validity data. Except for items written specifically for unique research populations, the casual generation of new scales is professionally irresponsible. The same careful attention researchers give to their basic experimental design should be invested in their choice of the scale they will use. At present one cannot determine whether the problems in research areas using self-esteem are conceptual or whether they are due to the diverse and unvalidated measures.

When possible, reviews in this chapter cover convergent validity (the extent to which a scale relates to supposedly similar measures), discriminant validity (the extent to which a scale does not tap irrelevant constructs), and predictive validity (the extent to which a scale predicts relevant criteria). The problem of establishing validity has been discussed by Campbell (1960), Campbell and Fiske (1959), Cronbach and Meehl (1955), Wylie (1961), and others. The general perspective taken here about validity is almost one of common sense. It requires much work to demonstrate that one has a valid measure of a trait, such as self-esteem, which cannot be

measured in any completely objective sense. Because of this problem some
critics (e.g., Mischel, 1968) have been able to suggest that basic personality dimensions may not in fact exist.

Viewed from a common sense perspective, problems like social desirability become straightforward. Once validity is established for a self-
esteem measure, if a measure of social desirability correlates with the
criterion or the measure, the social desirability scale becomes suspect.
The theoretical relationship between social desirability and self-esteem
is not always kept clear. It _is_ socially desirable to have high esteem,
and esteem may be generated by social reinforcement. However, people with
high esteem should have less need for social approval (i.e., less conformity).
The area of defensiveness is also unclear. High-esteem people probably
differ in quality of defenses rather than quantity (i.e., repression vs.
sensitization), but little decisive research has been done here.

When the theoretical issues are made clear, social desirability scales
can also be seen to have many problems. In the Campbell-Fiske sense, the
researcher would need valid measures of social desirability to distinguish
it from self-esteem. The statistical desirability scales,[4] like those of
Edwards, are confounded with adjustment. Moreover, the "lie-type" scales,
such as the Marlowe-Crowne, may discriminate among people on factors such
as the tendency to make sweeping generalizations, which may be irrelevant
to defensiveness or need for approval. Norman (1967) provides a conceptualization of social desirability which clarifies this concept.

People interested in self-esteem need not solve _all_ measurement problems. If a careful validation program is undertaken with the realization
that it is a multi-man-year project, self-esteem measurement can be put on

[4]Chosen because of endorsement rates (i.e., on statistical grounds).

a sound footing. Hundreds of items need to be tested in various formats against multi-determined criteria on large, cross replicated samples. Good criteria are difficult to justify, but past empirical and theoretical work has suggested many which may be valid if used in combination. Peer, teacher, or other "behavioral" ratings are the simplest adequate criteria. Other possible criteria are behaviors such as optimism, risk-taking, assertiveness, conformity, acceptance of others, rejection of false information about one-self (Gruen, 1960), anxiety, expression of aggression, and reactions to failure. Separate investigators could each use a battery of such criteria with particular esteem items. This can be done independently and some existing data could be used to select items for cross validation. There are problems with empirical item selection, but these can be overcome if results are cross replicated. In addition, internal item analyses are not ruled out before and after items are validated against internal criteria.

It may be optimistic to think that this sort of systematic validational work can be undertaken even by many people working over a number of years. Perhaps with this goal in mind, however, others will take up the challenge which seems too immense for one or two people. The procedures suggested here have been accessible to psychologists for over a decade. The basic item pool and knowledge are present several times over. Only a few new approaches to these problems have appeared since the early 1960's (e.g., Epstein, 1973). In 1961 several reviews and critiques appeared which could have led to the strategy suggested here (Crowne and Stephens, 1961; Lowe, 1961; Strong and Feder, 1961; and Wylie, 1961). While a few researchers investigated the problems they raised (Crowne et al., 1961; Strong, 1962), no programmatic measurement work seems to have ensued. Perhaps the tone of these criticisms discouraged interest in serious validation work.

Most of the following scales could provide a good start toward better measures using the strategy suggested here. Hopefully, the often critical tone of the reviews in this chapter will encourage the strengthening of measurement research in this area by implicitly suggesting ways in which each measure can be improved.

What Is Included

An attempt has been made to include all measures in the self-concept area which either have been used consistently in published reports or seem to have potential for further development. These include measures labeled self-esteem, ego strength, and self-acceptance, as well as many others.

Measures of three related constructs have not been included in this section. These are anxiety, internality-externality, and social desirability. Many self-esteem scales contain anxiety items, but a review of anxiety scales is beyond the scope of this section and the work with anxiety is well reviewed in volumes edited by Spielberger (1966, 1972). In general, it can be said that anxiety and self-esteem are highly negatively related (e.g., correlations in the -.60's are not unusual). The most used anxiety measures come from the MMPI (e.g., the Manifest Anxiety Scale, Taylor, 1953) and are widely available. Internality-externality (e.g., Rotter, 1966) was previously included in this section but has now expanded to its own chapter. While high esteem and internality are conceptually related, empirically the relationship has only been in the .30's (e.g., Fish and Karabenick, 1971). Social desirability is covered in the chapter on methodological scales. The high positive relationships between self-esteem and social desirability represent an embarrassment for both constructs which invites further research.

The previous self-esteem chapter (Shaver, 1969) included 19 self-esteem and related scales. Two were internality-externality scales now covered in Chapter 4. The present chapter includes 33 self-concept scales plus an annotated bibliography containing over 30 others. Eleven measures are covered in detail in both this and the previous edition, and six of the measures previously covered are in the annotated bibliography. The additional scales represent those which had been omitted from the previous edition (such as the Janis and Field scale) or new scales (such as Miskimins'). A rough attempt has also been made to present the scales in order of their quality even though in this area such an organization is both difficult and somewhat arbitrary. However, a rough ordering by quality has been achieved.

What is Recommended

The first 8 scales, in this author's opinion, represent the best of the current scales specifically designed to measure self-esteem. The next 17 scales represent measures which are more specialized and less focused on self-esteem or which have received less validation work. Most of these could become important scales with additional validation work. The last 8 scales represent constructs less directly related to self-esteem and which have potentially interesting relationships with self-esteem; some of these measures are excellent in their own right.

Several minor innovations in format are introduced in this chapter. Validity is broken down into Convergent, Discriminant, and Predictive categories along the general lines recommended by Campbell and Fiske (1959). Results and Comments are separated into Positive points, Negative points and Suggestions. The inclusion of a brief section annotating additional measures is also new. It is hoped that these changes will make this chapter more useful and complete for users.

A second type of change is that for many scales only a few sample items are presented. This is partly because several of the scales are sold commercially and partly to avoid the careless perpetuation of many scales which are not recommended for wide usage.

The assumption underlying this chapter is that most readers of this section want one good measure[5] and the 8 recommended scales provide a good selection. Personal experience and research (e.g., Chun et al., 1972) suggest that the choice of measures by most researchers bears no relationship to the quality of the measures, perhaps because it is often unclear which are the best measures in an area.

Overview of Scales Reviewed

In line with the strategy of presenting scales in rough order of perceived overall quality, the two most recommended scales-the Tennessee and Piers-Harris scales-are presented first. The first three scales are all widely used:

1. The Tennessee Self-Concept Scale (Fitts 1964)
2. The Piers-Harris Children's Self-Concept Scale (Piers 1969)
3. The Janis-Field Feelings of Inadequacy Scale (Eagly 1967)

Because the first two scales are marketed commercially only sample items can be presented here; the interested reader should order the manual and scale from the publisher. The Tennessee Self-Concept Scale, a 100-item form which includes a ten-item lie scale from the MMPI, has been administered to all but the youngest age groups. The carefully written and widely used Piers-Harris Scale is used with younger age groups. The

-----

[5]This volume is also used as an archival data source. Thus, some scales which are not available elsewhere are included even when they are not recommended.

main difference which makes these scales superior to others is the careful
work their creators have put into them. The Janis-Field Feelings of Inadequacy Scale presented next is probably the most widely used non-commer-
cial scale. It has been popular among persuasibility researchers despite
the ambiguities in the self-esteem and persuasibility area. The version
presented here, developed by Eagly and previously unpublished, has the
advantage of being balanced for response bias. Because of the wide use of
the Janis-Field version, some general validity information has accumulated.

The next two scales were developed for use with younger age groups
but have been widely used with adult samples as well:

4. Self-Esteem Scale (Rosenberg 1965)
5. Self-Esteem Inventory (Coopersmith 1967)

The Rosenberg Scale consists of ten items which measure self-worth or self-
acceptance rather directly. The main validity for the scale is construct
validity developed in Rosenberg's outstanding book. The Coopersmith Inventory was developed from a perspective similar to that of Rosenberg, however it taps many more aspects of self-esteem. The short form resulting
from an item analysis of the original 50-item form is presented here. It
has not previously been available in published form.

The following three scales represent the three main self-ideal discrepancy measures in the literature:

6. The Index of Adjustment and Values (Bills et al., 1951)
7. The Butler-Haigh Q-Sort (Butler and Haigh 1954)
8. The Miskimins Self-Goal-Other Discrepancy Scale (Miskimins 1971)

The first two are older measures dating from the period when this method
was popular, and the third is a relatively new and lesser known commercial
scale which seems to have great potential because of the sophisticated way
in which it is scored. The Bills Scale is essentially an adjective checklist using many different self-descriptive adjectives. It uses a clever

format to compactly measure self-ratings, self-acceptance, and self-ideal discrepancy, as well as optional generalized "other" ratings. The Butler-Haigh Q-Sort is the grandparent of Q-sorts. It measures many components of self-concept and many of its items would probably prove useful in a less time-consuming format. And in fact, both the Bills and Butler-Haigh measures have provided the basis for other scales. The brief and carefully developed Miskimins Scale is the one instrument for which discrepancy scores have proven to be more valuable than direct self-reports, probably because of the particular ratings dimensions included. The scale's main asset is the sophisticated scoring system developed around the idea of expressing an individual's esteem score relative to his other scores (i.e., ipsitized). This general scoring method could well prove valuable with other scales as well.

The four scales below are broad commercial inventories which measure more than just self-esteem.

9. The Personality Research Form (Jackson 1967)
10. The Jackson Personality Inventory (Jackson 1970)
11. The California Psychological Inventory (Gough 1956)
12. The Adjective Check List (Gough and Heilbrun 1965)

They are included for those who wish to measure several variables at once. The Personality Research Form and the Jackson Personality Inventory were developed by Jackson. The PRF does not contain a direct esteem scale, but esteem related scales in the PRF could be useful. The new JPI contains a direct self-esteem scale which emphasizes social behaviors. The widely used California Psychological Inventory contains several subscales which seem to be adequate measures of self-esteem. Many indices related to self-esteem can be derived from an individual's ratings on the 300 adjectives of the Adjective Checklist.

The next group of scales contains three older scales and one of more recent vintage:

13. Self-Perception Inventories (Soares and Soares 1965)
14. The Berger Self-Acceptance Scale (Berger 1952)
15. The Phillips Self-Acceptance Scale (Phillips 1951)
16. The Self-Activity Inventory (Worchel 1957)

The Soares' Self-Perception Inventories are currently used in educational settings. There are many variations covering several types of self and peer ratings. The Berger and Phillips self-acceptance scales are representative of those designed to test the relationship between self-acceptance and acceptance by others. Neither has been used much recently, but both are good sources of useful items. The Worchel Self-Activity, which contains some fairly unique items, was quite well validated at the time of its construction but has not received much validation since the early 1960's.

Attempts to improve measurement methodology are important in the following two scales:

17. The Self-Description Inventory (Cutick 1962)
18. The Sherwood Self-Concept Inventory (Sherwood 1962)

The Self-Description Inventory was devised by Cutick as part of a program of research directed by Diggory and has subsequently been expanded and used by Shrauger and Rosenberg. The rather specific referents of the items, the larger than usual response scale, and other such aspects of this scale make it somewhat unique; however, no work has been done to demonstrate whether these differences are useful. The Sherwood Self-Concept Inventory uses a realistic aspired-self rating instead of an ideal-self rating, unlabeled scales for respondents to define their own rating dimensions, and ratings of the importance of each item for total self-concept. Again, it has not been demonstrated that any of these innovations add to the validity of scores.

Included in the next three scales are two derived from the vast item pool of the MMPI which are still in common usage among those who use the MMPI; the third scale is previously unpublished:

19. The Repression-Sensitization Scale (Byrne 1963)
20. The Barron Ego Strength Scale (Barron 1953)
21. The Thomas-Zander Ego Strength Scales (Thomas and Zander 1960)

Interestingly, the two MMPI-derived scales have only 19 items keyed in common (out of 68 and 127 total), with two items actually keyed in opposite directions. The Byrne Repression-Sensitization Scale is not a self-esteem measure conceptually. Empirically, however, it has a close relationship to self-esteem and has stimulated considerable research. The Barron Ego Strength Scale is more directly related to self-esteem conceptually; however, it was empirically derived without cross validation and the evidence suggests that it is only tangentially related to self-esteem. The fact that many people are not aware of the unrepresentativeness of this scale has caused some unwarranted criticism of self-esteem as a construct; this is a good example of the misleading labeling in this area. The Thomas-Zander Ego Strength Scale has received some interesting validation. The scale represents an attempt to measure ego strength which is probably closer to self-esteem than the Barron Scale, while still retaining some interesting differences.

The next four scales stemmed generally from clinical concerns and have not been widely used:

22. The Body Cathexis Scale (Secord and Jourard 1953)
23. The Self-Report Inventory (Bown 1961)
24. The Twenty Statements (Who Am I?) Test (Kuhn and McPartland 1954)
25. The Who Are You Test (Bugental and Zelen 1950)

The Secord and Jourard Body Cathexis Scale is a very direct measure of satisfaction with various aspects of the physical self; it should be useful to investigators interested in this aspect of self-concept. Although the

Bown Self-Report Inventory has been used successfully as a self-esteem type measure, only six of the items are closely related to self-esteem. The Twenty Statements (Who Am I?) Test and the Who Are You Test each allow respondents to make up to twenty statements about themselves, which can then be classified for esteem-related content. Though this type of free response format has some appeal, its value for measuring self-esteem has not been demonstrated.

The remaining "measures" are of interest largely because of the various issues they raise. They generally point to measurement approaches which could be useful. These speculative reviews conform to the standard review format for measures and so a certain flexibility is sacrificed. It should prove interesting to explore more fully the relationships between self-esteem and some of these measures or approaches:

26. The Social Self-Esteem Scale (Ziller 1969)
27. The Personal Orientation Inventory (Shostrum 1968)
28. The Barclay Classroom Climate Inventory (Barclay 1972)

The Social Self-Esteem Scale devised by Ziller and others uses a unique topological approach to measuring self-concept. Because it does not relate to most other self-concept measures, it raises interesting questions. The Personal Orientation Inventory has been the measure of self-actualization. The relationship between self-actualization and self-esteem is positive but has yet to be fully explored. The Barclay Classroom Climate Inventory is designed to assess a school environment and to suggest strategies for overall change, as well as to provide ratings of each student. This scale attempts to measure far more than self-esteem but is included here because of interesting features such as a multi-method measurement approach.

The next two scales attempt to measure self-concept stability or consistency:

29. The Brownfain Self-Concept Stability Measure (Brownfain 1952)
30. Measure of Self-Consistency (Gergen and Morse 1967)

These constructs tend to be positively related to self-esteem. Tippitt and Silber (1965) report average correlations of .39 and .28 between several measures of self-esteem and self-stability. Stability of the self-concept should be of central interest to projects interested in changing self-esteem. In addition these concepts are of considerable interest in their own right (e.g., Gergen, 1968). The Brownfain self-concept stability measure and the Gergen and Morse self-consistency measure represent two of the many possible approaches to measuring stability or cognitive organization of the self-concept.

Three further measures complete the scale review. These are actually methods chosen to illustrate possible approaches for measuring behavioral and "unconscious" self-esteem:

31. The Duncan Personality Integration Scale (Duncan 1966)
32. The McDaniel Inferred Self-Concept Scale (McDaniel 1969)
33. The Unconscious Self-Evaluation Technique (Beloff and Beloff 1959)

The Duncan Personality Integration Scale and the McDaniel Inferred Self-Concept Scale are used here as examples of behavioral rating approaches. It would be valuable if all attempts to measure self-esteem included behavioral ratings of some kind. Various coding systems have attempted to measure "unconscious" self-esteem. A potentially exciting method of unobtrusively measuring self-concept involves a disguised presentation of the person's picture, handwriting, voice, and so forth. The method presented here was developed by Beloff and Beloff (1959) and involves the disguised presentation of a person's picture. As used by Taylor and Reitz (1968) this method has produced some interesting results. A test of this method against behavior or peer ratings might be especially informative.

Lastly, an annotated bibliography of thirty additional measures is appended which, along with Wylie's review of many more measures, will give the interested reader further exposure to self-concept measurement.

REFERENCES

Bailey, S. Independence and Factor structure of self-concept metadimensions. Journal of Counseling Psychology, 1970, 17, 425-430.

Berger, C.R. Sex differences related to self-esteem factor structure. Journal of Consulting and Clinical Psychology, 1968, 32, 442-446.

Block, J. and Thomas, H. Is satisfaction with self a measure of adjustment? Journal of Abnormal and Social Psychology, 1955, 51, 254-259.

Campbell, D.T. Recommendations for APA test standards regarding construct, trait or discriminant validity. American Psychologist, 1960, 15, 546-553.

Campbell, D.T. and Fiske, C.W. Convergent and discriminant validation by the multitrait-multimethod matrix. Psychological Bulletin, 1959, 56, 81-105.

Chun, K., Barnowe, J., Wykowski, K., Cobb, S., and French, J., Jr. Selection of psychological measures: quality or convenience. Proceedings, American Psychological Association, Hawaii, 1972, 15-16.

Cronbach, L., and Meehl, P. Construct validity in psychological tests. Psychological Bulletin, 1955, 52, 281-302.

Crowne, D. and Stephens, M. Self-acceptance and self-evaluative behavior: A critique of methodology. Psychological Bulletin, 1961, 58, 104-121.

Crowne, D., Stephens, M., and Kelly, R. The validity and equivalence of tests of self-acceptance. Journal of Psychology, 1961, 51, 101-112.

Epstein, S. The self-concept revisited: Or a theory of a theory. American Psychologist, 1973, 28, 404-416.

Finn, R. Effects of some variations in rating scale characteristics on the means and reliabilities of ratings. Educational and Psychological Measurement, 1972, 32, 255-265.

Fish, B. and Karabenick, S. Relationship between self-esteem and locus of control. Psychological Reports, 1971, 29, 784.

Gergen, K. Personal consistency and the presentation of self. The Self in Social Interaction, edited by C. Gordon and K. Gergen, New York: Wiley, 1968.

Gordon, C. and Gergen, K., (eds.) The self in social interaction. Vol. I: Classic and contemporary perspectives. New York: Wiley, 1968.

Gruen, W. Rejection of false information about oneself as an indication of ego identity. Journal of Consulting Psychology, 1960, 24, 231-233.

Hamilton, D. A comparative study of five methods of assessing self-esteem, dominance, and dogmatism. Educational and Psychological Measurement, 1971, 31, 441-452.

James, W. Principles of Psychology. New York: Holt, 1890, 2 vols.

Katz, P. and Zigler, E. Self-image disparity: A developmental approach. Journal of Personality and Social Psychology, 1967, 5, 186-195.

Levy, L.H. The meaning and generality of perceived and actual-ideal discrepancies. Journal of Consulting Psychology, 1956, 20, 396-398.

Lowe, C. Self-concept: Fact or artifact. Psychological Bulletin, 1961, 58, 325-336.

Matell, M. and Jacoby, J. Is there an optimal number of alternatives for Likert scale items? Study 1: Reliability and validity. Educational and Psychological Measurement, 1971, 31, 657-674.

Mischel, W. Personality and assessment. New York: Wiley, 1968.

Norman, W. On estimating psychological relationships: Social desirability and self-report. Psychological Bulletin, 1967, 67, 273-293.

Rotter, J. Generalized expectancies for internal versus external control of reinforcement. Psychological Monographs, 1966, 80, (1, Whole no. 609).

Shaver, P. Measurement of self-esteem and related constructs. In Measures of Social Psychological Attitudes by J.P. Robinson and P.R. Shaver, Ann Arbor, Mich.: Institute for Social Research, 1969.

Smith, P. A factor analytic study of the self-concept. Journal of Consulting Psychology, 1960, 24, 191.

Smith, P. A comparison of three sets of rotated factor analytic solutions of self-concept data. Journal of Abnormal and Social Psychology, 1962, 63, 326-333.

Snygg, D. and Combs, A. Individual behavior: A new frame of reference for psychology. New York: Harper, 1949.

Spielberger, C., ed. Anxiety and Behavior. New York: Academic Press, 1966.

Spielberger, C., ed. Anxiety: Current trends in theory and research. New York: Academic Press, 1972.

Stotland, E., and Dunn, R. Identification, "oppositeness," authoritarianism, self-esteem, and birth order. Psychological Monographs, 1962, 76, (9), 21.

Strong, D. A factor analysis study of several measures of self concept. Journal of Counseling Psychology, 1962, 9, 64-70.

Strong, D. and Feder, D. Measurement of the self-concept: A critique of the literature. Journal of Counseling Psychology, 1961, 8, 170-178.

Super, D., Starishevsky, R., Matlin, N., and Jordaan, J. Career development: Self concept theory. New York: College Entrance Examination Board, 1963.

Taylor, J.B. and Reitz, W.E. The three faces of self-esteem. Research Bulletin #80, Department of Psychology, University of Western Ontario, April, 1968.

Taylor, J. A personality scale of manifest anxiety. Journal of Abnormal and Social Psychology, 1953, 48, 285-290.

Tippett, J., and Silber, E. Self-image stability: The problem of validation. Psychological Reports, 1965, 17, 323-329.

Upshaw, H.S. and Yates, L.W. Self-persuasion, social approval, and task success as determinants of self-esteem following impression management. Journal of Experimental Social Psychology, 1968, 4, 143-152.

Watkins, D. and Park, J. The role of subjective importance in self-evaluation. Australian Journal of Psychology, 1972, 24, 209-210.

Weinberger, B. Achievement motivation and self-concept. Unpublished honors thesis. Ann Arbor, Mich.: University of Michigan, 1951.

Wilcox, Anne and Fritz, B. Actual-ideal discrepancies and adjustment. Journal of Counseling Psychology, 1971, 18, 166-169.

Wylie, Ruth. The Self Concept: Vol. 1. A review of methodological considerations and measuring instruments. Lincoln, Nebraska: University of Nebraska Press, in press.

Wylie, Ruth. The Self-Concept. Lincoln, Nebraska: University of Nebraska Press, 1961.

Wylie, Ruth. The present status of self theory. In Handbook of Personality Theory and Research, edited by E.F. Borgatta and W.W. Lambert, Chicago: Rand McNally, 1968.

TENNESSEE SELF-CONCEPT SCALE (Fitts 1964)

Variable   This is a self-report scale developed from a clinical perspective.
            It measures self-concept across many sub-areas, providing both an
            overall self-esteem score and a complex self-concept profile.

Description The scale was developed from a larger item pool derived from other
            scales and open-ended statements. The 90 statements retained were
            classified by seven clinical psychologists into 15 categories and
            positive and negative content with perfect agreement. The items
            fall into one of five general categories: physical self, moral-
            ethical self, personal self, family self, and social self. Each
            of these areas is in turn divided into statements of self-identity,
            self-acceptance, and behavior. Besides these 90 statements (evenly
            balanced for positivity-negativity), there are also 10 items from
            the MMPI lie scale.

            There are five response categories for each question, running from
            completely true (5) to completely false (1). The total positive
            score for the 90 items comprises the overall self-esteem measure,
            but the various subscores which were developed both conceptually
            and empirically add to the potential of the instrument. In addition
            to scores for the five areas already mentioned (i.e., social, family,
            physical, personal, and moral-ethical), a self-acceptance score
            across the five areas is available along with a variability score re-
            flecting differences in esteem across areas. Other scores consider
            distribution across answer categories, acquiescence bias, Personality
            Integration Score (contrasting health and pathology), and two new
            empirical scales, Number of Integrative Signs and a Self-Actualiza-
            tion Score. Empirical scales cover differences between psychiatric
            groups, subtle defensiveness, and so forth. Computer scoring is
            available from the publisher.

            Thus the instrument can provide a thorough clinical profile of a
            person's self-concept, and contains a useful variability index.

Sample   The norms in the manual are based on 626 people aged 12 through 68.
            However, subsequent research has used a remarkable variety of samples
            of respondents, including groups with personality pathology.

Reliability/ No data bearing on internal consistency are reported. Test-retest
Homogeneity reliability of the total positive score over two weeks was .92, with
            test-retest reliability of various subscores ranging between .70
            to .90.

Validity   Convergent: The scale correlated -.61 with the Butler-Haigh Q-sort
            in a well-conducted study by Leake (1970). It correlated -.70 with
            the Taylor manifest anxiety scale (Manual, 1965). Other correlations
            are reported with major self-esteem inventories. In a factor analy-
            sis by Vincent (1968), self-acceptance and personal self loaded with
            several similar measures, but on a different factor than the self-
            acceptance and self-control scales of the CPI.

Discriminant: The total score did not correlate strongly with the F scale (-.21, Manual, 1965). No correlation with social desirability has been reported (although it is likely that it would be fairly high since the desirability of most of the statements is clear).

Predictive: The scale has been found to relate to clinical indices of psychological "health," relations between many behaviors and self-esteem scores being discussed in the monographs. Most of the emphasis is on concerns of clinical psychologists, although some useful hints for behavior-esteem relationships among more normal individuals are contained in the monographs.

Location
The published scale and manual are available from Counselor Recordings and Tests, Box 6184-Acklen Station, Nashville, Tennessee 37212. Costs are: manual $.80; specimen sets, $1.25; keys, $.90; monographs $2.75 each. Dr. Fitts is located at the Dede Wallace Center, 2410 White Avenue, Nashville, Tennessee 37204. He maintains a bibliography and is interested in updating and compiling new information about the scale.

Administration
The form is self-administered and requires about 20 minutes.

Results & Comments
Positive Points: The scale has most of the positive attributes we would look for in a scale, and an active author. The use of several subscores should be encouraged to give a full picture of the self-concept. Fitts' own work integrating much of the unpublished research is now available in a monograph series (the most useful discussion of the scale is contained in Monograph 3) listed in the references. These can be purchased from the publisher.

Negative points. As mentioned above, social desirability is not controlled, although a lie scale makes it possible to invalidate certain protocols. Distinguishing items more or less susceptible to social desirability effects would constitute a most fruitful refinement of the scale. It appears that the items have not been modified or supplemented since 1955 or 1956.

In her new book, Wylie (in press) takes a much more negative view of this scale largely because of the non-independence of the subscores which can lead to overinterpretation of profiles. Evidence suggests that all subscores are not necessary (Gabel et al., 1973). Other reviews of this scale appear in Buros (1972).

Suggestions: Because this scale is so widely used in clinical practice, it seems appropriate to challenge it more than others. Further analyses of internal consistency and validity should be undertaken using non-clinical behavior criteria such as peer ratings, assertiveness, and goal setting. Reducing the effects of social desirability on items should also be possible.

This scale is worth improving. Surely in over fifteen years of use, data must exist identifying items that do not contribute to the scale which could be replaced by others. Coverage of additional sub-areas could also be included. Hopefully, workers in the area will take up the challenge to use this and other well-developed scales to build newer and better scales item by item. It would also be helpful if the existence of the monographs were more widely known (ads have since appeared in the APA Monitor) and if reviews of unpublished research occasionally appeared in major journals.

Feedback to author

Dr. Fitts is interested in obtaining reports from persons who use the scale.

References

Buros, O., (ed.) The seventh mental measurements yearbook. Highland Park, N.J.: The Gryphon Press, 1972, 364-370.

Fitts, W. Manual: Tennessee self-concept scale. Nashville, Tenn.: Counselor Recordings and Tests, 1964 and 1965.

Fitts, W. Interpersonal competence: The wheel model. (Monograph 2). Nashville, Tenn.: Counselor Recordings and Tests, 1970.

Fitts, W. and Hammer, W. The self concept and delinquency (Monograph 1). Nashville, Tenn.: Counselor Recordings and Tests, 1969.

Fitts, W., et al. The self concept and self-actualization. (Monograph 3). Nashville, Tenn.: Counselor Recordings and Tests, 1971. The best discussion of measurement with the scale in this series.

Fitts, W. The self concept and psychopathology (Monograph 4). Nashville, Tenn.: Counselor Recordings and Tests, 1972.

Fitts, W. The self concept and performance. (Monograph 5). Nashville, Tenn.: Counselor Recordings and Tests, 1972.

Fitts, W. The self concept and behavior: Overview and supplement (Monograph 7). Nashville, Tenn.: Counselor Recordings and Tests, 1972.

Gable, R., LaSalle, A., and Cook, K. Dimensionality of self perception: Tennessee self-concept scale. Perceptual and Motor Skills, 1973, 36, 551-560.

Leake, D. The measurement of self-esteem. Unpublished Masters Thesis, Ohio State University, 1970.

Thompson, W. Correlates of the self concept (Monograph 6). Nashville, Tenn.: Counselor Recordings and Tests, 1972.

Vincent, J. An exploratory factor analysis relating to the construct validity of self concept labels. Educational and Psychological Measurement, 1968, 28, 915-921.

Wylie, Ruth. The self concept: Vol. 1. A review of methodological considerations and measuring instruments. Lincoln, Nebraska: University of Nebraska Press, in press.

Sample items   Note: Because of commercial nature of the Tennessee Self-Concept Scale, only sample items can be reproduced here.

Items are answered on the following scale:

Completely false	Mostly false	Partly false and partly true	Mostly true	Completely true
1	2	3	4	5

1. I have a healthy body. (Physical)

25. I am satisfied with my moral behavior. (Moral)

38. I have a lot of self-control. (Personal)

57. I am a member of a happy family. (Family)

79. I am as sociable as I want to be. (Social)

Each of these items is keyed so that agreement indicates high self-esteem. Thus the total score possible for these five items would be 25. For other items where the scoring is reversed the scale would be reversed before the score was added. Each of the sample items has the sub-area of self-esteem which it represents noted after it.

THE PIERS-HARRIS CHILDREN'S SELF-CONCEPT SCALE (Piers 1969)

Variable
: This self-report scale was developed especially for work with children. Its items cover many areas of self-concept, particularly physical aspects, abilities and personality.

Description
: The original item pool was developed from Jersild's (1952) categories: physical characteristics and appearance, clothing and grooming, health and physical soundness, home and family, enjoyment of recreation, ability in sports and play, ability in school and attitudes toward school, intellectual abilities, special talents, "just me," and personality-character-inner resources-emotional tendencies. There was an original pool of 152 items and a 12 item lie scale. The 152 items were reduced to the final 80 items after two item analyses. In the process the 12 item lie scale was dropped because it didn't discriminate among grades.

The published scale consists of 80 yes-no items. They are clearly written and are balanced for acquiescence. In addition, they tend to be declarative statements, thus avoiding negatives or double negatives and contributing to clarity. In a factor analysis on 457 6th graders six interpretable factors emerged: 1) statements of behavior, 2) school related standing, 3) physical appearance, 4) anxiety, 5) social popularity, and 6) happiness. Some items loaded on up to three factors. Other comments about these factors are noted under "Results and Comments."

Sample
: During the original item analyses 15 classrooms of students in grades three through ten were used. Norms are presented for 1183 school children subsequently tested.

Reliability
: Using a preliminary 95 item scale, alpha coefficients[1] ranged from .78 to .93.

Test-retest stability was about .72 for four months for the 95 item scale and .77 for a large sample with the 80 item scale (two and four month intervals).

Validity
: Convergent: The manual cites largely unpublished information suggesting that the scale correlates positively with the Lipsitt self-concept scale (.68) and negatively with anxiety and similar measures (-.48 to -.69), as would be predicted.. More interestingly, teacher and peer ratings of self-concept, social effectiveness or superego strength correlated from .06 to .49 with scores.

Discriminant: Correlations with social desirability scores (manual, p. 16) ranged from .25 to .45. This is low for a scale which was not purposely constructed to avoid this source of contamination.

---

[1] Alpha is equivalent to the average of all split half coefficients for a test. Generally considered the lower bound of true reliability (Cronbach, L. Psychometrika, 1951, 16, 297-334.)

Predictive: Correlations with achievement and intelligence scores tend to be low and positive.

Interestingly, for a scale which underemphasizes family-parent items, self-esteem correlated .56 with the child's perception of each parent as loving (Manual, p. 15) and parental disagreement with regard to accepting-rejecting rearing practices was negatively related to self-esteem (-.24). In addition, peer acceptance over four years correlated .61 with self-esteem. Technically these later correlations are not predictions from self-esteem, though they can give us valuable information about self-esteem.

Location
Piers, Ellen, and Harris, Dale. The Piers-Harris Children's Self Concept Scale. Counselor Recording and Tests, Box 6184 Acklen Station, Nashville, Tennessee 37212, 1969.

Administration
Self-administered individually or in groups. Requires greater supervision below the third grade level. Suggested time of administration is 15-20 minutes.

Results and Comments
Positive points: Because the manual contains considerable relevant information for users, there is more information about this scale available than for most. In addition, it has many positive characteristics. The items are carefully written and the content is generally broad. The authors (Piers, 1969) seem aware of the many pitfalls which can hamper scales of this nature and hopefully will continue to improve the scale further to take them into account.

Negative points: There is very little work relating esteem to behavior and relations with the main criteria available (peer and teacher ratings) are played down. Hopefully, future research will look at behaviors which might be expected to relate to self-esteem such as assertiveness, conformity, risk-taking, expression of aggression, optimism, and so forth. The manual underplays the importance of the low convergence with teacher and peer ratings (.05 to .49) since "from the phenomenological point of view it is irrelevant whether the self-concept corresponds to ratings by others" (Piers, 1969, p. 6). Peer-type ratings are important since other types of construct validity can seldom partially control factors such as social desirability or intelligence. The utility of rating people both on phenomenological and behavioral esteem has been shown (e.g., Coopersmith, 1967). In addition, if self-esteem can have unconscious components, the congruence of self-report and behavior could contain valuable information about "true esteem." Of course, item analysis data are also lacking, as is the case on all self-esteem scales.

Suggestions: This should continue to be a useful scale for researchers. However, it is important to remember that for research purposes unchanging items and norms are not as valuable as improved scales. The following suggestions might be useful for future scale development:

1) The scale contains few items related to parents or family. This may be a content area worthy of further development in research with children. However, in light of two of the previously cited correlations, specific items may not be necessary to tap this dimension.

2) It seems possible that items reflecting cognitive organization would prove valuable (e.g., "I make up my mind easily").

3) Items that tend to have low loadings on several factors (e.g., 8, 49, 57) may reflect more general desirability than esteem. These items could be checked in itemetric analyses with old data and if true would recommend that items be anchored in specific content.

4) Breaking the scale down into areas is useful. However, the first factor essentially reflects reported goodness or badness (e.g., "I do many bad things"). This factor may not be useful for behavior predictions. If it related to teacher ratings but not peer ratings or more strongly to teacher ratings than other factors, this would suggest a halo effect due to teachers rating well-behaved children better.

5) Some empirical relations can be considered in selecting items without capitalizing on random variance. Although this process would be slow, it could build scales to predict specific behaviors. These scales could then enlarge the nomological network of findings by testing predictions concerning other behaviors.

References   Coopersmith, S. The antecedents of self-esteem. San Francisco: W.H. Freeman & Co., 1967.

Jersild, A. In search of self. Teachers College, Columbia University, Bureau of Publications, New York, 1952.

Piers, Ellen. Manual for the Piers-Harris Children's Self Concept Scale, Nashville, Tennessee: Counselor Recordings and Tests, 1969.

Piers, Ellen and Harris, D. The Piers-Harris Children's Self-Concept Scale. Nashville, Tenn. Counselor Recordings and Tests, 1969.

Sample   NOTE: Because of the commercial nature of this scale, only sample items can be reporduced here.

12. I am well behaved in school. (Factor 1, Behavior)

16. I have good ideas. (Factor 2, Intellectual)

54. I am good looking. (Factor 3, Physical)

74. I am often afraid. (Factor 4, Anxiety)

51. I have many friends. (Factor 5, Popularity)

2. I am a happy person. (Factor 6, Happiness)

Feedback   Dr. Piers is interested in obtaining reports from persons who
to Author   use the scale.

JANIS-FIELD FEELINGS OF INADEQUACY SCALE (Eagly 1967)

Variable	This scale was originally designed to measure feelings of inadequacy in studies relating to a person's persuasibility. The items generally concern esteem in social areas such as assertiveness.
Description	Because of its use by Janis and others in early persuasibility research (Hovland and Janis, 1959), this scale has seen wide usage. The original scale had 23 items of which all but two are keyed in the same direction. The revised version by Eagly presented here contains 20 items, answered on five-point Likert scales and balanced for response bias.

Some of the items derive from an earlier Janis article (1954). No information on construction is given. Items seem to rely on rational judgment for validity. No item analyses have been done by the Janis group. Janis' earlier work (1954), which served as a model for this scale, also generated the Rosenbaum and DeCharms (1960) scale which was modified by League and Jackson (1964) and has been used recently by Marcia (e.g., Marcia and Friedman, 1970) in relation to ego development. Berger (1968) constructed similar unpublished items.

Sample	The original Janis and Field sample consisted of 185 high school juniors. The scale has subsequently been used mainly with college students, by Eagly and by others.
Reliability/ Homogeneity	Eagly presents split-half reliabilities of .72 (1967) and .88 (1969) for two samples and a correlation of .54 between the positive and negative halves (Eagly 1967).

Taylor and Reitz (1968) estimated split-half reliability at .80 for the ten-item League and Jackson (1964) version.

Split-half reliability was .83 for the original scale. In an analysis of the original form, Skolnick and Shaw (1970) report an average interitem correlation of about .30, not counting items 3 and 4 which did not correlate well with the rest of the scale; item 4 is not in the Eagly version but item 3 appears as item 19.

Validity	<u>Convergent</u>: With an experiment intervening, the Eagly version correlated .84 with the Berger scale (Eagly, personal communication).

The Janis and Field version correlated .67 with the CPI esteem scale and .60 with self-ratings of esteem (Hamilton, 1971). It also correlated .45 with Barron ego strength and .41 with a discrepancy measure (Larsen and Schwendiman, 1969). The original scale correlated significantly with test anxiety (Hovland and Janis, 1959, p. 61).

<u>Discriminant</u>: Hamilton (1971) found low correlations with self-ratings of dominance and openmindedness, indicating some divergent validity (<u>r</u>'s vary between -.36 and .14).

Greenbaum (1966) reported a correlation of only .35 with the Marlowe-Crowne social desirability scale.

<u>Predictive</u>: Occasionally the scale has weakly predicted persuasibility (Hovland and Janis, 1959, p. 61); however, there is considerable ambiguity in the area. Hamilton (1971) found correlations of .24 and .27 with peer ratings of self-esteem and dominance, and -.09 with openmindedness, suggesting something beyond a halo effect.

Location The original measure is in <u>Personality and Persuasibility</u>, Hovland, C. and Janis, I., (eds.). New Haven Connecticut: Yale University Press, 1959. However, the unpublished version presented here is recommended because of its balancing for acquiescence.

Administration The form is self-administered and should take 10-15 minutes.

Results and Comments <u>Positive points</u>: This scale has been used in a great deal of research and seems to have some validity despite its ambiguous performance in the persuasibility literature. Perhaps item analyses could be done on existing data.

<u>Negative points</u>: Very little thorough psychometric attention has ever been paid to this scale. It is a good illustration of scale use based more on popularity than on quality, which is understandable considering the usual lack of concern with measurement in the field.

<u>Suggestions</u>: The version presented here can form a solid basis for future scales, particularly as a measure of <u>social</u> self-esteem.

References Berger, C., Sex differences related to self-esteem factor structure. <u>Journal of Consulting and Clinical Psychology</u>, 1968, <u>32</u>, 442-446.

Eagly, Alice H. Involvement as a determinant of response to favorable and unfavorable information. <u>Journal of Personality and Social Psychology</u>, Monograph, Vol. 7, No. 3, November 1967 (Whole No. 643), 1-15.

Eagly, Alice H. Sex differences in the relationship between self-esteem and susceptibility to social influence. <u>Journal of Personality</u>, 1969, <u>37</u>, 581-591.

Greenbaum, C. Effect of situational and personality variables on improvisation and attitude change. <u>Journal of Personality and Social Psychology</u>, 1966, <u>4</u>, 260-269.

Hamilton, D. A comparative study of five methods of assessing self-esteem, dominance, and dogmatism. <u>Educational and Psychological Measurement</u>, 1971, <u>31</u>, 441-452.

Hovland, C. and Janis, I., (eds.) Personality and Persuasibility, New Haven, Conn.: Yale University Press, 1959.

Janis, I. Personality correlates of susceptibility to persuasion. Journal of Personality, 1954, 22, 504-518.

Larsen, K. and Schwendiman, G. Authoritarianism, self-esteem, and insecurity. Psychological Reports, 1969, 25, 229-230.

League, Betty Jo and Jackson, D. Conformity, veridicality, and self-esteem. Journal of Abnormal and Social Psychology, 1964, 68, 113-115.

Marcia, J.E. and Friedman, M.L. Ego identity status in college women. Journal of Personality, 1970, 38, 249-263.

Rosenbaum, M. and deCharms, R. Direct and vicarious reduction of hostility. Journal of Abnormal and Social Psychology, 1960, 60, 105-111.

Skolnick, P. and Shaw, J. Brief note on the reliability of the Janis and Field "Feelings of inadequacy" scale. Psychological Reports, 1970, 27, 732-734.

Taylor, J.B. and Reitz, W.E. The three faces of self-esteem. Research Bulletin #80, University of Western Ontario (Department of Psychology), April, 1968.

REVISED JANIS-FIELD SCALE

This scale has been used with a Likert format, but a semantic differential format would probably be easier and faster. Wording can be adjusted to fit each question:

e.g.,
Very often | Fairly often | Sometimes | Once in a great while | Practically never

I. Items keyed so that an affirmative response indicates low-esteem:

1. How often do you have the feeling that there is <u>nothing</u> you can do well?

2. When you have to talk in front of a class or a group of people your own age, how afraid or worried do you usually feel? (e.g., very afraid)

3. How often do you worry about whether other people like to be with you?

4. How often do you feel self-conscious?

5. How often are you troubled with shyness?

6. How often do you feel inferior to most of the people you know?

7. Do you ever think that you are a worthless individual?

8. How much do you worry about how well you get along with other people?

9. How often do you feel that you dislike yourself?

10. Do you ever feel so discouraged with yourself that you wonder whether anything is worthwhile?

II. Items keyed so that an affirmative response indicates high self-esteem:

1. How often do you feel that you have handled yourself well at a social gathering?

2. How often do you have the feeling that you can do everything well?

3. When you talk in front of a class or a group of people of your own age, how pleased are you with your performance? (e.g., very pleased)

4. How comfortable are you when starting a conversation with people whom you don't know? (e.g., very comfortable)

5. How often do you feel that you are a successful person?

6. How confident are you that your success in your future job or career is assured? (e.g., very confident)

7. When you speak in a class discussion, how sure of yourself do you feel?

8. How sure of yourself do you feel when among strangers?

9. How confident do you feel that some day the people you know will look up to you and respect you?

10. In general, how confident do you feel about your abilities?

Revised Janis-Field (Eagly 1967); unpublished revised measure is used here with permission of Eagly, A. H. Permission from the authors of the original measure in *Personality and Persuasibility*, edited by Hovland, C. and Janis, I., copyright 1959 by Yale University Press, was also obtained.

SELF-ESTEEM SCALE (Rosenberg 1965)

Variable
This scale measures the self acceptance aspect of self-esteem, originally developed for use with high school students.

Description
The scale consists of ten items answered on a four point scale from strongly agree to strongly disagree, although they are scored only as agreement or disagreement. Since all the items revolve around liking and/or approving of the self, the scale probably measures the self-acceptance aspect of self-esteem more than it does other factors.

The scale was designed specifically with brevity and ease of administration in mind. It was designed to be unidimsional which is both a strength and a limitation. Actual development of the items and scale is not discussed except that it was meant to be a Guttman scale. Persumably this means a larger pool of items was reduced by selecting items (and groups of items) which differed substantially in the numbers of people answering each way. Rosenberg (1965) reports on several other potentially interesting scales: self-stability, faith in people, and sensitivity to criticism.

Sample
A total of 5,024 high school juniors and seniors from 10 randomly selected New York schools make up the main sample reported by Rosenberg. The scale has been used in a wide variety of samples since then.

Reliability/
Homogeneity
A Guttman scale reproducibility coefficient of .92 was obtained. (See comments below.)

Silber and Tippett (1965) found a test-retest correlation over two weeks of .85 (N=28).

Validity
Convergent: Silber and Tippett (1965) found that the scale correlated from .56 to .83 with several similar measures and clinical assessment (N=44). The present author has found the scale scored for Guttman scalability correlated .59 with Coopersmith's Self-esteem Inventory and scored as ten items, .60. Lorraine Broll (personal communication) reports the following correlations: with the CPI self-acceptance scale .27 (N=643), and with a one item esteem scale .45 (N=643) and .66 (N=101).

Discriminant: Correlations with measures of self-stability were substantial (.21 to .53) but it is suggested (in the self-consistency section) that some covariance would be expected. Correlations with (1) stability of ratings of others, and (2) stability of perceptual performance were close to zero (Tippett and Silber, 1965).

Predictive: Rosenberg (1965) presents considerable data about the construct validity of both this measure and self-esteem in general. He relates positive self-esteem to many social and interpersonal consequences such as less shyness and depression, more assertiveness, and more extra-curricular activities. (Many, but fortunately not all, of the dependent measures were also self-reports.)

Location   Rosenberg, M., <u>Society and the Adolescent Self-Image</u>. Princeton, New Jersey: Princeton University Press, 1965. The scale also appeared earlier (Rosenberg, 1962a,b).

Administration   The form is self-administering and would take at most five minutes.

Results and Comments   <u>Positive points</u>: The scale is brief and thorough in measuring the self-acceptance factor of self-esteem. It has high reliability for such a short scale and can be used without the grouping of items necessary for the Guttman format.

<u>Negative points</u>: Not much recent work has been done with the scale and there is no central repository for information for potential users. The Guttman format for scales has been strongly criticized by Nunnally, (1967, p. 61-66) who argues that the small number of items and forced rectangular distribution of items in Guttman scales are artificial and likely to produce only gross, ordinal distinctions among people. Certainly, any empirical advantage of using a Guttman scale to measure self-esteem remains to be demonstrated.

<u>Suggestions</u>: This scale is a model short measure aimed at one aspect of self-esteem, making it similar to a sub-scale from a longer form. In lieu of further empirical work, those wishing a brief scale applicable to various ages could use a scale like this one or the appropriate sub-scale of a longer form.

References   Nunnally, J. <u>Psychometric theory</u>. New York: McGraw-Hill, 1967.

Rosenberg, M. Self-esteem and concern with public affairs. <u>Public Opinion Quarterly</u>, 1962, <u>26</u>, 201-211,(a).

Rosenberg, M. The dissonant religious context and emotional disturbances. <u>American Journal of Sociology</u>, 1962, <u>68</u>, 1-10,(b).

Rosenberg, M. Parental interest and children's self-conceptions. <u>Sociometry</u>, 1963, <u>26</u>, 35-49.

Rosenberg, M. <u>Society and the adolescent self-image</u>. Princeton, N.J.: Princeton University Press, 1965.

Silber, E. and Tippett, Jean. Self-esteem: Clinical assessment and measurement validation. <u>Psychological Reports</u>, 1965, <u>16</u>, 1017-1071.

Tippett, Jean and Silber, E. Self-image stability: The problem of validation. <u>Psychological Reports</u>, 1965, <u>17</u>, 323-329.

SELF-ESTEEM SCALE
(Numbers in parentheses refer to high self-esteem responses)

Items   1. Strongly   2. Agree   3. Disagree   4. Strongly
              agree   disagree

1. I feel that I'm a person of worth, at least on an equal basis with others. (1,2)

2. I feel that I have a number of good qualities. (1,2)

3. All in all, I am inclined to feel that I am a failure. (3,4)

4. I am able to do things as well as most other people. (1,2)

5. I feel I do not have much to be proud of. (3,4)

6. I take a positive attitude toward myself. (1,2)

7. On the whole, I am satisfied with myself. (1,2)

8. I wish I could have more respect for myself. (3,4)

9   I certainly feel useless at times. (3,4)

10. At times I think I am no good at all. (3,4)

For Guttman scaling, two or three correct out of items 1 through 3 are scored as one item, one or two correct of 4 and 5 as one item, and one or two correct of 9 and 10 as one item. It is easier and apparently as valid to score the scale as a simple additive scale.

SELF-ESTEEM INVENTORY (Coopersmith 1967)

Variable   This scale measures evaluative attitudes toward the self in several domains. It was originally devised for use with children, although the form presented here is a briefer unpublished scale recently used by Coopersmith with all ages.

Description   The original pool of items was drawn from Rogers and Dymond (1954) and original research. Five psychologists classified them as indicative of high or low esteem. Fifty items were finally selected on rational grounds and then reduced to 25 items from an item analysis of the responses to the longer form by 121 selected children as reported in Coopersmith (1967). The shorter form correlated over .95 with the longer form.

The items are short statements, generally answered "like me" or "unlike me." They were originally described as covering peers, parents, school, and personal interests.

The present author, using two college samples of over 300 and 200 S's, conducted two factor analyses indicating the scale to be multi-dimensional in nature. Four factors emerged labeled as: self-derogation, leadership-popularity, family-parents, and assertiveness-anxiety. The family-parents factors was the most stable and unambiguous.

In the original work (1967) a behavioral rating scale for teachers was used in conjunction with the self-ratings.

Sample   The original sample contained between 80 and 140 fifth and sixth graders. The scale has subsequently been used with many ages.

Reliability/   Taylor and Reitz (1968) found a .90 split-half reliability for the
Homogeneity long form. No data are available for the shorter form but it would probably be somewhat less stable due to the shorter length. The present author has found inter-item correlations for the short form to be quite low for college students; for example for 453 students the average (absolute) correlation was about .13.

A test-retest reliability for the original 50 item scale was reported as .88 over five weeks and .70 over three years (Coopersmith, 1967, p. 10).

Validity   Convergent: The present author has found correlations of .59 and .60 between the short form and the Rosenberg scale for college students (N about 300). Weinberg (personal communication) reports a correlation of .63 between the Soares scale and the longer Coopersmith scale and .60 between a derived picture test and the long scale (Getsinger, et al., 1972). Taylor and Reitz (1968) report a correlation of .45 between the CPI self-acceptance scale and the longer Coopersmith scale, and correlations of .42 to .66 with other scales. Ziller et al. (1969) found correlations for males of .46 with the Bills scale, .37 with the Cutick scale, and .02 with the Ziller scale; for females, the correlations were .17, .23 and .04 respectively.

Discriminant: Taylor and Reitz (1968) found correlations of .75 and .44 with the Edwards and the Marlowe-Crowne social desirability scales.

Predictive: Coopersmith (1967) builds a nomological net suggesting how positive self-esteem might develop. Briefly, he found that parents of high esteem children report high acceptance of the child, setting clear and explicated rules, setting positive examples, and providing an overall level of quality stimulation and interaction. The entire book builds an outline of how parents might constructively affect children's self-esteem. It would be useful if further work looked at parental variables other than self-report and tested the directionality of some of those relationships.

Location Coopersmith, S. **The Antecedents of Self-Esteem**. San Francisco: W.H. Freeman & Co., 1967.

Administration The form is self-administering and takes about ten minutes.

Results and Comments **Positive points**: The scale has the potential to measure discrete sub-areas (such as family or social) of esteem. Coopersmith (1967) provides more validation than exists for many scales. Many of the individual items could probably prove valuable in future refinements. With slight wording changes the scale can be used with all ages.

Negative points: No systematic validation work has been undertaken on the scale. The high correlations with social desirability must be considered a problem. No collection point of information for users exists.

Suggestions: This short scale has considerable flexibility in measuring the family, social, self-acceptance, and anxiety-assertiveness areas of the self-concept for various ages. However, the low inter-item correlations along with a tendency for some items to load on more than one factor suggests that some further addition and selection of items might be useful.

Feedback to Author Dr. Coopersmith (Dept. of Psychology, University of California at Davis) would appreciate hearing about work with the scale.

References
Coopersmith, S. **The antecedents of self-esteem**. San Francisco: W.H. Freeman & Co., 1967.

Getsinger, S., Kunce, J., Miller, D., and Weinberg, S. Self-esteem measures and cultural disadvantagement. **Journal of Consulting and Clinical Psychology**, 1972, **38**, 149.

Rogers, C. and Dymond, R. **Psychotherapy and personality change**. Chicago: University of Chicago Press, 1954.

Taylor, J. and Reitz, W. The three faces of self-esteem. Department of Psychology, the University of Western Ontario, Research Bulletin #80, April, 1968.

Ziller, R., Hagey, Joan, Smith, Mary Dell, and Long, Barbara. Self-esteem: a self-social construct. **Journal of Consulting and Clinical Psychology**, 1969, **33**, 84-95.

SELF-ESTEEM INVENTORY

Items are answered either "like me" or "unlike me." The high esteem response is indicated in parentheses after each item.

1. I often wish I were someone else. (Unlike me)

2. I find it very hard to talk in front of a group. (Unlike me)

3. There are lots of things about myself I'd change if I could.
   (Unlike me)

4. I can make up my mind without too much trouble. (Like me)

5. I'm a lot of fun to be with. (Like me)

6. I get upset easily at home. (Unlike me)

7. It takes me a long time to get used to anything new. (Unlike me)

8. I'm popular with people my own age. (Like me)

9. My family expects too much of me. (Unlike me)

10. My family usually considers my feelings. (Like me)

11. I give in very easily. (Unlike me)

12. It's pretty tough to be me. (Unlike me)

13. Things are all mixed up in my life. (Unlike me)

14. Other people usually follow my ideas. (Like me)

15. I have a low opinion of myself. (Unlike me)

16. There are many times when I'd like to leave home. (Unlike me)

17. I often feel upset about the work that I do. (Unlike me)

18. I'm not as nice looking as most people. (Unlike me)

19. If I have something to say, I usually say it. (Like me)

20. My family understands me. (Like me)

21. Most people are better liked than I am. (Unlike me)

22. I usually feel as if my family is pushing me. (Unlike me)

23. I often get discouraged at what I am doing. (Unlike me)

24. Things usually don't bother me. (Like me)

Self-Esteem Inventory (Coopersmith 1967). Copyright 1967 by W. H. Freeman and Company. Reprinted here with permission.

*25. I can't be depended on. (Unlike me)

Additional items which discriminated well (from the 50 item form):

14. I'm proud of my school work. (Like me)

24. I'm pretty happy. (Like me)

33. No one pays much attention to me at home. (Unlike me)

46. Kids pick on me very often. (Unlike me)

---

*This is a weak item for college students since less than 10 percent answer in the low esteem direction.

INDEX OF ADJUSTMENT AND VALUES (Bills et al. 1951)

Variable   This inventory measures self-ideal discrepancy as well as acceptance of self. This is one of a battery of devices measuring
affective components of education and learning.

Description   A total of 124 adjectives were taken from the Allport-Odbert
(1936) list of 17,953 traits, the same item pool which provided
adjectives for other personality forms (e.g., Cattell's 16 PF).
Subjects (N=44) rated themselves twice using these words. The
49 words showing the greatest test-retest stability over three
weeks were selected as the final test.

The 49 words are used by subjects for three ratings: first, they
rated how often the sentence "I am a (an) _____ person," is
applicable (self-rating). They then rated how they accepted themselves as described by the first rating (self-acceptance). Lastly,
they rated how often they would like the completed sentence, "I
would like to be a (an) _____ person" to be applicable (ideal
rating). These three ratings are made on five-point Likert scales
running from very much to very little. The first rating can be
used as a self-rating, the second rating is used as a self-
acceptance score, and the discrepancy of the self and ideal ratings
as an adjustment or self-esteem score. Ratings are also sometimes
made for "others."

There are four age level forms of the self-concept inventory (IAV);
parallel scales measuring feelings about school; a locus of responsibility scale (concerning the balance of decision making in the classroom between students and teacher), a Relationship Inventory, and a
parent inventory measuring parental attitudes toward school conditions. For the purposes of this section, only the self-concept measures will be examined with the focus on the adult form.

Sample   A sample of 44 college students were used for the original item
analysis. Other samples have been used subsequently.

Reliability   In the basic article (Bills, Vance and McLean, 1951), information
on reliability is given. Split-half self-acceptance reliability
was .91 (adjusted). Split-half reliability for the discrepancy
was .88. (The old manual [Bills, 1958] offers similar split-half
reliabilities for the self-acceptance and discrepancy scores with
larger samples.) For self-ratings the corrected reliability was .93.

Test-retest reliability was .83 for self-acceptance and .87 for the
discrepancy score. Test-retest reliabilities vary from .83 to .92
for six weeks, and .52 to .86 for sixteen weeks for the self ratings.

Validity   Convergent: The manual presents several low positive correlations
with similar measures. For the self-acceptance scores these range
from -.04 to .55 and for self-ideal discrepancy from -.08 to .56.
Other information would suggest that the higher correlations are
more common. Ziller et al. (1969) found correlations of .47 and .60

between the Bills self-acceptance score and the Coopersmith and Cutick measures for males. For females the correlations were only .17 and .29. Crowne, Stephens and Kelly (1961) found correlations from .34 to .59 with various other measures for the self-acceptance score. Spitzer et al. (1966) show similar findings.

Discriminant: Cowen and Tongas (1959) used grouped data to show that self-ratings and social desirability ratings were highly cor-related with self and ideal ratings on the Bills scale; the discre-pancy score was uncorrelated with social desirability. However, grouped responses and discrepancies are meaningless for understand-ing individual scores. Bills (1959) also questions this study.

Crowne, Stephens and Kelly (1961) found more realistic correlations of -.54 and -.47 between Edwards social desirability scores and the Bills self-acceptance and discrepancy scores for males; the correla-tions were -.57 and -.51 for females.

Predictive: The 1958 manual reviews several studies suggesting that individuals high in self-acceptance tend to be rated as having greater leadership potential by themselves and others. These people are generally categorized both with regard to their own self-accept-ance and their acceptance of others. (Those above the mean on both are generally rated higher.) People high in self-acceptance also tend to be more assertive in introducing themselves. Considerably more interesting data of this type are available, although the data tend to rely on self-reports.

Location	Bills, R., Vance, E. and McLean, O. An index of adjustment and val-ues. *Journal of Consulting Psychology*, 1951, 15, 257-261.
Administration	The scale is self-administering, and it becomes progressively more complicated as more ratings are made for each adjective. Average time should not be over 45 minutes.
Results and Comments	Positive points: The author has long been active in this area and his scale has been widely used. Much of the information which has been gathered will soon be available in a published manual from the College of Education, University of Alabama, University, Al. 35486. Dr. Bills' address is the same and he will know when the manual is available. The use of self-acceptance ratings with self-ratings the individual has made is quite clever. If self-acceptance is the prime focus, such a technique could be useful with any inventory.

Negative points: The self-ratings correlate about .74 and -.72 with the self-acceptance and discrepancy scores, (Bills, 1958). Likewise the self-acceptance score correlates -.60 with the discrepancy score. For another sample in the manual, these correlations are .90, -.83, and -.67. In light of this, the value of using the discrepancy and self-acceptance scores instead of simple self-ratings remains to be demonstrated. Most of the adjectives are positive in nature (Cowen and Tongas, 1959) which may cause a bias in ratings. In addition, the particular adjectives, while suitable for self-acceptance ratings, are not all relevant to self-esteem. Thus, it would be useful if a list based on item analyses were used, or the advantage of using the self-acceptance and discrepancy scores were demonstrated. The point has also been made elsewhere that single adjectives may not make the best "items" (Loehlin, 1967).

Suggestions: Data may exist to answer any problems raised here; hopefully, the new manual will answer these objections. As a measure of self-acceptance, only the social desirability problem is major. As a measure of self-esteem or adjustment, the discrepancy scores are not convincing and the list of adjectives could be improved for simple self-ratings. Interestingly, several variations of Bills' adjectives have been used for other esteem measures (e.g., the section on other esteem measures).

Feedback to Author	Dr. Bills requests that researchers contact him for permission to use the scale.

References

Allport, G. and Odbert, H. Trait-names: A psycho-lexical study. Psychological Monographs, 1936, 211.

Bills, R. Manual for the Index of Adjustment and Values. Auburn, Alabama: Alabama Polytechnical Institute, 1958.

Bills, R. Two questions: A reply to Cowen and Tongas. Journal of Consulting Psychology, 1959, 23, 366-367.

Bills, R., Vance, E. and McLean, O. An index of adjustment and values. Journal of Consulting Psychology, 1951, 15, 257-261.

Cowen, E. and Tongas, P. The social desirability of trait descriptive terms: Applications to a self-concept inventory. Journal of Consulting Psychology, 1959, 23, 361-365.

Crowne, D., Stephens, M., and Kelly, R. The validity and equivalence of tests of self-acceptance. Journal of Psychology, 1961, 51, 101-112.

Loehlin, J. Word meanings and self-descriptions: A replication and extension. Journal of Personality and Social Psychology, 1967, 5, 107-110.

Spitzer, S., Stratton, J., Fitzgerald, J., and Mach, B. The self concept: Test equivalence and perceived validity. Sociological Quarterly, 1966, 7, 265-280.

Ziller, R., Hagey, J., Smith, M., and Long, B. Self esteem: a self-social construct. Journal of Consulting and Clinical Psychology, 1969, 33, 84-95.

INDEX OF ADJUSTMENT AND VALUES

The respondent puts each of the following words into the following three sentences. Then he/she rates how descriptive the sentence is on a 1 to 5 scale.

A sample scale would be:

5	4	3	2	1
Very much				Very little

1. I am a (an) _____ person.

2. How do you accept yourself as described by the first rating?

3. I would like to be a (an) _____ person.

Adjective list

acceptable	democratic	merry	stable
accurate	dependable	mature	studious
alert	economical	*nervous	successful
ambitious	efficient	normal	*stubborn
*annoying	*fearful	optimistic	tactful
busy	friendly	poised	teachable
calm	fashionable	purposeful	useful
charming	helpful	reasonable	worthy
clever	intellectual	*reckless	broadminded
competent	kind	responsible	businesslike
confident	logical	*sarcastic	competetive
considerate	*meddlesome	sincere	*faultfinding
*cruel			

Scoring for the self ratings is in the socially desirable direction. Most of the words are positive. A higher rating indicates higher esteem for all the words except those marked with an asterisk (*).

BUTLER-HAIGH Q-SORT (Butler and Haigh 1954)

Variable   This scale was developed when the Q-sort method was just coming
                  into wide use. It was used to measure discrepancies between ratings
                  of "self" and "ideal self" of people undergoing counseling.

Description   There are 100 items on cards which respondents sort into nine piles
                  under two conditions: Once to describe themselves as they are and
                  once to describe their ideal selves. The items cover a variety of
                  areas of self-concept, such as self-acceptance, sexual esteem, an-
                  xiety, self-demands, poise, and other less central areas.

Sample   In the original work the sample consisted of 29 people going through
                  therapy, 15 of whom delayed the start of therapy for 60 days to act
                  as a motivational control group. Another 25 people who dropped out
                  acted as separate controls and an additional 23 non-clients acted as
                  partial controls. It has subsequently been used on other samples.

Reliability   None is presented by Butler and Haigh (1954). Wylie (1961, p. 50)
                  suggests that the 16 control subjects' total discrepancy scores have
                  a test-retest correlation of .78 (from Table on p. 66, Butler and
                  Haigh, 1954). (This author, however, found this correlation to be
                  .65.)

Validity   Convergent: Leake (1970) obtained a correlation of -.61 between the
                  Tennessee Scale and this Q-sort. Turner and Vanderlippe (1958) ob-
                  tained positive correlations with general activity (.50); ascendance
                  (.58); sociability (.36); emotional stability (.36); and thoughtful-
                  ness (.41) (using the Guilford-Zimmerman Scale for these measures).

                  Discriminant: The fact that the self-ideal correlation did not change
                  for non-therapy subjects, nor for subjects waiting for therapy, sug-
                  gests some discriminant validity (Butler and Haigh, 1954). The scale
                  did not correlate with Guilford-Zimmerman traits such as masculinity
                  and objectivity (Turner and Vanderlippe, 1958)

                  Predictive: The self-ideal correlations became higher with therapy.
                  Other work in the 1954 book also suggest some construct validity.

Location   Butler, J. and Haigh, G. Changes in the relation between self-
                  concepts and ideal concepts consequent upon client-centered counsel-
                  ing. In Psychotherapy and Personality Change, edited by Rogers and
                  Dymond. Chicago: University of Chicago Press, 1954, 55-75.

Administration   This Q-sort with 100 items takes about an hour and a half to complete.

Results and   Positive points: Many of the items seem worthwhile and could be used
Comments   in other formats. The early work did provide some evidence for the
                  validity of this approach.

                  Negative points: Though the Q-sort method constituted a definite
                  theoretical breakthrough when it was introduced, enough questions
                  about discrepancy measures remain unresolved to give pause before
                  using them in preference to direct self-reports. For example, the
                  combination of two scores may increase the error variance. Thus

any validity that this measure has may be based simply on the self-sorts alone.

Suggestions: In most cases where the same items have been used for self and discrepancy scores, the self scores have predicted various criteria at least as well (e.g., Bills and Worchel) except when the items were less directly relevant to self-esteem (Miskimins). Until the theoretical advantage of discrepancy measures is empirically demonstrated, there seems no reason to use them since they may even be less valid and are certainly more time consuming than simple self-ratings.

References Butler, J. and Haigh, G. Changes in the relation between self-concepts and ideal concepts consequent upon client-centered counseling. In Psychotherapy and Personality Change, edited by Rogers and Dymond. Chicago: University of Chicago Press, 1954, 55-75.

Leake, D. The measurement of self esteem. Unpublished Masters Thesis, Ohio State University, 1970.

Turner, R. and Vanderlippe, R. Self-ideal congruence as an index of adjustment. Journal of Abnormal and Social Psychology, 1958, 57, 202-206.

Wylie, R. The Self Concept. Lincoln, Nebraska: University of Nebraska Press, 1961.

Sample Items The complete list of items is available in Butler and Haigh (1954) and in the previous edition of this volume. The keyed responses for high esteem are given in parentheses.

I usually feel driven. (F)
I often kick myself for the things I do. (T)
Self-control is no problem with me. (T)
I despise myself. (F)

The actual items are listed on page 77 of the book. It is interesting to note that because no internal item analyses have been reported individual items may not relate to the total self-esteem scores as they are keyed.

MISKIMINS SELF-GOAL-OTHER DISCREPANCY SCALE (Miskimins 1971)

Variable   This scale was developed to measure self-concept from a clinical
                  perspective.

Description   In its latest simplified form subjects rate (1) themselves, (2)
                  their goal for themselves, and (3) how family and friends see them
                  on nine point bipolar scales. There are four scales (five in other
                  forms) for each of three standard areas plus four scales which each
                  individual labels with personally relevant constructs. The three
                  standard areas are general, social, and emotional. In order to con-
                  trol for factors such as differential uses of scales by respondents
                  and differential characteristics of items such as social desirability
                  or actual frequency of occurrence, the authors (Miskimins and Braucht
                  1971) suggest a "double centering" technique involving standization
                  first within subjects, then across subjects via an iterative process.
                  They domonstrate some useful applications with both simulated and
                  actual experimental data. For this standardization, the authors con-
                  centrate on the case where several scores are available for each sub-
                  ject as well as subjects' and judges' ratings of video taped others.
                  Variations are discussed below.

Sample   To develop the original items, six graduate students generated self-
                  descriptors. Five other judges sorted these into the three standard
                  areas. The six pairs of descriptors on which there was perfect agree-
                  ment were then administered to 71 undergraduates at Ohio State. These
                  answers were correlated with anxiety scores and were item analyzed
                  with the weakest item in each area being eliminated. Subsequent
                  samples have included college students and mental patients.

Reliability   In the initial item analysis all retained items correlated from .45
                  to .78 with the total score. With 63 subjects the self-ideal dis-
                  crepancy scores across the four areas correlated between .53 and
                  .69 with each other.

                  The total discrepancy score (20-item scale) had a 14 day test-retest
                  correlation of .87 (N=51 students). There are 27 further indices
                  that can be derived but with somewhat less stability.

Validity   Convergent: The 24-item scale correlated .54 with the Taylor Mani-
                  fest Anxiety scale. In a replication the 20-item scale correlated
                  .71 with the MAS. Many of the correlations with MMPI scales showed
                  expected convergence.

                  Discriminant: Correlations with the MMPI lie scale were low:
                  -.17 for the 20-item total discrepancy score.

                  Predictive: A sample of 20 normal persons had lower scores on the
                  scale than a group of matched mental patients. Some of the scores
                  also related to severity of pathology. Other research adding to the
                  general construct validity is reported in Miskimins and Braucht
                  (1971).

Location   Pricelist, scales, manual and scoring programs are available from the Rocky Mountain Behavioral Science Institute, P. O. Box 2037, Ft. Collins, Colorado 80521.

Administration   Self administered, taking about 15 minutes.

Results and Comments

Positive points: The book describing this scale is excellent in its broad discussion of many aspects of self-concept research (Miskimins and Braucht 1971). Interestingly, this measure does provide some justification for using the discrepancy component of the scores. Using manifest anxiety scores as a criterion, the discrepancy scores correlated much more highly than any simple self-ratings. This highlights an aspect of this scale which is both a strength and a limitation. The rating scales cover many dimensions which may not be the most salient for self-concept, such as good-bad manners. Thus, we would expect the discrepancy scores to be more relevant for self-concept than simple self-ratings for such dimensions.

However, most of the rating scales cover aspects of self that can be rated by observers. In the body of research for which this scale is being used one of the foci is clinical self-confrontation using videotape playbacks of subjects. Since subjects rate how others see them, and most of the rating dimensions are accessible to observers, objective comparisons can be made between subjects' and judges' ratings. This and other aspects of the self-confrontation can be useful both for the subjects and for measurement validation.

Negative points: Two arguments underlying the rationale of this scale are not compelling: (1) the review of previous measures from which it is decided that a new scale is necessary, and (2) the decision that the discrepancy format is to be used.

Using items which provided more valid self-ratings would probably lessen the value of the discrepancy scores. Twenty to thirty scores derived from twenty items can lead to overinterpretation.

Suggestions: Using less general items could lessen social desirability effects and improve the scope of the scale.

An aspect of this form which can be used with almost any scale is the application of standardization techniques to raw scores. If we want to study intra-individual variations in abilities (e.g., Broverman, 1962), methods of analysis which consider these intra-individual relations of abilities across people are necessary. The correlation coefficient is one such technique; however, it cannot control for differential use of the scales.

In the case where items were balanced for response bias these standardizations could be done at the item level, first within, and then across subjects. In other words, answers to items on a multipoint scale can be standardized within subjects and then the absolute value of the standardized scores could be used to assign scores for each item across subjects. Miskimins and Braucht present some validation of the value of their general technique and validation with other scales would be valuable. Variations of this type of scoring have also been covered by Willis (1960). This technique seems to be very logical and testable. However, there are many complications involved which each reader should consider for himself in more detail just as Miskimins and Braucht (1971) do. This general approach has also been discussed by Rosenberg (1962) and Mueller and Schuessler (1961).

References Broverman, D. Normative and ipsative measurement in psychology. Psychology Review, 1962, 69, 295-305.

Miskimins, R.W. and Braucht, G. Description of the self. Rocky Mountain Behavioral Science Institute, P. O. Box 2037, Fort Collins, Colorado 80521, 1971.

Mueller, J. and Schuessler, K. Statistical Reasoning in Sociology. Boston: Houghton Mifflin, 1961.

Rosenberg, M. Test factor standardization as a method of interpretation. Social Forces, 1962, 41, 53-61.

Willis, R. Manipulation of item marginal frequencies by means of multiple response items. Psychological Review, 1960, 67, 32-50.

Sample items Because the scale is commercial, only sample items are given. The high esteem choice is underlined. Individuals rate 1) themselves. 2) their goal for themselves, and 3) how others see them on scales like the following:

GENERAL

Good person ___ ___ ___ ___ ___ ___ ___ ___ ___ Bad person

SOCIAL

Have good
 manners ___ ___ ___ ___ ___ ___ ___ ___ ___ Have bad
                      manners

EMOTIONAL

 Sad ___ ___ ___ ___ ___ ___ ___ ___ ___ Happy

PERSONALITY RESEARCH FORM AND JACKSON PERSONALITY INVENTORY (Jackson 1967;
1970)

Variable   The Personality Research Form (Jackson, 1967) is a useful measure
of many personality variables. It contains no direct measure of
self-esteem, although the dominance and exhibition scales of the PRF
could be used as esteem scales. The newer Jackson Personality Inventory does include a self-esteem scale tapping socially relevant
esteem behaviors.

Description   The PRF dominance and exhibition scales each have 20 true-false
items. Because these are parallel forms, up to 40 items could be
used to measure each trait. The PRF was conceived within trait
theory as expressed by Murray (1938). The JPI esteem scale also has
20 items and is developed within the same framework; these items
deal largely with self-esteem in a social context.

Sample   The PRF scales have been used with many samples (such as college students) some of which are discussed in the manual. The JPI esteem scale
has been used less since it is not yet published.

Reliability   Odd-even and homogeneity coefficients are reported in the .80's for
the two PRI scales.

Both the PRF dominance and exhibition scales had test-retest reliabilities for one week of .88.

No estimate of reliability is available for the JPI.

Validity   Convergent: The PRF dominance and exhibition scales correlated .65
and .69 with the self-acceptance scale of the CPI.

Discriminant: The PRF scales exhibited low correlations with many
PRF and CPI scales. Items were originally selected partly to avoid
correlations with social desirability.

Predictive: Both peer and self ratings correlated impressively
(from .43 to .75) with the PRF scales. The JPI esteem scale correlated .66 with peer ratings.

Location   The PRF manual and scales are available from the publisher: Research
Psychologists Press, Inc., Goshen, New York. The JPI should be
available from the same publisher soon.

Administration   The entire PRF takes about 40 minutes to administer. The JPI should
take about an equal amount of time.

Results and   Positive points: Both the PRF and the JPI, having been carefully de-
Comments   veloped and validated, stand among the very best multi-trait scales
available.

Negative points: The PRF scales were not developed with self-esteem
in mind. The JPI esteem scale only covers one aspect of esteem.

<u>Suggestions</u>: For people interested in several personality variables the PRF and JPI can be recommended. For those interested mainly in self-esteem a more specialized measurement approach would probably prove more useful.

References   Jackson, D. <u>Personality research form manual.</u> Goshen, New York: Research Psychologists Press, Inc., 1967.

Jackson, D. <u>The Jackson Personality Inventory</u>. London, Canada: Author, 1970.

Murray, H. <u>Explorations in Personality</u>. Cambridge: Harvard University Press, 1938.

Sample Items   Sample JPI esteem items with the high esteem answers keyed:

27. I am usually quite confident when learning a new game or sport. (T)

299. I prefer to go to social functions with a group of people so as not to stand out. (F)

315. I find it easy to introduce people. (T)

CALIFORNIA PSYCHOLOGICAL INVENTORY (Gough 1956)

Variable   The CPI developed to measure socially relevant personality char-
             acteristics in healthy individuals. Most of the CPI "Class 1"
             scales relate to esteem, especially the self-acceptance scale.

Description The CPI is a 480 item true-false inventory, about half of whose
             items come from the MMPI. It contains many scales derived both ra-
             tionally and empirically. The class 1 scales on the CPI are all
             conceptually related to self-esteem; while none directly measure
             esteem, self-acceptance is most closely related. The other con-
             structs measured would be expected to be positively related to
             self-esteem and all are positively related to self-acceptance (.10
             to .60). They are: dominance, capacity for status, sociability,
             social presence, and sense of well-being. The social-presence and
             self-acceptance scales were developed using only rational judgments
             and item analyses. The others were empirically developed using
             "peer type" ratings as criteria in most cases.

             Various investigators have used different combinations of the above
             six scales as measures of self-esteem. According to the formula-
             tions considered here, self-acceptance is the closest to self-esteem
             and the others are likely to be less directly related. In a factor
             analysis of the CPI, self-acceptance, sociability, and dominance load-
             ed highest on the second factor -- .77, .76, and .78 respectively
             (Mitchell and Pierce-Jones, 1960). These three scales also corre-
             lated well with peer ratings according to Vingoe (1968).

Sample   Data from many kinds of samples are presented in the manual.

Reliability Taylor and Reitz (1968) found a split-half reliability for the
             self-acceptance scale of .67.

             The test-retest correlations for the dominance, self-acceptance,
             and sociability scales in the manual range from .64 to .84 for
             periods up to a year.

Validity   Convergent: Taylor and Reitz (1968) found that the self-acceptance
             scale correlated .45 with the Coopersmith measure and from .21 to
             .63 with other scales.

             Hamilton (1971) combined both the self-acceptance and social pre-
             sence scales to measure self-esteem. He found that this measure cor-
             related .67 with the Janis and Field measures, .26 with a discrepancy
             measure, .58 with self-ratings, and .24 with peer ratings.

             Interestingly, a study by Vincent (1968) showed that the self-
             acceptance and self-control scales of the CPI loaded on a different
             factor than did several similar scales including scales from the Cat-
             tell 16 PF and the Tennessee (Fitts) self-esteem scale. Because these
             scales emphasize "sociability" they may contain less of the "mental
             health" factor than many esteem scales. In unpublished work Lorraine
             Broll (personal communication) reports that with 643 female students

the self-acceptance scale correlated -.01 with the Rotter I-E scale, .27 with the Rosenberg self-acceptance scale, and .25 with a one-item esteem scale. These correlations are considerably lower than average.

Discriminant: In Taylor and Reitz (1968) the self-acceptance scale correlated only .07 with the Marlowe-Crowne social desirability scale but .40 with the Edwards social desirability scale. In the manual the three scales considered here correlated from .25 to .48 with the Edwards desirability scale. Many other correlations bearing on divergent validity appear in the manual.

Predictive: The Vingoe (1968) and Hamilton (1971) correlations with peer ratings provide evidence of some predictive validity. The manual presents similar data using ratings by principals and other observers of students, medical school applicants, and military men.

Location   The manual and scales are available from Consulting Psychologists Press, Inc., 577 College Avenue, Palo Alto, California 94305.

Administration   The entire CPI is self-administered and takes up to an hour.

Results and   Positive points: The CPI scales were carefully developed. Megargee
Comments   (1972) has reviewed considerable evidence supporting their validity.

Negative points: Because self-esteem is not the central focus of the CPI, some aspects of esteem may be omitted here.

Suggestions: For those who wish to measure many variables at once the self-acceptance, dominance, and sociability scales can be useful measures of self-esteem. For those interested only in esteem, however, other scales may cover more aspects of the construct.

References   Gough, H. CPI Manual. Consulting Psychologists Press, 577 College Avenue, Palo Alto, California, 1957.

Hamilton, D. A comparative study of assessing self-esteem, dominance, and dogmatism. Educational and Psychological Measurement, 1971, 31, 441-452.

Megargee, E. The California Psychological Inventory Handbook. San Francisco: Jossey-Bass, Inc., 1972.

Mitchell, J., Jr. and Pierce-Jones, J. A factor analysis of Gough's California Psychological Inventory. Journal of Consulting Psychology, 1960, 24, 453-456.

Taylor, J. and Reitz, W. The three faces of self-esteem. Research Bulletin #80, April, 1968, Psychology Department, University of Western Ontario.

Vincent, J. An exploratory factor analysis relating to the construct validity of self concept labels. Educational and Psychological Measurement, 1968, 28, 195-221.

Vingoe, F. Note on the validity of the California Psychological Inventory. <u>Journal of Consulting and Clinical Psychology</u>, 1968, <u>32</u>, 725-727.

Sample Items   High self-acceptance answers are in parentheses.

    4. A person needs to "show off" a little now and then. (T)

279. I often get disgusted with myself. (F)

ADJECTIVE CHECK LIST (Gough and Heilbrun 1965)

Variable   The adjective check list (ACL) can be used to obtain several indices related to self-esteem. Based on correlations with the California Personality Inventory (CPI) self-acceptance scale presented
in the manual (Gough and Heilbrun, 1965), the self-confidence, exhibition, and change scales are closest to self-esteem.

Description   The ACL consists of 300 adjectives of which people check as many as
they consider to be self-descriptive. These adjectives have been
collected and tested over a number of years. The self-confidence
index was developed by selecting self-descriptors of people rated
high and low on traits such as poise and self-confidence. The number of adjectives checked which indicate low self-confidence are
subtracted from those checked which are indicative of high confidence
Scores are also standardized according to the total number of adjectives checked.

Twenty-one other meausres have been derived from the ACL, including
defensiveness, achievement, and heterosexuality.

Sample   Basic psychometric data are based on a sample of 56 college males,
23 college females, 100 adult men, and 34 medical students. Other
samples have been used.

Reliability/ No data bearing on the homogeneity of the instrument are reported.
Homogeneity   Test-retest coefficients for the self-confidence scale varied from
.63 to .73 for periods from 10 weeks to 5 1/2 years. The authors
note that these are somewhat lower than average for scales such as
the CPI which are able to identify some types of persons who are less
stable, but single adjectives may also be less stable as self-
descriptors.

Validity   Convergent: Spitzer et al. (1966) found correlations for the self-
confidence scale with the Bills scale and a semantic differential
in the .40 to .50 range. The manual presents a correlation of .38
with the CPI self-acceptance scale.

Discriminant: The manual reports a correlation of .40 between the
self-confidence scale and the Edwards social desirability scale.

Predictive: Only indirect predictive validity can be obtained from
the manual.

Location   Gough, H. and Heilbrun, A. The Adjective Check List Manual. Consulting Psychologists Press, 577 College Avenue, Palo Alto, Cal.,
1965.

Administration The entire 300 adjectives can usually be completed in less than 15
minutes.

Results and   Positive points: The ACL has been widely used and was developed in
Comments   the outstanding tradition of the CPI. It is very efficient for measuring several variables.

<u>Negative points</u>: Common sense and research (Loehlin, 1961, 1967) suggest that a single adjective is more open to individualistic semantic interpretation than other forms of self-description.

The convergence with other meaures of esteem is not much higher than with social desirability, and test-retest reliability is not high. The empirical selection of items can lead to the measurement of traits other than those directly intended.

<u>Suggestions</u>: For investigators who use this scale to test multiple hypotheses, it is also possible to use it to measure self-esteem. However, it cannot be recommended as a central measure of self-esteem, since several more specific self-esteem scales are available.

References

Gough, H. and Heilbrun, A.B., Jr. <u>The Adjective Check List Manual</u>. Consulting Psychologists Press, 577 College Avenue, Palo Alto, California, 1965.

Loehlin, J. Word meanings and self-descriptions. <u>Journal of Abnormal and Social Psychology</u>, 1961, <u>62</u>, 28-34.

Loehlin, J. Word meanings and self-descriptions: A replication and extension. <u>Journal of Personality and Social Psychology</u>, 1967, <u>5</u>, 107-110.

Spitzer, S., Stratton, J., Fitzgerald, J., and Mach, B. The self concept: Test equivalence and perceived validity. <u>Sociological Quarterly</u>, 1966, <u>7</u>, 265-280.

Sample words

Indicative of high self-confidence	Indicative of low self-confidence
____ aggressive	____ anxious
____ assertive	____ fickle
____ confident	____ lazy
____ dominant	____ modest
____ energetic	____ reserved
____ independent	
____ persistent	

SELF-PERCEPTION INVENTORIES (Soares and Soares 1965)

Variable | These scales have been used largely for investigating the self-images of disadvantaged students, school age children, and student teachers.

Description | The self-ratings use bipolar scales with four points. Students rate themselves, how they think classmates see them, how teachers see them, how parents see them, and their ideal selves; there is also a peer rating form. For student teachers there are self-ratings and ratings of how they think they are perceived by the cooperating teacher and by the supervisor. Similar forms are available for the student teacher to be actually rated by the supervisor, cooperating teacher and students. High esteem is always the answer on the left of the scale.

For younger students the bipolar scales consist of short sentences; for older adolescents, adults, and student teachers the scales consist of adjectives (e.g., contented vs. worried). The flexible format of these scales allows easy ratings and combinations of ratings can be used to measure discrepancies and congruence between various self-self and self-other scales.

Sample | The samples used generally have been disadvantaged students, children, and student teachers as noted above.

Reliability | No data bearing on internal consistency are reported. Soares (personal communication) reports a preliminary test-retest reliability of .88 for self-ratings for an unspecified sample.

Validity | Convergent: Soares (personal communication) obtained a correlation of .68 with the Coopersmith inventory using an unspecified sample. Getsinger et al., 1972, report a similar correlation of .63 with the Coopersmith scale.

Discriminant: No data appear to be available.

Predictive: Only indirect evidence of predictive validity can be obtained from published reports in the references. The authors find disadvantaged children to have higher esteem (e.g., Soares and Soares, 1969).

Location | The scale apparently will be available commercially. Those who wish to use the scales should contact Drs. Louise and Anthony Soares, Department of Psychology, University of Bridgeport, Bridgeport, Connecticut 06602. They have copies of both the scales and several reports of applications presented at professional meetings and in published writings.

Administration | If several forms were all administered at once, administration should take about half an hour and would require some explanation.

Results and
Comments

<u>Positive points</u>: As used by the authors, the scales seem to give
useful scores. The fact that the authors are actively involved in
refining and updating the scales is encouraging.

<u>Negative points</u>: The use of single adjectives as end points of
scales may be ambiguous as suggested by Loehlin (1967). There seems
to have been no demonstration that these specific rating dimensions
are particularly relevent to self-concept. Similarly, no item analyses appear to have been done to investigate scale homogeneity or
clusters. The correlation with social desirability is uncontrolled
as is agreement response bias, since the answer on the left is always
scored as high esteem.

<u>Suggestions</u>: In interpreting the validity of both the scales and the
individual items, it would be helpful to compare the obtained self-
ratings with the ratings made by others. The "self as others see it"
versus others' actual ratings can provide validation since it tests
the accuracy of an individual's perceptions, which can confirm the
accuracy of his/her self-ratings. The potential correlations between "self as others see it" and others' ratings are higher than
those between simple self and peer ratings since peers do not have
perfect knowledge of the individual being rated. See Norman and Goldberg (1966) for an example. Existing data could probably be examined
to investigate this kind of question. In addition, item analyses
which looked at the relationship of some of the scale items with
self-esteem would be useful (e.g., item-total correlations). For
instance, the nature of the relationship between "deliberate-
impulsive" and self-concept might be difficult to predict except in
discrepancy form. Eliminating items which reflect only social desirability would also be useful. The scales could easily be balanced for
response bias.

References

Getsinger, S., Kunce, J., Miller, D., and Weinberg, S. Self-esteem
measures and cultural disadvantagement. <u>Journal of Consulting and
Clinical Psychology</u>, 1972, <u>38</u>, 149.

Loehlin, J. Word meanings and self-descriptions: A replication and
extension. <u>Journal of Personality and Social Psychology</u>, 1967, <u>5</u>,
107-110.

Norman, W. and Goldberg, L. Raters, ratees, and randomness in personality structure. <u>Journal of Personality and Social Psychology</u>,
1966, <u>4</u>, 681-691.

Soares, A. and Soares, Louise. Self-perceptions of culturally disadvantaged children. <u>American Educational Research Journal</u>, 1969,
<u>6</u>, 31-45.

Soares, A. and Soares, Louise. Critique of Soares and Soares' "Self-
perceptions of culturally disadvantaged children--a reply." <u>American
Educational Research Journal</u>, 1970, <u>7</u>, 631-635.

Soeares, A. and Soares, Louise. Comparative differences in the self-
perceptions of disadvantaged and advanced students. <u>Journal of
School Psychology</u>, 1971, <u>9</u>, 424-429.

Sample Items | considerate __X__ _____ _____ _____ selfish

deliberate __X__ _____ _____ _____ impulsive

tough __X__ _____ _____ _____ sensitive

Note: The answer on the left side is always high esteem.

EXPRESSED ACCEPTANCE OF SELF SCALE (Berger 1952)
SELF-ACCEPTANCE SCALE (Phillips 1951)

Variable   Both of these scales follow from a seminal study of Scheerer
                    (1949) which tested the clinical hypothesis that self and other ac-
                    ceptance are positively related. Other scales have been construct-
                    ed with the same intention (e.g., Fey, 1954), but are unavailable.

Description   Both scales appear to tap self-acceptance, particularly in social
                    contexts. Each item is answered on a five-point scale, running
                    from "not at all true" to "true." Both have usually been adminis-
                    tered concurrently with items measuring acceptance of others. Ber-
                    ger (1952) started with 47 items. The 36 items which best discrim-
                    inated between those who scored high and low on the scale were re-
                    tained. These items are approximately balanced for acquiescence.
                    The Phillips (1951) scale contains 25 items, for each of which a
                    negative answer indicates high self-acceptance.

Sample   The Berger scale has been administered to college students,
                    stutterers, adults, and others. The Phillips scale has been ad-
                    ministered to high school and college students as well as adults.

Reliability   Spearman-Brown estimates of reliability equalled or exceeded .75
                    for several samples using the Berger scale. Eagly (personal com-
                    munication) obtained a correlation of .91 between 16 items adminis-
                    tered before and 16 items after an experiment. For the Phillips
                    scale a five day test-retest correlation of .84 was obtained for
                    45 respondents.

Validity   Convergent: Onwake (1954) found that the Berger and Phillips scales
                    correlated .73. She also obtained correlations of .49 and .55 with
                    the Bills self-acceptance scale for the Berger and Phillips scales,
                    respectively. Eagly (personal communication) found a correlation
                    of .84 with the Janis-Field scale for 32 of the Berger items with
                    an experiment intervening.

                    Discriminant: Indirect evidence for the discriminant validity of
                    the Berger scale can be obtained from some published studies
                    (e.g., Berger, 1955).

                    Predictive: The prediction on which these scales were constructed
                    has been confirmed. Onwake (1954) found correlations of .37 between
                    the Berger self and other scales and .41 between the Phillips self
                    and other scales. Phillips (1951) found correlations of from .51
                    to .74 between self and other acceptance. Berger (1952) obtained
                    some group differences in self-acceptance which could support the
                    scales' validity. Judges' ratings of essays by twenty respondents
                    showed high correlations with the respondents' self-acceptance
                    scores.

Location   The Phillips scale is discussed in Phillips, E., Attitudes toward
                    self and others: A brief questionnaire report, Journal of Consult-
                    ing Psychology, 1951, 15, 79-81, but has not been previously avail-
                    able. The Berger scale is discussed in Berger, E.; The relations

between expressed acceptance of self and expressed acceptance of others, Journal of Abnormal and Social Psychology, 1952, 47, 778-782; in Berger, (1955); and was available in the previous edition of this volume.

Administration   Administration of either form should take less than twenty minutes.

Results and Comments

Positive points: Early scales such as these contain most of the basic work necessary for constructing a strong scale. The Berger scale has been tested more than the Phillips scale but both have evidenced some validity.

Negative points: Neither scale has received much systematic validation work. The Phillips scale would be especially likely to benefit from an item analysis.

Suggestions: These scales provide a good item pool for subsequent analyses. Since they are closely related conceptually and empirically, they could be appropriately analyzed together both for internal item selection and for analyses against external criteria such as peer ratings, assertiveness, and so forth.

References

Berger, E. The relations between expressed acceptance of self and expressed acceptance of others. Journal of Abnormal and Social Psychology, 1952, 47, 778-782.

Berger, E. Relationships among acceptance of self, acceptance of others, and MMPI scores. Journal of Counseling Psychology, 1955, 2, 279-284.

Fey, W. Acceptance of self and others, and its relationship to therapy readiness. Journal of Clinical Psychology, 1954, 10, 269-271.

Omwake, Katharine. The relation between acceptance of self and acceptance of others shown by three personality inventories. Journal of Consulting Psychology, 1954, 18, 443-446.

Phillips, E. Attitudes toward self and others: A brief questionnaire report. Journal of Consulting Psychology, 1951, 15, 79-81.

Scheerer, Elizabeth. An analysis of the relationship between acceptance of and respect for self and acceptance of and respect for others in ten counseling cases. Journal of Consulting Psychology, 1949, 13, 169-175.

SELF-ACCEPTANCE SCALES

Scales   Both scales use a five-point answer scale as follows:

Not at all true		Half true half false		Completely true
1	2	3	4	5

Berger Items

1. I'd like it if I could find someone who would tell me how to solve my personal problems. (High acceptance end of answer scale: (1)

2. I don't question my worth as a person, even if I think others do. (5)

3. When people say nice things about me, I find it difficult to believe they really mean it. I think maybe they're kidding me or just aren't being sincere. (1)

4. If there is any criticism or anyone says anything about me, I just can't take it. (1)

5. I don't say much at social affairs because I'm afraid that people will criticize me or laugh if I say the wrong thing. (1)

6. I realize that I'm not living very effectively, but I just don't believe I've got it in me to use my energies in better ways. (1)

7. I look on most of the feelings and impulses I have toward people as being quite natural and acceptable. (5)

8. Something inside me just won't let me be satisfied with any job I've done--if it turns out well, I get a very smug feeling that this is beneath me, I shouldn't be satisfied with this, this isn't a fair test. (1)

9. I feel different from other people. I'd like to have the feeling of security that comes from knowing I'm not too different from others. (1)

10. I'm afraid for people that I like to find out what I'm really like, for fear they'd be disappointed in me. (1)

11. I am frequently bothered by feelings of inferiority. (1)

12. Because of other people, I haven't been able to achieve as much as I should have. (1)

13. I am quite shy and self-conscious in social situations. (1)

14. In order to get along and be liked, I tend to be what people expect me to be rather than anything else. (1).

Self-Acceptance Scales reprinted here with permission of Berger, E. (Dr. Berger requests that researchers contact him at the University of Minnesota Counseling Center for permission to use his scale.)

15. I seem to have a real inner strength in handling things. I'm on a pretty solid foundation and it makes me pretty sure of myself. (5)

16. I feel self-conscious when I'm with people who have a superior position to mine in business or at school. (1)

17. I think I'm neurotic or something. (1)

18. Very often, I don't try to be friendly with people because I think they won't like me. (1)

19. I feel that I'm a person of worth, on an equal plane with others. (5)

20. I can't avoid feeling guilty about the way I feel toward certain people in my life. (1)

21. I'm not afraid of meeting new people. I feel that I'm a worthwhile person and there's no reason why they should dislike me. (5)

22. I sort of only half-believe in myself. (1)

23. I'm very sensitive. People say things and I have a tendency to think they're criticizing me or insulting me in some way and later when I think of it, they may not have meant anything like that at all. (1)

24. I think I have certain abilities and other people say so too. I wonder if I'm not giving them an importance way beyond what they deserve. (1)

25. I feel confident that I can do something about the problems that may arise in the future. (5)

26. I guess I put on a show to impress people. I know I'm not the person I pretend to be. (1)

27. I do not worry or condemn myself if other people pass judgment against me. (5)

28. I don't feel very normal, but I want to feel normal. (1)

29. When I'm in a group I usually don't say much for fear of saying the wrong thing. (1)

30. I have a tendency to sidestep my problems. (1)

31. Even when people do think well of me, I feel sort of guilty because I know I must be fooling them--that if I were really to be myself, they wouldn't think well of me. (1)

32. I feel that I'm on the same level as other people and that helps to establish good relations with them. (5)

33. I feel that people are apt to react differently to me than they would normally react to other people. (1)

34. I live too much by other people's standards. (1)

35. When I have to address a group, I get self-conscious and have difficulty saying things well. (1)

36. If I didn't always have such hard luck, I'd accomplish much more than I have. (1)

Phillips Items

1. My own decisions regarding problems I face do not turn out to be good ones. (1)

2. I find that I feel the need to make excuses or apologize for my behavior. (1)

3. If someone criticizes me to my face it makes me feel very low and worthless. (1)

4. I change my opinion (or the way I do things) in order to please someone else. (1)

5. I regret my own past action I have taken when I find that my behavior has hurt someone else. (1)

6. It worries me to think that some of my friends or acquaintances may dislike me. (1)

7. I feel inferior as a person to some of my friends. (1)

8. I have to be careful at parties and social gatherings for fear I will do or say things that others won't like. (1)

9. It bothers me because I cannot make up my mind soon enough or fast enough. (1)

10. I feel that I have very little to contribute to the welfare of others. (1)

11. I feel that I might be a failure if I don't make certain changes in my behavior (or my life). (1)

12. It takes me several days or longer to get over a failure that I have experienced. (1)

13. When meeting a person for the first time I have trouble telling whether he (or she) likes (or dislikes) me. (1)

14. I become panicky when I think of something I have done wrong (or might do wrong in the future). (1)

15. Although people sometimes compliment me, I feel that I do not really deserve the compliments. (1)

16. I regard myself as different from my friends and acquaintances. (1)

17. I keep still, or tell "little white lies" in the company of my friends so as not to reveal to them that I am different (or think differently) from them. (1)

18. My feelings are easily hurt. (1)

19. As I think about my past there are some points about which I feel shame. (1)

20. I think I would be happier if I didn't have certain limitations. (1)

21. I doubt if my plans will turn out the way I want them to. (1)

22. I think that I am too shy. (1)

23. In class, or in a group, I am unlikely to express my opinion because I fear that others may not think well of it (or of me). (1)

24. I criticize myself afterwards for acting silly or inappropriately in some situations. (1)

25. If I hear that someone expresses a poor opinion of me, I do my best the next time I see this person to impress him (or her) as favorably as I can. (1)

SELF-ACTIVITY INVENTORY (Worchel 1957)

Variable This scale was originally designed to measure the effectiveness of coping in areas relevant to adjustment for military flying. However, it has also been used as a general measure of self-concept adjustment.

Description The original item pool consisted of 91 statements designed to have subjects rate their needs, interests, and adequacy in relation to their ability to cope in the following areas considered relevant to adjustment for military flying: hostility, achievement, sexual relations, and dependency relations. The applicability of the statements was rated on separate five point scales for (1) self description, (2) ideal description, and (3) general description of others. Based largely on the even distribution of responses across rating categories, the items were reduced to the final set of 54 through administration to a college and Air Force sample. Self and self-ideal scores are the most used. The ratings for generalized others have been dropped for most uses. (Worchel, personal communication).

Sample The original samples consisted of 98 college students and 97 Air Force cadets. Further samples included 51 students who had sought or were referred to counselors.

Reliability/ Homogeneity Split-half reliabilities of .91, .84 and .89 have been obtained using the scale without items 16, 31 and 36 (Bryne et al., 1963). Test-retest reliabilities of .79, .72 and .78 for the self, ideal, and other ratings are presented in Worchel (1957).

Validity Convergent: Correlations with anxiety of .36 to .41 are reported for the self and self-ideal scores (Worchel, 1957). Correlations from .62 to .68 with the repression-sensitization scale have been found for these scores (Byrne et al., 1963). Strong (1962) factored the form along with several others and found satisfactory convergence.

Discriminant: No correlation with recall of incomplete tasks under task instructions was found (Worchel, 1957).

Predictive: Self-ideal correlations of .41 to .64 were found for two normal samples while only non-significant correlations were found for patients in consultatin. Recall of incomplete tasks (ratio) under ego-threat conditions was .28 with self-ratings. Subsequent studies cited in the references show high esteem people (low self-ideal discrepancy) to be more able to express aggression, more difficult to anger, and quicker to recover from anger. This seems to have face validity as a healthy pattern.

In one study, scores did not correlate with peer ratings of adjustment (Nebergall et al., 1959). However, neither did self-ratings of adjustment, which suggests that the population was unusual.

Location	Prior to its appearance here, the scale has only been available from the author at the University of Texas.
Administration	Depending on the number of ratings, the scale could take up to half an hour.
Results Comments	Positive points: Some validity has been demonstrated for the scale, particularly for the self-ratings. Some of the items tap areas of self which are not covered in other scales.

Negative points: The scale has been used in discrepancy form, an approach which has less demonstrated validity than the self-ratings above. More information is needed to justify use of this scale rather than more standard scales which have received more validation.

Suggestions: This scale raises some interesting questions that might be usefully examined in existing data. In order to score as being high in self-esteem, one essentially has to deny maladjustment on almost all items. Inter-item correlations would be worth investigating since some items, such as "takes extreme likes or dislikes to other people" or "feels sexually stimulated when reading or talking about sex,"[1] seem ambiguous in their relation to self-esteem (in other than discrepancy form).

While particular items may be weak, the areas covered seem somewhat broader than suggested by the description offered. For instance, anxiety or conformity factors might emerge if multidimensional analyses were performed.[2] More interesting, some of the items may be different enough from general scale items to warrant their further use in other scales.

Interestingly enough, it is the self-ideal discrepancy score that has been used in subsequent research, despite the evidence that self-ratings are more valid. For example, only self-ratings correlated with the behavioral criterion of recall of completed tasks. (This criterion, by the way, might be usefully developed further in combination with others). The author concluded (Worchel, 1957, p. 10) that "of the three scores. . . consistent results were obtained for only one, the self-rating score." While the evidence against this discrepancy score is not strong, the evidence would support Wylie's (1961) contention that simple self-ratings should be used until it is demonstrated that discrepancy scores are more valid.

References	Byrne, D., Barry, J., and Nelson, D. Relation of the revised repression-sensitization scale to measures of self-description. Psychological Reports, 1963, 13, 323-334.

---

[1] Byrne et al. (1963) note that this item (#36) as well as items 16 and 31 (which also refer to sex) have not been used in recent research.

[2] In unpublished factor analyses by D. Veldman and W. Griffitt up to 14 factors emerge with little replicability across sexes and analyses.

Nebergall, Nelda, Angelino, H., and Young, H. A validation study of the self-activity inventory as a predictor of adjustment. Journal of Consulting Psychology, 1959, 23, 21-24.

Rothaus, P., and Worchel, P. The inhibition of aggression under nonarbitrary frustration. Journal of Personality, 1960, 28, 108-117.

Strong, D. A factor analysis study of several measures of self concept. Journal of Counseling Psychology, 1962, 9, 64-70.

Veldman, D. and Worchel, P. Defensiveness and self-acceptance in the management of hostility. Journal of Abnormal and Social Psychology, 1961, 63, 319-325.

Worchel, P. Adaptability screening of flying personnel: Development of a self-concept inventory for predicting maladjustment. SAM, USAF, Randolph AFB, Texas, No. 56-62, 1957.

Worchel, P. Personality factors in the readiness to express aggression. Journal of Clinical Psychology, 1958, 14, 355-359.

Worchel, P. and McCormick, B. Self-concept and dissonance reduction. Journal of Personality, 1963, 31, 588-599.

Wylie, Ruth. The self-concept. Lincoln Nebraska: University of Nebraska Press, 1961.

SELF-ACTIVITY INVENTORY

The items are answered in the following way: respondent answers
each statement prefaced by "I am a person who:" using a one to
five scale.

Never	Seldom	Sometimes	Often	Very often
1	2	3	4	5

(Answers can also be given for ideal self and "the average person."
Dr. Worchel [personal communication] confirms that negative answers
represent high esteem in all cases despite the fact that a few items
such as number 42 would appear to be keyed true.)

1. ____ feels he must win an argument.

2. ____ plays up to others in order to advance his position.

3. ____ refuses to do things because he is not good at them.

4. ____ avoids telling the truth to prevent unpleasant consequences.

5. ____ tries hard to impress people with his ability.

6. ____ does dangerous things for the thrill of it.

7. ____ relies on his parents to help make decisions.

8. ____ has periods of great restlesssness that he must be on the go.

9. ____ seeks out others so they can listen to his troubles.

10. ____ gets angry when criticized by his friends.

11. ____ feels inferior to his friends.

12. ____ is afraid to try something new.

13. ____ gets confused when working under pressure.

14. ____ worries about his health.

15. ____ has difficulty in starting to get down to work.

16. ____ is dissatisfied with his sex like.

17. ____ bluffs to get ahead.

18. ____ feels uncomfortable in the presence of old women.

19. ____ goes out of his way to avoid an argument.

20. ____ makes quick judgments about other people.

Self-Activity Inventory reprinted here with permission of Worchel, P.

21. ____ wonders whether parents will approve of his actions.

22. ____ is bothered by thoughts about sex.

23. ____ is afraid to disagree with another person.

24. ____ ignores the feelings of others.

25. ____ feels angry when his parents try to tell him what to do.

26. ____ likes to gossip about the misfortunes and embarrassments of his friends.

27. ____ is awkward in his relationships with members of the opposite sex.

28. ____ is annoyed when asked to do a favor by a friend.

29. ____ takes disappointment so keenly that he can't put it out of his mind.

30. ____ resents the way he has been treated by his parents.

31. ____ feels guilty about his past sex life.

32. ____ suppresses or "bottles up" his feelings when angry with someone.

33. ____ worries about saying things that will hurt other people's feelings.

34. ____ holds grudges against those who have "hurt" him.

35. ____ feels resentful when bossed.

36. ____ feels sexually stimulated when reading or talking about sex.

37. ____ needs somebody to push him in order to get things done.

38. ____ feels hurt when ignored by superiors.

39. ____ fails to take the initiative in meeting people, arranging dates, etc.

40. ____ takes extreme likes or dislikes to other people.

41. ____ feels ill at ease when he is the only man in a group of girls.

42. ____ exerts a great deal of influence over most of his friends.

43. ____ dislikes lending things to his friends.

44. ____ upset when he feels he is not treated fairly.

45. ____ is nervous when he has to wait.

46. ____ would rather seek help from others on difficult things than to do it himself.

47. ____ worries about whether other people like him.

48. ____ gives in if anyone insists on a point.

49. ____ is critical of the behavior of most of his associates.

50. ____ looks for weaknesses in others.

51. ____ makes excuses for his behavior.

52. ____ worries about the opinions others have of him.

53. ____ feels jealous when others get ahead of him.

54. ____ places his faith in God when in trouble.

SELF DESCRIPTION INVENTORY (Cutick 1962; Diggory 1966; Shrauger 1970)

Variable
The original scale was devised by Cutick (1962) according to the following rationale summarized by Diggory (1966): "people evaluate themselves as goal-achieving instruments."

Description
The eight items used by Cutick and Diggory generally fall in the areas of winning respect from others, and the ability to make decisions and perform efficiently. The questions ask about a specific class of purposive activity common in people's experiences. The specific means of accomplishment are not specified, the response categories are not limited to yes, no or uncertain, and classes of activity can be added or deleted according to the situation (Diggory, 1966, pp. 277-278).

Shrauger and Rosenberg have lengthened the scale to 16 items, which cover the areas of physical skill, appearance, and school, in addition to the previous areas. The revised scale is approximately balanced for response bias. Each statement refers to functioning in a concrete area and is answered on a 0 to 100 percent scale.

Sample
College students have generally been employed in research with this scale.

Reliability/
Homogeneity
The test-retest reliability was .79 for both 87 males and 80 females over a three-month period (Shrauger, personal communication).

Validity
Convergent: Ziller et al. report correlations for the Cutick-Diggory version with the Bills scale of .60 (for males) and .29 (for females) and with the Coopersmith scale of .37 and .23. Shrauger (personal communication) reports correlations of .44 (for males) and .22 (for females) for the more recent longer version with the Bills acceptance score. The longer scale also correlated -.26 with the Rotter internality-externality scale (esteem related to internality) and -.42 with anxiety (high esteem related to low anxiety) for about 365 females.

Discriminant: The long scale correlated .20 with the Marlowe-Crowne social desirability scale for 365 females (Shrauger, personal communication).

Predictive: The original form gains some construct validity from the work summarized by Diggory (1966), particularly in the areas of goal setting and feedback. Additional construct validation for the new, longer scale comes from unpublished studies, as well as from published work listed in Shrauger and Rosenberg (1970) and Shrauger (1972).

Location
Diggory, J. Self-evaluation: Concepts and studies. New York: Wiley, 1966. (This contains the shorter version.)

Administration The scale should take about five minutes to administer.

Results and   <u>Positive points</u>: The attempt to anchor items in concrete behavior
Comments   seems worthwhile but deserves more testing.

                <u>Negative points</u>: The correlations with other scales are low
enough to suggest that more information about what is being measured is necessary. The even lower correlations for females may suggest that the task-oriented items of the scale do not reflect relevant sources of esteem for females as directly as for males.

                <u>Suggestions</u>: Since the revised scale is in active use, further information about the scale should accrue. Item analyses, and criterion analyses using peer ratings, could also be useful.

Feedback   Dr. Shrauger (Department of Psychology, State University) would ap-
to Author   preciate hearing about work with the scale. (He is in psychology
                at the State University of New York at Buffalo, 14226.)

References   Cutick, R. Self-evaluation of capacities as a function of self-
esteem and the characteristics of a model. Unpublished Ph.D. dissertation, University of Pennsylvania, 1962.

                Diggory, J. <u>Self-evaluation</u>: Concepts and studies. New York:
Wiley, 1966.

                Shrauger, J. Self-esteem and reactions to being observed by others. <u>Journal of Personality and Social Psychology</u>, 1972, <u>23</u>, 192-200.

                Shrauger, J. and Rosenberg, S. Self-esteem and the effects of success and failure feedback on performance. <u>Journal of Personality</u>, 1970, <u>38</u>, 404-417.

                Ziller, R., Hagey, Joan, Smith, Mary, and Long, Barbara. Self-esteem: A self-social construct. <u>Journal of Consulting and Clinical Psychology</u>, 1969, <u>33</u>, 84-95.

SELF DESCRIPTION INVENTORY - FORM R

The following questions ask you to assess your competence in various areas of performance. Indicate your responses to the following questions in the blank to the left of each question. Just give a number from 0 to 100 that shows how you feel about your ability. Zero would be "never" and a hundred would be "all the time." You can pick any number you want, just so it is closest to how you feel.

It is important that you try to answer each item <u>frankly</u> and honestly. Please read each question carefully and try to answer all the items.

_____ 1. When you try some new sport or physical activity, what percent of the time do you feel you have <u>not</u> mastered the skill as well as the average person? (-)*

_____ 2. When you face new situations which require fast decisions, what percent of the time can you make them effectively? (+)

_____ 3. When you try to reach important goals of any kind, what percent of the time do you feel you have really succeeded? (+)

_____ 4. When you are required to direct the activities of others, in what percent of the cases can you feel that you <u>fail</u> to receive the co-operation and respect of those directed? (-)

_____ 5. When you are attempting to get someone of the same sex to form a favorable impression of you, what percent of the time do you think you are <u>un</u>successful? (-)

_____ 6. What percentage of people of your own age and sex have a <u>more</u> pleasing personal appearance than you? (-)

_____ 7. In situations where it is necessary for you to speed up your performance in order to meet a deadline, in what percent of the cases can you do so without sacrificing the quality of your work? (+)

_____ 8. When you enter a new college course what percent of the time do you feel <u>un</u>certain that you will do as well as the average student? (-)

_____ 9. When doing things that interest you most, what percent of the time are you satisfied with your performance? (+)

_____10. When you are part of group activities, what pe cent of the time do your ideas and opinions influence the group? (+)

_____11. When put in a situation which is new and unfamiliar, what percent of the time do you feel you are <u>not</u> able to function adequately? (-)

_____12. When you have to take the initiative and act independently of others, what percent of the time can you handle things on your own? (+)

---

*Items for which a high percent indicates high esteem are labeled (+); those where a low percent indicates high esteem (-).

Self-Description Inventory reprinted here with permission of Shrauger, J.

_____16. When wise, careful judgment is needed about something, what per-
          cent of the time do you make sound judgment? (+)

SHERWOOD'S SELF-CONCEPT INVENTORY (Sherwood 1962)

Variable	This measure is based on Miller's Self-Identity Theory (1963). It introduces several methodological innovations in its attempts to test the theory.
Description	The scale is based on self-ratings across several dimensions. In addition it contains a measure of realistic or aspired self-ratings to replace ideal self-ratings. It also contains "open" scales which allow respondents to define their own dimensions for rating and an additional rating of the importance of each item to the total self-concept.

On the revised scales, people rate the importance of each item to their total self-concept immediately <u>after</u> each item, and no aspired self-ratings are made. These changes serve to considerably simplify the form's administration. There are now 15 bipolar dimensions with 11-point rating scales, plus three dimensions for which the endpoints are defined by each respondent.

Sample	The main sample used by Sherwood (1962) was 68 adults attending a two week National Training Laboratory "T group" session. College students also have been used.
Reliability/ Homogeneity	No data on internal consistency are reported.

For 57 psychology students the two week test-retest reliability was .82 for self-ratings and .78 for importance ratings. For the T-group participants these were lower as expected (.61 self, .55 importance).

Validity	<u>Convergent</u>: No evidence is available.

<u>Discriminant</u>: No evidence is available.

<u>Predictive</u>: Several interesting predictions concerning self-concept change have been confirmed.

Location	Sherwood, J.J. Self identity and self-actualization: A theory and research. Unpublished doctoral dissertation, The University of Michigan, 1962.
Administration	The simpler form should take less than half an hour.
Results and Comments	<u>Positive points</u>: Several methodologically sophisticated measurement techniques were introduced in this scale.

<u>Negative points</u>: None of the methodological techniques have been directly tested or validated, nor have any item analyses been performed. In addition, there is no central repository for information on the scale, which means that data on it will remain fragmented and unavailable.

Suggestions: The innovative measurement techniques introduced by this scale all deserve further testing and consideration. All have theoretical potential but have not been systematically compared to simpler methods. For instance, the only support for weighting items by importance instead of combining them additively comes from one study using the body cathexis scale.

The Sherwood scale contains an overall self-rating which could be used to test the validity of weighting items, although these techniques could probably be better tested with a scale which has been used and tested more extensively.

References   French, J.R.P., Jr., Sherwood, J.J., and Bradford, D.L. Change in self-identity in a management training conference. Journal of Applied Behavioral Science, 1966, 2, 210-218.

Miller, D. Identity, situation, and social interaction: The impact of social structure on motivation. In Psychology: A study of a science, edited by S. Koch, New York: McGraw-Hill, 1963, 6, 639-787.

Sherwood, J.J. Self identity and self-actualization: A theory and research. Unpublished doctoral dissertation, The University of Michigan, 1962.

Sherwood, J.J. Self identity and referent others. Sociometry, 1965, 28, 66-81.

Sherwood, J.J. Increased self-evaluation as a function of ambiguous evaluation by referent others. Sociometry, 1967, 20, 404-409.

Sherwood, J.J. Self-actualization and self-identity theory. Personality, 1970, 1, 41-63.

Scale   The following pairs of adjectives are anchors (i.e., at the end points) of 11-point scales. Each scale is followed by another 11-point scale labeled extremely important and extremely unimportant. Unlabeled scales are also included. The high esteem adjective is listed first here. They should be counterbalanced if used.

If the importance ratings are used the total esteem scores is the sum of each answer on a 0 to 10 scale multiplied by the importance rating on the 0 to 10 scale. Thus the total possible score for 19 items would be 1900.

1. Self-confident :__:__:__:__:__:__:__:__:__:__: Lack self-confidence

2. Tolerant of others :__:__:__:__:__:__:__:__:__:__: Critical of others

3. Able to do most things well :__:__:__:__:__:__:__:__:__:__: Unable to do most things well

Sherwood's Self-Concept Inventory is reprinted here with permission of author.

4.   Honest   :__:__:__:__:__:__:__:__:__:__:__: Dishonest

5.   Enthusi-   Unenthusi-
     astic   :__:__:__:__:__:__:__:__:__:__:__: astic

6.   Likable :__:__:__:__:__:__:__:__:__:__:__: Not likeable

7. Cooperative:__:__:__:__:__:__:__:__:__:__:__: Competitive

8.   Leader :__:__:__:__:__:__:__:__:__:__:__: Follower

9.   Moral   :__:__:__:__:__:__:__:__:__:__:__: Immoral

10. Satisfied :__:__:__:__:__:__:__:__:__:__:__: Frustrated

11.Intelligent :__:__:__:__:__:__:__:__:__:__:__: Unintelligent

12. Friendly :__:__:__:__:__:__:__:__:__:__:__: Unfriendly

13.   Calm   :__:__:__:__:__:__:__:__:__:__:__: Anxious

14.   Useful :__:__:__:__:__:__:__:__:__:__:__: Useless

15. Know myself   Don't under
      well :__:__:__:__:__:__:__:__:__:__:__: stand myself
                                      at all

16. _ _ _ _ _ :__:__:__:__:__:__:__:__:__:__:_ _ _ _ _ _

17. _ _ _ _ _ :__:__:__:__:__:__:__:__:__:__: _ _ _ _ _ _

18. _ _ _ _ _ :__:__:__:__:__:__:__:__:__:__: _ _ _ _ _ _

19. Finally, on this scale you are to rate your overall level of
    self-opinion or self esteem, that is, how high or low you pre-
    sently judge your total picture of yourself to be.

           High :__:__:__:__:__:__:__:__:__: Low

REPRESSION-SENSITIZATION SCALE (Byrne 1963)

Variable   This scale attempts to measure defensive style. Its strong empirical relation to self-esteem supports the theoretical connection between level of esteem and type of ego defenses.

Description   The scale is derived from the MMPI. The first version had 182 items. Further testing led to 127 cross-replicated items for a more homogeneous, slightly more valid scale. This scale attempts to measure an individual's chronic defensive mode. "The repressive extreme involves avoidance defenses, such as denial, while the sensitizing extreme refers to approach defenses, such as intellectualization" (Byrne et al., 1963).

Sample   College students and clinical samples have largely been used.

Reliability/   The 182 item scale had a split-half reliability of .88. For the revised scale a correlation of .94 for split-half reliability is reported.
Homogeneity

Test-retest reliabilities of .88 for the longer scale and .82 for the shorter version have been reported (Byrne, 1963).

Validity   <u>Convergent</u>: The longer scale has correlated .62 and .55 with self-ideal discrepancy using Worchel's scale. The revised form correlated .63 with discrepancy and .68 with simple (negative) self-description (Byrne et al., 1963). For 40 males, a correlation of .85 was found between repression-sensitization and a modified Janis and Field esteem scale (Frankel and Barrett, 1971); and it correlated with the various self-actualization subscales of the Personality Orientation Inventory from -.36 to -.75, with the highest correlation being found for self-regard (Foulds and Warehime, 1971). The scale correlated from .76 to .91 with the Manifest Anxiety Scale depending on how much of the item overlap (29) was eliminated from the two scales (Sullivan and Roberts, 1969).

<u>Discriminant</u>: For a sample of 136 patients (half psychiatric) the scale correlated -.45 with the Marlowe-Crowne social desirability scale (Feder, 1967). Bernhardson found a similar correlation of -.42 (1967).

<u>Predictive</u>: Clinical judges agreed with the keying of 90% of the revised items. Sensitizers showed somewhat more conflict with regard to emotional preferences (Byrne et al., 1963).

Location   Byrne, D., Barry, J., and Nelson, D. Relation of the revised repression-sensitization scale to measures of self-description. <u>Psychological Reports</u>, 1963, <u>13</u>, 323-334.

Administration Administered alone the items could take up to an hour to complete.

Results and   <u>Positive points</u>: This scale has been usefully applied in several research settings and represents a large item pool.
Comments

<u>Negative points</u>: The suggestion of Byrne et al., (1963) that the scale may measure social desirability should be considered. In general, the relation between defensiveness and self-esteem has not been fully explicated.

<u>Suggestions</u>: Byrne (1964) has reviewed most of the early work with this and similar scales. If the MMPI is not routinely applied, other scales may prove more directly related to self-concept. A valuable contribution in this area would be the construction of a shorter scale independent of social desirability. The recent tendency to use the Marlowe-Crowne social desirability scale in conjunction with this scale is a good start (e.g., Kahn and Schill 1971).

References

Bernhardson, C. Dogmatism, defense mechanisms, and social desirability responding. <u>Psychological Reports</u>, 1967, <u>20</u>, 511-513.

Byrne, D. Repression-sensitization as a dimension of personality. In <u>Progress in Experimental Personality Research</u>, edited by B. Maker, New York: Academic Press, 1964, <u>1</u>, 169-220.

Byrne, D. The repression-sensitization scale: Rationale, reliability, and validity. <u>Journal of Personality</u>, 1961, <u>29</u>, 334-349.

Byrne, D., Barry, J., and Nelson, D. Relation of the revised repression-sensitization scale to measures of self-description. <u>Psychological Reports</u>, 1963, <u>13</u>, 323-334.

Feder, Carol. Relationship of repression-sensitization to adjustment states, social desirability, and acquiescence response bias. <u>Journal of Consulting Psychology</u>, 1967, <u>31</u>, 401-406.

Foulds, M. and Warehime, R. Relationship between repression-sensitization and a measure of self-actualization. <u>Journal of Consulting and Clinical Psychology</u>, 1971, <u>36</u>, 257-259.

Frankel, A. and Barrett, J. Variations in personal space as a function of authoritarianism, self-esteem, and racial characteristics of a stimulus situation. <u>Journal of Consulting and Clinical Psychology</u>, 1971, <u>37</u>, 95-98.

Kahn, M. and Schill, T. Anxiety report in defensive and nondefensive repressors. <u>Journal of Consulting and Clinical Psychology</u>, 1971, <u>36</u>, 300.

Sullivan, P. and Roberts, L. Relationship of manifest anxiety to repression-sensitization on the MMPI. <u>Journal of Consulting and Clinical Psychology</u>, 1969, <u>33</u>, 763-764.

REPRESSION-SENSITIZATION SCALE

The scale is keyed so that high scores represent sensitization,
which is related to low esteem or low social desirability.

MMPI item numbers and keying for the 127 item scale are as follows:

3(F)	94(T)	158(T)	207(F)	304(T)	361(T)
7(F)	96(F)	159(T)	213(T)	305(T)	362(T)
8(F)	102(T)	160(F)	217(T)	316(T)	374(T)
10(T)	103(F)	162(T)	230(F)	321(T)	379(F)
15(T)	104(T)	163(F)	234(T)	322(T)	382(T)
22(T)	106(T)	164(F)	236(T)	336(T)	383(T)
26(T)	107(F)	165(T)	238(T)	337(T)	384(T)
32(T)	109(T)	171(T)	241(T)	340(T)	389(T)
36(F)	114(T)	172(T)	242(F)	342(T)	396(T)
41(T)	122(F)	175(F)	243(F)	343(T)	397(T)
43(T)	124(T)	178(F)	259(T)	344(T)	398(T)
44(T)	129(T)	179(T)	265(T)	345(T)	411(T)
51(F)	131(F)	180(T)	266(T)	346(T)	414(T)
52(T)	136(T)	182(T)	267(T)	349(T)	418(T)
55(F)	138(T)	186(T)	270(F)	352(T)	431(T)
57(F)	141(T)	188(F)	278(T)	353(F)	443(T)
67(T)	142(T)	189(T)	279(T)	356(T)	465(T)
76(T)	145(T)	190(F)	289(T)	357(T)	511(T)
86(T)	147(T)	191(T)	290(T)	358(T)	518(T)
88(F)	148(T)	192(F)	292(T)	359(T)	544(T)
89(T)	152(F)	201(T)	301(T)	360(T)	555(T)
93(T)					

Used here with permission.

EGO STRENGTH SCALE (Barron 1953)

Variable
The scale was devised empirically to differentiate those who improved with therapy from those who did not. Presumably those who respond to psychotherapy have higher ego strength.

Description
The scale consists of 68 items from the MMPI. One point is scored for each "ego strength" answer. The items were empirically selected using a sample of only 33 patients. They differentiated those who improved from those who did not after six months.

The areas covered by questions as labeled by Barron (and with alternative labels) are: 1) physical functioning and physiological stability (like denying the somatic aspect of manifest anxiety; 2) psychasthenia and seclusiveness (inverse of timidity and anxiety); 3) attitudes toward religion (contradictory, but generally nonbelief); 4) moral posture (like the disinhibition items on the stimulus seeking scale; Zuckerman, 1971); 5) sense of reality (denying strangeness, answering in the statistically socially desirable direction); (6) personal adequacy, ability to cope (some stimulus seeking or creativity, very little self-esteem); 7) phobias, infantile anxieties (denying unreasonable anxieties); and 8) miscellaneous.

Sample
The original sample consisted of 33 patients, 17 of whom improved and were used to empirically select items. Many other samples have been used subsequently.

Reliability/
Homogeneity
A split-half reliability of .76 has been reported (Barron, 1953)

A test-retest reliability of .72 has been reported (Barron, 1953).

Validity
Convergent: The scale correlated .24 with the California Psychological Inventory self-acceptance scale (Gough, 1969). Correlations of .39 and .45 are reported with other measures (Larsen and Schwendiman, 1969). It correlated only -.37 with manifest anxiety (Worell and Hill, 1962).

Discriminant: For both normals and patients correlations with several MMPI scales exceed .40.

Predictive: Correlations of the scale with staff ratings (at IPAR in Berkley Calif.) were: vitality (.28); drive (.41); self-confidence (.24); poise (.24); breadth of interest (.25); submissiveness (-.40); effeminancy (for men) (-.34); and intraceptiveness (-.34).

Several partial cross-validations have been obtained by correlating scores with success in therapy for other samples. These correlations have been .49 for 39 items, .54 for a curvilinear relationship, and .38 for the entire scale.

Location
Barron, F. An ego-strength scale which predicts response to psychotherapy. Journal of Consulting Psychology, 1953, 14, 327-333.

Administration
The scale should take about half an hour to complete.

Results and Comments	Positive points: The scale has demonstrated some validity.

Negative points: The scale correlates more highly with measures unrelated to ego strength than it does with self-esteem measures. The cross-validation work should have been done item-by-item. When one starts with 550 items (MMPI) and uses unreplicated empirical selection procedures, 27 1/2 items can be expected by chance to relate significantly to a criterion.[1] An example of the problems that can arise from empirical selection are the six religion items, which portray the high ego-strength individual as going to church almost every week but neither praying nor believing. While this is possible, it is more probable that the church attendance item would simply not replicate. There is also contradictory evidence that people with stronger religious values have higher self-esteem (Johnson, 1971).

Suggestions: This scale is really not a self-esteem scale as the construct is developed here. Even the items classified under personal adequacy and ability to cope show little relation to the concept of self-esteem. The scale seems to have some validity, but without more detailed analyses it is impossible to tell what is being measured.

An example of the possible improvements which could be obtained by item analyses is demonstrated in unpublished work by Zander and Thomas (1960). Selecting out 24 items[2] on the basis of their relation to a conceptualization of ego strength, they improved the correlation with an unpublished open-ended scale from .37 to .72. More importantly they obtained a significant difference in scores of patients in open wards versus closed wards not obtainable with the longer scale. While no one study or criterion can be conclusive, more of this kind of analysis (especially on the item level) needs to be done and reported.

References	Barron, F. An ego-strength scale which predicts response to psychotherapy. Journal of Consulting Psychology, 1953, 17, 327-333.

Barron, F. A correction. Journal of Consulting Psychology, 1954, 18, 150.

Block, J. On the number of significant findings to be expected by chance. Psychometrika, 1960, 25, 369-380.

Gough, H. California Psychological Inventory Manual. Palo Alto, California: Consulting Psychologists Press, Inc., 1969 (revised edition).

Johnson, M. The relationship of religious commitment to self-esteem. M.S. thesis, Brigham Young University, 1971.

---

[1]Block (1960) has empirically demonstrated that the traditional estimate of the number of significant items expected by chance is conservative. Using groups of about the size Barron used, about 2.5% of the items (13.75) would be significant by chance.

[2]The items were: 22, 32, 94, 95, 181, 187, 217, 221, 234, 236, 253, 270, 349, 359, 367, 380, 389, 488, 494, 525, 544, 555, 559, and 561.

Larsen, K. and Schwendiman, G. Authoritarianism, self-esteem, and insecurity. Psychological Reports, 1969, 25, 229-230.

Worell, L. and Hill, L. Ego strength and anxiety in discrimination conflict performance. Journal of Consulting Psychology, 1962, 26, 311-316.

Zander, A. and Thomas, E. The validity of a measure of ego strength. Unpublished manuscript, The University of Michigan, 1960.

Zuckerman, M. Dimensions of sensation seeking. Journal of Consulting and Clinical Psychology, 1971, 36, 35-52.

Scale

For those who wish to develop this scale further, the following are the MMPI items numbers and keys in the Barron areas:

1) **Psychological stability:** 2(T), 14(F), 34(F), 36(T), 43(F), 51(T), 153(T), 174(T), 187(T), 189(F), 341(F)

2) **Psychasthenia:** 100(F), 217(F), 234(T), 236(F), 241(F), 270(T), 344(F), 359(F), 384(F), 489(F)

3) **Attitudes toward religion:** 58(F), 95(T), 209(F), 420(F), 483(F), 488(F)

4) **Moral posture:** 94(F), 109(T), 181(T), 208(T), 231(T), 253(T), 355(T), 378(F), 410(T), 430(T), 548(F)

5) **Sense of reality:** 22(F), 33(F), 48(F), 62(F), 192(T), 251(F), 349(F), 541(F)

6) **Personal adequacy:** 32(F), 82(F), 132(F), 140(F), 244(F), 261(F), 380(T), 389(F), 544(F), 554(F), 555(F)

7) **Phobias:** 367(T), 494(F), 510(F), 525(F), 559(F)

8) **Miscellaneous:** 221(T), 421(T), 458(T), 513(T), 515(T), 561(F)

Items 515(T) and 43(F) are not classified as to area by Barron.

THOMAS-ZANDER EGO STRENGTH SCALES (Thomas and Zander 1960)

Variable   The authors were originally interested in measuring ego strength
                  as it related to susceptibility to group pressure.

Description   Ego strength is conceptualized in two parts. First is a person's
                  ability to be self-directing and to translate intentions consis-
                  tently into behavior (i.e., executive ability). Second is the
                  ability to control and discharge tension without disrupting other
                  psychological processes (i.e., tension control).

                  The first attempt at measurement involved the coding of open ended
                  self-referent statements. The form reviewed here has 27 items
                  answered true or false. The items were selected from a larger pool
                  of 48 items; 20 were thought to reflect both executive ability and
                  tension control, as well as more general functions. Seven of the
                  items formed a Guttman scale thought to reflect both executive
                  ability and tension control.

Sample   Adults, mental patients, and military men have been the major
                  groups sampled to date.

                  Two items are more often answered in the high ego strength direction
                  by men (12,16), one by women (18) (Jahnke et al., 1962).

Reliability   The 20 items and the 7-item scales intercorrelated .50. The median
                  inter-item correlation for the 10 tension control items was .14;
                  for the 9 executive ability items (item 20 was excluded because
                  of extreme distribution) it was .24; for the 10 tension control
                  items with the nine executive items, it was .17 (Zander et al.,
                  1957). Schussel (1968) reports a median item-total scale correla-
                  tion in the .40's for all 27 items.

                  Test-retest reliability for the 20 items was .81 over about one
                  week for 541 men. For 7 items the test-retest correlation was .72
                  (Zander and Thomas, 1960).

Validity   Convergent: LaMonaca and Berkun (1959) found a correlation of -.65
                  between the combined 27-item scale and the 50-item manifest anxiety
                  scale. Schussel (1968) found a median correlation in the .20's
                  for the items with the Tennessee esteem scale total score.

                  Discriminant: No data are available.

                  Predictive: Ego strength predicted to several behavioral variables,
                  an intriguing one being evasion of capture during a military exer-
                  cise (Zander and Thomas, 1960). It predicted open or closed ward
                  status better than the Barron scale.

Location   Zander, A. and Thomas, E. The validity of a measure of ego strength.
                  Unpublished paper, The University of Michigan, Institute for Social
                  Research, 1960.

Administration Less than 15 minutes should be required.

Results and   <u>Positive points</u>: This scale incorporates slightly different items
Comments   than the average self-esteem scale. It has shown some validity.

          <u>Negative points</u>: More information and analyses are necessary before
the scale can be considered well validated. The distinction between
tension control and executive ability has not been empirically
validated.

<u>Suggestions</u>: These items could be usefully incorporated into fur-
ther item analyses designed to construct better measures. The
authors have not distributed the scale more widely because of their
concern about social desirability confounding. Analyses examining
this matter would seem most worthwhile.

References   Jahnke, J., Crannell, C., and Morrisette, J. Norms for the Thomas
and Zander scale of ego strength. Unpublished paper, Miami University (Ohio), 1962.

LaMonaca, H., and Berkun, M. Some Army normative data on the 50-
item form of the Taylor manifest anxiety scale. U.S. Army Leadership Human Research Unit, Presidio of Monterey, California, 1959.

Schussel, R. An item analysis of diverse personality inventories
and their relation to risk-taking behavior. Unpublished Masters
Thesis, Miami University (Ohio), 1968.

Zander, A. and Thomas, E. The validity of a measure of ego strength.
Unpublished paper, The University of Michigan, Institute for Social
Research, 1960.

Zander, A., Thomas, E. and Natsoulas, T. Determinants of motivation
and performance under pressure. Research Center for Group Dynamics,
Institute for Social Research, The University of Michigan, 1957.

EGO STRENGTH SCALES

The items are keyed for high ego strength. The first 20 items were constructed as a general scale, the last 7 items as a Guttman scale. They
can be used together.

1. I am a very ambitious person. (T)

2. I am very stubborn and set in my ways. (F)

3. No one can change my beliefs in which I have strong faith. (T)

4. I frequently find myself worrying about the future. (F)

5. I frequently worry about things that never happen. (F)

6. I give everything I have to what I undertake to do. (T)

7. I am a calm person in almost any emergency. (T)

8. Often I feel tense without any good reason. (F)

9. I am restless or irritable when people make me wait for them. (F)

10. I am always self-reliant and independent in doing my work. (T)

11. I am one who likes actively to keep busy. (T)

12. I have an inferiority complex about my abilities to do things. (F)

13. I have strong beliefs which I will always stand by. (T)

14. One of my greatest troubles is that I cannot get down to work when
    I should. (F)

15. I can work in the midst of a number of distractions. (T)

16. Whenever I am upset I always get over it right away. (T)

17. Often I feel that my time is spent aimlessly. (F)

18. When I decide to do something, I go right to work on it. (T)

19. I don't like to have to work hard to get things done. (F)

20. I never persist at things very long without giving up. (F)

21. I have very definite, established goals in life which I intend to
    pursue at all costs. (T)

22. Often I find myself doing and saying things that turn out to be
    things that shouldn't have been done or said. (F)

Thomas-Zander Ego Strength Scale is used here with permission.

23. Sometimes I don't care whether I get anywhere in life or not. (F)

24. There are odd moments now and then when I suspect I might go to pieces. (F)

25. Every now and then I lose my temper when things go wrong. (F)

26. Every now and then I can't seem to make up my mind about things. (F)

27. I am one who <u>never</u> gets excited when things go wrong. (T)

BODY CATHEXIS SCALE (Secord and Jourard 1953)

Variable   This scale is an interesting example of an attempt to measure one
                 particular aspect of self-esteem--satisfaction with aspects of
                 the body.

Description   Forty physical characteristics are listed and subjects rate
                 their satisfaction with each on a five-point Likert scale. Fifty-
                 five general self-characteristics were also used in the original
                 work as a general self-esteem measure.

Sample   A total of 45 male and 43 female college students comprised the
                 main sample. Respondents who indicated almost complete satisfaction
                 were eliminated from further analysis.

Reliability   The corrected split-half reliability for the body esteem score was
                 .78 for males and .83 for females. No test-retest data are reported.

Validity   Convergent: Physical self-esteem and general esteem correlated .58
                 for males and .66 for females (Secord and Jourard, 1953). This was
                 generally replicated by Weinburg (1960). Physical esteem also
                 correlated moderately with anxiety. Johnson (1956) obtained corre-
                 lations of .66 for males and .79 for females between general esteem
                 and body esteem.

                 Discriminant: No data are available.

                 Predictive: The fact that general esteem and anxiety correlate more
                 highly with body esteem for females may add construct validity, under
                 the assumption that physical appearance is more important for females
                 in our culture.

Location   Secord, P., and Jourard, S. The appraisal of body-cathexis; body
                 cathexis and the self. Journal of Consulting Psychology, 1953, 17,
                 343-347.

Administration   Administration time for physical esteem should be less than 20 minutes.

Results and   Positive points: The scale is not unique in its concern with physi-
Comments   cal esteem, but it is unique in its concrete anchoring of ratings
                 through the specification of each aspect of physical well-being.
                 Validity is added by several studies (e.g., Johnson, 1956; Jourard
                 and Secord, 1955).

                 Negative points: No item analyses and little validity work have
                 been performed on the scale.

                 Suggestions: This is one area of esteem where criterion groups
                 might not be hard to find. For instance, work has been done with
                 athletic performance and nudists.

                 Interestingly, data from this scale comprise one of few instances in which the possible utility of weighting items by importance has been supported. The correlation between self-esteem and satisfaction with physical characteristics rated as important was .62; for physical characteristics not rated important the correlation was only .28 (Rosen and Ross, 1968). Watkins and Park (1972) have extended this.

This scale can easily be adapted to reflect physical esteem or acceptance of physical self, or some combination as in the original Likert scale. For particular purposes, specific scales can prove useful either alone or added to a more general scale.

References   Gunderson, E. K. Body size, self-evaluation, and military effectiveness. Journal of Personality and Social Psychology, 1965, 2, 902-906.

Johnson, L. Body cathexis as a factor in somatic complaints. Journal of Consulting Psychology, 1956, 20, 145-149.

Jourard, S. and Secord, P. Body-cathexis and the ideal female figure. Journal of Abnormal and Social Psychology, 1955, 50, 243-246.

Rosen, G. and Ross, A. Relationship of body image to self-concept. Journal of Consulting and Clinical Psychology, 1968, 32, 100.

Secord, P. and Jourard, S. The appraisal of body-cathexis; body cathexis and the self. Journal of Consulting Psychology, 1953, 17, 343-347.

Watkins, D. and Park, J. The role of subjective importance in self evaluation. Australian Journal of Psychology, 1972, 24, 209-210.

Weinburg, J. A further investigation of body-cathexis and the self. Journal of Consulting Psychology, 1960, 24, 277.

INSTRUCTIONS AND ITEMS

The following instructions and forty items are recommended by Dr. Secord. Several other forms of the scale have been used. Other items have included: fingers, wrists, breathing, exercise, ankles, neck, shape of head, eyes, skin texture, lips, teeth, forehead, sex (male or female), back view of head (Secord and Jourard, 1953) thighs, calves, nose length, and neck length (Jourard and Secord 1955). Johnson (1956) modified the instructions to encourage broader use of the answer categories.

On the following pages are listed a number of things characteristic of yourself or related to you. Consider each item listed and encircle the number of each item which best represents your feelings according to the following scale:

1. Have strong positive feelings.
2. Have moderate positive feelings.
3. Have no feeling one way or the other.
4. Have moderate negative feelings.
5. Have strong negative feelings.

Body-Cathexis Items Used in BC Scale

1.	hair	21.	width of shoulders
2.	facial complexion	22.	arms
3.	appetite	23.	chest (or breasts)
4.	hands	24.	appearance of eyes
5.	distribution of hair (over body)	25.	digestion
6.	nose	26.	hips
7.	physical stamina	27.	resistance to illness
8.	elimination	28.	legs
9.	muscular strength	29.	appearance of teeth
10.	waist	30.	sex drive
11.	energy level	31.	feet
12.	back	32.	sleep
13.	ears	33.	voice
14.	age	34.	health
15.	chin	35.	sex activities
16.	body build	36.	knees
17.	profile	37.	posture
18.	height	38.	face
19.	keeness of senses	39.	weight
20.	tolerance for pain	40.	sex organs

Feedback to Author   Dr. Jourard (University of Florida) would appreciate hearing about work with the scale.

Body Cathexis Scale (Secord and Jourard 1953). Copyright 1953 by the American Psychological Association. Reprinted here with permission.

SELF-REPORT INVENTORY (Bown 1961)

Variable

Responses are intended to reflect a person's phenomenological world. Self and total scores have been used to measure self-esteem or general adjustment. Spanish and French versions exist.

Description

The Bown self-report inventory is in its third revision. The present version is a 48-item scale with 5-point answers from "like me" to "unlike me." It contains eight 6-item scales with generally good internal consistency. In addition, total and intensity scores can be computed, and the relative positivity toward self versus others can be measured.

The self scale seems most closely related to self-esteem. The other scales involve rating others, children, authorities, work, parents, hope (i.e., optimism), and reality (an unreliable scale, $\alpha = .28$, perhaps involving healthy acceptance of life and death). Dr. Bown suggests that the work, reality and hope subscales are also centrally important to the self-concept.

Sample

A total of 2,321 freshmen students were used to obtain data on the form in 1963. Many other large samples have been used.

Reliability

The alpha coefficient for the 6-item self scale was .78; for the total scale an alpha value of .87 was recorded. Other subscale reliabilities ranged from .28 to .85. Split half reliabilities have ranged from .66 to .89 (Bown, personal communication).

Validity

Convergent: The subscores comprising the total score correlate from .06 to .47 with each other.

Discriminant: The self and total scores do not correlate with several intellectual and demographic variables.

Predictive: Self and total scores correlate slightly (.21 to .24) with confidence about college. Dr. Bown (personal communication) states that correlations of the scale with various criteria have often been in the .30 to .65 range.

Location

The total set of items is available in a preliminary form of the manual which includes the questions and other data from the author, Dr. Oliver Bown, R & D Center for Teacher Education, The University of Texas, Austin, Texas 78712. He also has an extensive bibliography of largely unpublished studies.

Administration

The 6-item self scale should only take a few minutes to administer. However, the subscales are not often used separately and the items are given here only as a sample or as part of future item pools.

Results and Comments

Positive points: The scale has been used by many people. The self items have face validity.

Negative points: Because the subscores are largely unrelated, it is difficult to interpret the meaning of the total score which has been used to indicate self-esteem and general adjustment.

Suggestions: This scale is a good example of those which are quite popular but not widely available. For example only 11 of 39 items on the bibliography are published. To make important data available, and because use is often based on availability, a book summarizing work with the scale would be important if the scale is to be more widely used.

References   Bown, O. The development of a self-report inventory and its function in a mental health assessment battery. American Psychologist, 1961, 16, 402.

Bown, O., Fuller, Frances, and Richek, H. A comparison of self-perceptions of prospective elementary and secondary school teachers. Psychology in the Schools, 1967, 4, 21-24.

Bown, O., and Richek, H. Mental health of junior college students. Junior College Journal, 1966-1967, 37, 18-21.

Bown, O., and Richek, H. The Bown self-report inventory (SRI): A quick screening instrument for mental health professionals. Comprehensive Psychiatry, 1967, 8, 45-52.

Bown, O., and Veldman, D. Scoring procedures and college freshman norms for the self-report inventory. University of Texas; unpublished manual, undated.

SELF-REPORT INVENTORY
Self Scale

All items except number 4 are keyed so that disagreement indicates high esteem. The means from the five point scale are included for each item (5 is highest esteem).

1. I don't seem to have very much basic respect for myself. (3.88)

2. I feel sour and pessimistic about life in general. (4.22)

3. Thinking back, in a good many ways I don't think I have liked myself very well. (3.51)

4. In almost every respect, I'm very glad to be the person I am. (4.26)

5. When I think about the kind of person that I have been in the past, it doesn't make me feel very happy or proud. (3.58)

6. I'd give a good deal to be very different than I am. (4.08)

Self-Report Inventory reprinted here with permission of Bown, O. (Dr. Bown requests that researchers contact him for permission to use the scale.)

TWENTY STATEMENTS (WHO AM I? WHO ARE YOU?) TEST (Kuhn and McPartland 1954; Bugental and Zelen 1950)

Variable   Self-attitudes are presumably tapped in a very phenomenological context.

Description   This test requests people to answer the question, "Who am I?" Kuhn and McPartland ask it twenty times in the earlier version; Bugental and Zelen ask it only three times. These responses are coded for proportion of self-derogating statements and scored for strength of self-derogation or self-positivity.

                    In addition, individuals can indicate how much they like each statement about themselves. There is also a salience score which is the number at which the first self-derogating statement appears. Other coding systems are possible.

Sample   This technique has been tried only with college students.

Reliability/   Kuhn and McPartland report at least adequate coding reliabilities,
Homogeneity   although data on internal consistency are not reported.

                    No test-retest data are reported.

Validity   Convergent: Spitzer et al. (1966) show correlations largely in the .20s and .30s with the Bills scale, the Adjective Check List, and a semantic differential scale.

                    Discriminant: No data are reported.

                    Predictive: No data are reported.

Location   Kuhn, M. and McPartland. An empirical investigation of self-attitudes. American Sociological Review, 1954, 19, 58-76; and Bugental, J. and Zelen, S., Investigations into the "self-concept," I. The W-A-Y technique. Journal of Personality, 1950, 18, 483-498.

Administration   The test can be completed in less than 15 minutes.

Results and   Positive points: The test has the theoretical advantage of allowing
Comments   people to define their own rating dimensions.

                    Negative points: There has been little empirical demonstration of any advantage over more structured measurement approaches to self-esteem. In addition, it correlates at a low level with existing self-esteem scales, although it was not particularly intended to correlate with them. It is least liked by respondents as a self-rating method (Spitzer et al., 1966).

                    Suggestions: It is interesting to discover the types of things that people report about themselves. For instance, people mention their social roles first and idiosyncratic descriptions later. However, this type of scale is likely to be of little use in measuring self-esteem, except perhaps as an adjunct to other methods, such as in the Sherwood or Miskimins' scales. While the format may "force" some individuals to reveal their true selves or "unconscious" esteem, the possibility does not seem strong.

References

Bugental, J. and Zelen, S. Investigations into the "self-concept." I. The W-A-Y technique. Journal of Personality, 1950, 18, 483-498.

Kuhn, M. and McPartland. An empirical investigation of self-attitudes. American Sociological Review, 1954, 19, 58-76.

Spitzer, S., Stratton, J., Fitzgerald, J., and Mach, Brigitte. The self concept: Test equivalence and perceived validity. Sociological Quarterly, 1966, 7, 265-280.

TWENTY STATEMENTS TEST

A sheet should be prepared asking "Who Am I" or "Who Are You" with space for up to 20 answers.

SOCIAL SELF-ESTEEM (Ziller 1969)

Variable   Self-esteem is conceptualized as relative to the social reality of the individual. The individual's level of esteem is a response to social stimuli and the level of esteem affects the type of response.

Description   The "self-esteem" measure itself consists of six circles arrayed horizontally, followed by a list of "people" such as a) doctor, b) father, c) a friend, d) a nurse, e) "yourself," or f) someone you know who is unsuccessful. There are six such lists which all include "yourself." One is instructed to place each "person" in a circle. The further to the left in the horizontal array one puts "yourself" the higher one's social self-esteem. (The form for children uses a vertical array of circles with the top indicating high "esteem.")

Social "self-esteem" is only one measure of self-other orientation that is measured by various topological scales. Others include: range and intensity of identification, power, marginality (in groups), openness, and inclusion (in groups.)

Sample   Ziller and others have used various samples from college students to politicians.

Reliability/
Homogeneity   Corrected split-half reliability has been in the .80s.

No test-retest data are reported.

Validity   <u>Convergent</u>: The scale does not relate well to other self-esteem measures (Ziller et al., 1969) or to internality-externality (Platt, Eisenman and Darbes, 1970). Ziller et al. (1969) report a correlation between the vertical and horizontal measure of .50 (p. 87). Grace Mack (1972), finds that the horizontal and vertical scores only correlated .25 for first graders and only .22 for fourth graders; in both cases, the bulk of these correlations was contributed only by black males for whom correlations were .67 and .45. For other groups there were no significant correlations.

<u>Discriminant</u>: In the Mack (1972) data, vertical measures of different traits often correlated higher than the vertical and horizontal measures of the same trait, suggesting both low discriminant validity and unexplained method variance.

<u>Predictive</u>: Considerable evidence is presented concerning the scale's relationship to various "criteria." Much of this is summarized in the review by Ziller et al. (1969) and some is also covered in an unpublished manuscript (Ziller, 1968). Sociometric stars have higher "esteem" than sociometric isolates. Political candidates who won an election rose in "self-esteem," those who lost fell. "Esteem" and frequency and consistency of verbal participation were positively related as were "esteem" and socioeconomic status. Normals have higher "esteem" than psychiatric patients, behavior problem children and physically handicapped adolescents.

Location   Ziller, R.; Hagey, Joan; Smith, Mary; and Long, Barbara. Self-esteem: A self-social construct. <u>Journal of Consulting and Clinical Psychology</u>, 1969, <u>33</u>, 84-95. Educational Testing Service is now distributing it.

Results and   <u>Positive points</u>: There is creative potential in this scale which
Comments   may repay careful investigation. The method is unobtrusive and considerable validity has been demonstrated.

<u>Negative points</u>: This measure does <u>not</u> tap self-esteem as self-esteem is ascertained by other measures. Hopefully, the presentation of this measure here will stimulate research to determine just what it does measure: for instance, does it reflect <u>unconscious</u> self-esteem?

Several problems must be taken into account before this measure is fully explicated. Carlson (1970), for example, considers the major problems to be 1) the failure of the scale to distinguish between the source and level of esteem, 2) a sex bias making it inapplicable for females, and 3) unintended cultural biases. If the sources of esteem are different in females (i.e., more socially based) and in other groups, this may inaccurately show up as different <u>levels</u> of esteem for these groups.

More methodological problems are raised by Ziller et al.'s (1969) article, by Froehle and Zerface (1971), and by other data. The use of the left to right format is by no means universal. Only 50% to 60% of subjects put unhappy, unsuccessful, or flunking "people" on the far right. The next most common category is the <u>far left</u>, indicating reversal of the scoring system 16 to 31 percent of the time. The other 10 to 46 percent of the placements in intermediate positions further add to the confusion (Ziller et al. 1969, p. 86). In addition to this built-in problem, Froehle and Zerface (1971) show that the order in which stimulus "people" are listed can significantly affect where they are placed in the circles. People listed first tend to be placed at the left and people listed last at the right. They also note reversals of the left-right rule. Unfortunately, Ziller et al. (1969) report that scoring esteem as the distance from an undesirable other is not satisfactory either.

<u>Suggestions</u>: With the present state of knowledge on this measure any user should plan attempts to add to the understanding of what is being measured by the scale.

It is interesting to note that Kahn (1969) uses a similar technique where people locate themselves, their ideal selves, the leader, and the loser. This seems to be functionally equivalent to the measure presented here though perhaps more obtrusive. It is part of a larger package charting the self-image described in Kahn (1969).

References   Carlson, Rae. On the structure of self-esteem. Comments on Ziller's formulation. <u>Journal of Consulting and Clinical Psychology</u>, 1970, <u>34</u>, 264-268.

Froehle, T. and Zerface, J. Social self-esteem: A further look. Journal of Consulting and Clinical Psychology, 1971, 37, 73, 74.

Kahn, T. C. An introduction to hominology -- the study of whole man. Springfield, Illinois: Charles C. Thomas, 1969.

Mack, Grace. Further analysis of the Ziller esteem data. Unpublished paper, Institute for Social Research, The University of Michigan, February, 1972.

Platt, J., Eisenman, R. and Darbes, A. Self-esteem and internal-external control: A validation study. Psychological Reports, 1970, 26, 162.

Ziller, R. Self-other orientation theory and measures. Unpublished manuscript, 1968, available from author at University of Florida.

Ziller, R.; Hagey, Joan; Smith, Mary; and Long, Barbara. Self-esteem: A self-social construct. Journal of Consulting and Clinical Psychology, 1969, 33, 84-95.

SOCIAL SELF-ESTEEM

Sets of six circles are accompanied by lists of six "people."

The six sets of social objects included in the adult form of the instrument are:

a) doctor, father, a friend, a nurse, yourself, someone you know who is unsuccessful;

b) doctor, father, friend, politician, yourself, an employer;

c) someone you know who is a good athlete, someone you know who is popular, someone you know who is funny, someone who knows a great deal, yourself, someone you know who is unhappy;

d) an actor, your brother or someone who is most like a brother, your best friend, yourself, a salesman, a politically active person;

e) someone you know who is cruel, a judge, a housewife, a policeman, yourself, your sister or someone who is most like a sister;

146

f) a defeated legislative candidate, the happiest person you know, someone you know who is kind, yourself, someone you know who is successful, the strongest person you know.

PERSONAL ORIENTATION INVENTORY (Shostrum 1968)

Variable   The purpose of the scale is to measure self-actualization as defined by Maslow (e.g., 1962). The self-actualized person is more fully functioning and lives a more enriched life than the average person.

Description   The Personal Orientation Inventory (POI) has 150 paired choice items. The main measure of self-actualization involves inner directedness and living in the present (time competence), but there are sub-scales for self-regard, self-acceptance, and other conceptions.

While self-esteem and self-actualization are not conceptually identical, there is a conceptual and empirical relationship. The present author's understanding of the conceptual relationship is as follows: one must have high self-regard and self-acceptance to be self-actualized; however, having high self-esteem does not guarantee self-actualization. This would suggest that low-esteem people would not be self-actualized and high-esteem people may or may not be. This relationship would lead to some correlation between self-esteem and self-actualization.

A stronger statement is contained in the summary of Fitts et al. (1971). They suggest that ". . . available data seem to support the conclusion that the self-concept [the Tennessee measure] is an adequate index of self-actualization in that self-concept shows a consistent relationship to behavioral competence and effective adjustment."

Sample   Norms and profiles are presented in the manual for several college groups and other samples.

Reliability   No data on internal consistency are reported. Test-retest correlations over one week for 48 college students were .84 and .71 for the major scores and .75 and .80 for the self-regard and self-acceptance subscores.

Validity   Convergent: Self-regard involves liking oneself for one's strengths and only correlates .21 with the self-acceptance subscale, which involves accepting one's weaknesses (p. 21, 1968 Manual).

The high correlations (self-regard -.75, self-acceptance -.54) with repression-sensitization suggests that these subscales are closely related to self-esteem; repressors are more actualized (Foulds and Warehime, 1971a).

Discriminant: The manual shows several nonsignificant correlations with Cattell's 16 P-F variables and other scales. Foulds and Warehime (1971b) found that under "fake good" instructions all scores went down except self-regard which went up.

Predictive: Considerable research suggests the overall POI scores have validity (see Shostrum, 1968, and Knapp, 1971 for reviews).

For instance self-actualization seems to be positively related to dormitory assistant effectiveness and ability to communicate empathic understanding in counseling.

Location	Shostrum, E. <u>EITS Manual for the Personal Orientation Inventory</u>. San Diego, California (92107): Educational and Industrial Testing Service, 1966, supplemented 1968.
Administration	Testing time is usually about 30 minutes.
Results and Comments	<u>Positive points</u>: This measure seems to have a place as <u>the</u> measure of self-actualization in the current literature. It has demonstrated acceptable reliability and validity.

<u>Negative points</u>: The scale could probably benefit from updated item analyses at this time. The lack of subscore independence can lead to overinterpretation. The scale is reviewed somewhat negatively in Buros (1972).

<u>Suggestions</u>: While there has been no emphasis on the esteem type scales in the POI measure, the self-regard subscale would appear to be a typical measure of self-esteem. Because of the emphasis on negative traits, the self-acceptance scale is probably somewhat less related to self-esteem than it might otherwise be. Further investigation of the relationship between self-actualization and self-esteem should prove useful in developing both concepts.

References

Buros, O., ed. <u>The seventh mental measurements yearbook.</u> Highland Park, N.J.: The Gryphon Press, 1972.

Fitts, W. et al. <u>The self concept and self-actualization.</u> Dede Wallace Center, Nashville, Tennessee, 1971, Monograph 3.

Foulds, M. and Warehime, R. Relationship between repression-sensitization and a measure of self-actualization. <u>Journal of Consulting and Clinical Psychology</u>, 1971, <u>36</u>, 257-259(a).

Foulds, M. and Warehime, R. Effects of a "fake good" response set on a measure of self-actualization. <u>Journal of Counseling Psychology</u>, 1971, <u>18</u>, 279-280(b).

Knapp, R. <u>The measurement of self-actualization and its theoretical implications.</u> San Diego, California: Educational and Industrial Testing Service, 1971.

Maslow, A. <u>Toward a psychology of being.</u> New York: Van Nostrand, 1962.

Shostrum, E. <u>EITS Manual for the Personal Orientation Inventory.</u> San Diego, California (92107): Educational and Industrial Testing Service, 1966, supplemented 1968.

Sample Items   Because of the commercial nature of the scale only sample items are
reproduced here. Respondent chooses a or b.

   7. a. I am afraid to be myself.
       b. I am not afraid to be myself. (high self-regard)

 72. a. I accept inconsistencies within myself. (high self-acceptance)
       b. I cannot accept inconsistencies within myself.

THE BARCLAY CLASSROOM CLIMATE INVENTORY (Barclay 1972)

Variable
This inventory is basically designed to assess the school environment and suggest strategies for change. Thus, it attempts to measure far more than self-esteem, but is included here because it does include self-concept measures and utilizes an interesting multi-method measurement approach.

Description
The inventory has been under development for over 10 years. It uses three sources of data: self-reports, peer ratings, and teacher ratings. Students (grades 3-6) rate their interest in various occupations, their skills in various tasks, and how much they like various things which might be used as reinforcers. Students then rate each other on the various skills, and the teacher rates all students by identifying adjectives as descriptive or non-descriptive of each student. The format of the test booklet is clever and the entire inventory is computer scored, yielding 32 scores and a simplified summary for each student. Computer scoring is required to score large numbers of students.

Sample
Over 2000 students in grades 3 to 6 were used in developing the inventory.

Reliability/
Homogeneity
Barclay (personal communication) reports counting 42 of 91 total correlations or reliability indices over .60 and all were significant. For the total scale, internal consistency is .58 for males and .50 for females.

Test-retest reliabilities in the Research Manual vary from .22 to .53. For the total score, test-retest is .39 for males and .48 for females. Data from the manual suggest that the teacher ratings are highly reliable (.75 to .90) while self-ratings vary from .21 to .80 and reliabilities for peer ratings over one year are .80 for males and .71 for females.

Validity
Convergent: Some data on convergent validity evidently exists although it was not fully available at the time of this review.

Discriminant: Data on discriminant validity are also expected shortly.

Predictive: Scores have been related to actual behavioral observations, and to intelligence and achievement test scores.

Location
A specimen set is currently available from Educational Skills Development, Inc., 431 South Broadway, Suite 313, Lexington, Kentucky 40508.

Results
and Comments
Positive points: This type of multi-method approach has great potential.

Negative points: A conceptual and utilitarian problem revolves around the use of interest ratings of various occupations. Besides being used as interest indicators, interest ratings are also used "to deter-

mine knowledge of the environment" (p. 47, 1972 Research Manual).
Thus, if a child indicated <u>no interest</u> in many occupations he would
be rated as having low knowledge of the environment. Perhaps another approach would prove more useful in assessing the child's
actual knowledge of the environment.

It has not been demonstrated that the full potentials of this multi-
method format have been realized. For instance, in addition to the
lack of individual item and scale validation and the questionable
use of time spent rating occupational interest, Norman (1963) has
provided a model of how teacher and peer ratings can be made more
quickly and with less bias by having people rated relative to each
other on each trait. This can be done only for extreme thirds, forc-
ing the scale to be fully used while obtaining a score for each individual without each person having to be rated separately.

<u>Suggestions</u>: Most of the research on the form is presented in global
terms. As the author notes, this form is almost made to order for
the Campbell-Fiske approach to validation, briefly discussed in the
introduction to this chapter.* Analyses of the various components
against each other as well as other criteria would be useful demonstrations that all the ratings are needed and to what extent they
covary. In addition to this kind of format analysis, a similar approach is useful on the item level to justify the inclusion of each
item on empirical as well as common sense grounds. For example, most
of the self-skill ratings have the advantage of being observable by
peers and emerge in a factor labeled self-esteem. However, self-
ratings of more subjective dimensions such as happiness might also
prove valuable if considered. Barclay's forthcoming tests of convergent and discriminant validity may clarify some of these issues.

Norman and Goldberg (1966) and Passini and Norman (1969) present a
method for calculating reliabilities and validity of peer ratings
which could be useful with this scale.

References   Hoffman, B. <u>The tyranny of testing</u>. New York: Collier Books, 1964.

Norman, W. Toward an adequate taxonomy of personality attributes:
Replicated factor structure in peer nomination personality ratings.
<u>Journal of Abnormal and Social Psychology</u>, 1963, <u>66</u>, 574–583.

Norman, W. and Goldberg, L. Raters, ratees, and randomness in personality structure. <u>Journal of Personality and Social Psychology</u>, 1966,
<u>4</u>, 589–691.

Passini, F. and Norman, W. Ratee relevance in peer nominations.
<u>Journal of Applied Psychology</u>, 1969, <u>53</u>, 185–187.

*An article by Topp and Barclay in *Educational and Psychological Measurement* (in press)
uses this approach.

SELF-CONCEPT STABILITY (Brownfain 1952)

Variable	Self-concept stability is defined as the discrepancy between rated self at its best and rated self at its worst.
Description	Brownfain (1952) used self-ratings on 9 and 10 point scales. Individuals rate their private selves, self at best, self at worst, and self as others see them. The sum of the absolute value of the discrepancy between the best and worst self ratings is the stability score (i.e., higher score indicates less stability of self).
Sample	Sixty-two college men provided the major data.
Reliability	The split-half reliability of the stability score was .93 (corrected). Split-half reliability for the self-ratings was .90 (corrected). No test-retest data were reported.
Validity	Convergent: No stability measures have been inter-correlated. However, stable people do have lower standard deviations of self-ratings.
	Discriminant: The stability score correlated -.25 with the F scale (i.e., highly stable people were slightly more rigid). The mean score of an item did not relate to the mean stability of that item, suggesting that any relationship between self-ratings and stability scores is not an artifact of a restriction of range.
	Predictive: People with greater stability tend to have greater self-esteem (.25). Stable people have "healthier" Gamin scores. Stables are more popular (peer ratings) and know more people in their housing group (self-reports).
Location	The items used for this specific set of self-ratings are in Brownfain, J., Stability of the self-concept as a dimension of personality, Journal of Abnormal and Social Psychology, 1952, 47, 597-606. However, any self-rating scale could follow the same procedure to arrive at a stability score.
Administration	Administration time will vary according to the form with which this technique is used. Using all three ratings should take about twice as long as simple self-ratings.
Results and Comments	Positive points: Several interesting predictions are supported in the original study.
	Negative points: This technique has been so little used that not much is known about its value.
	Suggestions: Investigations of the convergence of this measure with other stability measures would be interesting, as would be further development of the construct.

References   Brownfain, J. Stability of the self-concept as a dimension of personality. <u>Journal of Abnormal and Social Psychology</u>, 1952, <u>47</u>, 597-606.

Sample Items   Brownfain's subjects rated themselves on traits such as the following defined by brief paragraphs.

1. self-acceptance
2. manners
3. prestige

MEASURE OF SELF-CONSISTENCY (Gergen and Morse 1967)

Variable   This scale taps the perceived consistency and integration of the
            self-concept.

Description Respondents chose five negative and five positive self-descriptors
             from the lists provided. These are then listed across the bottom
             and side of a 10 x 10 matrix. Each pair of descriptors is then com-
             pared and the individual rates their degree of consistency from 0
             (generally compatible) to 3 (incompatible). These 45 ratings are
             summed, with a low score indicating high perceived self-consistency.

             The 34 self-descriptive adjectives were selected to reflect a variety
             of relevant traits from about 600 answers to the question "Who am
             I?" They were classified into the positive and negative categories
             by independent raters. The authors wanted a measure which was quick,
             subjective and free of social desirability.

Sample   A total of 129 male and 80 female undergraduates comprised the
            sample used by Gergen and Morse (1967).

Reliability/ No data on internal consistency are reported.
Homogeneity
              Test-retest stability for eight weeks was .73.

Validity   Convergent: No measures of consistency have been intercorrelated.

             Discriminant: Correlations with social desirability were not significant.

             Predictive: Self-consistency was negatively related to respondents'
             reports of discrepancies in how they are viewed by important others.
             Consistency was also negatively related to the perceived discrepancy
             between self-perceptions and the average of how they are actually
             viewed by significant others. The measure was positively related
             to several measures reflecting estimates of the stability of child-
             hood life.

             Consistent individuals also scored in the healthier direction on
             several CPI scales. Further construct validity comes from one
             published study (Morse and Gergen, 1970) where consistent others
             changed their self-ratings less as a result of social comparison.

Location   Gergen, K. and Morse, S. Self-consistency: Measurement and valida-
             tion. Proceedings of the 75th American Psychological Association
             Convention, 1967, 2, 207-208.

Administration Administration time should be about 20 minutes.

Results and   Positive points: This measure is very clever and has demonstrated
Comments   some interesting validity.

              Negative points: Perceived semantic similarity between trait
              descriptors which might differ systematically between individuals

is a possible form of response bias (e.g., Passini and Norman, 1966; Loehlin, 1967). The general tendency to perceive discrepancies between ratings is another potential source of response bias that could have affected several of the relationships which contributed to construct validity (e.g., Levy, 1956).

Suggestions: Further work with this measure would certainly be worthwhile.

The list of words might be usefully modified for specific purposes. If researchers wished to relate this scale more closely to self-esteem, descriptors such as optimistic and self-centered could be retained while other descriptors such as self-aware or unassertive could be substituted for words less relevant to self-esteem.

References

Gergen, K., and Morse, S. Self-consistency: Measurement and validation. Proceedings of the 75th American Psychological Association Convention, 1967, 2, 207-208.

Loehlin, J. Word meanings and self-descriptions: A replication and extension. Journal of Personality and Social Psychology, 1967, 5, 107-110.

Levy, L. The meaning and generality of perceived and actual-ideal discrepancies. Journal of Consulting Psychology, 1956, 20, 396-398.

Morse, S. and Gergen, K. Social comparison, self-consistency, and the concept of self. Journal of Personality and Social Psychology, 1970, 16, 148-156.

Passini, F. and Norman, W. A universal conception of personality structure? Journal of Personality and Social Psychology, 1966, 4, 44-49.

Scale

The positive and negative words used by Gergen and Morse were as follows:

Positive		Negative	
optimistic	studious	impatient	worrier
honest	considerate	self-conscious	moody
reliable	kind	rebellious	immature
sincere	friendly	quick-tempered	easily influenced
cautious	independent	lazy	gullible
practical	happy	envious	often feel
sensitive	tolerant	disorganized	misunderstood
idealistic	adventurous	guilt-ridden	stubborn
intelligent		self-centered	noisy

Five positive and five negative words are entered into a prepared 10 x 10 matrix by the respondents.

Feedback to Authors

Both Dr. Morse (New York University, 10003) and Dr. Gergen (Kyoto University, Kyoto, Japan) would appreciate hearing about work with the scale.

PERSONALITY INTEGRATION SCALE (Duncan 1966)

Variable
This scale measures personality integration as outlined by Jahoda (1958) and Seeman (1959). Personality integration essentially represents a state of optimal adjustment. It gains some objectivity by using peer ratings.

Description
Seven items were written to represent categories (and one subcategory) used by Jahoda to reflect positive mental health. These items reflected: 1) ability to express feelings, 2) self-understanding, 3) open mindedness, 4) handling anxiety, 5) sticking with beliefs, 6) forming deep relationships, and 7) overall success. Item 5 did not relate to the other six and was deleted.

Individuals who know each other (such as fraternity members) nominate three people who fit each of the above categories. Nominations are summed for each individual's score. The distribution of scores is skewed, with only a few individuals scoring high on the scale.

Sample
Residential college groups, such as fraternities and sororities, have been the groups used.

Reliability/
Homogeneity
Split-half reliabilities varied from .78 to .85.

Test-retest reliability for an unspecified period was .88 (Duncan, 1966).

Validity
Convergent: No correlations with similar scales have been calculated although some of the predictive validity data are relevant in this regard.

Discriminant: High scorers did not differ significantly on intelligence-type tests or on a creativity measure from a control group.

Predictive: When compared to a control group, people nominated as highly integrated rated themselves higher on the same scales, had generally higher self-esteem, were somewhat more internal, engaged in more activities, and had higher grades (Duncan, 1966; Seeman, 1966). They also tended to use more affective and positive terms concerning interpersonal relationships when describing a picture test (Hearn and Seeman, 1971).

Location
Duncan, C. A reputation test of personality integration. Journal of Personality and Social Psychology, 1966, 3, 516-524.

Administration
Administration requires groups of people who know each other, but it should be very easy and take about 15 minutes for the group.

Results and
Comments
Positive points: The validity data suggest that these ratings could usefully be related to self-esteem.

Negative points: Peer ratings are rather difficult logistically to collect.

<u>Suggestions</u>: The use of peer ratings can be a valuable validation and adjunct to self-report scales of esteem.

If it is possible to obtain the proper subjects it might be more valuable to collect more ratings and relate them to each area of esteem one is interested in, using procedures like those of Norman (1963).

References

Duncan, C. A reputation test of personality integration. <u>Journal of Personality and Social Psychology</u>, 1966, <u>3</u>, 516-524.

Hearn, C. and Seeman, J. Personality integration and perception of interpersonal relationships. <u>Journal of Personality and Social Psychology</u>, 1971, <u>18</u>, 134-143.

Jahoda, M. <u>Current concepts of positive mental health</u>. New York: Basic Books, 1958.

Norman, W. Toward an adequate taxonomy of personality attributes: Replicated factor structure. <u>Journal of Abnormal and Social Psychology</u>, 1963, <u>66</u>, 574-583.

Seeman, J. Personality integration in college women. <u>Journal of Personality and Social Psychology</u>, 1966, <u>4</u>, 91-93.

Seeman, J. Toward a concept of personality integration. <u>American Psychologist</u>, 1959, <u>14</u>, 633-637.

Items

Peers nominate three people who best fit each of the following descriptions:

1. Who are the persons who seem best able to express their feelings without hurting the feelings of others?

2. In your opinion who are the three persons in this group who seem to understand themselves best; that is, are aware of their short-comings and strengths?

3. Who are the ones who seem best able to keep an open mind and not jump to premature conclusions?

4. Who are the three persons who seem the most able to deal effectively with everyday tensions and anxieties?

5. [Who are the ones who are most likely to stick by their own values and beliefs, even when these may be somewhat unpopular?] This item did not relate to the other items and was deleted.

6. Which three persons seem capable of forming deeper and more pro-found relationships with others and seem to be genuinely concerned with other people?

7. Which persons seem to you to have been the most successful in all phases of their life: social, personal, educational, etc.?

Personality Integration Scale (Duncan 1966). Copyright 1966 by the American Psychological Association. Reprinted here with permission.

THE INFERRED SELF-CONCEPT SCALE (McDaniel 1969)

Variable
This scale measures self-concept as rated by observers, such as teachers. It attempts to avoid problems with self-reports such as distortions, language problems, and intelligence.

Description
The scale has several forms for different ages. Each contains 30 items which an observer rates on a 5-point scale from "never" to "always." The items mainly cover social relations.

A total of 100 items were presented to eight judges of diverse professional background. These items were largely derived from the literature and adapted for rating by the judges. Six of the eight judges agreed on the appropriateness of 37 items as representing self-concept. Seven redundant items were eliminated by the author.

Sample
The original sample consisted of 90 girls and 90 boys representing 90 different classrooms: there were 30 students from each grade one through six. The school districts were largely low income. Each of the 90 teachers rated 2 students. School counselors also rated each of the children in their school.

Reliability/
Homogeneity
Agreement between counselors and teachers for the total scores of the 180 students was .58. Agreements for scores on individual items were significant except for one item. Split-half reliabilities were .86, .86 and .90 for the ratings by counselors, teachers, and both combined. Coefficient alpha was .92 for counselors and .91 for teachers.

Test-retest stability for the total sample over six months was .66. These varied between .49 and .87 depending on demographic variables such as age, sex, and race.

Validity
Convergent: The agreement between judges for selecting items indicates some convergent validity.

Discriminant: Scores were unrelated to variables such as age. They were significantly but weakly related to intellectual-type variables (from .16 to .32).

Predictive: A measure of intellectual competency which subtracted the standardized IQ score from the standardized achievement score was negatively related to self-esteem. This suggests that over-achievers have lower behavioral esteem.

Location
McDaniel, E.L. A Manual for the Inferred Self-Concept Scale. Austin, Texas: San Felipe Press, Box 2085, Austin, Texas, 78767, 1969, reprinted 1970.

Administration
Time per individual rating might be as little as 5 minutes.

Results and
Comments
Positive points: This scale has received worthwhile systematic work and development.

Negative points: Data demonstrating that this method actually measures a useful variable are needed. Some of the items may not be relevant to self-concept despite judges' agreement. Children rated high and low need to be compared on assertiveness and other behaviors related to esteem. Self-ratings are also helpful.

Suggestions: This technique can be used with the items of any scale. Hopefully, further work will be done.

Reference   McDaniel, E.L. A manual for the Inferred Self-Concept Scale. Austin, Texas: San Felipe Press, Box 2085, Austin, Texas, 78767, 1969, reprinted 1970.

INFERRED SELF-CONCEPT SCALE

Sample items: Observers rate the accuracy of statements such as the following, using a 1-5 scale as shown.

Never	Seldom	Sometimes	Usually	Always
1	2	3	4	5

1. Enjoys working with others. (5 is high esteem)

11. Tries to dominate or bully. (1 is high esteem)

UNCONSCIOUS SELF-EVALUATION TECHNIQUE (Beloff and Beloff 1959)

Variable
This measure is more in the nature of a technique than of a scale. The technique attempts to measure "unconscious" self-esteem by having people judge the attractiveness of their own faces in relation to others. A stereoscope is required equipment for this technique as well as pictures of the individual.

Description
The use of the technique described there is largely taken from Beloff and Beloff (1959). They suggest that the distance between the eyes be equated across pictures so that faces can be merged by the individual. Subjects should not know that their own picture is in the experiment. Attractiveness ratings of the control pictures should be made by the subjects relative to their own attractiveness.

Subjects should have enough practice with the stereoscope to be able to merge two faces easily. Subjects then rate the attractiveness of visual mergers consisting of the following: two strangers which the subjects have rated as equal in attractiveness to themselves, one stranger and one self picture (again equated on preratings of attractiveness) and possibly two self pictures. High esteem is scored if the self-other composite is rated higher than the other-other composite. The self picture should be presented to the non-dominant eye. For further details see Beloff and Beloff (1959), Reitz and Thetford (1967), and Taylor and Reitz (1968).

Sample
Beloff and Beloff (1959) used 23 male and 29 female college students. Taylor and Reitz (1968) used 46 high school girls.

Reliability/
Homogeneity
Taylor and Reitz (1968) estimated a split-half reliability of .83 for this technique.

No test-retest data are reported.

Validity
Convergent: The measure correlated significantly, .29, with the Coopersmith scale and the Body Cathexis scale (Taylor and Reitz, 1968).

Discriminant: The measure did not correlate significantly with the Marlowe-Crowne social desirability scores (Taylor and Reitz, 1968).

Predictive: By dividing subjects on conscious self-esteem and this "unconscious" measure it was found that people high in conscious esteem and low on unconscious esteem had higher Marlowe-Crowne social desirability scores than the other groups ($p<.06$). This suggests that the two types of esteem measured together may be able to distinguish defensive respondents (Taylow and Reitz, 1968).

Location
Beloff, H. and Beloff, J. Unconscious self-evaluation using a stereoscope. Journal of Abnormal and Social Psychology, 1959, 59, 275-278.

Administration
A stereoscope and the camera equipment noted must be used. The procedure should take less than 15 minutes.

Results and Comments

Positive points: The technique is still exploratory, but seems to have considerable potential, especially to augment the current stock of measurement techniques which overemphasize self-report.

Negative points: This technique requires considerably more equipment and takes more time on an individual basis than paper and pencil measures.

Suggestions: At present, subjects who realize that they are part of the fusion picture must be discarded. If the exposure time could be shortened without sacrificing discrimination, recognition would probably be less (Taylor and Reitz, 1968, used 10 seconds). This general approach can also be used by presenting subjects with their voice or handwriting in a distorted form (e.g., Diller, 1954; Epstein, 1955). More information of this technique would be valuable.

References

Beloff, H. and Beloff, J. Unconscious self-evaluation using a stereoscope. Journal of Abnormal and Social Psychology, 1959, 59, 275-278.

Diller, L. Conscious and unconscious self-attitudes after success and failure. Journal of Personality, 1954, 23, 1-12.

Epstein, S. Unconscious self-evaluation in a normal and schizophrenic group. Journal of Abnormal and Social Psychology, 1955, 50, 65-70.

Reitz, W. and Thetford, P. Skin potential correlates and rating assessments of self-evaluation under different degrees of awareness. Perceptual and Motor Skills, 1967, 27, 631-638.

Taylor, J. and Reitz, W. The three faces of self-esteem. Research Bulletin #80, Department of Psychology, University of Western Ontario, April, 1968.

Other Self-Concept Measures

Following are thirty measures of esteem for which there does not seem
to be enough information or use to warrant full reviews. Most older measures are covered in Wylie (1961). Many new measures which are often used
only once or twice are probably just as good (or bad) as existing measures.
However, as mentioned in the introduction, even with the imperfections of
better known existing measures, the field would profit considerably if these
diverse efforts were concentrated on a few central measures until the challenge to spend concentrated efforts to construct better measures is taken up
by workers.

* * * * * * * *

Bennett, Virginia. Development of a self concept Q sort for use with elementary age school children. Journal of School Psychology, 1964, 3, 19-25.

   Items adapted from A. Hilden (unpublished) and Butler and Haigh. Easy
   to understand (for children and psychologists) and easy to administer.

Bennett, Virginia. Combinations of figure drawing characteristics related to
   the drawer's self concept. Journal of Projective Techniques and Personality Assessment, 1966, 30, 192-196.

   The same author who criticized simple use of this technique (i.e., size
   of drawing, 1964) find some possible esteem indicators but still suggests supplementary data.

Berman, J. and Brickman, P. Standards for attribution of liking: Effects
   of sex, self-esteem, and other's attractiveness. APA Proceedings, 1971,
   271-272.

   A nine-item forced choice scale to measure "dating esteem." As Berman
   notes (personal communication), social desirability is probably a strong
   confound. The weak dating-esteem results may stem from this.

Bledsoe, J. Self concepts of children and their intelligence, achievement, interests, and anxiety. Journal of Individual Psychology, 1964, 20, 55-58.

Thirty adjectives in a discrepancy format. Modified from Lipsitt's adaption of the Bills scale.

Block, J. The Q-sort method in personality assessment and psychiatric research. Springfield, Ill.: Thomas, 1961.

Seventy adjectives arranged into a rectangular seven category distribution. Can be scored for desirability or discrepancies. Designed with rectangular distribution so Ss can just choose same number of items for each category--makes for ease of administration. Of course, the Blocks' work is generally of high quality.

Bolea, A. and Felkner, D. The adolescent Q-sort. Institute for Child Study, University of Maryland, mimeograph, 1968.

Items derived from Jersild (1952). Used by R.C. Smith (Journal of Clinical Psychology, July 1972) as a moderator variable.

Campbell, A., Converse, R., Miller, W., and Stokes, D. The American voter. New York: Wiley, 1960.

Used in various forms in surveys of political behavior. Considered personal efficacy in this context. Seems to be self-confidence plus a little internality.

Crary, W. Note on the nature of self-regard. Psychological Reports, 1969, 24, 487-490.

The most recent version of this measure is 33 adjectives rated on a 6-point scale. This was originally modified from the Bills scale and was designed for ease and speed of administration. Scale unpublished.

Cromwell, R. and Meeker, Mary. Evaluation of personality development. Unpublished form.

Stems from Cromwell's 1967 chapter in Mental Retardation edited by Baumeister. For use with young children to rate progression of personality development. In later ages schizophrenic signs may be observed.

Fiedler, F. et al. Interrelations among measures of personality adjustment in nonclinical populations. Journal of Abnormal and Social Psychology, 1958, 56, 345-351.

One of the many studies which uses the Fiedler semantic differential scale. It has been useful.

Ghiselli, E. *Explorations in managerial talent.* Pacific Palisades, California: Goodyear Publishing, 1971.

Subjects mark adjectives, for some of which the relation to self-esteem could be questioned. Some validity information is presented by Korman who has used it. (Korman, A. Task success, task popularity and self-esteem as influences on task liking. *Journal of Applied Psychology*, 1968, 52, 484-490).

Gordon, I. *A test manual for the how I see myself scale.* The Florida Educational Research and Development Council, University of Florida, Gainesville 32601.

This could be an interesting scale. Composed of 40 (or 42, according to age) forced choice items covering a variety of areas.

Greenberger, Ellen, et al. Reports 108, 110, and 127, Center for Social Organization of Schools, John Hopkins University, 1971-1972.

The measurement of psychosocial maturity includes items from Coopersmith and other scales. With continued attention to basic psychometrics this project may produce good returns.

Hunt, S., Singer, K, and Cobb, S. Components of depression: Identified from a self-rating depression inventory for survey use. *Archives of General Psychiatry*, 1967, 16, 441-447.

Eleven items cover optimism/depression and competence. Many of the items have been used by the Institute for Social Research, The University of Michigan.

Johnson, J., Jr., Kenny, C., and Rien, E. Picture Test of Self-Concept. Consultants in Child Development, 5654 Chapman Avenue, Memphis, Tenn. 38117

This scale was developed especially for children with a mental age of eight or less. There are alternate forms for males and females and separate keys for white boys, black boys, white girls and black girls. Keying was done empirically with the high esteem answer designated as that chosen by the majority of each group of children. Normal children score higher than disturbed children. Further validation of the keys would be useful.

Kahn, T.C. An introduction to homonology, the study of the whole man. Springfield, Illinois: Thomas, 1969.

A novel series of measures which "chart" the self. No validity is claimed but it could be useful.

Leary, T. Interpersonal diagnosis of personality. New York: Ronald, 1957.

Uses an adjective check list to measure a personality theory based on
the idea that behavior is aimed at reducing anxiety and maintaining/
increasing self-esteem. Some items would reflect esteem and discrepancy measures are also derived. Dominance-submission and love-hate are
the main dimensions.

Lipsitt, L. A self-concept scale for children and its relation to the children's form of the manifest anxiety scale. Child Development, 1958, 29,
463-472.

Self-ideal adjective checklist measure similar to Bills' in format.
Self-ratings were more reliable (test-retest) and correlated higher
with anxiety than discrepancies.

Loevinger, Jane. The meaning and measurement of ego development. American
Psychologist, 1966, 21, 195-206.

The seven stages of ego development are presented in this and later
work as an all important variable in understanding the individual.

Luszki, Margaret and Schmuck, R. Pupil perceptions of parental attitudes toward school. Mental Hygiene, 1965, 49, 296-307.

Three sentence stems: a) "When I look in the mirror, I ...," b) "Sometimes I think I am ...," and c) "When I look at other boys and girls,
and then I look at myself, I feel ...." Given to 727 students, elementary to high school. Inter-item correlations of .36 to .58. 95 percent rater agreement for high and low self-ratings. Interesting brief
example of "free" response items.

Maslow, A. A test for dominance-feeling (self-esteem) in college women.
Journal of Social Psychology, 1940, 12, 255-270.

This test was validated slightly less formally than newer tests, but
it looks pretty good.

McClain, E. Self-description blank. Undated, unpublished.

Stemming from an Erikson stage framework. All the scales seem to
have some relation to esteem, e.g., autonomy. The author is at the
University of Tennessee.

Muller, D. and Leonetti, R. Primary self-concept scale test manual and scales.
National Consortia for Bilingual Education, 6745-A Calmont-West Freeway,
Fort Worth, Texas 76116, undated.

This approach does not require verbal skills since the respondent chooses
a picture like himself. The pictures are designed to reflect esteem

in several areas such as peer acceptance and success. Further work
from this group should be interesting.

Pervin, L. and Lilly, R. Social desirability and self-ideal self ratings on
the semantic differential. Educational and Psychological Measurement,
1967, 27, 845-853.

Self and ideal ratings and certainty, then rated importance of traits.
They found that the potency and activity dimensions are not as strongly influenced by social desirability as the evaluative dimension.

Quereshi, M. The development of the Michill Adjective Rating Scale (MARS).
Journal of Clinical Psychology, 1970, 26, 192-196.

Cross-replicating older data; 48 adjectives are presented which cover
the areas of unhappiness, extroversion, self-assertiveness, and productive persistence.

Schwartz, M. and Tangri, Sandra. A note on self-concept as an insulator
against delinquency. American Sociological Review, 1965, 30, 922-926.

Confirming and clarifying a finding by Reckless et al. (American
Sociological Review, 1956) that potential delinquents have lower esteem.
Used ten semantic differential evaluative scales.

Vitro, F. Self-perceived abilities inventory. Undated, unpublished.

This scale is currently undergoing development at the University
of Maine.

Watson, D. and Friend, R. Measurement of social-evaluative anxiety. Journal
of Consulting and Clinical Psychology, 1969, 33, 448-457.

Social avoidance and distress scale and a fear of negative evaluation
scale are presented in this article. A short version of the FNE scale
correlated .81 with the Janis and Field scale (Dr. Ronald Friend, personal communication, May 18, 1972). While relating only to social esteem, this scale may prove worthwhile.

Waldschmidt, R. Self-regard and other-regard scales. Unpublished, 1957.

Discrepancy measures of self-regard, perceived regard from others,
and regard for others. Thirty items scaled to spread out responses
reduced from sixty items. Available from Dr. Waldschmidt at Valparaiso
University.

Weinberger, B. Achievement motivation and self-concept. Undergraduate honors
thesis, University of Michigan, 1951.

This scale was used by Stotland et al. As noted in the introduction, it didn't correlate with other scales in one test. It's essententially a discrepancy measure using all positive traits.

Wylie, Ruth. The self concept. Lincoln, Nebraska: University of Nebraska Press, 1961.

This standard reference covers most tests used before 1960. In its new revision it should be comprehensive with regard to newer tests also.

CHAPTER 4 – INTERNAL-EXTERNAL LOCUS OF CONTROL[1]

Internal-external locus of control refers to the extent to which persons perceive contingency relationships between their actions and their outcomes. People who believe they have some control over their destinies are called "Internals"; that is, they believe that at least some control resides within themselves. "Externals," on the other hand, believe that their outcomes are determined by agents or factors extrinsic to themselves, for example, by fate, luck, chance, powerful others, or the unpredictable.

The locus of control construct derives from Rotter's social learning theory (Rotter, 1954). The present popularity of the construct can be partly credited to two of Rotter's students who developed scales for its measurement as an intrapersonal variable (James, 1957; Phares, 1955) and named the construct "internal-external locus of control" (James, 1957).

The amount of attention that behavioral scientists have recently given to the IE construct is of phenomenal proportions. There are now over a dozen tests for its measurement and five literature reviews (Joe, 1971; Lefcourt, 1966, 1971; Minton, 1967; Rotter, 1966). A published bibliography of works through 1969 (Throop and MacDonald, 1971) lists 339 references, over 50 percent of which appeared in 1968-1969. MacDonald's continuing bibliographic research shows that the entire body of IE literature increased over 30

---

[1] A. P. MacDonald, author of this chapter, can be reached at the Frank Porter Graham Child Development Center of the Child Development Research Institute, the University of North Carolina.

percent in 1970 alone (MacDonald, 1972). Presently known references for 1971-1972 indicate a continuing geometric progression.[2]

The popularity of the IE construct is doubtless due to its wide range of generalizability, and its social relevance (at a time when social relevance is the cry). It has been related to such diverse phenomena as achievement behavior (Coleman et al., 1966; McGee and Crandall, 1968; Harrison, 1968; Nowicki and Roundtree, 1971; Eppes, 1970; Bartel, 1969), birth control practices (Bauman and Udry, 1972; MacDonald, 1970; Keller et al., 1970; Williamson, 1970), minority group status (Battle and Rotter, 1963; Lefcourt, 1966), rioting (Berkowitz, 1972; Crawford and Naditch, 1970; Forward and Williams, 1970; MacDonald, 1972b; Ransford, 1968), reaction to disability (Lipp et al., 1968; Land and Vineberg, 1965; Koelle, 1971; MacDonald and Hall, 1969, 1971), conformity (Odell, 1959; MacDonald, 1972a), reaction to influence attempts (Biondo and MacDonald, 1971; Hjelle and Clouser, 1970; Ritchie and Phares, 1969), automobile seat belt use (Bridge, 1971), psychopathology (Smith et al., 1971). And the list continues.

All of the research points to the same conclusion: people are handicapped by external locus of control orientations. The prevailing belief is that it is desirable to change people, especially those who are not doing well in our society, in the direction of internality. Accordingly, researchers have begun to develop IE change techniques (Dua, 1970; Reimanis and Schaefer, 1970; Pierce et al., 1970; Coven, 1970). For a review of IE change techniques see MacDonald (1972c). Though in need of considerable refinement and detailed explication, these first efforts show promise.

---

[2] The author has prepared a 49-page annotated bibliography (dated June 1, 1972) of references to work done during 1971 and 1972 alone.

It is short-sighted to focus solely on changing one's IE expectancy, however. For some people, especially for members of certain minority groups, the belief that there is little connection between effort and payoff is often realistic. For such people, an effective program for changing control orientations must produce change in the individual and in his immediate social surroundings.

Over 50 percent of the locus of control literature can be summarized by saying that Internals and Externals occupy different positions on the instrumental-expressive behavior dimension. Internals engage in more instrumental goal-directed activity whereas Externals more often manifest emotional non-goal-directed responses. Such findings of course are consonant with locus of control theory.

Disproportionately fewer studies have been concerned with other important aspects of locus of control. It is expected that much data will be added to the literature in the next year or two regarding two areas especially: 1) antecedents and 2) the multidimensional nature of the IE construct.

Antecedents

Factors which affect the development of the internal-external control orientation may be broadly distinguished as either episodic or accumulative antecedents.

Episodic Antecedents. Episodic antecedents are those events, of relatively great import, which occur at a restricted point in time; e.g., the death of a loved one, a mining accident, an earthquake or other community disaster, a temporally contiguous series of accidents. One example of episodic change is reflected in the finding that young men who were unfavorably affected by the draft lottery shifted to more external orientations (McArthur, 1970). Another is Gorman's (1968) finding that students were more external than Rotter's norms on the day following the 1968 Democratic convention; the majority of the students had been McCarthy supporters and consequently had experienced considerable disillusionment. Future research may show similar reactions among those suddenly incapacitated by the onset of a severe physical disability, those who have experienced an unexpected large financial or property loss, and so on.

If one can discount the literature on counseling techniques (see MacDonald, 1972c, for a review) the author is not aware of much research that has linked discrete "real world" events to shifts toward internality. Such research findings might prove extremely helpful to those involved in designing locus of control change strategies.

Episodic changes are probably of little practical significance (though they may be theoretically important) since people are most likely to return to previously held IE levels with the passage of time. For example, Smith (1970) found that crisis patients showed a significant shift toward internality following crisis resolution. However, the effects of episodic changes will endure when internalizing or externalizing factors continue to present themselves. At that point episodic antecedents might fall more appropriately under the rubric "accumulative antecedents."

Accumulative Antecedents. Little research has been done concerning the continuous exposures that can affect the development of internal and external control orientations. Three important factors have been identified: 1) social discrimination (Lefcourt, 1966), 2) prolonged incapacitating disability (Land and Vineberg, 1965; Koelle, 1971), and 3) parental child-rearing practices. Present support for the first two of these as antecedents of control orientation comes more from inference than from direct demonstration. Evidence pertaining to parenting is somewhat better grounded, though more data obtained by direct observation of parent-child interactions are needed.

Research consistently shows that Internals and Externals were exposed to different childrearing practices. Internals come from warm, democratic homes, where nurturance is combined with principled discipline, predictable standards, and instrumental companionship. Externals describe their parents as higher in the use of physical punishment, affective punishment, deprivation of privileges, and overprotection (Chance, 1965; Cromwell, 1963; Davis and Phares, 1969; Epstein and Komorita, 1971; Katkovsky et al., 1967; MacDonald, 1971; see Ryckman and Sherman, 1972, for a review). In short, Internals were exposed to the kinds of parenting that foster the development of autonomy, superego, and achievement striving, whereas Externals were exposed to parenting that is conducive to the development of dependency, hostility, aggression, and a view that the world is controlling and malevolent. Perhaps those who were over-protected, with the absence of harsh punishment, view the world as controlling and benevolent.

Externalizing parent practices seem most likely to be used by parents who are themselves external, and internalizing practices by those who are internal. Consequently, one might question whether or not modeling enters into the acquisition of IE orientations. Research dealing with that question is presently unavailable, but would seem worth the effort.

While data pertaining to the development of control orientations during early infancy are lacking, researchers and theorists in that area have been studying the infant's attainment of external environmental control. Watson (1969) has developed a response-contingent apparatus (a mobile which the infant activates by pressure on a pneumatic pillow) which has produced some interesting effects on infants. The infants appear both to learn more rapidly and to show much pleasure about their ability to control the mobile.

While these experiments have been limited to demonstrating that the reinforcement of a particular response can change the probability of occurrence of that response, it has been suggested by Watson and Ramey (1972) that this early response-contingent experience may be crucial for the learning of a generalizable "set" for effectiveness. In short, the learning of a particular response-contingent relationship helps to establish the set that the child's actions can have consequences.

This research would suggest that the development of locus of control orientations might be considerably affected by the quality and quantity of environmental interactions during early infancy, that is, the amount of direct control that can be affected by the infant. It is perhaps no coincidence that, consistent with observed social class differences in locus of control, researchers (e.g., Kagan, 1969) are finding that lower-class infants are not exposed to the same amount of parental reinforcement stimuli as middle-class infants (e.g., not as much mother-child face-to-face contact, which has been found to be important for the conditioning of smiling, vocalization, etc., and which often occurs in response to overtures made by the infant). It also would seem that lower-class homes do not contain as many control-contingent gadgets as do middle-class homes.

Thus far, IE researchers have not investigated factors during early infancy as antecedents of control orientations. It is hoped that some of the suggestions offered here might help to stimulate research in that area.

Methodological Concerns

The Multidimensional Nature of IE. Application of factor analysis to Rotter's IE Scale (1966) and its variants have revealed the scale not to be unidimensional. Early factor analyses generated more than one factor, but the additional factors (beyond the first factor) accounted for little variance and involved no more than two or three items each (Franklin, 1963; Rotter, 1966). For example, Franklin (1963), using data obtained from 1,000 high school students, found one factor that accounted for 53 percent of the total scale variance, while none of the remaining factors contained more than one test item that loaded above .30.

More recent factor analyses suggest the Rotter IE scale to be more multi-dimensional in character. The most prominent study in this area was performed by Gurin et al. (1969). Since the multidimensional scale produced by these investigators is reproduced in this chapter in its entirety, discussion and description here need only be brief.

Gurin and her colleagues factor analyzed a pool of items consisting of the items from Rotter's IE Scale (Rotter, 1966) along with their own items designed to tap personal efficacy and beliefs about the operation of personal and external forces in race relations. Data were collected from students in attendance at various black colleges in the United States. Four factors were extracted: 1) Control Ideology, referring to the subject's belief about the extent to which people have control generally, 2) Personal Control, referring to the extent to which the subject believes in personal control (items with the highest loading were phrased in the first person, 3) System Modifiability, referring to control over racial discrimination, war, and world affairs, and 4) Race Ideology, containing the race-related items.[3]

It would naturally be questionable whether these results could be generalized beyond blacks, and recent evidence (Guttentag, 1972) does suggest that it may not be proper even to generalize to all blacks. Guttentag reports that the racially related factors obtained by Gurin et al. were found in her sample of blacks from Harlem, but not in another New York urban sample. Reconciliation of these differences must await further research and more careful inspection of Guttentag's results.

---

[3] The items in Factor IV were factored as a separate group, with four additional factors being generated: 1) Individual Collective Action, 2) Discrimination Modifiability, 3) Individual-System Blame, and 4) Racial Militancy.

Subsequent factor analyses (Guttentag, 1972; MacDonald and Tseng, 1971; Minton, 1972; Mirels, 1970) all confirm the multidimensionality of Rotter's scale. The two major factors found by Gurin et al. continue to repeat themselves, viz., Personal Control and Control Ideology. These factors also appear in James' Scale, which was used by Rotter and his colleagues to construct the present Rotter IE Scale (MacDonald and Tseng, 1971).

Two other questions have been raised regarding the multidimensionality of locus of control. Hersch and Scheibe (1967) have called attention to the fact that locus of control scores may reflect more than a view of the world as controlling. One may view the world as controlling and malevolent or as controlling and benevolent. Inspection of the external items on Rotter's scale suggests that they may be more affected by a malevolent than a benevolent world view. It will be recalled that the research on parental antecedents of locus of control uncovered the fact that Externals reported their parents had used harsh disciplinary techniques, but significant differences between Internals and Externals also appeared for protectiveness. As suggested earlier, perhaps Externals who were subjected to harsh discipline are more likely to view the world and powerful others as controlling and malevolent, and Externals who were overprotected are more likely to view the world and powerful others as benevolent.

Another concern is reflected in the work of Hanna Levenson (1972). She questions the wisdom of lumping fate, chance, and powerful others' expectancies together. Levenson proposes that our understanding and prediction might be considerably increased if each were studied separately. Accordingly, she has developed three new scales, comprising several items adapted from Rotter's IE Scale as well as a set of original items. Twenty-four items are used to produce three scales of eight items each in a Likert format. All statements are phrased in the first person. The "I" Scale measures the extent to which a person believes he has control over his life (e.g., "Whether or not I get to be a leader depends mostly on my ability"); the "P" Scale deals with powerful others (e.g., "I feel like what happens in my life is mostly determined by powerful people"); and the "C" Scale is concerned with chance (e.g., "To a great extent my life is controlled by accidental happenings"). Results thus far with the scale have been encouraging.[4]

As a consequence of the methodological findings and concerns, researchers are presently taking two approaches to IE testing and test development. Some researchers are attempting to develop unidimensional scales--such scales being consistent with Rotter's original interests and intent--presumably by avoiding situation-specific items. Others are more interested in multidimensional scales. It is probably fair to characterize social psychologists as a group as being especially interested in the latter. It is probably also fair to say that the scale produced by Gurin et al. is the best multidimensional scale presently available.

The reader might ask why so many researchers are in the business of IE scale construction. Why not take the Factor I items of Rotter's Scale as the unidimensional measure? Several reasons have been offered: 1) Rotter's scale has been shown to be affected by social desirability response bias (correlations between -.20 and -.70) as measured by the Marlowe-Crowne Social

---

[4] Although there is presently insufficient evidence available regarding the validity of Levenson's scales, correlations between the Marlowe-Crowne Social Desirability Scale and the 24 items in this scale have all been near zero (the highest being only .19). However, correlations between the total scores for the three scales and the Marlowe-Crowne SDS are not reported. Internal consistency figures for all three scales range between .62 and .78. Test-retest reliabilities for a one-week period were, .64 (I Scale), .74 (P Scale), and .78 (C Scale). The P and C scales were significantly related (r = .59), although neither scale was found to be related to the I Scale.

Desirability Scale (Altrocchi et al., 1968; Feather, 1967; Hjelle, 1971; MacDonald, 1972) and by Edward's Social Desirability Scale (Berzins et al., 1970; Cone, 1971); 2) Rotter's scale is not considered satisfactory for use with children and retarded subjects; 3) there is some dissatisfaction with the forced-choice format; and 4) some researchers would prefer a shorter scale.

Despite the problems with Rotter's IE Scale, it will most likely continue to be the measure of IE since it is so thoroughly entrenched in the literature. Consequently, it is included in this chapter in full.

Short Forms. Four short forms of IE scales have recently been developed. One (Valecha, 1972a, 1972b) is an 11-item scale closely resembling Rotter's scale. Norms are available on a national probability sample of 4,330 males from 16-26 years of age, and a factor analysis has been performed. Unfortunately, more information was not available at the time of this writing, although its having been developed only on males would be a liability since sex differences are becoming a significant part of the IE literature.

Two other scales developed for use with children are presented in the context of the reviews of the full scales from which they were developed. These short forms were created from the IARQ and Nowicki-Strickland Scales and are appended at the end of those scale reviews.

Similarly, the reader will find a short form of the James' IE Scale based on a factor analysis of the scale by MacDonald and Tseng (1971).

Forms for Children. The results of the "Coleman Report" (Coleman et al., 1966) made it inevitable that the interests of IE researchers and developmental, child, and educational psychologists would soon overlap. This development made the need for IE scales that were appropriate for children more salient.[5]

---

[5] Scales designed for children may also prove to be better measures of the control orientations of retarded adults and adults with reading difficulties.

While some of the scales discussed above can be used with teenagers, they were not specifically designed for that purpose.

Three IE scales seem most promising for use with children. The first, the Nowicki-Strickland Locus of Control Scale, has been found to be appropriate for children beyond the second grade. The second, the Stephens-Delys Reinforcement Contingency Interview (SDRCI), is usable with children from four to ten years of age. Both are designed to measure generalized expectancies. The third, the Intellectual Achievement Responsibility Questionnaire, is appropriate for children past the second grade, but it is relevant only to the academic situation.

The "free-response" nature of the Stephens-Delys Scale, which requires a scoring manual, makes it inappropriate for full review here.[6] Nevertheless, extended description of the Stephens-Delys Scale seems warranted because of certain of its promising measurement qualities.

The Stephens-Delys Reinforcement Contingency Interview (SDRCI) was designed as a multidimensional measure of IE particularly suitable for use with preschoolers and was first introduced in 1971.

The SDRCI supposedly can be administered to children from four to ten years of age and permits subscaling for teacher, mother, father (or parents combined or adults combined), and peers; subscores are also available for

---

[6] In the context of the "free response" nature of the Stephens-Delys Scale, two others should be mentioned briefly: 1) The Children's Picture Test of Internal-External Locus of Control (Battle and Rotter, 1963) is a projective device, difficult to administer to large groups, with incomplete data pertaining to reliability. Projective measures devised for use with adults are described in Dies (1968) and Keller et al. (1970). 2) The Bialer-Cromwell Locus of Control Scale for Children (Bialer, 1961; Gozali and Bialer, 1968), is a 23-item, orally administered, yes-no scale, developed for use with retarded children. Reported internal consistency reliabilities have been low, e.g., Bartel (1969) reported Kuder-Richardson coefficients for children from grades one, two, four, and six as .05, -.01, .28, and .34. Concern about reliability, along with the introduction of new tests with seemingly better psychometric properties, will probably result in less use of this scale.

self-reinforcement IE expectancies and for positive versus negative reinforcement IE expectancies.

The SDRCI is administered individually as a free-response structured interview. Each of the 40 questions, which in all take 10-25 minutes per child to administer, posits the occurrence of some reinforcing event or cue associated with increased probability of reinforcement (e.g., "What makes mothers smile?" or "What makes other kids angry?") and ask the child to supply a contingency for the occurrence of that event. Responses are coded according to whether they cite some internal behavior of the child (e.g., "When I play nice," or "When I break their things.") or some external type contingency ("When Daddy comes home," or "When it rains and they can't play outside."). There is one coding manual to aid scoring and another manual for classifying internal responses into different categories of instrumental behavior. Half of the questions deal with positive reinforcement and half with negative. Questions concern reinforcement from each of five reinforcement agents: self, peers, mother, father, and teachers (8 items each).

A factor analysis based on 575 second graders from four different Follow Through samples (black and white), one "traditional" ghetto school sample, and one open classroom white middle-class sample, has revealed no separate item factors which accounted for an appreciable proportion of response variance; indeed, the largest factor accounted for only 15 percent of the total test-variance (Stephens, 1972b). Subscales (positive/negative or separate reinforcement agent) intercorrelate highly, generally around .70, except for the self-reinforcement subscale.

Interrater reliability has been found to be quite high: Delys (1971) reports a coefficient of .98. Internal consistency (Kuder-Richardson formula 20) is reported at .82 for the group of 575 children described above (Delys,

1971). Test-retest reliability across a four-month interval was found to
be .62 (Stephens, 1972a).

With regard to discriminant validity, the SDRCI has been found to be
related fairly consistently with intelligence test scores of preschoolers
(Stephens, 1971). Evidence for convergent validity is inconsistent. Forty-
one children from two black and two white Head Start classes were found to
be significantly more external than 45 middle-class children from two
Montessori and two Parent Cooperative Nursery School classes (Stephens,
1971). The mean of the means for the disadvantaged children was 9.6 and
the average for the advantaged group was 14.2 (higher scores being associated
with internality).

Coleman et al. (1966) found that Oriental children were the only non-
white minority group members studied who were found to be more internal than
whites. This finding was replicated in a study of Chinese-American children
by Wang and Stephens (1971), although the researchers report that the findings
emerged more clearly for boys than for girls--i.e., Chinese-American boys
had higher internal control than the Anglo-American boys. The Chinese-
American girls showed no clear pattern, and beyond age 10 tended to be more
external than Anglo-American girls.[7]

Nonsignificant correlations between the SDRCI and the Nowicki-Strickland
Locus of Control Scale and the Intellectual Achievement Responsibility Questionnaire (IARQ) have been found consistently (Stephens, 1972a), although
the Nowicki-Strickland Scale has been found to correlate significantly with
the IARQ, Rotter's IE Scale, and Bialer's IE Scale (Nowicki and Strickland,

---

[7] It should be pointed out that sex differences are numerous in the IE
literature, and with the SDRCI they are more the rule than the exception.

1972). Consistent with the findings obtained with the other tests, internality as measured with the SDRCI has been found to increase with age among
preschoolers (Stephens, 1971).

The SDRCI needs considerably more investigation before certifying its
usefulness as an IE measure. Though interrater reliability is reportedly
high, no statement is available about the nature of the raters, the number
of raters, procedures, etc. Internal consistency and test-retest reliabilities do seem quite acceptable. Significant correlations with intelligence
tests, though inconsistent, leave open the question of discriminant validity,
and evidence for convergent validity is yet vague and inconsistent. Nevertheless, there is need for an IE test for preschoolers, and the SDRCI is the
most viable candidate presently available.

Alternative Formats. The forced-choice format initiated by Rotter and
maintained for use by Gurin et al. (1969) is a source of dissatisfaction
among some IE researchers. It is argued that it is difficult for some
subjects (particularly children) to respond to and that forced-choice formats
are more subject to a social desirability response set than are other formats.
True as these points may be, the present author (in MacDonald and Tseng, 1971)
has uncovered some findings which indicate the issue should remain open for
a time.

The observation that most of the non-forced-choice IE scales exclusively
or primarily consist of items worded in the external direction led us to try
to develop a balanced test, having an equal number of items phrased internally
and externally. Thus far, we have been unable to produce a set of items
worded in both directions that would constitute a unidimensional scale. Our
most recent effort consisted of 19 items (12 worded externally and 7 worded
internally) chosen after extensive item and factor analyses. Factor analysis
of this scale revealed two factors, one in which the items with the highest

loadings <u>in every case</u> were worded in the external direction and one in which the items with the highest loadings were worded in the internal direction, again <u>in every case</u>.

Among conceivable explanations, it may be that locus of control is best measured by externally worded items, in non-forced-choice formats. It may also be that internally worded items tap a different dimension than externally worded items. In any event, externally worded items dominate existing scales. Levenson's (1972) C and P Scales are made up entirely of externally worded items, whereas (consistent with our factor analytic results) her I Scale is made up of internally phrased items. Interestingly enough, it will be remembered (see footnote 4) that the I Scale does not correlate significantly with the C and P Scales, and the C and P Scales do not correlate with each other. James' IE Scale (unpublished 1963 revision) is made up entirely of 30 externally phrased items. Further, Nowicki and Strickland (1972) suggest two short forms of their test based upon a selection of items showing best correlations of total scores; about 80 percent of the items in each scale are externally phrased.

Consequently, the presently available non-forced-choice scales are basically measures of the extent to which individuals agree that their reinforcements are contingent upon external factors. The forced-choice scales, on the other hand, measure the extent to which subjects favor external over internal explanations. The exact meaning and resolution of this issue must await further research. Meantime, researchers may wish to consider the problem before choosing an IE scale from those now in the literature.

Rationale of Scale Presentation

The selection of the tests for inclusion in this chapter proved a difficult task. As noted above, projective and indirect measures, requiring elaborate scoring instructions, had to be excluded due to space limitations. Also, some of the most recent measures are not included due to the lack of sufficient information at this time.

The following scales are included in the order listed. The scales are presented in order first by the age group at which they are aimed (i.e., children's scales precede adult scales); "short forms" are either included within the presentation of the "parent" scale or are placed immediately after it. Secondly, the order of presentation reflects this author's personal recommendations; i.e., the Nowicki-Strickland scale is recommended over the Bialer-Cromwell scale and the Rotter scale over the 60-item James scale. It should also be pointed out that well-known scales that have not yet been published were given preference for inclusion. The first four scales then are geared for children:

1. The Intellectual Achievement Responsibility Questionnaire (IARQ) (Crandall et al., 1965).

2. The Modified Intellectual Achievement Responsibility Questionnaire (MIARQ) (Ringelheim et al., 1970).

3. A Locus of Control Scale for Children (Nowicki and Strickland, 1972).

4. The Bialer-Cromwell Children's Locus of Control Scale (Bialer, 1960).

The IARQ is a specialized scale designed to measure children's (grades three through twelve) beliefs in their control over and responsibility for intellectual academic success and failures. The scale has been carefully developed and there is an abundant literature of studies in which it has been used. The psychometric properties of the scale are quite acceptable. Short forms, recommended by the authors, are presented along with the longer parent form. Two 20-item short forms are suggested: one for third through fifth grade children and one for children in the sixth through the twelfth grades.

The MIARQ of Ringelheim et al. is essentially a shortened version of the IARQ--although it contains four more items than the short forms recommended by Crandall et al. The test, which has not been published elsewhere, is included here because its developers claim to have simplified the language level for use with the mentally retarded.

The Nowicki and Strickland Locus of Control Scale is a 40-item yes-no paper-pencil test that has been used extensively with subjects ranging from the third grade through college. Information on the scale's internal consistency reliability, test-retest reliability, and convergent and discriminant validity indicates it to be the best measure of locus of control as a generalized expectancy presently available for use with children. An additional positive feature of this scale is that Nowicki (personal communication) plans to prepare alternate forms for older subjects and preschool children. Recommended short forms are presented along with the full scale for school grades three through six and seven through twelve.

The Bialer-Cromwell scale was developed for retarded children. Curiously, though reliability seems acceptable for retarded samples, reliability coefficients obtained from normal samples have been very low. This fact, coupled with the lack of sufficient validity data, makes the scale difficult to evaluate or to recommend over the other scales for children, about which more information is available.

The final four scales are primarily for use with adults:

5. A Multidimensional IE Scale (Gurin et al., 1969).

6. Rotter's Internal-External Locus of Control Scale (Rotter, 1966).

7. Abbreviated 11-item Rotter IE Scale (Valecha, 1972).

8. James' Internal-External Locus of Control Scale (unpublished).

The Gurin et al. multidimensional IE scale is intended to measure specialized dimensions of internal-external locus of control, viz.,

(a) subject's belief about the extent to which people have control generally, (b) subject's belief about his own personal control, (c) subject's belief about the modifiability of the system, and (d) a factor called Race Ideology. The scale is the most fully developed multidimensional scale presently available--although some others have more recently arrived on the scene (Guttentag, 1972; Levenson, 1972).

The Rotter scale is the most widely used test in the locus of control literature. Although it has undergone recent methodological criticism regarding lack of unidimensionality and social desirability response bias, it will no doubt continue to be the most popular IE scale for some time. Defenders of the scale argue that factors beyond the first factor account for little of the total scale variance or that such factors contain too few items to be useful as reliable subscales. Furthermore, most of the correlations between Rotter's test and measures of social desirability response bias have been found to be low.

The Valecha scale is included for researchers who must restrict themselves to a short IE scale. It uses items from the Rotter scale. Too little information is presently available to evaluate its usefulness.

Though results of studies using the James scale are in the literature, this scale has not been previously published. Factor analysis has revealed one large general factor accounting for about 25 percent of the variance; factors beyond the first factor each accounted for about 5 percent of the variance (MacDonald and Tseng, 1971). A drawback of this scale is that it contains 60 items, only 30 of which are scored for the IE dimension. Those interested in a short measure of generalized expectancy might employ the 11 items found by MacDonald and Tseng (1971) to load highest on the first factor, although psychometric properties of this abbreviated scale need more careful investigation.

REFERENCES

Altrocchi, J., Palmer, J., Hellmann, R., and Davis, H. The Marlowe-Crowne, repressor-sensitizer, and internal-external scales and attribution of unconscious hostile intent. Psychological Reports, 1968, 23, 1229-1230.

Bartel, N. R. Locus of control and achievement in middle class and lower class children. Dissertation Abstracts International, 1969, 29, 2991.

Battle, E. S., and Rotter, J. B. Children's feelings of personal control as related to social class and ethnic group. Journal of Personality, 1963, 31, 482-490.

Bauman, K. E., and Udry, J. R. Powerlessness and regularity of contraception in an urban Negro male sample: A research note. Journal of Marriage and the Family, 1972, 34, 112-114.

Berkowitz, L. Frustrations, comparisons, and other sources of emotion arousal as contributors to social unrest. Journal of Social Issues, 1972, 28, 77-91.

Berzins, J. I., Ross, W. F., and Cohen, D. I. Skill versus chance activity preferences as alternative measures of locus of control: An attempted cross-validation. Journal of Consulting and Clinical Psychology, 1970, 35, 18-20.

Bialer, I. Conceptualization of success and failure in mentally retarded and normal children. Journal of Personality, 1961, 29, 303-320.

Biondo, J., and MacDonald, A. P., Jr. Internal-external locus of control and response to influence attempts. Journal of Personality, 1971, 39, 407-419.

Bridge, R. G. Internal-external control and seat belt use. Paper presented at Western Psychological Association, San Francisco, April, 1971.

Chance, J. E. Internal control of reinforcements and the school learning process. Paper presented at Society for Research in Child Development, Minneapolis, 1965.

Coleman, J. S., Campbell, E. Q., Hobson, C. J., McPartland, J., Mood, A. M., Weinfeld, F. D., and York, R. L. Equality of educational opportunity, Washington, D. C.: Government Printing Office, 1966 (Superintendent of Documents, Catalog No. FS 5.238:38001).

Cone, J. D. Locus of control and social desirability. Journal of Consulting and Clinical Psychology, 1971, 36, 449.

Coven, A. B. The effects of counseling and verbal reinforcement on the internal-external control of the disabled. _Dissertation Abstracts International_, 1970, _31_, 1006.

Crawford, T. J., and Naditch, M. Relative deprivation, powerlessness, and militancy: The psychology of social protest. _Psychiatry_, Washington, D.C., 1970, _33_, 208-223.

Cromwell, R. L. A social learning approach to mental retardation. In _Handbook of Mental Deficiency_ edited by N. L. Ellis. New York: McGraw-Hill, 1963, 41-91.

Davis, W. L., and Phares, E. J. Parental antecedents of internal-external control of reinforcement. _Psychological Reports_, 1969, _24_, 427-436.

Delys, P. Rationale, method, and validity of the SDRCI IE Measure for pre-school children. Paper presented at the American Psychological Association, Washington, D. C., 1971.

Dies, R. R. Development of a projective measure of perceived locus of control. _Journal of Projective Techniques and Personality Assessment_, 1968, _32_, 487-490.

Dua, P. S. Comparison of the effects of behaviorally oriented action and psychotherapy reeducation on introversion-extraversion, emotionality, and internal-external control. _Journal of Counseling Psychology_, 1970, _17_, 567-572.

Eppes, J. W. The effect of varying the race of the experimenter on the level of aspiration of externally controlled inner city school children. _Dissertation Abstracts Internal_, 1970, _31_, 912.

Epstein, R., and Komorita, S. S. Self-esteem, success-failure, and locus of control in Negro children. _Developmental Psychology_, 1971, _4_, 2-8.

Feather, N. T. Some personality correlates of external control. _Australia Journal of Psychology_, 1967, _19_, 253-260.

Forward, J. R., and Williams, J. R. Internal-external control and black militancy. _Journal of Social Issues_, 1970, _26_, 75-92.

Franklin, R. D. Youth's expectancies about internal versus external control of reinforcement related to _N_ variables. _Dissertation Abstracts_, 1963, _24_, 1684.

Gozali, J., and Bialer, I. Children's locus of control scale: Independence from response set bias among retardates. _American Journal of Mental Deficiency_, 1968, _72_, 622-625.

Gurin, P., Gurin, G., Lao, R. C., and Beattie, M. Internal-external control in the motivational dynamics of Negro youth. _Journal of Social Issues_, 1969, _25_, 29-53.

Guttentag, M. Locus of control and achievement in minority middle school children. Paper presented at Eastern Psychological Association, Boston, 1972.

Harrison, F. I. Relationship between home background, school success, and adolescent attitudes. Merrill-Palmer Quarterly, 1968, 14, 331-344.

Hjelle, L. A. Social desirability as a variable in the locus of control scale. Psychological Reports, 1971, 28, 807-816.

Hjelle, L. A., and Clouser, R. Internal-external control of reinforcement in smoking behavior. Psychological Reports, 1970, 26, 562.

James, W. H. Internal vs. external control of reinforcement as a basic variable in learning theory. Unpublished doctoral dissertation, Ohio State University, 1957.

Joe, V. C. Review of the internal-external control construct as a personality variable. Psychological Reports, 1971, Monograph Supplement 3-V28, 619-640.

Kagan, J. On class differences and early development. Paper presented at the American Association for the Advancement of Science, Boston, 1969.

Katkovsky, W., Crandall, V. C., and Good, S. Parental antecedents of children's beliefs in internal-external control of reinforcement in intellectual achievement situations. Child Development, 1967, 28, 765-776.

Keller, A. B., Sims, J. H., Henry, W. E., and Crawford, T. J. Psychological sources of "resistance to family planning." Merrill-Palmer Quarterly, 1970, 16, 286-302.

Koelle, W. H. A study to determine differences in locus of control orientation between the deaf and the non-deaf. Unpublished master's thesis, West Virginia University, 1971.

Land, S. L., and Vineberg, S. E. Locus of control in blind children. Journal of Exceptional Children, 1965, 31, 257-260.

Lefcourt, H. M. Internal versus external control of reinforcement: A review. Psychological Bulletin, 1966, 65, 206-220.

Lefcourt, H. M. Internal versus external control of reinforcement revisited: Recent developments. Unpublished paper (Research Report No. 27), University of Waterloo, 1971. To appear in Progress in Experimental Personality Research edited by B. A. Maher (Academic Press).

Levenson, H. Distinctions within the concept of internal-external control: The development of a new scale. Paper presented at American Psychological Association, Hawaii, 1972.

Lipp, L., Kolstoe, R., James, W. H., and Randall, H. Denial of disability and internal control of reinforcement: A study utilizing a perceptual defense paradigm. Journal of Consulting and Clinical Psychology, 1968, 32, 72-75.

MacDonald, A. P., Jr. Internal-external locus of control and the practice of birth control. Psychological Reports, 1970, 27, 206.

MacDonald, A. P., Jr. Internal external locus of control: Parental antecedents. Journal of Consulting and Clinical Psychology, 1971, 37, 141-147.

MacDonald, A. P., Jr. An Asch-type conformity scale with control for acquiescence response set, plus some findings concerning internal-external locus of control. Unpublished paper, West Virginia University, 1972. (a)

MacDonald, A. P., Jr. Black power. Unpublished paper, West Virginia University, 1972. (b)

MacDonald, A. P., Jr. Internal-external locus of control change technics. Rehabilitation Literature, 1972, 33, 44-47. (c)

MacDonald, A. P., Jr. Internal-external locus of control: A partial bibliography (II). Journal Supplement Abstract Service of A.P.A., Catalogue of Selected Documents in Psychology, 1972, 2, 68. (d)

MacDonald, A. P., Jr., and Hall, J. Perception of disability by the non-disabled. Journal of Consulting and Clinical Psychology, 1969, 33, 654-660.

MacDonald, A. P., Jr., and Hall, J. Internal-external locus of control and perception of disability. Journal of Consulting and Clinical Psychology, 1971, 36, 338-343.

MacDonald, A. P., Jr., and Tseng, M. S. Dimensions of internal versus external control revisited: Toward the development of a measure of generalized expectancy. Unpublished paper, West Virginia University, 1971.

McArthur, L. A. Luck is alive and well in New Haven: A serendipitous finding on perceived control of reinforcement after the draft lottery. Journal of Personality and Social Psychology, 1970, 16, 316-318.

McGhee, P. E., and Crandall, V. C. Beliefs in internal-external control of reinforcements and academic performance. Child Development, 1968, 39, 91-102.

Minton, H. L. Power as a personality construct. Progress in experimental personality research edited by B. Maher. Vol. 4, New York: Academic Press, 1967.

Minton, H. L. Internal-external control and the distinction between personal control and system modifiability. Paper presented at Midwestern Psychological Association, Cleveland, 1972.

Mirels, H. L. Dimensions of internal versus external control. _Journal of Consulting and Clinical Psychology_, 1970, _34_, 226-228.

Nowicki, S., Jr., and Roundtree, J. Correlates of locus of control in secondary school age students. _Developmental Psychology_, 1971, _4_, 477-478.

Nowicki, S., Jr., and Strickland, B. R. A locus of control scale for children. _Journal of Consulting and Clinical Psychology_, 1972, in press.

Odell, M. Personality correlates of independence and conformity. Unpublished master's thesis, Ohio State University, 1959.

Phares, E. J. Changes in expectancy in skill and chance situations. Unpublished doctoral dissertation, Ohio State University, 1955.

Pierce, R. M., Schauble, P. G., and Farkas, A. Teaching internalization behavior to clients. _Psychotherapy: Theory, Research, and Practice_, 1970, _7_, 217-220.

Ransford, H. E. Isolation, powerlessness, and violence: A study of attitudes and participation in the Watts riot. _American Journal of Sociology_, 1968, _73_, 581-591.

Reimanis, G., and Schaeffer, M. Effects of counseling and achievement motivation training on locus of reinforcement control. Paper presented at Eastern Psychological Association, Atlantic City, 1970.

Ritchie, E., and Phares, E. J. Attitude change as a function of internal-external control and communicator status. _Journal of Personality_, 1969, _37_, 429-443.

Rotter, J. B. _Social learning and clinical psychology_. New York: Prentice-Hall, 1954.

Rotter, J. B. Generalized expectancies for internal versus external control of reinforcement. _Psychological Monographs_, 1966, _80_, (1 Whole No. 609).

Ryckman, R. M., and Sherman, M. F. Interactive effects of locus of control and sex of subject on confidence ratings and performance in achievement-related situations. Paper presented at American Psychological Association, Hawaii, 1972.

Shaffer, S., Strickland, B. R., and Uhl, N. P. The relationship of individual difference measures to socioeconomic level and to discrimination learning. Paper presented at the Southeastern Psychological Association, New Orleans, 1969.

Smith, C. E., Pryer, M. W., and Distefano, M. K., Jr. Internal-external control and severity of emotional impairment among psychiatric patients. _Journal of Clinical Psychology_, 1971, _27_, 449-450.

Smith, R. E. Changes in locus of control as a function of life crisis resolution. _Journal of Abnormal Psychology_, 1970, _3_, 308-332.

Stephens, M. W. Cognitive and cultural determinants of early IE development. Paper presented at the American Psychological Association, Washington, D. C., 1971.

Stephens, M. W. Locus of control and intellectual development. U. S. Department of Health, Education, and Welfare (Grant No. MH21423-02) Progress Report for period 9/1/71 through 8/31/72, 1972. (a)

Stephens, M. W. The development of new measures of cognitive variables in elementary school children. U. S. Department of Health, Education, and Welfare, Final Report (Contract No. OEC-0-70-4952), 1972. (b)

Strickland, B. R. The prediction of social action from a dimension of internal-external control. Journal of Social Psychology, 1965, 66, 353-358.

Throop, W. E., and MacDonald, A. P., Jr. Internal-external locus of control: a bibliography. Psychological Reports, Monograph Supplement 1-V28, 1971, 175-190.

Valecha, G. K. Construct validation of internal-external locus of control as measured by an abbreviated 11-item I-E scale. Unpublished doctoral dissertation, Ohio State University, 1972. (a)

Valecha, G. K. Construct validation of internal-external locus of reinforcement related to work-related variables. Paper presented at American Psychological Association, Hawaii, 1972. (b)

Watson, J. S. Operant conditioning of visual fixation in infants under visual and auditory reinforcement. Developmental Psychology, 1969, 508-516.

Watson, J. S., and Ramey, C. T. Reactions to response-contingent stimulation in early infancy. Merrill-Palmer Quarterly, 1972, 18, 219-227.

Wang, D., and Stephens, M. W. Cultural factors and philosophical aspects of locus of control expectancies. Unpublished paper, Purdue University, 1971.

Williamson, J. B. Subjective efficacy and ideal family size as predictors of favorability toward birth control. Demography, 1970, 7, 329-339.

INTELLECTUAL ACHIEVEMENT RESPONSIBILITY QUESTIONNAIRE
(Crandall, Katkovsky, and Crandall 1965)

Variable

This measure taps a belief in one's own control over, and responsibility for, intellectual-academic successes and failures.

Description

The IARQ is composed of 34 forced-choice items. Each item stem describes a positive or negative achievement experience which routinely occurs in children's lives. Each stem is followed by one alternative stating that the event was caused by the child and another stating that the event occurred because of the behavior of someone else (parent, teacher, peer) in the child's environment. One half of the items measure the child's acceptance of responsibility for positive events, the other half deals with negative events. Thus, in addition to a total I (internal or self-responsibility) score, separate subscores can be obtained for beliefs in internal responsibility for successes (I+ score) and for failures (I- score).

The following relationships between the two IARQ subscale scores have been found (Crandall, Katkovsky, and Crandall, 1965).

Grade	N	Correlation of I+ with I-
3	102	.14
4	103	.11
5	99	.11
6	166	.38 (p < .001)
8	161	.40 (p < .001)
10	183	.40 (p < .001)
12	109	.17

A modified form of the IARQ (called the MIARQ) has recently been developed. Modifications are: 1) 24 instead of 34 items, 2) the language level is simplified, and 3) the test is preceded by two examples to insure understanding of the instructions (Ringelheim et al., 1970).

In her NIMH Progress Report Crandall (1968) reported upon the development of two 20-item short forms--one for third to fifth graders and one for sixth through twelfth graders. Each scale yields a total I score and I+ and I- 10-item subscale scores. Correlations between long- and short-form subscales are quite high: I+ = .90 and .89, I- = .91 and .88, for younger and older children respectively.

Sample

A variety of samples, ranging mostly from third through twelfth graders, has been studied. For convenience, two of these samples will be hereafter referred to by letter designations A and B.

Sample A consisted of 923 elementary and high school students drawn from five different schools. Included were students from a consolidated country school, a village school, a small-city school, a medium-city school, and a college laboratory school; there were 102 third graders, 103 fourth graders, 99 fifth graders, 166 sixth graders, 161 eighth graders, 183 tenth graders, and 109 twelfth graders (Crandall, Katkovsky, and Crandall, 1965; McGhee and Crandall, 1968).

Sample B consisted of 134 students drawn from schools in a small central Ohio town; there were 35 seventh graders, 54 seventh graders, and 45 tenth graders (McGhee and Crandall, 1968).

Reliability/ Homogeneity

Some data bearing on internal consistency are noted under Description. Other data are not reported.

Test-retest reliabilities (two-month interval) were established on subsamples from Sample A: grades three through five, r = .69 for total I (.66 for I+, and .74 for I-) and for ninth graders, r = .65 for total I (.47 for I+ and .69 for I-).

Validity

Convergent: IARQ scores were significantly related to report-card grades (in all academic courses averaged over two marking periods) for the Sample A children-- all grades combined. Those with higher IARQ scores had higher report-card averages, as shown by factorial analysis of variance. There was no significant sex difference or sex by IARQ interaction.

The same analysis was used for achievement test scores as dependent variables--the Iowa Test of Basic Skills for grades 3-5, and the California Achievement Test for grades 6, 8, and 12. The tests provided separate sub-scores for reading, math, and language, in addition to total scores. High internal subjects of both sexes had significantly higher achievement test scores than low internal subjects on all subtest achievement scores and total achievement scores. Though IARQ subscores were consistent for females, only the I- subscore showed significant differences for males.

The relation between IARQ scores and report-card averages was again tested in Sample B. Unlike the results of the first study, no significant differences were obtained for females, although the differences were consistently in the same direction. For the males, high total I and I- subjects had significantly higher grade averages.

Other findings: internality was associated with the amount of time boys chose to spend in intellectual activities during free play (r = .70) and the intensity with which they were striving in these activities (r = .66); these relations were not significant for girls (Crandall et al., 1962).

Discriminant: Correlations with intelligence test scores (Sample A) were found to be only moderate but reached significance due to the large samples employed. The California Test of Mental Maturity was the intelligence test used for grades 6, 8, 10, and 12. The Lorge-Thorndike was used for grades 3, 4, and 5. Correlations were .26 for the total I scale (.22 for I+ and .14 for I-) for 233 children from grades 3-5; and .16 for the total I scale (.14 for I+ and I-) for 503 children from grades 6, 8, 10, and 12.

Correlations with social desirability test scores have been found to be rather low. Of the six correlations between IARQ scores and scores on the Children's Social Desirability Scale (Crandall et al., 1964)--(i.e., CSD with I+, I-, and total I for the younger children, and the same tests of association for the older children)-- only two were significant. Among the younger children in the A Sample, I- scores related negatively to CSD scores (r = -.26) and among the older children I+ scores were positively associated with CSD responses (r = .15).

Location	Crandall, V. C., Katkovsky, W., and Crandall, V. J. Children's beliefs in their own control of reinforcements in intellectual-academic achievement situations. Child Development, 1965, 36, 91-109.
Administration	The scale has been orally administered to children below the sixth grade, and is self-administered for those above the sixth grade.
Comments	The IARQ is a carefully developed scale that shows acceptable reliability and evidence of divergent and convergent validity. Studies in which it has been used are too numerous to summarize here. Reports of results and an Intellectual Achievement Responsibility Bibliography can be obtained from Virginia C. Crandall, Department of Psychology, The Fels Research Institute, Yellow Springs, Ohio.

In view of the multidimensional nature of locus of control, factor analytic information would seem desirable. None has been reported for the IARQ, but Crandall (1968) states in her NIMH Progress Report that a factor analytic study of the IARQ is planned.

Little information is presently available regarding the Short Forms, but it appears they may be used with confidence; e.g., Crandall suggests they are less affected by social desirability response bias than the longer forms.

References

Crandall, V. C. Refinement of the IARQ Scale. NIMH Progress Report, December 1968, Grant No. MH-02238, 60-67.

Crandall, V. C., Katkovsky, W., and Crandall, V. J. Children's belief in their own control of reinforcements in intellectual-academic achievement situations. Child Development, 1965, 36, 91-109.

Crandall, V. J., Katkovsky, W., and Preston, A. Motivational and ability determinants of young children's intellectual achievement behaviors. Child Development, 1962, 33, 643-661.

McGhee, P. E., and Crandall, V. C. Beliefs in internal-external control of reinforcements and academic performances. Child Development, 1968, 39, 91-102.

Ringelheim, D., Bialer, I., and Morrissey, H. The relationship among various dichotomous descriptive personality scales and achievement in the mentally retarded: A study of the relevant factors influencing academic achievement at various chronological age levels. Final Report, Office of Education, Bureau of Research, February 1970, No. 6-2685, Grant No. OEG-0-8-062685-1762 (032).

INTELLECTUAL ACHIEVEMENT RESPONSIBILITY QUESTIONNAIRE

This questionnaire describes a number of common experiences most of you have in your daily lives. These statements are presented one at a time, and following each are two possible answers. Read the description of the experience carefully, and then look at the two answers. Choose the one that most often describes what happens to you. Put a circle around the "A" or "B" in front of that answer. Be sure to answer each question according to how you really feel.

If, at any time, you are uncertain about the meaning of a question, raise your hand and one of the persons who passed out the questionnaires will come and explain it to you.

1. If a teacher passes you to the next grade, would it probably be
   A. because she liked you, or
   +B. because of the work you did?

2. ^{ab}When you do well on a test at school, is it more likely to be
   +A. because you studied for it, or
   B. because the test was especially easy?

3. ^{ab}When you have trouble understanding something in school, is it usually
   A. because the teacher didn't explain it clearly, or
   −B. because you didn't listen carefully?

4. ^{a}When you read a story and can't remember much of it, is it usually
   A. because the story wasn't well written, or
   −B. because you weren't interested in the story?

5. ^{ab}Suppose your parents say you are doing well in school. Is this likely to happen
   +A. because your school work is good, or
   B. because they are in a good mood?

6. ^{ab}Suppose you did better than usual in a subject at school. Would it probably happen
   +A. because you tried harder, or
   B. because someone helped you?

7. When you lose at a game of cards or checkers, does it usually happen
   A. because the other player is good at the game, or
   −B. because you don't play well?

8. Suppose a person doesn't think you are very bright or clever.
   −A. can you make him change his mind if you try to, or
   B. are there some people who will think you're not very bright no matter what you do?

9.[ab] If you solve a puzzle quickly, is it
   A. because it wasn't a very hard puzzle, or
   +B. because you worked on it carefully?

10. If a boy or girl tells you that you are dumb, is it more likely
    that they say that
    A. because they are mad at you, or
    -B. because what you did really wasn't very bright?

11.[ab] Suppose you study to become a teacher, scientist, or doctor and you
    fail. Do you think this would happen
    -A. because you didn't work hard enough, or
    B. because you needed some help, and other people didn't give
        it to you?

12.[ab] When you learn something quickly in school, is it usually
    +A. because you paid close attention, or
    B. because the teacher explained it clearly?

13. If a teacher says to you, "Your work is fine," is it
    A. something teachers usually say to encourage pupils, or
    +B. because you did a good job?

14.[ab] When you find it hard to work arithmetic or math problems at
    school, is it
    -A. because you didn't study well enough before you tried them, or
    B. because the teacher gave problems that were too hard?

15.[ab] When you forget something you heard in class, is it
    A. because the teacher didn't explain it very well, or
    -B. because you didn't try very hard to remember?

16. Suppose you weren't sure about the answer to a question your teacher
    asked you, but your answer turned out to be right. Is it likely to
    happen
    A. because she wasn't as particular as usual, or
    +B. because you gave the best answer you could think of?

17.[a] When you read a story and remember most of it, is it usually
    +A. because you were interested in the story, or
    B. because the story was well written?

18.[a] If your parents tell you you're acting silly and not thinking
    clearly, is it more likely to be
    -A. because of something you did, or
    B. because they happen to feel cranky?

19.[ab] When you don't do well on a test at school, is it
    A. because the test was especially hard, or
    -B. because you didn't study for it?

20.[b] When you win at a game of cards or checkers, does it happen
    +A. because you play real well, or
    B. because the other person doesn't play well?

21.[ab] If people think you're bright or clever, is it
    A. because they happen to like you, or
 +B. because you usually act that way?

22. If a teacher didn't pass you to the next grade, would it probably be
    A. because she "had it in for you," or
 −B. because your school work wasn't good enough?

23.[ab] Suppose you don't do as well as usual in a subject at school. Would
this probably happen
 −A. because you weren't as careful as usual, or
    B. because somebody bothered you and kept you from working?

24.[a] If a boy or girl tells you that you are bright, is it usually
 +A. because you thought up a good idea, or
    B. because they like you?

25. Suppose you became a famous teacher, scientist, or doctor. Do you
think this would happen
    A. because other people helped you when you needed it, or
 +B. because you worked very hard?

26.[ab] Suppose your parents say you aren't doing well in your school work.
Is this likely to happen more
 −A. because your work isn't very good, or
    B. because they are feeling cranky?

27.[b] Suppose you are showing a friend how to play a game and he has
trouble with it. Would that happen
    A. because he wasn't able to understand how to play, or
 −B. because you couldn't explain it well?

28.[ab] When you find it easy to work arithmetic or math problems at school,
is it usually
    A. because the teacher gave you especially easy problems, or
 +B. because you studied your book well before you tried them?

29.[ab] When you remember something you heard in class, is it usually
 +A. because you tried hard to remember, or
    B. because the teacher explained it well?

30.[b] If you can't work a puzzle, is it more likely to happen
 −A. because you are not especially good at working puzzles, or
    B. because the instructions weren't written clearly enough?

31.[b] If your parents tell you that you are bright or clever, is it more
likely
    A. because they are feeling good, or
 +B. because of something you did?

32. Suppose you are explaining how to play a game to a friend and he
learns quickly. Would that happen more often
 +A. because you explained it well, or
    B. because he was able to understand it?

33.[b] Suppose you're not sure about the answer to a question your teacher asks you and the answer you give turns out to be wrong. Is it likely to happen
    A. because she was more particular than usual, or
-B. because you answered too quickly?

34.[a] If a teacher says to you, "Try to do better," would it be
    A. because this is something she might say to get pupils to try harder, or
-B. because your work wasn't as good as usual?

Note: Item numbers preceded by + are those items which comprise the I+ sub-scale. Those preceded by - comprise the I- subscale.

[a]Recommended Short Form for younger (grades 3-5) subjects. For I+ items r_{pb} to total subscale score (143 males and 132 females) _ .27, for I- items $r_{pb} \geq .36$.

[b]Recommended Short Form for older (grades 6-12) subjects. For I+ items r_{pb} to total subscale score (303 males and 316 females) _ .34, for I- items $r_{pb} \geq .34$.

MODIFIED INTELLECTUAL ACHIEVEMENT RESPONSIBILITY QUESTIONNAIRE
(Ringelheim, Bialer, and Morrissey, 1970)

Variable   This measure taps belief in one's own control over, and responsibility for, intellectual-academic successes and failures.

Description   The instrument, the MIARQ, is a modified form of the Intellectual Achievement Responsibility Questionnaire (Crandall et al., 1965) described on the preceding pages. It was developed specifically for retardates and differs from the original scale in three ways: 1) it contains 24 instead of 34 items, 2) the language level is simplified, and 3) instructions include two examples to insure that the task is understood.

As with the parent IRAQ, the MIARQ uses the forced-choice format, and in addition to a total I (internal or self-responsibility) score, separate subscores can be obtained for beliefs in internal responsibility for successes (I+ score) and for failures (I- score).

The following statistics were obtained from a sample of 215 educable mentally retarded children (Ringelheim et al. 1970):

Age	Mean	SD
9	11.6	3.1
11	13.7	3.1
13	14.6	3.6
15	16.3	2.7

Sample   The sample consisted of 215 educable mentally retarded children ranging in age from 9 to 15 years and drawn from public school, parochial school, and institutional settings. Subjects ranged in IQ from 45 to 82 and in mental age from 4 to 12.

Reliability/   A Cronbach Alpha of .58 was obtained from data taken from
Homogeneity   the above sample.

No retest reliability data are reported.

Validity   Convergent: No information is reported.

Discriminant: No information is reported.

Location   Ringelheim, D., Bialer, I., and Morrissey, H. The relation
ship among various dichotomous descriptive personality
scales and achievement in the mentally retarded: A study
of the relevant factors influencing academic achievement
at various chronological age levels. Final report, Office
of Education, Bureau of Research, February 1970, No. 6-2685,
Grant No. OEG-0-8-062685-1762 (032).

Administration The scale has been orally administered to mentally retarded
children. No doubt it should be orally administered to
such groups and to children below the sixth grade. It
would appear that it could be self-administered by children
in the sixth grade or higher.

Comments   Because of its recency, little can be said about the usefulness of this scale. However, as it has been built upon the
Intellectual Achievement Responsibility Questionnaire, it
seems reasonable to suppose that the MIARQ would have
similar psychometric properties (though it might have lower
reliability, due to reduction of length). If so, it may be
useful as a more readable short form of the IARQ.

References   Crandall, V. C., Katkovsky, W., and Crandall, V. J.
Children's beliefs in their own control of reinforcements
in intellectual-academic achievement situations. <u>Child
Development</u>, 1965, <u>36</u>, 91-109.

          Ringelheim, D., Bialer, I., and Morrissey, H. The relation-
ship among various dichotomous descriptive personality
scales and achievement in the mentally retarded: A study
of the relevant factors influencing academic achievement
at various chronological age levels. Final report, Office
of Education, Bureau of Research, February 1970, No. 6-2685,
Grant No. OEG-0-8-062685-1762 (032).

203

MODIFIED INTELLECTUAL ACHIEVEMENT RESPONSIBILITY QUESTIONNAIRE

This is not a test. I am trying to find out how kids your age think about certain things. I am going to ask you some questions and you pick the answer that best describes what happens to you or how you feel. If you want me to repeat a question, ask me. Do you understand? All right, listen carefully and answer.

Examples

1. Which do you like best
    a) apples or
    b) oranges

2. If you had a nickel what would you buy
    a) chocolate bar or
    b) lollipop

MIARQ SCALE

1. When you pass a test, is it
    +a) because you studied, or
    b) because it was easy?

2. When you find it hard to understand school work, is it
    a) because the teacher did not explain it enough, or
    -b) because you did not listen carefully?

3. If you can't remember a story, is it
    a) because the story wasn't good, or
    -b) because you just weren't interested?

4. If your parents tell you your school work is good, is it
    +a) because your work is really good, or
    b) because they feel good?

5. When you do better in school, is it
    +a) because you try hard, or
    b) because somebody helped you?

6. If another child says you are dumb, is it
    a) because they are mad at you, or
    -b) because you did something dumb?

7. If you lose a game that you are playing with another child, is it
    a) because he is very good at it, or
    -b) because you don't play well?

Modified Intellectual Achievement Responsibility Questionnaire (Ringelheim, Bialer, and Morrissey, 1970) is reprinted here with permission; requests to use or cite portions of the questionnaire should be directed to the authors and publisher of the questionnaire.

8. If you do a puzzle quickly, it is
    a) because it wasn't very hard, or
    +b) because you worked on it carefully?

9. When you learn quickly, is it
    +a) because you listen carefully, or
    b) because the teacher explains it well?

10. If your teacher says, "Your work is fine," is it
    a) because she says that to all the children, or
    +b) because you did a good job?

11. If you find arithmetic very hard to do, is it
    -a) because you didn't study enough, or
    b) because the teacher gives hard problems?

12. When you forget something the teacher said, is it
    a) because she didn't explain it well, or
    -b) because you didn't try to remember it?

13. If you remember a story, is it
    +a) because you were interested, or
    b) because the story was good?

14. If your parents say you are acting silly, is it
    -a) because of something you did, or
    b) because they feel mean?

15. When you don't pass a test, is it
    a) because the test was too hard, or
    -b) because you didn't study?

16. If you win a game that you are playing with another child, is it
    +a) because you play well, or
    b) because he isn't very good at it?

17. When you do poorly in school, is it
    -a) because you weren't careful, or
    b) because somebody kept you from working?

18. If another child says you are smart, is it
    +a) because you are really smart, or
    b) because they like you?

19. If your parents tell you your school work isn't good, is it
    -a) because your work isn't good, or
    b) because they feel bad?

20. If you find arithmetic easy to do, is it
    a) because the teacher gives easy problems, or
    +b) because you study hard?

21. When you remember something the teacher said, is it
    +a) because you tried hard to remember, or
    b) because the teacher explained it well?

22. If you can't do a puzzle, is it
    -a) because you aren't good at puzzles, or
     b) because the instructions weren't good?

23. If your parents say you are smart, is it
     a) because they are feeling good, or
     b) because you did something smart?

24. If your teacher says "your work isn't good," is it
     a) because she says this to everybody, or
    -b) because your work really wasn't good?

Check items

1. When you pass a test, is it
     b) because it was easy, or
    +a) because you studied?

2. When you find it hard to understand school work, is it
    -b) because you didn't listen carefully, or
     a) because the teacher didn't explain it enough?

Note: Items preceded by + are those items which comprise the I+ subscale.
Those preceded by − comprise the I− subscale.

A LOCUS OF CONTROL SCALE FOR CHILDREN
(Nowicki and Strickland 1972)

Variable

The scale taps locus of control as defined by Rotter (1966). The Nowicki-Strickland instrument was designed as a measure of generalized expectancies for internal versus external control of reinforcement among children.

Description

The Nowicki-Strickland Locus of Control Scale for Children is a 40-item paper-pencil test having Yes-No response mode. The test was developed from an item pool of 102 items. The 102 items were given to a group of nine clinical psychology staff members who were asked to answer the items in an external direction. Items were dropped for which there was not complete agreement among the judges, leaving 59 items. Item analysis reduced the test further to the present 40 items ($\underline{N}$ = 152 children ranging from the third through the ninth grades).

The authors suggest two short forms, one for grades 3-6, and another for grades 7-12. These short forms are derived from a subset of items in the complete scale.

An adult form of the Nowicki-Strickland Scale is presently being developed (Nowicki and Duke, 1972), as well as a pre-school version.

Sample

A variety of samples, ranging from third grade through college, has been used. The main sample consisted of 1017 children (mostly Caucasian) ranging from the third through twelfth grade in four different communities.

Reliability/
Homogeneity

Estimates of internal consistency via the split-half method corrected by the Spearman-Brown Prophesy Formula, are: $\underline{r}$ = .63 (grades 3-5); $\underline{r}$ = .68 (grades 6-8); $\underline{r}$ = .74 (grades 9-11); and $\underline{r}$ = .81 (grade 12). Approximate sample sizes for the first three groups are 300, and 87 for the grade 12 group.

Test-retest reliabilities sampled at three grade levels ($\underline{N}$'s not reported), six weeks apart, are .63 for the third grade, .66 for the seventh grade, and .71 for the tenth grade.

Validity

Convergent: Correlations with the Intellectual Achievement Responsibility Questionnaire (Crandall et al., 1965) were computed for 182 third grade and 171 seventh grade blacks. Correlations with I- were not significant. Correlations with I+ were significant for both groups: r = .31, and r = .51, respectively.

A correlation of .41 with the Bialer-Cromwell Scale (Bialer, 1961) was found in a sample of 29 children nine through eleven years of age.

Internality was found to increase with age:

	Males			Females		
Grade	Mean	Standard Deviation	Sample Size	Mean	Standard Deviation	Sample Size
3	18.0	4.7	(44)	17.4	3.1	(55)
4	18.4	3.6	(59)	18.8	3.6	(55)
5	18.3	4.4	(40)	17.0	4.0	(41)
6	13.7	5.2	(45)	13.3	4.6	(43)
7	13.2	4.9	(65)	13.9	4.2	(52)
8	14.7	4.4	(75)	12.3	3.6	(34)
9	13.8	4.1	(43)	12.3	3.8	(44)
10	13.1	5.3	(68)	13.0	5.3	(57)
11	12.5	4.8	(37)	12.0	5.2	(53)
12	11.4	4.7	(39)	12.4	5.1	(48)

Internality was significantly related to achievement test scores for the third, fifth through seventh, tenth and twelfth grade males, but not for females.

The authors note (statistics not reported) that significant relationships have been found between internality and higher grade point averages in a sample of twelfth graders and another of college students. They also cite a dissertation study (Roberts, 1971) which found significant correlations between internal locus of control and reading achievement for both sexes, and mathematical achievement for males (but not for females).

Discriminant: Nonsignificant correlations (not reported) with an abbreviated form (odd-numbered items only) of the Children's Social Desirability Scale (Crandall et al., 1965) were computed within each grade level.

Nowicki and Strickland (1972) report nonsignificant relationships between their scale and intelligence in one sample of twelfth graders and another sample of college students (statistics not reported).

Location   Nowicki, S., Jr. and Strickland, B. R. A locus of control scale for children. Journal of Consulting and Clinical Psychology, in press.

Administration   The test was administered orally, with each item read twice, to the sample of 1017 children. It has also been self-administered. The authors make no recommendations about method of administration.

Comments   This test has been developed carefully by researchers of solid reputation. Though of recent construction, it has been used in many studies. Results presently available indicate the scale to have adequate internal consistency and temporal consistency. Data relevant to divergent and convergent validity are encouraging. In short, it appears to be the best measure of locus of control as a generalized expectancy presently available for children.

The unidimensionality of the scale remains open to question, and must await the results of factor analyses.

Finally, inspection of the item correlations to the total score indicates that (as is generally true of IE scales) the "better" items are phrased externally. The bias is even more pronounced in the short forms where about 80 percent of the items are so phrased.

References   Bialer, I. Conceptualization of success and failure in mentally retarded and normal children. _Journal of Personality_, 1961, _29_, 303-320.

Crandall, V. C., Crandall, V. J., and Katkovsky, W. A children's social desirability questionnaire. _Journal of Consulting Psychology_, 1965, _29_, 27-36.

Crandall, V. J., Katkovsky, W., and Crandall, V. C. Children's belief in their own control of reinforcement in intellectual-academic situations. Child Development, 1965, _36_, 91-109.

Nowicki, S., Jr., and Duke, M. P. A locus of control scale for adults: An alternative to the Rotter. Unpublished paper, Emory University, 1972.

Nowicki, S., Jr. and Strickland, B. R. A locus of control scale for children. _Journal of Consulting and Clinical Psychology_, 1972, in press.

Roberts, A. The self-esteem of disadvantaged third and seventh graders. Unpublished doctoral dissertation, Emory University, 1971.

Rotter, J. B. Generalized expectancies for internal versus external control of reinforcement. _Psychological Monographs_, 1966, _80_ (1, Whole No. 609).

THE NOWICKI-STRICKLAND PERSONAL REACTION SURVEY

+1. Do you believe that most problems will solve themselves if you just don't fool with them?

(Yes)   No

2. Do you believe that you can stop yourself from catching a cold? (N)

* 3. Are some kids just born lucky? (Y)

4. Most of the time do you feel that getting good grades means a great deal to you? (N)

+5. Are you often blamed for things that just aren't your fault? (Y)

6. Do you believe that if somebody studies hard enough he or she can pass any subject? (N)

* +7. Do you feel that most of the time it doesn't pay to try hard because things never turn out right anyway? (Y)

8. Do you feel that if things start out well in the morning that it's going to be a good day no matter what you do? (Y)

* +9. Do you feel that most of the time parents listen to what their children have to say? (N)

* 10. Do you believe that wishing can make good things happen? (Y)

+11. When you get punished does it usually seem it's for no good reason at all? (Y)

+12. Most of the time do you find it hard to change a friend's (mind) opinion? (Y)

13. Do you think that cheering more than luck helps a team to win? (N)

*+14. Do you feel that it's nearly impossible to change your parent's mind about anything? (Y)

15. Do you believe that your parents should allow you to make most of your own decisions? (N)

*+16. Do you feel that when you do something wrong there's very little you can do to make it right? (Y)

*+17. Do you believe that most kids are just born good at sports? (Y)

Reprinted with permission of Nowicki, S., Jr., and Strickland, B. R. A Locus of Control Scale for Children. From an article of the same name in *Journal of Consulting and Clinical Psychology,* 40 (1973), pp 148-154 (Scale: 150-151). Copyright 1973 by the American Psychological Association, Inc., 1200 17th Street, N.W., Washington, D.C. 20036.

* 18. Are most of the other kids your age stronger than you are?. (Y)

*+19. Do you feel that one of the best ways to handle most problems is just not to think about them? (Y)

20. Do you feel that you have a lot of choice in deciding who your friends are? (N)

21. If you find a four leaf clover do you believe that it might bring you good luck? (Y)

22. Do you often feel that whether you do your homework has much to do with what kind of grades you get? (N)

*+23. Do you feel that when a kid your age decides to hit you, there's little you can do to stop him or her? (Y)

24. Have you ever had a good luck charm? (Y)

25. Do you believe that whether or not people like you depends on how you act? (N)

26. Will your parents usually help you if you ask them to? (N)

*+27. Have you felt that when people were mean to you it was usually for no reason at all? (Y)

+28. Most of the time, do you feel that you can change what might happen tomorrow by what you do today? (N)

*+29. Do you believe that when bad things are going to happen they just are going to happen no matter what you try to do to stop them? (Y)

30. Do you think that kids can get their own way if they just keep trying? (N)

*+31. Most of the time do you find it useless to try to get your own way at home? (Y)

32. Do you feel that when good things happen they happen because of hard work? (N)

*+33. Do you feel that when somebody your age wants to be your enemy there's little you can do to change matters? (Y)

34. Do you feel that it's easy to get friends to do what you want them to? (N)

*+35. Do you usually feel that you have little to say about what you get to eat at home? (Y)

*+36. Do you feel that when someone doesn't like you there's little you can do about it? (Y)

*+37. Do you usually feel that it's almost useless to try in school because most other children are just plain smarter than you are? (Y)

*+38. Are you the kind of person who believes that planning ahead makes things turn out better? (N)

*+39. Most of the time, do you feel that you have little to say about what your family decides to do? (Y)

40. Do you think it's better to be smart than to be lucky? (N)

---

*Items selected for abbreviated scale for grades 3-6.

+Items selected for abbreviated scale for grades 7-12.

BIALER-CROMWELL CHILDREN'S LOCUS OF CONTROL SCALE
(Bialer, 1960)

Variable   The Bialer-Cromwell Children's Locus of Control Scale was
designed to measure the extent to which a child character-
istically construes event outcomes (both positive and negative) as being contingent upon his own actions (i.e.,
internally controlled) rather than upon fate, chance,
objects, or other people (i.e., externally controlled).

Description   The scale consists of 23 questions verbally administered,
and so worded that for 18 items a "Yes" answer and for five
items a "No" answer is taken as indicating internal control.

Ringelheim, Bialer, and Morrissey (1970) report the following average scores by age obtained from 215 educable
mentally retarded children:

Age	Mean	SD
9	12.5	3.3
11	12.1	3.2
13	13.2	2.8
15	13.1	2.1

Bartel (1968) reports the following statistics were obtained
from almost 400 children of both sexes randomly selected
from four grades in a metropolitan school:

Grade	Mean	SD
1	12.8	2.4
2	13.5	2.4
4	13.0	2.8
6	15.0	2.8

Sample   A variety of samples has been administered the Bialer-Cromwell
scale; e.g., (a) 44 children of normal intelligence from
grades one through eight (ranging from 6 to 14 years of age)
and 45 educable mentally retarded children drawn from
special classes (ranging from 7 to 14 years of age) (Bialer,
1960, 1961); (b) 431 children taken from 16 classes, equally
divided among first, second, fourth, and sixth grades, and
randomly selected from one metropolitan school district
(Bartel, 1968); and (c) 98 males and 91 females, ranging in

age from 16 to 30 years and within IQ scores from 58 through 91, who were all enrolled in a vocational training program at the time of testing (Gozali and Bialer, 1968).

Reliability/
Homogeneity

A Cronbach Alpha coefficient of .38 was obtained from the sample of 215 educable mentally retarded children (IQ's from 45-82).

Bartel (1968) reports consistently low Kuder-Richardson coefficients across four grade levels: (a) .05 from 94 first graders, (b) -.01 from 102 second graders, (c) .28 from 99 fourth graders, and (d) .34 from 98 sixth graders.

"In data derived during the standardization of the scale [presumably Bialer, 1960], an adjusted split-half reliability of .86 was obtained. In subsequent studies, Miller (1960), utilizing 100 mentally retarded Ss, found an adjusted split-half reliability of .87; and McConnell (1962) obtained a test-retest reliability coefficient of .73 with 18 retarded Ss." (Ringelheim et al., 1970, p. 15).

A test-retest reliability coefficient (not identified) of .84 was obtained over one week from 60 subjects of both sexes, ranging in age from 17-28 years and in IQ from 59-87 (Gozali and Bialer, 1968).

Validity

Convergent: Bartel (1968) found both fourth- and sixth-grade lower-class children to be more external on the Bialer-Cromwell scale than their middle-class grade mates. Further, gains in Bialer-Cromwell scores from first to sixth grade were significant for middle-class, but not for lower-class, children.

"Lesyk (1968) evaluated the impact of a token economy, operant conditioning ward upon the behavior of female schizophrenics. Patients received tokens for behaving appropriately and cooperatively each day, and were asked to estimate the number of tokens they anticipated earning on each subsequent day. IE-related level of aspiration indices, the Bialer-Cromwell scale, and interview assessments of control expectancy were obtained pre- and post-operant training. After five weeks, patients made less expectancy shifts, fewer unusual shifts, and higher internal scores on Bialer's measure. In addition, those subjects with the highest ratings of positive behavior had the most internal Bialer-Cromwell scores, higher internal ratings derived from the interview, and fewer unusual shifts in their expectancies." (Lefcourt, 1971, pp. 41-42).

Consistent with other studies, Bialer (1961) found that internality increased with age among a group of 89 mentally retarded and normal children, regardless of retarded-normal classification.

Among children from the first through the sixth grade, Bialer-Cromwell scores have been found to correlate significantly with standardized achievement test scores, reading readiness scores, and teacher ratings of achievement (Bartel, 1968). The relationships were much more pronounced among middle- than lower-class children, however,

Perhaps on the negative side, nonsignificant correlations have been found between the Intellectual Achievement Responsibility Questionnaire (Crandall et al., 1965) and the Bialer-Cromwell scale among 72 Negro fifth-grade children (r = .15 for males and .26 for females) (Solomon et al., 1971).

Discriminant: Gozali and Bialer (1968) report nonsignificant correlations between the Bialer-Cromwell scale and the Agreement Response Scale (Couch and Keniston, 1960) and the Children's Social Desirability Questionnaire (Crandall et al., 1965).

Location   Bialer, I. Conceptualization of success and failure in mentally retarded and normal children. Ann Arbor: University Microfilms, 1960.

Administration   The scale traditionally has been orally administered. Though this procedure may be necessary with retardates and young children, it appears the test can be self-administered at older age levels. However, the user should bear in mind that no upper age limit has been specified.

Comments   It is evident that there is insufficient validity data pertaining to the Bialer-Cromwell scale. Further, reliability coefficients obtained from normal samples have been very low, though those obtained from retarded subjects are strikingly higher. In short, present data make the scale's usefulness difficult to evaluate.

References   Bartel, N. R. Locus of control and achievement in middle-class and lower-class children. Unpublished doctoral dissertation, Indiana University, 1968.

Bialer, I. Conceptualization of success and failure in mentally retarded and normal children. Ann Arbor: University Microfilms, 1960.

Bialer, I. Conceptualization of success and failure in mentally retarded and normal children. Journal of Personality, 1961, 29, 303-320.

Couch, A., and Keniston, K. Yeasayers and naysayers: Agreeing response set as a personality variable. Journal of Abnormal Social Psychology, 1960, 60, 151-174.

Crandall, V. C., Crandall, V. J., and Katkovsky, W. A.
Children's social desirability questionnaire. Journal of
Consulting Psychology, 1965, 29, 27-36.

Crandall, V. C., Katkovsky, W., and Crandall, V. J.
Children's belief in their own control of reinforcements
in intellectual-academic achievement situations. Child
Development, 1965, 36, 91-109.

Gozali, J., and Bialer, I. Children's locus of control
scale: Independence from response set bias among retardates.
American Journal of Mental Deficiency, 1968, 72, 622-625.

Lefcourt, H. M. Internal versus external control of
reinforcement revisited: Recent developments. Unpublished
paper (Research Report No. 27), University of Waterloo,
1971. To appear in B. A. Maher (Ed.) Progress in Experimental Personality Research (Academic Press).

Solomon, D., Houlihan, K. A., Busse, T. V., and Parelius,
R. J. Parent behavior and child academic achievement,
achievement striving and related personality characteristics.
Genetic Psychology Monographs, 1971, 83, 173.

BIALER–CROMWELL CHILDREN'S LOCUS OF CONTROL SCALE

This is not a test. I am just trying to find out how kids your age think about certain things. I am going to ask you some questions to see how you feel about these things. There are no right or wrong answers to these questions. Some kids say "Yes" and some say "No." When I ask the question, if you think your answer should be yes, or mostly yes, say "Yes." If you think the answer should be no, or mostly no, say "No." Remember, different children give different answers, and there is no right or wrong answer. Just say "Yes" or "No," depending on how you think the question should be answered. If you want me to repeat a question, ask me. Do you understand? All right, listen carefully, and answer "Yes" or "No."

(.31)*   1p.   When somebody gets mad at you, do you usually feel there is nothing you can do about it?

(.55)   2f.   Do you really believe a kid can be whatever he wants to be?

(.34)   3f.   When people are mean to you, could it be because you did something to make them be mean?

(.23)   4f.   Do you usually make up your mind about something without asking someone first?

(.26)   5f.   Can you do anything about what is going to happen tomorrow?

(.41)   6f.   When people are good to you, is it usually because you did something to make them be good?

(.38)   7f.   Can you ever make other people do things you want them to do?

(.46)   8f.   Do you ever think that kids your age can change things that are happening in the world?

(.55)   9f.   If another child was going to hit you, could you do anything about it?

(.53)   10f.   Can a child your age ever have his own way?

(.23)   11p.   Is it hard for you to know why some people do certain things?

(.37)   12f.   When someone is nice to you, is it because you did the right things?

(.64)   13f.   Can you ever try to be friends with another kid even if he doesn't want to?

(.37) 14f. Does it ever help any to think about what you will be when you grow up?

(.34) 15f. When someone gets mad at you, can you usually do something to make him your friend again?

(.41) 16f. Can kids your age ever have anything to say about where they are going to live?

(.37) 17f. When you get in an argument, is it sometimes your fault?

(.62) 18p. When nice things happen to you, is it only good luck?

(.31) 19p. Do you often feel you get punished when you don't deserve it?

(.37) 20f. Will people usually do things for you if you ask them?

(.35) 21f. Do you believe a kid can usually be whatever he wants to be when he grows up?

(.33) 22p. When bad things happen to you, is it usually someone else's fault?

(.42) 23f. Can you ever know for sure why some people do certain things?

---

*The figures in parentheses represent the item-total score point biserial correlation coefficients, attained during standardization for Bialer's dissertation (Bialer, 1960).

The letter "f" following an item number indicates that an answer of "Yes" is scored as internal control. The letter "p" signifies that an answer of "No" is scored as internal control.

MULTIDIMENSIONAL IE SCALE
(Gurin et al., 1969)

Variable

Rotter (1966) presented evidence that his internal-external locus of control scale was unidimensional. Using factor analysis, Gurin et al. have presented evidence that the scale may not be unidimensional, at least for black college students. Four factors were identified: (1) belief in one's personal control, (2) belief in the extent to which people have control generally, (3) belief about people's ability to exercise control over racial discrimination, war, and world affairs, and (4) a factor called Race Ideology which contained race-related items.

Description

The instrument is a modified form of Rotter's IE scale. It consists of the 23 items from Rotter's scale, three items from the Institute for Social Research Personal Efficacy Scale, and 13 items written especially to tap beliefs about the operation of personal and external forces in the race situation in the United States.

Factor analysis on data taken from over 1,000 black subjects of both sexes yielded the following four factors:

Factor I: (Control Ideology) contains items that seem to measure the respondent's beliefs about the role of internal and external forces in determining successes and failures of people in the culture at large.

Factor II: (Personal Control) contains five items, all phrased in the first person, indicating one's belief in one's own control. This factor is closest to Rotter's (1966) conceptual definition of "internal-external locus of control."

Factor III: (System Modifiability) contains items referring to control over racial discrimination, war, and world affairs.

Factor IV: (Race Ideology) contains items phrased in race-related terms. These items were factored as a separate group. That analysis yielded four factors: (I) Individual-Collective Action, (II) Discrimination Modifiability, (III) Individual-System Blame, and (IV) Racial Militancy.

Sample
: The sample on which the factor analysis was based contained 849 males and 846 females, half of a random sample from 12 predominantly Negro colleges in the United States. Other groups have been administered the form.

Reliability/
Homogeneity
: No information has been reported.

Validity
: Convergent: Data bearing on the validity of the various subscale distinctions are to be found in a few papers authored by members of the Michigan group (Forward and Williams, 1970; Gurin et al., 1969; Lao, 1970).

Forward and Williams administered Rotter's IE scale (Rotter, 1966) to black Detroit high school students before and after the Detroit riot. Following the work of Gurin et al., they divided the total score into "personal control" and "control ideology" subscale scores. Those who indicated a positive reaction to the riot were more internal on personal control. No differences were found for the total Rotter scale score or the control ideology subscale score.

Lao (using the Gurin et al. sample) computed scores for three of the factors identified by Gurin et al., namely (a) personal control, (b) individual-system blame, and (c) discrimination modifiability. In part, Lao reported:

"Not only did we find clear support for the expected [academic] competent behavior from students with high Personal Control, we also found that the ideology measure—Individual System Blame—was not related to competence. Discrimination was related to some competent behaviors, but the direction was inconsistent. In contrast, Individual-System Blame was the only predictor of innovative behavior in the social action arena. The other two expectancy variables—Personal Control and Discrimination Modifiability—bore little or no relationship to how innovative a student is." (Lao, 1970, p. 269).

Discriminant: No information has been reported.

Location
: Gurin, P., Gurin, G., Lao, R. C., and Beattie, M. Internal-external control in the motivational dynamics of Negro youth. Journal of Social Issues, 1969, 25, 29-53.

Administration
: The items can be self-administered in less than one half an hour. None of the samples have included children younger than adolescents.

Comments
: According to Gurin et al. (1969, pp. 35 and 41), the "...separation of self from other, or the personal and

the ideological levels, is not typical of factor analytic results from studies of white populations. Rotter and others report finding one general factor which includes both types of questions [i.e., questions phrased in the first and third person]."

Though this interpretation appeared plausible at the time it was made, new data call it into question. Guttentag (1972) administered the Gurin et al. items, along with items from other IE scales, to 980 black urban school children from grades 5-8. Factor analysis failed to show that items grouped themselves according to first or third person, or race. Further, recent factor analyses of the Rotter Scale (MacDonald and Tseng, 1971; Minton, 1972; Mirels, 1970) do reveal that Rotter's scale is multidimensional for white samples. The self-other (personal control-control ideology) distinction seems to be the most stable one to be uncovered in these analyses. It indeed appears that subjects do not project their own personal sense of control onto people generally.

Clearly, further data on this scale need to be collected. The subscales contain from two to thirteen items. Such brevity would lead one to suspect the reliabilities of these scales. Though information pertaining to reliability is certainly needed, none is apparent in the literature. Information pertaining to divergent validity is also absent from the literature.

It is hoped that future users of this test will attend to these problems of discriminant validity and reliability.

References

Forward, J. R., and Williams, J. R. Internal-external control and black militancy. Journal of Social Issues, 1970, 26, 75-92.

Gurin, P., Gurin, G., Lao, R. C., and Beattie, M. Internal-external control in the motivational dynamics of Negro youth. Journal of Social Issues, 1969, 25, 29-53.

Lao, R. C. Internal-external control and competent and innovative behavior among Negro college students. Journal of Personality and Social Psychology, 1970, 14, 263-270.

MacDonald, A. P., Jr., and Tseng, M. S. Dimensions of internal versus external control revisited: Toward the development of a measure of generalized expectancy. Unpublished paper, West Virginia University, 1971.

Minton, H. L. Internal-external control and the distinction between personal control and system modifiability. Paper presented at the Midwestern Psychological Association, Cleveland, May 6, 1972.

Mirels, H. L. Dimensions of internal versus external control. <u>Journal of Consulting and Clinical Psychology</u>, 1970, <u>34</u>, 226-228.

Rotter, J. B. Generalized expectancies for internal versus external control of reinforcement. <u>Psychological Monographs</u>, 1966, <u>80</u> (1 Whole No. 609).

MULTIDIMENSIONAL INTERNAL-EXTERNAL CONTROL SCALE

FACTOR I: CONTROL IDEOLOGY

1a. Without the right breaks one cannot be an effective leader.
 b. Capable people who fail to become leaders have not taken advantage of their opportunities.

2a. No matter how hard you try, some people just don't like you.
 b. People who can't get others to like them, don't understand how to get along with others.

3a. In the case of the well prepared student, there is rarely if ever such a thing as an unfair test.
 b. Many times exam questions tend to be so unrelated to course work that studying is really useless.

4a. Becoming a success is a matter of hard work, luck has little or nothing to do with it.
 b. Getting a good job depends mainly on being in the right place at the right time.

5a. Who gets to be the boss often depends on who was lucky enough to be in the right place first.
 b. Who gets to be boss depends on who has the skill and ability, luck has little or nothing to do with it.

6a. It is hard to know whether or not a person really likes you.
 b. How many friends you have depends upon how nice a person you are.

7a. Without the right breaks, one cannot be an effective leader.
 b. Getting people to do the right thing depends upon ability; luck has little or nothing to do with it.

8a. Sometimes I can't understand how teachers arrive at the grades they give.
 b. There is a direct connection between how hard I study and the grades I get.

9a. Knowing the right people is important in deciding whether a person will get ahead.
 b. People will get ahead in life if they have the goods and do a good job; knowing the right people has nothing to do with it.

10a. Leadership positions tend to go to capable people who deserve being chosen.
  b. It's hard to know why some people get leadership positions and others don't; ability doesn't seem to be the important factor.

Multidimensional IE Scale (Gurin et al. 1969) is reprinted here with permission. Requests to use or cite portions of the scale should be directed to the authors and publishers of the scale.

11a. People who don't do well in life often work hard, but the breaks just don't come their way.
  b. Some people just don't use the breaks that come their way. If they don't do well, it's their own fault.

12a. Most people don't realize the extent to which their lives are controlled by accidental happenings.
  b. There really is no such thing as "luck."

13a. People are lonely because they don't try to be friendly.
  b. There's not much use in trying too hard to please people, if they like you, they like you.

FACTOR II: PERSONAL CONTROL

14a. I have often found that what is going to happen will happen.
  b. Trusting to fate has never turned out as well for me as making a decision to take a definite course of action.

15a. What happens to me is my own doing.
  b. Sometimes I feel that I don't have enough control over the direction my life is taking.

16a. When I make plans, I am almost certain that I can make them work.
  b. It is not always wise to plan too far ahead because many things turn out to be a matter of good or bad fortune anyhow.

17a. In my case, getting what I want has little or nothing to do with luck.
  b. Many times we might just as well decide what to do by flipping a coin.

18a. Many times I feel that I have little influence over the things that happen to me.
  b. It is impossible for me to believe that chance or luck play an important role in my life.

FACTOR III: SYSTEM MODIFIABILITY

19a. As far as world affairs are concerned, most of us are the victims of forces we can neither understand nor control.
  b. By taking an active part in political and social affairs, the people can control world events.

20a. Racial discrimination is here to stay.
  b. People may be prejudiced but it's possible for American society to completely rid itself of open discrimination.

21a. One of the major reasons why we have wars is because people don't take enough interest in politics.
  b. There will always be wars, no matter how hard people try to prevent them.

22a. The racial situation in America may be very complex, but with enough money and effort, it is possible to get rid of racial discrimination.
  b. We'll never completely get rid of discrimination. It's part of human nature.

32a. Discrimination affects all Negroes. The only way to handle it is for Negroes to organize together and demand rights for all Negroes.
  b. Discrimination may affect all Negroes but the best way to handle it is for each individual Negro to act like any other American--to work hard, get a good education, and mind his own business.

ITEMS NOT LOADING ON ANY FACTOR

33a. Many of the unhappy things in people's lives are partly due to bad luck.
  b. People's misfortunes result from the mistakes they make.

34a. In the long run people get the respect they deserve in this world.
  b. Unfortunately, an individual's worth often passes unrecognized no matter how hard he tries.

35a. The idea that teachers are unfair to students is nonsense.
  b. Most students don't realize the extent to which their grades are influenced by accidental happenings.

36a. The average citizen can have an influence in government decisions.
  b. This world is run by the few people in power and there is not much the little guy can do about it.

37a. With enough effort, we can wipe out political corruption.
  b. It is difficult for people to have much control over the things politicians do in office.

38a. The so-called "white backlash" shows once again that whites are so opposed to Negroes getting their rights that it's practically impossible to end discrimination in America.
  b. The so-called "white backlash" has been exaggerated. Certainly enough whites support the goals of the Negro cause for Americans to see considerable progress in wiping out discrimination.

39a. If a Negro only tries hard enough, he can get ahead despite opposition from whites.
  b. It's true that an individual Negro can get ahead by hard work, but every Negro will sometime face discrimination or opposition that can't be solved by individual effort alone.

RACE-RELEVANT INTERNAL-EXTERNAL ITEMS

FACTOR I: INDIVIDUAL-COLLECTIVE ACTION

1a. The best way to handle problems of discrimination is for each
     individual Negro to make sure he gets the best training possible
     for what he wants to do.
 b. Only if Negroes pull together in civil rights groups and activities
     can anything really be done about discrimination.

2a. The best way to overcome discrimination is through pressure and
     social action.
 b. The best way to overcome discrimination is for each individual
     Negro to be even better trained and more qualified than the most
     qualified white person.

FACTOR II: DISCRIMINATION MODIFIABILITY

3a. Racial discrimination is here to stay.
 b. People may be prejudiced but it's possible for American society to
     completely rid itself of open discrimination.

4a. The so-called "white backlash" shows once again that whites are so
     opposed to Negroes getting their rights that it's practically
     impossible to end discrimination in America.
 b. The so-called "white backlash" has been exaggerated. Certainly
     enough whites support the goals of the Negro cause for Americans
     to see considerable progress in wiping out discrimination.

5a. The racial situation in America may be very complex, but with
     enough money and effort, it is possible to get rid of racial
     discrimination.
 b. We'll never completely get rid of discrimination. It's part of
     human nature.

FACTOR III: INDIVIDUAL-SYSTEM BLAME

6a. It's lack of skill and abilities that keeps many Negroes from
     getting a job. It's not just because they're Negro. When a Negro
     is trained to do something, he is able to get a job.
 b. Many qualified Negroes can't get a good job. White people with
     the same skills wouldn't have any trouble.

7a. Many Negroes who don't do well in life do have good training, but
     the opportunities just always go to whites.
 b. Negroes may not have the same opportunities as whites, but many
     Negroes haven't prepared themselves enough to make use of the
     opportunities that come their way.

8a. Many Negroes have only themselves to blame for not doing better in life. If they tried harder, they'd do better.
 b. When two qualified people, one Negro and one white, are considered for the same job, the Negro won't get the job no matter how hard he tries.

9a. The attempt to "fit in" and do what's proper hasn't paid off for Negroes. It doesn't matter how "proper" you are, you'll still meet serious discrimination if you're Negro.
 b. The problem for many Negroes is that they aren't really acceptable by American standards. Any Negro who is educated and does what is considered proper will be accepted and get ahead.

FACTOR IV: RACIAL MILITANCY

10a. Negroes would be better off and the cause of civil rights advanced if there were fewer demonstrations.
 b. The only way Negroes will gain their civil rights is by constant protest and pressure.

11a. Depending on bi-racial committees is just a dodge. Talking and understanding without constant protest and pressure will never solve problems of discrimination.
 b. Talking and understanding as opposed to protest and pressure is the best way to solve racial discrimination.

12a. Organized action is one approach to handling discrimination, but there are probably very few situations that couldn't be handled better by Negro leaders talking with white leaders.
 b. Most discriminatory situations simply can't be handled without organized pressure and group action.

13a. Discrimination affects all Negroes. The only way to handle it is for Negroes to organize together and demand rights for all Negroes.
 b. Discrimination may affect all Negroes but the best way to handle it is for each individual Negro to act like any other American-- to work hard, get a good education, and mind his own business.

ROTTER'S INTERNAL-EXTERNAL LOCUS OF CONTROL SCALE
(Rotter 1966)

Variable

Rotter (1966) defines internal-external locus of control in the following way:

"...an event regarded by some persons as a reward or reinforcement may be differently perceived and reacted to by others. One of the determinants of this reaction is the degree to which the individual perceives that the reward follows from, or is contingent upon, his own behavior or attributes versus the degree to which he feels the reward is controlled by forces outside of himself and may occur independently of his own actions. ...a perception of causal relationship need not be all or none but can vary in degree. When a reinforcement is perceived by the subject as following some action of his own but not being entirely contingent upon his action, then, in our culture, it is typically perceived as the result of luck, chance, fate, as under the control of powerful others, or as unpredictable because of the great complexity of the forces surrounding him. When the event is interpreted in this way by an individual, we have labeled this a belief in <u>external control</u>. If the person perceives that the event is contingent upon his own behavior or his own relatively permanent characteristics, we have termed this a belief in <u>internal control</u>."

In view of recent concerns about the multidimensional nature of the IE construct, the reader may wish to note that Rotter's definition of the construct deals only with a person's <u>perception</u> of <u>contingency</u> <u>relationships</u> between <u>his own behavior</u> and events which follow that behavior.

Description

The history of the development of the test is detailed in Rotter's (1966) monograph. In its present form, it consists of 23 question pairs, using a forced-choice format, plus six filler questions.

Internal statements are paired with external statements. One point is given for each external statement selected. Scores can range from zero (most internal) to 23 (most external).

The items are presented below along with their correlation to the total test score minus that item. The correlations were reported by Rotter (1966) for a sample of 400 subjects, 200 of each sex.

Normative data are reported by Rotter (1966). Using the means reported for a variety of samples, and those from samples not reported by Rotter (for a total N of 4,433), Owens computed the overall means for all groups combined: males, mean = 8.2 (SD = 4.0); females, mean = 8.5 (SD = 3.9); combined, mean = 8.3 (SD = 3.9).

Rotter (1966) reported that two factor analyses had been completed; one by himself and the other by Franklin (1963). The results were much the same. Each revealed one general factor which accounted for much of the total scale variance (53 percent in Franklin's analysis) and several additional factors which involved only a few items and which accounted for very little variance. More recent factor analyses (Gurin, et al., 1969; MacDonald and Tseng, 1971; Minton, 1972; Mirels, 1970) have shown the Rotter scale to be more multidimensional than the analyses of Rotter and Franklin. (Still, there is generally one factor that accounts for most of the variance, and often this factor has to do with one's belief in his own control—with items worded in the first person; a second factor that often emerges has to do with one's belief that people have control generally—items worded in the third person.)

Sample

The Rotter IE scale has been administered to numerous samples. For details, see Joe (1971), Lefcourt (1966, 1972), and Rotter (1966).

Reliability/ Homogeneity

An internal consistency coefficient (Kuder-Richardson) of .70 was obtained from a sample of 400 college students (Rotter, 1966).

For two subgroups of Rotter's (1966) sample test-retest reliability coefficients were computed, with a value of .72 for 60 college students, after one month (for males, $r = .60$; for females, $r = .83$). After two months, an r of .55 was obtained for 117 college students (for males, $r = .49$; for females, $r = .61$). Rotter suggests that part of the decrease after the two month period is due to differences in adminis-tration (group vs. individual).

Validity

Convergent: Over 50 percent of the internal-external locus of control investigations have employed the Rotter scale. It is not possible to list all of the findings here. Detailed literature reviews are available (Joe, 1971; Lefcourt, 1966, 1972; Minton, 1967; Rotter, 1966). The literature does indicate that there are individual dif-ferences in perception about one's control over one's destiny and that the Rotter scale is sensitive to these differences.

Discriminant: Rotter reports that correlations with the Marlowe-Crowne Social Desirability Scale range from -.07 to -.35. More recent studies have uncovered higher coefficients (Altrocchi et al., 1968; Feather, 1967; Hjelle, 1971; MacDonald, 1972)--ranging from -.20 to -.42. Additionally, correlations with Edward's Social Desirability Scales have been found to range between -.23 and -.70 (Berzins et al., 1970; Cone, 1971).

Correlations with measures of intelligence have ranged from .03 to -.22 (Rotter, 1966).

Location   Rotter, J. B. Generalized expectancies for internal versus external control of reinforcement. Psychological Monographs, 1966, 80 (1 Whole No. 609).

Administration   The scale is self-administered and can be completed in about 15 minutes. The scale has been most frequently used with college students, but has been used with adolescent and older subjects. No upper or lower age limits have been established.

Comments   The scale has been used in a number of interesting and important studies. The recent group of studies that find significant correlations with measures of social desirability response bias, along with those which have found the scale tapping more than one factor, have called the validity of the scale into question. However, when one considers that (a) the correlations with measures of social desirability response bias are typically low, and (b) results of factor analyses are varied and difficult to compare (e.g., the analysis performed by Gurin et al. [1969] included a number of items not found in Rotter's scale; it is difficult to assess the effect of those items on the analysis), one must conclude that methodological questions have been more effectively raised than answered.

As mentioned above, factor analyses have uncovered one factor (named "personal control") on which the items with the highest loadings are phrased in the first person. This group of items would appear to be reflecting and measuring the construct as it has been defined by Rotter (see the definition under "Variable" above).

Although this factor tends to account for most of the scale variance, a second factor--"control ideology" (which could as easily be called "control attribution"), in which the items are phrased in the third person--appears with some frequency. This factor seems to be indeed different from IE as defined by Rotter and does seem to be important in its own right.

It is clear that there are methodological problems to be resolved in the IE area and that Rotter's scale is not as "pure" as it was believed to be. However, until such time as the issues are resolved, Rotter's scale is still to be recommended as a measure of generalized IE expectancy.

References   Altrocchi, J., Palmer, J., Hellmann, R., and Davis, H.
The Marlowe-Crowne, repressor-sensitizer, and internal-
external scales and attribution of unconscious hostile
intent. Psychological Reports, 1968, 23, 1229-1230.

Berzins, J. I., Ross, W. F., and Cohen, D. I. Skill versus
chance activity preferences as alternative measures of locus
of control: An attempted cross-validation. Journal of
Consulting and Clinical Psychology, 1970, 35, 18-20.

Cone, J. D. Locus of control and social desirability.
Journal of Consulting and Clinical Psychology, 1971, 36,
449.

Feather, N. T. Some personality correlates of external
control. Australia Journal of Psychology, 1967, 19, 253-260.

Franklin, R. D. Youth's expectancies about internal versus
external control of reinforcement related to N variables.
Dissertation Abstracts, 1963, 24, 1684.

Gurin, P., Gurin, G., Lao, R. C., and Beattie, M. Internal-
external control in the motivational dynamics of Negro
youth. Journal of Social Issues, 1969, 25, 29-53.

Hjelle, L. A. Social desirability as a variable in the locus
of control scale. Psychological Reports, 1971, 28, 807-816.

Joe, V. C. Review of the internal-external control
construct as a personality variable. Psychological Reports,
1971, Monograph Supplement 3-V28, 619-640.

Lefcourt, H. M. Internal versus external control of reinforcement: A review. Psychological Bulletin, 1966, 65, 206-220.

Lefcourt, H. M. Internal versus external control of
reinforcement revisited: Recent developments. Unpublished
paper (Research Report No. 27), University of Waterloo, 1971.
To appear in Progress in experimental personality research
edited by B. A. Maher (Academic Press).

MacDonald, A. P., Jr. An Asch-type conformity scale with
control for acquiescence response set, plus some findings
concerning internal-external locus of control. Unpublished
paper, West Virginia University, 1972.

MacDonald, A. P., Jr., and Tseng, M. S. Dimensions of
internal versus external control revisited: Toward the
development of a measure of generalized expectancy.
Unpublished paper, West Virginia University, 1971.

Minton, H. L. Power as a personality construct. In Progress
in experimental personality research edited by B. Maher.
Vol. 4, New York: Academic Press, 1967.

Minton, H. L. Internal-external control and the distinction between personal control and system modifiability. Paper presented at Midwestern Psychological Association, Cleveland, 1972.

Mirels, H. L. Dimensions of internal versus external control. Journal of Consulting and Clinical Psychology, 1970, 34, 226-228.

Owens, D. A. Disability-minority and social learning. Unpublished Master's thesis, West Virginia University, 1969.

Rotter, J. B. Generalized expectancies for internal versus external control of reinforcement. Psychological Monographs, 1966, 80 (1 Whole No. 609).

INTERNAL VS. EXTERNAL CONTROL

(Correlations are those of each item with total score, excluding that item.)

1.a. Children get into trouble because their parents punish
them too much.
  b. The trouble with most children nowadays is that their   Filler
parents are too easy with them.

2.<u>a</u>. Many of the unhappy things in people's lives are partly
due to bad luck.   .26
  b. People's misfortunes result from the mistakes they make.

3.a. One of the major reasons why we have wars is because
people don't take enough interest in politics.
  <u>b</u>. There will always be wars, no matter how hard people
try to prevent them.   .18

4.a. In the long run people get the respect they deserve in
this world.
  <u>b</u>. Unfortunately, an individual's worth often passes
unrecognized no matter how hard he tries.   .29

5.a. The idea that teachers are unfair to students is nonsense.
  <u>b</u>. Most students don't realize the extent to which their
grades are influenced by accidental happenings.   .18

6.<u>a</u>. Without the right breaks one cannot be an effective leader. .32
  b. Capable people who fail to become leaders have not taken
advantage of their opportunities.

7.<u>a</u>. No matter how hard you try some people just don't like
you.   .23
  b. People who can't get others to like them don't understand how to get along with others.

8.a. Heredity plays the major role in determining one's
personality.
  b. It is one's experiences in life which determine what
one is like.   Filler

9.<u>a</u>. I have often found that what is going to happen will
happen.   .16
  b. Trusting to fate has never turned out as well for me as
making a decision to take a definite course of action.

10.a. In the case of the well prepared student there is rarely
if ever such a thing as an unfair test.

Rotter's Internal-External Locus of Control Scale (Rotter 1966) is reprinted here with
permission. Requests to use or cite portions of the scale should be directed to the author and
publisher of the scale.

   b. Many times exam questions tend to be so unrelated to course work that studying is really useless.   .24

11. a. Becoming a success is a matter of hard work, luck has little or nothing to do with it.
    b. Getting a good job depends mainly on being in the right place at the right time.   .30

12. a. The average citizen can have an influence in government decisions.
    b. This world is run by the few people in power, and there is not much the little guy can do about it.   .27

13. a. When I make plans, I am almost certain that I can make them work.
    b. It is not always wise to plan too far ahead because many things turn out to be a matter of good or bad fortune anyhow.   .27

14. a. There are certain people who are just no good.
    b. There is some good in everybody.   Filler

15. a. In my case getting what I want has little or nothing to do with luck.
    b. Many times we might just as well decide what to do by flipping a coin.   .29

16. a. Who gets to be the boss often depends on who was lucky enough to be in the right place first.   .31
    b. Getting people to do the right thing depends upon ability, luck has little or nothing to do with it.

17. a. As far as world affairs are concerned, most of us are the victims of forces we can neither understand, nor control.   .36
    b. By taking an active part in political and social affairs the people can control world events.

18. a. Most people don't realize the extent to which their lives are controlled by accidental happenings.   .31
    b. There really is no such thing as "luck."

19. a. One should always be willing to admit mistakes.
    b. It is usually best to cover up one's mistakes.   Filler

20. a. It is hard to know whether or not a person really likes you.   .27
    b. How many friends you have depends on how nice a person you are.

21. a. In the long run the bad things that happen to us are balanced by the good ones.   .15
    b. Most misfortunes are the result of lack of ability, ignorance, laziness, or all three.

22.a. With enough effort we can wipe out political corruption.
   b. It is difficult for people to have much control over the
      things politicians do in office.   .23

23.a. Sometimes I can't understand how teachers arrive at the
      grades they give.   .26
   b. There is a direct connection between how hard I study
      and the grades I get.

24.a. A good leader expects people to decide for themselves
      what they should do.
   b. A good leader makes it clear to everybody what their
      jobs are.   Filler

25.a. Many times I feel that I have little influence over the
      things that happen to me.   .48
   b. It is impossible for me to believe that chance or luck
      plays an important role in my life.

26.a. People are lonely because they don't try to be friendly.
   b. There's not much use in trying too hard to please
      people, if they like you, they like you.   .20

27.a. There is too much emphasis on athletics in high school.
   b. Team sports are an excellent way to build character.   Filler

28.a. What happens to me is my own doing.
   b. Sometimes I feel that I don't have enough control over
      the direction my life is taking.   .24

29.a. Most of the time I can't understand why politicians
      behave the way they do.   .11
   b. In the long run the people are responsible for bad
      government on a national as well as on a local level.

Note: Score is the total number of underlined choices (i.e., external
      items endorsed).

ABBREVIATED 11-ITEM ROTTER IE SCALE
(Valecha, 1972)

Variable

The scale measures internal-external locus of control as described by Rotter (1966).

Description

The scale is composed of 11 items from Rotter's Internal-External Locus of Control Scale (Rotter, 1966). Items were selected on the basis of being more general, adult-oriented, and work-related.

There is a change in the format of the items allowing for the measurement of intensity of feeling. After each choice between an a and b alternative, the respondents note whether that choice is "much closer" or "slightly closer" to their own opinion. Thus each question is scored by assigning a value of:

1 for an internal response much closer
2 for an internal response slightly closer
3 for an external response slightly closer
4 for an external response much closer

The theoretical range of scores is from 11 to 44, as a result of this change in format.

Sample

The scale was administered to a national probability sample of 4,330 males of 16-26 years of age in 1968. Of the 4,330 individuals interviewed 3,694 (87 percent) completed the scale in usable form, of whom 2,691 were whites and 1,003 blacks. Data were analyzed separately for blacks (median = 24.1) and whites (median = 22.1).

Reliability/
Homogeneity

No data are reported.

Validity

Convergent: Men in higher-status occupations scored higher in internality among whites, but the relationship was not significant among blacks.

Higher knowledge about the world of work (as measured by a 28-item occupational information test) was positively associated with internality among whites.

Internal whites with lower levels of education (12 years or less) made better progress on the job than externals. No differences were found among the more highly educated. The results also were not significant for blacks.

Discriminant: No data are reported.

Location   Valecha, G. K. Construct validation of internal-external locus of control as measured by an abbreviated 11-item IE scale. Unpublished doctoral dissertation, The Ohio State University, 1972.

Administration   The scale has been individually administered but appears to be usable in a group setting.

Comments   Too little information was available at the time of this writing. Sorely needed are statistics pertaining to internal consistency and stability reliabilities. Also, factor analysis would seem in order. Considering the fact that this scale is built on items from Rotter's IE Scale (Rotter, 1966), which has been shown to be related to social desirability response bias, investigation of its relation to a measure of social desirability response bias would also seem in order.

A serious limitation is the scale's having been used only with males. Given the number of studies showing IE sex differences, it is important to provide information pertaining to both sex groups.

Considering all of the above, it would appear risky to use the 11-item abbreviated scale at this time.

References   Rotter, J. B. Generalized expectancies for internal versus external control of reinforcement. Psychological Monographs, 1966, 80, (1 Whole No. 609).

Valecha, G. K. Construct validation of internal-external locus of control as measured by an abbreviated 11-item IE scale. Unpublished doctoral dissertation. The Ohio State University, 1972 (a).

Valecha, G. K. Construct validation of internal-external locus of reinforcement related to work-related variables. Paper presented at APA, Honolulu, Hawaii, 1972 (b).

Items   See items 1, 4, 5, 11, 12, 15, 16, 18, 21, 25, and 28 of the preceding scale.

All the items have the form of the following example:

Example:

_____ Statement closer to my opinion

[a] Many of the unhappy things in people's lives are partly due to bad luck.

[b] People's misfortunes result from the mistakes they make.

☐ Much closer

☐ Slightly closer

Abbreviated 11-Item Rotter IE Scale (Valecha 1972) is reprinted here with permission.

JAMES' INTERNAL-EXTERNAL LOCUS OF CONTROL SCALE
(James 1957)

Variable
The scale measures internal-external locus of control as described by Rotter (1966).

Description
The scale is a 1963 revision of that first developed by James (1957). It contains 60 items, of which 30 are "true" items and 30 are fillers (namely the odd numbered items). It should be noted that all of the items in James' scale are worded in the external direction.

The scale employs a Likert-type format. Response options for each item are <u>Strongly Agree</u> (3) to <u>Strongly Disagree</u> (0). Scores theoretically range from 0 (internal) to 90 (external). James reports that in practice the actual range in college populations he has tested varies between 8 and 82, with a mean of 37 and a standard deviation of 12.

MacDonald and Tseng (1971) factor analyzed responses to James' items, taken from 178 (105 male and 73 female) undergraduate students at West Virginia University. Varimax rotation yielded two factors for the total sample, four for males and five for females. Factor I accounted for 23 percent of the variance for the total sample; 22 percent for males and 28 percent for females. Factors beyond the first factor each accounted for about 5 percent of the variance.

Eleven of the 17 items that loaded highest on Factor I and three of the six that loaded highest on Factor II were common to both sexes (i.e., loaded higher than $\pm$ .30). Factor I (i.e., the 11 items common to both sex groups) might be viewed as a generalized measure of locus of control in that it contained items that reflect the acceptance or rejection of the idea that outcomes are contingent upon (a) luck (items: 6, 10, 26, 30, 42, and 54), (b) fate (items: 36, 50, and 56), and (c) powerful others (items: 20 and 52). Factor II (items: 16, 18, and 60) seems to reflect support for the notion that life is ambiguous, confusing, and unpredictable.

Sample
A variety of samples has been used. As is generally the case, college students have been the most widely-used samples.

Reliability/ Homogeneity	James (personal communication) reports split-half reliabilities ranging from .84 to .96. Retest reliabilities vary from .71 (one year period) to .86 (3 month period). See also, James and Steele, 1968.
Validity	Convergent: MacDonald (unpublished study done at West Virginia University in 1971) administered both Rotter's IE scale (Rotter, 1966) and the James scale (1963 revision) to 171 (103 male and 68 female) undergraduate students enrolled in an introductory sociology class. The two scales intercorrelated at .64 for the total sample (.61 for males and .71 for females). However, the relationship should be interpreted with the knowledge that the James scale was used as the stimulus to the development of Rotter's scale. Though the two instruments differ in format (Rotter's being a forced-choice scale), they do share some common items. Too few studies have been done to speculate much about the validity of the James scale. Of those done, relationships have been weak or nonsignificant, and in some cases the results have been opposite to those predicted (James and Steele, 1965; Lipp et al., 1968). Discriminant: Nonsignificant correlations with the Marlowe-Crowne Special Desirability Scale have been referred to (James, Woodruff, and Werner, 1965), but the actual coefficients have not been reported.
Location	The scale, copyrighted by James, has not been previously published and is reproduced here with his permission.
Administration	The scale may be filled out individually or self-administered in groups. Though reference is made to use with college students, no lower age limit has been reported.
Comments	The James scale appears to have satisfactory internal consistency and retest reliabilities. Further, it seems to have a simpler factor structure than Rotter's scale—in the sense that a more general first factor has been found which accounts for an appreciable amount of the total variance and for which there is a significant number of items (11) common to both sex groups. All of the items are worded in the external direction, which is generally true of the nonforced-choice IE scales. The implications of this format are not now clear and must await further more detailed IE test analysis. No information is presently available regarding the effect of the 30 filler items. A user might reasonably consider removing the filler items. For those interested

in a short form of the James scale, factor analysis
(MacDonald and Tseng, 1971) suggests the following 11
items: 6, 10, 20, 26, 30, 36, 42, 50, 52, 54, and 56.

References

James, W. H. Internal versus external control of
reinforcement as a basic variable in learning theory.
Unpublished doctoral dissertation, Ohio State
University, 1957.

James, W. H. and Steele, B. J. Internal control of
reinforcement and resistance to extinction in operant
learning. Paper presented at the Midwestern Psychological
Association Meetings, Chicago, Illinois, May 1968.

James, W. H., Woodruff, A. B., and Werner, W. Effect
of internal and external control upon changes in smoking
behavior. Journal of Consulting Psychology, 1965, 29,
127-129.

Lipp, L., Kolstoe, R., and James, W. Denial of disability
and internal control of reinforcement: A study using a
perceptual defense paradigm. Journal of Consulting and
Clinical Psychology, 1968, 32, 72-75.

MacDonald, A. P., Jr., and Tseng, M. W. Dimensions of
internal versus external control revisited: Toward the
development of a measure of generalized expectancy.
Unpublished paper, West Virginia University, 1971.

Rotter, J. B. Generalized expectancies for internal
versus external control of reinforcement. Psychological
Monographs, 1966, 80, (1 Whole No. 609).

JAMES' INTERNAL-EXTERNAL
LOCUS OF CONTROL SCALE

Below are a number of statements about various topics. They have been collected from different groups of people and represent a variety of opinions.
There are no right or wrong answers to this questionnaire; for every statement there are large numbers of people who agree and disagree. Please
indicate whether you agree or disagree with each statement as follows:

Circle SA if you strongly agree
Circle A if you agree
Circle D if you disagree
Circle SD if you strongly disagree

Please read each item carefully and be sure that you indicate the response
which most closely corresponds to the way which you personally feel.

1. I like to read newspaper editorials whether I agree with them or not.

        SA   A   D   SD

2. Wars between countries seem inevitable despite efforts to prevent
    them.

3. I believe the government should encourage more young people to make
    science a career.

4. It is usually true of successful people that their good breaks far
    outweighed their bad breaks.

5. I believe that moderation in all things is the key to happiness.

6. Many times I feel that we might just as well make many of our
    decisions by flipping a coin.

7. I disapprove of girls who smoke cigarettes in public places.

8. The actions of other people toward me many times have me baffled.

9. I believe it is more important for a person to like his work than
    to make money at it.

10. Getting a good job seems to be largely a matter of being lucky
    enough to be in the right place at the right time.

11. It's not what you know but who you know that really counts in
    getting ahead.

James' Internal-External Locus of Control Scale (James 1957) is reprinted here with permission.
Requests to use or cite portions of the scale should be directed to the author and publisher of the scale.

12. A great deal that happens to me is probably just a matter of chance.

13. I don't believe that the presidents of our country should serve for more than two terms.

14. I feel that I have little influence over the way people behave.

15. It is difficult for me to keep well-informed about foreign affairs.

16. Much of the time the future seems uncertain to me.

17. I think the world is much more unsettled now than it was in our grandfathers' times.

18. Some people seem born to fail while others seem born for success no matter what they do.

19. I believe there should be less emphasis on spectator sports and more on athletic participation.

20. It is difficult for ordinary people to have much control over what politicians do in office.

21. I enjoy reading a good book more than watching television.

22. I feel that many people could be described as victims of circumstances beyond their control.

23. Hollywood movies do not seem as good as they used to be.

24. It seems many times that the grades one gets in school are more dependent on the teachers' whims than on what the student can really do.

25. Money shouldn't be a person's main consideration in choosing a job.

26. It isn't wise to plan too far ahead because most things turn out to be a matter of good or bad fortune anyhow.

27. At one time I wanted to become a newspaper reporter.

28. I can't understand how it is possible to predict other people's behavior.

29. I believe that the U.S. needs a more conservative foreign policy.

30. When things are going well for me I consider it due to a run of good luck.

31. I believe the government has been taking over too many of the affairs of private industrial management.

32. There's not much use in trying to predict which questions a teacher is going to ask on an examination.

33. I get more ideas from talking about things than reading about them.

34. Most people don't realize the extent to which their lives are controlled by accidental happenings.

35. At one time I wanted to be an actor (or actress).

36. I have usually found that what is going to happen will happen, regardless of my actions.

37. Life in a small town offers more real satisfactions than life in a large city.

38. Most of the disappointing things in my life have contained a large element of chance.

39. I would rather be a successful teacher than a successful businessman.

40. I don't believe that a person can really be a master of his fate.

41. I find mathematics easier to study than literature.

42. Success is mostly a matter of getting good breaks.

43. I think it is more important to be respected by people than to be liked by them.

44. Events in the world seem to be beyond the control of most people.

45. I think that states should be allowed to handle racial problems without federal interference.

46. I feel that most people can't really be held responsible for themselves since no one has much choice about where he was born or raised.

47. I like to figure out problems and puzzles that other people have trouble with.

48. Many times the reactions of people seem haphazard to me.

49. I rarely lose when playing card games.

50. There's not much use in worrying about things...what will be, will be.

51. I think that everyone should belong to some kind of church.

52. Success in dealing with people seems to be more a matter of the other person's moods and feelings at the time rather than one's own actions.

53. One should not place too much faith in newspaper reports.

54. I think that life is mostly a gamble.

55. I am very stubborn when my mind is made up about something.

56. Many times I feel that I have little influence over the things that happen to me.

57. I like popular music better than classical music.

58. Sometimes I feel that I don't have enough control over the direction my life is taking.

59. I sometimes stick to difficult things too long even when I know they are hopeless.

60. Life is too full of uncertainties.

Score only even numbered items as follows: SA = 3, A = 2, D = 1, and SD = 0. High scores are associated with higher externality.

CHAPTER 5 - ALIENATION AND ANOMIA

The concept of alienation has become one of the most widely used and misused terms of our time. While the scales in this chapter afford us considerable insight into this phenomenon in society, we shall see that major methodological problems remain to limit their basic utility.

These scales come from the realms of both sociology and psychology, but mainly from sociology. In sociology the topic is often subsumed (from Durkheim) under the heading of "anomie," although the first thing a sociologist in the area will want to impress on his audience is that anomie refers to a property of a social system and hence cannot be directly measured by the attitudes of single individuals. Therefore one encounters the use of the related terms "anomia" and "anomy" in connection with attitude measurement in this area.

There are fourteen scales in this chapter that relate to such concepts:

1. Anomy Scale (McClosky and Schaar 1965)
2. Anomia Scale (Srole 1956)
3. Powerlessness (Neal and Seeman 1962)
4. Political Alienation (Olsen 1969)
5. Alienation via Rejection (Streuning and Richardson 1965)
6. Purpose-in-Life Test (Crumbaugh 1968)
7. Alienation Scale (Dean 1961)
8. Alienation (Middleton 1963)
9. Political Alienation (Horton and Thompson 1962)
10. Alienation (Nettler 1957)
11. Anomie Scale (Hyman, Wright and Hopkins 1960)
12. Helplessness (Gamson 1961)
13. Alienation (Davids 1955)
14. Alienation Within a Social System (Clark 1959)

Most of these scales, and especially the most widely-used two, suffer from a major fault that needs correction--the lack of control over agreement response set. None of the items in either the McClosky and Schaar or Srole scale is keyed in the negative direction. In one cross-section study Lenski and Leggett (1960) included the Srole item:

"It's hardly fair to bring children into the world, the way things look for the future."

Later in the same interview schedule, they asked respondents to agree or disagree with the statement:

"Children born today have a wonderful future to look forward to."

While a logician could argue that the two statements are not exact opposites of each other, a basic inconsistency in orientation does exist between the two statements. In point of fact, Lenski and Leggett found that more than two-thirds of their respondents who agreed with the first statement also agreed with the second. Blue-collar respondents and black respondents were most likely to exhibit this inconsistent response pattern and hence to seriously call into question the traditional finding that both groups express greatest alienation. Actually, however, one does find this result holding true for those who agree with the first statement and disagree with the second, although the differences are greatly reduced:

	White Collar	Blue Collar	White	Negro
Agree with first	4%	15%	8%	25%
Agree with first and disagree with second	2%	5%	3%	6%

In other words, if the Lenski-Leggett data can be generalized, they suggest that one is more likely to risk overestimating the number of alienated individuals in a sample using the Srole scale than to risk making incorrect inferences about which variables are associated with alienation. Nevertheless more extended research needs to be done on the validity of such a generalization. In the meantime, researchers need to be especially cautious in estimating the size of the alienated segment of the population using these questions (this general caution probably applies to all attitude measures, but this is one area where researchers often speculate incorrectly about the large number of alienated persons in society).

Of the fourteen scales in this chapter, that of McClosky and Schaar has produced the greatest variety of correlates. The McClosky-Schaar study provides some of the strongest arguments for the contention that there exists considerable overlap in the concepts developed in the separate chapters of the present volume. Specifically, McClosky and Schaar find their anomy scale to relate to life satisfaction (Chapter 2), aspects of self-esteem (Chapter 3), extreme political beliefs (Chapter 6), aspects of authoritarianism (Chapter 5), trust in people (Chapter 8), and some methodological scales (Chapter 10). The scale, however, does not have impressive internal consistency and thus far has yet to undergo a full test of validity, in the sense of correlation with some observed behavior (although this is probably true of most scales in this chapter). The authors do note that the astonishing number of attitudinal variables that relate to this scale are not affected when controls for acquiescence, social status, or status frustration are controlled.

The Srole scale has undoubtedly been applied in the widest variety of separate research studies (over 25 such studies are noted in the sociological literature up to 1965 by Bonjean et al., 1967). The scale has consistently related as hypothesized to socio-political attitudes and background variables, such as social status (although note the arguments two paragraphs previously). The internal consistency and unidimensionality of the scale seem well established, although both of these facets may be spuriously affected by agreement response set. (In Bonjean et al., pp. 34-35, Srole is quoted as feeling that negative wordings of these items would be accepted by everyone; the reader might want to examine the negative items provided by Christie in our scale review of Srole.) As was the case with the McClosky-Schaar scale, normative data from cross-section populations are available for the Srole scale.

The powerlessness scale of Neal and Seeman draws its items from the internal-external control scale of Rotter, which is reviewed in the previous chapter. The item content for the powerlessness scale deals with control over societal and economic problems rather than personal problems. The authors present data to support their argument that the scale taps an aspect of alienation not reflected in Srole's anomia scale, although the two are moderately correlated. The scale has been used in a variety of research studies and its internal consistency and validity seem well established. Items are in forced-choice format to prevent the operation of agreement response set. The reader may also be interested in the normlessness scales that have been developed in this same research program.

The Olsen political alienation scale makes an interesting distinction between feelings of incapability and feelings of discontent--the first referring to alienation imposed on the individual (measured by the Survey Research Center political efficacy scale), the second to an attitude reached by the individual. Empirical evidence for the need of such a distinction is not compelling, as the two scales both intercorrelate highly and show largely the same pattern of correlations with background variables (although there is some evidence for feelings of discontent to characterize the older middle class and, for incapability, those of lower social status). Both scales do predict to political participation. However, the internal consistency of the items is not high and they appear liable to agreement response set.

The Streuning-Richardson study, in addition to supporting the unidimensionality of the five-items in the Srole scale, provides eleven other items that appear to tap the same domain (unfortunately again none of these are worded in the negative direction). This study was mainly methodological and hence haphazard sampling was employed and no evidence regarding validity is advanced. It was found that even though separate factors of alienation and authoritarianism were isolated by factor analysis, scores on the two factors did correlate .41.

Crumbaugh's purpose-in-life test, which appears to be an extension of a semantic differential type approach, was developed from clinical psychological experience. In fact, one validation of this test consists of its ability to separate successfully functioning individuals in society from individuals diagnosed as neurotic. While such differentiation is statistically significant, it is not as large as one might imagine such differences to be. More impressive are the correlations of test scores with ratings of ministers and psychiatrists. The test does correlate significantly with depression and anomia scales.

The alienation scale of Dean attempts to isolate three separate components of powerlessness, normlessness, and social isolation. The three components do intercorrelate significantly, but the social isolation scale correlates lower with authoritarianism than the other two (which may make the effort at component separation worthwhile). The author has confirmed hypotheses about voting behavior in subsequent studies using the scale (although these effects do not hold when controlled for social status).

The Middleton scale is similar in that it is built largely upon Seeman's conceptual distinction between five types of alienation. The items (one for each type of alienation) have relatively high internal consistency but again are liable to agreement response set. No evidence for validity is available but the author has found dramatic differences between whites and Negroes with these items.

The Horton and Thompson measure separates two facets of alienation:

powerlessness and power consciousness. The second facet appears to predict whether citizens would vote at all, and if they did, the first facet then predicted a "no" vote on a referendum. No reliability data are presented for these very short scales.

The Nettler scale contains a number of both interesting and questionable features. Most interesting are the novel content areas (mass culture, family and religion, in addition to the usual area of politics) and the fact that the scale was validated by the use of a known group of "aliens." However, the specific items suffer from wording peculiarities, e.g., "Are you interested in having children? (Or would you be at the right age?);" and the quantitative evidence for the essential homogeneity of items is not compelling. The scale would seem to tap an upper-middle class alienation (an active disgust), rather than the usual content of previous scales (a sort of passive malaise) and may be useful for researchers interested in such a distinction.

Hyman et al.'s anomie scale also introduces some new item content into this attitude area. However, it has yet to be tested on any large-scale sample, and no data on its reliability or validity are available. The most successful of Gamson's "helplessness" items (in terms of predicting opposition to fluoridation) were drawn from the Survey Research Center political efficacy scale (reviewed in Measures of Political Attitudes).

The final two scales of Davids and of Clark seem applicable only to limited populations. The Davids items have only been applied to a sample of 20 undergraduates at Harvard and one wonders if even this group found the items to be highly esoteric. It is interesting to see that the author's alienation scale was composed of measures of five initially separate intellectual dispositions (egocentricity, distrust, pessimism, anxiety, and resentment) which were later combined because of their high intercorrelations.

The scale scores for the 20 individuals were validated against how they were judged by clinical psychologists along these dimensions.

The Clark scale was developed for use with members of an agricultural cooperative, which somewhat delimits its applicability. The items appear to have adequate internal consistency, and impressive data bearing on the scale's validity are reported. The reader may want to refer to two similar "alienation from work" scales that are presented in our volume of occupational attitudes.

For a comprehensive effort at measurement of children's alienation and involvement in the school setting, Rhea et al. (1966) is recommended.

References:

Bonjean C., Hill, R. and McLemore, S. Sociological measurement. San Francisco: Chandler, 1967.

Lenski, G. and Leggett, J. Caste, class, and deference in the research interview, American Journal of Sociology, 1960, 65, 463-467.

Rhea, B., Williams, R., Minisce, R., and Rhea, D. Measures of child involvement and alienation from the school program. Chestnut Hill, Mass.: Dept. of Sociology, Boston College, 1966.

ANOMY (McClosky and Schaar 1965)

Variable   Anomy is defined as normlessness. The traditional sociological model
(e.g., Durkheim)--assuming that social conditions give rise to
specified feelings (anomie) which in turn result in certain be-
haviors--is revised to give equal weight to psychological variables
as a cause of anomie.

Description   The authors' intention was to examine those dimensions of personality
which are likely to result in an individual's feelings of anomy. The
nine-item anomy scale was one of several measures included in a large
questionnaire. Answers to each item were either "agree" or "disagree,"
with one point given for each agree response. Scores ranged from 0-9.
Those scoring 6-9 were highly anomic, 3-5 was the middle group, and
0-2 were low or non-anomic. The following distribution of scores was
obtained in the two samples.

	National Sample	Minnesota Sample
Low (0-2)	26%	38%
Medium (3-5)	39%	34%
High (6-9)	35%	28%
	100%	100%

(For those with low education, 61 percent of the national sample and
50 percent of the Minnesota sample scored high on the anomy scale.
The overall correlation between anomy and education was -.43.)

The original source(s) of the items is not given. Through preliminary
screening and pre-testing, a large pool of items was reduced and given
to a sample of 273 Minnesota adults. Their responses were examined
for internal consistency, subjected to a Guttman reproducibility procedure, and finally reduced to 9 items.

Sample   There were two samples. One was a cross-section of the population of
Minnesota, designed by the Minnesota Poll in 1955, with an N of 1082.
The other was a national sample drawn and administered by Gallup Poll
in 1958 with an N of 1484.

Reliability   The corrected split-half reliability coefficient for the scale was .76.
As a measure of unidimensionality, the reproducibility coefficient for the
national sample was .80, and on another national sample of 3020
"political influentials" the reproducibility coefficient was .83.

Validity   The scale was also judged by several groups of graduate students in
political science and psychology, and by 40 Fellows at the Center
for Advanced Study in the Behavioral Sciences (Stanford). For each
item, the proportion of affirmative judgments (i.e., that the item
does embody some aspect of anomy) was high enough to satisfy the
authors. (This proportion is not stated in the article.) A further
indication (still indirect) of validity is indicated in the table
of correlations with other variables given below:

	National (N = 1484)	Minnesota (N = 1082)
Alienation	.60	.58
Bewilderment	NA	.62
Pessimism	.50	.43
Political Impotence	.54	.55
Political Cynicism	.59	.62
Life Satisfaction	-.41	-.39

Location   McClosky, H. and Schaar, J. H. Psychological dimensions of anomy. *American Sociological Review*, 1965, <u>30</u> (1), 14-40.

Administration   The questionnaire was self-administered. After an interviewer explained how it should be filled out, it was left with the respondent, who completed it and returned it by mail. The Minnesota questionnaire was composed of 512 items, and the national study contained 390 items.

Results and Comments   It is generally hypothesized that anomic feelings result when socialization and the learning of social norms are impeded, and that three psychological factors may impede the learning of these norms: cognitive factors, emotional factors, and an individual's beliefs and opinions. The authors summarize their results as follows:

> "In order to determine the efficacy of psychological, as opposed to sociological, factors in producing anomie three groups of measures were correlated with anomic feeling. It was found that individuals whose cognitive capacity was deficient (as indicated by high scores on Mysticism and Acquiescence; and low scores on Education, Intellectuality and Awareness) tended to score high on anomie. It was also found that individuals predisposed to maladjustive emotional states (such as inflexibility, strong anxiety and aggression, and low ego strength) are high on anomie. Finally, those individuals who held extreme beliefs and had a rejective attitude towards people were also found to be high on anomie. All of these correlations were strong and in the predicted direction."

The extent of these differences is examined quantitatively in the table on the next page.

Most importantly, all of these results are insignificantly affected when controls for measures of acquiescence, social status, and status frustration are imposed. The authors conclude:

> "...it may be defensible to conceptualize anomy as a unique disease that afflicts men in certain kinds of societies. Anomy, in sum, may be only one of many symptoms expressing a negativistic, despairing outlook both on one's own life and on the community in which one lives."

Relations between Anomy and Various Measures

	National Sample Anomy			Minnesota Sample Anomy		
	High	Medium	Low	High	Medium	Low
COGNITIVE FUNCTIONING						
Low Intellectuality	55	35	10 = 100%	52	33	15 = 100%
Low Awareness		Not asked		46	36	18
High Mysticism		Not asked		47	34	19
High Acquiescence	65	30	5	57	33	10
PSYCHOLOGICAL INFLEXIBILITY						
High Intolerance of Ambiguity	56	35	9	45	35	20
High Rigidity	52	34	14	39	36	25
High Obsessiveness	46	36	18	34	36	30
High Inflexibility	67	27	6	48	41	11
ANXIETY						
High Manifest Anxiety		Not asked		52	35	13
High Disorganization		Not asked		52	33	15
Bewilderment		Not asked		61	27	12
EGO-STRENGTH						
High Guilt	64	30	6	52	35	13
Low Self-Confidence		Not asked		44	32	24
High Need Inviolacy	62	31	7	50	33	17
Low Life Satisfaction	51	36	13	45	33	22
High Alienation	62	33	5	59	27	14
High Status Frustration	61	32	7	56	28	16
High Pessimism	60	33	7	55	30	15
High Political Futility	62	31	6	61	28	11
Low Dominance	57	34	9	51	36	13
Low Social Responsibility	59	30	11	54	32	14
AGGRESSION						
High Hostility	62	32	6	53	33	14
High Paranoia	63	33	4	57	31	12
High Intolerance for Human Frailty	54	34	12	46	35	19
High Contempt for Weakness	57	34	9	49	36	15
EXTREME BELIEFS						
High Totalitarianism	65	30	5	48	34	18
High Fascist Values		Not asked		49	30	31
High Left Wing	73	25	2	69	24	7
High Right Wing	71	26	3	70	26	4
MISANTHROPY						
Low Tolerance	52	35	13	41	36	23
Low Faith in People		Not asked		49	30	21
High Calvinism	47	42	11		Not asked	
High Elitism	50	36	14	46	34	20
High Ethnocentrism	58	35	7	54	34	12
TOTAL SAMPLE	26	39	35 = 100%	38	34	28 = 100%

Anomy

	Percent Who Agree National Sample (N = 1484)
1. With everything so uncertain these days, it almost seems as though anything could happen.	82
2. What is lacking in the world today is the old kind of friendship that lasted for a lifetime.	69
3. With everything in such a state of disorder, it's hard for a person to know where he stands from one day to the next.	50
4. Everything changes so quickly these days that I often have trouble deciding which are the right rules to follow.	49
5. I often feel that many things our parents stood for are just going to ruin before our very eyes.	48
6. The trouble with the world today is that most people really don't believe in anything.	44
7. I often feel awkward and out of place.	37
8. People were better off in the old days when everyone knew just how he was expected to act.	27
9. It seems to me that other people find it easier to decide what is right than I do.	27

Reprinted with permission of McClosky, H. and Schaar, J. H. Anomy in "Psychological Dimensions of Anomy," *American Sociological Review,* 30 (1963), pp 14-40. Copyright 1965 by the American Sociological Association, 1001 Connecticut Avenue, N.W., Washington, D.C. 20036.

ANOMIA (Srole 1956)

Variable   Anomia is viewed as an individual's generalized, pervasive sense of
                social malintegration or "self-to-others alienation" (vs. self-to-
                other's belongingness).

Description   The scale consists of five items, each one measuring one aspect of
                anomia. They are presented as opinion statements, with possible
                answers of "agree," "disagree," and "can't decide." Only an
                unequivocal "agree" receives a score of 1. The possible range of
                scores, therefore, is 0-5. The distribution of the sample of 401
                is given here in percent (average = 2.1) along with data on random
                sample of 981 Los Angeles adults (average 1.7) in 1961 (Miller and
                Butler 1966).

Score		Anomia (Springfield)	Anomia (Los Angeles)
(Low)	0	16%	29%
	1	25	24
	2	20	17
	3	21	14
	4	13	9
(High)	5	5	7
	Total	100%	100%

Sample   The sample was drawn from Springfield, Mass. Since the study measured
                attitudes toward minority groups, members of minority groups were
                themselves excluded and the sample was limited to white, Christian,
                native born residents who were mass-transit riders. The sampling
                design combined random selection with age-sex quotas. There were 401
                people between the ages of 16-69 (average being 40.3 years).

Reliability   The unidimensionality of the anomia scale was assessed by the proce-
                dures of latent structure analysis, and found to satisfy the criteria.
                In addition, in a study in New York City, it was determined that the
                anomia scale satisfied the requirements of a Guttman-type scale.
                No quantitative estimates or test-retest data are reported, although
                subsequent researchers (Streuning and Richardson, 1965; Miller and
                Butler, 1966) have demonstrated the essentially unidimensionality
                of these items by factor analytic criteria. Miller and Butler report
                the following item intercorrelation matrix (Pearson's r) for a random
                cross-section of Los Angeles adults in 1961:

	1	2	3	4	5
Item 1	X				
2	.21	X			
3	.25	.28	X		
4	.20	.28	.40	X	
5	.30	.29	.46	.36	X

Bell (1957) found that the items had a coefficient of reproducibility
of .90 and coefficient of scalability of .65.

Validity   The author noted that the full validity had yet to be established
                  but added:

> "A clue to its validity is found in a datum from the current
> NYC study, involving a geographic probability sample of
> 1660 resident adults. A single indicator of latent suicide
> tendency was the agree-disagree item: 'You sometimes can't
> help wondering whether anything is worthwhile anymore.' The
> correlation between this item and the Anomia scale scores is
> expressed by a tetrachoric coefficient of .50."

Bell (1957) found the anomia scale to relate significantly to social
isolation.

Location   Srole, L.   Social integration and certain corollaries.
                  American Sociological Review, 1956, 21, 709-716.

Results and   The hypothesis that anomia is related to the formation of negative
Comments   attitudes toward minorities was confirmed in the Springfield sample,
                  the Pearson correlation between anomia and negative attitudes towards
                  minorities being .43. These results held when controlled for social
                  status.

                  When scores on authoritarianism are partialled out, the correlation
                  is reduced from .43 to .35, indicating that the relationship between
                  anomia (A) and minority attitudes (M) is independent of the personality
                  trends measured by authoritarianism (F).

                  Holding A constant and investigating the relationship between F and
                  M, however, reduces the correlation between F and M from .29 to .12.
                  It could be concluded therefore that the correlation between F and M
                  is partially due to anomia.

                  Anomia was found to be inversely related ($r = -.30$) to socioeconomic
                  status. Consistent with this, Rose (1962) applied the items to 71
                  heads of organizations in Minnesota and found that only 3 percent of
                  them agreed with any of the Srole items vs. 20 percent of a cross-
                  section sample of married people in Minneapolis-St. Paul. Angell
                  (1962) also found a significant negative correlation between the
                  anomia scale and occupational status ($r = -.25$), income ($-.19$),
                  and education ($-.33$) in a cross-section of Detroit residents.
                  Older people ($r = .16$) and Negroes ($r = .25$) were also found to score
                  higher on the scale.

                  Lenski and Leggett (1960) present a strong case that the scale in
                  its present format is highly susceptible to agreement response set.
                  Richard Christie (personal communication) reports that the following
                  five negatively worded items may be useful in offsetting this response
                  set:

                  1. Most people can still be depended upon to come through in a pinch.
                  2. If you try hard enough, you can usually get what you want.
                  3. Most people will go out of their way to help someone else.

4. The average man is probably better off today than he ever was.
5. Even today, the way that you make money is more important than how much you make.

Four of the five items were originally devised by Srole, although no further psychometric data on their use is reported.

Srole (personal communication) reports that translations of the scale into simple Spanish and simple English (for use with low SES people) are avaiable from Dr. Stanley Lehmann at the Department of Psychology at New York University. The scale has also been translated into French.

References

Angell, R. Preferences for moral norms in 3 problem areas, American Journal of Sociology, 1962, 67, 650-672.

Bell, W. Anomia, social isolation and class structure, Sociometry, 1957, 20, 105-116.

Lenski, G. and Leggett, J. Caste, class, and déference in the research interview, American Journal of Sociology, 1960, 65, 463-467.

Miller, C. and Butler, E. Anomia and eunomia: a methodological evaluation of Srole's Anomia scale, American Sociological Review, 1966, 31, 400-405.

Rose, A. Alienation and participation, American Sociological Review, 1962, 27, 834-838.

Streuning, E. and Richardson, A. A factor analytic exploration of the alienation, anomia and authoritarianism domain, American Sociological Review, 1965, 30, 768-776.

Anomia
(Score 1 for agreement with each item)

	% Agreement (Miller and Butler 1966)
1. There's little use writing to public officials because they often aren't really interested in the problems of the average man.	39

Agree   Disagree

2. Nowadays a person has to live pretty much for today and let tomorrow take care of itself.	29
3. In spite of what some people say, the lot of the average man is getting worse, not better.	33
4. It's hardly fair to bring children into the world with the way things look for the future.	23
5. These days a person doesn't really know whom he can count on.	50

Four new items in the enlarged anomia scale are:

6. Most people really don't care what happens to the next fellow.

7. Next to health, money is the most important thing in life.

8. You sometimes can't help wondering whether anything is worthwhile.

9. To make money there are no right and wrong ways anymore, only easy and hard ways.

The wording of the first of the five original items has been slightly changed to read: Most public officals (people in public offices) are not really interested in the problems of the average man.

Reprinted with permission of Srole, L. Anomia, in "Social Integration and Certain Corollaries," *American Sociological Review,* 21 (1956), pp 709-716. Original copyright 1953 by Harper and Brothers, New York.

POWERLESSNESS (Neal and Seeman 1964)

Variable

The measure used here defines powerlessness as "low expectancies for control of events," with the events being in terms of mass society (e.g., control over politics, the economy, etc.).

Description

The scale consists of seven forced-choice items, which were reduced from an original pool of 50 items via pre-testing (actually 12 items were employed in this study but only 7 were found to be scalable). The items were originally devised to measure the individual's psychological orientation toward how much (internal) control he had over events in his environment vs. the view that these were outside his control (external). The scale was apparently developed through the joint efforts of sociologist Shepard Liverant and psychologist Julian Rotter at Ohio State University. Experience with these items has been developed from their use in a number of research studies (see below). One point is given for each response in the powerless (i.e., external) direction, making scores range from 0 (high power) to 7 (high powerlessness). The average score for the random sample of males in Columbus was 2.70.

Sample

The sample consisted of 609 male respondents (out of 1094 contacted by mail) chosen at random from the Columbus, Ohio city directory. Subsequent data collected from about a tenth of the 47 percent of the sample who did not return the mail questionnaires revealed that their powerlessness scores were no different than those who did respond.

Reliability/
Homogeneity

This seven item scale had a coefficient of reproducibility of .87. Neal and Rettig (1963) report for the same sample that ten of the original twelve items had factor loadings over .30 and seven loadings over .50 (which indicate inter-item correlations of about .15-.35). Using many of the same items, Seeman and Evans (1962) report a split-half reliability of .70 and Neal (1959) a reproducibility coefficient of .866.
No test-retest stability data have been reported.

Validity

As hypothesized, members of work-related organizations exhibited less powerlessness (2.54) than those who were unorganized (2.94). The results held for manual workers and for "mobility-oriented" non-manual (i.e., white-collar) workers, but not for white-collar workers who were not mobility-oriented.

Use of the Srole anomia scale did not result in such a clear pattern of findings. Neal and Rettig (1963) report that factor analysis revealed the anomia scale to be essentially independent of the power-lessness scale, although earlier Neal (1959) had reported a .32 correlation between anomia and an earlier version of the powerlessness scale. In their latest discussion of the relation of the two concepts (and many other alienation concepts), Neal and Rettig (1967) conclude that alienation can be seen as either unidimensional or multidimensional depending on one's level of analysis.

Location	Neal, A. and Seeman, M. Organizations and powerlessness: a test of the mediation hypothesis, <u>American Sociological Review</u>, 1964, <u>29</u>, 216-225.
Administration	The present items were administered as part of a mail questionnaire.
Results and Comments	The authors report the following very small differences in powerlessness by social mobility:

	Non-Manual	Manual
Downwardly mobile	2.71	2.73
Stationary	2.44	2.87
Upwardly mobile	2.66	2.77

These data indicate practically no resultant feelings of powerlessness as a result of social mobility. One downwardly-mobile group did show quite high powerlessness (3.86)--those non-manuals, who were mobility-oriented but unorganized.

In an earlier study, Neal (1959) studied the relation between powerlessness and normlessness and found: "The maximum likelihood for both powerlessness and normlessness was found among older, downwardly mobile, manual workers who reject mobility values. By way of contrast, the least likelihood for both powerlessness and normlessness was found among the younger, stationary, non-manual workers who are mobility oriented."

Seeman and Evans (1962) found powerlessness to predict tuberculosis patients' lack of knowledge concerning their illness but not dissatisfaction with their medical care.

Neal and Rettig (1963 and 1967) found another aspect of alienation, normlessness, to be essentially independent of powerlessness and anomia and to be itself composed of two separate factors, political and economic. The items comprising the two factors were:

<u>Political Normlessness</u> (The Necessity of Force and Fraud in Government)

1. Those running our government must hush up many things that go on behind the scenes, if they wish to stay in office.
2. Having "pull" is more important than ability in getting a government job.
3. In order to get elected to public office, a candidate must make promises he does not intend to keep.
4. Those elected to public office have to serve special interests (e.g., big business or labor as well as the public's interest).
5. In getting a job promotion, some degree of "apple polishing" is required.
6. In getting a good paying job, it's necessary to exaggerate one's abilities (or personal merits).
7. In order to have a good income, a salesman must use high pressure salesmanship.

Economic Normlessness (The Necessity of Force and Fraud in Business)

1. Success in business and politics can easily be achieved without taking advantage of gullible people.*
2. In getting a good paying job, it's necessary to exaggerate one's abilities (or personal merits).
3. In order to have a good income, a salesman must use high pressure salesmanship.
4. For a strike to be effective, picket line violence is necessary.
5. One can be successful in business without compromising moral principles.*
6. A newspaper can build up its circulation without making news events (i.e., crime stories) seem more sensational than they really are.*

*Reverse scoring.

References

Neal, A. Stratification concomitants of powerlessness and normlessness. Unpublished Ph.D. dissertation, Ohio State University, 1959.

Neal, A. and Rettig, S. Dimensions of alienation among manual and non-manual workers, American Sociological Review, 1963, 28, 599-608.

Neal, A. and Rettig, S. On the multidimensionality of alienation, American Sociological Review, 1967, 32, 54-63.

Rotter, J., Seeman, M., and Liverant, S. Internal vs. external control of reinforcements: a major variable in behavior theory, in N. Washburne (ed.), Decisions, values, and groups, Vol. 2, London: Pergammon Press, 1962, 473-516.

Seeman, M. and Evans, J. Alienation and learning in hospital setting, American Sociological Review, 1962, 27, 772-782.

THE POWERLESSNESS SCALE
(* powerless response)

This is a survey to find out what the public things about certain events which we face in our society. Each item consists of a pair of statements. Please select the one statement of each pair (and only one) which you more strongly believe to be true. Be sure to check the one you actually believe to be more nearly true, rather than the one you think you should check or the one you would like to be true. This is a measure of personal belief; obviously, there are no right or wrong answers. Again, be sure to make a choice between each pair of statements.

1.   I think we have adequate means for preventing run-away inflation.
  * There's very little we can do to keep prices from going higher.

2. * Persons like myself have little chance of protecting our personal interests when they conflict with those of strong pressure groups.
   I feel that we have adequate ways of coping with pressure groups.

3.   A lasting world peace can be achieved by those of us who work toward it.
  * There's very little we can do to bring about a permanent world peace.

4. * There's very little persons like myself can do to improve world opinion of the United States.
   I think each of us can do a great deal to improve world opinion of the United States.

5. * This world is run by the few people in power, and there is not much the little guy can do about it.
   The average citizen can have an influence on government decisions.

6. * It is only wishful thinking to believe that one can really influence what happens in society at large.
   People like me can change the course of world events if we make ourselves heard.

7. * More and more, I feel helpless in the face of what's happening in the world today.
   I sometimes feel personally to blame for the sad state of affairs in our government.

Discarded Items

8.   By studying the world situation, one can greatly increase his political effectiveness.
  * Whether one likes it or not, chance plays an awfully large part in world events.

9. * The international situation is so complex that it just confuses a person to think about it.
   Active discussion of politics can eventually lead to a better world.

264

10. * Wars between countries seem inevitable despite the efforts of men to
       prevent them.
       Wars between countries can be avoided.

11.   Those who do not vote are largely responsible for bad government.
     * There's little use for me to vote, since one vote doesn't count very
       much anyway.

12.   With enough effort we can wipe out political corruption.
     * Some political corruption is a necessary evil of government.

(Neal and Rettig's (1967) factor analysis shows low loadings for item 1, and
high loadings for item 8 and 9, indicating that some rearrangements of items
to be included or discarded is desirable.)

POLITICAL ALIENATION (Olsen 1969)

Variable   Alienation is conceptualized as being of two distinct types: attitudes
                         of incapability and attitudes of discontentment.

Description   The author contends that the failure to distinguish these two types of
                         alienated attitudes have considerably restricted the value of research
                         in this area. Included under feelings of incapability (where aliena-
                         tion is imposed involuntarily upon the person by the social system)
                         are such attitudes as guidelessness, powerlessness, and normlessness.
                         The four items measuring incapability were drawn from the Survey
                         Research Center political efficacy scale. One point is given for
                         each statement with which the respondent agrees. Scale scores there-
                         fore run from 0 (highly capable) to 4 (highly incapable). Average
                         score for the sample was 1.29, with 36 percent of the sample classified
                         as incapable (score 2, 3 or 4).

                         The author constructed his own four item scale to measure discontent-
                         ment, whereby alienation is voluntarily chosen by the individual as
                         an attitude toward the system. In counter-distinction to the atti-
                         tudes of incapability, feelings subsumed here are dissimilarity,
                         dissatisfaction, and disillusionment. Again one point is given for
                         each agree response, with scores running from 0 (no discontent) to
                         4 (high discontent). Average score for the sample was 1.19, with
                         35 percent of the sample classified as discontented (score 2, 3 or 4).

Sample   A total of 154 respondents were interviewed, out of an original 200
                         selected by random methods in 1965 from the city directory for two
                         census tracts in Ann Arbor, Michigan. One of the tracts was lower
                         middle class, the other upper middle class.

Reliability/   The coefficient of reproducibility for the incapability scale was
    Homogeneity   .893 and for the discontent scale .921. The two scales do correlate
                         rather highly (eta = .46) but the author considers them as distinct.
                         No test-retest data are reported.

Validity   The following differences in political participation were noted for
                         the Incapability Scale.

	Low	High
Political media exposure	80%	56%
Political discussion	66%	28%
Voting participation	69%	60%
Political Involvement	60%	24%

These differences were not as pronounced for the Discontent Scale
(especially voting) as the author expected, since discontent is seen
as more of an upper middle class phenomenon.

	Low	High
Political media exposure	80%	68%
Political discussion	59%	40%
Voting participation	69%	72%
Political involvement	47%	28%

Location   Olsen, M. Two categories of political alienation, <u>Social Forces</u>, 1969, <u>47</u>, 288-299.

Results and   The author feels that the most significant findings of the study were
Comments   differences by party affiliation and voting behavior. Over 80 percent
of people scoring high on the incapability scale and low on the discontent scale voted Democratic in 1960 and 1964 vs. about 20 percent
of those scoring low on incapability and high on discontentment.

Both measures were highly inversely related to respondent's education, occupation and income. The following average scores for education were obtained.

	Incapable	Discontent
Some college or more	.96	.98
High school graduate	1.60	1.38
High school not complete	2.29	1.81

Unlike incapability, however, which characterized the disadvantaged, discontent was prevalent among the "old middle class."

POLITICAL ALIENATION

Political incapability/futility scale

1. I believe public officials don't care much what people like me think.

   Agree   Disagree

2. There is no way other than voting that people like me can influence actions of the government.

3. Sometimes politics and government seem so complicated that I can't really understand what's going on.

4. People like me don't have any say about what the government does.

Discontentment or cynicism with politics

1. These days the government is trying to do too many things, including some activities that I don't think it has the right to do.

   Agree   Disagree

2. For the most part, the government serves the interests of a few organized groups, such as business or labor, and isn't very concerned about the needs of people like myself.

3. It seems to me that the government often fails to take necessary actions on important matters, even when most people favor such actions.

4. As the government is now organized and operated, I think it is hopelessly incapable of dealing with all the crucial problems facing the country today.

Reprinted with permission of Olsen, M. Political Alienation in *Social Forces,* 47 (1969), pp 288-299. Copyright 1969 by the University of North Carolina Press, Box 2288, Chapel Hill, N.C. 27514.

ALIENATION VIA REJECTION (Streuning and Richardson 1965)

Variable
: This set of items emerged as the first factor from a factor analysis of three related attitude domains.

Description
: The scale consists of 16 items of the six-point Likert format. Five of the items are from the Srole scale (see scale description above). A number of sources were used to provide a pool of 300 from which the final 68 were chosen: half came from the scales of Adorno, Davids, Srole and others; the rest were derived from the concepts and theories of Durkheim, Fromm, Marx, May, Merton and Camus' novel The Stranger. No further explanation is given of the method of selection.

Sample
: The sample of 442 people was provided a wide range of possible alienation scores. Sub-groups of the sample were as follows: 68 inmates of "criminally insane" ward, 49 long-term male mental patients, 31 hospitalized female mental patients, 39 institutionalized juvenile delinquents, 47 male mental patients ready for discharge, 30 persons over 75 years of age, 17 relatives of mental patients, 68 college undergraduates, 73 adult education students.

Reliability:
: Internal consistency coefficients (Spearman-Brown) for the alienation factor was .86 (for the purposelessness scale it was .65).

Validity
: No data bearing on the validity of this scale are reported.

Results and Comments
: The authors note that similar factor analyses using young undergraduates show distinct facets of this scale (e.g., cynicism) emerging as separate factors.

Scores on the alienation factor in the present study correlated as follows with scores on the other eight factors that emerged from the factor analysis.

Factor (Number of items)	Correlation
Emotional distance (4)	.49
Authoritarianism (8)	.41
Purposelessness (6)	.36
Self-determinism (5)	.34
Family authority (6)	.12
Trust and optimism (12)	-.10
Conventionality (4)	-.12
Religious orthodoxy (6)	-.14

The reader may find of interest the items in two of the three scales that correlated highest with alienation.

Emotional Distance

17. It is almost impossible for one person to really understand the feelings of another.

19. In this fast-changing world, with so much different information available, it is difficult to think clearly about many issues.

24. There will always be a great lack of understanding between the older and younger generations.

60. Parents often expect too much of their children.

Purposelessness

21. Too many people in our society are just out for themselves and don't really care for anyone else.

55. There are many people who don't know what to do with their lives.

56. Many people in our society are lonely and unrelated to their fellow human beings.

57. Many people are unhappy because they do not know what they want out of life.

58. In a society where almost everyone is out for himself, people soon come to distrust each other.

59. Everyone should have someone in his life whose happiness means as much to him as his own.

Alienation via Rejection

1. These days a person doesn't really know who he can count on.

   1.Strongly 2.Agree 3.Not sure   4.Not sure but 5.Disagree 6.Strongly
     agree   but prob-   probably   disagree
                         ably agree   disagree

2. There is not much chance that people will really do anything to make this country a better place to live in.

3. Success is more dependent on luck than real ability.

4. Nowadays a person has to live pretty much for today and let tomorrow take care of itself.

5. It is hard to figure out who you can really trust these days.

6. It's hardly fair to bring children into the world with the way things look for the future.

7. In spite of what some people say, the lot of the average man is getting worse.

8. There's little use writing to public officials because they aren't really interested in the problems of the average man.

9. There are so many ideas about what is right and wrong these days that it is hard to figure out how to live your life.

10. So many people do things well that it is easy to become discouraged.

11. Things are changing so fast these days that one doesn't know what to expect from day to day.

12. Most people don't realize how much their lives are controlled by plots hatched in secret by others.

14. Few people really look forward to their work.

15. Our country has too many poor people who can do little to raise their standard of living.

16. It is usually best to tell your superiors or bosses what they really want to hear.

18. People will do almost anything if the reward is high enough.

Alienation via Rejection (Streuning and Richardson, 1965) is reprinted here with permission.
Requests to use or cite portions of the scale should be directed to the authors of the scale.

PURPOSE-IN-LIFE TEST (Crumbaugh 1968)

Variable

This attitude scale is designed to measure the degree to which a person experiences a sense of meaning and purpose in life.

Description

The scale was devised to test Viktor Frankl's thesis that when meaning in life is not found, the result is existential frustration (or among mental patients, noögenic neurosis). The Purpose-in-Life Test (PIL) is made up of 20 items rated from 1 (low purpose) to 7 (high purpose). Total scores therefore range from 20 (low purpose) to 140 (high purpose). Average scores tend to skew toward the purposeful end of the scale, as noted for the following samples.

Sample

The following non-representative samples were interviewed in the present study.

Normal	N	Average score	(s.d.)
Successful businessmen and professionals	230	118.9	(11.3)
Active and leading Protestant parishoners	142	114.3	(15.3)
College undergrads	417	108.5	(14.0)
Indigent hospital patients	16	106.4	(14.5)
Psychiatric			
Neurotics, outpatient	225	93.3	(21.7)
Neurotics, hospitalized	13	95.3	(18.4)
Alcoholics, hospitalized	38	85.4	(19.4)
Schizophrenics, hospitalized	41	96.7	(16.1)
Psychotics, hospitalized	18	80.5	(17.5)

All the above respondents were white and from the area of Columbus, Georgia. A group of 11 hospitalized Negro schizophrenics had an average score of 108.0.

Reliability/
Homogeneity

A split-half correlation of .85 was reported for 120 parishoners. No test-retest data are reported.

Validity

The average scores reported above give some support for the scale's validity. Within each of the two samples, PIL scores correlated .47 with ministers' ratings (for the parishoner sample) and .38 with therapist ratings (for the outpatient sample).

Location

Crumbaugh, J. Cross-validation of purpose-in-life test based on Frankl's concepts, Journal of Individual Psychology, 1968, 24, 74-81.

Results and
Comments

The PIL scale correlated significantly only with the depression scale of the MMPI (r = -.65). It also correlated about .40 with the Srole anomia scale. There is considerable overlap therefore with the constructs of depression and anomia (although the scale author does not agree with this conclusion).

The author concludes that low correlations with income and education "imply that either education or income alone do not assure the attainment of meaning in life," although he did not appear to examine the full range of socioeconomic status. No consistent sex differences are reported.

It is estimated by Frankl that about 20 percent of the clinic-load in mental health units fall into the noögenic neurosis syndrome.

The Purpose in Life Test

For each of the following statements, circle the number that would be most nearly true for you. Note that the numbers always extend from one extreme feeling to its opposite kind of feeling. "Neutral" implies no judgment either way. Try to use this rating as little as possible.

1. I am usually:

    1   2   3   4   5   6   7

    completely bored   (neutral)   exuberant, enthusiastic

2. Life to me seems:

    7   6   5   4   3   2   1

    always exciting   (neutral)   completely routine

3. In life I have:

    1   2   3   4   5   6   7

    no goals or aims at all   (neutral)   very clear goals and aims

4. My personal existence is:

    1   2   3   4   5   6   7

    utterly meaningless, without purpose   (neutral)   very purposeful and meaningful

5. Every day is:

    7   6   5   4   3   2   1

    constantly new and different   (neutral)   exactly the same

6. If I could choose, I would:

    1   2   3   4   5   6   7

    prefer never to have been born   (neutral)   like nine more lives just like this one

7. After retiring, I would:

    7   6   5   4   3   2   1

    do some of the exciting things I have always wanted to   (neutral)   loaf completely the rest of my life

8. In achieving life goals I have:

    1   2   3   4   5   6   7

    made no progress whatever   (neutral)   progressed to complete fulfillment

9. My life is:

    1   2   3   4   5   6   7

    empty, filled only with despair   (neutral)   running over with exciting good things

10. If I should die today, I would feel that my life has been:

    7   6   5   4   3   2   1

    very worthwhile   (neutral)   completely worthless

Reprinted with permission of Crumbaugh, J. Purpose-in-Life Test in *Journal of Individual Psychology,* 24 (1968), pp 74-81. Copyright 1968 by the American Society of Adlerian Psychology, Inc., c/o Heinz Lansbacker, University of Vermont, John Dewey Hall, Burlington, Vermont 05401.

11. In thinking of my life, I:

      1   2   3   4   5   6   7

often wonder why I exist   (neutral)   always see a reason for
my being here

12. As I view the world in relation to my life, the world:

      1   2   3   4   5   6   7

completely confuses me   (neutral)   fits meaningfully with
my life

13. I am a:

      1   2   3   4   5   6   7

very irresponsible person   (neutral)   very responsible person

14. Concerning man's freedom to make his own choices, I believe man is:

      7   6   5   4   3   2   1

absolutely free to make all   (neutral)   completely bound by limita-
life choices   tions of heredity and
environment

15. With regard to death, I am:

      7   6   5   4   3   2   1

prepared and unafraid   (neutral)   unprepared and frightened

16. With regard to suicide, I have:

      1   2   3   4   5   6   7

thought of it seriously as   (neutral)   never given it a second
a way out   thought

17. I regard my ability to find a meaning, purpose, or mission in life as:

      7   6   5   4   3   2   1

very great   (neutral)   practically none

18. My life is:

      7   6   5   4   3   2   1

in my hands and I am   (neutral)   out of my hands and controlled
in control of it   by external factors

19. Facing my daily tasks is:

      7   6   5   4   3   2   1

a source of pleasure and   (neutral)   a painful and boring
satisfaction   experience

20. I have discovered:

      1   2   3   4   5   6   7

no mission or purpose in life   (neutral)   clear-cut goals and a
satisfying life purpose

ALIENATION SCALE (Dean 1961)

Variable

The variable is alienation, defined and measured through three separate components: powerlessness, normlessness and social isolation.

Description

Beginning with 139 items gleaned from the literature, 7 judges (instructors and assistants in the department of sociology at Ohio State University), were requested to judge each item as to whether it specifically and exclusively referred to each of the 3 sub-scale concepts. It was necessary for at least 5 of the 7 judges to agree, for an item to be retained. The result was 9 items in the final scale for powerlessness, 6 for normlessness, and 9 for social isolation.

The alienation scale is composed of the sum of 24 items presented in standard 5-point Likert format from 4 (strongly agree) to 0 (strongly disagree); five of the items are worded in the reverse direction. Scale scores can thus vary between 0 (lowest alienation) to 96 (highest alienation). The following normative data are reported.

Sample	Total	Powerless	Normless	Isolation
Columbus men (N=384)	36.6 (s.d.=13.5)	13.7	7.6	11.8
Prot. college women (N=75)	36.3	12.7	7.6	14.9
Cath. college women (N=65)	30.2	10.9	3.6	15.2

No reason is given for the lack of correspondence between total scale scores and the sum of the three components.

Scores form a normal curve of distribution, with scores extending almost the entire possible range.

Sample

Data were collected in Columbus, Ohio, from 4 of the 19 wards of that city, selected by criteria related to voting incidence and socioeconomic variables, as part of the author's study of political apathy. Precincts and individuals were selected by random sampling. The questionnaire was sent to 1108 individuals and 433 responded (38.8 percent). Of these, a final sample of 384 gave usable replies.

Reliability

The reliability of the subscales, tested by the split-half method and corrected by the Spearman-Brown prophecy formula, was as follows: Powerlessness: .78, Normlessness: .73, Social Isolation: .84, and the total Alienation scale, with items rotated to minimize a possible halo effect, had a reliability of .78.

The intercorrelations among the alienation scale components are:

	Normlessness	Social Isolation	Alienation
Powerlessness	.67	.54	.90
Normlessness	x	.41	.80
Social Isolation		x	.75

Validity   This alienation scale correlated in the .30's with Srole's scale and Nettler's scale. It was hypothesized 1) that alienation and each of its components would correlate negatively with social status (as measured by North-Hatt Occupational Prestige Scale, amount of education, and income), 2) that advancing age would be positively correlated with alienation, and 3) that rural background and alienation would correlate negatively. While in most instances the hypotheses were sustained at levels of significance (.01 and .05), the correlation coefficients were considered too low to predict the degree of alienation from an individual's score on the 5 social factors. Status correlated negatively at about -.20, and the correlation coefficient for age and alienation was +.12.

It was suggested that much more research would be necessary to empirically validate the concept of alienation.

Location   Dean, D. Alienation: its meaning and measurement, American Sociological Review, Oct. 1961, 26 (5), 753-758.

Administration   Self-administered questionnaire.

Results and Comments   The components of Dean's scale were correlated with Adorno's authoritarianism scale and the results were as follows (with a pretest sample of 73 college students):

Powerlessness and authoritarianism:	.37
Normlessness and authoritarianism:	.33
Social isolation and authoritarianism:	.23
Alienation and authoritarianism:	.26

The author speculated that his variable might be a situation-relevant variable, rather than a personality trait, so that a person might score high on alienation in political activity, but low in religion. He also speculated that alienation might be a syndrome, rather than a unitary phenomenon.

In a subsequent study, Dean (1966) found that while his scale(s) predicted vote against a school levy, they were less powerful predictors than age and socioeconomic status.

Reference   Dean, D. Alienation and negative voting on a school levy. Paper read at the 61st Annual Meeting of American Sociological Association, Miami Beach, Florida, September 1966.

Public Opinion Questionnaire

Below are some statements regarding public issues, with which some people agree and others disagree. Please give us your own opinion about these items, i.e., whether you agree or disagree with the items as they stand.

Please check in the appropriate blank, as follows:

```
_____  A   (Strongly Agree)
_____  a   (Agree)
_____  U   (Uncertain)
_____  d   (Disagree)
_____  D   (Strongly Disagree)
```

Powerlessness Items

2. I worry about the future facing today's children.

    __A   __a   __U   __d   __D

6. Sometimes I have the feeling that other people are using me.

9. It is frightening to be responsible for the development of a little child.

13. There is little or nothing I can do towards preventing a major "shooting" war.

15. There are so many decision that have to be made today that sometimes I could just "blow up."

18. There is little chance for promotion on the job unless a man gets a break.

20. We're so regimented today that there's not much room for choice even in personal matters.

21. We are just so many cogs in the machinery of life.

23. The future looks very dismal.

Normlessness Items

4. The end often justifies the means.

7. People's ideas change so much that I wonder if we'll ever have anything to depend on.

10. Everything is relative, and there just aren't any definite rules to live by.

12. I often wonder what the meaning of life really is.

16. The only thing one can be sure of today is that he can be sure of nothing.

19. With so many religions abroad, one doesn't really know which to believe.

Social Isolation Items

1. Sometimes I feel all alone in the world.

3. I don't get invited out by friends as often as I'd really like.

*5. Most people today seldom feel lonely.

*8. Real friends are as easy as ever to find.

*11. One can always find friends if he shows himself friendly.

*14. The world in which we live is basically a friendly place.

17. There are few dependable ties between people any more.

*22. People are just naturally friendly and helpful.

24. I don't get to visit friends as often as I'd really like.

* Reversed items.

ALIENATION (Middleton 1963)

Variable
Drawing heavily upon the conceptual distinctions made by Seeman, the author conceives of six types of alienation: powerlessness, normlessness, meaninglessness, cultural estrangement, social estrangement, and work estrangement.

Description
The six items in the scale (one for each type of alienation) are presented in agree-disagree format, agreement with each item indicating alienation. While the author does not analyze his items in terms of a scale, he does report that 28% of whites do not agree with any of five items (excluding the cultural item) and only 1% agree with all of them. The corresponding proportions for Negroes were 6% and 28% respectively.

Sample
The sample consisted of a random sample of 256 persons over 20 years of age drawn at random from a small city in central Florida in the summer of 1962. A special supplementary sample of 50 Negroes was also interviewed.

Reliability/
Homogeneity
The following inter-item correlations (Yule's Q, which yields values considerably higher than the standard product-moment formulas) were obtained:

	P.	Me.	No.	SE	WE	CE
Powerless	X					
Meaningless	.58	X				
Normless	.61	.59	X			
Social Estrangement	.54	.46	.48	X		
Work Estrangement	.57	.81	.67	.71	X	
Cultural Estrangement	.06	.17	.31	.08	.20	X

With the cultural item excluded, a coefficient of reproducibility of .90 was attained.

No test-retest data are reported.

Validity
No data bearing on validity are reported.

Location
Middleton, R. Alienation, race, and education. American Sociological Review, 1963, 28, 973-977.

Results and
Comments
The most striking results were differences noted between whites and Negroes, which held up when controlled for education.

	Whites (less than high school)		Negroes (less than high school)	
1. Powerless	40%	(57)	70%	(73)
2. Meaningless	48	(80)	71	(76)
3. Normless	16	(22)	55	(59)
4. Social Estrangement	27	(37)	60	(39)
5. Work Estrangement	18	(33)	66	(67)
6. Cultural Estrangement	34	(42)	35	(73)

ALIENATION

1. There is not much that I can do about most of the important problems that we face today. (Powerlessness)

   Agree   Disagree

2. Things have become so complicated in the world today that I really don't understand what is going on. (Meaninglessness)

   Agree   Disagree

3. In order to get ahead in the world today, you are almost forced to do some things which are not right. (Normlessness)

   Agree   Disagree

4. I am not much interested in the TV programs, movies, or magazines that most people seem to like. (Cultural Estrangement)

   Agree   Disagree

5. I often feel lonely. (Social Estrangement)

   Agree   Disagree

6. I don't really enjoy most of the work that I do, but I feel that I must do it in order to have other things that I need and want. (Estrangement from Work)

   Agree   Disagree

Reprinted with permission of Middleton, R. Alienation in "Alienation, Race, and Education," *American Sociological Review,* 28 (1963), pp 973-977. Copyright 1963 by the American Sociological Association, 1001 Connecticut Ave., N.W., Washington, D.C. 20036.

POLITICAL ALIENATION (Horton and Thompson 1962)

Variable
This instrument attempts to measure political alienation, which is seen as having two separate aspects: powerlessness, and consciousness of potentially menacing power.

Description
The object of the development of this scale was to have a measure for determining if political negativism was a consequence of political alienation. The scale consists of four items, two measuring each aspect of alienation. Three of these items are of the agree-disagree type. The other item is in a multiple choice format. Neither the source, nor method of construction of the items is described.

The powerlessness items were weighted equally for scoring. Those individuals who identified themselves as belonging in the last two categories of item one and agreeing with item two were deemed powerless. The power conscious were those who agreed with both of the awareness of power items.

Sample
Four hundred voters were selected by non-probability methods from two upstate New York communities after school-bond proposals had been defeated (1957 and 1958). In one town, at least five interviews were drawn from each of the school districts. In the other town, "a number of interviews were gathered proportionate to the total number of eligible voters in each election district."

Reliability
No reliability data are reported.

Validity
No data bearing directly on validity are reported, although the results (see below) would argue for the scale's validity.

Location
Horton, J. and Thompson, W. Powerlessness and political negativism: a study of defeated local referendums, American Journal of Sociology, 1962, 67 (5), 485-493.

Results and Comments
The data show that those who scored high on alienation were considerably more likely to vote against the referenda than those who scored low. In the university town 86 percent of the alienated individuals voted negatively as opposed to 25 percent of the non-alienated. In the company town the corresponding figures were 88 percent and 31 percent. Middle and upper class respondents were less likely to vote "No" than were lower or working class individuals, but the difference was only half as great as that between alienated and unalienated groups. Being a taxpayer increased the likelihood of voting at all, but degree of alienation dictated the direction of voting. From a consideration of their data the authors concluded that "the evidence thus supports the contention that, among the powerless who were power conscious, voting against the referendums may have been an expression of political protest, a vote against the local powers-that-be."

POLITICAL ALIENATION

(*Powerless response)

Powerlessness:

1. People have different ideas of just how they fit into community affairs.
    Would you say that you are:

    1. A person who contributes to community decisions.
    2. A person who is active, but not one of the decision makers.
    *3. Just an ordinary person in the community.
    *4. Not a part of the community at all.

2. It doesn't matter which party wins the elections, the interests of the little
    man don't count.

    *Agree   Disagree   Don't know

Awareness of Power:

(For the Corning, New York sample)

1. Corning-Glass and Ingersoll-Rand run the show in this area.

    *Agree   Disagree

2. The school board is just as much a special interest group as any other group
    in town.

    *Agree   Disagree

(For the Ithaca, New York sample)

1. The University people run the show in Ithaca.

    *Agree   Disagree

2. The school board is just as much a special interest group as any other group
    in town.

    *Agree   Disagree

Reprinted with permission of Horton, J. and Thompson, W. Political Alienation in "Powerlessness
and Political Negativism: A Study of Defeated Local Referendums," *American Journal of Sociology*, 67
(1962), pp 485-493. Original copyright 1960 by the Williams and Wilkins Company.

ALIENATION (Nettler 1957; 1964)

Variable   Alienation is defined as the subjective feeling of estrangement from society and the culture it carries. For some of the items this definition should be restricted to "American society and the culture it carries."

Description   Nettler's original (1957) scale consisted of 17 dichotomous items, scored either 2 (non-alienated) or 1 (alienated). The possible range of scores was from 17 (alienated) to 34 (non-alienated).

A revised version of the scale (Nettler, 1964) contains four subscales: vs. mass culture (4 items), vs. familism (4 items), a-religiosity (3 items), and a-politicism (4 items). These four subscales can be combined to yield a total score useful for group ordering purposes, but Nettler advises against using this score for individual assessment.

Sample   The items were originally constructed on the basis of in-depth interviews with 37 "known aliens"--persons who felt they were well described by literary characterizations of alienation (e.g., the writings of Edmund Wilson and George Santayana).

These people's scale scores were compared with the scores of 515 anonymous respondents, described as follows:
  a. 41 enlisted men
  b. 22 members of an enlisted men's wives' club
  c. 42 members of the Hotel, Restaurant and Bartenders' Union.
  d. 12 members of the Fish Cannery Workers' Union
  e. 27 members of the Hod Carriers and Laborers' Union
  f. 97 Naval Officers
  g. 11 members of the PTA
  h. 12 adult volunteers
  i. 251 students - Monterey Peninsula College (about half of these in the evening school)

The four revised subscales (1964) were administered to "265 western Canadian subjects."

Reliability/   For 162 of the original respondents (1957) the coefficient
Homogeneity of reproducibility was .87.

For the 265 western Canadians (1964) the coefficients for the four subscales were as follows: mass culture, .88; familism, .87; a-religiosity, .94; a-politicalism, .92.

Nettler (personal communication, 1969) warns: "These scales are restricted in their unidimensionality by time and population and it is advisable to re-scale them when new populations are being evaluated."

Validity

The mean score for the original 515 people was 28.6 (s.d. = 2.9). The mean score for the 37 "known aliens" was 17.05 (s.d. not given but must be extremely small because 17 is the lowest possible score).

Nettler's concept of alienation is not claimed to be synonymous with Srole's concept of anomia but the two were expected to be related, and for "345 subjects" the Pearson correlation coefficient between the two measures was +.31. For "83 subjects" Nettler's scale correlated +.25 with Rosenberg's misanthropy scale.

Location

Nettler, G. A measure of alienation. American Sociological Review, 1957, 22, 670-677.

Nettler, G. Scales of alienated attitude, revised. Mimeographed, Department of Sociology, University of Alberta, 1964.

Results and Comments

This scale seems to reflect middle class discontent rather than working class apathy. References for related studies are given in Bonjean et al. (1967).

Reference

Bonjean, C. et al. Sociological Measurement. San Francisco: Chandler, 1967.

ALIENATION

(Items added in 1964 are starred; those omitted in 1964 appear at the end of the list.)

Vs. Mass Culture:
1. Do you read <u>Reader's Digest</u>? (No)
2. Do national spectator sports (football, baseball, hockey) interest you? (No)
*3. "Our public education is in pretty sorry shape." Do you agree or disagree? (Agree)
4. Do you enjoy TV? (No)

Vs. Familism:
5. Are you interested in having children? (Or would you be at the right age?) (No)
6. For yourself, assuming you could carry out your decision or do things over again, do you think a single or married life would be more satisfactory? (Single)
7. If people really admitted the truth, they would agree that children are more often a nuisance than a pleasure to their parents. (Agree)
8. Do you think most married people lead trapped (frustrated or miserable) lives? (Yes)

A-Religiosity:
9. Do you believe human life is an expression of divine purpose, or is it only the result of chance and evolution? (Chance)
10. Do you think religion is mostly myth or mostly truth? (Myth)
11. Do you participate in church activities? (No, or rarely)

A-Politicalism:
12. Do you vote in national elections? (Or would you if of voting age?) (No)
*13. Are you generally interested in local (municipal and provincial or state) elections? (No)
14. Looking backward, did the last national election in the United States (between Kennedy and Nixon) interest you? (No)
*15. In the long run, and with some rare exceptions, who gets elected or doesn't hasn't the slightest influence upon social welfare. (Agree)

Omitted in 1964 version:

1. What do you think of the new model American automobiles? (Disapprove)
2. Do you think you could just as easily live in another society - past or present? (Yes)
3. Do you think most politicians are sincerely interested in the public's welfare, or are they more interested in themselves? (Themselves)
4. "Life, as most men live it, is meaningless." Do you agree or disagree? (Agree)
5. "Most people live lives of quiet desperation." Do you agree or disagree? (Agree)

Reprinted with permission of Nettler, G. Alienation in "A Measure of Alienation," *American Sociological Review,* **22** (1957), pp 670-677. Copyright 1957 by the American Sociological Association.

ANOMIE (Hyman, Wright and Hopkins 1962)

Variable
This scale was devised to summarize a person's views on the extent to which there are norms of proper conduct in our society which are still recognized and subscribed to by many people.

Description
The source and manner of selection of the items is not reported. The scale consists of eight items for which (except for one reversed item) agreement was scored as 2, disagreement as a 0. Don't know and no answer received scores of 1. Summing produced scores running from 0 (lowest anomie) to 16 (highest anomie). Median score (at the beginning of encampment) was 3.5.

Sample
The respondents all attended the Encampment for Citizenship in New York and California.which brings together about a hundred dedicated young (mainly between the ages of 18 and 20) persons each summer in an equalitarian program designed to increase skills in democratic living. Studies during the sessions of 1955, 1957 and two separate camps in 1958 yielded a total sample of 364.

A battery of scales was administered each year of the study on the first day of the Encampment, at the end of the six week session and six weeks afterwards. In addition the 1955 group was tested four years later.

Reliability
No reliability data are reported

Validity
No validity data are reported.

Location
Hyman, H., Wright, C,, and Hopkins, T. Applications of methods of evaluation. Berkeley and Los Angeles: University of California Press, 1962.

Results and Comments
The authors' primary concern was the evaluation of change of attitudes related to prejudice. The anomie scale was only a minor part of the study. Correlations between the various scales are not reported and change scores as a result of encampment were not large.

Here are two sets of results of median anomie scores:
a) Beginning of camp (3.5) vs. end of camp (2.3) vs. six weeks after camp (2.9)
b) End of encampment 1955 (2.1) vs. four years later 1959 (2.3)

ANOMIE

(*Reversed item)

Most people cannot be trusted.

     Agree   Disagree   ?

*Since 1890 people's ideas of morality have changed a lot, but there are still some absolute guides to conduct.

Nobody cares whether you vote or not except the politicians.

Nobody cares whether you attend church or not except the clergy.

People talk a lot about being decent to Negroes and other minority groups, but when it comes right down to it, most people don't really care how you treat these groups.

Cheating on income taxes is nobody's business but the government's.

What really made Dr. Salk work so hard on the polio vaccine was the thought of the money or fame he would get.

Kinsey made his name with his report on sexual behavior, and the hope of publicity was what really led him to study sex in the first place.

Anomie Scale in Hyman, H., Wright, C., and Hopkins, T., *Applications of Methods of Evaluation* (1962); originally published by the University of California Press; reprinted here by permission of The Regents of the University of California.

HELPLESSNESS (Gamson 1961)

Variable
Beginning with Seeman's five variations of alienation, Gamson selects two, powerlessness and meaninglessness, and combines them under the label of helplessness.

Description
The purpose of the study was to examine the attitudes that distinguish whose who voted in favor of fluoridation in Cambridge, Mass. and those who opposed it. From a larger group of statements (several of which were taken from a Political Efficacy Scale developed at the Survey Research Center, according to a footnote in the article), 5 items were selected as appropriate. Through item analysis, two clusters resulted: Nos. 1, 2 and 3; and Nos. 4 and 5.

Sample
From an initial probability sample of 190 registered voters living in one Cambridge, Mass. precinct, 141 interviews were completed (74 percent). This sample was primarily lower-middle, working class, 71 percent Catholic, and mostly second or third generation Irish and Italian.

Reliability
No data bearing on reliability are reported.

Validity
No data bearing on validity are reported.

Location
Gamson, W. The fluoridation dialogue: is it an ideological conflict?, Public Opinion Quarterly, 1961, 25, 526-537.

Results and Comments
On the first three statements: 32 percent of strong and moderate proponents of fluoridation (weak opponents and proponents were not included in results) agreed with all three statements, while 62 percent of opponents agreed with all three.

Controlling for age, education and income of head of household did not change the relationship between feelings of helplessness and attitude toward fluoridation. "With only one nonsignificant exception, opponents are more likely than proponents to agree with each of the first three statements in every age, education, and income category."

HELPLESSNESS

Statement	Percent Who Agree with Statement	
	Proponents	Opponents
1. Public officials don't really care about what people like me think.	40	68
2. Sometimes politics and government seem so complicated that a person like me can't really understand what's going on.	71	91
3. Human nature being what it is, there will always be war and conflict.	76	94
4. Very little of what we read in newspapers and magazines can really be trusted.	36	46
5. With the types of rockets and weapons used nowadays, it would be easy for some official to push a button and plunge us into war.	56	45

ALIENATION (Davids 1955)

Variable   Alienation was defined by high scores on "five interrelated dispositions: egocentricity, distrust, pessimism, anxiety and resentment."

Description   The scale consists of 50 items from an "Affect Questionnaire" which
contains 80 statements (10 relating to each of the total of eight
dispositions: optimism, trust and sociocentricity included with the
five making up the alienation syndrome). Some of the items were
drawn from a number of sources such as Stevenson's The Home Book of
Quotations and Murray's Explorations in Personality; others were orig-
inated by the experimenters. There is no explanation as to how the
final items were selected from the original pool. The items (which
used a scale of 1 to 6 running from strongly disagree to strongly agree)
tapping the eight dispositions were systematically randomized for administration.

Sample   Subjects were 20 Harvard undergraduates enrolled in a large introductory
course in psychology. They volunteered to participate in the experi-
ment in return for payment.

Reliability   No test of item reliability is mentioned in this article although the
correlation of the five areas making up the alienation scale were as
follows:

	Egocentricity	Distrust	Pessimism	Anxiety
Egocentricity	X			
Distrust	.75	X		
Pessimism	.76	.84	X	
Anxiety	.67	.86	.82	X
Resentment	.54	.58	.59	.58

The correlations with the sociocentricity and trust dispositions also
tended to be quite significant. Only the optimism area failed to show
significant correlation.

Validity   Prior to acceptance the respondents were given two brief personal
interviews by a clinical psychologist, interceded by their writing of a
detailed autobiography. The rank order of the subjects by the psychologist
in terms of ego structure was correlated with their rank order on the
alienation scale. The resulting correlation (tau = -.41) was significant at the .01 level.

Location   Davids, A.   Alienation, social apperception, and ego structure,
Journal of Consulting Psychology, 1955, 19, 21-27.

Administration   The items were given in a self-administered questionnaire.

Results and   The author generated five hypotheses which he tested using his data.
Comments   First treated by the data was the hypothesis that people who are high on
alienation will be less accurate in their social apperceptions than

those who are low on alienation. The rank order correlation was found
to be in the predicted direction but did not reach the .05 level of
significance (tau = .14). This result led to the formulation of the
hypothesis that those who are low on alienation will perceive others
as being low; and those who are high will perceive others as being
high. The author felt this hypothesis was confirmed by a tau of .45
($p < .01$). Also confirmed were the author's hypotheses that students
who are high on alienation show a greater negative discrepancy between
their own ratings and those they attributed to the average student
and that those who score high on alienation show the greatest discrepancy between their own values and those they attribute to their
"ideal" person.

ALIENATION

Following are the first eight statements as they appear on the Affect Questionnaire (the remaining 72 items are not reported).

1. The most profound happiness is reserved for those who are capable of selfless dedication to a cause.

   | Strongly Agree | Agree | Slightly Agree | Slightly Disagree | Disagree | Strongly Disagree |

2. No longer can a young man build his character and his hopes on solid ground: civilization is crumbling, the future is dreadfully uncertain, and his life hangs by a thread.

3. People will be honest with you as long as you are honest with them.

4. A man who never gets angry at anything or anyone is not likely to be treated with respect.

5. There are days when one awakes from sleep without a care in the world, full of zest and eagerness for whatever lies ahead of him.

6. Beneath the polite and smiling surface of man's nature is a bottomless pit of evil.

7. There are times when it is absolutely necessary to use other people as tools in the accomplishment of a purpose.

8. The real substance of life consists of a procession of disillusionments, with but few goals that are worth the effort spent in reaching them.

ALIENATION WITHIN A SOCIAL SYSTEM (Clark 1959)

Variable   This scale measures alienation, defined as "The degree to which a man
           feels powerless to achieve the role he has determined to be rightfully
           his in specific situations...." or "the discrepancy between the power
           a man has and what he believes he should have."

Description   The scale consists of items which were developed for use with members
              of an agricultural cooperative. One of the items consists of an
              interviewer's rating, the other four are closed-ended questions.

              The scores for the sample described below ranged from 4 to 20, with
              an average of 11.1 (s.d. = 3.1).

Sample   The sample consisted of 361 members of an agricultural cooperative
         randomly selected from the total membership of 3,000.

Reliability/   Evidence for the unidimensionality of the scale is provided by the
  Homogeneity item-total score correlations for the five items of .62, .82, .64,
               .80, and .74. A Guttman reproducibility coefficient of 93.4 percent
               was obtained. The coefficient of reliability, computed by the split-
               half method, is .70.
               No test-retest data are reported.

Validity   Evidence bearing on validity is given by the following correlations
           between alienation and respondent reports:

           1.) Member's satisfaction in the organization = -.62
           2.) Participation in the organization   = -.37
           3.) Knowledge-dgree to which member is
               informed about the organization   = -.30

           Evidence concerning the basic validity of these three criteria is
           also reported.

Location   Clark, J.   Measuring alienation within a social system, American
           Sociological Review, 1959, 24 (6), 849-852.

ALIENATION

(Number in parentheses refer to score assigned to each code)

a. Interviewee's statement of who actually owns the cooperative.
    Farmer-members (0)   Non-farm businessmen and others (4)

b. Interviewee's statement of how much influence he feels he has in the cooperative.
    Very much (0)   Quite a bit (1)   Some (2)   Very little (3)   None at all (4)

c. Interviewee's statement of how much "say" he feels members should have about how the cooperative is run.
    Less say (0) About the same (2) More say (4)

d. Interviewee's statement of the extent to which he feels a part owner of the cooperative.
    Very much (0)   Quite a bit (1)   Some (2)   Not very much (3)   None at all (4)

e. Interviewer's rating of the interviewee's feeling of belonging to or identification with the cooperative.
    Very much (0)   Quite a bit (1)   Some (2)   Little (3)   None at all (4)

CHAPTER 6 - AUTHORITARIANISM, DOGMATISM AND RELATED MEASURES

Systematic research on the authoritarian personality syndrome, as conceived by Adorno and others (1950) in a famous series of studies at the University of California, has been continuing for two decades. Few concepts have received so much attention in the literature of the social sciences. There are at least two reasons for continued interest in this area. First, the concept of authoritarianism represents an attempt to link deepseated personality dispositions with the socially significant forms of belief and social behavior involved in adhering to a rigid and dogmatic ideology and in discriminating against out-groups. Especially in the early years after World War II, but obviously still today, the motivation of intolerant, ethnocentric, rigid, and authority-dependent persons is of great practical as well as theoretical significance. Hence "authoritarianism" is an important variable for psychologists, sociologists, and political scientists. Second, in The Authoritarian Personality, Adorno et al. offered not only a general theoretical framework for understanding authoritarianism but also a scale to measure it that could be used in studies as diverse as laboratory experiments and nationwide sample surveys (the well-known F, for potential Fascism, Scale).

Since the publication of The Authoritarian Personality several criticisms have been leveled both at the theory advanced to explain authoritarianism and the methods used to identify it (summarized in Christie and Jahoda, 1954; and in Kirscht and Dillehay, 1967). We shall briefly consider the most important problems in order to explain the several scales now in existence which are considered to be relatives of the F Scale.

1. Ideological Content. The F Scale was designed primarily to tap fascistic proclivities--i.e., personality characteristics which make a person

susceptible to an extremely rightist or conservative political program--although it was hoped that it would also be able to identify authoritarianism regardless of specific ideological beliefs. Roger Brown (1965) has suggested that interest in measuring "authoritarianism of the left" grew as the Western nations became less concerned with the threat of Fascism and increasingly alert to the rise of Communism. Both ideologies were characterized as authoritarian ("anti-democratic"), but as lying at opposite ends of an assumed left-to-right ideological continuum. Also, several psychologists began to realize the importance of authoritarianism in totally apolitical social situations, such as school classrooms, and this instigated the development of more specialized and less ideological measures.

Three major attempts have been made to design scales that tap anti-democratic tendencies of a person without restriction to elements of a rightist political ideology. The first attempt was made by Eysenck (1954), who factor-analyzed forty items selected from published scales in the literature and extracted two orthogonal factors, "radical-conservative" and "toughminded-tenderminded." Eysenck has argued (1956a and 1956b) that Communists and Fascists both appear high on toughmindedness--which he sees as related to authoritarianism--although the Communists are radical and the Fascists con-servative. This interpretation, while intuitively plausible and perhaps esthet-ically pleasing, has been seriously challenged because of Eysenck's questionable handling of data (Rokeach and Hanley, 1956; Christie, 1956a and 1956c).

A second approach has been offered by Rokeach (1960) who designed scales to measure "dogmatism"--theoretically a characteristic of people with "closed minds" independent of their particular ideology--and "opinionation," another characteristic of closed-minded individuals who, according to Rokeach, accept or reject other people on the basis of opinion-similarity. Although several relevant studies have been done (Rokeach, 1960; see also the reviews by Kirscht and Dillehay, 1967; Ehrlich and Lee, 1969; and Vacchiano, Strauss, and Hochman, 1969), it is still not clear whether the Dogmatism Scale is sufficiently distinct from the F Scale to settle the debate concerning "authoritarianism of the left." Indications are, however, that radical leftists do show signs of rigid adherence to in-group authorities and intolerance of different opinions, even though they usually do not exhibit other signs of right-wing authoritarianism, such as ethnocentrism and traditional family ideology.

The third take-off from research employing the F Scale was prompted not only by dissatisfaction with ideological limitations of the scale, but also by the consistent finding of a negative relationship between F Scale scores and level of education or socioeconomic status (Christie, 1954). Christie expressed a major conclusion from his review of such findings as follows:

> Recent research clearly indicates that (the F Scale) is highly correlated (negatively) with measures of education and social status. Thus it is excellent for the study of those who are of little political effectiveness but is not extremely discriminating when applied to those who are high in status and are involved in the power processes of society. Recent research in the area of political and other organizational forms of behavior has revived interest in those who make decisions and wield power in the formulation of problems to be decided. These are not the sorts of individuals who make high scores on the F Scale (Christie, 1956b, pp. 1-2).

Work stimulated by this problem has yielded several versions of a "Machiavellianism Scale" designed to measure manipulative tendencies in people who fill leadership roles and to tap "Machiavellianism" as a personality trait in members of more general populations. Because the resulting scale correlates only weakly with the F Scale and appears to measure fairly general attitudes toward other people in social situations, it is discussed at length in Chapter 8, which deals with attitudes toward other people.

2. <u>Elements of the Authoritarian Syndrome</u>. Several characteristics of

the "authoritarian mind" or personality were isolated by Adorno et al.; these included anti-Semitism, ethnocentrism, political and economic conservatism, idealization of parents and self, anti-intraception (avoidance of introspection), rigid conception of sex roles, concern for status, and a cognitive style characterized by rigidity and intolerance of ambiguity. These characteristics have suggested hundreds of hypotheses for later studies using the F Scale in conjunction with other paper-and-pencil survey measures or in laboratory experiments. Some of these studies attest to the validity of the original conception of the authoritarian "syndrome," while others contribute further questions or more confusion. To date it is still impossible to offer a concise, coherent picture of the authoritarian personality, and it is quite possible that much fruitful work could be done using only parts of the syndrome rather than the range represented by the F Scale (see Kirscht and Dillehay, 1967, for a comprehensive review of the literature and an excellent summary of the "dimensions of authoritarianism"). Consequently, we shall include some scales in this chapter which have been developed to measure specific facets of the authoritarian syndrome as it is presently conceived, even though not all of them have been closely tied empirically to the original work on the F Scale.

3. _Acquiescence Response Set_. The Anti-Semitism, Ethnocentrism, and F scales of the California study, as well as Rokeach's Dogmatism Scale, were all worded in such a way that endorsement of an item yielded a higher score. There was, therefore, a strong possibility that high scorers were displaying not only, say, fascistic predispositions but also a tendency to agree with questionnaire items in general (see, e.g., Cronbach, 1946; Couch and Kenniston, 1960).

Interest in this methodological problem has absorbed considerable research energy in the last several years, sometimes seeming to dwarf theoretical interest

in authoritarianism itself--especially since some investigators went so far
as to conclude that acquiescence and authoritarianism were essentially
synonomous.[1] More recently, however, the importance of acquiescence as an
explanation for research findings in the area of authoritarianism has been
questioned (Rorer, 1965; Block, 1965; Campbell et al., 1967; Rokeach, 1967;
Samelson and Yates, 1967; Bock et al., 1969).

Rokeach (1967), for instance, showed that a respondent might agree
with oppositely worded statements in an authoritarian scale for three reasons:
1) because of response bias or acquiescence; 2) because he tells the truth
when responding to the original items but lies when responding to reversed
items; 3) because he has a weak need for cognitive consistency. The first
explanation is independent of content, whereas the last two take content into
account. The last two are plausible, says Rokeach, since a "high F" person
may agree with prodemocratic items because such statements are supposedly
normative in this culture, while also agreeing with antidemocratic items
because he is an authoritarian personality. Rokeach then presents evidence
that content is important in explaining numerous research findings in the
dogmatism area, and that a response-bias interpretation is highly implausible
in most of these cases.

Samelson and Yates (1967) present a slightly different argument for the
possible endorsement of both a statement and its opposite. They show that
unless an item and its opposite have the same neutral point (say, on a 7-point
Likert scale), it will be possible to agree--or disagree, depending on how the
response distributions overlap--with supposedly opposite statements. Furthermore,

----

[1]For example, Bass (1955) claimed acquiescence accounted for 60 percent
of F variance and Peabody (1964) decided it might determine 75 percent of the
answers to all items; Couch and Kenniston even suggested F might be used as a
criterion measure for acquiescence.

this need not involve any lapse in logic or "cognitive consistency." In a detailed analysis of earlier studies purporting to establish the existence of an agreement response set, and with the presentation of new data supporting their explanation, Samelson and Yates give convincing evidence that double-agreements are often reasonable. Of course, this does not rule out the possible influence of acquiescence in some cases, but it makes it much more difficult to have strong faith in the overwhelming influence of acquiescence in authoritarianism research.

Obviously this issue cannot be settled here. Having alerted the reader to it, we shall mention it repeatedly in presenting the various scales. Some of the scales in this chapter have been constructed specifically to avoid contamination by acquiescence response bias.[2] Nevertheless, it is worthwhile to bear in mind that no one yet knows how important response biases are in determining results in studies using authoritarianism scales and, while methodological care is always advisable, it is our opinion that enough theoretically interesting research has been done in this domain to justify further substantive studies. Incapacitation from fear that acquiescence will eventually be found to "explain" the behavior of supposed authoritarians could easily hinder progress in an important research field.

In this chapter, scales are grouped into four rough categories: (A) variants of the F Scale; (B) components of the F syndrome, according to the California studies; (C) Eysenck's factor scales; and (D) scales related to Rokeach's conception of closed-mindedness. Related research on "religious authoritarianism" is discussed in Chapter 9 (containing measures of religiosity).

---

[2]The often-cited and used Bass and Christie reversed, or negative-worded, F Scale items are included in the write-up of the California F Scale in the present chapter.

A. <u>The F Scale, its variants, and highly similar measures</u>. Under this
heading the following scales are to be discussed:

1. The California F Scale (Adorno <u>et al</u>. 1950)
2. A New F Scale (Webster <u>et al</u>. 1955)
3. Forced Choice F Scale (Berkowitz and Wolkon 1964)
4. Forced Choice F Scale (Schuman and Harding c. 1962)
5. Balanced F Scale (Athanasiou 1968)
6. Shortened F for Political Surveys (Janowitz and Marvick 1953)
7. Four-Item F Scale (Lane 1955)
8. Ten-Item F Scale (Survey Research Center 1952)
9. Pensacola Z Scale (Jones 1957)
10. Fascist Attitudes Scale (Stagner 1936)
11. Unlabeled Fascist Attitudes (Edwards 1941)

They are difficult to list in a precise evaluative order, because a
variety of different criteria led to the inclusion of these particular scales.
The original F Scale is listed first because it has historical prominence and
is often treated as a benchmark for validation of new scales. The Webster
Scale is a useful large pool of items of the California F type which can be
sampled for the construction of new scales or can be factor-analyzed in studies
of components of the F syndrome.

The two forced-choice scales of Berkowitz and Wolkon and Schuman and
Harding were constructed to eliminate acquiescence biases, as was the balanced
scale reported by Athanasiou. The balanced scale is not completely satisfactory,
since--as is often the case--reversed items are not as well correlated with
original items as one would like. The forced-choice scales reduce this problem
by presenting an item and its reverse together, clearly indicating to the
respondent that they are meant to be logical opposites on some dimension.
This procedure may well reduce the validity of the scales, however--and this
is the opinion of Schuman and Harding--by making a rational choice of something
that is theoretically supposed to be affective and irrational.

The scales reported by Janowitz and Marvick and by Lane, as well as the
Survey Research Center items, tend to stress components of authoritarianism

that are most likely to be related to political attitudes and behavior, such as power-orientation. Political researchers will probably want to consider these most closely.

The Pensacola Z Scale was constructed in an attempt to measure the personality predispositions that make up the authoritarian syndrome without mentioning political content. The items are worded in a more personal way, similar to the format of standard personality tests. The scale is only moderately correlated (.43) with the F Scale, so there is some question about its adequacy as a substitute for that scale. Nevertheless, in personality studies--especially where anxiety, hostility, dependency, and rigidity as components of authoritarianism are expected to be important--the Z Scale may be useful.

Finally, the Stagner and the Edwards scales are included primarily for historical interest. They were published before the better-known work on authoritarianism came out, and thus demonstrate further the interest of social scientists around World War II in psychological correlates of adherence to a fascist ideology.

B. Scales related to authoritarianism according to the theory evolved in the California Study, such as intolerance of ambiguity, status-concern, and traditionalism regarding the family.

    12. Anti-Semitism (Levinson and Sanford 1944)
    13. Traditional Family Ideology (Levinson and Huffman 1955)
    14. Status-Concern Scale (Kaufman 1957)
    15. Rigidity Scale (Rehfisch 1958)
    16. RAPH Scale (Meresko et al. 1954)
    17. Rigidity Scale (Wesley 1953)
    18. Intolerance of Ambiguity (Budner 1962)
    19. Intolerance of Ambiguity (Martin and Westie 1959)
    20. Desire for Certainty Test (Brim 1955)
    21. Ethnocentric Democracy Scale (Hyman et al. 1962)

These scales could be supplemented almost indefinitely by political and racial attitude measures related to authoritarianism. Many of these have been collected in a companion volume, <u>Measures of Political Attitudes</u> (Robinson, Rusk and Head, 1968). For example, that volume includes the California Study scales entitled Political-Economic Conservatism and Ethnocentrism, as well as several more recent scales along these lines. In the present chapter we have included only a few illustrative measures of components of the authoritarian syndrome.[3]

C. <u>Eysenck's R and T Factor Scales</u>. As mentioned above, Eysenck claimed to have discovered one contentless authoritarianism dimension, tender-tough-mindedness, and an orthogonal content dimension, radicalism-conservatism. Although these particular scales need refinement and perhaps even replacement, the ideas behind them are quite interesting and worthy of further research.

22. Toughmindedness (<u>T</u>) Scale (Eysenck 1954)

D. <u>Scales related to Rokeach's conception of closed-mindedness</u>. The notion of dogmatism was advanced by Rokeach as a suitable way to conceptualize <u>general</u> authoritarianism, as opposed to the rightist authoritarianism measured by the California F Scale. Several studies indicate the success of this effort. For example, Plant (1960) found the Dogmatism Scale to be a better measure of general authoritarianism than F in a large student population. Hanson (1968) found that F measures right authoritarianism while D measures general authoritarianism. In a factor-analytic study, Kerlinger and Rokeach (1966) discovered a "common core" of authoritarianism underlying both F and D Scales, but a second-order factoring revealed differences between the scales with D appearing to be more general. The exact connection between dogmatism

---

[3]The reader interested in racial prejudice and its relation to authoritarianism may be interested in the extensive work by Gough (1951 a, b, c and d). For further research on status concern see the several papers by Seeman and his colleagues (e.g., Silberstein and Seeman, 1959; Neal and Seeman, 1964; Seeman, Rohan, and Argeriou, 1966). Levinson has constructed several scales related to authoritarianism, e.g., the Custodial Mental Illness Ideology Scale (Gilbert and Levinson, 1956), the Religious-Conventionalism Scale (Levinson, 1954), and the Internationalism Scale (Levinson, 1957).

and authoritarianism needs to be studied further in non-college populations, however.

In this chapter, the basic Rokeach scales will be presented, along with two short versions of the D Scale.

23. Dogmatism Scale (Rokeach 1956)
24. Short Dogmatism Scale (Schulze 1962)
25. Short Dogmatism Scale (Troldahl and Powell 1965)
26. Opinionation Scale (Rokeach 1956)
27. Intellectual Conviction Scale (Rokeach and Eglash 1956)

The Schulze version of the D Scale was constructed on the basis of college student responses, and thus would be suitable where a short measure of dogmatism is needed in classroom studies. Troldahl and Powell (1965) found, however, that only two of Schulze's items were among the top ten in field studies of more general populations. Thus the Troldahl and Powell scale should be of most interest to field researchers who need a short dogmatism scale.

For readers interested in a good, up-to-date summary of research on dogmatism we recommend Vacchiano et al. (1969).

References:

Adorno, T. W., Frenkel-Brunswik, Else, Levinson, D. J., and Sanford, R.N. The authoritarian personality. New York: Harper, 1950.

Bass, B. M. Authoritarianism or acquiescence? Journal of Abnormal and Social Psychology, 1955, 51, 616-623.

Block, J. The challenge of response sets. New York: Appleton-Century-Crofts, 1965.

Bock, R., Dicken, C., and Van Pelt, J. Methodological implications of content-acquiescence correlations in the MMPI, Psychological Bulletin, 1969, 71, 127-139.

Brown, R. The authoritarian personality. Chapter 10 in Social psychology. New York: Free Press, 1965.

Campbell, D., Siegman, C., and Rees, M. Direction-of-wording effects in the relationship between scales, Psychological Bulletin, 1967, 68, 293-303.

Christie, R. Authoritarianism re-examined, in R. Christie and Marie Jahoda (Eds.), Studies in the scope and method of "The authoritarian personality." New York: Free Press, 1954.

_____. Eysenck's treatment of the personality of communists, Psychological Bulletin, 1956, 53, 411-430. (a)

_____. The 'Likertization of Machiavelli,' a progress report. Dittoed manuscript, 1956. (b)

_____. Some abuses of psychology, Psychological Bulletin, 1956, 53, 439-451. (c)

_____ and Jahoda, Marie (Eds.), Studies in the scope and method of "The authoritarian personality." New York: Free Press, 1954.

Couch, A. and Kenniston, K. Yea sayers and nay sayers: agreeing response set as a personality variable, Journal of Abnormal and Social Psychology, 1960, 60, 151-174.

Cronbach, L. J. Response sets and test validity, Educational and Psychological Measurement, 1956, 6, 475-494.

Ehrlich, H. J. and Lee, D. Dogmatism, learning, and resistance to change, Psychological Bulletin, 1969, 71, 249-260.

Eysenck, H. J. The psychology of politics. London: Routledge and Kegan Paul, 1954.

_____. The psychology of politics: a reply, Psychological Bulletin, 1956, 53, 177-182. (a)

Eysenck, H. J. The psychology of politics and the personality similarities between Fascists and Communists, Psychological Bulletin, 1956, 53, 431-438. (b)

Gilbert, D. and Levinson, D. Ideology, personality, and institutional policy in the mental hospital, Journal of Abnormal and Social Psychology, 1956, 53, 263-271.

Gough, H. G. Studies of social intolerance: I. Some psychological and sociological correlates of anti-semitism, Journal of Social Psychology, 1951, 33, 237-246. (a)

_____. Studies of social intolerance: II. A personality scale for anti-semitism, Journal of Social Psychology, 1951, 33, 247-256. (b)

_____. Studies of social intolerance: III. Relationship of prejudice scale to other variables, Journal of Social Psychology, 1951, 33, 257-262. (c)

_____. Studies of social intolerance: IV. Related social attitudes, Journal of Social Psychology, 1951, 33, 262-269. (d)

Hanson, D. J. Dogmatism and authoritarianism, Journal of Social Psychology, 1968, 76, 89-95.

Kerlinger, F. and Rokeach, M. The factorial nature of the F and D scales, Journal of Personality and Social Psychology, 1966, 4, 391-399.

Kirscht, J. P. and Dillehay, R. C. Dimensions of authoritarianism: a review of research and theory. Lexington: University of Kentucky Press, 1967.

Levinson, D. The inter-group workshop: Its psychological aims and effects, Journal of Psychology, 1954, 38, 103-126.

_____. Authoritarian personality and foreign policy, Journal of Conflict Resolution, 1957, 1, 37-47.

Neal, A. G., and Seeman, M. Organizations and powerlessness: a test of the mediation hypothesis, American Sociological Review, 1964, 29, 216-226.

Peabody, D. Models for estimating content and set components in attitude and personality scales, Educational and Psychological Measurement, 1964, 24, 255-269.

Plant, W. T. Rokeach's dogmatism scale as a measure of general authoritarianism, Psychological Reports, 1960, 6, 164.

Robinson, J. P., Rusk, J. G., Head, K. B. Measures of political attitudes. Ann Arbor: Survey Research Center, Institute for Social Research, 1968.

Rokeach, M. Authoritarianism scales and response bias: comment on Peabody's paper, Psychological Bulletin, 1967, 67, 349-355.

_____. The open and closed mind. New York: Basic Books, 1960.

Rokeach, M. and Hanley, C. Eysenck's tender-mindedness dimension: a critique, Psychological Bulletin, 1956, 53, 169-176.

Rorer, L. G. The great response-style myth, Psychological Bulletin, 1965, 63, 129-156.

Samelson, F. and Yates, J. F. Acquiescence and the F Scale: old assumptions and new data, Psychological Bulletin, 1967, 68, 91-103.

Seeman, M., Rohan, D., and Argeriou, M. Social mobility and prejudice: a Swedish replication, Social Problems, 1966, 14, 188-197.

Silberstein, F. B. and Seeman, M. Social mobility and prejudice, American Journal of Sociology, 1959, 65, 258-264.

Troldahl, V. C. and Powell, F. A. A short-form dogmatism scale for use in field studies, Social Forces, 1965, 44, 211-214.

Vacchiano, R. B., Strauss, P. S. and Hochman, L. The open and closed mind: a review of dogmatism, Psychological Bulletin, 1969, 71, 261-273.

CALIFORNIA F SCALE (Adorno et al. 1950)

Variable
    The F Scale was designed to measure ethnic prejudice and "prefascist tendencies" simultaneously, without mentioning minority groups by name. Both of these characteristics come under the heading of authoritarian or "implicit antidemocratic" trends in a personality.

Description
    The authors conceived of the authoritarian personality syndrome as comprising the following nine variables: conventionalism, authoritarian submission, authoritarian aggression, anti-intraception, superstition and stereotype, power and "toughness", destructiveness and cynicism, projectivity, and sex (Adorno et al., 1950, p. 228). The F Scale was not constructed by the method of selecting items from a large pool on a statistical basis; rather, each one was written specifically for the original scale on the basis of the authors' previous experience and theoretical considerations. Each item was meant to be related to both prejudice and one or more of the 9 personality variables listed above. In addition, each item had to be indirect and had to reflect a balance between irrationality and objective truth.

    Form 78 contained 38 Likert-type items. The respondent indicated his degree of agreement or disagreement on a +3 to -3 scale, with the neutral point excluded. These scale points were then converted to the appropriate values from +1 to +7 by adding +4 to each response--except for 3 items (12, 20, 28) scored in the reverse direction because they expressed unprejudiced views. Thus, a high positive score reflected a high degree of authoritarianism. Item analysis according to the discriminatory power (D.P.) technique (Murphy and Likert, 1938) yielded an average D.P. of 1.80 which, although low, indicated that the items in general yield statistically significant differences between respondents having total scores in the high and low quartiles. 16 D.P.'s were above 2.00, 18 between 1.00 and 1.99, and 4 below 1.00.

    Form 60 contained 34 items, 15 of which were newly devised for this scale. The remaining 19 were the best from Form 78 (with some minor changes in wording). Item analysis yielded a mean D.P. of 2.15 for these 34 items. 3 D.P.'s were above 3.00, 18 between 2.00 and 2.99, 12 between 1.00 and 1.99, and one below 1.00.

    Form 40/45, containing 30 items, was meant to be an improved and shorter version of the F Scale. 7 items from Form 60 were dropped and 3 new ones were added. The mean D.P. for these 30 items, all of which differentiated significantly between high and low quartiles, was 2.85. One D.P. exceeded 4.00, 11 were between 3.00 and 3.99, 16 were between 2.00 and 2.99, and 2 were between 1.00 and 1.99.

Sample   Form 78 was administered to the following 4 groups:

Group A:	U.C. public speaking class women	140
Group B:	U.C. public speaking class men	52
Group C:	U.C. extension psychology class women	40
Group D:	Professional women	63
	TOTAL N FOR FORM 78	295

Form 60 was administered to the following groups:

Group I:	University of Oregon student women	47
Group II:	University of Oregon & University of California student women	54
Group III:	University of Oregon and University of California student men	57
Group IV:	Oregon service club men	68
Group V:	Oregon service club men	60
	TOTAL N FOR FORM 60	286

Form 45 and 40 were administered to the following groups:

George Washington University women	132
California service club men	63
Middle class men	69
Middle class women	154
Working class men	61
Working class women	53
Los Angeles men	117
Los Angeles women	130
Testing class women	59
San Quentin men prisoners	110
Psychiatric clinic women	71
Psychiatric clinic men	50
Employment service men veterans	106
Maritime school men	343
TOTAL N FOR FORMS 45 and 40	1518

Reliability   The reliability (split-half) of Form 78 over all groups was .74. Group reliabilities ranged from .56 to .88. Form 60 had a reliability of .87 over all groups tested with group reliabilities ranging from .81 to .91. Forms 45 and 40 had a reliability of .90 over all groups tested. Individual group means varied from .81 to .97.

Validity   For all groups receiving Form 78, the F Scale correlated .53 with the AS Scale, .65 with the E Scale and .54 with the PEC Scale. For all groups taking form 60, the F Scale correlated

.69 with the E Scale and .34 with the PEC Scale. The F Scale correlated .73 with the E Scale and .52 with the PEC Scale for groups receiving form 45. For all groups taking form 40, the F Scale correlated .77 with the E Scale and .61 with the PEC Scale.

For Form 78, the D.P.s of the items were computed using high and low quartiles on the A-S Scale in addition to the D.P.'s computed using high and low quartiles on the F Scale. Seventeen items have a significant relationship to the A-S Scale, that is D.P.'s greater than 1.00. Four items have negative D.P.'s ranging from -.08 to -1.18. The remaining items have D.P.'s falling between 0 and .99. The mean D.P. using the AS Scale is .89. For Form 60, the D.P. of each item was computed using high and low quartiles of the E Scale. The average D.P. was 1.53. There were 28 items with significant D.P.'s, that is, D.P.'s over 1.00. The remaining D.P.'s were between .38 and .99. None was negative. There is no evidence that the items representing each of the variables comprising the authoritarian personality exist as item clusters. When every item on form 45 (N=517 women) was correlated with every other, the correlation ranged from .11 to .24. However, the items representing any one variable did not correlate with one another any better than they did with items representing other variables.

The overall item mean scores of Mack and Larry, two men who in extensive interviewing expressed Authoritarian and Democratic ideas respectively, were 4.31 and 2.95 (on Form 45 with an average D.P. of 1.80). Although the item mean scores of Mack and Larry definitely differ, both scores would barely be included in the extreme quartiles from which the D.P.'s are calculated.

Location   Adorno, T. et al. The authoritarian personality, New York: Harper, 1950.

Administration This scale is self administered. The amount of time required would depend on the form used (Figure roughly 1/2 minute per item). A subject's score is the sum of the converted responses (see description section). Scores are most often expressed in terms of item mean scores which are calculated by dividing sum score by the number of items.

Results and
Comments   The mean item scores for all groups taking Form 78 was 3.71, with group means ranging from 3.43 to 3.94. For groups receiving Form 60, the overall item mean was 3.50; group means ranged from 3.25 to 3.82. For forms 40 and 45 the mean was 3.84 with groups means ranging from 4.19 to 4.39.

As noted above, there was no statistical clustering of items into the 9 personality variables theoretically comprising the authoritarian

syndrome. This finding, despite high reliabilities for total
scale scores, calls into question the existence of a true "syndrome"
of separable traits and raises important issues about the
dimensions of authoritarianism (Kirscht and Dillehay, 1967).

Form 45 of the F Scale was correlated with Form 45 of the E Scale
(10 items), with a subset of 5 items concerning minority groups
in general, and with the remaining 5 items expressing prejudice
against Jews and Negroes (N=399). The F Scale correlated notably
higher with the minority group items than with the four anti-
Semitic and one anti-Negro items (r=.63 and .53, respectively).
A similar result was obtained by comparing correlations between
E and F with correlations between F and A-S. Thus, it would
appear that the F Scale is more closely related to measures of
general ethnocentrism than to attitudes toward particular ethnic
groups (particularly the Jews).

Because the F Scale has been criticized for containing a large
majority of positively worded items--thus confounding acquiescence
with authoritarianism, we have included here two lists of item
reversals (Bass, 1955; Christie, et al., 1958). There is
considerable disagreement about the appropriateness of such items
for measuring authoritarianism, however, especially since they
appear to have lower reliabilities than the positively worded
items (see Kirscht and Dillehay,1967, for a complete discussion).

References

Bass, B.M., Authoritarianism or acquiescence?, Journal of Abnormal
and Social Psychology, 1955, 51, 616-623.

Christie, R., Havel, J. and Seidenberg, B., Is the F Scale irreversible?, Journal of Abnormal and Social Psychology, 1958, 56, 143-149.

Kirscht, J.P. and Dillehay, R.C., Dimensions of authoritarianism:
a review of research and theory, Lexington: University of Kentucky
Press, 1967.

Murphy, G. and Likert, R., Public opinion and the individual,
New York: Harper, 1938.

THE F SCALE

Form 78
(* Reversed Scored)

2. Although many people may scoff, it may yet be shown that astrology can explain a lot of things.

3. America is getting so far from the true American way of life that force may be necessary to restore it.

6. It is only natural and right that women be restricted in certain ways in which men have more freedom.

9. Too many people today are living in an unnatural, soft way; we should return to the fundamentals, to a more red-blooded, active way of life.

10. It is more than a remarkable coincidence that Japan had an earthquake on Pearl Harbor Day, December 7, 1944.

* 12. The modern church, with its many rules and hypocrisies, does not appeal to the deeply religious person; it appeals mainly to the childish, the insecure, and the uncritical.

14. After we finish off the Germans and Japs, we ought to concentrate on other enemies of the human race such as rats, snakes, and germs.

17. Familiarity breeds contempt.

19. One should avoid doing things in public which appear wrong to others, even though one knows that these things are right.

* 20. One of the main values of progressive education is that it gives the child great freedom in expressing those natural impulses and desires so often frowned upon by conventional middle class society.

23. He is indeed contemptible who does not feel an undying love, gratitude, and respect for his parents.

24. Today everything is unstable; we should be prepared for a period of constant change, conflict, and upheaval.

* 28. Novels or stories that tell about what people think and feel are more interesting than those which contain mainly action, romance, and adventure.

30. Reports of atrocities in Europe have been greatly exaggerated for propaganda purposes.

31. Homosexuality is a particularly rotten form of delinquency and ought to be severely punished.

32. It is essential for learning or effective work that our teachers or bosses outline in detail what is to be done and exactly how to go about it.

35. There are some activities so flagrantly un-American that, when responsible officials won't take steps, the wide-awake citizen should take the law into his own hands.

38. There is too much emphasis in college on intellectual and theoretical topics, not enough emphasis on practical matters and on the homely virtues of living.

39. Every person should have a deep faith in some supernatural force higher than himself to which he gives total allegiance and whose decisions he does not question.

42. No matter how they act on the surface, men are interested in women for only one reason.

43. Sciences like chemistry, physics, and medicine have carried men very far, but there are many important things that can never be understood by the human mind.

Reprinted with permission of Adorno, T. and Harper & Row, Publishers, Inc. The California F Scale in *The Authoritarian Personality*, New York: Harper & Row, 1950.

46. The sexual orgies of the old Greeks and Romans are nursery school stuff compared to some of the goings-on in this country today, even in circles where people might least expect it.
47. No insult to our honor should ever go unpunished.
50. Obedience and respect for authority are the most important virtues children should learn.
53. There are some things too intimate or personal to talk about even with one's closest friends.
55. Although leisure is a fine thing, it is good hard work that makes life interesting and worthwhile.
56. After the war, we may expect a crime wave; the control of gangsters and ruffians will become a major social problem.
58. <u>What</u> a man does is not so important so long as he does it well.
59. Human nature being what it is, there will always be war and conflict.
60. Which of the following are the most important for a person to have or to be? <u>Mark X the three most important</u> *
  ____Artistic and sensuous
  ____Popular, good personality
  ____Drive, determination, will power
  ____Broad, humanitarian outlook
  ____Neatness and good manners
  ____Sensitivity and understanding
  ____Efficiency, practicality, thrift
  ____Intellectual and serious
  ____Emotional expressiveness, warmth, intimacy
  ____Kindness and charity
65. It is entirely possible that this series of wars and conflicts will be ended once and for all by a world-destroying earthquake, flood or other catastrophe.
66. Books and movies ought not to deal so much with the sordid and seamy side of life: they ought to concentrate on themes that are entertaining or uplifting.
67. When you come right down to it, it's human nature never to do anything without an eye to one's own profit.
70. To a greater extent than most people realize, our lives are governed by plots hatched in secret by politicians.
73. Nowadays when so many different kinds of people move around so much and mix together so freely, a person has to be especially careful to protect himself against infection and disease.
74. What this country needs is fewer laws and agencies, and more courageous, tireless, devoted leaders whom the people can put their faith in.
75. Sex crimes, such as rape and attacks on children, deserve more than mere imprisonment; such criminals ought to be publicly whipped.
77. No sane, normal, decent person could ever think of hurting a close friend or relative.

* The scoring key for this item is not reported, although, since the item is supposed to tap conventionalism, the "popular," "drive," "neatness," and "efficiency" replies would probably be scored in the authoritarian direction.

THE F SCALE

Form 60

Conventionalism: Rigid adherence to conventional, middle-class values.
1. Obedience and respect for authority are the most important virtues children should learn.
6. A person who has bad manners, habits, and breeding can hardly expect to be liked and accepted by decent people.
53. One main trouble today is that people talk too much and work too little.

Authoritarian submission: Submissive, uncritical attitude toward idealized moral authorities of the ingroup.
1. See above.
7. Science has carried man very far, but there are many important things that can never possibly be understood by the human mind.
11. Every person should have complete faith in some supernatural power whose decisions he obeys without question.
23. Young people sometimes get rebellious ideas, but as they grow up they ought to get over them and settle down.
29. No sane, normal, decent person could ever think of hurting a close friend or relative.
32. What this country needs most, more than laws and political programs, is a few courageous, tireless, devoted leaders in whom the people can put their faith.
44. In order for us to do good work, it is necessary that our bosses outline carefully what is to be done and exactly how to go about it.

Authoritarian aggression: Tendency to be on the lookout for, and to condemn, reject and punish people who violate conventional values.
6. See above.
17. An insult to our honor should never go unpunished.
19. What youth needs most is strict discipline, rugged determination, and the will to work and fight for family and country.
22. The trouble with letting everybody have a say in running the government is that so many people are just naturally stupid or full of wild ideas.
34. Sex crimes, such as rape and attacks on children, deserve more than mere imprisonment; such criminals ought to be publicly whipped, or worse.
39. There is hardly anything lower than a person who does not feel a great love, gratitude, and respect for his parents.
49. Most of our social problems would be solved if we could somehow get rid of the immoral, crooked, and feebleminded people.
53. See above.
58. Homosexuals are nothing but degenerates and ought to be severely punished.

Anti-intraception: Opposition to the subjective, the imaginative, and tender-minded.
16. When a person has a problem or worry, it is best for him not to think about it, but to keep busy with more cheerful things.
30. Some cases of feeblemindedness are caused by overstudy.
45. Nowadays more and more people are prying into matters that should remain personal and private.
53. See above.

Sex: Exaggerated concern with sexual "goings-on."
34. See above.
52. See above.
58. See above.

THE F SCALE

Forms 45 and 40

Conventionalism: Rigid adherence to conventional, middle-class values.
1. Obedience and respect for authority are the most important virtues children should learn.
12. A person who has bad manners, habits, and breeding can hardly expect to get along with decent people.
37. If people would talk less and work more, everybody would be better off.
41. The businessman and the manufacturer are much more important to society than the artist and the professor.

Authoritarian submission: Submissive, uncritical attitude toward idealized moral authorities of the ingroup.
1. See above.
4. Science has its place, but there are many important things that can never possibly be understood by the human mind.
8. Every person should have complete faith in some supernatural power whose decisions he obeys without question.
21. Young people sometimes get rebellious ideas, but as they grow up they ought to get over them and settle down.
23. What this country needs most, more than laws and political programs, is a few courageous, tireless, devoted leaders in whom the people can put their faith.
42. No sane, normal decent person could ever think of hurting a close friend or relative.
44. Nobody ever learned anything really important except through suffering.

Authoritarian aggression: Tendency to be on the lookout for, and to condemn, reject, and punish people who violate conventional values.
12. See above.
13. What youth needs most is strict discipline, rugged determination, and the will to work and fight for family and country.
19. An insult to our honor should always be punished.
25. Sex crimes, such as rape and attacks on children, deserve more than mere imprisonment; such criminals ought to be publicly whipped, or worse.
27. There is hardly anything lower than a person who does not feel a great love, gratitude, and respect for his parents.
34. Most of our social problems would be solved if we could somehow get rid of the immoral, crooked, and feebleminded people.
37. See above.
39. Homosexuals are hardly better than criminals and ought to be severely punished.

Anti-intraception: Opposition to the subjective, the imaginative, and tenderminded.
9. When a person has a problem or worry, it is best for him not to think about it, but to keep busy with more cheerful things.
31. Nowadays more and more people are prying into matters that should remain personal and private.
37. See above.
41. See above.

<u>Superstition and stereotypy</u>: The belief in mystical determinants of the individual's fate; the disposition to think in rigid categories.

4. See above.
8. See above.
16. Some people are born with an urge to jump from high places.
26. People can be divided into two distinct classes: the weak and the strong.
29. Some day it will probably be shown that astrology can explain a lot of things.
33. Wars and social trouble may someday be ended by an earthquake or flood that will destroy the whole world.

<u>Power and "Toughness"</u>: Preoccupation with the dominance-submission, strong-weak, leader-follower dimension; identification with power figures, overemphasis upon the conventionalized attributes of the ego; exaggerated assertion of strength and toughness.

2. No weakness or difficulty can hold us back if we have enough will power.
13. See above.
19. See above.
22. It is best to use some prewar authorities in Germany to keep order and prevent chaos.
23. See above.
26. See above.
38. Most people don't realize how much our lives are controlled by plots hatched in secret places.

<u>Destructiveness and cynicism</u>: Generalized hostility, vilification of the human.

6. Human nature being what it is, there will always be war and conflict.
43. Familiarity breeds contempt.

<u>Projectivity</u>: The disposition to believe that wild and dangerous things go on in the world: the projection outwards of unconscious emotional impulses.

18. Nowadays when so many different kinds of people move around and mix together so much, a person has to protect himself especially carefully against catching an infection or disease from them.
31. See above.
33. See above.
35. The wild sex life of the old Greeks and Romans was tame compared to some of the goings-on in this country, even in places where people might least expect it.
38. See above.

<u>Sex</u>: Exaggerated concern with sexual "goings-on."

25. See above.
35. See above.
39. See above.

BASS REVERSALS

Astrology will never explain anything.

Sex criminals such as those who rape and attack children should be treated as sick people, not publicly whipped or worse.

A sane, normal decent person might have to hurt a close friend or relative.

Young people sometimes get rebellious ideas. As they grow up they ought to try to carry them out and not be content to get over them and settle down.

Weaknesses and difficulties can hold us back; will power is not enough.

Our lives are not at all controlled by plots hatched in secret places.

Decent people can get along with a person who has bad manners, habits and breeding.

Human nature being what it is, universal peace will come about eventually.

Familiarity does not breed contempt.

If people would discuss matters more before acting, everybody would be better off.

What a youth needs most is to be free to make up his own mind, to be flexible and to work and fight for what he considers right personally even though it might not be best for his family and country.

Nowadays, not enough investigating of personal and private matters is done.

The artist and the professor are much more important to society than the businessman and the manufacturer.

Because of science, it will be possible for the human mind to understand most important things.

Self-reliance, respect for democracy and lack of need to submit to authority are the most important virtues children should learn.

Many fine people honestly could never bring themselves around to feeling a great love, gratitude, and respect for their parents.

Some of the goings-on in this country, even in places where people might least expect it, are tame compared to the wild sex life of the Greeks and Romans.

A person does not have to worry about catching an infection or disease just because many different kinds of people move around and mix together a great deal nowadays.

Reprinted with permission of Bass, B. M. Bass Reversals scale in "Authoritarianism or acquiescence?" *Journal of Abnormal and Social Psychology,* 51 (1955), pp 616-623. Copyright 1955 by The American Psychological Association, Inc., 1200 17th Street, N.W., Washington, D.C. 20036.

Homosexuals are not criminals and should not be punished.

People cannot be divided into two distinct classes, the weak and the strong.

When a person has a problem or worry, it is best for him to think about doing something about it, not be distracted by more cheerful things.

What this country needs most, more than a few courageous, tireless devoted leaders in whom the people can put their faith, is better laws and political programs.

An insult to our honor should be studied, not punished.

No people are born with an urge to jump from high places.

No person should have complete faith in some supernatural power whose decisions he obeys without question.

CHRISTIE REVERSALS

It is highly unlikely that astrology will ever be able to explain anything.

Sex crime, such as rape and attacks on children, are signs of mental illness; such people belong in hospitals rather than in prison.

It's only natural for people to sometimes have thoughts about hurting a close friend or relative.

If it weren't for the rebellious ideas of youth there would be less progress in the world.

There are many difficulties a person cannot overcome no matter how much will power he has.

Many people have too great a fear of plots hatched in secret by politicians.

People should be willing to overlook failures in manners and unpleasant personal habits in other people.

Human nature doesn't make war inevitable; man may some day establish a peaceful world.

You may dislike a person very much, but the chances are that if you get to know him well you'll have more respect for him.

It would be a good thing if people spent more time thinking and talking about ideas just for the fun of it.

In the long run it is better for our country if young people are allowed a great deal of personal freedom and are not strictly disciplined.

There are times when it is necessary to probe into even the most personal and private matters.

The artist and the professor are probably more important to society than the businessman.

The findings of science may some day show that many of our most cherished beliefs are wrong.

One of the most important things children should learn is when to disobey authorities.

Most honest people admit to themselves that they have sometimes hated their parents.

In spite of what you read about the wild sex life of people in important places, the real story is about the same in any group of people.

Reprinted with permission of Christie, R., Havel, J., and Seidenberg, B. Christie Reversals scale in "Is the F Scale Irreversible?" *Journal of Abnormal and Social Psychology*, 56 (1958), pp 143-159. Copyright 1958 by The American Psychological Association, Inc., 1200 17th Street, N.W., Washington, D.C. 20036.

Even though people of all sorts mix together nowadays, you don't have to worry very much about catching an infection or disease.

It's nobody's business if someone is a homosexual as long as he doesn't harm other people.

It doesn't make much sense to divide people into groups like the weak and the strong; too many people are strong in some ways and weak in others.

When a person has a problem or worry, it is best to face it and try to think it through, even if it is so upsetting that it keeps him from concentrating on other things.

It is more important for this country to have a just legal and political system than a series of trustworthy leaders, however, courageous, tireless, and devoted they might be.

Insults to our honor are not always important enough to bother about it.

An urge to jump from high places is probably the result of unhappy personal experiences rather than something inborn.

It's all right for people to raise questions about even the most sacred matters.

A NEW F (AUTHORITARIANISM) SCALE
(Webster, Sanford & Freeman 1955)

Variable	This scale was designed to measure the authoritarian or potentially anti-democratic personality as it was conceived in the California study (Adorno et al., 1950).
Description	This scale is composed of 123 true-false items. In constructing the scale, the authors administered the E and F Scales together with 677 true-false items from various personality tests. 178 of the 677 items were reported to have sufficient correlation with the F Scale and enough variance to comprise a new scale. These 178 items were then narrowed down to 123. The procedure for selecting the 123 is not described. The scale was cross-validated on a new sample the following year. All scale items had validates of .05 in both samples and .01 in at least one of the samples. The authors classified the items into the following categories: punitive morality, authoritarian submission, conventionality, religious fundamentalism, anti-intraception, ego-alien symptomatology, lack of self confidence, projectivity, cynicism, romanticism, circumscribed aggression, and sense of victimization.
	13 of the 149 items listed are scored as false and the remaining items are scored as true. A high score indicates a high degree of authoritarianism.
Sample	The two samples consisted of 441 college freshmen and 402 college freshmen, respectively.
Reliability	The reliability coefficient for the first sample was .88. No reliability coefficient for the second sample was given.
Validity	In the first sample, the 123 item scale correlated .78 with the F Scale and .53 with the E Scale (E and F Scales correlated .59 in this sample). For the second sample, this scale correlated .74 with the F Scale. The estimated correlation with the F Scale if both samples were pooled using the 149 items would exceed .74.
Location	Webster, H., Sanford, N., and Freeman, M., A new instrument for studying authoritarianism in personality, Journal of Psychology, 1955, 40, 73-85.
Administration	This scale is self administered and requires an estimated 30 minutes to complete.

Results and
Comments

The original 32-item F Scale was believed, by the authors, to
be too short to encompass all of the 30 to 40 variables that
had come to be used in describing the authoritarian personality.
The present scale was proposed to remedy this situation. The
authors also felt that more successful attempts to factor analyze
a measure of the authoritarian personality could be made with a
longer scale.

Unlike the original F Scale, this scale was composed solely by
empirical methods. It is thus interesting to note the close
correspondence between the original nine personality variables
supposed to comprise the authoritarian personality and the
categories used by the authors to classify the items in this
new scale. The authors state that the new scale is less
ideological and more personality-centered than the F Scale.
The authors also felt that the present scale would be less
dependent upon the immediate cultural environment of the subject
than the original F Scale since the new items are much less
concerned with social relations, politics, or economics.

Unfortunately, only thirteen of the new items are false from
the authoritarian point of view. Consequently, the contribution
of acquiescence to a high positive score is an important
consideration, both in using the scale and in interpreting
correlations between it and the various scales used in the
California study.

Reference

Adorno, T. et al. The authoritarian personality, New York:
Harper, 1950.

A NEW F (AUTHORITARIANISM) SCALE

A. COMPULSIVENESS

1. Orderliness, carefulness, liking for routine

T   I always see to it that my work is carefully planned and organized.

T   I always like to keep my things neat and tidy and in good order.

T   I find that a well ordered mode of life with regular hours is congenial to my temperment.

T   I like to have a place for everything and everything in its place.

T   I do not like to see people carelessly dressed.

T   It bothers me when something unexpected interrupts my daily routine.

T   I would rather be a steady and dependable worker than a brilliant but unstable one.

T   I like to plan a home study schedule and then follow it.

T   I prefer a man to be dressed carefully rather than casually or carelessly.

T   I am very careful about my manner of dress.

2. Rigidity

T   Once I have my mind made up I seldom change it.

3. Intolerance of ambiguity

T   I often wish people would be more definite about things.

T   I don't like to undertake any project unless I have a pretty good idea as to how it will turn out.

T   I don't like things to be uncertain and unpredictable.

T   It is annoying to listen to a lecturer who cannot seem to make up his mind as to what he really believes.

T   Our thinking would be a lot better off if we would just forget about words like "probably", "approximately", and "perhaps".

T   People who seem unsure and uncertain about things make me feel uncomfortable.

T   Perfect balance is the essence of all good composition.

T   Straightforward reasoning appeals to me more than metaphors and the search for analogies.

T   I don't like modern art.

B. PUNITIVE MORALITY (AUTHORITARIAN AGGRESSION)

T   I am in favor of a very strict enforcement of all laws, no matter what the consequences.

T   Every family owes it to the city to keep their sidewalks cleared in the winter and their lawn mowed in the summer.

T   I would disapprove of anyone's drinking to the point of intoxication at a party.

T   I get pretty discouraged with the law when a smart lawyer gets a criminal free.

Reprinted with permission of Webster, H., Sanford, N., and Freeman, M. A New F (Authoritarianism) Scale, in "A New Instrument for Studying Authoritarianism in Personality, *Journal of Psychology,* **40** (1955), pp 73-85. Copyright 1955 by The Journal Press.

A NEW F (AUTHORITARIANISM) SCALE (Continued)

T   Lawbreakers are almost always caught and punished.

T   Every wage earner should be required to save a certain part of his income each month so that he will be able to support himself and his family in later years.

T   The trouble with many people is that they don't take things seriously enough.

T   I set a high standard for myself, and I feel others should do the same.

T   There must be something wrong with a person who is lacking in religious feeling.

T   Divorce is practically never justified.

T   No man of character would ask his fiancee to have sexual intercourse with him before marriage.

C. AUTHORITARIAN SUBMISSION

1. Exaggerated respect for parents

T   One of my aims in life is to accomplish something that would make my mother proud of me.

T   Parents are much too easy on their children nowadays.

T   Children should associate more with children and less with their elders.

T   It is a pretty callous person who does not feel love and gratitude towards his parents.

F   At times I have very much wanted to leave home.

2. Exaggerated respect for the state, laws, and prevailing moral agents

T   Disobedience to the government is never justified.

T   Army life is a good influence on most young men.

T   It is the duty of a citizen to support his country, right or wrong.

T   Only a fool would try to change our American way of life.

F   Politically I am probably something of a radical.

T   Communism is the most hateful thing in the world today.

3. Identification with power

T   It's a good thing to know people in the right places so you can get traffic tags, and such things, taken care of.

T   I would dislike being a member of a leaderless group.

T   When I take a new job, I like to be tipped off on who should be gotten next to.

T   I like to know some important people because it makes me feel important.

D. CONVENTIONALITY

1. Self-righteous moralism

T I think I am stricter about right and wrong than most people.
T I always tried to make the best school grades that I could.
T I never make judgments about people until I am sure of the facts.
T I am known as a hard and steady worker.
T I prefer men who are never profane.
T I never attend a sexy show if I can avoid it.
T I have been inspired to a program of life based on duty which I have since carefully followed.
T It is usually a good thing to be frank.

2. Conformity

T I would be uncomfortable in anything other than fairly conventional dress.
T A person should adapt his ideas and his behavior to the group that happens to be with him at the time.
T Before I do something I try to consider how my friends will react to it.
T I would be uncomfortable if I accidentally went to a formal party in street clothes.
F I dislike men who always follow the usual social conventions (manners, customs, etiquette, etc.).
F I like unconventional language.
T I dislike a man who is frequently blunt in his speech.

3. Preference for traditional feminine role

T I would never play cards (poker) with a stranger.
T Women should not be allowed to drink in cocktail bars.
F I think I would like to drive a racing car.
T I would like to be a nurse.
F I would like to be a journalist.
T Kindness and generosity are the most important qualities for a wife to have.
T I dislike women who disregard the usual social or moral conventions.
T I like the sweet "feminine" type of girl as my friend.
T I used to like drop-the-hankerchief.

E. RELIGIOUS FUNDAMENTALISM

T I feel sure that there is only one true religion.
F In religious matters, I believe I would have to be called an agnostic.
T I believe in a life hereafter.
T I pray several times every week.

326

T   Everything is turning out just like the prophets of the Bible said it would.
T   I go to church almost every week.
T   I believe in the second coming of Christ.
T   I am very religious (more than most people).
T   I believe there is a Devil and a Hell in afterlife.

F. ANTI-INTRACEPTION

1. Emotional suppression

T   A strong person doesn't show his emotions and feelings.
F   I am fascinated by fire.
T   Human passions cause most of the evil in the world.

2. Ideational suppression

T   When a person has a problem or worry it is best for him not to think about it.
T   I must admit that I have at times been worried beyond reason over something that really did not matter.
T   Something exciting will almost always pull me out of it when I am feeling low.

3. Anti-intellectual attitudes

T   I get sort of annoyed with writers who go out of their way to use strange and unusual words.
T   The best theory is the one that has the best practical applications.
T   I enjoy detective or mystery stories.

G. EGO-ALIEN SYMPTOMATOLOGY

F   I almost never blush.
T   I wish I could be as happy as others seem to be.
F   I can read a long while without tiring my eyes.
F   When I leave home I do not worry about whether the door is locked and the windows closed.
T   At times I have fits of laughing and crying that I cannot control.
T   I have more trouble concentrating than others seem to have.
T   Sometimes some unimportant thought will run through my mind and bother me for days.
T   I often think, "I wish I were a child again."
T   It makes me nervous to have to wait.

H. LACK OF SELF-CONFIDENCE

T   Even the idea of giving a talk in public makes me afraid.
T   It is pretty easy for people to win arguments with me.
T   It is hard for me to find anything to talk about when I meet a new person.

F I like to talk before groups of people.
T Clever, sarcastic people make me feel very uncomfortable.
T I have a tendency to give up easily when I meet difficult problems.
T I prefer team games to games in which one individual competes against another.
F I am an important person.
T I certainly feel useless at times.
T I frequently have to fight against showing that I am bashful.

I. PROJECTIVITY

1. Personal projectivity

T I am bothered by people outside, on streetcars, stores, etc., watching me.
T I have often felt that strangers were looking at me critically.

2. Impersonal projectivity

T The future is too uncertain for a person to make serious plans.
T I dread the thought of an earthquake.
T A large number of people are guilty of bad sexual conduct.
T It is better never to expect much; in that way, you are rarely disappointed.

J. CYNICISM

T I don't blame anyone for trying to grab all he can get in this world.
T Most people will use somewhat unfair means to gain profit or an advantage rather than lose it.
T Only a fool would ever vote to increase his own taxes.
T Most people inwardly dislike putting themselves out to help other people.
T People pretend to care more about one another than they really do.
T The man who provides temptation by leaving valuable property unprotected is about as much to blame for its theft as the one who steals it.
T Most people make friends because friends are likely to be useful to them.
T A person does not need to worry about other people if only he looks after himself.
T There will always be war as long as there are men.
T I feel that it is certainly best to keep my mouth shut when I'm in trouble.
T I think a great many people exaggerate their misfortunes in order to gain the sympathy and help of others.
T I dream frequently about things that are best kept to myself.
T I do not blame a person for taking advantage of someone who lays himself open to it.
T The average person is not able to appreciate art and music very well.

T It's no use worrying my head about public affairs; I can't do anything about them anyhow.

T If several people find themselves in trouble, the best thing for them to do is to agree upon a story and stick to it.

K. ROMANTICISM

T In most ways the poor man is better off than the rich man.

T There is something noble about poverty and suffering.

T One of the marks of superior things in nature is that they develop from within rather than from without.

T An invention which takes jobs away from people should be suppressed until new work can be found for them.

L. CIRCUMSCRIBED AGGRESSION

1. Overt but safe aggression

T I must admit that I enjoy playing practical jokes on people.

T There are certain people whom I dislike so much that I am inwardly pleased when they are catching it for something they have done.

T I like to poke fun at people.

T I sometimes tease animals.

2. Inhibited and transformed aggression

T Animals should not be used in experiments if it is known that they will die as a result of it.

T Men who look as though they could be brutal are repelling to me.

T The thought of being in an automobile accident is very frightening to me.

M. SENSE OF VICTIMIZATION

T Teachers often expect too much work from the students.

T I have had more than my share of things to worry about.

T I feel that I have often been punished without cause.

T I have often had to take orders from someone who did not know as much as I did.

T My way of doing things is apt to be misunderstood by others.

T My mother or father often made me obey even when I thought that it was unreasonable.

T People often disappoint me.

T My parents have often disapproved of my friends.

T Police cars should be specially marked so that you can always see them coming.

FORCED CHOICE F SCALE (Berkowitz and Wolkon 1964)

Variable

This scale was designed to measure authoritarianism as defined by the California study (Adorno et al, 1950) while avoiding two problems encountered with previous scales: 1) acquiescence response set and 2) inadequate counterbalancing which yields unreliability and perhaps multidimensionality.

Description

The authors presented each positively worded F Scale item along with its reversal. The respondent was instructed to select one statement of the pair and indicate the extent to which he agreed with it relative to its opposite. Three levels of agreement were provided: "slightly more", "somewhat more", and "a great deal more". Thus there were six scale points, three levels of agreement for each of the two alternatives. These were scored from 1 to 7, with 4 representing the absent midpoint.

Twenty-five items which appear in the original F Scale and also in both Bass' and Christie's sets of negatively phrased items were selected.[1] These 75 items, 25 originals and two sets of reversals, arranged in random order, comprise Form I. From the items in Form I, two forced-choice scales were constructed. Form II (FCC) used the original items paired with Christie's reversals; each pair constituted an item. The items appeared in random order. Form III (FCB) was exactly the same as the previous one, except the Bass reversals were coupled with the original F statement. Stems appeared in the exact same random order used in Form II. In each forced choice form (FC), for 13 randomly chosen items, the original statement from the F Scale preceded its reversal, while in the other 12 items, the reversal came first. The original F+ statements appeared first in the same items of each FC form. In short, the only difference between the two forms used was in the set of reversed items employed in the pairing .

Sample

The various forms were administered to two major groups. The first comprised 153 Junior College students, who received the tests in the following different orders:

    Condition 1 (N=51): Form II (FCC) followed by Form I
    Condition 2 (N=54): Form I followed by Form III (FCB)
    Condition 3 (N=48): Form III (FCB) followed by Form I,
                          followed by Form II (FCC)

The second sample included 135 students attending the summer school of the College of Liberal Arts of Boston University, who received the questionnaires in four different orders.

    Condition 1 (N=25): Form I followed by Form II (FCC)
    Condition 2 (N=23): Form I followed by Form III (FCB)
    Condition 3 (N=43): Form II (FCC) followed by Form I
    Condition 4 (N=44): Form III (FCB) followed by Form I

---

[1]See the write-up of the original F Scale in this chapter which also lists the Bass and Christie reversals.

For this sample, Form I was reduced from 75 to 50 items by eliminating the Bass reversals.

Reliability   The following reliability coefficients were obtained after combining across conditions. In each case the largest possible number of cases was used.

(Hoyt) Reliabilities of Scales

	Junior College Sample		Liberal Arts Sample	
Scale	Reliability	N	Reliability	N
F+	.68	153	.79	135
CF-	.60	153	.66	135
BF-	.53	153	-	-
FCC	.59	99	.69	68
FCB	.41	102	.71	67

The reliabilities of the reversed scales are larger than usually obtained, probably due to the length of the scales (CF- and BF-).

Validity   Scores obtained on the various forms were correlated with those from the original F Scale. To the extent that the new scales measure the same thing as the F Scale, these correlations should be high. The results are presented in table form below.

Validity (correlation with F+) of scales

	Junior College Sample		Liberal Arts Sample	
Scale	Validity	N	Validity	N
CF-	.33	153	.48	135
BF-	.34	153	-	-
FCC	.74	99	.84	68
FCB	.69	102	.83	67

Notice that both forced-choice scales yielded higher correlations with F+ than did the two F- scales. In addition, the FC scores correlated highly with F- scores. Thus, the authors reason, "the forced-choice form predicts well to both a measure confounded with agreement response set and another confounded with disagreement response set (while the two do not correlate as highly with each other). This seems to suggest that the FC format is relatively insensitive to each of these opposing response tendencies".

There was, however, some indication that order of presentation affected responding. Stems in which F+ preceded F- correlated only between .24 and .54 with items constructed in the reverse order. Nevertheless, this did not cause the items to exhibit differential association with F+ scores.

Location   Berkowitz, N.H. and Wolkon, G.H. A forced choice form of the F scale-free of acquiescent response set. Sociometry, 1964, 27, 54-65.

Administration This scale is self administered; each form of 25 items requires an estimated 15-20 minutes to complete.

Results and
Comments   The forced-choice technique appears to be one of the best solutions to the problem of agreement set. This scale correlates highly with F+ and F- subscales of balanced forms, although these subscales usually do not correlate highly with each other. This may be due in part to a change in the meaning of the negative items in the presence of their authoritarian opposites. One of the problems encountered in constructing negative items has been the difficulty of determining what changes were needed to create psychological opposition in statements that had several logical opposites. Perhaps putting the opposites together makes the implied underlying dimension more salient to the subject.

The authors discuss the difficulty of validating a new scale against an old one of questionable validity (i.e., the original F Scale), and suggest that further exploration of their scale needs to be done in studies of behavior. It is possible, as mentioned in the introduction to this chapter, that a forced choice scale makes rational considerations too salient, thus decreasing the validity of a scale designed to measure "deep" and irrational personality tendencies. This is little more than a conjecture, however. Only further empirical work will determine its worth.

References   Adorno, T. W. et al. The authoritarian personality. New York: Harper, 1950.
Bass, B. M. Authoritarianism or acquiescence? Journal of Abnormal and Social Psychology, 1955, 51, 616-623.
Christie, R., Havel, Joan, and Seidenberg, B. Is the F scale irreversible? Journal of Abnormal and Social Psychology, 1958, 56, 143-159.

FORM II (Forced Choice Christie)

(* Included on short form)

*1. a. It is highly unlikely that astrology will ever be able to explain anything.
     b. Someday it will probably be shown that astrology can explain a lot of things.

2.   a. Sex crimes, such as rape and attacks on children, are signs of mental illness; such people belong in hospitals rather than in prison.
     b. Sex criminals such as those who rape and attack children, deserve more than mere imprisonment: such criminals ought to be publicly whipped, or worse.

3.   a. No sane, normal, decent person could ever think of hurting a close friend or relative.
     b. It's only natural for people to sometimes have thoughts about hurting a close friend or relative.

*4. a. If it weren't for the rebellious ideas of youth there would be less progress in the world.
     b. Young people sometimes get rebellious ideas, but as they grow up they ought to get over them and settle down.

5.   a. There are many difficulties a person cannot overcome no matter how much will power he has.
     b. No weakness or difficulty can hold us back if we have enough will power.

6.   a. Many people have too great a fear of plots hatched in secret by politicians.
     b. Most people don't realize how much of our lives are controlled by plots hatched in secret places.

7.   a. A person with bad manners, habits, and breeding can hardly expect to get along with decent people.
     b. People should be willing to overlook failures in manners and unpleasant personal habits in other people.

8.   a. Human nature doesn't make war inevitable; man may some day establish a peaceful world.
     b. Human nature being what it is there will always be war and conflict.

9.   a. Familiarity breeds contempt.
     b. You may dislike a person very much, but the chances are that if you get to know him well you'll have more respect for him.

*10. a. It would be a good thing if people spent more time thinking and talking about ideas just for the fun of it.
     b. If people would talk less and work more, everybody would be better off.

*11. a. What a youth needs most is strict discipline, rugged determination, and the will to work and fight for family and country.
     b. In the long run it is better for our country if young people are allowed a great deal of personal freedom and are not strictly disciplined.

*12. a. Nowadays more and more people are prying into matters that should remain personal and private.
    b. There are times when it is necessary to probe into even the most personal and private matters.

*13. a. The businessman and the manufacturer are much more important to society than the artist and the professor.
    b. The artist and the professor are probably more important to society than the businessman.

14. a. Science has its place, but there are many important things that can never possibly be understood by the human mind.
    b. The findings of science may some day show that many of our most cherished beliefs are wrong.

*15. a. Obedience and respect for authority are the most important virtues children should learn.
    b. One of the most important things children should learn is when to disobey authorities.

*16. a. Most honest people admit to themselves that they have sometimes hated their parents.
    b. There is hardly anything lower than a person who does not feel great love, gratitude, and respect for his parents.

*17. a. The wild sex life of the old Greeks and Romans was tame compared to some of the goings-on in this country, even in places where people might least expect it.
    b. In spite of what you read about the wild sex life of people in important places, the real story is about the same in any group of people.

18. a. Even though people of all sorts mix together nowadays, you don't have to worry very much about catching an infection or disease.
    b. Nowadays when so many different kinds of people move around and mix together so much, a person has to protect himself especially carefully against catching an infection or disease from them.

*19. a. It's nobody's business if someone is a homosexual as long as he doesn't harm other people.
    b. Homosexuals are hardly better than criminals and ought to be severely punished.

20. a. People can be divided into two distinct classes, the weak and the strong.
    b. It doesn't make much sense to divide people into groups like the weak and the strong; too many people are strong in some ways and weak in others.

*21. a. When a person has a problem or worry, it is best to face it and try to think it through, even if it is so upsetting that it keeps him from concentrating on other things.
    b. When a person has a problem or worry, it is best for him not to think about it, but to keep busy with more cheerful things.

22. a. It is more important for this country to have a just legal and political system than a series of trustworthy leaders, however, courageous, tireless, and devoted they might be.
    b. What this country needs most, more than laws and political programs, is a few courageous, tireless, devoted leaders in whom the people can put their faith.

23. a. An insult to honor should always be punished.
    b. Insults to our honor are not always important enough to bother about it.

24. a. Some people are born with an urge to jump from high places.
    b. An urge to jump from high places is probably the result of unhappy personal experiences rather than something inborn.

*25. a. Every person should have complete faith in some supernatural power whose decisions he obeys without question.
    b. It's all right for people to raise questions about even the most sacred matters.

FORM III (Forced Choice Bass)

(* Included in short form)

*1. a. Astrology will never explain anything.
     b. Someday it will probably be shown that astrology can explain a lot of things.

2. a. Sex criminals such as those who rape and attack children should be treated as sick people, not publicly whipped or worse.
    b. Sex criminals such as those who rape and attack children, deserve more than mere imprisonment: such criminals ought to be publicly whipped, or worse.

3. a. No sane, normal, decent person could ever think of hurting a close friend or relative.
    b. A sane, normal decent person might have to hurt a close friend or relative.

*4. a. Young people sometimes get rebellious ideas. As they grow up they ought to try to carry them out and not be content to get over them and settle down.
     b. Young people sometimes get rebellious ideas, but as they grow up they ought to get over them and settle down.

5. a. Weaknesses and difficulties can hold us back; will power is not enough.
    b. No weakness or difficulty can hold us back if we have enough will power.

6. a. Our lives are not at all controlled by plots hatched in secret places.
    b. Most people don't realize how much of our lives are controlled by plots hatched in secret places.

7. a. A person with bad manners, habits, and breeding can hardly expect to get along with decent people.
    b. Decent people can get along with a person who has bad manners, habits and breeding.

8. a. Human nature being what it is, universal peace will come about eventually.
    b. Human nature being what it is, there will always be war and conflict.

9. a. Familiarity breeds contempt.
    b. Familiarity does not breed contempt.

*10. a. If people would discuss matters more before acting, everybody would be better off.
     b. If people would talk less and work more, everybody would be better off.

*11. a. What a youth needs most is strict discipline, rugged determination, and the will to work and fight for family and country.
     b. What a youth needs most is to be free to make up his own mind, to be flexible and to work and fight for what he considers right personally even though it might not be best for his family and country.

*12. a. Nowadays more and more people are prying into matters that should remain personal and private.
 b. Nowadays, not enough investigating of personal and private matters is done.

*13. a. The businessman and the manufacturer are much more important to society than the artist and the professor.
 b. The artist and the professor are much more important to society than the businessman and the manufacturer.

14. a. Science has its place, but there are many important things that can never possibly be understood by the human mind.
 b. Because of science, it will be possible for the human mind to understand most important things.

*15. a. Obedience and respect for authority are the most important virtues children should learn.
 b. Self-reliance, respect for democracy and lack of need to submit to authority are the most important virtues children should learn.

*16. a. Many fine people honestly could never bring themselves around to feeling a great love, gratitude, and respect for their parents.
 b. There is hardly anything lower than a person who does not feel great love, gratitude, and respect for his parents.

*17. a. The wild sex life of the old Greeks and Romans was tame compared to some of the goings-on in this country, even in places where people might least expect it.
 b. Some of the goings-on in this country, even in places where people might least expect it, are tame compared to the wild sex life of the Greeks and Romans.

18. a. A person does not have to worry about catching an infection or disease just because many different kinds of people move around and mix together a great deal nowadays.
 b. Nowadays when so many different kinds of people move around and mix together so much, a person has to protect himself especially carefully against catching an infection or disease from them.

*19. a. Homosexuals are not criminals and should not be punished.
 b. Homosexuals are hardly better than criminals and ought to be severely punished.

20. a. People can be divided into two distinct classes, the weak and the strong.
 b. People cannot be divided into two distinct classes, the weak and the strong.

*21. a. When a person has a problem or worry, it is best for him to think about doing something about it, not be distracted by more cheerful things.
 b. When a person has a problem or worry, it is best for him not to think about it, but to keep busy with more cheerful things.

22. a. What this country needs most, more than a few courageous, tireless devoted leaders in whom the people can put their faith, is better laws and political programs.
    b. What this country needs most, more than laws and political programs, is a few courageous, tireless, devoted leaders in whom the people can put their faith.

23. a. An insult to honor should always be punished.
    b. An insult to our honor should be studied, not punished.

24. a. Some people are born with an urge to jump from high places.
    b. No people are born with an urge to jump from high places.

*25. a. Every person should have complete faith in some supernatural power whose decisions he obeys without question.
     b. No person should have complete faith in some supernatural power whose decisions he obeys without question.

FORCED CHOICE F SCALE (Schuman and Harding c. 1962)

Variable
This scale is quite similar to that of Berkowitz and Wolkon, and was designed to eliminate acquiescence biases from the California F Scale.

Description
For a large study of racial prejudice (see Schuman and Harding 1963 and 1964 for partial results) the authors desired a relatively short authoritarianism scale free from response bias. In an initial pretest, 24 of the 30 original F items were paired with the Christie et al. (1958) reversals. The ten "best" were selected using two criteria: the ability of the item to discriminate between individuals high and low on the Ethnocentrism Scale, and a fairly even distribution of responses. A second pretest included a sample of college students and a mixed group of adults.

Scoring is accomplished as follows. The response alternative taken from the California F Scale is always considered "High" (H) and the matching Christie reversal "Low" (L). When the high alternative is chosen, an associated response of "Very sure" is scored 7, "Moderately sure," 6, and "Not very sure," 5. When the low alternative is chosen, "Very sure" is scored 1, and so on. Failure to respond is scored 4.

Sample
The samples for the pretests were described only as stated above. For their main study, Schuman and Harding surveyed two groups, a heterogeneous quota sample of 229 Boston adults and a sample of 112 girls from a northern Catholic college.

Reliability/
Homogeneity
Pooling the pretest samples (total N = 94), a split-half reliability check was made yielding a corrected coefficient of .67. In the two main samples, the reliabilities were only .48 (general sample) and .39 (college sample). These low figures should not be taken simply as "low reliability"; a test-retest study needs to be done. Probably the low split-half coefficients indicate multi-dimensionality.

Validity
The authors report somewhat lowered validity of this scale due to the forced choice format: "...we do have the impression that the paired alternative item encourages conscious reflection and considered choice, and that this format probably reduces the influence on responses of unconscious personality trends. Thus we believe there is some loss of validity...."

Nevertheless, moderate to high correlations were obtained with several theoretically related variables, e.g., ethnocentrism, anti-internationalism, traditional family ideology, custodial attitude toward mental illness, conformity, and prejudice--thus lending evidence for the construct validity of the paired alternatives scale.

Location	Schuman, H. and Harding, J. Indirect measures of prejudice. Unpublished manuscript, c. 1962.
Administration	This scale should take only about 10 minutes to complete.
Results and Comments	Schuman and Harding were hesitant to recommend this scale for further use because of its relatively low split-half reliability and apparently decreased validity (in comparison with non-forced choice measures). The scale has not been previously published. Nevertheless, it represents an important methodological approach which could perhaps be used more effectively with more items (to increase reliability). Anyone wishing to use this item format might also want to run a test-retest correlation pretest study to determine whether reliability in this sense is satisfactory.

It would be useful to find out whether the apparently lowered validity is due to elimination of agreement bias or to the increased salience of rational deliberation, or both.

References	Christie, R., Havel, J. and Seidenberg, B. Is the F Scale irreversible? _Journal of Abnormal and Social Psychology_, 1958, _56_, 143-149.

Schuman, H. and Harding, J. Prejudice and the norm of rationality, _Sociometry_, 1964, _27_, 353-371.

Schuman, H. and Harding, J. Sympathetic identification with the underdog, _Public Opinion Quarterly_, 1963, _27_, 230-241.

ITEMS

In the list below GS means general sample and SCS means college sample. For each item pair response distributions, mean score, correlation with the total scale and N are presented. Alternatives in the authoritarian direction are preceded with an H.

1. L It would be a good thing if people spent more time thinking and talking about ideas just for the fun of it.

   H If people would talk less and work more, everybody would be better off.

	1	2	3	4	5	6	7	Mean	Av. Total Scale r	N
GS	47	31	6	1	9	47	82	4.63	.13	223
SCS	38	25	7	1	6	13	16	3.14	.03	106

2. H There is hardly anything lower than a person who does not feel a great love, gratitude, and respect for his parents.

   L Most honest people admit to themselves that they have sometimes hated their parents.

	1	2	3	4	5	6	7	Mean	Av. Total Scale r	N
GS	38	38	22	2	13	22	88	4.49	.13	223
SCS	13	27	2	0	4	20	40	4.66	.11	106

3. L.Insults to our honor are not always important enough to bother about.

   H An insult to our honor should always be punished.

	1	2	3	4	5	6	7	Mean	Av. Total Scale r	N
GS	59	50	25	1	10	33	45	3.59	.12	223
SCS	17	29	15	1	11	16	17	3.72	.03	106

4. L It's only natural for people to sometimes have thoughts about hurting a close friend or relative.

   H No sane, normal, decent person could ever think of hurting a close friend or relative.

	1	2	3	4	5	6	7	Mean	Av. Total Scale r	N
GS	39	61	18	2	7	34	62	4.02	.10	223
SCS	30	33	16	0	5	13	9	2.92	.07	106

5. H Young people sometimes get rebellious ideas, but as they grow up they ought to get over them and settle down.

   L If it weren't for the rebellious ideas of youth there would be less progress in the world.

	1	2	3	4	5	6	7	Mean	Av. Total Scale r	N
GS	36	42	10	6	15	75	39	4.36	.09	223
SCS	22	22	10	2	9	28	13	3.85	.10	106

6. H Human nature being what it is, there will always be war and conflict.

   L Human nature doesn't make war inevitable; man may some day establish a peaceful world.

GS	39	79	11	0	11	48	35	3.67	.09	223
SCS	18	37	8	0	2	25	16	3.66	.03	106

7. H What the youth needs most in strict discipline, rugged determination, and the will to work and fight for family and country.

   L In the long run it is better for our country if young people are allowed a great deal of personal freedom and are not strictly disciplined.

GS	9	17	6	0	16	62	113	5.85	.08	223
SCS	5	5	2	0	15	24	55	5.90	.07	106

8. H A person who has bad manners, habits, and breeding can hardly expect to get along with decent people.

   L People should be willing to overlook failures in the manners and unpleasant personal habits in other people.

GS	21	39	12	1	16	60	74	4.92	.06	223
SCS	6	5	5	1	19	33	37	5.54	.04	106

9. L There are times when it is necessary to probe into even the most personal and private matters.

   H. Nowadays more and more people are prying into matters that should remain personal and private.

GS	39	50	20	1	15	54	44	4.08	.05	223
SCS	14	13	7	1	10	19	42	4.93	.09	106

10. H No weakness or difficulty can hold us back if we have enough will power.

   L There are many difficulties a person cannot overcome no matter how much will power he has.

GS	40	52	12	2	10	41	66	4.24	.01	223
SCS	14	16	8	0	7	31	30	4.73	.03	106

BALANCED F SCALE   (Athanasiou   1968)

Variable   This scale was designed to measure authoritarianism as conceived
                   in the California study (Adorno et al., 1950) using equal
                   numbers of positively and negatively worded items.

Description   The author selected 14 stereopathic (positively worded) and 14
                   nonstereopathic ("reversed") six-point Likert-type items from an
                   unpublished list developed by Christie and his associates. The
                   28 items were chosen on the basis of item analyses "against two
                   internal criteria using a sample of Peace Corps Volunteers"
                   (Smith, 1965). Stems which correlated positively with total score
                   and negatively with "an indicator of agreement set" and which were
                   not clearly concerned with religion and politics were retained.
                   Scores on the stereopathic and nonstereopathic segments of the
                   scale have ranged from -.18 to -.62 and have always been negative.

                   This 28-item scale was used in a study of the differences between
                   college students who transferred out of engineering and those who
                   continued through college as engineering majors. It was hypothesized
                   that the transfer students would score lower on authoritarianism.

Sample   The sample included 347 engineering students and 111 students who,
                   by their sophomore year, had transferred out of engineering. All
                   were males. 98% were between 19 and 21 years of age. The modal
                   residential area of their families was suburban and 71% had
                   fathers whose occupational category was rated middle class or
                   above. The religious break-down of the sample was reported:
                   Protestants 63%, Catholics 20%, Jews 8%, and atheists or
                   agnostics 9%.

Reliability   A test-retest study including 8 male and 11 female students
                   yielded a coefficient of stability of .86 over a two-week period.

Validity   Validity is indirectly indicated by the findings reported below.

Location   Athanasiou, R. Technique without mystique: A study of
                   authoritarianism in engineering students. Educational and
                   Psychological Measurement, 1968, 28, 1181-1188.

Administration   This scale is self-administered and requires an estimated 20
                   minutes to complete.

Results and
Comments   All but 4 items (9, 11, 23, 27) discriminated between "engineers"
                   and transfers. The two groups also differed on a number of other
                   variables theoretically related to authoritarianism: Transfers
                   were more likely to be non-Christians, less likely to attend
                   religious services, more likely to be only children, more likely
                   to have foreign born parents, more likely to have a mother with

high education and a job, and more likely to have a high verbal
SAT score. On a seven-point scale administered before these
young men entered college, transfers as compared to "engineers"
rated themselves as significantly more spontaneous than rigid,
more politically liberal than conservative, more "open" than
"closed", and more unconventional than conventional.

The correlation between stereopathic and nonstereopathic segments
of the scale was -.31 for engineers and -.18 for transfers. A
large negative coefficient would indicate lack of response bias,
therefore the relatively low figures obtained suggest that the
problem of item reversal has not been completely overcome.
Moreover, in terms of proportional reduction in variance, the
stereopathic items proved to be better predictors of transfer
behavior than the nonstereopathic items.

The average item mean score on the nonstereopathic items was 3.82
for "engineers" and 4.00 for transfers, indicating mild acceptance
of liberal positions in both groups. For the stereopathic items,
the average item means were 2.90 and 2.44 for "engineers" and
transfers, respectively, indicating stronger rejection of the
authoritarian position by the transfers.

References Adorno, T. et al. The authoritarian personality, New York: Harper,
1950.

Smith, M.B. An analysis of two measures of "authoritarianism"
among Peace Corps teachers, Journal of Personality, 1965, 33, 513-535.

BALANCED F SCALE

Items to which "engineers" indicated greater agreement than did "transfers."
(p < .01) These items are all from the S subscale. Responses ranged from 1 = strongly disagree to 6 = strongly agree.

2. What our youth need most is strict discipline, rugged determination, and the will to work and fight for family and country.

3. The minds of today's youth are being hopelessly corrupted by the wrong kind of literature.

6. One of the best assurances for peace is for us to have the biggest bomb and not be afraid to use it.

12. Sex crimes, such as rape and attacks on children, deserve more than mere imprisonment; such criminals ought to be publicly whipped or worse.

13. Drunks and degenerates who end up in the gutter on skid row deserve their fate because of their lack of moral fibre.

14. There may be a few exceptions, but, in general, members of a racial group tend to be pretty much alike.

16. The poor will always be with us.

17. It usually helps the child in later years if he is forced to conform to his parents' ideas.

18. A sexual pervert is an insult to humanity and should be punished severely.

21. The worst danger to real Americanism during the last fifty years has come from foreign ideas and agitators.

22. A child ought to be whipped at once for any sassy remark.

24. Most homosexuals are hardly better than criminals and ought to be severely punished.

25. Army life is a good influence on most young men.

Items to which "transfers" indicated greater agreement than did "engineers."
(p < .01) These items are from the N subscale.

1. Many modern paintings have both beauty and purpose.

4. Most censorship of books or movies is a violation of free speech and should be abolished.

7. Sex offenders should be treated with expert care and understanding rather than punishment.

Reprinted with permission of Athanasiou, R. Balanced F Scale in *Educational Psychological Measurement*, 28 (1968), pp 1181-1188. Copyright 1968 by G. Frederick Kuder, Box 6907, College Station, Durham, N.C. 27708.

10. What a youth needs most is the flexibility to work and fight for what he considers right personally even though it might not be best for his family and country.

28. As young people grow up they ought to try to carry out some of their rebellious ideas and not be content to get over them and settle down.

Items to which "transfers" indicated greater agreement than did "engineers." $(p < .05)$

5. Science declines when it confines itself to the solution of immediate practical problems.

8. One of the most important things for children to learn is when to question authority.

15. Poverty can be eliminated.

19. Strict discipline of children often interferes with the development of self-direction and personal responsibility.

20. Almost everyone has at some time hated his parents.

26. It is the duty of a citizen to criticize or censure his country whenever he considers it to be wrong.

Items which did not discriminate between engineers and transfers.

9. Human nature doesn't make war inevitable for man will some day establish a peaceful world. (N)

11. It is only natural and right for each person to think that his family is better than any other. (S)

23. It would probably be best to discourage feeble-minded people from having children. (N)

27. Without the friendly cooperation of many other nations, the United States probably could not survive for very long. (N)

SHORTENED F FOR POLITICAL SURVEYS
(Fillmore 1950; Janowitz and Marvick 1953)

Variable

This shortened F Scale emphasizes two of the several components of the authoritarian syndrome, chosen because they seemed relevant to political attitudes and behavior: (1) authoritarian submission, "a tendency in an individual to adopt an uncritical and submissive attitude toward the moral authorities that are idealized by his in-group;" and (2) power and toughness, "a preoccupation with con-siderations of strength and weakness, domination and subservience, superiority and inferiority."

Description

Fillmore (1950) chose several items from the original F Scale (Adorno et al. 1950) and modified them slightly for use in an attitude sur-vey in the Philadelphia area. Six of these were used in 1950 by the Survey Research Center (SRC) in an ongoing national study of public opinion regarding U.S. foreign policy. Results from this study were reported by Janowitz and Marvick (1953) and will be the basis for the present description of the scale. (Note: All of the items from the ten-item pool used in SRC studies are reported in a scale description below along with response frequencies from a national survey in 1952.)

A six-point Likert scale was used to assess degree of agreement-disagreement with each of the six statements. An analysis was per-formed to discover whether political self-confidence and participa-tion were related to authoritarianism, and to see what the social origins of political authoritarianism might be.

For this purpose respondents were put in one of three authoritarianism categories--high, medium, and low, according to the following scheme:

Two criteria were used: cumulative score on all six questions, and ratio of agree to disagree responses. Numerical equivalents from 1 to 6 were assigned to responses ranging from strong agreement to strong disagreement. A low cumulative score for all six responses--a score of less than 19--was necessary in order to be classed as a high authoritarian while a high cumula-tive score--a score of at least 25--was necessary for classifica-tion as low authoritarian. The intermediate group thus included persons whose scores ranged from 19 through 24.

In addition, in order to be classified as low authoritarian, a res-pondent had to have disagreed with four of the six items; to be clas-sified as high authoritarian, he had to agree with four. Only a very few respondents failed to fit both criteria simultaneously.

Sample

In November 1949 the SRC interviewed a national cross-sectional area probability sample regarding foreign policy. Fifty-eight percent (341) were reinterviewed in May 1950 and given the authoritarianism measure. This was not quite a random sub-sample of the original sample, because only "consistent" scorers on a measure of isolationism were eligible for the May study. Janowitz and Marvick do not say how large this "consistent" group was.

At about the same time, another study, concerned with economic attitudes, included the same authoritarianism scale (N = 1227). The authors state: "It is of central importance that in every single relevant social relationship the findings based on the second sample population confirmed the conclusions based on the first sample population--the political attitude survey sample."

The classification system already described yielded the following breakdowns:

	Political Survey		Economic Survey		Total	
	No.	%	No.	%	No.	%
High Authoritarian	107	32	262	23	369	25
Intermediate	117	34	437	39	554	38
Low Authoritarian	117	34	430	38	547	37

Reliability

No direct information on test-retest reliability or on item-test correlations appears in the article by Janowitz and Marvick.

Validity

Several of the research findings support the conception of authoritarianism put forward by Adorno and his colleagues. For example, three variables (education, age, and income) interact to predict authoritarianism. The highest scores were obtained by older, poorly educated persons in the lower halves of the middle and lower classes. Presumably these are the most frustrated. Moreover, authoritarianism predicts a number of the voters' conservative attitudes as well as non-voting behavior--also presumed to be signs of frustration.

Location

Janowitz, M. and Marvick, D. Authoritarianism and political behavior. Public Opinion Quarterly, 1953, 17, 185-201.

Fillmore, F.H. Authoritarianism and leadership. Philadelphia: Stephenson Brothers, 1950.

Administration

Although no time is mentioned by the authors, this scale would probably take only about five minutes to complete.

Results and Comments

Since only one of the six items is worded negatively, the issue of response bias, discussed in the introduction to this chapter, should be kept in mind. Otherwise, the scale seems to be reasonable for political survey use, being short, understandable, and of demonstrated usefulness. Recall, however, that it explicitly taps only two dimensions of the authoritarian syndrome. Research directed toward other dimensions would obviously require additional items or one of the other scales presented in this chapter.

The authors' conclusion is worth quoting as a summary of their results:

"... the application to nation-wide samples of the techniques used in this study indicates the feasibility of considering personality tendencies as dimensions of American political behavior. At least three conclusions underline the desirability of continued study of these personality tendencies in different political situations: (a) Personality tendencies measured by the authoritarian scale served to explain political behavior at least as well as those other factors traditionally included in political and voting behavior studies (age, education, class); (b) It was possible to locate in the national population a number of social groupings characterized by very high and very low authoritarian reactions...; (c) The incidence of authoritarianism not only was significantly related to political isolationism and to feelings of political ineffectiveness, but also to non-voting. Authoritarianism was helpful in explaining candidate preferences."

References   Adorno, T. et al.   The authoritarian personality. New York: Harper, 1950.

SHORTENED F FOR POLITICAL SURVEYS

<u>Items</u> (Note: Only the last is reverse-scored.)

1. Human nature being what it is, there will always be war and conflict.

2. A few strong leaders could make this country better than all the laws and talk.

3. Women should stay out of politics.

4. Most people who don't get ahead just don't have enough will power.

5. An insult to your honor should not be forgotten.

6. People can be trusted.

FOUR-ITEM F SCALE (Lane   1955)

Variable   Lane analyzed data collected by the Survey Research Center for a
            study of political attitudes and behavior (post-election, November
            1952). Instead of using all ten items included in this survey (the
            ten-item scale appears in the next section of the present chapter;
            many of the results of the survey are reported in Campbell, Gurin,
            and Miller, 1954), Lane decided to construct a scale that would
            satisfy Guttman criteria, thus increasing the likelihood of uni-
            dimensionality. After some experimentation, four items were chosen
            which, at the same time, seemed to measure authoritarianism and to
            satisfy the requirements for a Guttman scale.

Description The three of the four items are the same used by Janowitz and Marvick
            (1953; also see summary in the present chapter). The remaining item
            (the first in the list below), although available to Janowitz and
            Marvick also, was omitted from their analysis because so many people
            agreed with it. In constructing a Guttman scale, Lane used the item
            for just this reason.

            The four items, along with the associated response distributions
            from a random national sample in 1952, are as follows:

            1. What young people need most of all is strict discipline by their
               parents. (agree: 76%; disagree: 25%; NA: 1%)

            2. Most people who don't get ahead just don't have enough will power.
               (agree: 64%; disagree: 35%; NA: 1%)

            3. A few strong leaders could make this country better than all the
               laws and talk. (agree: 51%; disagree: 48%; NA: 1%)

            4. People sometimes say that an insult to your honor should not be
               forgotten. Do you agree or disagree with that? (agree: 25%;
               disagree: 73%; NA: 2%)

            Respondents actually had two degrees of agreement and two of dis-
            agreement from which to choose (e.g., "agree quite a bit;" "agree
            a little"), but Lane collapsed these categories in computing the
            percentages reported above. Throughout his article, he discusses
            "high" versus "low" authoritarians without saying precisely how
            respondents were classified.

Sample   The 585 respondents were a subgroup chosen randomly from a random
            stratified sample of American adults in 1952.

Reliability The four-item Guttman scale yielded a coefficient of reproducibility
            of 90.4. The coefficients of error for each question were as fol-
            lows: 1 - 7.6; 2 - 12.7; 3 - 12.0; and 4 - 7.4.

Validity	Since the items were modified versions of original F scale items, they would obviously correlate at least moderately with other close relatives of the original scale. Beyond this, there was evidence for construct validity in several of the findings reported by Lane (see summary below).
Location	Lane, R. E. Political personality and electoral choice. American Political Science Review, 1955, XLIX, 173-190.
Administration	This scale would take only a few minutes to self-administer.
Results and Comments	Again, as in most of the F scales, one should notice that all four items are positively stated, i.e. in such a way that agreement is always scored as authoritarianism. See the introduction to this chapter for a discussion of this problem.

Obviously, the scale is extremely short, making it attractive to large-scale survey researchers but, at the same time, perhaps reducing its reliability and certainly its coverage of all the dimensions included in the original F Scale. Nevertheless, Lane says in an appendix to his book, Political Ideology (1962), that the four-item scale is better as a measure of authoritarianism than the longer, balanced ten-item version used by Campbell et al. (1960) and by Lane in his 1962 study.

Using the four-item scale, Lane reached the following conclusions:

"Taking the authoritarian syndrome for illustrative purposes, we have shown its influence upon political participation... in terms of a sense of political efficacy and the effect of multiple group membership ... The Republicanism of the authoritarians was due partly to a greater traditional identification with the Republican party, which in turn could be traced partly to disidentification with the underdog groups seen as allied to the Democratic party. The better-educated authoritarians' position on Korea is in accord with what would be expected of people with this personality characteristic (intolerance of ambiguity about the outcome) and is in accord with the position of the Republican party; and the same is true of their position on the welfare state. With respect to their candidate orientation, authoritariansim seems to inhibit criticism of General Eisenhower but not to be associated with praise of the General in personal terms."

References	Campbell, A., Converse, P.E., Miller, W.E., and Stokes, D.E. The American voter. New York: Wiley, 1960. Campbell, A., Gurin, G., and Miller, W.E. The voter decides. Evanston, Ill.: Row, Peterson, 1954. Janowitz, M. and Marvick, D. Authoritarianism and political behavior. Public Opinion Quarterly, 1953, 17, 185-201. Lane, R.E. Political ideology. New York: Free Press, 1962.

TEN-ITEM F SCALE (Survey Research Center 1952)

Because the two scales just described were based on the ten items used in the 1952 post-election survey of the Survey Research Center, they are included here along with the response distributions obtained from a national cross-section of 585 adults.

N	Code
	Q. 36. Now, I'd like to read some of the kinds of things people tell me when I interview them, and ask you whether you agree or disagree with them. I'll read them one at a time, and you just tell me whether you agree or disagree with them, and whether you agree or disagree a little or quite a bit.

Q. 36a. Human nature being what it is, there must always be war and conflict.

205	1. Agree quite a bit
128	2. Agree a little
86	4. Disagree a little
150	5. Disagree quite a bit
9	9. DK
7	-. NA
585	

Q. 36b. What young people need most of all is strict discipline by their parents.

285	1. Agree quite a bit
153	2. Agree a little
82	4. Disagree a little
50	5. Disagree quite a bit
5	9. DK
10	-. NA
585	

Q. 36c. A few strong leaders could make this country better than all the laws and talk.

190	1. Agree quite a bit
92	2. Agree a little
96	4. Disagree a little
187	5. Disagree quite a bit
12	9. DK
8	-. NA
585	

N	Code

Q. 36d. Most people who don't get ahead just don't have enough will power.

236	1. Agree quite a bit
130	2. Agree a little
104	4. Disagree a little
102	5. Disagree quite a bit
7	9. DK
6	-. NA
585	

Q. 36e. Women should stay out of politics.

99	1. Agree quite a bit
75	2. Agree a little
119	4. Disagree a little
278	5. Disagree quite a bit
6	9. DK
8	-. NA
585	

Q. 36f. People sometimes say that an insult to your honor should not be forgotten. Do you agree or disagree with that?

78	1. Agree quite a bit
66	2. Agree a little
175	4. Disagree a little
247	5. Disagree quite a bit
7	9. DK
12	-. NA
585	

Q. 36g. People can be trusted.

261	1. Agree quite a bit
173	2. Agree a little
71	4. Disagree a little
66	5. Disagree quite a bit
2	9. DK
12	-. NA
585	

N	Code

Q. 36h. One main trouble today is that people talk too much and work too little.

293	1. Agree quite a bit
148	2. Agree a little
72	4. Disagree a little
62	5. Disagree quite a bit
6	9. DK
4	-. NA
585	

Q. 36i. Sex criminals deserve more than prison; they should be whipped publicly or worse.

172	1. Agree quite a bit
60	2. Agree a little
112	4. Disagree a little
215	5. Disagree quite a bit
14	9. DK
12	-. NA
585	

Q. 36j. It is only natural and right that women should have less freedom than men.

47	1. Agree quite a bit
76	2. Agree a little
90	4. Disagree a little
361	5. Disagree quite a bit
3	9. DK
8	-. NA
585	

Ten-Item F Scale (Survey Research Center 1952) from 1952 post-election survey; reprinted here with permission.

PENSACOLA Z SCALE (Jones 1957)

Variable

This scale attempts to measure authoritarianism by using personal items instead of those with specific social or political content found on the F Scale. Due to the strong association between the term "authoritarianism" and the F Scale, the author has chosen to call the dimension of personality measured by the Pensacola Z Scale "heteronomy". The scale is composed of four factors: Anxiety, Hostility, Dependency, and Rigidity.

Description

Four inventories, the Taylor Manifest Anxiety Scale, the Wesley Manifest Rigidity Scale, the Guilford-Zimmerman Temperment Survey, and the Thurstone Temperment Schedule were administered to the subjects in addition to the F Scale. The factors of Anxiety, Hostility and Rigidity were found to have the strongest and the most unambiguous relation to the authoritarian personality (as measured by the F Scale). Solely on a priori grounds, the author chose to add a fourth factor, dependency, to these three. Fifty forced choice items were then written for each factor. These 200 items and the F Scale were then administered to a new sample. To be included on the final test, an item had to meet three criteria: 1) the item had to relate to the F Scale in the theoretically expected direction, 2) less than 85% of the subjects had to answer the item in the same way, 3) the correlation of the item with the F Scale had to be significant at the .20 probability level or better. The final scale is composed of 66 forced choice items, of which 19 measure Dependency, 20 Rigidity, 15 Anxiety, and 12 Hostility.

The item analysis showed 20 items with a significance level of .20, 11 with .10, 20 with .05 and 15 with .01.

One point is scored for each authoritarian (or heteronomous) response. Thus, the range of scores is from 0 to 66 with high scores indicating high heteronomy.

Sample

All subjects used in the construction of this test were Naval Aviation Cadets. The cadets were single, between 18 and 25 years of age, and came from all sections of the country. Approximately 20% came from the fleet and had all graduated from high school. The remainder came from civilian life and had all had at least two years of college. The mean F score per item for these cadets was 3.90 (with a S.D. of .75) which, the author states does not differ greatly from the values reported in The Authoritarian Personality. In the construct of the test, a total of 411 cadets received the F Scale and the Taylor Manifest Anxiety Scale. 211 received the F Scale and the Wesley Manifest Rigidity Scale. 628 received the Guilford-Zimmerman Temperment Survey and the F Scale. 304 received the Thurstone Temperment Schedule and the F Scale. A sample of 306 cadets received the pool of 200 items and the F Scale.

Reliability   For a sample of 187 cadets, the test-retest coefficient over a 24 hour period was .87. The test-retest coefficient was .74 when 123 cadets were tested and retested four weeks later.

Validity   Cross-validation using a sample of 311 cadets yielded a correlation of +.43 between the Z Scale and the F Scale. When two samples of enlisted personnel were given the Pensacola Z Scale and the General Classification Test, the correlations between the two scales were -.28 and -.17 indicating a negative relationship between the Pensacola Z Scale and scholastic aptitude.

Location   Jones, M.B., The Pensacola Z Survey: A study in the measurement of authoritarian tendency, Psychological Monographs, 1957, 71, Whole No.45.

Administration   This scale is self administered. Less than 30 minutes are needed for the subject to complete the scale. A subject's score is computed by adding one point for each "authoritarian" response.

Results and
Comments

An advantage of the Z Scale is that it is not "fakable". The scale was tested for fakability in two ways. Two distinct groups received the 66 items, one group getting the standard instructions, and the other group getting instructions to check what they thought was the best answer regardless of whether or not it applied to them. The 66 items were administered twice to a third group, once with the usual instructions and once with instructions to give the "best" answer. Instructions to "fake" did not alter the test scores significantly in either of these two testing situations.

Although this scale appears to have face validity, its construct validity is open to question. The scale is supposedly a measure of authoritarianism (or heteronomy, to use the author's term). There is evidence that there are four clusters of items corresponding to the four original factors (the average item between-group correlation is .03 while the average within-group correlation is .10.) However, it is questionable whether these four factors, Anxiety, Hostility, Dependency and Rigidity, tap the same dimension of personality tapped by the F Scale. Sanford summarized the several hypothetical clusters of authoritarianism around which the F Scale was based as follows: conventionalism, authoritarian submission, authoritarian aggression, anti-intraception superstition and stereotype, power and toughness, destructiveness and cynicism, projectivity, and sex.

There is another reason why these two scales might not be measuring the same personality dimension. The direct personal items of the Z Scale may elicit a different response set from the subject than the indirect items with socio-political content of the F Scale. The author reports a correlation of .43 for the two scales which, although adequate, is not as high as it might be. In a sample of 766 cadets, the mean of the Z Scale was 35.51 and the standard deviation was 6.33.

References   Jones, M. B. Note on authoritarianism, confinement, and scholastic aptitude. _Psychological Reports_, 1956, _2_, 461-464.

Jones, M. B. The Pensacola Z Survey: a study in the measurement of authoritarian tendency. _Psychological Monographs_, 1957, _71_, No. 452.

Sanford, N. The approach of the authoritarian personality, in J. L. McCary (ed)., _Psychology of personality: six modern approaches_, New York: Logos Press, 1956, p. 1.

THE PENSACOLA Z SCALE

In this test you will find pairs of statements having to do with personal characteristics. One member of the pair is labeled A and the other B. You are to select from each pair the statement that BEST describes you. Consider the example shown below.

   1. A) You are attractive.
     B) You are strong.

If you think "You are strong" describes you better than "You are attractive", you would put a mark under B on your answer sheet.

If you marked B on your answer sheet, it would not necessarily mean that you are extremely strong or that you are not attractive. It would mean that ON THE WHOLE, "You are strong" describes you better than "You are attractive".

Be sure that you select ONE statement from EVERY pair. You are not permitted to omit any pair of statements. Mark your answers on your answer sheet starting with number 1 and continuing through number 66. You should finish the test in approximately 15 minutes.

1. A) You are too friendly for your own good. (r)
   B) Your opinions are often incorrect.

2. A) Taking advantage of a person sexually makes you feel bad.
   B) You have no scruples in sex.   (H)

3. A) You are anxious.   (a)
   B) You are conceited.

4. A) To you life is a jungle.   (A)
   B) To you life is a bowl of cherries.

5. A) You day-dream politically.
   B) You don't formulate opinions about issues over which you have no control.   (d)

6. A) In political activities you confine your efforts to group action.   (d)
   B) In political activities you frequently indulge in individual endeavor.

7. A) You like a tightly organized group.   (d)
   B) You like a loosely organized group.

8. A) You haven't made any mistakes in your life.
   B) You can't get the mistakes you have made out of your mind.   (a)

9. A) There are some people you could never feel for.   (H)
   B) Sometimes you feel a real compassion for everyone.

10. A) You like instructions to be specific.   (d)
    B) You like instructions to be general.

THE PENSACOLA Z SCALE
(Continued)

11. A) You are sexually appealing.
    B) You are faithful.   (D)

12. A) You are responsible for most of your troubles.
    B) You sometimes get confused without any reason.   (a)

13. A) You frequently laugh at yourself.
    B) You don't like your favorite habits ridiculed.   (r)

14. A) You frequently get away with murder.
    B) People often blame you for things you didn't do.   (a)

15. A) You are not attracted to prudish people.
    B) You are not attracted to unkempt people.   (r)

16. A) You want badly to "belong".   (D)
    B) You don't care whether you "belong" or not.

17. A) You like a clean, neat house.   (R)
    B) You like good food.

18. A) You can never forget that love is more than just sex.   (R)
    B) You can take pleasure in sex as sex.

19. A) You are always on the lookout for new ways of attacking a problem.
    B) In general, you find the tried-and-true methods work best.   (r)

20. A) You are rebellious.
    B) You like discipline.   (D)

21. A) You don't like to gamble on getting a good break.   (a)
    B) You usually figure on getting a good break.

22. A) You get more credit than you deserve.
    B) You get less credit than you deserve.   (a)

23. A) You get into scraps you didn't start.   (a)
    B) When you get into trouble it is almost always your fault.

24. A) Most everybody lets you know directly what they think of you.
    B) Some people are secretly trying to get the better of you.   (h)

25. A) You positively like to be different from your immediate associates.
    B) Being different from your immediate associates makes you uncomfortable.   (D)

26. A) People are either your friends or your enemies.   (r)
    B) People are rarely either real friends or real enemies.

THE PENSACOLA Z SCALE
(Continued)

27. A) Your hardest battles are with other people rather than with yourself.　　(h)
    B) You are cocky.

28. A) You could like anyone if you tried.
    B) There are some people you know you could never like.　　(H)

29. A) You are forgetful.
    B) You have a meticulous memory.　　(R)

30. A) There are some people you would like to tell off.　　(h)
    B) You are occasionally taken in.

31. A) People criticize you unjustly.　　(a)
    B) People give you more breaks than you deserve.

32. A) You are charming.
    B) You are firm and resolute.　　(R)

33. A) Disappointments affect you so little that you seldom think about them twice.
    B) Your daydreams are often about things that can never come true.　　(A)

34. A) You would like to counsel a friend on his personal problem.
    B) You would like to give first aid to a friend.　　(d)

35. A) You collect things.　　(R)
    B) You lose things.

36. A) You like haphazard living.
    B) You like routine.　　(R)

37. A) Stuffed-shirts amuse you.
    B) Stuffed-shirts get under your skin.　　(h)

38. A) You keep calm in an emergency.
    B) You can obey orders.　　(d)

39. A) You are difficult to please.
    B) You like to do favors.　　(D)

40. A) You are aware of dripping water in the kitchen.　　(r)
    B) You are not observant.

41. A) You don't mind a coward.
    B) You can't stand a coward.　　(h)

42. A) You just can't stay mad even when you think you should.
    B) There are some people you would like to take apart.　　(H)

THE PENSACOLA Z SCALE
(Continued)

43. A) You admire spontaneity in people.
    B) You admire efficiency in people.   (R)

44. A) You don't particularly like to march.
    B) You like to march with a group you feel proud to belong to.   (d)

45. A) You need someone in whom you can confide completely.   (D)
    B) You are selfish.

46. A) You play fair.   (D)
    B) You are an individualist.

47. A) There are some magazines to which you particularly turn for the
       substantiation of your political ideas.   (d)
    B) Your political ideas tend to be peculiar to yourself.

48. A) You can't help feeling antagonistic to people who hold important opinions
       radically different from yours.   (h)
    B) You like a lot of people who disagree with you violently on important issues.

49. A) Your interest in general principles occasionally gets you up in the clouds.
    B) You are a stickler for precision.   (R)

50. A) You have felt so sorry for someone you have cried.
    B) You have gotten so mad you cried.   (h)

51. A) Yours is a quick and ready sympathy.
    B) You are stern.   (H)

52. A) You are independent.
    B) You are loyal.   (D)

53. A) You are talkative.
    B) Often you're sure you've forgotten something important.   (A)

54. A) You would be happier if you felt more secure.   (a)
    B) You would be happier if you were less gullible.

55. A) You never change your basic beliefs.   (r)
    B) All your beliefs are open to debate.

56. A) You follow your conscience.
    B) You have ethical standards which you follow.   (d)

57. A) You are very proud of your membership in some groups   (d)
    B) You don't go for groups.

THE PENSACOLA Z SCALE
(Continued)

58. A) You are indifferent to most people.
    B) You like or you dislike people.   (r)

59. A) You don't worry about physical disorders.
    B) Sometimes you figure you're a sure thing for ulcers.   (a)

60. A) You are dogmatic.   (R)
    B) You are sloppy.

61. A) There are some people you admire so much you would not question their
        opinions.   (D)
    B) You don't admire anybody very much.

62. A) Concerning your past actions you figure, "If I did it, it can't be too bad."
    B) If you had your life to live over, there would be a lot of things you'd do
        differently.   (A)

63. A) You admire careful, rigorous thinking.   (r)
    B) You admire brilliant, penetrating thinking.

64. A) The details of life are important to you.   (R)
    B) You are often thoughtless.

65. A) You are well coordinated.   (r)
    B) You seek new opinions.

66. A) You are self-confident.
    B) You are a good Joe.   (A)

One point is scored for each response with a letter in parenthesis after it.

These letters refer to further subscales that can be built from the full 197 items.
There are 40 items that form subscales that tap each of four traits (or 160 items)
and they are marked with capital letters as follows:

> D -- Dependency
> R -- Rigidity
> A -- Anxiety
> H -- Hostility

Items marked with small letters fall into one of these domains but are not part
of one of the 40 item subscales.

FASCIST ATTITUDES SCALE (Stagner 1936)

Variable	This scale represents one of the earliest attempts to measure "attitudes of sympathy for fascism." Stagner realized that mentioning fascism explicitly would evoke normative anti-fascist responses, so he attempted to disguise the true purpose of the scale. This was, then, an early attempt to do what Adorno and his colleagues did years later--devise a subtle scale to measure authoritarian predispositions in personality.
Description	Fascist documents were reviewed to discover the key characteristics of German and Italian Fascism. Seven more or less distinct concepts were found: nationalism, or opposition to internationalism; imperialism; militarism; racial antagonism; anti-radicalism; middleclass-consciousness, "which may be defined as a superior attitude toward the working class"; and the benevolent despot or strong-man philosophy of government. Thirty-five opinion statements were gathered from various sources (or devised by Stagner) to illustrate these concepts. In order to disguise the purpose of the study, fascism was never mentioned, and 15 extra statements about general economic conditions were intermingled with the 35 fascism items. The resulting questionnaire was administered in true-false format with the hopefully deceptive title, "Opinions about the Depression." One point was given for each "pro-fascist" response.
Sample	Respondents were 224 college students in three middle-western institutions. Scores for the three groups were as follows:

	$\underline{N}$	Median	Mean	S.D.
A	91	15	16.9	5.18
B	71	15	16.7	5.75
C	62	21	20.8	3.88

	Group A came mostly from working class families. Group B came from a large university. Their mean scores were not significantly different. Group C "is from an expensive institution attended by well-to-do young people whose leanings are very conservative." The mean from this group was reliably different from the other two. There was no significant sex difference.
Reliability	The correlation between items 1-21 and 22-50 was .77 (corrected) for 91 students from Group A. Although moderately high, this suggests non-unidimensionality--not a surprising finding considering the heterogeneous sources of items.
Validity	Only the reasonable pattern of group results was offered as evidence for validity.
Location	Stagner, R. Fascist attitudes: an exploratory study, Journal of Social Psychology, 1936, 6, 309-319.
Administration	The scale is self-administered. With the filler items, about half an hour would be needed to complete it.

364

Results and
Comments

In an attempt to find out more about the characteristics of high and low responders, and to determine whether there was a single, general "pro-fascist" attitude underlying high scores, Stagner took the 46 highest and 46 lowest scorers and computed a critical ratio for each item based on the endorsement percentage difference between these two groups. The result is shown below, where the items are organized into three sets according to critical ratio.

Looking at the best items, Stagner concluded:

The essence of the general "pro-fascist" attitude which seems to be indicated by this study lies in the attitude of class superiority taken by many individuals toward the elements of the population which are below them in an economic and industrial sense. The anti-radical attitude is also markedly involved, and nationalism and racial antagonism are manifested.

FASCIST ATTITUDES SCALE

Items receiving a C.R. of 5.00 or more
(The numbers at the left show the position of each statement in the mimeographed scale.)

3. Recovery has been delayed by the large number of strikes.
4. The U.S. should stop immigration to give American workers more jobs.
8. If we buy European made goods, we make the depression in this country last longer.
11. Building a bigger navy would give men jobs and protect our foreign markets, so that should be done.
12. Most labor trouble happens only because of radical agitators.
13. The unemployed should be given military training so our country could be protected in time of war.
16. The people who complain most about the depression wouldn't take a job if you gave it to them.
21. Any able-bodied man could get a job right now if he tried hard enough.
23. Most people on relief are living in reasonable comfort.
24. We must protect our trade in the Philippines against the Japanese.
27. The government must first balance the budget.
28. CCC camps where the boys learned military discipline and self-control would be a good idea.
30. The president was justified in protecting U. S. interests in Cuba.
34. Labor unions are all right, but we can't have strikes.
37. The U. S. should make these European countries pay off their war debts.
42. While raising the standard of living we must safeguard property rights as guaranteed by the Constitution.
43. Unemployment insurance would saddle us with a nation of idlers.
46. These unemployed organizations are just a bunch of chronic complainers.

Items receiving a C.R. between 3.00 and 4.99

7. What we need is a strong president who will make people cooperate for recovery.
10. Recognition of Soviet Russia was a big mistake.
14. Capital and labor should get together for a fair wage and a fair profit.
15. The sales tax is an unfair way of raising relief money.
17. We must all sacrifice a little to build a strong American nation.
18. The president was all right until he became influenced by communistic ideals.
33. The formation of big trusts bankrupted many small businesses and so brought on the depression.
39. If the government didn't meddle so much with business everything would work out all right.
40. We should consider our duty to our country first in this time of crisis.
44. America has plenty of plans--what it needs is strong men who are willing to work for recovery.
45. If we have unemployment, we should deport the excess workers back to their home countries.
47. The NRA would have worked if so many strikes hadn't been organized.
48. People should not be allowed to vote unless they are educated and intelligent.

Reprinted with permission of Stagner, R. Fascist Attitudes Scale in "Fascist Attitudes: An Exploratory Study," *Journal of Social Psychology*, 6 (1936), pp 309-319. Copyright 1936 by Clark University.

366

Items receiving a C.R. of 3.00 or less

1. Conditions are likely to get better in 1935.
2. The farmers have been hit harder than the city workers.
5. The depression has caused an increase in crime.
6. This country should try to get more foreign markets so as to increase prosperity.
9. Many workers have been unemployed for five years through no fault of their own.
19. What we need is more international cooperation, not less.
20. Prosperity would come back if we could show businessmen that they could invest money at a profit.
22. Munitions makers probably don't have near as much to do with starting wars as the papers claim.
25. Italy has taken the wrong way out of the depression.
26. We will always have depressions.
29. The average person isn't intelligent enough to vote his way out of the depression.
31. Inflation would solve most of the problems of the depression.
32. There is no excuse for depressions.
35. The Wall Street bankers brought on the depression to clean up on the little fellows.
36. If we had stayed out of the World War, we would never have had this depression.
38. We'd get out of the depression quicker if we had a strong intelligent man with full power to run things.
41. The collapse in 1929 was due primarily to overproduction.
49. The U. S. ought to demand its fair share of trade with China.
50. What we need is more businesslike government.

UNLABELED FASCIST ATTITUDES (Edwards 1941)

Variables	This scale is designed to measure fascist attitudes, and differs from other fascism scales by omitting reference to such basic elements of the attitude as militarism and nationalism. Instead, the items are concerned with topics about which the fascist point of view is more subtle and less anti-democratic (such as birth control, education, status of women, and status of religion).
Description	The final scale consists of 22 five-point Likert-type items. Statements concerning various aspects of fascism were selected from earlier studies by Stagner, Gundlack, and others; and from the writings of Childs, Mann, and Kolnai. The statements were rated as either pro- or anti-fascist by five judges and discarded if found to be ambiguous. The remaining 26 statements were subjected to an item analysis which determined the median ratings on each item for the 16 highest and the 16 lowest scores. Four items with critical ratios of less than 2.00 were eliminated from the final scale.
	Total score is the sum of item scores, and response values range from 5, for strongly agree, to 1, for strongly disagree; thus indicating agreement with fascist attitudes. For the final scale (22 items) the range of possible scores is from 22 to 110.
Sample	The original 91 subjects were students in general psychology classes at the University of Akron. The revised 22 item scale was administered to 146 students at Ohio University and a new group of 97 at the University of Akron. This group of 243 contained 89 males and 154 females. Range of obtained scores was 25-87.
Reliability/ Homogeneity	The split-half reliability coefficient (corrected) for the sample of 91 on the 26 item scale was .93. The split-half reliability coefficient (corrected) was .84 for the sample of 243 on the 22 item scale.
Validity	Very few data from which to judge the validity of this scale are reported. No correlation coefficients between this scale and any other independent measure of fascism are given. The ability of the 22 items to discriminate between high and low scoring subjects provides an internal consistency check.
Location	Edwards, A., Unlabeled fascist attitudes, Journal of Abnormal and Social Psychology, 1941, 36, 579-582.
Administration	This scale is self-administered and requires an estimated 15 minutes to complete.

Results and
Comments

Further analysis of the sample of 243 yielded the following results: the variability of the scores was greater among juniors and seniors than among freshmen and sophomores (critical ratio of difference = 2.88); variability is greater among those 21 and over than among those 18 and under (critical ratio difference = 2.88); and Independents score lower than either Republicans or Democrats (critical ratio difference = 3.29 and 3.01, respectively).

In a study (1944), the author administered his scale to a sample described as 250 Akron, Ohio residents aged 20-67, earning incomes of under $1000 to over $20,000 per year. He obtained a split-half reliability of .84 (corrected) for this sample, and found that subjects falling in the lowest of three socioeconomic groupings achieved the lowest means on the attitude scale, with middle and high socioeconomic status groups following in order. Below are some of the means of the groups studied:

Classification	Mean
Age	
20-29	56.6
30-39	57.4
40-49	64.7
50-65	67.4
Status	
Housewives	66.7
Social workers	51.3
Elementary school teachers	54.5

This scale, although constructed prior to 1941, is still of interest because the dimension of fascism, which it attempts to measure, is closely related to the dimension now called authoritarianism. Many of the items on this scale bear a close resemblance to items found on the F Scale. The underlying assumption upon which claims for the validity of this measure are based, that an attitude of fascism is revealed in opinions concerning a variety of topics, is also found in the theoretical conception of "the authoritarian personality," where this term implies a syndrome of various personality traits manifested in different ways but stemming from a common core.

Reference

Adorno, T. W. et al. The authoritarian personality, New York: Harper and Row, 1950.

Edwards, A. L. The signs of incipient fascism, Journal of Abnormal and Social Psychology, 1944, 39, 301-316.

UNLABELED FASCISM SCALE

1. Children should be taught to be more obedient and to have more respect for authority by the public schools.

    _____ I strongly agree with this statement

    _____ I agree with this statement

    _____ I am uncertain about this statement

    _____ I disagree with this statement

    _____ I strongly disagree with this statement

2. Whatever best serves the interests of government is generally right.

*3. The public schools should place more emphasis upon physical training and loyalty and less upon the development of intellectual functions.

*4. Everyone should have the full liberty of propagandizing for what he believes to be true.

5. The masses of people are capable of determining what is and what is not good for them.

6. America has reached a higher state of civilization than any other country in the world and as a consequence has a culture which is superior to any other.

*7. People should be given the opportunity to hear all sides of a question, regardless of how controversial it is.

8. Over 10% of the population is incapable of democratic participation in government by reason of their lack of inherited abilities.

9. Generally speaking, women are less intelligent and efficient than men.

10. The superior people in any culture are justified in dominating national affairs by force if necessary, because of the very fact that they are superior.

*11. Many people who claim they believe in democracy have unconscious prejudices and attitudes which would make them sympathetic to a fascist movement.

12. Because many of the minor political parties merely confuse national issues, all political parties except the two major ones should be abolished.

13. The right to vote should be restricted to those individuals who have a specified amount of private property and therefore have a direct concern in the welfare of the country.

Reprinted with permission of Edwards, A. Unlabeled Fascist Attitudes in *Journal of Abnormal and Social Psychology*, 36 (1941), pp 579-582.

14. A large percent of the taxes which citizens pay is wasted in an effort to educate individuals who are not capable or worthy of being educated.

15. The right of the working classes to call a general strike should be abolished because it is a potential threat to democracy and is not in the general interest of society.

16. Patriotism and loyalty to one's country are more important than one's intellectual convictions and should have precedence over them.

17. A standing army of 2,000,000 men or over is necessary for our national defense at all times.

18. Government should attempt to persuade people to have more children and if necessary restrict birth control information for the benefit of our national defense.

19. In the national interest, private schools should either be abolished or restricted in their teachings so that the control of education is largely in the hands of the federal government.

20. Regardless of who our next president is, he must be a strong intelligent man and be given full power to run things in the interest of the people.

21. Certain religious sects whose beliefs do not permit them to salute the flag, should either be forced to conform or else be abolished.

22. There will always be superior and inferior races in the world and in the interests of all concerned it is best that the superior continue to dominate the inferior.

23. Our foreign markets are a vital necessity to our prosperity and must be protected at all costs.

24. Women have more ability and are more efficient at tasks around the home and as a result their rightful place is in the home and not in the business world.

25. Minor forms of military training such as drill, marching, and simple commands should be made a part of the elementary school educational program.

26. Academic freedom is all right in principle, but instructors in high schools and colleges should not be allowed to express their convictions concerning their subject matter.

* These items were not included in the revised scale, since it was found that they failed to discriminate between subjects with low total scores and those with high total scores.

ANTI-SEMITISM (A-S) SCALE (Levinson and Sanford 1944)

Variable
This scale is designed to measure anti-Semitism, which the authors defined as "an ideology, that is, as a relatively organized, relatively stable system of opinions, values, and attitudes concerning Jews and Jewish-Gentile relations."

Description
The scale consists of 52 six-point Likert-type items, and is divided into the following five sub-scales:

1). Jews as personally offensive (PO)-12 items
2). Jews as socially threatening (ST)-10 items
3). Attitudes about what should be done to or against Jews (A)-16 items
4). Jews as being too seclusive (S)-8 items
5). Jews as being too intrusive (I)-8 items

A few items were included on more than one sub-scale. The final scale also included 4 "neutral" items (N) which were not part of any of the sub-scales. The sub-scales are not intended to be received as representing the theoretical components of anti-Semitism or as statistically independent measures. But merely as being convenient ways of grouping items. Nonetheless, each sub-scale does seem to measure a fairly definable aspect of anti-Semitism.

The original 52 items on the total Anti-Semitism Scale were formulated especially for that scale. The items were not designed to tap the violent anti-Semitic feelings, but rather the more widely spread tempered anti-Semitic feelings.

The discriminatory power (DP) of each of the 52 items was computed for the first group of subjects. Four items were less than 2.0, 15 were between 2.0 and 3.0, and 33 were greater than 3.0. The discriminatory power of each of the 52 items was computed for the second group of subjects. The average DP was 2.85. Five items were above 4.0, 21 were between 3.0 and 3.9, 15 were between 2.0 and 2.9, and 11 were between 1.2 and 1.9. For the third group of subjects, the average DP on the 10-item form of the A-S Scale was 3.68, with two items between 2.0 and 3.0, 4 items between 3.0 and 4.0, and 4 items over 4.0.

Response choices were coded +3 to -3 for strong agreement to strong disagreement (the neutral point, 0, was omitted). Scoring is accomplished by adding +4 to each response and then summing the values. Scores have a possible range of 52 to 364. A high score indicates high anti-Semitism.

A 10-item form of the A-S Scale is also available. The 10 items were selected from the original 52 on a statistical and a theoretical basis. Items selected had to have adequate DP's. An attempt was made to cover the 5 sub-scales and keep duplication of content at a minimum.

Sample

Group 1 consisted of 77 female students in introductory psychology classes at the University of California. Group 2 consisted of 144 female students in introductory psychology at the University of California. This group included 19 members of major minority groups such as Jews, Negroes, and Chinese. Group 3 received only the 10-item form. This group consisted of 140 women in a public speaking class, 52 men in the same class, 40 adult women in an extension class in psychology, and 63 professional women including nurses, teachers, and social workers.

Reliability

For group 1, the split-half reliability was .98 (corrected). The average interrelation among the sub-scales was .79; the correlation with the total scale of the "offensive", "threatening", and "attitudes" sub-scales were .96, .94, and .93, respectively.

For group 2, the split-half reliability (with parts I and II administered a week apart) was .92. The average intercorrelation among the sub-scales was .79; the correlation with the total scale of the "offensive", "threatening", and "attitudes" sub-scales was .92, .93, and .94, respectively.

For group 3, reliabilities of .89 to .94 with an average of .92 were obtained.

Validity

The scale was administered to 13 non-Jewish graduate students and faculty members of the Department of Psychology who responded naively under normal test conditions. This criterion group composed of people who possessed liberal social attitudes and who openly opposed chauvanism and prejudice, achieved scores ranging from 57-120 and a mean of 86.0.

When group 1 (77 women) was broken down into various sub-groups, the following results were obtained: Republicans had higher scores than Democrats (critical ratio, 2.81). Protestant sectarians and Catholics had higher scores than the non-religious and non-sectarian "Protestants" (critical ratio 4.90). Sorority members had higher scores than non-members (critical ratio 4.57).

Further evidence for the validity of this scale is found in two case studies. It was found that the item responses reflected accurately the attitudes expressed in the case study interviews. The prejudiced man had an item mean score of 4.6 while the man who revealed very little prejudice had an item mean score of 1.2.

Location   Levinson, D.J. and Sanford, R.N., A scale for the measurement
                    of anti-Semitism , Journal of Psychology, 1944, 17, 2, 339-370.

Administration   This scale is self-administered, and requires an estimated 25
                    minutes to complete.

Results and   Group 1 had a mean score of 158.17, SD 67.3. Group 2 had an
Comments   item mean score of 2.7, SD 1.11. Group 3 had an item mean
                    score of 3.16, SD 1.41 (10-item scale).

                    All of the items are negative, that is, they express unfavorable
                    and hostile attitudes toward the Jews. The authors felt that
                    positive items would elicit the "self-righteous" tolerance response
                    set demanded by democratic ideology, whereas negative items could
                    be formulated which would not be obviously anti-Semitic and thus
                    not violate "democratic" ideals. The main argument against the
                    use of all negative items is that the subject's score will be
                    influenced by his tendency to "agree" or "disagree" independently
                    of the variable being measured.

                    This scale deals with what the author terms "pseudo-democratic"
                    rather than openly anti-democratic attitudes. Consequently, those
                    people who insist that they are not prejudiced and preface their
                    anti-Semetic statements with "I'm not prejudiced, but..." will
                    score highly on this test, in addition to those few who openly
                    express violent prejudice.

                    The 52-item form of the A-S Scale correlated .80 with the total
                    E Scale (for group 2). The short form of the A-S Scale correlated
                    .68 with the short form of the E Scale (for group 3). The short
                    form of the A-S Scale correlated .43 with the short form of the
                    PEC Scale (for group 3). The short form of the A-S Scale
                    correlated .53 with the short form of the F Scale (for group 3).

Reference   Adorno,T. et al.The authoritarian personality, New York: Harper
                    & Brothers, 1950.

ANTI-SEMITISM SCALE

This is an investigation of general public opinion concerning Jewish people. The following are statements with which some people agree and others disagree.

Questionnaire A

1). Jews seem to prefer the most luxurious, extravagant, and sensual way of living. (PO)

2). The Jews must be considered a bad influence on Christian culture and civilization. (ST)

3). In order to maintain a nice residential neighborhood it is best to prevent Jews from living in it. (A)

4). A major fault of the Jews is their conceit, overbearing pride, and their idea that they are a chosen race. (PO)

5). One trouble with Jewish businessmen is that they stick together and connive, so that a Gentile doesn't have a fair chance in competition with them. (ST & I)

6). Colleges should adopt a quota system by which they limit the number of Jews in fields which have too many Jews now. (A)

7). No matter how Americanized a Jew may seem to be, there is always something basically Jewish underneath, a loyalty to Jewry and a manner that is never totally changed. (PO)

8). Jewish power and control in money matters is far out of proportion to the number of Jews in the total population. (ST)

9). A step toward solving the Jewish problem would be to prevent Jews from getting into superior, profitable positions in society, for a while at least. (A)

10). Districts containing many Jews always seem to be smelly, dirty, shabby, and unattractive. (PO)

11). There are too many Jews in the various federal agencies and bureaus in Washington, and they have too much control over our national policies. (T & I)

12). The Jewish problem is so general and deep that one often doubts that democratic methods can ever solve it. (A)

13). There are a few exceptions, but in general Jews are pretty much alike. (PO)

14). Jews tend to lower the general standard of living by their willingness to do the most menial work and to live under standards that are far below average. (ST)

15). It is wrong for Jews and Gentiles to intermarry. (A)

16). The Jews should not pry so much into Christian activities and organizations nor seek so much recognition and prestige from Christians. (PO & I)

17). Much resentment against Jews stems from their tending to keep apart and to exclude Gentiles from Jewish social life. (S)

18). It is best that Jews should have their own fraternities and sororities since they have their own particular interests and activities which they can best engage in together, just as Christians get along best in all-Christian fraternities. (A)

19). One thing that has hindered the Jews from establishing their own nation is the fact that they really have no culture of their own; instead, they tend to copy the things that are important to the native citizens of whatever country they are in. (I)

20). The Jews should give up their un-Christian religion with all its strange customs (kosher diet, special holidays, etc.) and participate actively and sincerely in the Christian religion. (S)

21). It is sometimes all right to ban Jews from certain apartment houses. (A)

22). One big trouble with Jews is that they are never contented, but always try for the best jobs and the most money. (N)

23). Jews tend to remain a foreign element in American society, to preserve their old social standards and to resist the American way of life. (S)

24). Anyone who employs many people should be careful not to hire a large percentage of Jews. (A)

25). Jews go too far in hiding their Jewishness, especially such extremes as changing their names, straightening noses, and imitating Christian manners and customs. (I)

26). There is little doubt that Jewish pressure was largely responsible for the U.S. getting into the war with Germany. (N)

Questionnaire S

1). The Jews should make sincere efforts to rid themselves of their conspicuous and irritating faults, if they really want to stop being persecuted. (PO)

2). Wars show up the fact that the Jews are not patriotic or willing to make sacrifices for their country. (ST)

3). It would hurt the business of a large concern if it had too many Jewish employees. (A & I)

4). There is something different and strange about Jews; one never knows what they are thinking or planning, nor what makes them tick. (PO)

5). Jews may have moral standards which they apply in their dealings with others, but with Christians they are unscrupulous, ruthless, and undependable. (ST)

6). The best way to eliminate the Communist menace in this country is to control the Jewish element which guides it. (A)

7). The trouble with letting Jews into a nice neighborhood is that they gradually give it a typically Jewish atmosphere. (PO & I)

8). The Jew's first loyalty is to Jewry rather than to his country. (ST)

9). In order to handle the Jewish problem, the Gentiles must meet fire with fire and use the same ruthless tactics with the Jews that the Jews use with the Gentiles. (A)

10). I can hardly imagine myself marrying a Jew. (PO)

11). Jews seem to have an aversion to plain hard work; they tend to be a parasitic element in society by finding easy, nonproductive jobs. (ST)

12). It is not wise for a Christian to be seen too much with Jews, as he might be taken for a Jew, or be looked down upon by his Christian friends. (A)

13). One general fault of Jews is their overaggressiveness, a strong tendency always to display their Jewish looks, manners, and breeding. (PO & S)

14). There seems to be some revolutionary streak in the Jewish makeup as shown by the fact that there are so many Jewish Communists and agitators. (ST)

15). One of the first steps to be taken in cleaning up the movies and generally improving the situation in Hollywood is to put an end to Jewish domination there. (A)

16). Jews should be more concerned with their personal appearance, and not be so dirty, smelly, and unkempt. (PO)

17). The Jewish districts in most cities are results of the clannishness and stick-togetherness of Jews. (S)

18). Most hotels should deny admittance to Jews, as a general rule. (A)

19). The true Christian can never forgive the Jews for their crucifixion of Christ. (I)

20). Jewish millionaires may do a certain amount to help their own people, but little of their money goes into worthwhile American causes. (S)

21). Jewish leaders should encourage Jews to be more inconspicuous, to keep out of professions and activities already overcrowded with Jews, and to keep out of the public notice. (A)

22). There is little hope of correcting the racial defects of the Jews, since these defects are simply in their blood. (N)

23). The Jews keep too much to themselves, instead of taking the proper interest in community problems and good government. (S)

24). It would be to the best interests of all if the Jews would form their own nation and keep more to themselves. (A)

25). When Jews create large funds for educational or scientific research (Rosewald, Heller, etc.) it is mainly due to a desire for fame and public notice rather than a really sincere scientific interest. (I)

26). On the whole, the Jews have probably contributed less to American life than any other group. (N)

Short Form   Form 78

11). Anyone who employs many people should be careful not to hire a large percentage of Jews. (A)

16). One trouble with Jewish businessmen is that they stick together and connive, so that a Gentile doesn't have a fair chance in competition. (ST & S)

21). The Jewish districts in most cities are results of the clannishness and stick-togetherness of Jews. (S)

26). Persecution of the Jews would be largely eliminated if the Jews would really make sincere efforts to rid themselves of their harmful and offensive faults. (PO)

33). Jewish leaders should encourage Jews to be more inconspicuous, to keep out of the professions and activities already overcrowded with Jews, and keep out of the public notice. (A)

40). I can hardly imagine myself marrying a Jew. (PO)

49). The trouble with letting Jews into a nice neighborhood is that they gradually give it a typically Jewish atmosphere. (PO & I)

62). No matter how Americanized a Jew may seem to be, there is always something different and strange, something basically Jewish underneath. (PO)

69). There may be a few exceptions, but, in general, Jews are pretty much alike. (PO)

72). There are too many Jews in the various federal agencies and bureaus in Washington, and they have too much control over our national policies. (ST & I)

TRADITIONAL FAMILY IDEOLOGY SCALE (Levinson and Huffman 1955)

Variable
This scale is designed to assess differences in family ideology along an autocratic-democratic continuum and is based on five personality factors: conventionalism, authoritarian submission, exaggerated masculinity and femininity, extreme emphasis on discipline, and a moralistic rejection of impulse life.

Description
This scale is composed of 40 six-point Likert-type items, each of which was intended to represent as many of the five factors as possible. The theoretical basis of the authoritarian-democratic personality dimension is described in The Authoritarian Personality (Adorno et al., 1950). These five factors are not regarded as being statistically or conceptually independent. No further information about the source of the items or the selection of those composing the final scale is given. Of the scale items, 34 were regarded as autocratic and six as democratic. Responses to each item were given a value on a scale ranging from +3 (strong agreement) to -3 (strong disagreement) and were converted into item scores by the addition of +4.

Scoring was reversed for the democratic items. The range of scores was 40-280, with a high score indicating adherence to a traditional autocratic family ideology. For convenience, the mean score per item (1-7), computed by dividing the total score by 40, was multiplied by 10 to yield a range of scores from 10 to 70. The item DP's averaged 2.0 and varied from .04 to 3.5.

Sample
The sample contained 109 adults in evening classes in psychology at Cleveland College, 67 men and 42 women between the ages of 20 and 40, either full-time students of college age or part-time students from various occupational groups.

Reliability/
Homogeneity
The (corrected) split-half reliability for the Traditional Family Ideology scale (TFI) was .84. Further data are reported under Results and Comments.

Validity
In an item analysis, it was found that the discriminating power of five of the items did not achieve the five percent significance level. The TFI Scale was correlated with two shortened forms of the E and F Scales (which statistically approximated their longer original forms) yielding values of .65 and .73, respectively.

As with the E and F Scales, TFI scores varied from high to low across religious denominations in the following order: Catholic, Protestant, Jewish, and "unaffiliated." TFI scores increased, on the average, with church attendance. On four projective questions concerning various family roles and practices, the responses of the lowest and the highest scoring quarters on the TFI were compared, and "authoritarian" vs. "equalitarian" scoring categories were formulated. The results indicated that the categories which differentiate high and low scorers reflect the variables on which the TFI Scale was originally constructed.

Location	Levinson, D. and Huffman, P. Traditional family ideology and its relation to personality, Journal of Personality, 1955, 23, 251-273.
Administration	Estimated administration time is about 25 minutes.
Results and Comments	The mean for the sample of 109 was 33.3 (s.d.=7.8), which is slightly on the democratic side of the theoretically neutral point of 40. An abbreviated 12-item form of the TFI Scale (items starred twice on the 40 item scale below) was presented to five groups (total of 507 subjects) in Boston. The group means averaged 32.6 (the s.d.'s 10.7). In these groups, the TFI Scale correlated .6 with the E Scale, .7 with the F Scale, and .5 with a religious conventionalism scale.

The following table presents specific data for the 12 item scale administered to these 5 groups:

				Correlation with		
Group	N	Mean	s.d.	E	F	RC
1. Harvard Summer Session	84	28.3	11.3	.68	.75	.56
2. Boston University Sophomores	236	34.0	9.6	.59	.66	.45
3. Boston University Freshmen	76	35.7	11.1	.77	.70	.67
4. Registered Nurses	46	30.2	10.5	.50	.62	.51
5. Student Nurses	65	34.8	10.9	.65	.61	.13
Over-all	507	32.6	10.7	.65	.67	.46

The Harvard summer session group had a 6-week test-retest reliability of .93 and a split-half reliability on the initial test of .92.

The authors' hypothesis that individuals are relatively consistent in their tendency to take a democratic or an autocratic stand in various ideological spheres is supported by the significant correlations between the TFI Scale and the E and RC (Religious Conventionalism) Scales. It appears that an individual's family ideology overlaps with his ideological views of other social institutions. The significant correlations obtained between the TFI Scale and the F Scale demonstrate a close relationship between the democratic-autocratic continuum of family ideology and the equalitarian-authoritarian continuum of personality.

Reference	Adorno, T. et al. The authoritarian personality. New York: Harper, 1950.

TRADITIONAL FAMILY IDEOLOGY SCALE

Item Mean	D.P.	
		A. Parent-child relationships: child-rearing techniques
4.0	3.5	39. A child should not be allowed to talk back to his parents, or else he will lose respect for them. (II, IV)
3.2	3.1	40. There is a lot of evidence such as the Kinsey Report which shows we have to crack down harder on young people to save our moral standards. (IV, V)
3.8	2.9	58. There is hardly anything lower than a person who does not feel a great love, gratitude, and respect for his parents. (II)
2.9	2.8	33. A well-raised child is one who doesn't have to be told twice to do something. (II, IV)
4.4	2.4	56. A woman whose children are messy or rowdy has failed in her duties as a mother. (II, V)
4.2	2.2	15. It isn't healthy for a child to like to be alone, and he should be discouraged from playing by himself. (I, V)
2.7	2.1	22. If children are told much about sex, they are likely to go too far in experimenting with it. (I, V)
3.5	2.0	57. A child who is unusual in any way should be encouraged to be more like other children. (I, V)
4.2	1.8	45. The saying "Mother knows best" still has more than a grain of truth. (I, II)
3.5	1.7	9. Whatever some educators may say, "Spare the rod and spoil the child" still holds, even in these modern times. (IV)
2.5	1.5	21. It helps the child in the long run if he is made to conform to his parents' ideas. (II, IV)
3.3	0.9	*3. A teen-ager should be allowed to decide most things for himself. (II, IV)

*Agreement with these items is given a low score, disagreement a high score.

The numbers in parentheses at the end of each item refer to the personality variables they are thought to tap. The numbers are given here for their possible suggestive value; it is not assumed that any item is a "pure" expression of any variable. The variables are named as follows: I. Conventionalism; II. Authoritarian Submission; III. Exaggerated Masculinity and Femininity; IV. Extreme Emphasis on Discipline; V. Moralistic Rejection of Impulse Life.

Reprinted with permission of Levinson, D. and Huffman, P. Traditional Family Ideology Scale in "Traditional Family Ideology and Its Relation to Personality," *Journal of Personality,* **23 (1955), pp 251-273. Copyright 1955 by Duke University Press, Box 6697, College Station, Durham, N.C. 27708.**

Item Mean	D.P.	
1.8	0.9	*27. In making family decisions, parents ought to take the opinions of children into account. (II, IV)
6.1	0.7	51. It is important to teach the child as early as possible the manners and morals of his society. (I)
2.2	0.0	*52. A lot of the sex problems of married couples arise because their parents have been too strict with them about sex. (IV, V)

B. Husband and wife roles and relationships

Item Mean	D.P.	
3.7	3.2	31. Women who want to remove the word obey from the marriage service don't understand what it means to be a wife. (II, III)
3.5	3.0	20. Some equality in marriage is a good thing, but by and large the husband ought to have the main say-so in family matters. (III)
4.5	2.6	28. One of the worst problems in our society today is "free love," because it mars the true value of sex relations. (I, V)
3.9	1.9	34. It is only natural and right for each person to think that his family is better than any other. (I, II)
3.7	1.8	4. A marriage should not be made unless the couple plans to have children. (I, V)
3.5	2.3	38. A man who doesn't provide well for his family ought to consider himself pretty much a failure as husband and father. (I, III)
3.8	2.2	14. Faithlessness is the worse fault a husband could have. (I, III)
3.6	1.3	44. In choosing a husband, a woman will do well to put ambition at the top of her list of desirable qualities. (III)
1.3	0.7	7. A wife does better to vote the way her husband does, because he probably knows more about such things. (II)
1.6	0.6	8. It is a reflection on a husband's manhood if his wife works. (III, V)
1.9	0.6	*43. Women should take an active interest in politics and community problems as well as in their families. (I, III)

Item Mean	D.P.		

C. General male-female relationships; concepts of masculinity and femininity

3.6	3.1	46.	A man can scarcely maintain respect for his fiancee if they have sexual relations before they are married. (III)
3.4	3.0	50.	It goes against nature to place women in positions of authority over men. (II, III)
2.8	2.9	37.	It is a woman's job more than a man's to uphold our moral code, especially in sexual matters. (III)
2.6	2.7	49.	The unmarried mother is morally a greater failure than the unmarried father. (III)
4.2	2.6	26.	The most important qualities of a real man are strength of will and determined ambition. (III)
3.0	2.6	25.	Women can be too bright for their own good. (II, III)
3.0	2.2	*10.	Women have as much right as men to sow wild oats. (III, V)
2.6	2.0	16.	Petting is something a nice girl wouldn't want to do. (III, V)
3.0	2.0	13.	Women think less clearly than men and are more emotional. (III)
3.8	1.4	1.	Almost any woman is better off in the home than in a job or profession. (I, III)
2.0	1.4	32.	It doesn't seem quite right for a man to be a visionary; dreaming should be left to women. (III, V)
4.1	1.2	*19.	Even today women live under unfair restrictions that ought to be done away with. (II, III)
3.7	0.9	2.	It's a pretty feeble sort of man who can't get ahead in the world. (III)

D. General values and aims

4.6	3.3	55.	The family is a sacred institution, divinely ordained. (I, II)

AN ABBREVIATED TRADITIONAL FAMILY IDEOLOGY SCALE (FORM FERPT)

1. Some equality in marriage is a good thing, but by and large the husband ought to have the main say-so in family matters.

2. If children are told much about sex, they are likely to go too far in experimenting with it.

3. Women who want to remove the word obey from the marriage service don't understand what it means to be a wife.

4. The most important qualities of a real man are determination and driving ambition.

5. A child should never be allowed to talk back to his parents, or else he will lose respect for them.

6. A man should not be expected to have respect for a woman if they have sexual relations before they are married.

7. It is somehow unnatural to place women in positions of authority over men.

8. The family is a sacred institution, divinely ordained.

9. A woman whose children are at all messy or rowdy has failed in her duties as a mother.

10. If a child is unusual in any way, his parents should get him to be more like other children.

11. There is hardly anything lower than a person who does not feel a great love, gratitude, and respect for his parents.

12. The facts on crime and sexual immorality show that we will have to crack down harder on young people if we are going to save our moral standards.

STATUS-CONCERN SCALE (Kaufman 1957)

Variable	This scale attempts to measure directly attitudes toward status and mobility, that is, the value placed on symbols of status and in the attainment of higher status. It was hypothesized that concern with status would vary directly with anti-Semitism.
Description	The scale consists of ten Likert-type items. No information concerning the selection of the final items was given. Response format is a six-point agreement-disagreement continuum requiring response on a +3 (agreement) to -3 (disagreement) scale with 0 omitted. Responses are converted into item scores by the addition of +4 to each response value. Range of possible scores is 10-100 with high scores indicating high concern with status.
Sample	The scale was administered to 213 non-Jewish college undergraduates from a "middle-class" population.
Reliability/ Homogeneity	The split-half reliability corrected for double length was .78. The author states that the items did not meet the 90 percent reproducibility criterion for a Guttman scale.
Validity	The differences between the item means of high and low scores were significant at the .01 level for each item. The Status-Concern (SC) Scale correlated .71 with the F Scale and .66 with the Anti-Semitism Scale for the sample of 213. The F Scale correlated .53 with the AS Scale. However, with SC Scale held constant, the AS Scale correlated .12 with the F Scale, a non-significant correlation.
Location	Kaufman, W. C. Status, authoritarianism, and anti-semitism, American Journal of Sociology, 1957, 62, 379-382.
Administration	An estimated time of less than ten minutes is needed to complete this scale.
Results and Comments	In this particular sample, concern for status was more closely related to anti-Semitism than was authoritarianism, and the relationship between authoritarianism and anti-Semitism seemed to be largely explained by their mutual relationship to status-concern.
	This study took an interesting approach to the relationship between status, mobility, and prejudice. In most related studies correlations are hypothesized between actual status and prejudice. Here an attempt was made to measure attitudes toward status and mobility. Similar studies have been done by Seeman and his associates (e.g., Silberstein and Seeman, 1959; Seeman et al., 1966) and, as in Kaufman's study, the results suggest that such attitudes are more important than actual status.

386

References

Adorno, T. W. et al. The authoritarian personality. New York: Harper, 1950.

Silberstein, F. B and Seeman, M.   Social mobility and prejudice, American Journal of Sociology, 1959, 65, 258-264.

Seeman, M., Rohan, D., and Argeriou, M.   Social mobility and prejudice: a Swedish replication, Social Problems, 1966, 14, 188-197.

STATUS-CONCERN SCALE

1. The extent of a man's ambition to better himself is a pretty good indication of his character.

    Strongly   Agree   Slightly   Strongly   Disagree   Slightly
    Agree   Agree   Disagree   Disagree

2. In order to merit the respect of others, a person should show the desire to better himself.

3. One of the things you should consider in choosing your friends is whether they can help you make your way in the world.

4. Ambition is the most important factor in determining success in life.

5. One should always try to live in a highly respectable residential area, even though it entails sacrifices.

6. Before joining any civic or political association, it is usually important to find out whether it has the backing of people who have achieved a respected social position.

7. Possession of proper social etiquette is usually the mark of a desirable person.

8. The raising of one's social position is one of the more important goals in life.

9. It is worth considerable effort to assure one's self of a good name with the right kind of people.

10. An ambitious person can almost always achieve his goals.

Reprinted with permission of Kaufman, W. C. Status-Concern Scale in "Status, Authoritarianism, and Anti-Semitism," *American Journal of Sociology,* 62 (1957), pp 379-382. Copyright 1957 by the University of Chicago.

RIGIDITY SCALE (Rehfisch 1958)

Variable

This scale is designed to measure personality rigidity which is characterized by the following qualities: (a) constriction and inhibition, (b) conservatism, (c) intolerance of disorder and ambiguity, (d) observational and perserverative tendencies, (e) social introversion, (f) anxiety and guilt.

Description

The scale consists of 39 true-false items. The original pool of 957 items included items from the MMPI and the California Psychological Inventory and items specially constructed for this scale. These items were administered to subjects who had been rated on a number of personality variables, including rigidity by IPAR (Institute for Personality Assessment and Research) staff members.

The final items were selected on the basis of their ability to discriminate between the quartiles rated highest and lowest on rigidity among the entire criterion sample revealed 20 items discriminating significantly at the .01 level, 18 at the .05 level, and one at the .06 level.

Cross validation for two preliminary forms of the scale was accomplished by the following procedure. The first preliminary scale was constructed from the responses of the quartiles rated highest and lowest on rigidity among 80 graduate students, 80 medical students, and 20 Air Force captains. A cross validation coefficient of .35 (two-tailed test: $p < .01$) was obtained by correlating scores on this scale with rigidity ratings (for a sample of 60 Air Force captains not used in constructing this preliminary scale). A second preliminary scale was constructed on the basis of the responses of these 60 Air Force captains. The scores of 70 medical school applicants on the second preliminary scale were correlated with their IPAR staff ratings on various personality variables. The following results were obtained: (a) in interpersonal situations tends to be a good listener or spectator .54; (b) constriction .51; (c) tends toward over-controls of his needs and impulses... delays gratification unnecessarily .44; (d) manifest anxiety .39; (e) has a readiness to feel guilty .36; (f) tends to delay or avoid decision..33; (h) tends to ruminate and have obsessive thoughts .30; (i) is uncomfortable with uncertainties and complexities .30; (j) follows routine in living, is orderly .28; (k) rigidity .19.

Negative correlations are with (a) is self-indulgent -.51; (b) fluency of ideas -.45; (c) verbal fluency -.40; (d) impulsivity -.35; (e) originality -.35.

One point is assigned for each "rigid" response yielding a range of scores from 0 to 39. A high score indicates high rigidity.

Sample

The following groups served as subjects for the construction of this scale: 80 graduate students from the University of California, 80 senior medical students from the University of California, 70 applicants to the University of California Medical School, and 100 Air Force captains. The total number of subjects was 330. All subjects were male.

Reliability/
  Homogeneity

A new sample of 60 Air Force captains was used to determine reliability. Corrected split-half reliability was .72.

Validity

The number of IPAR staff members rating each subject varied but was never fewer than five and averaged eight. Interrater reliability, computed by an analysis of variance technique, ranged, across the samples, from .50 to .81 and averaged .73.

In addition to the cross validation discussed above, further cross validation data were obtained from an item analysis of IPAR staff ratings for each subject on the Gough Adjective Check List. An adjective composite for each of the 70 Medical School applicants was then constructed from adjectives checked by three or more staff members. The adjective composite for the 18 highest and 18 lowest scorers on the second preliminary rigidity scale were compared. The following adjectives were found to differentiate significantly (.05 level) between high and low scorers.

Adjectives more often checked by high scorers: anxious, conscientious, conservative, deliberate, dependent, gentle, inhibited, mild, moderate, modest, painstaking, peaceable, quiet, reserved, retiring, serious, shy, sincere, submissive, thorough, timid, withdrawn, worrying.

Adjectives more often checked by low scorers: active, adaptable, aggressive, argumentative, assertive, clear-thinking, confident, curious, demanding, energetic, independent, irritable, organized, outgoing, outspoken, painful, poised, quick, resourceful, self-centered, self-confident, self-seeking, sociable, spontaneous, talkative, versatile.

Location

Rehfisch, J.M., A scale for personality rigidity , Journal of Consulting Psychology, 1958, 22, 10-15.

Administration

Estimated administration time is 20 minutes.

Results and
Comments

For a sample of 343 Air Force captains and 70 medical school applicants, the mean on the Rigidity Scale was 15.77 (s.d. 5.21).

The author states that the low correlation between the Rigidity (Ri) Scale and the rigidity ratings (.19) could be a result of either error in the scale or error in the ratings. However, because the correlations of the scale with the ratings of other traits along the rigidity-flexibility dimension were as expected, the author feels that the accuracy or the comprehensiveness of the rigidity ratings could be open to question.

In another study using two samples of Air Force captains the author found the Ri Scale to be significantly positively related (at the .01 level) to the MMPI scales of social introversion and anxiety and significantly negatively related (at the .01 level) to the K Scale and rules of ego-strength and leadership. The author also found negative correlations of equal significance between the Ri Scale and a scale of the CPI measuring sociability, social presence, interest in scholastic achievement, and intellectual efficiency.

Further research needs to be done to see how the items in this instrument relate to the apparently similar measures of dogmatism, authoritarianism, intolerance of ambiguity, intolerance, and so on.

Reference

Rehfisch, J.   Some scale and test correlates of a personality rigidity scale, Journal of Consulting Psychology, 1958, 22, 372-374.

THE RI (RIGIDITY) SCALE

Anxiety and Constriction in Social Situations

1.	I usually don't like to talk much unless I am with people I know very well.	True*	False
2.	I like to talk before groups of people.	True	False*
3.	It is hard for me to start a conversation with strangers.	True*	False
4.	I would like to be an actor on the stage or in the movies.	True	False*
5.	It is hard for me to act natural when I am with new people.	True*	False
6.	I feel nervous if I have to meet a lot of people.	True*	False
7.	I usually feel nervous and ill at ease at a formal dance or party.	True*	False
8.	When I work on a committee I like to take charge of things.	True	False *
9.	I usually take an active part in the entertainment at parties.	True	False*
10.	I am a better talker than listener.	True	False*
11.	I try to remember good stories to pass them on to other people.	True	False*
12.	I am embarrassed with people I do not know well.	True*	False
13.	A strong person doesn't show his emotions and feelings.	True*	False

Need for a stable, orderly, predictable environment; perseverative tendencies

14.	I must admit that it makes me angry when other people interfere with my daily activity.	True*	False
15.	I find that a well-ordered mode of life with regular hours is congenial to my temperment.	True*	False
16.	It bothers me when something unexpected interrupts my daily routine.	True*	False
17.	I don't like to undertake any project unless I have a pretty good idea as to how it will turn out.	True*	False
18.	I find it hard to set aside a task that I have undertaken, even for a short time.	True*	False
19.	I don't like things to be uncertain and unpredictable.	True*	False

Slowness in coming to a decision--compulsive doubting

20.	I am very slow in making up my mind.	True*	False
21.	At times I feel that I can make up my mind with unusually great ease.	True	False *

Conservatism and conventionality

22.	I must admit I try to see what others think before I take a stand.	True*	False
23.	I do not like to see women smoke.	True*	False
24.	I would be uncomfortable in anything other than fairly conventional dress.	True*	False
25.	I keep out of trouble at all costs.	True*	False

26. It wouldn't make me nervous if any members of my family got into trouble with the law.   True   False*
27. I must admit that I would find it hard to have for a close friend a person whose manners or appearance made him somewhat repulsive, no matter how brilliant or kind he might be.   True*   False
28. I would certainly enjoy beating a crook at his own game.   True   False*
29. I would like the job of a foreign correspondent for a newspaper.   True   False*

Self-doubt and sensitivity to negative criticism.

30. I get very tense and anxious when I think other people are disapproving of me.   True*   False
31. I am certainly lacking in self-confidence.   True*   False
32. Criticism or scolding makes me very uncomfortable.   True*   False

Misanthropy and parsimony

33. Most people inwardly dislike putting themselves out to help other people.   True*   False
34. I am against giving money to beggars.   True*   False
35. Many of the girls I knew in college went with a fellow only for what they could get out of him.   True*   False

Emphatic concern with work and study

36. I always follow the rule: business before pleasure.   True*   False
37. I get disgusted with myself when I can't understand some problem in my field, or when I can't seem to make any progress on a research problem.   True*   False

Miscellaneous

38. I have never been made especially nervous over trouble that any members of my family have gotten into.   True*   False
39. I have no fear of spiders.   True*   False

---

* Indicates rigid response.

RAPH SCALE (RIGIDITY OF ATTITUDES REGARDING PERSONAL HABITS)
(Meresko, Rubin, Shontz and Morrow 1954)

Variable
This scale is designed to measure rigidity as manifested by attitudes concerning personal habits. The authors define psychological rigidity as a person's resistance or lack of readiness to be influenced by motivationally relevant stimulation in such a way as to adjust to his environment as effectively as his behavior-repertory permits.

Description
The RAPH Scale consists of 20 six-point Likert-type items. The 20 items can be grouped according to which of two aspects of rigidity they reflect. The first, opposition to change as such, includes traditionalism, rule-riddeness, opposition to any change of judgment and opposition to any change of plans. The second aspect is intolerance of ambiguity, either regarding a specific situation or regarding plans or expectation for the future. Some items reflect both aspects.

In constructing the scale from an original 32 items, 12 items were excluded by an item analysis. No further information pertaining to the construction of this scale was given.

A subject score is the sum of the numerical values assigned to each of his responses, 0-6, with the value 3 being a neutral category indicating omission of response. All items are positively scored except 1 and 14. The range of possible scores is from 0 to 120 with a high score indicating high rigidity.

Sample
The sample used for constructing this scale was a group of 60 undergraduate college students, otherwise undescribed.

Reliability/
Homogeneity
The corrected odd-even reliability coefficient on the original sample was .75. On a sample of 188 college students given the final 20-item scale, the corrected odd-even reliability coefficient was .78. Every item on the final scale showed a significant correlation with total scale scores.

Validity
No information directly pertaining to validity was reported.

Location
Meresko, R., Rubin, M., Shontz, F.C., and Morrow, W.R., Rigidity of attitudes regarding personal habits and its ideological correlates, Journal of Abnormal and Social Psychology, 1954, 49, 89-93.

Administration
This test is self-administered. To complete this test, an estimated 15 minutes would be required.

Results and
Comments

The 32 preliminary items correlated .82 with a 20-item form of the F Scale for the sample of 60. The final form of the RAPH Scale correlated .62 with the same form of the F Scale for a sample of 188. For this same sample, all 20 items showed discriminatory power beyond the .01 level.

The main purpose of the article from which this scale was taken was to test hypotheses regarding the attitudes of American college students. Consequently, a minimum amount of information regarding the RAPH Scale itself (which was constructed to help test the hypotheses) was reported. No test-retest reliability coefficients are reported and, as noted above, there is almost no information given about construction procedures, subjects, or item-analysis.

More information about validity is needed for this scale, as well as a better understanding of the overlap between rigidity (as measured by this scale), "intolerance of ambiguity" (theoretically a characteristic of authoritarian personalities), and other dimensions of authoritarianism.

THE RAPH SCALE
(* Reversed items)

(a) Traditionalism

6. In whatever one does, the "tried and true" ways are always
the best.

| Strongly
Agree | Agree | Slightly
Agree | Slightly
Disagree | Disagree | Strongly
Disagree |

(b) Rule-riddeness

5. A self-respecting person should never permit himself to relax his
vigilance over personal habits; seemingly minor lapses can easily
grow into complete breakdown of self-discipline.

9. The rules of logic are the rules of life.

10. If I had a new car, I'd always keep it nicely cleaned and polished.

11. "A place for everything and everything in its place" is a pretty
good motto to live by.

15. One of the major aims of education should be to give us a few
simple rules of behavior to apply in every situation.

16. The biggest advantage man possesses over lower animals is his
ability to regulate himself and live by definite and unchanging
rules of conduct.

19. Every person should live by a few good and unchanging rules of
conduct; that way he can never go wrong.

(c) Opposition to any change of judgment

8. It's a good idea to have a strong point of view about things
because that makes it easier to decide what's wrong or right.

17. A person who seldom changes his mind can usually be depended upon
to have sound and reliable judgment on matters of importance.

18. Once a person makes up his mind about something he should stick to
his conclusion instead of repeatedly rehashing the question.

(d) Opposition to any change of plans

* 1. I rather like the idea of having friends drop in unexpectedly
at odd hours.

Reprinted with permission of Meresko, R., Rubin, M., Shontz, F. C., and Morrow, W. R. RAPH
Scale in "Rigidity of Attitudes Regarding Personal Habits and Its Ideological Correlates," *Journal of
Abnormal and Social Psychology*, 49 (1954), pp 89-93. Copyright 1954 by the American Psychological
Association.

2. I dislike doing anything just on the spur of the moment.

4. Few things are more upsetting than a sudden unexpected change of plans.

7. I never start anything I can't finish.

13. Once a person starts going off his budget, even by small amounts, he's on the road to financial difficulty.

20. The only way to make sure that things get done right is to set up a definite and fixed schedule and never depart from it.

(e) Intolerance of ambiguity manifested in specific situations

3. I don't much like the kind of painting that doesn't tell a story or doesn't portray something in a clear, unambiguous fashion.

(f) Intolerance of ambiguity regarding expectations or plans for the future

12. The best way to enjoy a vacation is to plan every detail carefully before you leave.

* 14. I rather like the idea of having my meals at odd hours and of going to bed when the mood strikes me.

RIGIDITY SCALE (Wesley 1953)

Variable

Wesley defines rigidity as the "tendency to persist in responses that may previously have been suitable in some situation or other but that no longer appear adequate to achieve current goals or to solve current problems."

Description

The Wesley Rigidity Scale consists of 67 items, 50 of which are used to measure rigidity. The remaining 17 items used as filler items, are taken from the Minnesota Multiphase L, F, and P+ Scales. The subject responds "true" or "false" to each item indicating whether or not the statement applies to himself. He receives one point for every rigid answer (see list of items for rigid answer key). The 50 rigidity items were selected from a pool of 90 which the author drew from various personality tests (notably the Gough-Sanford Rigidity Scale) or constructed herself. Five clinical psychologists rated each item in the pool on the degree of rigidity it expressed. The 50 items selected were judged by all five judges to express a high degree of rigidity.

Sample

The original sample receiving the test was an unspecified number of undergraduates taking psychology courses. From this group, the following three groups were selected for Wesley's study on the basis of their scores on the Wesley Rigidity Scale and the "Manifest Anxiety Scale."

1) Rigid Group: 21 subjects who scored in the upper tenth of the Rigidity Scale (28 and above) and below the 60th percentile of the Anxiety Scale.

2) Anxious Group: 21 subjects who scored in the upper tenth of the Anxiety Scale and below the median (23) on the Rigidity Scale.

3) Normal Group: 30 subjects scoring below the median on both scales.

All subjects received a T Score of 50 or less on the L Scale of the MMPI.

Reliability

No reliability data were given, other than the fact that the five clinical psychologists rated all 50 items as "high."

Validity

The three groups selected for the study were required to learn a card sorting task resembling the Wisconsin Card-Sorting Test, which involves the formation of concepts and the shifting of the concepts. When the scores on this task were corrected for differences in rate of original learning, the rigid group took significantly longer to shift sets on subsequent series and gave significantly more preservative responses. Thus, rigidity as measured by this scale seems to be related to a behavioral measure of this concept (as defined by Wesley and quoted above).

398

Location
Wesley, Elizabeth. Perseverative behavior, manifest anxiety, and rigidity, <u>Journal of Abnormal and Social Psychology</u>, 1953, <u>48</u>, 129-134.

Administration
The test of 67 items would take approximately 25 minutes for a subject to complete. He receives one point for each rigid answer given in response to the 50 items that comprise the scale (see item list for rigid response key).

Results and Comments
In a separate study by Wrightsman (private communication), 207 subjects received this scale. His subjects had a mean of 22.16 and an s.d. of 6.13. The ability of this scale to discriminate among different amounts of "rigidity" seems open to question. If the upper divide is 28 and above and the median is 23 (according to Wesley's data) then 40 percent of his subjects have scored between 23 and 28 on a 50 point scale.

The relationship between the sort of rigidity measured by this scale and dogmatism or authoritarianism remains to be studied. Looking at the items, however, points up at least some overlap-- notice, for example, the mention of church-attendance, duty, sexual freedom for women, and conventionalism. Also Rokeach has reported relevant evidence, thought not based on this particular scale (1948; 1960).

References
Rokeach, M. Generalized mental rigidity as a factor in ethnocentrism, <u>Journal of Abnormal and Social Psychology</u>, 1948, <u>43</u>, 259-278.

Rokeach, M. <u>The open and closed mind</u>. New York: Basic Books, 1960.

RIGIDITY SCALE

+	I am often the last one to give up trying to do a thing.	True* False
+	There is usually only one best way to solve most problems.	True* False
+	I prefer work that requires a great deal of attention to detail.	True* False
+	I often become so wrapped up in something I am doing that I find it difficult to turn my attention to other matters.	True* False
	I prefer doing one thing at a time to keeping several projects going.	True* False
+	I dislike to change my plans in the midst of an undertaking.	True* False
+	I never miss going to church.	True* False
	I would like a position which requires frequent changes from one kind of task to another.	True False*
+	I usually maintain my own opinions even though many other people may have a different point of view.	True* False
+	I find it easy to stick to a certain schedule, once I have started on it.	True* False
	I believe women ought to have as much sexual freedom as men.	True False*
+	I do not enjoy having to adapt myself to new and unusual situations.	True* False
+	I prefer to stop and think before I act even on trifling matters.	True False*
	I would not like the kind of work which involves a large number of different activities.	True* False
+	I try to follow a program of life based on duty.	True* False
	I have kept a careful diary over a period of years.	True* False
	My interests tend to change quickly.	True False*
+	I usually find that my own way of attacking a problem is best, even though it doesn't always seem to work in the beginning.	True* False
	I dislike having to learn new ways of doing things.	True* False
	I like a great deal of variety in my work.	True False*
+	I am a methodical person in whatever I do.	True* False
	I am usually able to keep at a job longer than most people.	True* False

Reprinted with permission of Wesley, E. Rigidity Scale in "Perseverative Behavior, Manifest Anxiety, and Rigidity," *Journal of Abnormal and Social Psychology,* 48 (1953), pp 129-134. Copyright 1953 by the American Psychological Association.

RIGIDITY SCALE (Continued)

+	I think it is usually wise to do things in a conventional way.	True*	False
+	I always finish tasks I start, even if they are not very important.	True*	False
	People who go about their work methodically are almost always the most successful.	True*	False
	When I have undertaken a task, I find it difficult to set it aside, even for a short time.	True*	False
+	I often find myself thinking of the same tune or phrases for days at a time.	True*	False
+	I have a work and study schedule which I follow carefully.	True*	False
+	I usually check more than once to be sure that I have locked a door, put out the light, or something of the sort.	True*	False
+	I have never done anything dangerous for the thrill of it.	True*	False
	It is always a good thing to be frank.	True*	False
	I have a habit of collecting various kinds of objects.	True*	False
	I have taken a good many courses on the spur of the moment.	True	False*
+	I believe that promptness is a very important personality characteristic.	True*	False
	My interests change very quickly.	True	False*
	It is the slow, steady worker who usually accomplishes the most in the end.	True*	False
+	I am always careful about my manner of dress.	True*	False
	I usually dislike to set aside a task that I have undertaken until it is finished.	True*	False
	I am inclined to go from one activity to another without continuing with any one for too long a time.	True	False*
	I prefer to do things according to a routine which I plan myself.	True*	False
+	I always put on and take off my clothes in the same order.	True*	False

---

* Answers that show rigidity
+ Items taken from the Gough-Sanford Rigidity Scale, an adaption of which is included in the well-known California Personality Inventory.

Note: The copy of Wesley's items made available to us only contained 41, rather than 50, items.

INTOLERANCE OF AMBIGUITY (Budner 1962)

Variable   Intolerance of ambiguity is defined as "the tendency to perceive (i.e., interpret) ambiguous situations as sources of threat;" tolerance of ambiguity as "the tendency to perceive ambiguous situations as desirable." Ambiguity arises in situations characterized by novelty, complexity, or insolubility. Threat responses include repression and denial, anxiety and discomfort, destructive behavior and avoidance behavior. Budner classifies these responses under four headings: phenomenological submission and denial, and operative (behavioral) submission and denial.

Description   An initial pool of 33 items, conforming to the three types of ambiguous situations and four kinds of threat responses mentioned above, were administered in three pretests (in six-point Likert form). Only items yielding a Pearson r of .35 or higher were included in the final scale. Ten positively worded and eight negatively worded items met this criterion; two of the positive were dropped to yield a balanced 16-item scale (presented below). Scoring is accomplished by assigning 7 to strong agreement, 1 to strong disagreement, and so on, then adding across all items. (Notice that negatively-worded items are scored in the reverse direction.)

Samples   Pretest

1. Two introductory sociology classes (combined) in the adult education division of a private university in New York City (N = 35).

2. An evening session class in graduate business administration at a university in New York City (N = 37).

3. Two elective classes in education (combined) at one of the municipal colleges in New York City (N = 45).

Further study

Sample	Mean	Variance	Reliability	N
4. An introductory psychology class, all freshmen, at a college in New York City suburbs (N = 50)	50.9	103.4	.62	50
5. An evening introductory psychology class in the same school (N = 57)	53.0	99.9	.49	57
6. Two elective sociology classes (combined) at a private women's college in New York City (N = 41)	43.3	56.5	.47	41
7. Two classes of engineering students (combined) in a required social studies course at a municipal college in New York City (N = 58)	48.9	81.5	.43	58
8. Two advanced classes in sociology (combined) at a private college in New York City (N = 33)	49.3	62.9	.57	33

Sample	Mean	Variance	Reliability	N
9. A group of first-year student nurses at a local hospital in New York City (N = 34)	51.9	87.2	.42	34
10. Two classes in a special English course (combined) at one of the elite high schools in New York City (N = 62)	48.2	66.1	.40	62
11. The first-year class at an eastern medical school (N = 79)	44.6	86.8	.62	79
12. The second-year class at the same school (N = 75)	44.8	68.3	.45	75
13. The third-year class at the same school (N = 75)	44.3	63.4	.46	75
14. The first-year class at a midwestern medical school (N = 83)	45.0	60.4	.39	83
15. The second-year class at the same school (N = 80)	44.0	71.5	.49	80
16. The third-year class at the same school (N = 86)	46.5	69.2	.51	86

Reliability   Reliabilities reported above were computed by Cronbach's alpha formula (Guilford 1954). A 17th sample of 15 graduate students was used in a test-retest study over a period of two to four weeks, and a correlation of .85 was obtained. Although the alpha reliabilities appear lower than the more common split-half coefficients, the instrument seems to have acceptable reliability considering its probable multidimensionality.

Validity   A measure of acquiescence or "agreement response set" did not yield significant correlations with Budner's scale, nor did Edwards' Scale of Social Desirability.

From sample #7 above, scores on three other tolerance of ambiguity scales were obtained: Coulter Scale (Eysenck 1954), Walk Scale (O'Connor 1952), Princeton Scale (Saunders 1955). They correlate as follows:

	1. Present Scale	2. Princeton[a] Scale	3. Coulter[b] Scale	4. Walk[c] Scale
1.	--	.50*	.36*	.54*
2.		--	.17	.34*
3.			--	.47*
4.				--

[a] Taken from Saunders, 1955

[b] Taken from Eysenck, 1954

[c] Taken from O'Connor, 1952

* $\leq$ .05

Other validity studies, involving interjudge agreement on ratings of respondents' intolerance of ambiguity, also supported the validity of the Budner scale.

Finally, in a long series of correlational studies the ambiguity scale was found to correlate with conventionality, belief in divine power, attendance at religious services, dogmatism about one's religious beliefs, and favorable attitudes toward censorship. The scale also correlated moderately with F (a balanced version constructed by Christie, Havel, and Seidenberg, 1958) as follows:

Intolerance of Ambiguity and Authoritarianism

	r	N
4. Suburban day	.19	50
5. Suburban night	.35*	57
6. Women's college	.35*	41
7. Municipal college	.17	58
8. Private college	.42*	33
9. Nursing students	.25	34
11. First-year eastern medical students	.26*	79
12. Second-year eastern medical students	.31*	75
13. Third-year eastern medical students	.55*	75

*$p < .05$

Location	Budner, S. Intolerance of ambiguity as a personality variable. Journal of Personality, 1962, 30, 29-50.
Administration	This scale is self-administered and would take between 10 and 15 minutes to complete.
Results and Comments	This appears to be a good scale for measuring intolerance of ambiguity as it was conceptualized by the early writers on authoritarianism. Its moderate correlation with the Christie F Scale suggests trait overlap, but not complete congruence. Intolerance of ambiguity is most likely just one of several characteristics that contribute to high F scores.

The reader interested in empirical correlates of Budner's scale, mentioned briefly under "validity" above, should consult his article. It is quite long and includes detailed information about several interesting correlational studies. Also, Budner's dissertation (1960) may be of interest. |
| References | Budner, S. An investigation of intolerance of ambiguity. Unpublished doctoral dissertation, Columbia University, 1960.

Christie, R., Havel, Joan, and Seidenberg, B. Is the F scale irreversible? Journal of Abnormal and Social Psychology, 1958, 56, 143-159. |

Eysenck, H.J. The psychology of politics. London: Routledge and Kagan Paul, 1954.

Guilford, J.P. Psychometric methods, 2nd ed. New York: McGraw-Hill, 1954.

O'Connor, Patricia. Ethnocentrism, 'intolerance of ambiguity,' and abstract reasoning ability. Journal of Abnormal Psychology, 1952, 47, 526-530.

Saunders, D.H. Some preliminary interpretive material for the PRI. Research memorandum 55-15. Educational Testing Service, October, 1955.

INTOLERANCE OF AMBIGUITY

	Designed to tap[a]	
	Type of Response	Type of Situation

Positive items:

1. An expert who doesn't come up with a definite answer probably doesn't know too much	PD	I
2. There is really no such thing as a problem that can't be solved	PD	I
3. A good job is one where what is to be done and how it is to be done are always clear	OS	C
4. In the long run it is possible to get more done by tackling small, simple problems rather than large and complicated ones	OS	C
5. What we are used to is always preferable to what is unfamiliar	PS	N
6. A person who leads an even, regular life in which few surprises or unexpected happenings arise, really has a lot to be grateful for.	PS	N
7. I like parties where I know most of the people more than ones where all or most of the people are complete strangers.	PS	N
8. The sooner we all acquire similar values and ideals the better.	OD	C

Negative items:

9. I would like to live in a foreign country for a while.	PS	N
10. People who fit their lives to a schedule probably miss most of the joy of living.	PS	C
11. It is more fun to tackle a complicated problem than to solve a simple one.	PS	C
12. Often the most interesting and stimulating people are those who don't mind being different and original.	PS	C
13. People who insist upon a yes or no answer just don't know how complicated things really are.	PD	C
14. Many of our most important decisions are based upon insufficient information.	PD	I
15. Teachers or supervisors who hand out vague assignments give a chance for one to show initiative and originality.	OS	C
16. A good teacher is one who makes you wonder about your way of looking at things.	OS	C

---

[a] Codes are as follows:

Type of response	Type of situation
PD - phenomenological denial	I - insolubility
OS - operative submission	C - complexity
PS - phenomenological submission	N - novelty
OD - operative denial	

INTOLERANCE OF AMBIGUITY SCALE (Martin and Westie 1959)

Variable
: This scale was designed to measure intolerance of ambiguity as conceptualized in the original work on the authoritarian syndrome (e.g., Frenkel-Brunswik, 1949; 1951). According to this conceptual scheme, intolerant and authoritarian persons tend to perceive dimensionalized stimuli as absolutely dichotomized, to seek unambiguous solutions for complex problems, to demonstrate rigid, categorical thinking, and so on.

Description
: In a study of prejudice toward Negroes, Martin and Westie (1959) attempted to characterize the "tolerant personality"----one who is neither extremely negative or extremely positive in his attitudes. Tolerance was assessed with Westie's (1953) Summated Difference Scales; two groups were selected from 429 initial respondents----41 who were relatively neutral (tolerant) and 59 who were conspicuously prejudiced against Negroes. These groups were then compared on several other dimensions, including intolerance of ambiguity.

The scale used for this latter dimension contains eight items, each scored along a five-point agree-disagree continuum (Likert-type). Scoring is accomplished simply by summing across items.

Sample
: The sampling universe for this study was all "white adults (21 years of age or older) residing within the city limits of Indianapolis in blocks containing no Negro residents." From 429 initial respondents who completed a short prognostic scale (used to avoid detailed interviews of too many prejudiced respondents), 41 qualified as "tolerant" and 59 were chosen who had high prejudice scores.

Reliability
: No information given.

Validity
: The intolerance of ambiguity scale bears close resemblance to several items on the original F Scale, thus suggesting relevant face validity. Further, the scale significantly distinguished between the tolerant and prejudiced respondents ($p < .001$) and correlated as follows with related measures:

CORRELATION MATRIX OF SCALE SCORES OF TOLERANT SUBJECTS (N=41)

Scale	1	2	3	4	5	6	7
1 Nationalism	X	.22	.39*	.01	.28	.41*	.10
2 Intolerance of ambiguity		X	.37*	-.01	.34*	.32*	.48*
3 Superstition-pseudo-science			X	.24	.40*	.31*	.36*
4 Threat-competition				X	.17	-.08	.28
5 "F"					X	.56*	.62*
6 Religiosity						X	.48*
7 Child rearing							X

* Significantly different from zero at the .05 level.

CORRELATION MATRIX OF SCALE SCORES OF PREJUDICED SUBJECTS (N=59)

Scale	1	2	3	4	5	6	7
1 Nationalism	X	.32*	.32*	.22	.28*	.12	.19
2 Intolerance of ambiguity		X	.54*	.62*	.72*	.13	.29
3 Superstition-pseudo-science			X	.52*	.58*	.02	.14
4 Threat-competition				X	.70*	-.08	.30*
5 "F"					X	.14	.28*
6 Religiosity						X	.22
7 Child rearing							X

* Significantly different from zero at the .05 level.

Location   Martin, J.G. and Westie, F.R. The tolerant personality, American Sociological Review, 1959, 24, 521-528.

Administration   This scale would take only about five minutes to complete.

Results and
  Comments   The findings of this research were quite consistent with the original work by Adorno, et al., (1950) on authoritarianism. Specifically, tolerant persons do differ significantly on several components of an authoritarian "syndrome", including intolerance of ambiguity. (The other "components" are listed in the correlation tables above. The measure of religiosity is discussed later in Chapter 9 of this volume.) The Martin and Westie scale, however, could use further study, especially with regard to reliability. Also, it would be useful to see how it relates to the other measures of intolerance and cognitive rigidity presented in the present chapter.

References   Adorno, T.W., et al. The authoritarian personality. New York: Harpers, 1950.

Frenkel-Brunswik, Else. Intolerance of ambiguity as an emotional and perceptual personality variable, Journal of Personality, 1949, 18, 108-143.

Frenkel-Brunswik, Else. Personality theory and perception. In R.R. Blake and G.V. Ramsey (eds.), Perception: An approach to personality. New York: Ronald, 1951, pp. 356-419.

Westie, F.R. A technique for the measurement of race attitudes, American Sociological Review, 1953, 18, 73-78.

INTOLERANCE OF AMBIGUITY SCALE

1. There are two kinds of people in the world: the weak and the strong.

   Strongly agree   Agree   Undecided   Disagree   Strongly disagree

2. A person is either a 100% American or he isn't.

3. A person either knows the answer to a question or he doesn't.

4. There are two kinds of women: the pure and the bad.

5. You can classify almost all people as either honest or crooked.

6. First impressions are very important.

7. It doesn't take very long to find out if you can trust a person.

8. There is only one right way to do anything.

DESIRE FOR CERTAINTY TEST (Brim 1955)

Variable
This scale was constructed to measure individual differences in motivation for certainty. It is closely related conceptually to "intolerance of ambiguity" as this is viewed by researchers on authoritarianism (see especially Else Frenkel-Brunswik 1949; 1951). (Some important qualifications regarding empirical similarity are mentioned below in "Results and Comments.")

Description
The Desire for Certainty Test comprises 32 statements about every-day events; e.g., "The chances that an American citizen will believe in God are about ____ in 100." Respondents place a probability value in the blank space in each such sentence. In addition, they indicate their confidence in each estimate by rating it on a five-point certainty scale from 1 (very sure) to 5 (not sure at all).

The statements included four from each of eight different subject-matter areas: education, recreation, politics, economics, religion, health, family, transportation and communication. Half were in agreement with generally accepted American values, half were not. Each had a different estimated true probability value drawn from a set of 32 values between 1 and 46 or 54 and 99. Combinations of the three criteria--subject matter, value-agreement, and true probability-- were determined randomly, and then a statement was written to conform to each particular combination of these criteria.

Scoring is based on the assumption that a strong desire for certainty will be expressed by two tendencies: 1) to select probability values close to the extremes of 0 and 100; and 2) to express confidence in these extreme choices. Thus, the authors took the distance of each probability estimate from its nearest end point (0 or 100) and multiplied this value by its certainty score (very sure = 1; not sure at all = 5). The products were then summed over all 32 test items. Notice that by this procedure a low score indicates a high desire for certainty.

Sample
Reliability and validity information was reported for several different groups of college students, all of whom were enrolled in introductory sociology courses. (The tests were administered during class periods.)

Reliability/ Homogeneity
For one group of students (N = 50), a corrected split-half reliability coefficient of .81 was obtained.

Validity
For 500 students the test scores "appeared" normally distributed. For a sub-sample of 200 there was no relationship between test scores and "standard socioeconomic variables." For a subsample of 100 there was no relationship with intelligence (r = -.07; the intelligence measure was not specified). Notice, however, that since all respondents were college students the range of SES and intelligence variables was not as great as would be found in a more general sample.

A study by Brim and Hoff (1957) offers construct validity for the scale. "Desire for certainty" was found to be significantly related to extreme responding on several measures, including a variety of attitude scales and judgments of roommates' personality traits. In an experiment some subjects were frustrated in an attempt to achieve perceptual order and clarity, while others were "satisfied" in this attempt. A third (control) group received no manipulation. There were significant differences between all groups on the Desire for Certainty Test, with the "frustrated" group showing the strongest "desire."

Finally, it should be noted that a marginally significant <u>curvilinear</u> relationship was obtained between this test and the original F Scale (see Results and Comments below).

Location   Brim, O.G., Jr.   Attitude content - intensity and probability expecta-
                tions.   <u>American Sociological Review</u>, 1955, <u>20</u>, 68-76.

Administration No time estimate was mentioned by Brim, but the test would probably
                take about 20 minutes for self-administration.

Results and   It is not clear whether this test measures intolerance of ambiguity
Comments   as conceived by Frenkel-Brunswik (1949, 1951), because instead of
                obtaining a linear relationship with F scores, as did Frenkel-Brunswik,
                Brim found a curvilinear relationship. This suggests that respon-
                dents who are on one extreme or the other of the authoritarianism scale
                are also at the extremes on the Desire for Certainty Test. Clearly,
                this relationship deserves further study because of its possible con-
                nection with the issues of dogmatism independent of ideological con-
                tent and general response biases.

                It is worth noting again that Brim and Hoff used only college student
                samples, so their finding of no relationship between desire for cer-
                tainty and education or SES needs further study in other groups.

                The successful experimental manipulation of "desire for certainty"
                lends credence to the validity of the theoretical notions behind
                Brim's scale, and makes further understanding of the relationship
                between authoritarianism, intolerance for ambiguity, and desire for
                certainty a fruitful topic for further work.

References   Brim, O. and Hoff, D.   Individual and situational differences in
                desire for certainty. <u>Journal of Abnormal and Social Psychology</u>,
                1957, <u>54</u>, 225-229

                Frenkel-Brunswik, Else.   Intolerance of ambiguity as an emotional
                and perceptual personality variable.   <u>Journal of Personality</u>, 1949,
                <u>18</u>, 108-143.

                Frenkel-Brunswik, Else.   Personality theory and perception.   In
                R.R. Blake and G.V. Ramsey (eds.), <u>Perception: an approach to
                personality</u>, New York: Ronald, 1951, 356-419.

DESIRE FOR CERTAINTY

1. <u>The chances that</u> an adult American male will earn at least $4000 a year <u>are about</u> .... in 100.

2. <u>The chances that</u> a student entering law school will quit before getting his law degree <u>are about</u> .... in 100.

3. _____ frequent thumbsucking during childhood will make teeth stick out (cause buck teeth) _____.

4. _____ the president of the United States will be a man without a college education _____.

5. _____ a major league baseball team will win the pennant if it is in first place July 4th _____.

6. _____ a sexual pervert will have a low intelligence (IQ 80 or less) _____.

7. _____ a highschool graduate will go on to a freshman year in college _____.

8. _____ a couple getting married this year will later have divorce _____.

9. _____ an American male now at the age of 40 will live beyond the age of 55 _____.

10. _____ an American family will live in a place without a telephone _____.

11. _____ an American family will own its own home _____.

12. _____ the telephone number you call will be busy _____.

13. _____ an American citizen will believe in God _____.

14. _____ a varsity football player in an American university will be subsidized (given money for his football ability) _____.

15. _____ an American city of over 50,000 people will have a chapter of the League of Women Voters _____.

16. _____ the governor of a state will be elected for a second term in office _____.

17. _____ a son will go into the same kind of work as his father _____.

18. _____ a man 70 years old will need financial help from someone to support himself _____.

19. _____ spanking a child will make him tell the truth next time _____.

20. _____ an American-born baby will get a poor and inadequate diet during his first year of life _____ .

21. _____ an adult male will stay home instead of going to church on Sunday _____ .

22. _____ a sixth grade teacher in the public schools will be a man _____ .

23. _____ a child whose parents are divorced will be neurotic _____ .

24. _____ in the United States that a girl will be married before the age of 17 _____ .

25. _____ a world's champion boxer comes from a poor family _____ .

26. _____ an American citizen will be bilingual (speak two languages) _____ .

27. _____ a five card deal will have two cards of the same kind (one pair) _____ .

28. _____ a man with a broken neck will die _____ .

29. _____ a crime in the United States will be solved (someone arrested and convicted for it) _____ .

30. _____ the number of auto accidents in a year will be higher than for the year just before _____ .

31. _____ a small business (for examples, gas station, motel) will fail within 2 years after starting _____ .

32. _____ the person one marries will have the same religion _____ .

ETHNOCENTRIC DEMOCRACY (Hyman, Wright and Hopkins 1962)

Variable   The items in this scale reflect the degree to which a person rejects practices in democratic countries.

Description   The scale consists of nine descriptions of practices in democracies. The respondent is asked to judge whether each practice is "thoroughly democratic," "undemocratic but tolerable," or "thoroughly undemocratic." One point is scored for each "thoroughly undemocratic" response, and hence scores run from 0 (low ethnocentrism) to 9 (high ethnocentrism). Median score for the sample in question was around 3.1 before "encampment."

Sample   The sample consisted of 364 young persons who attended the "Encampment for Citizenship" in 1955-58. These young people were chosen to attend the camp because of their democratic orientations and leadership qualities in order to improve upon these skills.

Reliability/   No reliability data are reported.
Homogeneity

Validity   No validity data are reported.

Location   Hyman, H., Wright, C. and Hopkins, T. Application of methods of evaluation. Berkeley, Cal.: University of California Press, 1962.

Results and   Median scores after encampment were about 2.9, which was not a
Comments   significant change.

This scale is included here because of the potentially fruitful approach it represents. Much further work on it is required.

ETHNOCENTRIC IMAGE OF DEMOCRACY

In some democracies there are certain customs or laws which you personally might or might not regard as democratic. Look over the following list and check whether each practice appears thoroughly democratic, somewhat undemocratic but tolerable in a democracy, or thoroughly undemocratic in your personal opinion:

1. In Australia, every citizen is required by law to vote.

   This practice seems to me: thoroughly democratic, undemocratic but tolerable, thoroughly undemocratic.

2. Until recently, in Sweden, most babies were automatically registered as members of the Lutheran Church, the state religion.

3. Until recently, in Sweden, the amount of alcohol that a person could buy each month was regulated by law.

4. In France, you must pay for a license in order to have a radio set in your home.

5. In the United States, all children must be vaccinated against small-pox.

6. In Great Britain, under the law, doctors no longer collect their fees from patients but bill the government.

7. In Norway, any Jesuit is prohibited by law from entering the country.

8. In Japan, all school children wear uniforms.

9. In the United States, one may legally have only one husband or wife at a time.

TOUGHMINDEDNESS (T) SCALE (Eysenck 1954)

Variable	This scale was not constructed as a measure of a specific personality variable but rather emerged from an attempt to discern the primary dimensions underlying people's social attitudes and beliefs. Factor analysis yielded two basic dimensions which the author has labeled "radicalism-conservatism" and "tendermindedness-toughmindedness."
Description	The original scale was composed of 40 five-point Likert-type items chosen from a pool of 500 attitude items. All items in the literature were included "which had been shown to have high saturations on any factor isolated by any method whatever." A factor analysis was carried out using Burt's Summation Method. The first factor, accounting for 18 percent of the variance, was labeled "radicalism-conservatism," and included 14 items; put together, these make up the R Scale. An orthogonal dimension emerged, accounting for 8 percent of the variance and labeled "tendermindedness-toughmindedness," which is assessed by the 14-item T Scale. Eleven of the 14 items in the T Scale are identical to those in the R Scale.
	One point was awarded for agreement (of either degree) with the response key (see below) and a zero for disagreement or a neutral answer.
Sample	This scale was administered to 750 respondents: 250 were conservatives, 250 liberals, and 250 socialists. They were matched for sex and age (over or under 30); all were middleclass, urban Britishers. This group was obtained by Eysenck's students from contacts with family and friends, so it is not necessarily representative.
Reliability	The two scales (R and T) were divided randomly into halves (labeled R_1, R_2 and T_1, T_2 in the list below). The split-half correlation for the entire sample was .81 for the R Scale and .64 for the T Scale.
Validity	One rough index of validity was obtained by having students rate what they thought relatives and friends should answer. These agreed 98 percent with the actual ratings, but were probably contaminated by discussion with respondents, and so on.
	In his 1954 book, Eysenck cites evidence that the T Scale is related to independent measures of introversion-extroversion. This supports his view that, whereas the R Scale measures attitude-content, the T Scale measures the effect of underlying personality dynamics on social attitudes.
Location	Eysenck, H. J. Primary social attitudes: I. The organization and measurement of social attitudes, _International Journal of Opinion and Attitude Research_, 1947, 1, 49-84.
	Eysenck, H. J. _The psychology of politics._ London: Routledge and Kegan Paul, 1954.

Administration   The scale would take about 10 minutes to complete.

Results and   In 1956, after the digestion of Eysenck's 1954 book, two sets of
Comments   heated attacks on it appeared in the Psychological Bulletin, one
                  set by Rokeach and Hanley (1956 a, b) and the other by Christie
                  (1956 a, b). Eysenck replied to both (1956 a, b). The main
                  criticisms included improper computations, unrepresentative sampling,
                  unusual scoring techniques, and faulty interpretation of data. The
                  last is most significant because it challenges Eysenck's interesting
                  claim that Communists and Fascists--representatives of both ends of
                  the R dimension--are about equally high on toughmindedness, a
                  characteristic similar to authoritarianism and related to
                  extroversion. Recapitulating this discussion is beyond the scope
                  of this book, but we recommend that anyone planning to use this
                  scale as it stands read it. Overall, it is our belief that
                  Eysenck's (1954) theoretical position is interesting enough to
                  encourage further work, even though improvement of both the T and
                  R Scales may be necessary. The R Scale is further described in
                  our main volume, Measures of Political Attitudes.

References   Christie, R.   Eysenck's treatment of the personality of communists,
                  Psychological Bulletin, 1956, 53, 411-430. (a)

                  Christie, R.   Some abuses of psychology, Psychological Bulletin,
                  1956, 53, 439-451. (b)

                  Eysenck, H. J.   The psychology of politics: a reply, Psychological
                  Bulletin, 1956, 53, 177-182. (a)

                  Eysenck, H. J.   The psychology of politics and the personality
                  similarities between fascists and communists, Psychological Bulletin,
                  1956, 53, 431-438. (b)

                  Rokeach, M. and Hanley, C.   Eysenck's tendermindedness dimension:
                  a critique, Psychological Bulletin, 1956, 53, 169-176. (a)

                  Rokeach, M. and Hanley, C.   Care and carelessness in psychology,
                  Psychological Bulletin, 1956, 53, 183-186. (b)

TOUGHMINDEDNESS SCALE

(Agreement with R+ items indicates Radicalism)
(Agreement with T- items indicates Toughmindedness)

1. Colored people are innately inferior to white people R_2- T_2-

3. War is inherent in human nature. R_2- T_2-

5. Persons with serious hereditary defects and diseases should be compulsorily sterilized. T_1-

8. In the interests of peace, we must give up part of our national sovereignty. R_1+ T_1+

9. Sunday-observance is old-fashioned, and should cease to govern our behavior. R_2+ T_2-

10. It is wrong that men should be permitted greater sexual freedom than women by society. T_2+

12. Ultimately, private property should be abolished, and complete socialism introduced . R_2+

13. Conscientious objectors are traitors to their country, and should be treated accordingly. T_1-

15. The laws against abortion should be abolished. R_1+ T_1-

16. Only by going back to religion can civilization hope to survive. R_2- T_2+

23. Divorce laws should be altered to make divorce easier. R_2+ T_1-

26. Crimes of violence should be punished by flogging. R_1-

27. The nationalization of the great industries is likely to lead to inefficiency, bureaucracy, and stagnation. R_1-

28. It is right and proper that religious education in schools should be compulsory. R_1- T_1+

29. Men and women have the right to find out whether they are sexually suited before marriage (e.g., by companionate marriage). R_1+ T_2-

36. The death penalty is barbaric, and should be abolished. R_2+ T_2+

39. The Japanese are by nature a cruel people. R_1- T_1-

Reprinted with permission of Eysenck, H. J. Toughmindedness (T) Scale in "Primary Social Attitudes: The Organization and Measurement of Social Attitudes," *International Journal of Opinion and Attitude Research,* 1 (1947), pp 49-84; and in *The Psychology of Politics* (London: Routledge and Kegan Paul, 1954).

DOGMATISM SCALE (Rokeach 1956)

Variable

This scale is designed to measure individual differences in openness or closedness of belief systems. Rokeach states that the extent to which a person's belief system is open is "the extent to which the person can receive, evaluate, and act on relevant information received from the outside on its own intrinsic merits, unencumbered by irrelevant factors in the situation arising from within the person or from the outside". (Rokeach, 1960, p. 57)

Description

This scale has been revised several times in an attempt to improve the reliability and also to make use of the refinements in the theoretical formulation. (The attached copy of items includes forms D & F). Form D is composed of 66 6-point Likert-type items. Form E is composed of the 40 best items from these 66. A total of 89 items were used throughout the various revisions. Each item had to go beyond any specific belief content and penetrate the structure of how the belief was held. People who dogmatically hold viewpoints as diverse as Communism, Capitalism, or Catholicism, should all score on one end of the continuum on the D Scale.

The items on forms D & E can be grouped according to a variety of categories. These categories are listed on the attached copy of the items. Responses were scored along a + 3 to -3 agree-disagree scale, with the 0 point excluded. These scores were converted to a 1 to 7 scale by adding the constant 4 to each score. The range of possible scores is from 66-462 on form D, and from 40-280 on form E. A high score indicates a high degree of dogmatism.

Subjects

Form A was administered to 202 MSU students. 207 students in New York City colleges received form B. Form C was given to the 207 New York City college students and to two groups of MSU students, 153 and 186. Form D was administered to 137 students at University College in London. 80 students at Birbeck College (England) and 60 English workers received form E.

Reliability

The following split-half reliabilities were obtained for the different forms.

Corrected Reliability of Successive Forms of the Dogmatism Scale

Form	Number of Items	Group	N	Reliability	M	SD
A	57	MSU I	202	.70	182.50	26.20
B	43	N.Y. Colleges	207	.75	141.35	27.21
C	36	(N.Y. Colleges	207	.84)*	120.00	19.46
		MSU II	153	.73	126.92	20.14
		MSU III	186	.71	128.34	19.17
D	66	English Colleges I	137	.91	219.10	28.30
E	40	English Colleges II	80	.81	152.80	26.20
		English Workers	60	.78	175.80	26.00

*Based upon a rescoring of the 36 best items out of the 43 items in form B.

Validity   The following table presents the results of an item analysis on forms D and E.

Item Analysis of the Dogmatism Scale, Form D

Items	Total Group (N=137) M	Highs (N=37) M	Lows (N=37) M
A. Based upon the structure of dogmatism.			
*1. U.S. and Russia have nothing in common.	2.88	3.43	2.16
2. Communism & Catholicism have nothing in common.	3.54	4.32	2.68
3. My principles are different from most others.	3.51	3.70	3.14
4. People bring up irrelevant issues.	5.99	6.46	5.81
*5. Belief in democracy run by most intelligent.	4.72	5.60	3.92
*6. Belief in free speech, but not for all.	4.16	5.11	3.27
7. Force is wrong, but sometimes necessary.	3.89	4.54	3.51
8. Masses intelligent, but also stupid.	5.64	6.11	5.00
*9. Worst crime is to attack those of similar beliefs.	2.74	3.30	1.76
*10. Guard against subversion from within.	3.96	4.78	2.81
*11. Groups tolerating diverse opinions can't exist.	3.35	4.32	2.19
*12. Better knowledge of beliefs than disbeliefs.	4.99	5.65	4.14
13. Certain "isms" really the same, not different.	4.59	5.19	4.08

Table (Continued)

Items	Total Group (N=137) M	Highs (N=37) M	Lows (N=37) M
*14. To know what's going on, rely on leaders.	3.80	5.46	3.08
*15. Reserve judgment until you hear leaders' opinion.	5.20	5.70	4.32
*16. Pick friends who believe as you do.	3.98	5.08	2.68
17. Don't waste money on reading opposing views.	3.42	3.76	2.97
18. Keep young people away from confusing books.	3.02	3.65	2.76
*19. Present unhappy. The future is what counts.	3.15	3.81	2.35
20. To progress, return to glorious past.	1.58	1.73	1.38
21. For happiness in future, present injustice necessary.	4.57	5.35	4.22
*22. To accomplish mission, gamble all or nothing.	5.04	5.84	4.35
*23. Most people don't understand what's going on.	4.70	5.43	3.51
*24. Most people don't know what's good for them.	4.10	5.16	2.81
25. Nothing new under the sun.	3.12	3.81	2.38
26. If you understand, it's easy to predict future.	2.72	3.19	2.27
27. Force necessary to advance ideal.	3.71	4.43	3.11
B. Based upon formal content of dogmatism.			
*28. Just a handful of great thinkers.	4.85	5.87	3.60
*29. I hate some people because of what they stand for.	3.07	3.35	1.95
*30. A man without a cause hasn't lived.	4.52	5.51	3.27
*31. Life meaningful when there is devotion to cause.	5.34	6.14	4.19
*32. There is only one correct philosophy.	2.66	4.11	1.97
*33. Person believing in too many causes is "wishy-washy".	3.20	4.32	2.54
*34. To compromise is to betray own side.	2.78	3.32	1.95
*35. In religion, we should not compromise.	2.58	3.46	1.92
*36. To consider only one's own happiness is selfish.	4.21	5.41	3.62
*37. To compromise is to appease.	2.23	2.95	1.70
*38. Two kinds of people; those for, those against truth.	2.58	3.97	1.57
*39. My blood boils when others won't admit they're wrong.	4.66	5.30	3.87
*40. One who thinks of own happiness beneath contempt.	4.17	4.97	3.57

Table (Continued)

Items	Total Group (N=137) M	Highs (N=37) M	Lows (N=37) M
*41. Most printed ideas aren't worth paper printed on.	3.52	4.73	2.73
42. I'm too critical of others' ideas.	4.81	5.30	4.19

C. Based upon the function of dogmatism.

Items	Total Group (N=137) M	Highs (N=37) M	Lows (N=37) M
*43. Man on his own is helpless and miserable.	3.43	4.92	2.41
*44. World is a lonesome place.	3.23	3.89	2.41
*45. Most people don't give a "damn" for others.	3.75	4.57	2.81
*46. I want to find someone to solve my problems.	3.61	4.43	2.10
*47. Natural to fear future.	3.79	4.81	1.61
*48. So much to do, so little time to do it in.	5.86	6.49	1.01
*49. Once I get wound up, I can't stop.	3.34	3.73	2.43
*50. I repeat myself to make sure I'm understood.	3.50	4.30	2.78
*51. I don't listen.	3.44	3.92	2.78
52. I interrupt others to put across my own views.	4.43	4.78	3.65
*53. Better be dead hero than live coward.	3.26	4.05	2.60
54. Hardest battles are with myself.	4.70	5.38	3.84
55. I'm no good.	4.60	5.38	3.84
56. I'm afraid people will find out what I'm really like.	2.83	3.49	1.97
*57. Secret ambition is to become a great man.	5.02	5.97	5.16
*58. Main thing in life is to do something important.	4.22	5.38	3.32
*59. If given chance I'd benefit world.	5.51	6.43	4.81
60. Greatness more important than happiness.	2.05	2.89	1.97
61. People won't practice what they preach.	5.55	5.97	5.16
62. Most people failures and the system is responsible.	3.31	3.62	2.70
63. Strangers look at me critically.	4.10	5.22	3.35
64. Only natural to have guilty conscience.	3.35	4.65	2.46
65. People say insulting things about me.	2.68	3.78	2.03
66. I'm talked about.	3.25	4.22	2.76

*Item retained in final 40-item scale.

The following table presents the intercorrelation among Dogmatism, Authoritarianism, and Ethnocentrism. (D, F, and E, respectively.)

Group	N	D,F	F,E[a]	D,E	(D,F) E
MSU I	202	.67	.56	.36	.61
N.Y. Colleges Jewish sub-sample	131	.61	.60	.49	.42
MSU II	153	.61	.58	.33	.54
MSU III	186	.54	.64	.31	.47
English Colleges I	137	.57	.58	.39	.46
English Colleges II	80	.62	.62	.32	.57
English Workers	60	.77	.56	.53	.67

[a] There were 21 Jews in the English colleges I group, 11 Jews in the English Colleges II group, one Jew in the English worker group. These Ss were excluded in computing the correlations between F and E, and between D and E (N=116, 69, 59, respectively).

The following table compares different political groups in England on the Dogmatism Scale and other variables.

Comparisons Among Various Political Groups in England on Opinionation, Dogmatism, F and E

Group	N	Left Opinion-ation	Right Opinion-ation	Total Opinion-ation	Dogmatism	F Scale	Ethnocentrism[a]	
		M	M	M	M	M	M	N
1. Conservatives	54	56.15	83.04	139.20	258.76	115.51	29.94	51
2. Liberals	22	68.67	68.18	136.85	242.91	98.40	24.75	16
3. Attleeites	27	76.78	59.15	135.94	252.60	101.79	22.74	13
4. Bevanites	19	96.52	44.52	141.05	249.78	90.37	23.50	14
5. Cummunists	13[b]	107.86	46.62	154.48	261.62	82.93	16.50	10

[a] The N on which the mean E scores are based are 51, 16, 23, 14, and 10 for groups 1,2,3,4, and 5, respectively. Jewish Ss were excluded from these computations.

[b] The N for the English Colleges I is 137. Seven of these gave "other" political affiliations (e.g., Anarchist, Trotskyite, ex-Communist, Celtic Alliance). Five of the 13 Communists were from English Colleges II, and the full 60-item Dogmatism Scale was scored (form D) for these five Ss for purposes of the present analysis.

Different religious groups in the New York college students and the MSU students are compared regarding their scores on the Dogmatism Scale and other variables.

Comparisons Among Various Religious Groups in the
New York Colleges Group on
Opinionation, Dogmatism, F and E

Group	N	Left Opinion-ation	Right Opinion-ation	Total Opinion-ation	Dogmatism	F Scale	Ethnocentrism
		M	M	M	M	M	M
1. Catholic	46	58.26	86.37	144.64	147.38	105.24	26.52
2. Protest-ants	24	56.71	88.84	145.55	138.34	95.80	25.00
3. Jews	131	70.18	76.41	146.59	139.53	94.73	20.32
4. None	6	94.35	61.01	155.36	147.20	93.69	18.67

Comparisons Among Various Religious Groups
In the MSU I Group on
Opinionation, Dogmatism, F and E

Group	N	Left Opinion-ation	Right Opinion-ation	Total Opinion-ation	Dogmatism	F Scale	Ethnocentrism
		M	M	M	M	M	M
1. Catholics	42	58.43	94.71	153.14	191.10	109.79	34.31
2. Protest-ants	145	58.47	86.41	144.88	180.10	99.24	29.99
3. None	15	67.73	76.67	144.40	174.60	91.60	24.27

Dogmatism and F Scale scores were both correlated with 2 measures of liberalism-conservatism (the PEC Scale and a measure derived from the Opinionatism Scale).

The Dogmatism and F Scales in Relation to Liberalism-Conservatism

Group	N	Correlations between D and		Correlations between F and		Correlation between
		P.E.C.	(R.O.-L.O.)[a]	P.E.C.	(R.O.-L.O.)	P.E.C. and (R.O.-L.O.)
MSU I	202	.13	.13	.22	.28	.38
N.Y. Colleges	207	.11	.04	.43	.37	.58
MSU II	153	.20	.13	.29	.21	.30
MSU III	186	.28	.17	.40	.35	.49
English Colleges I	137	b	.12	-	.36	-
English Colleges II	80	-	-.03	-	.31	-
English Workers	60	-	.11	-	.15	-

[a]Right-opinionation score minus left-opinionation score. Positive differences indicate a rightist orientation; negative differences indicate a leftist orientation.
[b]The P.E.C. Scale was not employed in the English research.

In addition to the above, an attempt was also made to validate this scale by the method of "known groups." In the first study professors "nominated" high and low dogmatic students from graduate students working with them (a variety of different fields was used). No differences in either Dogmatism or Opinionation were found between the highs and the lows. In the second study, graduate students in psychology were asked to "nominate" other graduate students (outside the field of psychology) as being high or low in Dogmatism. The highs scored significantly higher on both Dogmatism and Opinionation. However the highs also scored significantly higher on the E and F Scales. Consequently, the statement that the D and O Scales measure general authoritarianism and intolerance as compared with the authoritarianism and intolerance of the right measured by the F and E scales, is not supported by the data.

Location: Rokeach, M., Political and religious dogmatism: an alternative to the authoritarian personality, Psychological Monograph, No. 425, 1956, 70, No. 18.

Administration: This test is self administered. An estimated 30 minutes would be needed to complete form D and 20 minutes to complete form E.

Results and
Comments:

The author constructed this scale to be a measure of general
authoritarianism, or closed mindedness. This scale differs from the
F scale in that general authoritarianism is viewed as concerning
the way an individual adheres to a belief and not the specific
content of that belief. The author claims that the F Scale is
concerned with the specific content of a belief, that is
authoritarianism of the right, fascism, etc.

The general trends in the data tend to support the author's
distinction between the variables measured by his scales and those
measured by the California scales. The fact that the correlations
between D and E are consistently smaller than the correlations
between F and E, and the fact that the correlations between D and F
are only slightly reduced when E is held constant, lead the author
to conclude that the D Scale measures differences in authoritarianism
independent of the degree of ethnic intolerance. Dogmatism
correlated negligibly with liberalism-Conservatism in every group
tested. These correlations are always smaller than those between
the F Scale and Liberalism-Conservatism.

From these results, the author concludes that the D Scale comes
closer to measuring general authoritarianism than does the F Scale.
Dogmatism correlates positively with both right and left
opinionation which are negligibly or sometimes negatively correlated
with each others. The E and F scales correlate relatively high
with right opinionation, but negligibly or negatively with left
opinionation. In every sample Dogmatism correlates more highly with
total opinionation than with either left or right. The E, F, and
P.E.C. scales correlate less with total opinionation than with right
opinionation. These results all indicate that the author's scale
has accomplished the purpose for which it was constructed.

References:

Rokeach, M. Political and religious dogmatism: an alternative to
the authoritarian personality, Psychological Monograph, No. 425,
1956, 43, p. 70, no. 18.

Rokeach, M. The open and closed mind, New York: Basic Books,
1960.

DOGMATISM SCALE

Form D - consists of all following items
Form E - contains * items
A. ISOLATION WITHIN AND BETWEEN BELIEF AND DISBELIEF SYSTEMS.
A.1. Accentuation of differences between the belief and the disbelief systems.

*1. The United States and Russia have just about nothing in common.
 2. Communism and Catholicism have nothing in common.
 3. The principles I have come to believe in are quite different from those
     believed in by most people.

A.2. The perception of irrelevance.

 4. In a heated discussion people have a way of bringing up irrelevant issues
     rather than sticking to the main issue.

A.3. The coexistence of contradictions within the belief system.

*5. The highest form of government is a democracy and the highest form of democracy
     is a government run by those who are most intelligent.
*6. Even though freedom of speech for all groups is a worthwhile goal, it is
     unfortunately necessary to restrict the freedom of certain political groups.
 7. While the use of force is wrong by and large, it is sometimes the only way
     possible to advance a noble ideal.
 8. Even though I have a lot of faith in the intelligence and wisdom of the common
     man I must say that the masses behave stupidly at times.

B. RELATIVE DEGREES OF DIFFERENTIATION OF THE BELIEF AND THE DISBELIEF SYSTEM.
B.1. Relative amount of knowledge possessed.

*9. It is only natural that a person would have a much better acquaintance with
     ideas he believes in than with ideas he opposes.

B.2. Differentiation within the disbelief system.

10. There are certain "isms" which are really the same even though those who
     believe in these "isms" try to tell you they are different.

C. SPECIFIC CONTENT OF PRIMITIVE BELIEFS.
C.1. Beliefs regarding the aloneness, isolation, and helplessness of man.

*11. Man on his own is a helpless and miserable creature.
*12. Fundamentally, the world we live in is a pretty lonesome place.
*13. Most people just don't give a "damn" for others.
*14. I'd like it if I could find someone who would tell me how to solve my
      personal problems.

C.2a. Beliefs regarding the uncertainty of the future.

*15. It is only natural for a person to be rather fearful of the future.

C.2b. <u>A feeling of urgency.</u>

*16. There is so much to be done and so little time to do it in.

C.2c. <u>Compulsive repetition of ideas and arguments.</u>

*17. Once I get wound up in a heated discussion I just can't stop.
*18. In a discussion I often find it necessary to repeat myself several times to make sure I am being understood.
*19. In a heated discussion I generally become so absorbed in what I am going to say that I forget to listen to what others are saying.
 20. In a discussion I sometimes interrupt others too much in my eagerness to put across my own point of view.

C.3a. <u>Need for martyrdom.</u>

*21. It is better to be a dead hero than a live coward.

C.3b. <u>Conflict within the self.</u>

 22. My hardest battles are with myself.

C.3c. <u>Self-depreciation.</u>

 23. At times I think I am no good at all.
 24. I am afraid of people who want to find out what I'm really like for fear they'll be disappointed in me.

C.4. <u>Self-aggrandizement as a defense against self-inadequacy.</u>
C.4a. <u>Concern with power and status.</u>

*25. While I don't like to admit this even to myself, my secret ambition is to become a great man, like Einstein, or Beethoven, or Shakespeare.
*26. The main thing in life is for a person to want to do something important.
*27. If given the chance I would do something of great benefit to the world.
 28. If I had to choose between happiness and greatness, I'd choose greatness.

C.4b. <u>Moral self-righteousness.</u>

 29. It's all too true that people just won't practice what they preach.

C.5. <u>Paranoid outlook on life</u>.

 30. Most people are failures and it is the system which is responsible for this.
 31. I have often felt that strangers were looking at me critically.
 32. It is only natural for a person to have a guilty conscience.
 33. People say insulting and vulgar things about me.
 34. I am sure I am being talked about.

D. FORMAL CONTENT OF THE INTERMEDIATE BELIEF REGION.
D.1a. <u>Beliefs in positive and negative authority</u>.

*35. In the history of mankind there have probably been just a handful of really great thinkers.
*36. There are a number of people I have come to hate because of the things they stand for.

D.1b. Belief in a cause.

*37. A man who does not believe in some great cause has not really lived.
*38. It is only when a person devotes himself to an ideal or cause that life
      becomes meaningful.
*39. Of all the different philosophies which exist in this world there is probably
      only one which is correct.
*40. A person who gets enthusiastic about too many causes is likely to be a pretty
      "wishy-washy" sort of person.
*41. To compromise with our political opponents is dangerous because it usually
      leads to the betrayal of our own side.
*42. When it comes to differences of opinion in religion we must be careful not
      to compromise with those who believe differently from the way we do.
*43. In times like these, a person must be pretty selfish if he considers primarily
      his own happiness.
 44. To compromise with our political opponents is to be guilty of appeasement.

D.2.   Intolerance.
D.2a. Toward the renegade.

*45. The worst crime a person could commit is to attack publicly the people who
      believe in the same thing he does.
*46. In times like these it is often necessary to be more on guard against ideas
      put out by people or groups in one's own camp than by those in the opposing
      camp.
*47. A group which tolerates too many differences of opinion among its own members
      cannot exist for long.

D.2b. Toward the disbeliever.

*48. There are two kinds of people in this world: those who are for the truth
      and those who are against the truth.
*49. My blood boils whenever a person stubbornly refuses to admit he's wrong.
*50. A person who thinks primarily of his own happiness is beneath contempt.
*51. Most of the ideas which get printed nowadays aren't worth the paper they are
      printed on.
 52. I sometimes have a tendency to be too critical of the ideas of others.

E. INTERRELATIONS AMONG PRIMITIVE, INTERMEDIATE, AND PERIPHERAL BELIEFS.
E.1. Tendency to make a party line change.

*53. In this complicated world of ours the only way we can know what's going on is
      to rely on leaders or experts who can be trusted.
*54. It is often desirable to reserve judgment about what's going on until one has
      had a chance to hear the opinions of those one respects.

E.2. Narrowing: selective avoidance of contact with facts, events, etc. incongruent
      with one's belief-disbelief system.

*55. In the long run the best way to live is to pick friends and associates whose
      tastes and beliefs are the same as one's own.
 56. There's no use wasting your money on newspapers which you know in advance are
      just plain propaganda.
 57. Young people should not have too easy access to books which are likely to
      confuse them.

F. ATTITUDE TOWARD THE PAST, PRESENT, AND FUTURE.

*58. The present is all too often full of unhappiness. It is only the future that counts.
 59. It is by returning to our glorious and forgotten past that real social progress can be achieved.
 60. To achieve the happiness of mankind in the future it is sometimes necessary to put up with injustices in the present.

G. KNOWING THE FUTURE.

*61. If a man is to accomplish his mission in life it is sometimes necessary to gamble "all or nothing at all."
*62. Unfortunately a good many people with whom I have discussed important social and moral problems don't really understand what's going on.
*63. Most people just don't know what's good for them.
*64. There is nothing new under the sun.
 65. To one who really takes the trouble to understand the world he lives in, it's an easy matter to predict future events.

H. BELIEF IN FORCE AS A WAY TO REVISE THE PRESENT.

 66. It is sometimes necessary to resort to force to advance an ideal one strongly believes in.

SHORT DOGMATISM SCALE (Schulze 1962)

Variable This scale was designed to measure dogmatism as conceived by Rokeach (1960) with fewer items than appear in the original scale (40).

Description Guttman's scalogram analysis was used to select the ten items from Rokeach's D-Scale which best met the criteria of unidimensionality, item consistency, and reproducibility. Two samples were used to test the validity of the resulting 10-item scale (D_{10} Scale).

Sample The first sample consisted of one hundred questionnaires which were randomly selected from 227 administered by Bonier (1957) in a study of the relationship between time perspective and dogmatism. (The subjects presumably were college students.) The second sample comprised 172 students in introductory sociology at Michigan State University.

Reliability The D_{10} yielded a reproducibility coefficient (CR) of .83. Although not as high as the .90 which Guttman recommended, this CR was claimed to be as high as one could get using a 10-item subset of the D-Scale. The author attributes the low CR to the intrusion of variables such as anxiety, rigidity, authoritarianism, self-rejection and paranoia. Hence, this scale is not unidimensional but neither is the original D-Scale.

Validity Two indicants of validity were reported, the correlation between the D and D_{10} scales and the correlation between the latter and measures of anxiety. Fruchter, Rokeach, and Novak (1958) have reported that "dogmatism was found to have factorial content in common with anxiety".

In the first sample, D and D_{10} correlated .76, and D_{10} correlated .19 with the Heineman (1953) anxiety scale. The 40-item D-scale correlated .32 with this measure of anxiety.

In the second sample, D and D_{10} correlated .73, but when the overlapping items were removed from D this fell to .46. The correlation between D_{10} and the Welch (1952) anxiety scale was .29; between the 40-item D-scale and Welch anxiety, .37; and between the nonoverlapping 30 items and anxiety .35.

Location Schulze, R.H.K., A shortened version of the Rokeach Dogmatism Scale, Journal of Psychological Studies, 1962, 13, 93-97.

Administration This scale is self-administered and should take less than 10 minutes to complete. For suitable instructions, see those used with the D-Scale.

Results and
Comments

Although this scale has adequate credentials, it would be
worthwhile to explore its utility in further detail before
relying heavily upon it. In both of the samples tested the 10
items were included in a large questionnaire which contained the
remainder of the D-Scale items and an anxiety scale. Part of the
evidence for validity could be based on a consistent set that
would not be maintained were the 10 items to stand along. Also,
test-retest measures should be obtained to indicate the reliability
of such a short scale.

References

Bonier, R.J., A study of the relationship between time perspective
and open-closed belief systems , Unpublished Master's thesis,
Michigan State University, 1957.

Fruchter, B., Rokeach, M., and Novak, E., A factorial study of
dogmatism, opinionation, and related scales , Psychological
Reports, 1958, 4, 19-22.

Heineman, C.E., A Forced Choice Form of Taylor Anxiety Scale ,
Journal of Consulting Psychology, 1953, 17, 447-454.

Rokeach, M., The open and closed mind, New York: Basic Books,
1960.

Welch, G.S., An Anxiety Index and an internalization ratio for
the MMPI, Journal of Consulting Psychology, 1952, 16, 65-72.

SHORT DOGMATISM SCALE

(The ten items are listed in descending order of "difficulty", i.e., the smallest number of respondents agreed with the first).

1. Fundamentally, the world we live in is a pretty lonesome place.

2. It is often desirable to reserve judgment about what's going on until one has a chance to hear the opinions of those one respects.

3. A person who thinks primarily of his own happiness is beneath contempt.

4. In the history of mankind there have probably been just a handful of really great thinkers.

5. Most people just don't know what's good for them.

6. Once I get wound up in a heated discussion I just can't stop.

7. The worst crime a person can commit is to attack publicly the people who believe in the same thing he does.

8. In this complicated world of ours the only way we can know what is going on is to rely upon leaders or experts who can be trusted.

9. In the long run the best way to live is to pick friends and associates whose tastes and beliefs are the same as one's own.

10. While I don't like to admit this even to myself, I sometimes have the ambition to become a great man like Einstein, or Beethoven, or Shakespeare.

SHORT DOGMATISM SCALE (Troldahl and Powell 1965)

Variable   This scale was designed to reduce the length of Rokeach's (1960)
            dogmatism scale so that it could be included in survey studies. The
            authors were also interested in discovering whether Schulze's (1962)
            D_{10} Scale , developed from college student samples, could be
            considered appropriate for more heterogeneous samples.

Description The 40-item dogmatism scale was included in an interview survey of
            Boston suburbanites and also in a field study in Lansing, Michigan.
            In the Boston study interviewers read the items to respondents
            and asked two questions: whether they agreed or disagreed, and
            then how much they agreed or disagreed in the following terms:

                    Agree   Disagree

            1. Agree a little   1. Disagree a little
            2. Agree on the whole   2. Disagree on the whole
            3. Agree very much   3. Disagree very much

            "Don't know" responses were coded as zeros.

            In the Lansing study the scale was self-administered, but the same
            answer categories were used. The authors used the Boston study to
            select the best items to be included in shorter scales, and then
            cross-validated these items with the Lansing results. The items
            finally selected for inclusion had to meet the following criteria:
             1) Average item-total score correlation coefficients were
            computed for each item, weighing the interview and self-administered
            versions equally (and employing Fisher's Z transformation). The
            20 items selected were listed in order according to the coefficients.
             2) An item was selected only if its item-total score correlation
            reached or exceeded .30 in each study. 3) One item meeting
            these criteria was dropped because it seemed difficult for people
            to understand in the interview study.

Sample   The Boston sample included 227 suburbanites who subscribed to a
            county agricultural newspaper. In the Lansing study respondents
            were 84 adults sampled by quota-control and stratified by social
            status.

Reliability/ In the Boston study a "corrected" split-half reliability coefficient
Homogeneity of .84 was obtained for the 40-item scale. Item-total score
            correlations ranged from .18 to .59, with seven of .50 or above and
            19 of .40 or above. Short forms of the scale, containing 10, 15 and
            20 items, were selected on the basis of these correlations.

On the basis of the Lansing cross-validation, the following reliabilities are approximated for each version of the scale:

40 items	.84
20 items	.79
15 items	.73
10 items	.66

Validity The short forms scores were correlated with total 40-item scores in each sample studied, yielding the following results:

	Original Boston Data	Lansing Cross-Validation
10-item vs. 40-item score	.88	.79
15-item vs. 40-item score	.91	.73
20-item vs. 40-item score	.95	.94

Location Troldahl, V.C., and Powell, F.A. A short-form dogmatism scale for use in field studies. Social Forces, 1965, 44, 211-214.

Administration This scale is self-administered and takes about 45 seconds per item to complete, hence $7^{1}/2$, $11^{1}/4$, and 15 minutes for the 10-, 15-, and 20-item versions, respectively. In the list below the first 10 items comprise the 10-item scale; the first 15, the 15-item scale.

Results and Comments This study serves to emphasize the importance of sampling in the construction of a scale: Only 2 of Schulze's 10 items, selected on the basis of college student's scores, fell among the best 10 in the present field research.

The authors suggest that the 20-item scale can be used without reluctance in field studies, while the shorter forms should be used only where a relatively gross estimate of dogmatism is required.

Unfortunately, no information on validity other than correlations with the total dogmatism scale scores is given. Hence, this scale's relationships to anxiety and other theoretically relevant variables and behaviors remain to be explored.

References Rokeach, M. The open and closed mind. New York: Basic Books, 1960.

Schulze, R.H.K. A shortened version of the Rokeach dogmatism scale. Journal of Psychological Studies, 1962, 13, 93-97.

SHORT-FORM DOGMATISM SCALE

		Average R of Item vs. Total Score

1. In this complicated world of ours the only way we can know what's going on is to rely on leaders or expects who can be trusted. .60

2. My blood boils whenever a person stubbornly refuses to admit he's wrong. .59

3. There are two kinds of people in this world: those who are for the truth and those who are against the truth. .59

4. Most people just don't know what's good for them. .56

5. Of all the different philosophies which exist in this world there is probably only one which is correct. .56

6. The highest form of government is a democracy and the highest form of democracy is a government run by those who are most intelligent. .54

7. The main thing in life is for a person to want to do something important. .53

8. I'd like it if I could find someone who would tell me how to solve my personal problems. .52

9. Most of the ideas which get printed nowadays aren't worth the paper they are printed on. .51

10. Man on his own is a helpless and miserable creature. .51

11. It is only when a person devotes himself to an ideal or cause that life becomes meaningful. .49

12. Most people just don't give a "damn" for others. .48

13. To compromise with our political opponents is dangerous because it usually leads to the betrayal of our own side. .47

14. It is often desirable to reserve judgment about what's going on until one has had a chance to hear the opinions of those one respects. .47

15. The present is all too often full of unhappiness. It is only the future that counts. .45

16. The United States and Russia have just about nothing in common. .44

17. In a discussion I often find it necessary to repeat myself several times to make sure I am being understood.   .43

18. While I don't like to admit this even to myself, my secret ambition is to become a great man, like Einstein, or Beethoven, or Shakespeare.   .43

19. Even though freedom of speech for all groups is a worthwhile goal, it is unfortunately necessary to restrict the freedom of certain political groups.   .42

20. It is better to be a dead hero than to be a live coward.   .37

OPINIONATION SCALE (Rokeach   1956)

Variable   The Opinionation Scale was designed to measure general intolerance,
                or the extent to which we accept others because they agree with
                our opinions and reject others because they disagree with our
                opinions.

Description   The final forms of the scale, form C, used in the U.S., and form
                Ce, used in England, both consist of 40 six-point Likert-type
                items. These two forms are essentially the same as the two earlier
                forms, forms A and B, in that half of the items are classed as
                "opinionated" rejection (speaker rejects particular belief and
                therefore rejects all those who accept it) and half are classed as
                "opinionated acceptance" (speaker holds certain belief and therefore
                accepts all those who accept it). To keep the scale free from any
                specific ideological content, half of the items in each item group
                were designed to tap right opinionation and the remainder, left
                opinionation. The final tests contain four groups of ten statements
                each: opinionated rejected-right opinionation, opinionated rejected-
                left opinionation, opinionated acceptance-right opinionation, and
                opinionated acceptance-left opinionation. Responses to forms C and
                Ce were scored along a +3 to -3 agree-disagree continuum with the 0
                point excluded. These scores were converted to a 1 to 7 scale by
                adding the constant 4 to each answer. The scores can range from
                40 to 280. High scores indicate a high degree of opinionation.

                Form A contained 20 pairs of statements, each pair containing one
                left-opinionated statement and the corresponding right-opinionated
                statement. The subject rated these statements on the usual six-
                point Likert Scale. Form B contained the best 16 pairs from form
                A. These items were rated on a three point agree-disagree scale.

Sample   Form A was administered to 202 Michigan State University students
                and 207 students from New York University, form B was administered
                to 153 Michigan State University students, form C was administered
                to 186 Michigan State University students, and form Ce was
                administered to 137 students at University College, London, to 80
                students at Birkbeck College, England, and to 60 English workers.

Reliability/   The following table presents the obtained reliabilities for the
Homogeneity   different forms of the Opinionation Scale.

Corrected Reliabilities of the Total Opinionation Scale (T.O.),
Left Opinionation (L.O.), Right Opinionation (R.O.),
And Liberalism-Conservatism (R.O.-L.O.)

Form	Number of items	Group	N	T.O.	L.O.	R.O.	R.O.- L.O.	Correlation between L.O. & R.O.
A	40	MSU I	202	.67	.64	.67	.66	-.22
B	32	N.Y. Colleges	207	.75	.74	.77	.83	-.51
C	40	MSU II	153	.68	.39	.68	.50	.09
Ce	40	English Colleges I	137	.75	.89	.88	.93	-.65
		English Colleges II	80	.75	.90	.86	.93	-.61
		English Workers	60	.75	.91	.91	.94	-.62

Validity   The following table presents the results of an item analysis of form C for the Michigan State University group of 186.

Item Analysis of the Opinionation Scale,
Form C for the MSU III Group

Items	Total Group (N=186) M	Highs (N=47) M	Lows (N=47) M
Left Opinionation, Opinionated Rejection			
1. Pro-Roosevelt	5.35	5.75	4.68
2. No race differences	3.92	4.92	3.06
3. Pro Truman's Fair Deal	2.31	2.92	1.66
4. Anti-loyalty oaths	3.94	4.04	3.70
5. Russia not imperialistic	4.13	4.72	3.77
6. Anti-real estate interests	3.20	4.17	2.30
7. Government & education not Red-infiltrated	1.86	2.15	1.43
8. Anti-universal military training	2.22	2.89	1.77
9. Anti-government support of religion	5.02	5.72	3.94
10. Anti-McCarthy	2.99	3.62	2.57
Left Opinionation, Opinionated Acceptance			
11. Pro-Rosenbergs	2.39	2.40	2.77
12. Anti-MacArthur	2.61	3.00	2.32
13. Anti-big business	3.93	4.30	3.49
14. Pro-social security	2.28	2.55	1.87
15. Anti-Congressional investigating committees	2.80	2.96	2.36

Table (Continued)

Items	Total Group (N=186) M	Highs (N=47) M	Lows (N=47) M
16. Anti-American Legion	2.08	2.28	1.70
17. Pro-soak-the-rich taxes	2.51	3.38	2.06
18. Rich getting richer, poor getting poorer	2.32	2.72	1.72
19. Capitalism causes depressions and wars	2.12	2.72	1.72
20. Anti-Hoover	3.14	4.04	2.38
Right Opinionation, Opinionated Rejection			
21. Anti-socialized medicine	3.92	5.23	2.94
22. Pro-Eisenhower	4.04	4.55	3.47
23. Reds yell about civil rights	3.33	4.38	2.38
24. Anti-Labor	4.55	5.38	3.21
25. Anti-Democratic Party	4.38	4.79	4.11
26. Pro-God	4.31	5.15	3.68
27. Anti-government ownership of utilities	3.23	4.13	2.13
28. U.S. no warmonger	4.75	5.38	4.23
29. Anti-socialism	3.44	4.55	2.36
30. Anti-Red China	4.14	4.77	3.66
Right Opinionation, Opinionated Acceptance			
31. U.S. rearms to stop aggression	4.40	5.19	3.94
32. Prejudice removable by education	5.74	6.00	5.45
33. U.S. should send military aid	2.67	2.98	2.30
34. Pro-Churchill	4.92	5.45	4.66
35. U.S. rearms to preserve freedom	4.69	5.30	4.04
36. Pro-Chiang Kai Shek	3.49	4.51	2.75
37. U.N. a failure	1.93	2.36	1.36
38. Businessman contributes most to society	3.85	4.45	2.98
39. Pro-Franco	4.49	5.00	3.70
40. Alger Hiss a traitor	4.62	5.13	3.75

The following table presents the obtained correlations of Left, Right, and Total Opinionation with the Dogmatism Scale, the F Scale, the E Scale, and the PEC Scale.

Left, Right, and Total Opinionation: Correlation with Other Variables

Group	N	Dogmatism and--			F Scale and--			Ethnocentrism[a] and--			P.E.C. Scale[b] and--		
		Left Opin.	Right Opin.	Total Opin.	Left Opin.	Right Opin.	Total Opin.	Left Opin.	Right Opin.	Total Opin.	Left Opin.	Right Opin.	Total Opin.
MSU I	202	.22	.40	.51	.11	.53	.54	-.08	.50	.37	-.20	.41	.19
N.Y. Colleges	207	.20	.23	.43	-.08	.56	.50	-.22	.62	.43	-.39	.60	.25
MSU II	153	.20	.31	.34	.12	.46	.45	-.02	.44	.41	-.10	.26	.21
MSU III	186	.24	.42	.47	.12	.55	.49	.01	.50	.39	-.18	.48	.26
English Colleges I	137	.17	.38	.61	-.27	.64	.40	-.21	.58	.38	-	-	-
English Colleges II	80	.25	.25	.55	-.06	.56	.46	-.22	.49	.20	-	-	-
English Workers	60	.22	.43	.63	.18	.47	.63	-.18	.59	.50	-	-	-

[a] The N's for the English Colleges I, II, and English Worker samples are 116, 69, and 59 respectively, since Jewish Ss were omitted.

[b] Not given in England.

The following tables present the mean scores achieved, by different religious groupings on right, left, and total opinionation in adding to other tests.

Comparisons Among Various Religious Groups in the MSU I Group on Opinionation, Dogmatism, F and E

Group	N	Left Opinion-ation	Right Opinion-ation	Total Opinion-ation	Dogmatism	F Scale	Ethnocentrism
		M	M	M	M	M	M
1. Catholic	42	58.43	94.71	153.14	191.10	109.79	34.31
2. Protest-ants	145	58.47	86.41	144.88	180.10	99.24	29.99
3. None	15	67.73	76.67	144.40	174.60	91.60	24.27

Comparisons Among Various Religious Groups In the New York Colleges Group on Opinionation, Dogmatism, F and E

Group	N	Left Opinion-ation	Right Opinion-ation	Total Opinion-ation	Dogmatism	F Scale	Ethnocentrism
		M	M	M	M	M	M
1. Catholics	46	58.26	86.37	144.64	147.38	105.24	26.52
2. Protest-ants	24	46.71	88.84	145.55	138.34	95.80	25.00
3. Jews	131	70.18	76.41	146.59	139.53	94.73	20.32
4. None	6	94.35	61.01	155.36	147.20	93.69	18.67

The following procedure was used to decide if a statement should be labeled "left" or "right". A given statement was considered "right" if it could be placed to the "right" of its ideological opposite. The statement of its ideological opposite could then be considered "left". To check this means of classifying statements, two colleagues were asked to rate each statement as either "left" or "right". Both men agreed 100% with the author.

Location	Rokeach, M. Political and religious dogmatism, an alternative to the authoritarian personality , <u>Psychological Monographs</u>, 1956, <u>43</u>(18), 70.
Administration	Estimated administration time is 20 minutes.
Results and Comments	The following table presents the means and s.d. achieved by the different groups of subjects on the different forms.

Means and Standard Deviations on
Left, Right, and Total Opinionation

Form	Number of items	Group	N	Left Opinionation		Right Opinionation		Total Opinionation	
				M	s.d.	M	s.d.	M	s.d.
A	40	MSU I	202	59.20	11.95	87.25	13.75	146.45	16.03
		N.Y. Colleges	207	66.67	17.28	79.61	18.39	146.28	17.69
B	32	MSU II	153	1.16	1.32	5.75	3.13	6.91	3.56
C	40	MSU III	186	61.17	11.94	80.84	14.60	142.01	18.94
C_E	40	English Colleges I	137	77.77	21.80	67.23	21.30	145.00	17.80
		English Colleges II	80	76.60	23.00	62.55	17.90	139.15	17.90
		English Workers	60	75.40	25.50	80.85	25.70	156.25	19.40

While the E (Ethnocentrism) Scale is considered to be a measure of intolerance of the right, this scale is designed to be a measure of general intolerance . The <u>Opinionation Scale</u> contains a broad range of topics and attempts to assess the structure of one's intolerance rather than its specific content.

One of the more interesting findings of this investigation is the difference in correlations between the Left- and Right-Opinionation Scales for different samples. Michigan State University students had correlations of -.22, .09, .00. New York University students had correlations of -.51. English groups had correlations of -.65, -.61, and -.62. This finding would suggest that there are sharp differences in organization of attitudes among these three groups, regarding the left-right dimension.

Reference	Rokeach, M. <u>The open and closed mind,</u> New York: Basic Books, 1960.

OPINIONATION SCALE
British version - Form C$_E$

Opinionated Rejection - Left

1. It is quite stupid to say that the Bevanites follow the Communist line.
2. A person must be pretty stupid if he still believes in differences between races.
3. There are two kinds of people who opposed the Labour Government post-war programme: the selfish and the stupid.
4. A person must be pretty shortsighted if he thinks that the Conservatives represent the best interest of the British people.
5. It is the people who believe everything they read in the papers who are convinced that Russia is pursuing a ruthless policy of imperialist aggression.
6. It is mainly those who support the viewpoint put out by the landlord who believe that rents should be increased.
7. A person must be pretty gullible if he really believes that the Communists have actually infiltrated into the teaching profession.
8. It's mostly those who want a third World War who want to rearm Western Germany.
9. It is very foolish to advocate government support of religious education.
10. Only a simple-minded fool would think that the present Colonial Secretary is interested in Freedom.

Opinionated Rejection - Right

21. It is simply incredible that anyone should believe that Dr. Jagan had the interest of the people of British Guiana at heart.
22. A person must be very ignorant if he thinks that Churchill is going to let big business run this country.
23. It's the Communists and fellow travellers who are always bringing up the issue of freedom for the Colonies.
24. It's the fellow travellers or Communists who are always going on about the right to strike.
25. It is foolish to think that the Labour party is really the party of the common man.
26. You just can't help but feel sorry for the person who believes that the world could exist without a Creator.
27. It's usually the trouble-makers who talk about state ownership.
28. Only a misguided idealist would believe that the Soviet Union is for peace.
29. It's mostly the noisy radicals who try to tell us that we will be better off under socialism.
30. It's the agitators and left-wingers who want to get Red China into the United Nations right away.

Opinionated Acceptance - Left

11. It's perfectly clear to any thinking person that the execution of the Rosenbergs has done the United States more harm than good.
12. Any person with even a brain in his head knows that it would be dangerous to let our country be run by men like Lord Beaverbrook.
13. The truth of the matter is this: It is big business which wants to continue the cold war.

14. Make no mistake about it! The best way to achieve security is for the government to guarantee full employment.
15. It's perfectly clear to all decent people that all this fuss about communism does more harm than good.
16. Thoughtful persons know that the Tories are not really interested in democracy.
17. It's perfectly clear to any thinking person that the way to solve our financial problems is by soak-the-rich taxation.
18. It's all too true that the rich are getting richer and the poor are getting poorer.
19. History clearly shows that it is the private enterprise system which is at the root of depression and wars.
20. Anyone who truly understands America will tell you that the sooner we stop following in their footsteps the better off we will be.

Opinionated Acceptance - Right

31. Any intelligent person can plainly see that the real reason Britain is spending so much for defense is to stop aggression.
32. Plain common sense tells you that nationalization of industry has gone far enough.
33. Anyone who is really for democracy knows very well that the only way for Britain to avoid revolution and civil war is to support American foreign policy.
34. History will clearly show that Churchill's victory over the Labour Party in 1951 was a step forward for the British people.
35. The American re-armament program is clear and positive proof that they are willing to make sacrifices to preserve their freedom.
36. This much is certain: The only way is to wipe out the Mau Mau terrorists.
37. It's already crystal clear that the United Nations is a failure.
38. A study of British history clearly shows that it is the British merchant who has contributed most to our society.
39. Even a person of average intelligence knows that to defend ourselves against aggression we should welcome any kind of help--including Franco's.
40. Anyone who knows what's going on will tell you that the Foreign Office diplomats who disappeared in 1952 were traitors to their country.

OPINIONATION SCALE
Form C - American Version

Opinionated Rejection - Left

1. It's just plain stupid to say that it was Franklin Roosevelt who got us into the war.
2. A person must be pretty stupid if he still believes in differences between races.
3. There are two kinds of people who fought Truman's Fair Deal Program: the selfish and the stupid.
4. A person must be pretty short-sighted if he believes that college professors should be forced to take special loyalty oaths.
5. It's the people who believe everything they read in the papers who are convinced that Russia is pursuing a ruthless policy of imperialist aggression.
6. It's mainly those who believe the propaganda put out by the real estate interests who are against a federal slum clearance program.
7. A person must be pretty gullible if he really believes that the Communists have actually infiltrated into government and education.
8. It's mostly those who are itching for a fight who want a universal military training law.
9. It is very foolish to advocate government support of religion.
10. Only a simple-minded fool would think that Senator McCarthy is a defender of American democracy.

Opinionated Rejection - Right

21. It's simply incredible that anyone should believe that socialized medicine will actually help solve our health problems.
22. A person must be pretty ignorant if he thinks that Eisenhower is going to let the "big boys" run this country.
23. It's the fellow travellers or Reds who keep yelling all the time about labor's right to strike.
24. It's the radicals and labor racketeers who yell the loudest about labor's right to strike.
25. It is foolish to think that the Democratic Party is really the party of the common man.
26. You just can't help but feel sorry for the person who believes that the world could exist without a Creator.
27. It's usually the trouble-makers who talk about government ownership of public utilities.
28. Only a misguided idealist would believe that the United States is an imperialist warmonger.
29. It's mostly the noisy liberals who try to tell us that we will be better off under socialism.
30. It's the agitators and left-wingers who are trying to get Red China into the United Nations.

Opinionated Acceptance - Left

11. It's perfectly clear that the decision to execute the Rosenbergs has done us more harm than good.
12. Any person with even a brain in his head knows that it would be dangerous to let our country be run by men like General MacArthur.

13. The truth of the matter is this! It is big business which wants to continue the cold war.
14. Make no mistake about it! The best way to achieve security is for the government to guarantee jobs for all.
15. It's perfectly clear to all decent Americans that Congressional committees which investigate communism do more harm than good.
16. Thoughtful persons know that the American Legion is not really interested in democracy.
17. It's perfectly clear to all thinking persons that the way to solve our financial problem is by a soak-the-rich program.
18. It's all too true that the rich are getting richer and the poor are getting poorer.
19. History clearly shows that it is the private enterprise system which is at the root of depressions and wars.
20. Anyone who's old enough to remember the Hoover days will tell you that it's a lucky thing Hoover was never re-elected.

Opinionated Acceptance - Right

31. Any intelligent person can plainly see that the real reason America is rearming is to stop aggression.
32. Plain common sense tells you that prejudice can be removed by education, not legislation.
33. Anyone who is really for democracy knows very well that the only way for America to head off revolution and civil war in backward countries is to send military aid.
34. History will clearly show that Churchill's victory over the Labour Party in 1951 was a step forward for the British people.
35. The American rearmament program is clear and positive proof that we are willing to sacrifice to preserve our freedom.
36. This much is certain! The only way to defeat tyranny in China is to support Chiang Kai-Shek.
37. It's already crystal-clear that the United Nations is a failure.
38. A study of American history clearly shows that it is the American businessman who has contributed most to our society.
39. Even a person of average intelligence knows that to defend ourselves against aggression we should welcome all help--including Franco's Spain.
40. Anyone who knows what's going on will tell you that Alger Hiss was a traitor who betrayed his country.

INTELLECTUAL CONVICTION SCALE (Rokeach and Eglash, 1956)

Variable   This scale is designed to distinguish people with intellectual convictions or rational beliefs from those with dogmatic convictions or beliefs held on other than logical rational grounds.

Description   The scale consists of 20 six-point Likert-type items. It is based on the assumption that persons with strong intellectual convictions will reject statements of acceptably rational beliefs when such statements are supported by unacceptable reasons or rationalizations.

In a preliminary study, 52 "intellectual conviction" statements were administered to 101 subjects. The 20 most discriminating items were retained for the final scale. No further information about the selection of these items was given. The response alternatives required expression of agreement or disagreement on a scale ranging from +3 to -3 with 0 excluded. Negative scores were eliminated by the addition of +4 to each item score. Possible range of total scores is thus 20-140, with a high score indicating less intellectual conviction.

Sample   All subjects were college sophomores in social science or introductory psychology classes. One hundred and one received the original 52 items. Two samples of 153 and 186 received the final 20 items, along with other tests designed to measure authoritiarianism, rigidity, dogmatism, ethnocentrism, opinionation, political-economic conservatism, and anxiety. (Scales used were thosed constructed by the authors of California Study, and by Gough, Rokeach, and Welsh).

Reliability/   The split-half reliability for the sample of 101 on the 52 items
Homogeneity   was .93 (corrected). The corrected reliability for the two samples of 153 and 186 on the 20 item scale was .76 and .73, respectively.

Validity   The Intellectual Conviction Scale was correlated with the other measures administered as shown in the following table.

	Study I (N=153)	Study II (N=186)
Intellectual Conviction	.76*	.73*
Authoritarianism (F Scale)	-.71	-.61
Rigidity	-.59	-.40
Einstellung (Luchins Test)	-.27**	
Dogmatism	-.55	-.46
Ethnocentrism	-.49	-.35
Opinionation--Total Scale	-.46	-.52
Right Opinionation	-.49	-.52
Left Opinionation	-.08	-.19
Opinionated Rejection	-.41	-.44
Opinionated Acceptance	-.39	-.46
Conservatism (Right Opinionation-Left Opinionation)	-.24	-.28
Conservatism (PEC Scale)	-.38	-.26
Anxiety	-.38	-.24

   * Corrected by Spearman-Brown formula.
  ** Point bi-serial correlation (N=72).

All correlations were negative and significant at the .05 level.
Notice that the Intellectual Conviction Scale correlated -.27 with
the Einstellung Problem Test. This correlation is of special interest
since these problems are a "behavioral" measure of "mental set"
rather than a "paper and pencil" measure as are the other scales
used to assess validity.

Location   Rokeach, M. and Eglash, A., A scale for measuring intellectual
conviction, Journal of Social Psychology, 1956, 44, 135-141.

Administration Estimated administration time is ten minutes.

Results and
Comments   Despite the evidence for the reliability and validity of this
scale, it does have one potentially serious limitation. By the
very nature of the scale's items, it does no more than identify
instances where a rationalization is accepted. In short, if
agreement with the scale may be a good criterion for the absence
of intellectual conviction, disagreement with the scale items does
not necessarily indicate the presence of intellectual conviction.
The assumption that individuals rejecting an item have done so
only because they do not accept the rationalization supporting
that item may not be correct. The authors acknowledge that
validating one scale against another which uses the same
measuring techniques is not as meaningful a validation as one
would desire. The obtained correlations could be the result
of intelligence or response set. The low but statistically
significant correlation of the scale with the Einstellung Problems,
an independent measure of mental set, is good supporting validation
evidence.

Even considering its limitations, this scale is based on an interesting theoretical notion, and further research to determine the possible SES and response set biases involved in score interpretations can easily be carried out.

INTELLECTUAL CONVICTION SCALE

1. The reason we should show consideration for others is that they will reciprocate and show consideration for us.

2. Radio and TV programs should employ only loyal Americans, so as not to lose their audiences.

3. What is wrong with socialization, as seen in England, is that it results in severe rationing.

4. The reason you should not criticize others is that they will turn around and criticize you.

5. The American economic and political system is preferable to the Russian, because the Soviet system means long hours at poor wages.

6. The fallacy in Hitler's theories is shown by the fact that, after all, he lost the war.

7. The reason that criticism is a poor policy is that it prevents you from making and keeping friends.

8. Do unto others as they do unto you.

9. It's better not to talk about people behind their back, because sooner or later it gets back to them, and you get a reputation as a gossip.

10. Negroes deserve equal treatment, because there is as yet no scientific evidence showing there there is any real difference in body odors.

11. The fact that God exists is proven by the fact that so many millions of people believe in Him.

12. The trouble with Communism is that, in all of human history, it has never worked.

13. Taxation without representation is wrong because sooner or later people rebel.

14. If a man fails to practice what he preaches, there's something wrong with what he preaches.

15. You should only criticize others when you are above reproach yourself.

16. The reason it's better to let people make up their own mind is because they won't follow your advice anyway.

17. Whether it's all right to manipulate people or not, it is certainly all right when it's for their own good.

18. Appreciation of others is a healthy attitude, since it is the only way to have them appreciate you.

Reprinted with permission of Rokeach, M. and Eglash, A. Intellectual Conviction Scale in *Journal of Social Psychology,* 44 (1956), pp 135-141. Copyright 1956 by The Journal Press, 2 Commercial Street, Provincetown, Mass. 02657.

INTELLECTUAL CONVICTION SCALE (Continued)

19. Generosity is a healthy way of life, because he who casts his bread upon the waters shall have it returned ten-fold.

20. Whether one approves of filibustering or not, it is all right if it's for a good cause.

CHAPTER 7 - OTHER SOCIO-POLITICAL ATTITUDES

By and large, the scales in this chapter belong in our major volume,

Measures of Political Attitudes. It can be seen by the recent dates of these

scales, however, that they became available (or came to our attention) only

after this volume was in print. On the other hand the first three scales are

more social-psychological than political in nature. The seven scales are:

1. National Involvement Scales (DeLamater et al. 1968)
2. Beliefs about Distribution of Power (Form and Rytina 1969)
3. Social Responsibility Scale (Berkowitz and Lutterman 1968)
4. New Left Scale (Christie et al. 1969)
5. Radicalism-Conservatism (Comrey and Newmeyer 1965)
6. Inputs to the Political System (Milbrath 1968)
7. Opinion Leadership (Scheuch 1960)

The DeLamater et al. scales have the most advanced underlying theoreti-

cal rationale of the four. However, their internal consistency seems quite

low and it is unclear from the study results to date whether the scales

really provide any more than an insightful description of class and/or

educational differences in the ways in which individuals identify themselves

with their country. Nevertheless, the author's scales do considerably ad-

vance our understanding of these processes and some of the basic tenets of

public opinion that may flow from them.

The Form and Rytina measure actually consists of a single question, in

which the respondent is asked to choose which of three descriptions most

aptly fits the way in which power in America is distributed. The three

descriptions follow the basic philosophies of Reisman, Marx or Mills. While

the Reisman (or pluralist) view is endorsed by most respondents, especially

the better educated and more affluent, their replies to other questions

indicate that these beliefs are inconsistent with other political beliefs.

The social responsibility scale of Berkowitz and Lutterman follows

closely from earlier measures of this phenomenon devised by Harris and by

Gough. The present scale benefits from having been applied to a state-wide probability sample in which a number of impressive correlations with a wide variety of associated behaviors and attitudes were obtained. The items in the scale have been constructed so as to allow for control of agreement response set.

The new left scale of Christie et al. is still in process of development but if present campus behavior continues it is likely to receive wide application in the years to come. The scale items show relatively high internal consistency and satisfactory validity on the small sample of students to whom they have been applied. Many of the items, however, seem likely to become time-bound and culture-bound to the college-aged youth of the late 1960's.

The Comrey-Newmeyer scale of radicalism-conservatism suffers from many of the liabilities of measures of this variable that were discussed in Measures of Political Attitudes. However compared to many of these measures, the one of Comrey and Newmeyer contains better written and less-dated items, items split into parallel forms (with an extremely high correlation between forms), a sophisticated item-analytic basis, and content from a variety of areas. On the other hand, the authors present no validational data.

The final two scales clearly belong in Chapter 11 of Measures of Political Attitudes, which is devoted to measures of political participation.

The Milbrath scale of "inputs to the political system" consists of general participation in politics, making it more similar to the Woodward-Roper and Matthews-Prothro scale in Chapter 11 than to the scales of Campbell, et al. and Robinson which deal with activity during a specific campaign. Milbrath's scale is a promising start in the direction of a multidimensional measure of political participation. As yet, however, exact scoring instructions and norms on the instrument as a scaling device are not available. Milbrath does present some interesting data on the scale's reliability and relative freedom from agreement response set.

Scheuch's opinion leadership scale is based more on evidence of associated political activity than on actual opinion leadership. That is, the scale assumes that greater participation in associations and greater use of the mass media will result in an individual's being an opinion leader. There is sound research evidence to substantiate this assumption (and Scheuch himself presents data showing a fairly strong relationship between participation and political knowledge). However, evidence relating this measure to reported or observed opinion leadership is needed before a proper evaluation of this scale is possible.

NATIONAL INVOLVEMENT SCALES
(DeLamater, Katz, and Kelman 1968)

Variable   The scales attempt to separate three mechanisms by which an individual can be nationalistic: symbolic (by national symbols), normative (by rewards and sanctions), and functional (by material benefits).

Description   The three mechanisms follow from Katz and Kahn's (1966) distinction between the major means by which a role system is integrated: through values, norms, and roles. In terms of some of the different orientations that are hypothesized as being associated with each role:

Attitude toward:	Symbolic	Normative	Functional
1. Flag, leaders, etc.	strong and positive	mild positive	low
2. Role of an "American"	most important to learn and low tolerance for deviation	as important as other roles	in terms of political and social responsibilities
3. Criticism of American way of life	defensive and hostile		tolerated if in the national interest
4. Extending American way of life	approve	disapprove because want to preserve	only if in other countries' national interest
5. Policies that might weaken U.S. power	oppose	accept if agreed upon by national leaders	support if in national interest
6. Involvement in political life		passive (as reflected in their political apathy	active (as reflected in their greater participation)

Initially, 15-20 items tapping each orientation were included in the interview schedule, but only those were included which either (a) correlated at the .05 level with one other item or (b) seemed on an a priori basis to tap the aspect in question. Eight items remained in the symbolic and normative scales, and six in the functional scale. Items on each scale employ a variety of question formats. The score categories and the percentage of the sample falling into each score category are as follows:

Score category	Symbolic		Normative		Functional	
High	5-8	(28%)	4-5	(19%)	3-5	(26%)
High-Medium	3-4	(28%)	3	(23%)	2	(23%)
Low-Medium	1-2	(22%)	1-2	(38%)	1	(35%)
Low	-4-0	(22%)	-4-0	(20%)	0	(16%)
		100%		100%		100%

Sample

A probability sample of 129 residents of Ann Arbor, Michigan. People affiliated with the University of Michigan were excluded from the sample.

Reliability/ Homogeneity

The following average inter-item correlation coefficients (phi) were obtained:

Symbolic: .16
Normative: .11
Functional: .08

Values of .17 are significant at the .05 level for this size sample. The correlation between the three scales was:

	Sym	Norm	Func
Symbolic	X		
Normative	.19	X	
Functional	-.11	-.11	X

Validity

As might be expected, there was a strong relation between education and type of role involvement. While 84% of the Functional group had been to college, only 40% of the Normative group and 0% of the Symbolic group had attended college. The same relation held in terms of fathers' education--47% of the Functional group had fathers who had been to college vs. 30% of Normatives and 14% of Symbolics. Other indirect evidence of validity is provided by the verbal behavior of the various types of respondents when asked open-ended questions about political issues and events. For example, the Symbolic group was especially likely to report strong affect (e.g., anger, sorrow) as their reaction to the assassination of President Kennedy. These people also placed highest values on children's learning to be "good Americans" and were least tolerant of deviation from role prescriptions (e.g., by not believing in God, or being an ex-Communist). On the other hand, the Normative group (mainly working-class) were most likely to feel that violators of norms are not "good" Americans, in mentioning interpersonal morality as something "a person ought to do to be a good American." They are most likely also to accept government policies that are generally agreed upon.

Finally the Functional group were better informed politically, most likely to stress helping one's fellow man as a value in child-rearing, more favorable toward the United Nations, more favorable toward disarmament and international negotiation, and least likely to do nothing if a dictatorship came to power in this country.

458

Location   DeLamater, J., Katz, D., and Kelman, H. On the nature of national
                 involvement: a preliminary study in an American community. Unpub-
                 lished paper available from the first author at Department of
                 Sociology, University of Wisconsin.

Results and   As the authors note, this is a pilot study conducted with a relatively
Comments   small sample. Undoubtedly, controls for education (possible with a
                 larger sample) would result in considerably attenuated relations from
                 those found here. For now, these scales still comprise a most in-
                 teresting way of conceptualizing educational differences in the man-
                 ner in which people identify themselves with their country.

                 The major author has expanded his study of nationalism into Yugo-
                 slavia and work on this study is in progress. He has added a fourth
                 form of commitment, namely Ideological (Sample item: How should
                 income in the country be distributed?).

Reference   Katz, D. and Kahn, R. The social psychology of organizations. New
                 York: Wiley, 1966.

SYMBOLIC COMMITMENT SCALE

Questions and Codes	Response Distribution (w=129) %	Scoring

Item 1: "Suppose a person criticizes the government in time of national crisis. In your opinion, could he be a good American?"

Could be; Yes	63.6	0
Depends: on kind of criticism, nature of crisis	17.8	0
No, unqualified	16.3	1

Item 2: "Suppose a person doesn't stand when the Star Spangled Banner is being played. Do you think he could be a good American?"

Yes, unqualified	32.6	-1
Yes, if he had a reason--physical, religious	33.3	0
No, qualified	4.7	1
No, unqualified	24.0	2

Item 3: "Do you happen to own a flag?"

Yes	54.3	1
No	39.5	0
Other; once did, NA	6.2	0

-(For those who own flag) "Do you ever display it on national holidays?"

Always; yes	26.4	1
Usually; sometimes	8.6	1
Never; no	17.8	0
Other; inappropriate	47.2	0

Item 4: "Some observers have complained that the American public nowadays does not pay proper respect to the American flag. Would you agree or disagree with this complaint?"

Agree	46.5	1
Disagree	45.0	0
Other	8.5	0

Item 5: "What would you think of an American who says that he takes no particular pride in our armed forces?"

Approve; he has a right to say that	14.0	-1
Indifferent; nothing; don't know	10.0	0
Disapprove, general	33.3	1
Disapprove: not a good American	33.3	0
Other	9.3	0

Reprinted with permission of DeLamater, J., Katz, D., and Kelman, H. National Involvement Scales in "On the Nature of National Involvement: A Preliminary Study in an American Community," unpublished paper available from the first author at Department of Sociology, University of Wisconsin.

Item 6: "Imagine the American Peace Corps comes up in a
conversation between yourself and a foreigner and
he laughs at it. How do you think you would react
when this occurs--would you regard this as an
insult, or a sign of poor taste, or a personal
opinion to which he is entitled?"

An insult	10.1	1
A sign of poor taste	16.3	0
An opinion to which he is entitled	61.2	0

Item 7a: "How would you feel if a foreigner criticized
racial segregation in the U.S.?"

7b: "How would you feel if a foreigner attacked the
free enterprise system?"

	Item 7a %	Item 7b %	Scoring
An insult; poor taste; would be mad	17.1	29.5	1**
He is wrong; would argue with him	5.4	24.8	0
Depends: where he's from, what he says	7.8	1.6	0
An opinion to which he's entitled	31.0	20.2	0
Would like to talk to him	1.6	7.0	0
He is right; would agree with him	26.4	3.1	0
Other	10.9	13.9	0

**One point only if coded in this category on both items

Item 8: "How do you feel about the following quotation:
Do you strongly agree, slightly agree, slightly disagree,
or strongly disagree? 'Whereas some people feel that
they are citizens of the world, that they belong
to mankind and not to any one nation, I, for my part,
feel that I am first, last, and always an
American.'"

Strongly agree	58.9	1
Slightly agree	21.7	0
Slightly disagree	8.5	-1
Strongly disagree	7.8	-2

NORMATIVE COMMITMENT SCALE

Questions and Codes	Response Distribution (%)	Scoring
Item 1: "What do you think a person ought to do in order to be a good American?"		
Mentioned formal requirements: vote, pay taxes, serve in Army, support constitution.	34.9	1
Did not mention the above	65.1	0
Item 2: "What do you think a person ought to do in order to be a good American?"		
Mentioned conformity to norms: obey laws, be honest, stay out of trouble, do the right things, be loyal, live properly, live a clean life, etc.	37.2	1
Did not mention the above	62.8	0
Item 3: "Some people say that a person should go along with whatever his country does even if he disagrees with it. How do you feel about that?"		
Agree, unqualified; he should	15.5	1
He should go along with majority	9.3	1
Has no choice, has to go along	10.1	1
Depends: on the issue, the person	13.2	0
Disagree: he has a right to criticize	38.8	0
Disagree: government could be wrong	8.5	-1
Item 4: "Suppose a law was passed raising income taxes by fifty percent. Would you pay the tax without question, refuse to pay if a good many other people refused, or refuse regardless of what others did?"		
Pay without question	62.8	1
Refuse if others did	17.8	0
Refuse regardless	7.8	-1

Item 5: "Suppose a law was passed requiring all
citizens to be fingerprinted and to
carry identity cards. Would you obey
without question, not obey if a good many
others also refused to obey, or not obey
regardless of what others did?"

Obey without question	82.9	1
Refuse if others did	4.7	0
Refuse regardless	7.8	-1

Items
6-8: "Here is a list of things that a government
might ask its citizens to do.

    a. First, go through this list and tell me
       which things the government should
       require people to do.
    b. Now go through the list and tell me which
       of these things you think the government
       should encourage people to do, but which
       they have a right to refuse if they prefer
    c. Finally, go through the list and pick out
       those things which you think the government
       should leave completely to the individual."

Item 6: "Serve in the armed forces."

Government should require people to	78.3	0
Government should encourage people to	17.8	-1
Government should leave to the individual	2.3	-2

Item 7: "Pay taxes."

Government should require people to	95.3	0
Government should encourage people to	3.1	-1
Government should leave to the individual	.8	-2

Item 8: "Send their children to school."

Government should require people to	90.7	0
Government should encourage people to	8.5	-1
Government should leave to the individual	.8	-2

FUNCTIONAL COMMITMENT SCALE

Questions and Codes	Response Distribution (%)	Scoring
Item 1: "What are some of the things that particularly remind you that you are an American?"		
Mentioned opportunity: affluence, standard of living, free enterprise; accomplishment, progress	28.7	1
Did not mention the above	70.5	0
Item 2: "What do you think a person ought to do in order to be a good American?"		
Mentioned participation: be informed, participate in public affairs, use citizenship rights; take part in community, vote intelligently, etc.	42.6	1
Did not mention the above	57.4	0
Item 3: "Are there any people you know or have heard about who you think are not good Americans?"		
Mentioned apathetic persons: people who don't appreciate what they have, our opportunities; people who don't accept their responsibilities as citizens.	6.2	1
Did not mention the above	93.8	0
Item 4: "What do you think people mean when they talk about the American way of life?"		
Mentioned affluence: high standard of living, free enterprise, freedom (defined in terms of consumption), security, happiness	42.6	1
Did not mention the above	57.4	0
Item 5: "What do you think are the most important things that make America different from other countries?"		
Mentioned opportunity: advancement, chance to get ahead	14.7	1
Did not mention the above	83.7	0
Item 6: "What do you think are the most important things that make America different from other countries?"		
Mentioned affluence: high standard of living, ease of living, convenience; modern civilization; industrialization; free enterprise	31.0	1
Did not mention the above	67.4	0

BELIEFS ABOUT THE DISTRIBUTION OF POWER
(Form and Rytina, 1969)

Variable

This attitude item taps whether individuals believe that power in the United States is distributed according to the positions advocated by David Riesman (political pluralism), C. Wright Mills (a power elite), or Marxists (control by big business).

Description

The task for the respondent is to pick one of the three formulations of how power is distributed in this country. The following distribution was obtained:

Pluralistic	63%
Elitist	19%
Economic dominance	18%
	100%

Statements of the employee and managerial society were originally included but later dropped because so few respondents considered them meaningful.

Sample

The sample consisted of a cross-section of 186 respondents in Muskegon, Michigan, plus supplementary samples of poor and rich respondents bringing the total sample up to 354. These people were interviewed sometime in the mid-1960's.

Reliability/
Homogeneity

No reliability data are reported, although only test-retest measures would be appropriate.

Validity

No data bearing directly on validity are reported. However, the authors feel that the fact that the pluralistic belief is reported more often by those with higher incomes supports their presupposition that this view would be expected from people who get more rewards from the system. On the other hand, the authors note that although higher income respondents reported belief in the pluralist ideology, very few rejected the task of selecting which interest groups were most powerful when asked to give such ratings. (Such ratings would constitute a violation of the pluralistic conception of politics.)

Location

Form, W. and Rytina, J. Ideological beliefs on the distribution of power in the United States. American Sociological Review, 1969, 34, 19-31.

Results and
Comments

Larger differences were found in ideological beliefs by education than by the factors of income or race. The pluralistic view was endorsed by 73% of college graduates but only 33% of those who had not completed grade school. This view was held by 55% of the poor and 65% of the rich.

Those choosing the economic dominance model varied from 40% of the less than grade school educated to 8% of college graduates. Negroes (37%) were much more likely to take this view than whites (18%) and poor whites (23%) more than rich whites (12%).

As noted above, separate questions dealing with which of twelve interest groups ought to have most influence over the way things were run in Washington were also included in this study. While espousing the pluralist ideology, only 38% of the better educated said that all groups should have equal say vs. 52% of the least educated. Close to 15% of the college-educated and 30% of the rich said that big business ought to be most powerful vs. well under 10% of the poor and middle income groups, or the less-educated.

In terms of who had most actual power at the time (ed. note: during a Democratic administration), over 50% of the rich and college-educated said labor unions vs. about 25% of the rest of the sample.

DISTRIBUTION OF POWER SCALE

I am going to read you three ways in which people think that power in this country is distributed. Which of these, in your opinion, is the most accurate description?

(Riesman)   No one group really runs the government in this country. Instead, important decisions about national policy are made by a lot of different groups such as labor, business, religious, and educational groups, and so on. These groups influence both political parties, but no single group can dictate to the others, and each group is strong enough to protect its own interests.

(Mills)   A small group of men at the top really run the government in this country. These are the heads of the biggest business corporations, the highest officers in the Army, Navy, and Air Force, and a few important senators, congressmen and federal officials in Washington. These men dominate both the Republican and Democratic parties.

(Marx)   Big businessmen really run the government in this country. The heads of the large corporations dominate both the Republican and Democratic parties. This means that things in Washington go pretty much the way big businessmen want them to.

SOCIAL RESPONSIBILITY SCALE (Berkowitz and Lutterman 1968)

Variable   This scale attempts to assess a person's traditional social responsibility, an orientation toward helping others even when there
is nothing to be gained from them.

Description   Six of the eight items in the SRS scale are drawn from a social responsibility scale for children derived by Harris (1957); these in
turn are similar to items constructed earlier by Gough et al. (1952).
The items in the present scale are especially tied into traditional
values and are therefore likely to have essentially a conservative
individualist theme. The scale is also conceived of as a polar
opposite of alienation.

The items were given in straightforward Likert scale format, with
five response options from strongly agree through strongly disagree.
Four items are worded in the responsible direction, the other four
in the opposite direction. No further scoring instructions are
given but the following distribution of scores along the scale are
reported:

	Middle Class	Working Class		TOTAL
High	24	42	=	35
Middle	37	35	=	36
Low	39	23	=	29
	100%	100%		100%

Sample   The SRS scale was administered to a statewide probability sample of
766 Wisconsin adults in early fall, 1963. Response rate was 88%.

Reliability/   The scale was constructed on the basis of item analyses with samples of
  Homogeneity   college students. The internal consistency of the scale in the
present sample was "very satisfactory", although no statistical data
are reported. No test-retest data were apparently collected.

Validity   Most of the following behavioral correlates are based on respondent
descriptions and therefore cannot be considered as completely objective estimates of validity. Among both working class and middle
class respondents, those scoring high on the SRS scale were more
likely to:

1. Make financial contributions to an educational or religious
   institution

2. Be active in organizations or church work

3. Show great interest in national and local politics and to
   be active politically

4. To vote in elections and know the names of candidates for
   office.

However, high SRS people were also more likely to oppose more government involvement in problems in unemployment and to oppose extending social security.

Location   Berkowitz, L. and Lutterman, K. The traditionally socially responsible personality. Public Opinion Quarterly, 1968, XXXII, 169-185.

Results and   High SRS scorers among both middle and working class respondents
Comments   tended to affiliate more with the Republican party. This result held even when controlled for city size, except for the rural working class.

% Republican	Low SRS	High SRS
Middle class, urban	42	49
Middle class, rural	43	60
Working class, urban	14	30
Working class, rural	45	42

It was concluded that "all in all, high scorers on SRS generally were least inclined to deviate from the political traditions of their class and community."

High SRS types however were not "other-directed conformists" in the sense that they were less likely (than those with low SRS) to place a high value on being well-liked or popular as important things for children to learn, and more likely to place a high value on thinking for oneself. High SRS people in the working class were less likely than low SRS people to disagree with the view that big business was too powerful.

It is reported that SRS is strongly associated with education, but the authors note that college students, homogeneous on this factor, evidence behaviors in experiments congruent with their SRS scores. Finally, all of these results run counter to McClosky's (1958) description of conservatives as alienated and hostile.

References   Gough, H.; McClosky, H.; and Meehl, P. A personality scale for social responsibility. Journal of Abnormal and Social Psychology, 1952, 47, 73-80.

Harris, D. A scale for measuring attitudes of social responsibility in children. Journal of Abnormal and Social Psychology, 1957, 55, 322-326.

McClosky, H. Conservatism and personality. American Political Science Review, 1958, 55, 27-45.

Social Responsibility Scale (SRS)
(* responsible reply)

1. It is no use worrying about current events or public affairs; I can't do anything about them anyway.

   Strongly agree   Agree   Undecided   *Disagree   *Strongly disagree

2. Every person should give some of his time for the good of his town or country.

   *Strongly agree   *Agree   Undecided   Disagree   Strongly disagree

3. Our country would be a lot better off if we didn't have so many elections and people didn't have to vote so often.

   Strongly agree   Agree   Undecided   *Disagree   *Strongly disagree

4. Letting your friends down is not so bad because you can't do good all the time for everybody.

   Strongly agree   Agree   Undecided   *Disagree   *Strongly disagree

5. It is the duty of each person to do his job the very best he can.

   *Strongly agree   *Agree   Undecided   Disagree   Strongly disagree

6. People would be a lot better off if they could live far away from other people and never have to do anything for them.

   Strongly agree   Agree   Undecided   *Disagree   *Strongly disagree

7. At school I usually volunteered for special projects.

   *Strongly agree   *Agree   Undecided   Disagree   Strongly disagree

8. I feel very bad when I have failed to finish a job I promised I would do.

   *Strongly agree   *Agree   Undecided   Disagree   Strongly disagree

Reprinted with permission of Berkowitz, L. and Lutterman, K. Social Responsibility Scale in "The Traditionally Socially Responsible Personality," *Public Opinion Quarterly*, 32 (1968), pp 169-185. Copyright 1968 by Columbia University Press.

NEW LEFT SCALE (Christie et al. 1969)

Variable

This scale is an exploratory attempt to measure agreement with the principles exposed by the under-30 New Left, mainly concerning discontent with the existing social order.

Description

A total of 62 items were derived from open-ended responses of Columbia students arrested during spring 1968 demonstrations as well as from various New Left publications (items referring to tactics were deliberately excluded). Of these, 56 items correlated at the .05 level with total scale scores.

Items are given in Likert-scale format from 1 (strongly disagree), through 4 (no opinion), and up to 7 (strongly agree). Items are worded in both pro-Left and anti-Left directions.

Sample

A total of 153 freshmen at Columbia participated in this first phase of instrument construction. These freshmen were recruited from a pool of 254 who returned questionnaires (out of 700 entering freshmen). Efforts were made to ensure that the 153 would contain a proportionate number of radical students. (It turned out that 30% of these students had participated in politically relevant activities.)

Reliability/
Homogeneity

Average item-test correlations for the 20 best items was .54 (comparable F scale items had an average of .33). No test-retest data have been reported.

Validity

The following average scores (from 1, anti-Left, to 7, pro-Left) were obtained from students according to their degree of participation in civil rights and peace movements:

No activity (N = 54)	3.2
Moderate activity (N = 36)	3.3
High activity (N = 40)	4.4

Location

Christie, R.; Friedman, L.; and Ross, A. The New Left and its ideology. Unpublished paper, Department of Social Psychology, Columbia University.

Administration

The items should take less than 30 minutes to complete. Note that the average scores (noted on the following description of items) of negatively-worded items have the reverse interpretation of the positive items.

Results and
Comments

This scale is still in process of development. Interested researchers may find that the first 10 or 20 items will be sufficient for their research purposes.

The following average item scores for students with preferences with 1968 political candidates was as follows:

Nixon, Reagan, Wallace (N = 25)	3.1
Humphrey, Johnson (N = 17)	3.1
Rockefeller, Kennedy, McCarthy (N = 56)	3.5
McCarthy alone (N = 15)	3.7
Cleaver, Gregory (N = 18)	4.3

NEW LEFT SCALE

(in order of item-scale correlation)
* agree response scored anti-Left

	Average Likert score	r_{iRS} [a]
1. "The Establishment" unfairly controls every aspect of our lives; we can never be free until we are rid of it. Strongly Agree 1 2 3 4 5 6 7 Strongly Disagree	3.2	.75
2. You can never achieve freedom within the framework of contemporary American society.	3.3	.69
3. The United States needs a complete restructuring of its basic institutions.	4.2	.68
4. A mass revolutionary party should be created.	3.1	.65
5. Authorities must be put in an intolerable position so they will be forced to respond with repression and thus show their illegitimacy.	5.0	.62
6. The solutions for contemporary problems lie in striking at their roots, no matter how much destruction might occur.	3.8	.58
7. Disruption is preferable to dialogue for changing our society.	4.2	.55
8. Even though institutions have worked well in the past, they must be destroyed if they are not effective now.	4.2	.55
9. The structure of our society is such that self-alienation is inevitable.	4.1	.52
10. Sexual behavior should be bound by mutual feelings, not by formal and legal ties.	6.1	.51
11. A problem with most older people is that they have learned to accept society as it is, not as it should be.	5.2	.51
12. The bureaucracy of American society makes it impossible to live and work spontaneously.	3.7	.50
*13. Radicals of the left are as much a threat to the rights of the individual as are the radicals of the right.	4.9	-.49

[a] r_{iRS} is the product-moment correlation of each subject's score on each item (i) with his total score on the 62-item New Left Scale.

Reprinted with permission of Christie, R., Friedman, L., and Ross, A. New Left Scale in "The New Left and Its Ideology," unpublished paper, Department of Social Psychology, Columbia University.

	Average Rating	r_{iRS}
14. While man has great potential for good, society brings out primarily the worst in him.	3.8	.47
15. The processes of rebuilding society are of less immediate importance than the processes of destroying it.	1.7	.47
16. The political structure of the Soviet Union is more like that of the United States than that of Red China.	3.7	.46
17. The streets are a more appropriate medium for change in our society than printing presses.	2.9	.46
*18. Competition encourages excellence.	4.8	-.46
19. Marriage unfairly restricts one's personal freedom.	3.1	.46
*20. The right to private property is sacred.	3.9	-.46
21. No one should be punished for violating a law which he feels is immoral.	2.7	.45
*22. The courts are a useful vehicle for responsible change.	4.7	-.44
*23. There are legitimate channels for reform which must be exhausted before attempting disruption.	5.8	-.43
24. You learn more from ten minutes in a political protest than ten hours of research in a library.	2.9	.43
*25. Although our society has to be changed, violence is not a justified means.	4.6	-.42
*26. Society needs some legally based authority in order to prevent chaos.	5.7	-.42
*27. Representative democracy can respond effectively to the needs of the people.	4.6	-.42
*28. Police should not hesitate to use force to maintain order.	2.5	-.41
29. Real participatory democracy should be the basis for a new society.	4.7	.41
*30. If people worked hard at their jobs, they would reap the full benefits of our society.	2.5	-.40
31. Groups with a formal structure tend to stifle creativity among their members.	4.3	.40

474

	Average Rating	r_{iRS}
32. A social scientist should not separate his political responsibilities from his professional role.	4.1	.40
33. People should not do research which can be used in ways which are contrary to the social good.	3.3	.40
*34. Abrupt reforms in society usually lead to such a severe backlash that they will be self-defeating.	4.3	-.40
*35. Traditions serve a useful social function by providing stability and continuity.	4.7	-.39
*36. The very existence of our long-standing social norms demonstrates their value.	2.4	-.37
37. If the structure of our society becomes non-repressive, people will be happy.	3.6	.37
38. The distinction between public and private life is unnecessary.	2.8	.36
*39. Compromise is essential for progress.	5.1	-.35
40. Extensive reform in society only serves to perpetuate the evils; it will never solve problems.	2.6	.34
*41. Voting must be a pragmatic rather than moral decision.	3.5	-.33
*42. Anyone who violates the law for reasons of conscience should be willing to accept the legal consequences.	5.3	-.33
*43. It is possible to modify our institutions so that the blacks can be incorporated on an equal basis into our contemporary society.	4.7	-.31
44. Although men are intrinsically good, they have developed institutions which force them to act in opposition to their basic nature.	3.4	.30
45. Educational institutions should espouse political doctrines.	2.4	.28
*46. Change in our society should be based primarily on popular elections.	4.2	-.26
*47. A minority must never be allowed to impose its will on the majority.	3.7	-.25
*48. Spontaneity is often an excuse for irresponsibility.	4.4	-.24

	Average Rating	r_{iRS}
49. An individual can find his true identity only by detaching himself from formal ideologies.	4.4	.24
*50. Being put in positions of leadership brings out the best in men.	3.6	-.24
51. Political factions cannot cooperate with each other without sacrificing their integrity.	2.9	.23
52. It is more important that people be involved in the present rather than concerned with the past or the future.	3.9	.23
53. A commitment to action is more socially relevant than a commitment to any specific philosophy.	4.1	.22
*54. Commitment to a meaningful career is a very important part of a man's life.	5.7	-.21
*55. One's personal life can be kept separate from one's political life.	3.1	-.20
*56. A group without a clear-cut pattern of leadership cannot function effectively.	4.9	-.18
57. Freedom of expression should be denied to racist and neo-fascistic movements.	1.9	.15
*58. Provocation of the police should only be a by-product, not a goal, of mass action.	5.7	.12
*59. A liberal society is more conducive to revolutionary change than is a fascistic one.	3.9	-.12
*60. We must strive for the democratization of decision-making bodies within the existing government.	5.4	-.11
61. The only way to combat violence is to use violent means.	2.1	.09
62. You should always be candid with your friends even though you may hurt their feelings.	3.9	.04

RADICALISM - CONSERVATISM (Comrey and Newmeyer 1965)

Variable   This scale was derived from factor analyses of twenty-five socio-political attitude variables.

Description   A total of 120 items tapping the 25 variables were rated on nine-point Likert scales from 1 (agree very strongly) through 9 (disagree very strongly). When these items were formed into indices of the 25 variables and factor analyzed, 9 factors emerged. When factor scores for these nine factors were themselves factor analyzed, the primary "second-order" factor was comprised of five of the nine first-order factors (welfare-state, punitiveness, nationalism, religion, and racial tolerance). Out of the original 120 items, 67 loaded on this major second-order factor called radicalism-conservatism.

From these 67 items, two parallel forms (A and B) of 30 items each were constructed. Scores thus can vary between 30 (radical) to 270 (conservative) on both forms. For the sample below the average score on Form A was 159.0 (s.d. = 41.3) and for Form B, 158.4 (s.d. = 41.8) and the distribution of scores was "approximately normal" around these average scores.

Sample   A total of 212 volunteers from universities, organizations, and randomly-selected blocks in Los Angeles participated in the study. The volunteers were two-thirds male and had a median age of 29 and a median 15 years of education. Less than 10% professed extreme political beliefs.

Reliability/   For this sample, Forms A and B correlated .96, although this estimate
Homogeneity   would be somewhat less if applied to a new sample.

Validity   No data bearing on validity are reported.

Location   Comrey, A. and Newmeyer, J. Measurement of radicalism-conservatism. Journal of Social Psychology, 1965, 67, 357-369.

Results and   The authors note close resemblance between factors found in British
Comments   studies (Religionism, Humanitarianism, Nationalism) and three of the factors extracted in this study (Religion, Punitiveness, Nationalism). Moreover they predict that the British results would yield the same single factor, if a second-order factor analysis were performed.

The reader will note that the instrument contains items from only 13 of the 25 variables originally investigated by the authors. The 12 variables not included in the final scale are: population control, pay based on ability, partisanship, rapid social change, fatalism, traditional moral values, fascism, respect for age, indoctrination, belief in people, cultural ethnocentrism, and education for adjustment.

RADICALISM - CONSERVATISM SCALE

Form A

(*Reversed item)

(Religiosity) 1. Every child should have religious instruction.
Agree very strongly 1 2 3 4 5 6 7 8 9 Disagree very strongly

2. God exists, in the form in which the Bible describes him.

3. This country would be better off if religion had a greater influence in daily life.

4. All people alive today are the descendants of Adam and Eve.

(Pacifism) *5. This country should disarm regardless of whether or not other countries do.

*6. If my country had been destroyed, I still would not push the button to wipe out the attacking enemy nation.

7. Our country should be engaged constantly in research to develop superior weapons for our national defense.

(Welfarism) *8. The average man today is getting less than his rightful share of our national wealth.

*9. The government should guarantee every citizen enough to eat.

(Anti-Unionism) 10. Many large unions have officers with criminal records.

11. Most unions do not elect officers by honest, secret-ballot elections.

(Weak Federal Government) 12. Central government should run only those things which cannot be run effectively at the local level.

13. The federal government has too much power over citizens and local government.

14. Greater decentralization of power would be better for this country.

15. A greater degree of government control over business would result in a weakening of this country's economy.

(Moral Censorship) 16. If a man is showing a sex movie to friends in his own home, the police should stop it.

17. Every city should prevent the sale of objectionable books.

18. Sexual relations between unmarried people should be illegal.

19. The police should hunt down homosexuals and put them in jail.

Reprinted with permission of Comrey, A. and Newmeyer, J. Radicalism-Conservatism in "Measurement of Radicalism-Conservatism," *Journal of Social Psychology*, 67 (1965) pp 357-369. Copyright 1965 by The Journal Press.

(Contraception) *20. Abortion should be legalized.

(Racial Toler- *21. Employers should be prevented by law from hiring
ance)   only people of their own race.

(Severe Treat- 22. Criminals convicted of three separate felonies
ment of Crimi-   should never be released.
nals)   23. In our country, the sentences handed out to crimi-
                    nals are usually too light.

(Capital   24. A mentally ill man who attacks and kills a little
Punishment)   girl should be executed.
                25. A gunman who kills someone in an armed robbery
                    should receive the death sentence.

(Service to   26. Every able bodied male should willingly serve for
Country)   a period of time in his country's military service.
                27. A man who is ready to die for his country deserves
                    the highest honor.

(World Govern- *28. The United States should work peacefully for a
ment)   strong world government.
                *29. The United States should be willing to surrender
                    some of its rights to strengthen the United Nations.

(Service to the *30. Laws which benefit the people are more important
Individual)   than laws which strengthen the nation.

Form B

(Religiosity)   1. School teachers should believe in God.
                 2. It should be against the law to do anything which
                    the Bible says is wrong.
                 3. Moses got the ten commandments directly from God.
                 4. All the miracles described in the Bible really
                    happened.

(Pacifism)   *5. Under no circumstances should our country use
                    nuclear bombs against anybody.
                *6. I would rather have a foreign power take over our
                    country than start another world war to stop it.
                 7. Our country should prepare to employ every avail-
                    able weapon to destroy any major power that seriously
                    attacks us.

(Welfarism)   *8. It is the responsibility of the government to take
                    care of people who can't take care of themselves.
                *9. If the government must go deeper in debt to help
                    people, it should do so.

(Anti-Unionism) 10. Most unions try to prevent the efficient use of labor.
11. Many union leaders use threats and violence to keep themselves in power.

(Weak Federal Government) 12. The federal government should not interfere in the affairs of individual states unless absolutely necessary.
13. The strength of this country today is largely a product of the free enterprise system.
14. Regulation of business by government usually does more harm than good.
15. When something is run by the government, it is apt to be inefficient and wasteful.

(Moral Censorship) 16. Motion pictures which offend any sizeable religious group should be banned.
17. Public libraries should contain only books which are morally sound.
18. A woman who has sexual relations with a man for money should go to jail.
19. More restrictions should be imposed to prevent young people from having sexual relations before marriage.

(Contraception) *20. Birth control devices should be made readily available to anyone who wants to use them.

(Racial Tolerance) *21. Marriages between persons of different races should be socially acceptable.

(Severe Treatment of Criminals) 22. Teenage hoodlums should be punished severely.
23. Our laws give too much protection to criminals.

(Capital Punishment) 24. A dictator who orders the extermination of thousands of innocent people should be executed for his crimes.
25. Someone who plans and carries out the murder of his or her spouse should be executed.

(Service to Country) 26. If called upon to do so, a citizen should be willing to sacrifice his life for his country.
27. Patriotism is one of the great virtues.

(World Government) *28. The United States eventually should give up its military power to a strong world government.
*29. Present nations should become states within an all powerful world government.

(Service to the Individual) *30. The welfare of the individual is more important than the welfare of the country.

INPUTS TO THE POLITICAL SYSTEM (Milbrath 1968)

Variable   This measure of general political participation is based
                on the premise that "beliefs are important determinants
                of the political behavior of ordinary citizens."

Description   There are a total of 21 inputs to the political system.
                In this investigation, each of these inputs was listed
                separately on a card and the respondent was told to place
                each statement into one of four piles headed:

                    Things you do regularly   (4)
                    Things you do fairly often   (3)
                    Things you seldom do   (2)
                    Things you never do at all   (1)

                The numbers in parentheses refer to the numerical value
                associated with each response.

                In addition to sorting the 21 cards under this "real"
                condition, respondents were also asked to place the
                statements under an "ideal" condition into one of the
                following four categories:

                    Things you feel it is essential to do   (4)
                    Things you have an important responsibility to do   (3)
                    Things you have some responsibility to do   (2)
                    Things you feel you have no responsibility to do   (1)

Sample   An unspecified sample of about 960 residents of the
                Buffalo, New York area were interviewed. Of these,
                about 260 were Negro and about 700 white.

Reliability/   The author reports the following factors emerging from a
Homogeneity   factor analysis of the 21 items:

                    1) Party and Campaign Participation (Items 1, 9, 10,
                       13, 14, and 19)
                    2) Protest and Question (Items 4, 5, 6, and 17)
                    3) Teach Children (Items 11, 15, and 18)

                The following inter-item correlation matrix is reported
                for five of the items in the first factor:

	1	9	10	14	19
1) Participate between elections	X	.60	.31	.44	.48
9) Take part in campaign		X	.39	.49	.46
10) Engage in discussions			X	.52	.27
14) Inform others				X	.35
19) Join political party					X

Validity	No data bearing directly on validity are reported. The author presents the following findings which indirectly relate to validity.

1) The substantial correlations (in the .30 to .60 range) between responses on the real and ideal card sorts.

2) A substantial correlation (tau-beta = .57) between the card sort and an open-ended question on the same topic.

3) Some laudable evidence on the lack of systematic bias due to agreement response set.

Location	Milbrath, L. The nature of political beliefs and the relationship of the individual to the government. The American Behavioral Scientist. November-December 1968, XII, 28-36.

Administration	The real and ideal sorts together take about 10 minutes to administer. The author does not give any special instructions for scoring the items as if they comprised a scale. This is true both for all 21 items and those subsets which comprise the factors discussed above under Reliability/Homogeneity.

Results and Comments	In addition to inputs, Milbrath has constructed a similar set of 23 statements dealing with "outtakes from the political system." Respondents also sort these statements into four "real" piles and four "ideal" piles. The statements and piles are listed below after the input items.

Milbrath offers the following tentative generalizations from this study:

"Most people are plugged into the political system in at least a minimal way; they pay taxes, they are loyal, they try to keep informed, they try to vote, and they try to teach their children to be good citizens. More than half of the people feel that their duty as a citizen ends there. Interestingly, people who take this minimal view of their political inputs are somewhat more likely than others to wish to confine governmental outputs (outtakes) to standard old-fashioned governmental duties such as keeping public order (minimal inputs and minimal outtakes are significantly correlated).

"A minority of people feel some responsibility to take an active role in politics and an even smaller percentage actually do so. Conventional participation by this minority seems to have kept the political system functioning reasonably adequately up to now. For a very small

group, non-conventional participation (demonstrations
and riots) may be used, Negroes being somewhat more
willing to do this than Whites. In fact, our data show
that Negroes are somewhat more likely than Whites to
use both conventional and non-conventional means of
political participation. Negroes seem to be developing
a sense of racial identity and a sense of political
skill and effectiveness that they did not possess a few
years ago. At the same time one can see from the outtakes data that Negroes are much less happy with the
performance of the political system than are Whites
while also believing that the system has greater responsibility to do things for them than the Whites are
likely to request.

"One could expect, then, in the near future of American
city politics that Negroes will act increasingly as a
tight bloc, using both conventional and un-conventional
tactics, trying to get the political system to do many
things that more conventional and traditional Whites
will think inappropriate for government to do. The
conflict will be intense and emotional and may significantly transform the nature of government and the way
that citizens relate to their government."

INPUTS TO THE POLITICAL SYSTEM

INPUTS TO THE POLITICAL SYSTEM	MEAN SCORES				TOTAL SAMPLE REAL-IDEAL CORRELATIONS
	Negro		White		
	Real	(Ideal)	Real	(Ideal)	
1. Participate in a political party between elections as well as at election time	1.72	(2.21)	1.69	(2.06)	.47
2. Keep informed about politics	2.75	(2.96)	3.01	(3.14)	.50
3. Vote in elections	3.46	(3.59)	3.39	(3.68)	.41
4. Send messages of support to political leaders when they are doing well	1.62	(2.24)	1.64	(2.22)	.38
5. Send protest messages to political leaders when they are doing badly	1.52	(2.19)	1.50	(2.13)	.38
6. Protest both vigorously and publicly if the government does something that is morally wrong	1.83	(2.43)	1.88	(2.28)	.43
7. Join in public street demonstrations	1.39	(1.56)	1.12	(1.21)	.59
8. Riot if necessary to get public officials to correct political wrongs	1.23	(1.43)	1.10	(1.19)	.44
9. Take an active part in political campaigns	1.69	(2.20)	1.58	(1.99)	.48
10. Engage in political discussion	2.34	(2.52)	2.40	(2.26)	.50
11. Teach my children the importance of give and take in the democratic way of life	3.11	(3.24)	3.09	(3.38)	.52
12. Pay all taxes	3.72	(3.69)	3.81	(3.79)	.37
13. Be a candidate for public office	1.23	(1.44)	1.14	(1.42)	.33
14. Inform others in my community about politics	2.10	(2.30)	1.91	(2.13)	.52
15. Teach my children to participate in politics beyond voting	2.15	(2.59)	2.05	(2.65)	.49
16. Have undivided loyalty and love for my country	3.67	(3.59)	3.71	(3.70)	.48
17. Question the legitimacy of regulations issued by authorities before obeying them	2.12	(2.25)	2.19	(2.36)	.51
18. Personally see to it that my children understand and accept the responsibilities of citizenship	3.14	(3.36)	3.15	(3.49)	.47
19. Join and support a political party	2.33	(2.63)	2.17	(2.49)	.48
20. Be a calming and informing influence in my own community	2.48	(2.71)	2.30	(2.63)	.51
21. Actively support community organizations	2.64	(2.96)	2.52	(2.76)	.51
	N = about 260		N = about 700		

Inputs to the Political System in "The Nature of Political Beliefs and the Relationship of the Individual to the Government," by Lester W. Milbrath is reprinted from *American Behavioral Scientist*, Volume XII, No. 2 (Nov-Dec 1968) pp 31-32 by permission of the Publisher, Sage Publications, Inc., Beverly Hills, Calif.

POLITICAL OUTTAKES

1. Being careful in using public money and trust

2. Taking actions that make me proud of my country

3. Taking actions that make me proud of my city

4. Trying to even out differences in wealth and prestige

5. Arranging things so it is easy for citizens to move from place to place, job to job, class to class

6. Providing a chance to make a good living

7. Seeing to it that every man who wants a job can have a job

8. Insuring equal opportunity for citizens to participate in making political decisions

9. Providing protection and security

10. Providing public order: for example, traffic regulations

11. Securing civil rights and liberties for all

12. Providing justice for all

13. Providing national system of health insurance for people of all ages

14. Making it possible for a person to be heard when he feels he has something to say

15. Competently handling foreign affairs

16. Providing welfare services

17. Provide courts for resolving conflicts between private parties

18. Providing strong leadership

19. Arranging things so that business is left alone

20. Providing free university education for all who can qualify

21. Intervening to stop an individual or group from persecuting another individual or group

22. Providing stability in society even if it means slowing down the role of progress

23. Make it possible for a person with the means to live where he wishes to live.

POLITICAL OUTTAKES (Continued)

Real Sort Piles

1. Things the government does a <u>very</u> effective job of providing
2. Things the government does a <u>moderately</u> effective job of providing
3. Things the government is <u>not</u> <u>very</u> effective in providing
4. Things the government does <u>ineffectively</u> or not at all

Ideal Sort Piles

1. Things you feel it is <u>essential</u> for the government to do
2. Things the government has an <u>important</u> responsibility to do
3. Things the government has <u>some</u> responsibility to do
4. Things you believe the government should <u>not</u> attempt to do <u>at all</u>

OPINION LEADERSHIP (Scheuch 1960)

Variable — This tentative index of opinion leadership was developed on a West German sample.

Description — The intention of the scale was "to separate a presupposed proportion of roughly 10% of the adult population who can be considered active in the sense of opinion moulding." Two sets of criteria make up the scale:
  a) political and organizational participation and
  b) exposure to the mass media
Individuals who were active politically and heavy users of the mass media were designated as opinion leaders, the others being categorized as either "leaders" or "apathetic." Using this scheme, 12% of the sample scored as opinion leaders, 33% as leaders, and 55% as apathetic.

Sample — An unspecified sample of 1843 persons in West Germany were interviewed for empirical data on the scale.

Reliability/ Homogeneity — The following table shows the relation between the two criteria used in the index for the sample of 1843 respondents:

| | Participation | | |
Media Used	Very Active	Active	Inactive
4	62	73	79
3	94	117	124
2	106	130	236
1	60	122	281
0	17	71	271

The correlation (Yule's Y) between these two criteria is .45.

Validity — No data bearing directly on the validity of the scale are reported, although a definite relation between participation and amount of information was found. While 39% of those who were "very active" scored as very well informed, only 5% of those qualifying as "inactive" scored as very well informed.

Location — Scheuch, E. Determination of opinion leadership. Unpublished paper available from the author who is at the Department of Sociology, Köln University, West Germany.

Administration — The following scoring scheme for participation was employed, with the number of respondents in the sample giving the response pattern in parentheses.

Functionaries	Classification	(N)
Association members who attend meetings	Very active	(61)
Association members who do not attend meetings	Very active	(24)
Non-members who attend meetings	Very active	(19)
Non-members who do not attend meetings	Active	(15)

Non-office holders		
Association members who attend meetings	Very active	(235)
Association members who do not attend meetings	Active	(259)
Non-members who attend meetings	Active	(239)
Non-members who do not attend meetings	Inactive	(991)

This leads to a distribution of participation with 18% scored as very active, 28% active, and 54% inactive.

The following scoring scheme for opinion leadership was employed:

	Participation		
Media Used	Very Active	Active	Inactive
4	opinion leader	opinion leader	leader
3	opinion leader	leader	leader
2	leader	leader	apathetic
1	leader	apathetic	apathetic
0	apathetic	apathetic	apathetic

The specific questions used to measure media usage are not reported in this article.

I. PARTICIPATION

1.) Do you perhaps pursue any other kind of activity or hold any other kind of office outside your job--such as listed on this card?

As councillor in rural areas,
    city councillor, or county representative
In a refugee organization
In a professional or trade organization
As village or county selectman
6.7%   As a representative on the shop committee
In a trade union
In a political party
In a youth organization
In a fraternity
In a business organization
6.8%   In a voluntary association or club
86.5%   None of this

1a.) (If "none of this") --or do you perhaps pursue some similar activity or office which is not listed here?

0.6%	Yes
85.9%	No

2.) About now often do you attend meetings or gatherings at which also economic or political questions are discussed?

3%		Frequently
7%	27%	Occasionally
17%		Rarely
73%		Never

3.) Are you a member of a club, association, trade union or political party?

20%		Member of voluntary association
12%	35%	Member of trade union
3%		Member of a political party
69%		No membership

II. MEDIA USAGE

(Exact questions are not reported)

Reprinted with permission of Scheuch, E. Opinion Leadership in "Determination of Opinion Leadership," unpublished paper available from the author at the Department of Sociology, Koln University, West Germany.

CHAPTER 8 - VALUES

The empirical investigation of values remains an isolated area within the field of social psychology, although it is usually assumed important in this field. In the related disciplines of anthropology, sociology and philosophy it has received considerable attention. This chapter contains a brief review of the historical development of empirical instruments to measure values and a discussion of a few of the important theoretical issues currently left unsettled.

In the 1930's a number of similar value scales appeared in the literature. Of these, the Allport-Vernon Study of Values (1931) emerged as the most popular instrument and, as Dukes (1955) noted in a review of studies of values, "...it has (since) received widespread, sometimes uncritical usage." A perusal of three key reviews of the literature on values -- Cantril and Allport (1933), Duffy (1940), and Dukes (1955) -- clearly indicates the dominance of this scale. In order to gain some perspective on values research, it is worthwhile to look briefly at some of the other scales developed during the same period as the Study of Values, although few have been employed by later investigators and none will be given detailed presentation in this chapter.

Lurie (1937) carried out a factor analysis of items based on Spranger's (1928) work and obtained factors differing from Allport and Vernon's, but he failed to validate these adequately. Van Dusen et al. (1939) constructed a Likert-type inventory based on the previous conceptions of Spranger and Lurie. Maller and Glaser's (1939) Interest-Values Inventory was founded in part upon Thurstone's (1931) factor analysis of the Strong Vocational Interest Blank and in part upon the earlier work of Allport and Vernon and of

Lurie. Four value categories were proposed: social, economic, theoretic, and aesthetic. Harding (1941, 1944) developed two more value assessment tests based on five different value areas, each of them sub-divided into two antithetical categories. Finally, Wickert (1940) constructed a test to assess the relative strengths of nine personal "goal-values."

Most of these instruments conceived of values as personal goals or interests rather than as moral imperatives. Perhaps all were influenced directly or indirectly by Spranger's contention that there were various "types of men" who could be identified by their dominant interests. Although these early efforts at scale construction have been largely ignored, the theory and techniques evolved during their development may still be of interest to the reader about to undertake a serious assessment of personal values.

During the two or three decades in which these early attempts were made to characterize human values, anthropologists and sociologists for the most part (rather than psychologists) have made the major contributions in the conceptualization of values. Anthropologists have examined culture patterns and life styles; sociologists have studied ideologies and mores, while psychologists have tended to focus on more narrowly circum-scribed constructs such as attitudes, motives, valences, and cathexes.

No doubt the reasons for largely ignoring values within psychology are varied and complex, but two seem particularly salient. The first has to do with psychologists' desire to define their discipline as a part of the larger enterprise of scientific research, with its emphasis on rigorous objective methods. Patterning themselves after physicists, differentiating themselves from philosophers, many psychologists consider value judgements

to be outside the boundaries of an empirical discipline. They seem to have
confused _making_ value judgements,which is incompatible with scientific objectivity, with studying objectively _how_ _other_ _people_ _make_ _them_ -- a phenomenon as amenable to psychological study, in principle, as other forms of
human learning and choice.

Related to this was a more reasonable view: that because values were
based on irrational or inexpressable feelings they were not accessible to
available psychometric techniques. Thurstone (1954; 1959) disputed this
claim, saying that the problem of developing a subjective metric was manage-
able with existing measurement procedures. Catton (1954) offered specific
demonstrations of three methods for eliciting information about six "infinite" or ultimate values -- choosing between paired alternatives, selecting the "most infinite" value, and rating values according to ultimacy
or importance -- and these were found to intercorrelate almost perfectly.
Even when the measurement issue is settled in principle, however, there remains
another difficulty related to the nature of values conceived as deep, irrational
forces: their resistance to manipulation in laboratory experiments. Unlike
more superficial attitudes, values are assumed to be central to the way an
individual structures his world and defines himself and thus are not subject
to experimental change. Although this problem seems to have encouraged
psychologists to avoid the study of values, more recent work -- for example
Rokeach (1968) -- indicates that it is not insurmountable.

The second major problem, once the psychological study of values is
accepted as legitimate, is to find a fruitful conceptual or theoretical
framework from which to initiate research. The rubric "values" has included
everything from utilities in decision theory (Becker and McClintock, 1967)
to preferred "ways of life" (Morris, 1956). A brief review of a few con-

ceptualizations of the value domain will provide a general background for the discussion of specific scales included in the present chapter.

Adler (1956) outlined four approaches to the definition of values which, taken in combination, exhaust most of the conceptual possibilities. First, values may be considered as absolutes, existing as "eternal ideas" or as parts of the "mind of God." Second, values may be thought to inhere in objects, as the potential of those objects to satisfy needs or desires. Third, values may be seen as present in man (or men), as preferences held by people (whether learned, innate, or both). Finally, values may be conceptualized in terms of action, and this is the view adopted by Adler: that knowing what people do is all that can be known objectively about what they value. Equating values with behavior may, however, present more problems than it solves; for which, if not all, actions then represent values? How can a reasonable class of values be isolated for study?

For most psychologists Adler's third definition is preferred. "Value" then becomes a hypothetical construct -- a kind of "meta-attitude" -- not directly accessible to observation but inferable from verbal statements and other behaviors and useful in predicting still other observable and measurable verbal and nonverbal behavior.

Among social scientists who have attempted to classify values, Kluckhohn (1951) has offered one of the most comprehensive analyses. Values[1] are categorized in terms of the several dimensions: modality; content, including three categories -- aesthetic, cognitive, and moral; generality; intensity and other dimensions. Explication of these dimensions and of

---

[1] Kluckhohn proposes the following definition: "A value is a conception, explicit or implicit, distinctive of an individual or characteristic of a group, of the desirable which influences the selection from available modes, means, and ends to action."

Kluckhohn's provocative essay would take us beyond the scope of the present chapter. However, Kluckhohn has written one of the most complete and sophisticated attempts to arrive at adequate _conceptual_ definitions and integration, and his work is recommended to anyone seeking a theoretical foundation for research on values.

Another way of classifying values has been proposed by Morris (1956). Actual preferences among real alternatives are called _operative_ values. Ideal conceptions of what should be or actual choices that people feel ought to be made are _conceived_ values. Means-end relationships are _object_ values; the preferred means to a particular end may be operative or conceived. Operative values are studied by observing preferential _behavior_ (similar to the approach chosen by Adler), conceived values by the relationship between symbols and preferential behavior. Object values have yet to be satisfactorily operationalized in Morris' work.

Still others have divided values into moral, aesthetic, and social classes--moral values involving a personal sense of "ought," social values containing a sense of "ought" regarding maintenance of the collective welfare, and aesthetic values being a matter of "taste" (preference for certain kinds of sensations).

Philosophical distinctions in the study of values have also been utilized. Included among those which have influenced psychological conceptions are the differences between intrinsic (inseparable from an object or situation) and extrinsic values; between instrumental (means) and inherent or terminal (ends) values (e.g., see the discussion of Rokeach's work later in this chapter); implicit (known only to the subject) and explicit (known to outside observers) values. Factor analysis may reveal empirical dimensions of value initially known to neither respondent nor researcher. Additional conceptual and theoretical work on values has been done by Perry (1926), Lepley (1949), Pepper (1958), Maslow (1959), and Catton (1959).

From all the positions reviewed so far, it is possible to collect a fairly comprehensive list of value characteristics which must eventually be included in an adequate theoretical framework. These include distinctions between values that are individual and collective, explicit and implicit, and that fall into five broad categories: 1) telic, referring to ultimate means and ends; 2) ethical, dealing with good and evil; 3) aesthetic, defining beauty and ugliness; 4) intellectual (or epistomological), outlining how truth is to be known; and 5) economic, dealing with definitions of both preferences and the preferable in the realm of social exchange. These categories seem exhaustive but not mutually exclusive. Operationalizing them successfully presents a formidable challenge.

Measuring Values

To the social psychologist, the theoretical distinctions and numerous conceptual classes may reduce to these simpler notions when it comes to operations. The value realm consists of enduring and central clusters of beliefs, thoughts, and feelings which influence or determine important evaluations or choices regarding persons, situations, and ideas (propositions). Values differ operationally from attitudes only in being fewer in number, more general, central and pervasive, less situation-bound, more resistant to modification and perhaps tied to developmentally more primitive or dramatic experiences. Values influence judgements and actions beyond an immediate or specific situation or goal by providing an abstract frame of reference for perceiving and organizing experience and for choosing among courses of action. When pressed for a decision, then, about where attitude shades into value, the attitude researcher is usually at a loss for criteria more definite than those suggested above.

Within this chapter a small sample of instruments claimed to measure values are presented in detail. These were selected with several characteristics in mind: recency, inclusiveness, diversity, and relevance to empirical social psychology. All the scales presented were either developed or revised within the last 20 years.[2] Nevertheless, some of these incorparate earlier work -- for example, Rettig and Pasamanick (1959) employ items developed by Crissman in 1927. Only scales or instruments tapping general values were selected. Those dealing only with achievement, occupational, religious, and other unidimensional values were omitted.[3] Changes in values as a result of psychotherapy or college attendance are not reviewed here (see, respectively, Rosenthal, 1955, and Newcomb and Feldman, 1968), nor are value measures designed specifically for children (Hawkes, 1952) or for high school students (Asher, 1954).

The scales to be presented in the following pages were based on several

---

[2] The Psychological Abstracts, Sociological Abstracts, and Social Sciences and Humanities Index from 1949 to 1969 provided the major sources for these scales. For the period 1920-1949 only the Psychological Abstracts were consulted.

[3] For occupational measures see our companion volume, Robinson et al. (1968); for a study of the aesthetic value see Cohen (1941); references for measures of achievement values are listed in Bonjean, et al. (1967). American "core" values are discussed by Gruen (1966).

Measures of values based on hypothetical situations are discussed by Carter (1956) and by Stoffer and Toby (1951). For a comparison of verbal and behavioral value measures see Grace and Grace (1952). An excellent introduction to the problems of relating verbally assessed values and attitudes to behavior can be found in Brown (1965, Ch. 8).

different definitions of "value"; each represents a slightly different

approach to the problem of measurement. Included are:

1. Study of Values (Allport, Vernon, and Lindzey 1960)
2. Test of Value Activities (Shorr 1953)
3. Survey of Interpersonal Values (Gordon 1960)
4. Personal Value Scales (Scott 1965)
5. Value Profile (Bales and Couch 1969)
6. Dimensions of Values (Withey 1965)
7. Changes in Moral Values (Rettig and Pasamanick 1959)
8. Inventory of Values (Ewell 1954)
9. Value Survey (Rokeach 1968)
10. Ways to Live (Morris 1956)
11. Variations in Value Orientations (Kluckhohn and Strodtbeck 1961)
12. Social Values Questionnaire (Perloe 1967)

A problem common to authors of all these scales is proper specifi-

cation of the universe from which value items are to be sampled. When one

chooses to assess basic values, items either selected or written must be

neither too general nor too specific. If too general, the items may elicit

only cultural cliches; individual differences in value systems will be

missed. If too specific, the items may tap constructs better labeled

more specifically as attitudes, beliefs, motives, etc.

Another common problem is to overlook the important theoretical and

methodological distinction between values as "what is preferred" vs.

"what is preferable" -- what is desired as opposed to what ought to be

desired. In some cases there may be little difference. For example, in

a study by Scott (1965) it was shown that most college students expected

others to hold the same ultimate values as they did, and others were

judged on the basis of conformity to these personal values. Moreover, the

extensive literature on cognitive dissonance indicates that when a person

is induced to make a choice, he generally comes to see the chosen alter-

native as increasingly preferable. (Festinger, 1957; Abelson et al., 1968)

Nevertheless, the relationship between what is desired by an individual or by a group concensus and what is held by individuals or groups to be the morally proper choice should not be prejudged.[4]

The scales presented in this chapter are organized loosely according to this distinction -- values as choice vs. values as the standards by which choices ought to be made. It should be kept in mind, however, that this is not a distinction considered by many of the authors, and some of the scales do not fit perfectly into either category.

Values as What is Desired

The Allport-Vernon-Lindzey Study of Values ascertains relative preferences for six different kinds of ideas and activities: theoretical, economic, aesthetic, social, political, and religious. This instrument has been used most often to type college students according to their dominant interests. A few questions are couched in terms of "should" or "ought," but, in general, personal preferences are what is measured.

Shorr's Test of Value Activities assesses the intensity with which an individual avoids or shows interest in four kinds of activities: theoretical, social, aesthetic, and economic. It is similar to the Study of Values but does not force a respondent to choose one activity at the expense of another.

Gordon's Interpersonal Values survey also appears to measure what is desired, although here the "objects" of value are social-psychological states (support, conformity, recognition, independence, benevolence, and leadership) important to the respondent. The line between values and central

---

[4]Philosophers point to the so-called "positivistic fallacy" of equating the desired with the desirable, of viewing the majority preference as the worthy preference.

personality traits here becomes very hazy. Operationally there appears
to be little difference, for example, between personality, attitude, and
value survey measures of conformity or independence.

Values as what ought to be desired

Scott is primarily concerned with judgements of college students of
rightness/wrongness and goodness/badness in the area of interpersonal relations.
For this purpose, Scott's instruments appear to be among the most sophisticated and comprehensive in the recent literature.

The Bales and Couch Value Profile also focuses on values related to
social interaction. Unlike Scott, who conceived of his several value
dimensions and then designed items for each, Bales and Couch factor analyzed
a pool of items and turned up four useful empirical dimensions. The Withey
instrument is based on the most important items from this Value Profile. It
is included here because data from a representative national sample, when
factored, yielded the same four dimensions as the Value Profile -- acceptance
of authority, expression vs. restraint, equalitarianism, and individualism --
thus adding considerable support to the reliability of this dimensional
scheme.

The measures designed by Rettig and Pasamanick and by Ewell tap what
is more commonly called morality. Acts such as cheating on exams, lying
under certain conditions, using birth control methods, and so on are judged
according to whether they are right or wrong. This is a direct method for the
assessment of personal values as expressed in norms governing behavior.

Scales Based on a Mixed Conception of Values

In Rokeach's Value Survey respondents are instructed to rank order 18 terminal and 18 instrumental values -- ends and means -- in terms of their importance as guiding principles. Although this procedure is exceptionally simple, Rokeach has already produced interesting results in value-change and behavior-change experiments using the Survey. For some discussion of these and for an enlightening conceptual exploration of beliefs, attitudes, values, and their systematic relations, see his recent book (Rokeach, 1968).

Morris' Ways to Live scale contains 13 complex paragraphs which include values both as what is desired and as what should be preferred. Instructions ask the respondent what he prefers, but some data have been gathered by asking the respondent what he feels he ought to prefer. This instrument is particularly useful in comparing value differences among distinct social groups, and has been used in extensive cross-cultural research.

Also of particular relevance to cross-cultural investigations is the interview questionnaire proposed by Kluckhohn and Strodtbeck, who based their research on the assumption that people in all cultures have to face the same fundamental problems and so must develop normative and preferential ways to deal with these. Although their measures need much further work, this seems to be a productive beginning at combining the insights of psychologists, sociologists, and anthropologists.

Perloe's work contains both conceptions of values, with one of his four factor dimensions running from acceptance of a moral obligation to emphasis on individual preference with reference to behavior toward secondary groups.

REFERENCES

Abelson, R. P.; Aronson, E.; McGuire, W.; Newcomb, T. M.; Rosenberg, M. J.;
and Tannenbaum, P. H. (eds.). Theories of cognitive consistency: a source book.
Chicago: Rand McNally, 1968.

Adler, F. The value concept in sociology. American Journal of Sociology, 1956,
62, 272-279.

Allport, G. W. and Vernon, P. E. A study of values. Boston: Houghton Mifflin,
1931 (revised 1951 in collaboration with G. Lindzey).

Asher, E. J., Jr. An investigation of the relationship between attitudes of
high school students toward ethical practices and several environmental
variables. Ph.D. dissertation, Purdue University, 1954. Ann Arbor:
University Microfilms, Inc., Pub. No. 9853.

Becker, G. M. and McClintock, C. G. Value: behavioral decision theory
in Annual review of psychology (P. R. Farnsworth et al., eds.), 18,
Palo Alto, Calif.: Annual Reviews, Inc. 1967,   239-286.

Bonjean, C. M., Hill, R. J. and McLemore, S. D. Sociological measurement.
San Francisco: Chandler Publishing Company, 1967.

Brown, R. Social psychology. New York: Free Press, 1965.

Cantril, H. and Allport, G. W. Recent applications of The study of values.
Journal of Abnormal and Social Psychology, 1933, 38, 259-273.

Carter, R. E. An experiment in value measurement. American Sociological Review,
1956, 21, 156-163.

Catton, W. R. Exploring techniques for measuring human values. American
Sociological Review, 1954, 19, 49-55.

_____. A theory of value. American Sociological Review, 1959, 24, 310-317.

Cohen, J. B. A scale for the measurement of attitude toward the aesthetic value.
Journal of Psychology, 1941, 12, 75-79.

Crissman, P. Temporal changes and sexual differences in moral judgments.
Journal of Social Psychology, 1942, 16, 29-38.

_____. Temporal changes and sexual differences in moral judgments. University
of Wyoming Publication 15, 1950, 57-68.

Duffy, E. A critical review of investigations employing the Allport-Vernon
study of values and other tests of evaluative attitude. Psychological
Bulletin, 1940, 37, 597-612.

Dukes, W. F. Psychological studies of values. Psychological Bulletin, 1955,
52, 24-50.

Festinger, L. A theory of cognitive dissonance. Evanston, Ill.: Row, Peterson, 1957.

Grace, G. L. and Grace, H. A. The relationship between verbal and behavioral measures of value. Journal of Educational Research, 1952, 46, 123-131.

Gruen, W. Composition and some correlates of the American core culture. Psychological Reports, 1966, 18, 483-486.

Harding, L. W. Value-type problemmaire and value-type generalizations test. Columbus, Ohio: College of Education, Ohio State University, 1941.

_____. A value-type generalizations test. Journal of Social Psychology, 1944, 19, 53-79.

Hawkes, G. R. A study of personal values of elementary school children. Educational and Psychological Measurement, 1952, 12, 654-663.

Kluckhohn, C. Values and value-orientations in the theory of action: an exploration in definition and classification, in T. Parsons and E. Shils, (eds.), Toward a general theory of action. Cambridge, Mass.: Harvard University Press, 1951, 388-433.

Lepley, R. (ed.). Value: a cooperative inquiry. New York: Columbia University Press, 1949.

Lurie, W. A. A study of Spranger's value types by the method of factor analysis. Journal of Social Psychology, 1937, 8, 17-37.

Maller, J. B. and Glaser, E. M. The interest-values inventory for high school and college students and adults. New York: Bureau of Publications, Teachers College, Columbia University, 1939.

Maslow, A. (ed.). New knowledge in human values. New York: Harper and Brothers Publishers, 1959.

Morris, C. Varieties of human value. Chicago: University of Chicago Press, 1956.

Newcomb, T. and Feldman, K. The impacts of colleges upon their students. Ann Arbor, Michigan: University of Michigan, Institute for Social Research, 1968.

Pepper, S. C. The sources of value. Berkeley: University of California Press, 1958.

Perry, R. G. General theory of value. New York: Longmans, Green & Co., 1926.

Rettig, S. and Pasamanick, B. Changes in moral values among college students: a factorial study. American Sociological Review, 1959, 24, 856-863.

Robinson, J., Athanasiou, R. and Head, K. Measures of occupational attitudes and occupational characteristics. Ann Arbor: Institute for Social Research, 1968.

Rokeach, M. Beliefs, attitudes and values. San Francisco: Jossey-Bass, 1968.

Rosenberg, M. Occupations and values. Glencoe, Illinois: The Free Press, 1957.

Rosenthal, D. Changes in some moral values following psychotherapy. Journal of Consulting Psychology, 1955, 19, 431-437.

Scott, W. A. Values and organizations. Chicago: Rand McNally & Company, 1965.

Spranger, E. Types of men. Translated from the 5th German edition of Lebensformen by P.J. Pigors. Halle: Max Niemeyer Verlag, 1928. American agent: Stechert-Hafner, Inc., New York.

Stoffer, S. and Toby, J. Role conflict and personality. American Journal of Sociology, 1951, 56, 395-406.

Thurstone, L. L. A multiple factor study of vocational interests. Personality Journal, 1931, 10, 198-205.

_____. The measurement of values. Psychological Review, 1954, 61, 47-58.

_____. The measurement of values. Chicago: University of Chicago Press, 1959.

VanDusen, A. C., Wimberly, S. and Mosier, C. I. Standardization of values inventory. Journal of Educational Psychology, 1939, 30, 53-62.

Wikert, F. A test for personal goal-values. Journal of Social Psychology, 1940, 11, 259-274.

STUDY OF VALUES (Allport, Vernon and Lindzey 1960)

Variable First developed in 1931, the Study of Values assesses the relative
importance of six basic interests or personality motives: theoretical, economic, aesthetic, social, political, and religious. This
classification is based on Spranger's Types of Men. Described in
terms of men, the six values are elaborated as follows:

1) The theoretical man most values the discovery of truth. He is
   empirical, critical, and rational, aiming to order and systematize
   his knowledge.

2) The economic man most values that which is useful. He is interested in practical affairs, especially those of business, judging
   things by their tangible utility.

3) The aesthetic man most values beauty and harmony. He is concerned
   with grace and symmetry, finding fulfillment in artistic experiences.

4) The social man most values altruistic and philanthropic love. He
   is kind, sympathetic, unselfish, valuing other men as ends in themselves.

5) The political man most values power and influence. He seeks leadership, enjoying competition and struggle.

6) The religious man most values unity. He seeks communion with the
   cosmos, mystically relating to its wholeness.

Description The test is composed of 45 items, 30 of which are forced choice (Part
I), and 15 of which require rank ordering of 4 alternatives (Part II).
In Part I the subject can express a strong or weak preference for
his choices by the way he distributes three points. Thus, a strong
preference for alternative a over alternative b would be indicated by
marking alternative a as 3 and marking alternative b as 0. A slight
preference for a over b would be indicated by marking a as 2 and b
as 1, etc. Each value is represented by 10 of the 60 possible answers. In Part II the subject rank orders 4 statements from 1 to 4,
where 4 indicates greatest preference. Again each value is represented 10 times in the 60 possible answers. Scores are obtained by summing
item scores and adding or subtracting correction figures.

Sample About 1,400 students from a number of colleges were used in devising
and refining the original test. The test has since been administered
to thousands of people, primarily college students. (See, for example,
references in Newcomb and Feldman (1968), p. 321.) New norms provided
in the 1960 edition are based on 1,816 college students.

Reliability	Split-half reliabilities (N = 100) show Spearman-Brown product moment correlations ranging from .84 (theoretical) to .95 (religious). A Z transformation provides a mean reliability coefficient of .90. A final item analysis (N = 780 male and female subjects at 6 different colleges) indicates that every item is positively correlated at the .01 level with the total score for its value. Testretest reliabilities after one month (N = 34, 1951) and after two months (N = 53, 1957) range from .84 to .93 for the economic and religious scales, respectively, for the 1957 sample. For the 1951 study, .89 was the Z transformed mean repeat reliability coefficient; for the 1957 study, this figure was .88. In a recent study (Hilton and Korn 1964), the Study of Values was administered 7 times to 30 subjects at monthly intervals. Repeat reliability r's ranged from .74 (political scale) to .89 (religious scale).
Validity	Much external validation has been done on this test. Two surveys review issues of validation for the 1931 form: Cantril and Allport (1933) and Duffy (1940). Indirect validation is suggested by findings such as those of Newcomb (1943) which indicate that values change in the direction predicted by a particular kind of college education. The scale does distinguish among groups differing in occupation, religion, and other interests in predicted ways. There are many studies showing correlations between the scales and other variables such as group memberships, occupational and educational choices. Researchers interested in different assessments of validity for the different scales or for the test as a whole should consult the literature (see, for example, Hunt 1968).
Location	Allport, G., Vernon, P., Lindzey, G. Study of values. (3rd edition.) Test booklet and manual. Boston: Houghton Mifflin Co., 1960.
Administration	The test is self-administered, requiring, according to the authors, about 20 minutes to complete. The test is also self-scoring, and both taking and scoring the test can be completed within 1 hour. Norms are provided for men and women so that the subject can interpret his own profile of values.
Results and Comments	This test is so widely used that an adequate summary is beyond the scope of this review (see references in Mental Measurements Yearbooks (1959, 1965) and in Newcomb and Feldman 1968). It has been used in vocational guidance, counseling, and a variety of areas of research, some of which are referenced in the manual.

Limitations of this instrument are also well known. This scale measures only the relative strength of each value; thus, a high score on one scale necessitates a corresponding reduction on one or more of the other scales. This is not necessarily a deficiency in the test, but it is a fact that both must not be forgotten in evaluating scores and may make interpretation difficult by imposing negative correlations and making prediction more troublesome. For example, someone moderately religious but disinterested in the other five areas could score higher on the religious scale than the very religious person with strong interests in the other five areas. Another limitation is that the test is standardized on college students who are primarily in liberal arts. A systematic sampling of colleges has not been completed, and despite some studies of non-collegiate groups, there is still insufficient data to allow for generalization beyond this narrow range of subjects. Furthermore, the test vocabulary is difficult enough to require a fairly high level of education, although less complex, but equivalent, versions have been written (Levy, 1958). The revised 1951 form simplified and updated the 1931 version, improved item diagnostic power, shortened and modified the scoring system, increased the test reliability and offered new norms. The social value was redefined to measure altruistic love or philanthropy rather than the broader conception of Spranger. Spranger had included love in any form in the social value. The 3rd edition, 1960, makes changes in the manual and score sheet only, not in the test itself. More normative data are also provided. The new scoring system requires the subject to check boxes in the test booklet. Correlations between the revised and old forms after a 2 week interval were, according to the manual, "significantly high" for a sample of 50 college men. Nevertheless, the meaning of the scores may be different: the redefined social value correlated only $r = .31$ with the old form; other correlations ranged from .45 (political) to .75 (religious).

In sum, this test looks at the relative importance of 6 areas of interest or values. It measures preferences, not what ought to be preferred. Internal consistency and split-half reliability for group use are adequate, and scores do consistently relate as predicted by the theory. It is easy to administer and, not without reason, in spite of the criticisms and limitations noted, is one of the best and certainly the most ubiquitous of scales of values.

References

Buros, O. Fifth mental measurements yearbook and Sixth mental measurements yearbook. Princeton, New Jersey. Gryphon Press, 1959 and 1965.

Cantril, H. and Allport, G. Recent applications of the study of values. Journal of Abnormal and Social Psychology, 1933, 28, 259-273.

Duffy E. A critical review of investigations employing the Allport-Vernon study of values and other tests of evaluative attitudes. Psychological Bulletin, 1940, 37, 597-612.

Hilton, T. and Korn, J. Measured change in personal values. Educational and Psychological Measurement, 1964, 24, 609-622.

Hunt, R. The interpretation of the religious scale of the Allport-Vernon-Lindzey study of values. Journal for the Scientific Study of Religion, 1968, 7, 65-77.

Levy, J. Readability level and differential test performance: a language revision of the study of values. Journal of Educational Psychology, 1958, 49, 6-12.

Newcomb, T. Personality and social change: attitude formation in a student community. New York: Dryden Press, 1943.

506

Newcomb, T. and Feldman,K. The impacts of colleges upon their students.
Ann Arbor, Michigan: Institute for Social Research, 1968.

Spranger, E. Types of men. Translated from the 5th German edition of
Lebensformen by P.J. Pigors. Halle: Max Niemeyer Verlag, 1928. American
agent: Stechert-Hafner, Inc., New York.

STUDY OF VALUES SCALE

Sample Items

Part I (30 questions--choose one answer and note strength of preference)

1. The main object of scientific research should be the discovery of truth rather than its practical application.

   (a) Yes   (b) No

4. Assuming that you have sufficient ability, would you prefer to be:

   (a)   a banker?
   (b)   a politician?

15. At an exposition, do you chiefly like to go to the buildings where you can see:

   (a) new manufacturing products?
   (b) scientific (e.g., chemical) apparatus?

Part II (15 questions--rank order highest preference with a 4, next highest with a 3, next with a 2, and least preferred with a 1)

3. If you could influence the educational policies of the public schools of some city, would you undertake

   _____   a. to promote the study and participation in music and fine arts?
   _____   b. to stimulate the study of social problems?
   _____   c. to provide additional laboratory facilities?
   _____   d. to increase the practical value of courses?

12. Should one guide one's conduct according to, or develop one's chief loyalties toward

   _____   a. one's religious faith?
   _____   b. ideals of beauty?
   _____   c. one's occupational organization and associates?
   _____   d. ideals of charity?

TEST OF VALUE ACTIVITIES (Shorr 1953)

Variable   This scale assesses the intensity with which individuals hold
                  four kinds of values: theoretical, social, aesthetic and economic-
                  political. The scales are similar to those of Allport, Vernon and Lindzey's
                  Study of Values, but no religious scale was included on the assump-
                  tion that the scores on this scale may represent, as Super (1949)
                  suggested, answers showing "neither deep religious feeling nor intel-
                  lectual doubts concerning religion". Furthermore, in Shorr's
                  measure the economic and political scales are combined.

Description   Numerous items covering a broad range of activities were gathered.
                  Each item was then rated by 11 judges familiar with tests and theories
                  of values on an 11 point scale of intensity of interest ranging from
                  avoidance to great interest. Twenty questions for each scale, total-
                  ing 80 items, of minimum variability were selected; each scale value
                  from 1 to 11 was represented by two items. No negative questions
                  were used, and all items with a median scale-value from 1.00 to 1.75
                  were given a value of 1. The same procedure was used throughout;
                  thus, a 2.65 score would be given a value of 2.

Sample   The sample consisted of 389 females--126 college sophomores, 263 high
                  school seniors--and 352 males--121 college sophomores, 231 high school
                  seniors.

Reliability   Split-half reliability for each scale was easily computed since each
                  scale had two items of the same weight. The reliability coefficients
                  obtained from the scores of 126 female college sophomores were .84
                  (theoretical), .82 (aesthetic), .78 (economic-political), and .72
                  (social scale).

Validity   No measures of validity are reported.

Location   Shorr, J. The development of a test to measure the intensity of
                  values, Journal of Educational Psychology, 1953, 44, 266-274.

Administration   The test is self-administered, and should take under five minutes
                  to complete.

Results and   No significant differences were found between college sophomores
Comments   and high school seniors, but sex differences were found on all
                  four scales. This scale is useful in that it measures intensity
                  of different kinds of values rather than only the relation of one
                  set of values to another. Whether or not this scale represents
                  a wider range of value-relevant items that the Allport-Vernon Study
                  of Values (which it was meant to improve) is a moot question. The
                  lack of data on validity is an unfortunate omission. Anyone
                  wanting to use this measure in a large study should explore its
                  validity first.

References   Allport, G., Vernon, P., and Lindzey, G. Study of values (revised edition). Boston: Houghton Mifflin Co., 1951.

Super, D. Appraising vocational fitness. New York: Harper, 1949.

Each item in the scale is coded as follows:
    A - theoretical
    B - economic-political
    C - aesthetic
    D - social

Total scores for each area are calculated by summing for each "yes" response, the number associated with the response on the scale items below. Taking the A (theoretical) scale as an example, if the respondent replies Yes only to A items 19, 58 and 60, his total score on the theoretical dimension would be 6 (2 + 3 + 1). The following percentile norms developed on the above sample are to be used in interpreting scale scores.

PROFILE SHEET

% PERCENTILE	THEORETICAL	ECON-POLITICAL	AESTHETIC	SOCIAL
100	110	110	110	110
90	85	89	83	90
80	74	76	69	80
70	66	67	60	73
60	54	56	47	65
50	45	49	39	56
40	39	38	32	47
30	31	30	26	39
20	21	21	20	33
10	11	12	12	25
1	0	0	0	4

MALE ⟶ (N=352) (50 percentile row)

% PERCENTILE	THEORETICAL	ECON-POLITICAL	AESTHETIC	SOCIAL
100	110	110	110	110
90	74	70	96	96
80	60	54	88	88
70	48	46	79	82
60	40	39	69	77
50	32	32	62	72
40	25	25	54	67
30	19	21	46	59
20	14	17	36	52
10	8	11	22	39
1	0	1	3	0

FEMALE ⟶ (N=389) (50 percentile row)

THEORETICAL - A high score indicates that the individual prefers and considers most worthwhile those activities which involve a problem-solving attitude and are related to investigation, research, and scientific curiosity.

<u>ECONOMIC-POLITICAL</u> - A high score indicates that an individual prefers and considers most worthwhile those activities which involve the accumulation of money and the securing of executive power.

<u>AESTHETIC</u> - A high score indicates that an individual prefers and considers most worthwhile those activities which involve art, music, dance and literature.

<u>SOCIAL</u> - A high score indicates that an individual prefers and considers most worthwhile those activities which involve service and help to people, and which exhibit a definite desire to respond and be with people socially.

A Test of Value Activities

<u>Direction</u>: Read each statement in turn then circle both the <u>number and letter</u> appearing next to either yes or no that best indicates your feeling of like or dislike for the activity described. <u>Be sure to answer each question.</u> A sample response is as follows:

"Enjoy eating ice cream"   (2A) Yes 2A No

1.	Meet new people and get acquainted with them.	5D Yes	5D No
2.	Take a car load of children for an outing.	6D Yes	6D No
3.	Serve as a companion to an elderly person.	7D Yes	7D No
4.	Like to be with people despite their physical deformities.	8D Yes	8D No
5.	Work with a group to help the unemployed.	9D Yes	9D No
6.	Work with labor and management to help solve their conflicts.	10D Yes	10D No
7.	Go with friends to a movie.	4D Yes	4D No
8.	Help distribute food at a picnic.	3D Yes	3D No
9.	Play checkers with members of your family.	2D Yes	2D No
10.	Make a phone call for movie reservations.	1D Yes	1D No
11.	Collect specimens of small animals for a zoo or museum.	5A Yes	5A No
12.	Do algebra problems.	6A Yes	6A No
13.	Develop an international language.	7A Yes	7A No
14.	Do an experiment with the muscle and nerve of a frog.	8A Yes	8A No
15.	Study the various methods used in scientific investigations.	9A Yes	9A No
16.	Do research on the relation of brain waves to thinking.	10A Yes	10A No
17.	Visit a research laboratory in which small animals are being tested in a maze.	4A Yes	4A No
18.	Plan the defense and offense you are to use before a tennis game.	3A Yes	3A No
19.	Read the biography of Louis Pasteur.	2A Yes	2A No
20.	See moving pictures in which scientists are heroes.	1A Yes	1A No
21.	Judge entries in a photo contest.	5C Yes	5C No
22.	Sketch action scenes on a drawing pad.	6C Yes	6C No
23.	Participate in a summer theatre group.	7C Yes	7C No
24.	Compare the treatment of a classical work as given by two fine musicians.	8C Yes	8C No
25.	Mould a statue in clay.	9C Yes	9C No
26.	Be a ballet dancer.	10C Yes	10C No
27.	Be a sign painter.	4C Yes	4C No
28.	Plant flowers and shrubbery around a home.	3C Yes	3C No
29.	Listen to "jive" and "jazz" records.	2C Yes	2C No
30.	Play the juke box.	1C Yes	1C No
31.	Lead a round-table discussion.	5B Yes	5B No
32.	Be a chairman of an organizing committee.	6B Yes	6B No
33.	Buy a run-down business and make it grow.	7B Yes	7B No
34.	Borrow money in order to "put over" a business deal.	8B Yes	8B No
35.	Run for political office.	9B Yes	9B No
36.	Own and operate a bank.	10B Yes	10B No
37.	Be a bank teller.	4B Yes	4B No
38.	Take a course in Business English.	3B Yes	3B No
39.	Major in commercial subjects in school.	2B Yes	2B No
40.	Collect luncheon money at the end of a school cafeteria line.	1B Yes	1B No
41.	Send a letter of condolence to a neighbor.	5D Yes	5D No
42.	Help people to be comfortable when traveling.	6D Yes	6D No

Reprinted with permission of Shorr, J. **Test of Value Activities** in "The Development of a Test to Measure the Intensity of Values," *Journal of Educational Psychology,* **44** (1953) pp 266-274.

43.	Belong to several social agencies.	7D Yes	7D No
44.	Treat wounds to help people get well.	8D Yes	8D No
45.	Help an agency locate living places for evicted families.	9D Yes	9D No
46.	Be a medical missionary to a foreign country.	10D Yes	10D No
47.	Attend a dance.	4D Yes	4D No
48.	Dine with classmates in the school cafeteria.	3D Yes	3D No
49.	Play checkers.	2D Yes	2D No
50.	Ride in a bus to San Francisco or a neighboring city.	1D Yes	1D No
51.	Be a laboratory technician.	5A Yes	5A No
52.	Be a scientific farmer.	6A Yes	6A No
53.	Develop new kinds of flowers in a small greenhouse.	7A Yes	7A No
54.	Solve knotty legal problems.	8A Yes	8A No
55.	Develop improved procedures in a scientific experiment.	9A Yes	9A No
56.	Develop new mathematical formulas for research.	10A Yes	10A No
57.	Look at the displays on astronomy in an observatory exhibit.	4A Yes	4A No
58.	Visit the fossil display at a museum.	3A Yes	3A No
59.	Keep a chemical storeroom or physical laboratory.	2A Yes	2A No
60.	Sell scientific books.	1A Yes	1A No
61.	Judge window displays in a contest.	5C Yes	5C No
62.	Collect rare and old recordings.	6C Yes	6C No
63.	Be an interior decorator.	7C Yes	7C No
64.	Make a comparative study of architecture.	8C Yes	8C No
65.	Write a new arrangement for a musical theme.	9C Yes	9C No
66.	Paint a mural.	10C Yes	10C No
67.	Visit a flower show.	4C Yes	4C No
68.	Make and trim household accessories like lamp shades, etc.	3C Yes	3C No
69.	Dance to a fast number.	2C Yes	2C No
70.	Paint the kitchen with colors of your choice.	1C Yes	1C No
71.	Install improved office procedures in a big business.	5B Yes	5B No
72.	Plan business and commercial investments.	6B Yes	6B No
73.	Be an active member of a political group.	7B Yes	7B No
74.	Address a political convention.	8B Yes	8B No
75.	Operate a race track.	9B Yes	9B No
76.	Become a U. S. Senator.	10B Yes	10B No
77.	Purchase supplies for a picnic.	4B Yes	4B No
78.	Live in a large city rather than a small town.	3B Yes	3B No
79.	Work at an information desk.	2B Yes	2B No
80.	Be a private secretary.	1B Yes	1B No

SURVEY OF INTERPERSONAL VALUES (Gordon 1960)

Variable   This test is designed to measure the relative importance
            ascribed to each of six factored interpersonal value dimen-
            sions. These values include both the subject's relations with
            others and others with him. The six dimensions are 1) sup-
            port--being treated with understanding, encouragement, kind-
            ness and consideration; 2) conformity--doing what is socially
            correct, accepted and proper; 3) recognition--being admired,
            looked up to, considered important and attracting favorable
            notice; 4) independence--being able to do what one wants to
            do, making one's own decisions, doing things in one's own way;
             5) benevolence--doing things for other people, sharing and
            helping; 6) leadership--being in charge of others, having
            authority or power.

Description This is a brief, forced choice test instrument. There are 30
            groups of 3 statements in each group in this test; within each
            triad, each of the three statements presented reflects an in-
            terpersonal value. The respondent checks the statement most
            and least important to him. The items within each triad have
            been, according to the manual, equated for social desirability.
            Responses are scored by hand by using a punched overlay stencil.

Sample   The sample was developed on 232 subjects, and this form, as well as 4
            succeeding revisions were given to a number of high school, college,
            industrial and other adult samples.

Reliability Test-retest reliability coefficients range from .78 to .89 for
            the six value scores; median value is $r = .84$. The Kuder-
            Richardson reliability results range from .71 to .86; median
            estimate is $r = .82$.

            Norms are available for college and high school males and
            females, although there is no explanation of who was selected
            or how this selection was done. College norms are based on
            samples from 12 different universities and colleges throughout
            the country. High school norms are based on 4 schools in Cali-
            fornia.

Validity   The manual supplement (1963) suggests that test users validate
            the SIV for the particular situation in which it is to be used.
            The results of over 25 studies illustrating the use of the SIV
            are presented. The SIV has been used as a predictor of job
            and educational success, as a way of examining cross-cultural
            differences, and as a way to measure change resulting from
            educational or other changes. For example, one study using
            this scale (Gordon and Mensch 1962) on 208 medical students
            concluded that there was a downward trend in benevolence from
            freshmen to senior students. Decrease in this kind of value has
            often been noted in other studies of medical students (Eron
            1955; and Becker and Geer ,1958).

Location	Gordon, L. _Survey of interpersonal values_. Chicago: Science Research Associates, 1960; supplementary revised manual, 1963.
Administration	The test is self-administered and should take about 15-20 minutes to complete.
Results and Comments	A comprehensive discussion of the development of the SIV is lacking. It is not clear how the items were initially selected, and the factor analysis is not presented in sufficient detail. However, the manual is clear and pertinent. Although some studies of dubious value are included in the review summaries, most studies support the usefulness of this instrument, and correlations between the SIV and other tests are of interest. The items are transparent and may invite faking. Norms on non-academic populations will increase the usefulness of this instrument, as will additional research. Nevertheless, it has potential use in personnel selection and counseling and a variety of other areas, but the caveat of the author concerning validation must be kept in mind.

References	Becker, H. and Geer, B. The fate of idealism in medical school. In E.G. Jaco, (ed.), _Patients, Physicians and Illness_, Glencoe, Illinois: Free Press, 1958, Ch. 32.
	Eron, J. Effects of medical education on medical students. _Journal of Medical Education_, 1955, 10, 559-566.
	Gordon, L. and Mensch, I. Values of medical students at different levels of training. _Journal of Educational Psychology_, 1962, 53, 48-51.

Survey of Interpersonal Values

Instructions

In this booklet are statements representing things that people consider to be important to their way of life. These statements are grouped into sets of three. This is what you are asked to do: Examine each set. Within each set, find the ONE STATEMENT of the three which represents what you consider to be most important to you. Blacken the space beside that statement in the column headed M (for most). Next, examine the remaining two statements in the set. Decide which one of these statements represents what you consider to be least important to you. Blacken the space beside that statement in the column headed L (for least).

For every set you will mark one statement as representing what is most important to you, one statement as representing what is least important to you, and you will leave one statement unmarked...

Sample items

	M	L
To be in a position of not having to follow orders	☐	☐
To follow rules and regulations closely	☐	☐
To have people notice what I do	☐	☐
To be able to do pretty much as I please	☐	☐
To be in charge of some important project	☐	☐
To work for the good of other people	☐	☐
To have others approve of what I do	☐	☐
To make decisions for the group	☐	☐
To share my belongings with other people	☐	☐
To have people admire me	☐	☐
To always do the approved thing	☐	☐
To be able to leave things lying around if I wish	☐	☐

PERSONAL VALUE SCALES (Scott 1965)

Variable

Scott defined personal values as follows: "a personal value
(or moral ideal) is any individual's conception of an ideal
relationship between people--a state of affairs that he considers ultimately, absolutely, and universally good. A value
is...identified, not by its content..., but by the attitude
of the person toward it. No matter what state a given individual,
regards as ultimately, absolutely, and universally good, that
state constitutes, for him, a value."

Description

Scott developed scales to measure personal values in a study of
University of Colorado fraternities and sororities. The following 12 were chosen in part because they seemed a priori to
be relevant to Greek student organizations, in part because
most were mentioned in a preliminary open-ended survey (Scott
1959): 1) intellectualism, 2) kindness, 3) social skills
(being charming, popular, etc.), 4) loyalty (to one's group),
5) academic achievement, 6) physical development, 7) status
leadership), 8) honesty, 9) religiousness, 10) self-control,
11) creativity, and 12) independence.

Up to a dozen statements were written for each value area, and
these were administered to "try-out samples of students," usually of about 200 in size. Item analysis resulted in the elimination of all but four to six items for each scale.

The resulting instrument was administered to a sample of general
psychology students to test for homogeneity within each scale.
The results are reported under Reliability below.

The final instrument requires a respondent to check one of the
following categories in response to each value statement: Always Admire, Depends on Situation, Always Dislike. In most
cases "Always Admire" is scored 1, and the other two responses
are scored 0 (the only exceptions are the few reversed items,
for which "Always Admire" and "Depends" are scored 0). Total
scores for each value are obtained by summation.

Because Scott needed a relatively short instrument, he used
this 60 item questionnaire despite its having only moderate
reliability. Following this research, however, he designed additional items for each scale, which we have included in the list
reported below. These additional items also provide a control
for agreement response set, a possible bias inherent in the original instrument.

Sample

For the pretest phases of Scott's research, respondents were
University of Colorado students, usually selected in an unspecified manner, although for the test-retest stability study general
psychology students were used.

For the major research project, the sample consisted of the members of six fraternities and four sororities, plus a control group--representative of the entire undergraduate body--containing 108 independents and 64 Greeks. Over 900 subjects were tested.

In developing the longer version of the values instrument, Scott employed a sample of students taking general psychology (N = 254).

Reliability

As a measure of reliability Scott used Cronbach's (1951) coefficient alpha. In the following list, the first coefficient refers to alpha for the short scales, the second to two-week test-retest stability of the short scales, the third to alpha for the long scales, and the fourth to the correlation of each long scale with its corresponding original scale.

Intellectualism (.68, .64, .82, .66); kindness (.66, .68, .85, .76); social skills (.70, .74, .87, .76); loyalty (.71, .58, .89, .79); academic achievement (.69, .68, .82, .75); physical development (.77, .74, .89, .81); status (.65, .70, .83, .67); honesty (.61, .74, .80, .75); religiousness (.78, .77, .88, .81); self-control (.68, .72, .85, .78); creativity (.64, .66, .84, .62); independence (.55, .73, .82, .74). Notice that in each case alpha is considerably higher for the longer scale. The correlations between the original scales and their lengthened counterparts are less than perfect, probably for at least two reasons: reduction of agreement biases and slight alterations in content.

Validity

Concurrent validity was assessed by asking a group of students (N = 208) to rate the items for "rightness" or "wrongness" (right, wrong, or neither) and according to "how other people should feel" (should admire the trait, should dissapprove the trait, people might differ in their opinion on the matter). The items were also rated according to admirability to self. The intercorrelations between these three assessments were quite high.

Another attempt to infer validity involved asking a group of students (N = 218) to say how bothered they would be if each value were transgressed (e.g., for intellectualism, "if you were unable to read any books or magazines for several weeks, how would you feel: would not bother me at all...would bother me a lot"). Correlations between scale scores and transgression scores were statistically significant in nine of 12 cases (exceptions were loyalty, status, and creativity--which may have been the most difficult to propose transgressions for).

Finally, known group validation was attempted with several scales. For example, Jesuit seminarians scored higher on religiousness than male students at the University of Colorado; members of the Women's Physical Education Club scored higher than a cross-section of university women; art majors scored higher on creativity; members of the University Players Club, reputed to be nonconformists, scored higher on independence; high grade-point students scored higher than academically mediocre students on the academic achievement scale.

Location   Scott, W. *Values and organizations: a study of fraternities and sororities.* Chicago: Rand McNally, 1965.

Administration Both versions of the values instrument are self-administered. The 60-item version would take about half an hour to complete, while the 240-item version would take something over an hour.

Results and   Considerable care was exercised in developing the Personal
Comments   Value Scales. (See his earlier study developing a way to assess both values and ideologies; Scott 1959.) For student populations similar to Scott's (from a large state university) and for purposes similar to his (measuring several values important to students) these scales are recommended. Even for other groups most of Scott's items would appear to be applicable; only a few, such as "studying hard to get good grades in school," seem to be "student specific."

Scott's research on Greek organizations confirmed several interesting hypotheses; for example, that a student's initial values are useful in predicting whether he will join such an organization, that these organizations do tend to recruit new members with values similar to those of old members, and that the sociometric ratings a person receives from others depend in part on the rater's values. There were several more such findings--collectively supporting the construct validity of Scott's scales and the worth of including personal values among a list of important social psychological variables.

For an interesting study relating personal values to international values or ideology, see Scott (1960).

References   Cronbach, L. Coefficient *alpha* and the internal structure of tests. *Psychometrika*, 1951, 16, 297-334.

Scott, W. Empirical assessment of values and ideologies. *American Sociological Review*, 1959, 24, 299-310.

Scott, W. International ideology and interpersonal ideology. *Public Opinion Quarterly*, 1960, 24, 419-435.

VALUE SCALES

Instructions

Please read over the following statements, and for each one indicate (by a check in the appropriate space) whether it is something you <u>always admire</u> in other people, or something you <u>always dislike</u>, or something that <u>depends on the situation</u> whether you admire it or not.

Examples:

Always Admire	Depends on Situation	Always Dislike	
1. _____	_____	_____	Having a strong intellectual curiosity.
2. _____	_____	_____	Creating beautiful things for the enjoyment of other people.

(Items preceded by an asterisk were included in both short and long versions of the instrument. Items in parentheses were included in the short but not the long version. All other items appeared only in the long version.)

Intellectualism

Direct-scored items

*Having a keen interest in international, national, and local affairs.
*Having a strong intellectual curiosity.
*Developing an appreciation of the fine arts--music, drama, literature, and ballet.
*Having an active interest in all things scholarly.
 Having cultural interests.
 Striving to gain new knowledge about the world.
 Enjoying books, music, art, philosophy, and sciences.
 Keeping abreast of current events.
 Knowing what's going on in the world of politics.
 Keeping up with world news through regular reading or by watching informative programs.
 (Being an intellectual.)

Reverse-scored items

Having restricted and narrow interests.
Having no knowledge of current events.
Being interested only in one's work.

Personal Value Scales in *Values and Organizations* by William A. Scott; copyright 1965 by Rand McNally and Company, Chicago, pp 245-257. Reprinted by permission of Rand McNally College Publishing Company.

Having no opinions about the world situation.
Knowing only one's specialty.
Having little interest in arts, theater, music, and other cultural
        activities.
Being uninterested in national and world affairs.
Showing little interest in the finer things of life.
Ignoring what goes on in the world around one.
Reading only things that don't pose any intellectual challenge.

Kindness

Direct-scored items

*Being kind to people, even if they do things contrary to one's beliefs.
*Helping another person feel more secure, even if one doesn't like him.
*Helping another achieve his own goals, even if it might interfere with
        your own.
*Turning the other cheek, and forgiving others when they harm you.
 Being considerate of others' feelings.
 Finding ways to help others less fortunate than oneself.
 Being utterly selfless in all one's actions.
 Having a deep love of all people, whoever they are.
 Going out of one's way to help someone new feel at home.
 Being concerned about the happiness of other people.

Reverse-scored items

Looking out for one's own interests first.
Ridiculing other people.
Being selfish.
Ignoring the needs of other people.
Revenging wrongs that other people have done to one.
Being unable to empathize with other people.
Hurting other people's feelings.
Making jokes at the expense of other people.
Letting each person go it alone, without offering help.
Refusing any aid to people who don't deserve it.

Social Skills

Direct-scored items

*Being well mannered and behaving properly in social situations.
*Dressing and acting in a way that is appropriate to the occasion.
*Being able to get people to cooperate with one.
*Being poised, gracious, and charming under all circumstances.
 Always doing the right thing at the right time.
 Being informed in proper etiquette.

Being able to plan social functions smoothly.
Being popular with everyone.
Always behaving properly in public.
Being concerned about what kind of impression one makes on others.
(Being able to get along with all kinds of people, whether or not they
    are worthwhile.)
(Being the person in the group who is the most popular with the oppo-
    site sex.)

Reverse-scored items

Being a social isolate.
Dressing sloppily.
Displaying unpleasant personal habits in public.
Interrupting others while they are talking.
Constantly making social blunders.
Talking constantly and attracting attention to oneself.
Having bad manners.
Being discourteous.
Being unable to act in a way that will please others.
Being ignorant of the rules of proper behavior.

Loyalty

Direct-scored items

*Defending the honor of one's group whenever it is unfairly criticized.
*Working hard to improve the prestige and status of one's groups.
*Helping organize group activities.
 Attending all meetings of one's groups.
 Upholding the honor of one's group.
 Supporting all activities of one's organizations.
 Doing more than one's share of the group task.
 Performing unpleasant tasks, if these are required by one's group.
 Remembering one's group loyalties at all times.
 Taking an active part in all group affairs.
 (Treating an attack on one's group like an attack on oneself.)
 (Concealing from outsiders most of one's dislikes and disagreements
        with fellow members of the group.)
 (Doing all one can to build up the prestige of the group.)

Reverse-scored items

Betraying one's group to outsiders.
Letting other people do all the work for the group, and not getting
        involved oneself.
Letting people get away with unfair criticism of one's group.
Being unconcerned with what other people think about one's group.
Being uncooperative.
Failing to support group functions.

Paying little attention to what the members of one's group think.
Criticizing one's own group in public.
Getting by with as little involvement in organizations as possible.
Not taking one's group memberships seriously.

Academic Achievement (Grades)

Direct-scored items

*Studying hard to get good grades in school.
*Working hard to achieve academic honors.
 Trying hard to understand difficult lectures and textbooks.
*Striving to get the top grade-point average in the group.
*Studying constantly in order to become a well educated person.
 Being studious.
 Getting the top grade on a test.
 Treating one's studies as the most important thing in college life.
 Doing well in school.
 Priding oneself on good grades.

Reverse-scored items

Being content with a "gentlemanly C" grade.
Making fun of academic grinds.
Being satisfied with poor grades.
Priding oneself on being able to get by in school with little work.
Not doing well in one's coursework.
Not letting studies interfere with one's college life.
Doing one's best to avoid working hard in a course.
Being proud of poor grades.
Paying no attention to lectures and textbooks that are difficult.
Taking snap courses that don't require any work.

Physical Development

Direct-scored items

*Being graceful and well coordinated in physical movements.
*Taking good care of one's physical self, so that one is always healthy.
*Being good in some form of sport.
*Developing physical strength and agility.
 Developing an attractive body that others will admire.
 Having a good figure or physique.
 Having good muscular coordination.
 Being a well developed outdoors type who enjoys physical activity.
 Keeping in good physical shape.
 Exercising regularly.

Reverse-scored items

Being physically weak and puny.
Being an indoor type, and avoiding outdoor activities.
Being poorly proportioned physically.
Being uninterested in sports.
Being listless and uninterested in strenuous activity.
Being awkward in bearing and walk.
Being unable to do anything that requires physical effort.
Being unskilled in any form of athletics.
Ignoring one's own physical condition.
Avoiding any form of exercise.

Status

Direct-scored items

*Being respected by people who are themselves worthwhile.
*Gaining recognition for one's achievements.
*Being in a position to direct and mold others' lives.
 Making sure that one is respected.
 Doing what one is told.
 Being in a position to command respect from others.
 Having all the respect that one is entitled to.
 Being dignified in bearing and manner.
 Being looked up to by others.
 Enjoying great prestige in the community.
 (Having the ability to lead others.)
 (Showing great leadership qualities.)

Reverse-scored items

Acting beneath one's dignity.
Not being able to do anything better than other people.
Not being recognized for one's true worth.
Being in a subordinate position.
Having little effect on other people's actions.
Being unable to exert any influence on things around one.
Failing to develop contacts that could improve one's position.
Being content with an inferior position all one's life.
Associating with worthless people.
Not taking pride in one's achievements.

Honesty

Direct-scored items

*Never cheating or having anything to do with cheating situations, even
        for a friend.

*Always telling the truth, even though it may hurt oneself or others.
*Never telling a lie, even though to do so would make the situation
         more comfortable.
 Sticking up for the truth under all circumstances.
 Always representing one's own true thoughts and feelings honestly.
 Speaking one's mind truthfully, without regard for the consequences.
 Testifying against friends, if need be, in order that the truth be
         known.
 Presenting oneself completely and honestly, even if it is unnecessary
         to do so.
 Going out of one's way to bring dishonest people to justice.
 Volunteering information concerning wrongdoing, even if friends are
         involved.

Reverse-scored items

*Helping a close friend get by a tight situation, even though one may
         have to stretch the truth a bit to do it.
 Taking things that don't belong to one.
 Telling white lies.
 Deceiving others.
 Using others' property without asking permission.
 Telling falsehoods in order to help other people.
 Helping a friend through an examination.
 Using a false ID card to get into restricted places.
 Stealing when necessary.
 Being dishonest in harmless ways.

Religiousness

Direct-scored items

*Being devout in one's religious faith.
*Always living one's religion in his daily life.
*Always attending religious services regularly and faithfully.
*Avoiding the physical pleasures that are prohibited in the Bible.
*Encouraging others to attend services and lead religious lives.
 Saying one's prayers regularly.
 Seeking comfort in the Bible in time of need.
 Adhering to the doctrines of one's religion.
 Having an inner communication with the Supreme Being.
 Having faith in a Being greater than man.

Reverse-scored items

 Being an atheist.
 Denying the existence of God.
 Paying little attention to religious matters.
 Treating man, rather than God, as the measure of all things.

Abstaining from trivial religious rituals.
Not falling for religious mythology.
Taking a skeptical attitude toward religious teachings.
Seeking scientific explanations of religious miracles.
Treating the Bible only as an historical or literary work.
Regarding religions as crutches for the primitive peoples of the world.

Self-control

Direct-scored items

*Practicing self-control.
*Replying to anger with gentleness.
*Never losing one's temper, no matter what the reason.
*Not expressing anger, even when one has a reason for doing so.
 Suppressing hostility.
 Keeping one's feelings hidden from others.
 Suppressing the urge to speak hastily in anger.
 Hiding one's feelings of frustration from other people.
 Keeping one's hostile feelings to himself.
 Not getting upset when things go wrong.
 (Always being patient with people.)

Reverse-scored items

Losing one's temper easily.
Showing one's feelings readily.
Telling people off when they offend one.
Expressing one's anger openly and directly when provoked.
Getting upset when things don't go well.
Letting others see how one really feels.
Letting off steam when one is frustrated.
Swearing when one is angry.
Becoming so angry that other people know about it.
Letting people know when one is annoyed with them.

Creativity (Originality)

Direct-scored items

*Being able to create beautiful and artistic objects.
*Developing new and different ways of doing things.
*Constantly developing new ways of approaching life.
*Inventing gadgets for the fun of it.
 Trying out new ideas.
 Being original in one's thoughts and ways of looking at things.
 Always looking for new roads to travel.
 Doing unusual things.
 Creating unusual works of art.
 Being an innovator.

(Creating beautiful things for the enjoyment of other people.)
(Devoting one's entire energy to the development of new theories.)

Reverse-scored items

Doing routine things all the time.
Not having any new ideas.
Always doing things in the same way.
Enjoying a routine, patterned life.
Doing things the same way that other people do them.
Abiding by traditional ways of doing things.
Repeating the ideas of others, without any innovation.
Working according to a set schedule that doesn't vary from day to day.
Painting or composing or writing in a traditional style.
Keeping one's life from changing very much.

Independence

Direct-scored items

Being a freethinking person, who doesn't care what others think of
        his opinions.
*Being outspoken and frank in expressing one's likes and dislikes.
Being independent.
Standing up for what one thinks right, regardless of what others think.
Going one's own way as he pleases.
Being a non-conformist.
Being different from other people.
Encouraging other people to act as they please.
*Thinking and acting freely, without social restraints.
Living one's own life, independent of others.
(Being independent, original, non-conformist, different from other
        people.)

Reverse-scored items

*Conforming to the requirements of any situation and doing what is ex-
        pected of one.
Going along with the crowd.
Acting in such a way as to gain the approval of others.
Keeping one's opinions to himself when they differ from the group's.
Being careful not to express an idea that might be contrary to what
        other people believe.
Always basing one's behavior on the recognition that he is dependent
        on other people.
Acting so as to fit in with other people's way of doing things.
Always checking on whether or not one's intended actions would be
        acceptable to other people.
Never acting so as to violate social conventions.
Suppressing one's desire to be unique and different.
(Working and living in harmony with other people.)

VALUE PROFILE (Bales and Couch 1969)

Variable   This general purpose inventory of values was developed for inter-
                  personal relations research. A value statement "in the concrete
                  interaction context is a statement of the basis of an existing
                  norm, or a proposal for the basis of a new norm." Factor analysis
                  yielded four orthogonal factors: acceptance of authority, need-
                  determined expression vs. value-determined restraint, equalitar-
                  ianism, and individualism.

Description   This questionnaire contains 252 items, each of which is a sen-
                  tence that is evaluated on a 7 point scale, from strongly disagree
                  to strongly agree. Six categories of agreement were used. A
                  weight of 4, the mean value, was utilized in cases where there
                  was no response. Items were obtained by recording group discus-
                  sions, and by examining several books. Although neither random
                  nor systematic, this sampling procedure was an attempt to repre-
                  sent as many value areas as possible. 163 items were obtained
                  from subjects' conversations; 11 from the Allport-Vernon-Lindzey
                  Study of Values; 30 items from one of the author's a priori classi-
                  ficatory scheme of ideological issues in small groups. 16 items
                  were based on the work of Florence Kluckhohn; 120 items from
                  Morris' Ways to Live. Other questionnaires, scales, and descriptions
                  relating to values and personality provided additional items, in
                  particular those associated with Adorno et al.'s Authoritarian
                  Personality and Henry Murray's Explorations in Personality. For
                  the factor analysis the 252 items were reduced in number. Items
                  which did not discriminate among subjects were eliminated as were
                  items that overlapped so that the factor analysis was based on
                  the intercorrelations of 144 variables.

Sample   The major sample was composed of Harvard undergraduates who
                  answered a newspaper advertisement. Some Harvard faculty, gradu-
                  ate students, and Radcliffe undergraduates also participated,
                  making a total of 388 respondents. About 80 Bennington College students.
                  and 80 officer candidates at Maxwell Airforce Base were tested,
                  bringing the total sample size to 552.

Reliability   The range of factor loadings for authoritarianism is .56 to .76,
                  for need expression .29 to .62, for equalitarianism .35 to .57,
                  and for individualism .28 to .49. This would indicate average inter-
                  item correlations in the .40's for the authoritarian items and in
                  the high teens for the other scales. No test-retest data are re-
                  ported.

Validity   No validity measures are reported.

Location   Bales, R. and Couch, A. The value profile: a factor analytic
                  study of value statements. Sociological Inquiry, 1969, 39, 3-17.

Administration   The test is self-administered. The authors do not note its dura-
                  tion, but it should probably take from 25-40 minutes to complete.

Results and
Comments

Despite the unfortunate lack of information on tests for
validity,this scale is useful because it is extremely comprehensive, seemingly representing a very large domain of value positions on which people differ. The authors note that "the underlying factor space seems to be congruent with that obtained by
Morris and others..." This, in fact, seems to be the case, but
more detailed comparisons are necessary. Since various rotations
give various factors, the underlying space should be the basis of
comparisons made.

The value profile seems easy to use for a variety of respondents.
It appears to be an instrument of much utility, although this possibility cannot be adequately evaluated from the information
available in the article reviewed.

References

Adorno, T. et al. The authoritarian personality. New York: Harper,
1950.

Allport, G., Vernon, P., and Lindzey, G. Study of values. (revised
edition), Boston: Houghton Mifflin, 1951.

Bales, R. Interaction process analysis, a method for the study of
small groups. Cambridge, Mass.: Addison-Wesley, 1950.

Kluckhohn, Florence. Dominant and substitutive profiles of cultural
orientation, Social Forces, 1950, 28, 376-394.

Morris, C. Varieties of human value. Chicago: University of Chicago
Press, 1956.

Murray, H. et al. Explorations in personality. New York: Oxford
University Press, 1938.

VALUE PROFILE

Directions:

This questionnaire is designed to measure the extent to which you hold each of several general attitudes or values common in our society. On the following pages you will find a series of general statements expressing opinions of the kind you may have heard from other persons around you. After each statement there is a set of possible responses as follows:

| Strongly Disagree | Disagree | Slightly Disagree | Slightly Agree | Agree | Strongly Agree |

You are asked to read each of the statements and then to circle the response which best represents your immediate reaction to the opinion expressed. Respond to each opinion as a whole. If you have reservations about some part of a statement, circle the response which most clearly approximates your general feeling.

VP Scale Factor I

Acceptance of Authority

1. Obedience and respect for authority are the most important virtues children should learn.

2. There is hardly anything lower than a person who does not feel a great love, gratitude, and respect for his parents.

3. What youth needs most is strict discipline, rugged determination, and the will to work and fight for family and country.

4. You have to respect authority and when you stop respecting authority, your situation isn't worth much.

5. Patriotism and loyalty are the first and the most important requirements of a good citizen.

6. Young people sometimes get rebellious ideas, but as they grow up they ought to get over them and settle down.

7. A child should not be allowed to talk back to his parents, or else he will lose respect for them.

8. The facts on crime and sexual immorality show that we will have to crack down harder on young people if we are going to save our moral standards.

9. Disobeying an order is one thing you can't excuse -- if one can get away with disobedience, why can't everybody?

10. A well-raised child is one who doesn't have to be told twice to do something.

Reprinted with permission of Bales, R. and Couch, A. Value Profile in *Sociological Inquiry*, 39 (1969), pp 3-17. Copyright 1969 by Sociological Inquiry, 252 Bloor Street, W., Toronto 5, Ontario, Canada.

VP Scale Factor II

Need-determined Expression vs. Value-determined Restraint

1. Since there are no values which can be eternal, the only real values are those which meet the needs of the given moment.

2. Nothing is static, nothing is everlasting, at any moment one must be ready to meet the change in environment by a necessary change in one's moral views.

3. Let us eat, drink, and be merry, for tomorrow we die.

4. The solution to almost any human problem should be based on the situation at the time, not on some general moral rule.

5. Life is something to be enjoyed to the full, sensuously enjoyed with relish and enthusiasm.

6. Life is more a festival than a workshop or a school for moral discipline.

7. The past is no more, the future may never be, the present is all that we can be certain of.

8. Not to attain happiness, but to be worthy of it, is the purpose of our existence.   (reverse scored)

9. No time is better spent than that devoted to thinking about the ultimate purposes of life.   (reverse scored)

10. Tenderness is more important than passion in love.   (reverse scored)

VP Scale Factor III

Equalitarianism

1. Everyone should have an equal chance and an equal say.

2. There should be equality for everyone -- because we are all human beings.

3. A group of equals will work a lot better than a group with a rigid hierarchy.

4. Each one should get what he needs -- the things we have belong to all of us.

5. No matter what the circumstances, one should never arbitrarily tell people what they have to do.

6. It is the duty of every good citizen to correct anti-minority remarks made in his presence.

7. Poverty could be almost entirely done away with if we made certain basic changes in our social and economic system.

8. There has been too much talk and not enough real action in doing away with racial discrimination.

9. In any group it is more important to keep a friendly atmosphere than to be efficient.

10. In a small group there should be no real leaders -- everyone should have an equal say.

VP Scale Factor IV

Individualism

1. To be superior a man must stand alone.

2. In life an individual should for the most part "go it alone," assuring himself of privacy, having much time to himself, attempting to control his own life.

3. It is the man who stands alone who excites our admiration.

4. The rich internal world of ideals, of sensitive feelings, of reverie, of self knowledge, is man's true home.

5. One must avoid dependence upon persons or things, the center of life should be found within oneself.

6. The most rewarding object of study any man can find is his own inner life.

7. Whoever would be a man, must be a non-conformist.

8. Contemplation is the highest form of human activity.

9. The individualist is the man who is most likely to discover the best road to a new future.

10. A man can learn better by striking out boldly on his own than he can by following the advice of others.

DIMENSIONS OF VALUES (Withey 1965)

Variable	These short scales are used to tap four basic dimensions of value.
Description	The items were taken from the four basic value dimensions of Bales and Couch (see previous scale). The three highest loading items on each factor of this instrument were adapted for use on a nation-wide study of public civil defense practices to observe whether such behavior could be explained by value orientations.

The items are given in straightforward Likert format from 1 (strongly agree) to 5 (strongly disagree), and therefore all scales run from 3 (high agreement with value) to 15 (low agreement with value). Average scores for the nationwide sample were:

Acceptance of authority	5.5
Need-determined expression	8.3
Equalitarianism	7.5
Individualism	7.2

Sample	The sample consisted of a nationwide probability sample of 1475 adult Americans interviewed in the fall of 1961.
Reliability	In an unpublished paper Robinson performed one factor analysis on the twelve items which essentially replicated the four dimensional structure originally obtained by Bales and Couch. The factor loadings were smaller than those obtained originally. Average inter-item correlations for the items in the various scales varied between .10 and .33. No test-retest data were collected.
Validity	No data bearing directly on validity were collected, although some of the findings reported below suggest some construct validity.
Location	Withey, S. The U.S. and the U.S.S.R.: a report of the public's perspective on United States - Russian relations in late 1961, in D. Bobrow (ed.) Components of defense policy Chicago: Rand McNally, 1965, 164-174. (also available in Survey Research Center monograph series 30)
Administration	The test is self administered and should take under five minutes to complete.
Results and Comments	The items in their present format were highly susceptible to agreement response set, especially for this cross-section sample (whose rates of agreement were noticeably higher than those obtained in Bales and Couch's relatively well-educated sample). This is reflected by the fact that only one item (#6) out of the twelve received more disagreement than agreement and by the intercorrelation matrix showing only three negative coefficients out of the sixty-six

inter-item correlations. One factor analysis actually yielded a
single factor on which all items loaded positively.

Withey found the small minority of people who had built atomic
shelter facilities (or who planned to build such facilities) to be
rather more authoritarian. He also found the authoritarians describing
the "cold war" in terms of Russia "acting like a delinquent" in a
"fight between two ways of life", while rejecting the conflict's
origins as "a lack of mutual understanding".

While contamination attributable to agreement response set precludes
definitive conclusions, it is interesting to note that agreement with
the authoritarian items was highest for this cross-section sample,
while the "expression" items received highest endorsement in the Bales-
Couch sample. In terms of relative rates of agreement, the better-
educated were more likely to agree with the authoritarian items than
any other (although in absolute terms they were the group least likely
to agree with these items). Change in the wording of item 4 (original wording, "It is the man who starts off bravely on his own
who excites our admiration") resulted in its loading higher on the
authoritarian factor than the original individualism factor.

Dimensions of Value

Here are some statements about some of the things that some people believe and others don't. Would you tell me whether you agree or disagree with the statement I read, and whether you feel strongly about it or only fairly sure. If you don't know how you feel, say so.

Acceptance of authority	Average[*]	(s.d.)
1. Young people sometimes get rebellious ideas, but as they grow up they ought to get over them.	1.9	(.7)

Strongly Agree   In between; Disagree Strongly
Agree   Don't know;   Disagree
               Mixed

5. You have to respect authority and when you stop respecting authority, your situation isn't worth much.	1.8	(.7)
9. Obedience and respect for authority are the most important things in character that children should learn.	1.8	(.8)

Need-determined expression (vs. Value-determined restraint)

2. The solution to almost any human problem should be based on the situation at the time, not on some general idea of right or wrong.	2.6	(1.0)
6. Do what you want to do that's fun and worry about the future later.	3.7	(1.0)
10. Since no values last forever, the only real values are those that fit the needs of right now.	3.0	(1.1)

Equalitarianism

3. A group of people that are nearly equal will work a lot better than one where people have bosses and ranks over one another.	2.9	(1.1)
7. Everyone should have an equal chance and an equal say in most things.	2.1	(1.1)
11. Everyone should have what he needs, the important things we have belong to all of us.	2.5	(1.0)

Individualism

4. We should all admire a man who starts out bravely on his own.	1.9	(.7)

---

[*] Where 1 = strongly agree and 5 = strongly disagree.

		Average	(s.d.)
8.	In life a person should for the most part "go it alone," working on his own and trying to make his own life.	2.9	(1.1)
12.	One should not depend on other persons or things, the center of life should be found inside oneself.	2.4	(1.0)

Reprinted with permission of Withey, S. Dimensions of Value in "The U.S. and the U.S.S.R: A Report of the Public's Perspective on United States-Russian Relations in Late 1961," *Components of Defense Policy,* edited by Bobrow, D. (Chicago: Rand McNally, 1965), pp 164-174. Copyright 1965 by Rand McNally, Box 7600, Chicago, Illinois 60680.

CHANGES IN MORAL VALUES (Rettig and Pasamanick 1959)

Variable   This study compares the moral values of a sample of college students with similar data gathered by Crissman (1942, 1950). Subjects evaluate the "rightness" or "wrongness" of several acts.

Description   Since the authors were interested in the change of moral judgments over time they used a questionnaire Crissman had given to college populations in 1929, 1939, and 1949. The questionnaire consists of 50 items describing behaviors which are evaluated on a 1 - 10 point scale of morality. These instructions preceded the questions:

> This questionnaire presents 50 acts or situations which you are to evaluate in terms of "rightness" or "wrongness" ranging from 1 to 10. Encircle the 1 if the item seems least wrong or not wrong at all, and the 10 if the item is judged most wrong or "wrongest" possible. Use the in-between numbers for in-between degrees of "wrongness," the higher the number the more wrong it becomes.

Sample   The sample was 489 freshmen and sophomore students in an elementary sociology course at Ohio State University, 204 males and 285 females.

Reliability   The Kuder-Richardson reliability coefficient was .93. No other information about reliability was reported.

Validity   No measure of validity is reported for this instrument. Crissman does not report the validity of his scale in the several published reports of its use. That a meaningful pattern of results has been obtained with this instrument over a period of thirty years may, however, be interpreted as some measure of validity.

Location   Rettig, S. and Pasamanick, B. Changes in moral values among college students: a factorial study, American Sociological Review, 1959, 24, 856-863.

Rettig, S. and Pasamanick, B. Changes in moral values over three decades 1929-1958, Social Problems, 1959, 6, 320-328.

Administration This questionnaire is self-administered and should take about a half hour to complete.

Results and   A Thurstone factor analysis of the 1958 data yielded six factors
Comments   from the 50 item intercorrelation matrix--basic morality, religious morality, family morality, "puritanical morality," exploitative-manipulative morality, and economic morality. The data indicate increased severity of those moral standards associated with the sanctity of individual life and with democratic governing procedure, and a simultaneous decrease in the severity of judgments of immoral collective acts. The findings are provocative: in 1958 it is "more acceptable to use a poison gas on the civilian enemy than it is to forge a check or to commit adultery."

538

A lack of stability of responses is readily apparent. The average judgment changes 6.5 ranks over the 30 years, and, according to the authors, moral values seem to change with socio-economic conditions.

However, the various college samples differed in terms of region, age, class, and religion, so obtained differences may be in part a factor of intitially different populations, rather than actual changes in moral values over time. An important question that remains to be investigated is the generality of these findings.

A later study by the authors (1960) considered changes in moral values in relation to age. They have also studied the effect of class (1961) and have begun comparisons with subjects of other cultural backgrounds (1962) and among subjects of different generations (1966). This scale covers a wide variety of behaviors and is one of the few on which there is extensive longitudinal data.

References

Crissman, P., Temporal changes and sexual differences in moral judgments, _Journal of Social Psychology_, 1942, _16_, 29-38.

Crissman, P., Temporal changes and sexual differences in moral judgments, _University of Wyoming Publications_, July 1950, _15_, 57-68.

Rettig, S. and Pasamanick, B., Differences in the structure of moral values of students and alumni, _American Sociological Review_, 1960, _25_, 550-555.

Rettig, S. and Pasamanick, B., Moral value structure and social class, _Sociometry_, 1961, _24_, 21-35.

Rettig, S. and Pasamanick, B., Invariance in factor structure of moral value judgments from American and Korean college students, _Sociometry_, 1962, _25_, 73-84.

Rettig, S., Relation of social systems to intergenerational changes in moral attitudes, _Journal of Personality and Social Psychology_, 1966, _4_, 409-414.

Thurstone, L., _Multiple-factor analysis_. Chicago: University of Chicago Press, 1947.

Moral Values

1. Killing a person in defense of one's own life: 1 2 3 4 5 6 7 8 9 10

2. Kidnapping and holding a child for ransom:

3. Having sex relations while unmarried:

4. Forging a check:

5. Habitually failing to keep promises:

6. Girls smoking cigarettes:

7. An industry maintaining working conditions for its workers known to be detri-
    mental to their health:

8. A doctor allowing a badly deformed baby to die when he could save its life but
    not cure its deformity:

9. A legislator, for a financial consideration, using his influence to secure the
    passage of a law known to be contrary to public interest:

10. Testifying falsely in court when under oath:

11. Betting on horse races:

12. A nation dealing unjustly with a weaker nation over which it has power:

13. A jury freeing a father who has killed a man for rape against his young daughter:

14. Living beyond one's means in order to possess luxuries enjoyed by friends and
    associates:

15. Bootlegging under prohibition law:

16. Having illicit sex relations after marriage:

17. Driving an automobile while drunk but without accident:

18. A prosperous industry paying workers less than a living wage:

19. Holding up and robbing a person:

20. Not giving to charity when able:

21. Not taking the trouble to vote at primaries and elections:

22. A strong commercial concern selling below cost to crowd out a weaker competitor:

23. Falsifying about a child's age to secure reduced fare:

24. A student who is allowed to grade his own paper reporting a higher grade than the
    one earned:

25. Not giving to support religion when able:

26. Keeping over-change given by a clerk in mistake:

27. Copying from another's paper in a school examination:

28. Speeding away after one's car knocks down a pedestrian:

29. Charging interest above a fair rate when lending money:

30. Falsifying a federal income tax return:

31. Buying bootleg liquor under prohibition law:

32. Married persons using birth-control devices:

33. Seeking divorce because of incompatibility when both parties agree to separate (assuming no children):

34. Depositing more than one ballot in an election in order to aid a favorite candidate:

35. Living on inherited wealth without attempting to render service to others:

36. Taking one's own life (assuming no near relatives or dependents):

37. Using profane or blasphemous speech:

38. Being habitually cross or disagreeable to members of one's own family:

39. Seeking amusement on Sunday instead of going to church:

40. Refusing to bear arms in a war one believes to be unjust:

41. Advertising a medicine to cure a disease known to be incurable by such a remedy:

42. Misrepresenting the value of an investment in order to induce credulous persons to invest:

43. Taking money for one's vote in an election:

44. Newspapers treating crime news so as to make hoodlums and gangsters appear heroic:

45. A man having a vacant building he cannot rent sets it on fire to collect insurance:

46. Nations at war using poison gas on the homes and cities of its enemy behind the lines:

47. Slipping out secretly and going among people when one's home is under quarantine for a contagious disease:

48. A man deserting a girl whom he has got into trouble without himself taking responsibility:

49. Disbelieving in God:

50. A man not marrying a girl he loves because she is markedly his inferior socially and in education:

Reprinted with permission of Rettig, S. and Pasamanick, B. Changes in Moral Values in "Changes in Moral Values among College Students: A Factorial Study," *American Sociological Review*, 24 (1959), pp 856-863. Copyright 1959 by American Sociological Association, 1001 Connecticut Ave., N.W., Washington, D.C. 20036.

INVENTORY OF VALUES (Ewell 1954)

Variable
: This inventory was designed to measure moral rigidity regarding several kinds of social relationships: sexual, social, legal and religious, family, and business relationships.

Description
: The final instrument contained 100 statements describing acts to be judged "always right," "generally right," "neither right nor wrong," "generally wrong," or "always wrong." Five subscales were designed to measure the areas mentioned above (under "Variable"). Each sub-scale contained 20 items. The 100 items included were taken from a list of 205 statements submitted by members of the Psychology Department at the VA Hospital in Lyons, New Jersey. These 205 statements were rated, using the rightness categories, by 75 attendants at the hospital. Only items yielding nearly even distributions across the three rigidity classes ("always," "generally," "neither") were retained for the 100 item final version. For final scoring, an "always" response was scored 2; a "generally," scored 1; and a "neither," scored 0. Subscale scores were computed by addition.

Sample
: The subjects for Ewell's dissertation research were 90 patients from two veterans' hospitals. They were all WWII veterans, Catholics, between 20 and 50 years old, white males, and none had received intensive psychotherapy. He formed three groups: 30 "nonpsychiatrics," suffering only physical disabilities; 30 psychiatric patients who had received privilege cards and 30 "non-privileged" psychiatric patients showing more severe functional symptoms and kept under tighter security. Age and education levels were reported as follows:

	Mean age	Mean years education
Non-psychiatric	31.47	11.53
Privileged	31.07	11.57
Non-privileged	32.37	11.83

Reliability
: A split-half measure of reliability yielded a coefficient of .90.

Validity
: Nothing other than face validity was claimed for this instrument.

Location
: Ewell, A.H., Jr. The relationship between the rigidity of moral values and the severity of functional psychological illness: a study with war veterans of one religious group. Doctoral dissertation, New York University, 1954. Ann Arbor: University Microfilms, Inc., Publ. No. 8002.

Administration
: This test is self-administered and should take from 10-15 minutes to complete.

Results and Comments
: This instrument is included here primarily because the concept of moral rigidity and its operationization seemed worth further consideration. Also, Ewell seems to have chosen an interesting and diverse set of items that may be of use to other researchers, especially those concerned with samples of the general public rather than college students. It must be clear, however, that the present inventory has not been factor analyzed, and there is nothing more than face validity claimed either for the items or for the five supposed subscales.

INVENTORY OF VALUES SCALE

This inventory consists of a number of things which people might do, some of which some people regard as right and some of which some people regard as wrong. In the list of statements below, you are to check each statement in one of five columns.

If you consider a statement to represent something which is always right, you should check Column 1. If you consider the statement to represent something that is usually but not always right, you should check Column 2. If you consider the statement to represent something which is neither right nor wrong, you should check Column 3. If you consider the statement to represent something which is usually but not always wrong, you should check Column 4. If you consider the statement to represent something which is always wrong, you should check Column 5.

Please answer every item. There is no time limit on answering these questions.

1. To crash a party you have not been invited to.

1	2	3	4	5
Always Right	Generally Right	Neither Right nor Wrong	Generally Wrong	Always Wrong
_____	_____	_____	_____	_____

2. To gamble.

3. To use slugs in pin-ball machines.

4. To take "sick leave" when you want to go to a baseball game.

5. To belong to secret societies.

6. To make huge profits.

7. To be a pacifist.

8. To defend a Negro.

9. To get mad enough to hit your brother.

10. To get a divorce.

11. To use birth control methods.

12. To pass counterfeit money which was passed to you.

Reprinted with permission of Ewell, A. H., Jr. Inventory of Values in "The Relationship between the Rigidity of Moral Values and the Severity of Functional Psychological Illness: A Study with War Veterans of One Religious Group," doctoral dissertation, New York University, 1954. Copyright held by University Microfilms, Ann Arbor; publication no. 8002.

13. To take advantage of mistakes in a contract.

14. To encourage sterilization.

15. To go to church regularly.

16. To have some sort of sexual expression at least every day.

17. To play the stock market.

18. To "bill and coo" with your wife in the presence of your children.

19. For a man to be an interior decorator.

20. To sneak something through customs.

21. Not to have any sexual experiences before marriage.

22. To confess your sins.

23. To kill an enemy soldier.

24. To play with a woman's breasts.

25. To read "dirty" stories.

26. To lie about the speed you were doing when you hit the other car.

27. To tell your mother-in-law off.

28. To abandon a burning building before seeing that others are safe.

29. To talk back to your supervisor.

30. To get on the good side of your supervisor.

31. To have a mistress.

32. To hide the defects of your car when you sell it so as to get as much as possible for it.

33. To eat with your fingers.

34. To have your parents live with your family.

35. To bribe a cop to avoid a ticket.

36. To buy something you can't afford.

37. To gossip.

38. To go through a red light.

39. To exaggerate damages or loss in settling an insurance claim.

40. To go to a prostitute.

41. To tell your children about sex.

42. To whip your children.

43. To buy things that are embargoed which are still available.

44. For a girl to be a tomboy.

45. To follow the saying "Finders keepers, losers weepers."

46. To use profanity.

47. To get a parking ticket fixed.

48. To display affection for a man openly.

49. To cash in on the reputation of your family to get a job.

50. To look at "dirty" pictures.

51. To ask your boss for a raise.

52. To let your wife run the family's money.

53. To allow your daughter to marry someone you do not like.

54. To criticize how the government is run.

55. To allow your 8-year old son and 6-year old daughter to sleep in the same room.

56. To force an older child to give in to a younger child.

57. To take the blame for a co-worker's mistake.

58. To lie to a policeman.

59. To take the blame for a buddy's mistake.

60. To answer your child's questions about sex, childbirth, etc.

61. To go swimming nude.

62. To avoid orgasm until the woman is ready.

63. To undersell a competitor.

64. To experiment with various positions for sex.

65. To get a job by pull.

66. To get drunk.

67. To exaggerate your business experience to get a better job.

68. For a boy to be a sissy.

69. To have a two year old child sleep in the same room as his parents.

70. To tell "fish stories."

71. To try to take another man's girl away from him.

72. To use contraceptives.

73. To urinate outside.

74. To belch openly.

75. To take drugs.

76. To agree always with your boss because you need the job.

77. To pad an expense account.

78. To go to banned movies.

79. To kill an enemy prisoner.

80. To go into bankruptcy to avoid paying debts.

81. To let your 6-year old son dress up in his mother's clothes.

82. To have extra-marital intercourse.

83. To have sex in any but the usual way.

84. To follow a book on bringing up children.

85. To play golf on Sunday.

86. To lend your brother money.

87. To masturbate.

88. To go on wild-cat strikes.

89. To play the horses.

90. To be seen undressed by others of the opposite sex.

91. To get an erection by thinking about a girl.

92. To take your employer's customers away from him by going into business yourself.

93. To allow your 5-year old son and 6-year old daughter to take a bath together.

94. To be a conscientious objector.

95. To allow an 18-year old daughter to kiss her boyfriend.

96. To allow your wife to have dinner with another man when you are away from home.

97. To allow your children to play on your neighbor's property.

98. To defend a Jew.

99. To exceed the speed limit.

100. To offer someone advice even if he doesn't ask for it.

101. To copy from someone else's examination paper.

102. To pay for something you break.

103. To keep the temperature low in your tenant's apartment to save fuel.

104. To tell your son it is wrong to masturbate.

105. To carry life insurance.

106. To tell a buddy his wife is unfaithful.

107. To buy a drink for a minor.

108. To turn in to lost and found a wallet you find someone has left on a bus.

VALUE SURVEY (Rokeach 1968)

Variable
This instrument assesses a respondent's hierarchical arrangement of two kinds of values: instrumental and terminal. Instrumental values refer to preferable modes of conduct; terminal, to preferable end states of existence.

Description
Subjects rank order 18 alphabetically listed terminal values along a dimension of the relative importance of each of these values to themselves. On the next page, they then rank order 18 alphabetically listed instrumental values, again in terms of relative personal importance. Each value is printed on a gummed label. Subjects are instructed to arrange and rearrange the order of the labels until they determine the ordering which best represents the relative importance of each value to them.

Sample
Rokeach's ongoing research in this area has included samples of 50 policemen, 141 unemployed whites, 28 unemployed blacks, 75 Calvinist students, 298 students in a Michigan State University psychology class, and an unspecified number of other subjects.

Reliability
Test-retest reliabilities, after seven weeks, are reported in the .60's for form A, the initial form composed of 12 instrumental and 12 terminal values. Test-retest reliabilities, after seven weeks, are reported in the .70's for form D, the final version of 18 instrumental and 18 terminal values.

Validity
How the values were initially selected and modified is not reported. Only predictive validity is noted: the rank order of the terminal value salvation highly predicts church attendance. The relationship between the average relative positions of the values equality and freedom differentiates among those who are "sympathetic and have participated" (freedom ranked #1, equality #3), "sympathetic but have not participated" (freedom ranked #1, equality #6) and "unsympathetic" (freedom ranked #2, equality #11) to civil rights demonstrations. Additional data provide some validation: salvation was ranked 1st among 12 terminal values by Lutheran ministers and students in a Calvinist college, but it was typically ranked last by Jewish students and those expressing no religious preference.

Location
Rokeach, M. Beliefs, attitudes, and values. San Francisco: Jossey-Bass, Inc., 1968. (See Chapter 7, Organization and change within value-attitude systems, 156-178.)

Administration
The test is self-administered and may take from 10 minutes to a half hour to complete.

Results and Comments
The distinction between terminal and instrumental values is useful in delineating types of values. Nevertheless, terminal values may sometimes function as means to attain other values. For example, loving in a mature way may be seen as the instrumental means to happiness. For some, being intellectual (an instrumental value) may be instead a preferable end state of existence and therefore a

terminal value. Rokeach is concerned with the functional relationships among values, attitudes and their respective systems. He describes these elements as hierarchically arranged within an individual,
with terminal values being both the smallest in number and the most
central or inclusive. Positing that individuals strive for consistency both within and among the several sub-systems, Rokeach suggests
that change may be induced by exposing an individual to the states of
inconsistency already existing in his own value system. Thus a subject who ranks freedom first and equality last "may be revealing something about himself that others might interpret as anti-democratic or
logically inconsistent or, even, as hypocritical." Rokeach has experimental evidence indicating that when this inconsistency is pointed out,
subjects tend to change their rank ordering of these and other values.

In a recent lecture at the Institute for Social Research (Spring 1969),
Rokeach reported that calling attention to such inconsistencies can also
induce behavioral changes. In one study, for example, experimental
subjects (college students) were asked to notice where they had ranked
freedom and equality relative to each other, and then an experimenter
suggested that people who rank freedom high relative to equality seem
to value their own freedom more than they value the freedom of others.
In a control group this was not mentioned. Three months later all
subjects received membership invitations from the NAACP, and it was
found that significantly more experimental than control subjects paid
to join this civil rights organization in response to their invitation.

It is worth noting, in addition, that subjects were asked to answer a
question about how dissatisfied they were with their ratings following
the experimenter's interpretation of the relative placements of freedom
and equality. And, as anticipated, the more dissatisfied were more
likely to show behavioral changes later. This suggests that some people
have a satisfactory way to justify placing freedom above equality and
they therefore experience little dissonance when the apparent inconsistency is pointed out. In fact, Rokeach has shown by content-analyzing
the writings of political figures that rightist ideologists firmly hold
such views, whereas leftists tend to stress equality at the relative
expense of freedom.

Finally, note that Rokeach's test forces the subject to order one value
at the expense of the other, since the relative rather than the absolute
importance of each value is sought. It is therefore impossible to know
whether, for a given individual, the values are equally spaced along
the importance continuum, or cluster together at a few points (e.g., a
few being very important and all others being generally irrelevant).

VALUE SURVEY SCALE

Instructions

On the next page are 18 values listed in alphabetical order. Your task is to arrange them in order of their importance to YOU, as guiding principles in YOUR life. Each value is printed on a gummed label which can be easily peeled off and pasted in the boxes on the left-hand side of the page.

Study the list carefully and pick out the one value which is the most important for you. Peel it off and paste it in Box 1 on the left.

Then pick out the value which is second most important for you. Peel it off and paste it in Box 2. Then do the same for each of the remaining values. The value which is least important goes in Box 18.

Work slowly and think carefully. If you change your mind, feel free to change your answers. The labels peel off easily and can be moved from place to place. The end result should truly show how you really feel.

Reprinted with permission of Rokeach, M. Value Survey in *Beliefs, Attitudes, and Values* (San Francisco: Jossey-Bass, Inc., 1968). Copyright 1968 by Jossey-Bass, Inc., 615 Montgomery Street, San Francisco, Calif. 94111.

1		A COMFORTABLE LIFE a prosperous life
2		AN EXCITING LIFE a stimulating, active life
3		A SENSE OF ACCOMPLISHMENT lasting contribution
4		A WORLD AT PEACE free of war and conflict
5		A WORLD OF BEAUTY beauty of nature and the arts
6		EQUALITY brotherhood, equal opportunity for all
7		FAMILY SECURITY taking care of loved ones
8		FREEDOM independence, free choice
9		HAPPINESS contentedness
10		INNER HARMONY freedom from inner conflict
11		MATURE LOVE sexual and spiritual intimacy
12		NATIONAL SECURITY protection from attack
13		PLEASURE an enjoyable, leisurely life
14		SALVATION saved, eternal life
15		SELF-RESPECT self-esteem
16		SOCIAL RECOGNITION respect, admiration
17		TRUE FRIENDSHIP close companionship
18		WISDOM a mature understanding of life

When you have finished, go to the next page.

Below is another list of 18 values. Arrange them in order of importance, the same as before.

1		AMBITIOUS hard-working, aspiring
2		BROADMINDED open-minded
3		CAPABLE competent, effective
4		CHEERFUL lighthearted, joyful
5		CLEAN neat, tidy
6		COURAGEOUS standing up for your beliefs
7		FORGIVING willing to pardon others
8		HELPFUL working for the welfare of others
9		HONEST sincere, truthful
10		IMAGINATIVE daring, creative
11		INDEPENDENT self-reliant, self-sufficient
12		INTELLECTUAL intelligent, reflective
13		LOGICAL consistent, rational
14		LOVING affectionate, tender
15		OBEDIENT dutiful, respectful
16		POLITE courteous, well-mannered
17		RESPONSIBLE dependable, reliable
18		SELF-CONTROLLED restrained, self-disciplined

WAYS TO LIVE (Morris 1956)

Variable   This scale measures conceptions of the good life. The 13 ways to live include values promulgated by the major religious and philosophical systems. Briefly characterized, the ways are as follows:

1. preserve the best that man has attained

2. cultivate independence of persons and things

3. show sympathetic concern for others

4. experience festivity and solitude in alternation

5. act and enjoy life through group participation

6. constantly master changing conditions.

7. integrate action, enjoyment and contemplation

8. live with wholesome, carefree enjoyment

9. wait in quiet receptivity

10. control the self stoically

11. meditate on the inner life

12. chance adventuresome deeds

13. obey the cosmic purposes

Description   The Ways to Live document consists of 13 paragraphs describing different notions of what is good in life. The respondent rates each way on a 1-7 Likert-type scale in terms of how much this is the kind of life he personally would like to live. He then rank orders all 13 ways along the same dimension. The first seven ways were developed by combining various strengths of the three basic components of personality Morris had delineated in Paths of Life. These three components of personality are buddhistic, dionysian and promethian. The three components yielded six patterns, and a seventh possibility, that of all three components being approximately equal in strength, was added. After testing these seven ways on several hundred college students, Morris added three more ways as a result of their responses. Several years later, the last three ways were added in order to include more extreme alternatives. All the alternatives are positive in tone, concerned with "healthy" values only.

A factor analysis of the data from 250 male college students yielded five factors: social restraint and self-control (positive loadings on ways 1 and 10; negative, on way 4), enjoyment and progress in action (positive loadings on ways 12, 5, and 6; negative, on way 2), withdrawal and self-sufficiency (positive loadings on ways 11 and 2; negative, on way 5), receptivity and sympathetic concern (positive loadings on ways 13 and 9) and self-indulgence or sensuous enjoyment (positive loadings on ways 8 and 4; negative, on way 13).

Sample   The 13 alternative form of this instrument has been used (pri-
                    marily with college students) in the United States, India, China,
                    Japan, Italy, Norway, Canada, England and other countries.
                    2,015 college men and 831 college women, primarily in liberal
                    arts, were tested in the United States from 1945-1952. Data
                    from China were gathered in 1948 from 523 male and 220 female
                    students. In India, between 1949 and 1950, 724 male and 410
                    female students were tested. Samples from the U.S., India and
                    China were the most extensive.

Reliability   The estimated repeat reliability rate for college students is
                    .85, although no rigorous investigation has yet been undertaken.
                    Twenty college students, after a three week interval, showed an
                    average product-moment correlation of .87. Thirty college students,
                    after a 14 week interval, showed a correlation of .78. For 56
                    college women, rank-order correlations taken three weeks apart
                    on the first six ways averaged .93. The ways themselves (based on
                    21 students after a three week interval) have a mean reliability of
                    .67.

Validity   There is no information on the extent to which respondents, prior
                    to taking the test, saw the ways as distinctly different, con-
                    ceptually clear and unambiguous. Morris notes: "It is merely
                    believed that the thirteen alternatives, because of the conside-
                    rations mentioned in the construction of the document, do represent
                    a good sample of the regions in such a space, thus providing a
                    valid instrument in the technical sense of the term." Validation
                    seems to refer only to statistical procedure, and not to any other
                    kinds of validity, a most unfortunate omission. (See Winthrop,
                    1961 for an excellent critical review of the validity and other
                    problems of this test.)

Location   Morris, C. Varieties of human value. Chicago: University of
                    Chicago Press, 1956.

Administration   The test is self-administered and may take from one half to one
                    hour to complete. The paragraphs are long and complex, perhaps
                    necessitating several re-readings before evaluations can be made.

Results and   Morris notes that three major results have emerged: "...the
Comments   attainment of a cross-cultural interval scale for measuring
                    values, the isolation of five value dimensions that appear (with
                    minor variations) in the three main cultural samples (e.g., United
                    States, China and India); and the accumulation of a body of evidence
                    supporting in its totality a field conception of values." Further-
                    more, the five value dimensions have been found in the six cul-
                    tures reported in this book, with factors A and B being the most
                    favored in all cultures, although in each culture each way was
                    selected as most preferred by some respondents. (See Morris, 1951,
                    for more cross cultural data.) Way 7 is most preferred by students
                    in the United States. Morris presents a plethora of statistical
                    information; unfortunately the results are presented in a variety
                    of ways -- as factors, first choice, scale values, etc. -- and

often neither integrated nor interpreted sufficiently. Discussion of scaling procedures and other methodology may be found in Morris and Jones (1955).

This brief summary cannot do justice to Morris' work; most of the book explicates the determinants -- social, psychological, biological and ecological -- of conceived values. Numerous measures ranging from somatotype to beliefs have been employed to assess these determinants (see Jones and Morris, 1956).

A major problem with this instrument is the complexity and abstract quality of each paragraph. Both positive and negative imperatives, preferences, cliches, specific activities and even poetry (way 6 suggests life tends"...to become sickled o'er with the pale cast of thought") may be found, in differing combinations in these paragraphs. The phrasing is often so lacking in rigor and clarity that precisely <u>what</u> the subject was responding to becomes unclear. (See Osgood, Ware, and Morris', 1961, use of the semantic differential to tap connotative meanings.) In short, very abstract rich stimuli are presented and only a simple response is asked. Dempsey and Dukes (1966) using a Q-sort technique to assess the coherence of these paragraphs found discordancy (negative within-path inter-item <u>r</u>'s) in 11 of the paths. They prepared both a revised form eliminating discordant statements and a shortened form that may well be helpful to those interested in, but critical of, the Ways to Live instrument. (See Gorlow and Barocas for another Q-sort of the Ways to Live which yielded clusters different from those of Morris.)

The scales do overlap a great deal: reflection and self-knowledge elements are found in ways 2, 4, 11 and, negatively, in ways 5 and 6. The value of intellectual activities is neglected, and since some items in all statements are normatively appropriate cliches or even shibboleths it is strange that respondents are expected to utilize a scale ranging from "I like it very much" to "I <u>dislike</u> it very much."

In sum, Morris has amassed an impressive collection of data of multidisciplinary interest. The test is a careful and creative effort, and his main conclusions are adequately supported.

References   Dempsey, P. and Dukes, W. Complex value stimuli: an examination and revision of Morris's <u>Paths</u> <u>of</u> <u>Life</u>, <u>Educational</u> <u>and</u> <u>Psychological</u> <u>Measurement</u>, 1966, <u>26</u>, 871-882.

Gorlow, L. and Barocas, R. Value preferences and interpersonal behavior, <u>Journal</u> <u>of</u> <u>Social</u> <u>Psychology</u>, 1965, <u>66</u>, 271-80.

Jones, L. and Morris, C. Relations of temperment to the choice of values, <u>Journal</u> <u>of</u> <u>Abnormal</u> <u>and</u> <u>Social</u> <u>Psychology</u>, 1956, <u>53</u>, 346-349.

Morris, C. Comparative strength of life-ideals in Eastern and Western cultures. In Moore, C. (ed.) <u>Essays</u> <u>in</u> <u>East-West</u> <u>philo</u>-

sophy. Honolulu: University of Hawaii Press, 1951, 353-370.

Morris, C. Paths of life. New York: Harper, 1942; 2nd edition, New York: Braziller, 1956.

Morris, C. and Jones, L. Value scales and dimensions, Journal of Abnormal and Social Psychology, 1955, 51, 523-535.

Osgood, C., Ware, E., and Morris, C. Analysis of the connotative meanings of a variety of human values as expressed by American college students, Journal of Abnormal and Social Psychology, 1961, 62, 62-73.

Winthrop, H. Psychology and value: a critique of Morris' approach to evaluation as behavior, The Journal of General Psychology, 1959, 61, 13-37.

WAYS TO LIVE

Instructions: Below are described thirteen ways to live which various persons at various times have advocated and followed.

Indicate by numbers which you are to write in the margin how much you yourself like or dislike each of them. Do them in order. Do not read ahead.

Remember that it is not a question of what kind of life you now lead, or the kind of life you think it prudent to live in our society, or the kind of life you think good for other persons, but simply the kind of life you personally would like to live.

Use the following scale of numbers, placing one of them in the margin alongside each of the ways to live:

> 7 I like it very much
> 6 I like it quite a lot
> 5 I like it slightly
> 4 I am indifferent to it
> 3 I dislike it slightly
> 2 I dislike it quite a lot
> 1 I dislike it very much

WAY 1: In this "design for living" the individual actively participates in the social life of his community, not to change it primarily, but to understand, appreciate, and preserve the best that man has attained. Excessive desires should be avoided and moderation sought. One wants the good things of life but in an orderly way. Life is to have clarity, balance, refinement, control. Vulgarity, great enthusiasm, irrational behavior, impatience, indulgence are to be avoided. Friendship is to be esteemed but not easy intimacy with many people. Life is to have discipline, intelligibility, good manners, predictability. Social changes are to be made slowly and carefully, so that what has been achieved in human culture is not lost. The individual should be active physically and socially, but not in a hectic or radical way. Restraint and intelligence should give order to an active life.

WAY 2: The individual should for the most part "go it alone," assuring himself of privacy in living quarters, having much time to himself, attempting to control his own life. One should stress self-sufficiency, reflection and meditation, knowledge of himself. The direction of interest should be away from intimate associations with social groups, and away from the physical manipulation of objects or attempts at control of the physical environment. One should aim to simplify one's external life, to moderate those desires whose satisfaction is dependent upon physical and social forces outside of oneself, and to concentrate attention upon the refinement, clarification, and self-direction of oneself. Not much can be done or is to be gained by "living outwardly." One must avoid dependence upon persons or things; the center of life should be found within oneself.

WAY 3: This way of life makes central the sympathetic concern
for other persons. Affection should be the main thing in life, affection that is free from all traces of the imposition of oneself upon
others or of using others for one's own purposes. Greed in possessions,
emphasis on sexual passion, the search for power over persons and things,
excessive emphasis upon intellect, and undue concern for oneself are to
be avoided. For these things hinder the sympathetic love among persons
which alone gives significance to life. If we are aggressive we block
our receptivity to the personal forces upon which we are dependent for
genuine personal growth. One should accordingly purify oneself, restrain
one's self-assertiveness, and become receptive, appreciative, and helpful with respect to other persons.

WAY 4: Life is something to be enjoyed--sensuously enjoyed, enjoyed with relish and abandonment. The aim in life should not be to
control the course of the world or society or the lives of others, but
to be open and receptive to things and persons, and to delight in them.
Life is more a festival than a workshop or a school for moral discipline.
To let oneself go, to let things and persons affect oneself, is more important than to do--or to do good. Such enjoyment, however, requires
that one be self-centered enough to be keenly aware of what is happening
and free for new happenings. So one should avoid entanglements, should
not be too dependent on particular people or things, should not be self-
sacrificing; one should be alone a lot, should have time for meditation
and awareness of oneself. Solitude and sociality together are both necessary in the good life.

WAY 5: A person should not hold on to himself, withdraw from
people, keep aloof and self-centered. Rather merge oneself with a
social group, enjoy cooperation and companionship, join with others in
resolute activity for the realization of common goals. Persons are social
and persons are active; life should merge energetic group activity and
cooperative group enjoyment. Meditation, restraint, concern for one's
self-sufficiency, abstract intellectuality, solitude, stress on one's
possessions all cut the roots which bind persons together. One should
live outwardly with gusto, enjoying the good things of life, working
with others to secure the things which make possible a pleasant and
energetic social life. Those who oppose this ideal are not to be dealt
with too tenderly. Life can't be too fastidious.

WAY 6: Life continuously tends to stagnate, to become "comfortable,"
to become sickled o'er with the pale cast of thought. Against these tendencies, a person must stress the need of constant activity--physical action, adventure, the realistic solution of specific problems as they appear, the improvement of techniques for controlling the world and society.
Man's future depends primarily on what he does, not on what he feels or
on his speculations. New problems constantly arise and always will arise.
Improvements must always be made if man is to progress. We can't just
follow the past or dream of what the future might be. We have to work
resolutely and continually if control is to be gained over the forces
which threaten us. Man should rely on technical advances made possible
by scientific knowledge. He should find his goal in the solution of his
problems. The good is the enemy of the better.

WAY 7: We should at various times and in various ways accept something from all other paths of life, but give no one our exclusive allegiance. At one moment one of them is the more appropriate; at another moment another is the most appropriate. Life should contain enjoyment and action and contemplation in about equal amounts. When either is carried to extremes we lose something important for our life. So we must cultivate flexibility, admit diversity in ourselves, accept the tension which this diversity produces, find a place for detachment in the midst of enjoyment and activity. The goal of life is found in the dynamic integration of enjoyment, action, and contemplation, and so in the dynamic interaction of the various paths of life. One should use all of them in building a life, and no one alone.

WAY 8: Enjoyment should be the keynote of life. Not the hectic search for intense and exciting pleasures, but the enjoyment of the simple and easily obtainable pleasures: the pleasures of just existing, of savory food, of comfortable surroundings, of talking with friends, of rest and relaxation. A home that is warm and comfortable, chairs and a bed that are soft, a kitchen well stocked with food, a door open to the entrance of friends--this is the place to live. Body at ease, relaxed, calm in its movements, not hurried, breath slow, willing to nod and rest, grateful to the world that is its food--so should the body be. Driving ambition and the fanaticism of ascetic ideals are the signs of discontented people who have lost the capacity to float in the stream of simple, carefree, wholesome enjoyment.

WAY 9: Receptivity should be the keynote of life. The good things come of their own accord, and come unsought. They cannot be found by resolute action. They cannot be found in the indulgence of the sensuous desires of the body. They cannot be gathered by participation in the turmoil of social life. They cannot be given to others by attempts to be helpful. They cannot be garnered by hard thinking. Rather do they come unsought when the bars of the self are down. When the self has ceased to make demands and waits in quiet receptivity, it becomes open to the powers which nourish it and work through it; and sustained by these powers it knows joy and peace. To sit alone under the trees and the sky, open to nature's voices, calm and receptive, then can the wisdom from without come within.

WAY 10: Self-control should be the keynote of life. Not the easy self-control which retreats from the world, but the vigilant, stern, manly control of a self which lives in the world, and knows the strength of the world and the limits of human power. The good life is rationally directed and holds firm to high ideals. It is not bent by the seductive voices of comfort and desire. It does not expect social utopias. It is distrustful of final victories. Too much cannot be expected. Yet one can with vigilance hold firm the reins to his self, control his unruly impulses, understand his place in the world, guide his actions by reason, maintain his self-reliant independence. And in this way, though he finally perish, man can deep his human dignity and respect, and die with cosmic good manners.

WAY 11: The contemplative life is the good life. The external world is no fit habitat for man. It is too big, too cold, too pressing. Rather it is the life turned inward that is rewarding. The rich internal world of ideals, of sensitive feelings, of reverie, of self-knowledge is man's true home. By the cultivation of the self within, man alone becomes human. Only then does there arise deep sympathy with all that lives, an understanding of the suffering inherent in life, a realization of the futility of aggressive action, the attainment of contemplative joy. Conceit then falls away and austerity is dissolved. In giving up the world one finds the larger and finer sea of the inner self.

WAY 12: The use of the body's energy is the secret of a rewarding life. The hands need material to make into something: lumber and stone for building, food to harvest, clay to mold. The muscles are alive to joy only in action, in climbing, running, skiing and the like. Life finds its zest in overcoming, dominating, conquering some obstacle. It is the active deed which is satisfying, the deed adequate to the present, the daring and adventuresome deed. Not in cautious foresight, not in relaxed ease does life attain completion. Outward energetic action, the excitement of power in the tangible present--this is the way to live.

WAY 13: A person should let himself be used. Used by other persons in their growth, used by the great objective purposes in the universe which silently and irresistibly achieve their goal. For persons and the world's purposes are dependable at heart, and can be trusted. One should be humble, constant, faithful, uninsistent. Grateful for the affection and protection which one needs, but undemanding. Close to persons and to nature, and secure because close. Nourishing the good by devotion and sustained by the good because of devotion. One should be a serene, confident, quiet vessel and instrument of the great dependable powers which move to their fulfillment.

Instructions for ranking your preferences: Rank the thirteen ways to live in the order you prefer them, putting first the number of the way to live you like the best, then the number of the way you like next best, and so on down to the number of the way to live you like the least:

Final Word: If you can formulate a way to live you would like better than any of the thirteen alternatives, please do so....

VARIATIONS IN VALUE ORIENTATIONS (Kluckhohn and Strodtbeck 1961)

Variable   This study attempts to develop an interview instrument to measure
                the dominant and variant value orientations found in 5 different
                cultures. The definition of "value orientation" is:

                        Value orientations are complex but definitely patterned
                        (rank-ordered) principles, resulting from the transactional
                        interplay of three analytically distinguishable elements
                        of the evaluative process--the cognitive, the affective,
                        and the directive elements--which give order and direction
                        to the ever-flowing stream of human acts and thought as
                        these relate to the solution of "common human problems."

                The five common human problems and their postulated solutions are
                presented in the following chart:

Orientation	Postulated Range of Variations		
human nature	Evil	Neutral	Mixture of Good & Evil	Good
	mutable / immutable	mutable / immutable	mutable / immutable
man-nature	Subjugation to Nature	Harmony with Nature	Mastery over Nature
time	Past	Present	Future
activity	Being	Being-in-becoming	Doing
relational	Lineality	Collaterality	Individualism

                These notions have been developed and revised in several papers of
                Florence Kluckhohn.

Description   Twenty-two items were selected to assess the ordering of solutions
                to four orientations; time and financial limitations obviated examina-
                tion of the human nature orientation. Each item was expected to be
                a familiar type of life situation. Respondents chose among alterna-
                tives which were based on theoretical notions of what the three
                variations for each orientation would be.

Sample	Limitations of time, financial resources, and other difficulties also necessitated a small sample. (1) A Spanish-American community. The total population of this community was selected, since there were only 25 adult members. Two men did not complete the schedule; thus the number interviewed was 23 (12 women and 11 men). (2) A Mormon group. Eleven men and nine women were randomly selected. The procedure involved dividing the names of all people over the age of 20 according to sex and using random numbers to select 10 names from each of the two groups. An error in interpretation caused the sample to be composed of 11 men and 9 women. The (3) Texan group and the (4) Navaho group were sampled in the same way as the Mormon group, resulting in a sample of 10 men and 10 women in each group. In addition, a full alternate Navaho sample was drawn because the need for substitutions was anticipated. Twenty-two respondents were used in the final analysis. (5) Zuni community. A random sample was not drawn. The 11 men and 10 women interviewed were a close network of adults who shared frequent face-to-face interaction and close kinship ties.
Reliability	There is no report of reliability. The authors note, "concerning that aspect of reliability which means consistency of response over time, we expected the 'general question' method to produce more reliable results than a method which depended upon the use of situationally specific questions. But we were not able to put this expectation to the empirical test of repeated questioning."
Validity	The authors suggest that the simultaneous testing of the same items in the various cultural samples constitutes some measure of validity. Thus a lack of pattern in the responses of only one or two groups may be attributed to true cultural inconsistency, rather than to the poor quality of the question. Extensive ethnographic data tended to support the findings of the schedule and many of the predicted relationships.
Location	Kluckhohn, Florence and Strodtbeck, F. Variations in value orientations. Evanston, Illinois: Row, Peterson, and Company, 1961.
Administration	The amount of time necessary for this interview will probably vary greatly. The sentences among which a respondent must choose are often long and complex and may need repetition for some subjects, thus extending the length of the interview.
Results and Comments	This study is based on several interesting assumptions: there are a limited number of common human problems; all peoples at all times must find some solution to these problems; a limited range of different solutions is possible; and all solutions are not only present at all times in all societies but also differentially preferred. Each of these assumptions needs further refinement and empirical verification. It is not clear that the five problems suggested are exhaustive; for example, might not conceptions of space be another common human problem? Furthermore, a more precise specification both of which solutions become preferred by which groups or subgroups and of why change in these preferences occurs is necessary.

Significant within-culture regularities and significant between
culture differences were found. Unfortunately the data were insufficient for an analysis of the variation within each of the
cultures. This is particularly unfortunate because one of the
most important contributions of this book is to point to the existence of permitted and required variant orientations, thus recognizing the heterogeneity of values. Some between culture results
are troublesome: Is the consistency found among the Zuni a statement about their values or about the measures used? How can the
Texas and Mormon groups have similar profiles when the ethnographic
data shows great differences? (The answer to this question seems
to be that the interview does not ask for the intensity of degree
to which a value is held.) Furthermore, as the authors recognize,
items seem to have more than one orientation present. Items 16
and 17 to test relational values have elements of time and activity
orientations too. Of interest is the graphic method analysis employed to show levels of significance among the alternative solutions to a particular orientation. The problem of lack of reliability
data is particularly serious, both because of the usual problems of
translating the same concept into several languages, and because the
items are long and complex, and may have been troublesome to many
respondents. Despite all the above criticisms, the specification
of these value orientations has great potential utility for assessing the values of individuals in different groups or subgroups.
Psychologists may well wish to modify the interview in a variety of
ways, perhaps developing a questionnaire, perhaps by adding items,
perhaps by finding ways to assess degree of valuation, but the comprehensiveness and generality suggested by the five value orientations
and the possible variations is attractive indeed.

References

Kluckhohn, Florence. Dominant and substitute profiles of cultural
orientations: their significance for the analysis of social stratification. Social Forces, 1950, 28, 376-394.

Kluckhohn, Florence. Dominant and variant value orientations.
in C. Klukholn and H. Murray (eds.), Personality in Nature, Society
and Culture (2nd edition). New York: Alfred A. Knopf, 1953. Pp.
342-357.

VARIATIONS IN VALUE ORIENTATIONS SCALE

1. Job Choice   activity: Items A1 and A2

   A man needed a job and had a chance to work for two men. The two
bosses were different. Listen to what they were like and say which
you think would be the best one to work for.

A   One boss was a fair enough man, and he gave somewhat higher
(Doing)   pay than most men, but he was the kind of boss who insisted
           that men work hard, stick on the job. He did not like it
           at all when a worker sometimes just knocked off work for a
           while to go on a trip or to have a day or so of fun, and he
           thought it was right not to take such a worker back on the
           job.

B   The other paid just average wages but he was not so firm.
(Being)   He understood that a worker would sometimes just not turn
           up--would be off on a trip or having a little fun for a
           day or two. When his men did this he would take them back
           without saying too much.

                            (Part one)

Which of these men do you believe that it would be better to work for
in most cases?

Which of these men would most other _____ think it better to work for?

                            (Part two)

Which kind of boss do you believe that it is better to be in most cases?

Which kind of boss would most other _____ think it better to be?

2. Well Arrangements   relational: Item R1

   When a community has to make arrangements for water, such as drill a
well, there are three different ways they can decide to arrange things
like location, and who is going to do the work.

A   There are some communities where it is mainly the older or
(Lin)   recognized leaders of the important families who decide the
           plans. Everyone usually accepts what they say without much
           discussion since they are the ones who are used to deciding
           such things and are the ones who have had the most experience.

Reprinted with permission of Kluckhohn, F. and Strodtbeck, F. Variations in Value Orientations in *Variations in Value Orientations* (Westport, Connecticut: Greenwood Press, 1973).

B
(Coll)
There are some communities where most people in the group have a part in making the plans. Lots of different people talk, but nothing is done until almost everyone comes to agree as to what is best to be done.

C
(Ind)
There are some communities where everyone holds to his own opinion, and they decide the matter by vote. They do what the largest number want even though there are still a very great many people who disagree and object to the action.

Which way do you think is usually best in such cases?

Which of the other two ways do you think is better?

Which way of all three ways do you think most other persons in _____ would usually think is best?

3. Child Training

time: Item T1

Some people were talking about the way children should be brought up. Here are three different ideas.

A
(Past)
Some people say that children should be taught well the traditions of the past (the ways of the old people). They believe the old ways are best, and that it is when children do not follow them too much that things go wrong.

B
(Pres)
Some people say that children should be taught some of the old traditions (ways of the old people), but it is wrong to insist that they stick to these ways. These people believe that it is necessary for children always to learn about and take on whatever of the new ways will best help them get along in the world of today.

C
(Fut)
Some people do not believe children should be taught much about past traditions (the ways of the old people) at all except as an interesting story of what has gone before. These people believe that the world goes along best when children are taught the things that will make them want to find out for themselves new ways of doing things to replace the old.

Which of these people had the best idea about how children should be taught?

Which of the other two people had the better idea?

Considering again all three ideas, which would most other persons in _____ say had the better idea?

4. Livestock Dying

One time a man had a lot of livestock. Most of them died off in
different ways. People talked about this and said different things.

A
(Subj)
Some people said you just can't blame a man when things
like this happen. There are so many things that can and do
happen, and a man can do almost nothing to prevent such losses
when they come. We all have to learn to take the bad with
the good.

B
(Over)
Some people said that it was probably the man's own fault
that he lost so many. He probably didn't use his head to
prevent the losses. They said that it is usually the case
that men who keep up on new ways of doing things, and really
set themselves to it, almost always find a way to keep out
of such trouble.

C
(With)
Some people said that it was probably because the man had
not lived his life right--had not done things in the right
way to keep harmony between himself and the forces of nature
(i.e., the ways of nature like the rain, winds, snow, etc.).

Which of these reasons do you think is most usually true?

Which of the other two reasons do you think is more true?

Which of all three reasons would most other persons in _____ think
is usually true?

5. Expectations about Change

(a. 20-40 Age Group)

Three young people were talking about what they thought their families would have one day as compared with their fathers and mothers.
They each said different things.

C
(Fut)
The first said: I expect my family to be better off in the
future than the family of my father and mother or relatives
if we work hard and plan right. Things in this country usually get better for people who really try.

B
(Pres)
The second one said: I don't know whether my family will
be better off, the same, or worse off than the family of my
father and mother or relatives. Things always go up and
down even if people do work hard. So one can never really
tell how things will be.

A
(Past)
The third one said: I expect my family to be about the same
as the family of my father and mother or relatives. The
best way is to work hard and plan ways to keep up things as
they have been in the past.

Which of these people do you think had the best idea?

Which of the other two persons had the better idea?

Which of these three people would most other _____ your age think had the best idea?

(b. 40-up Age Group)

Three older people were talking about what they thought their children would have when they were grown. Here is what each one said.

C
(Fut)
One said: I really expect my children to have more than I have had if they work hard and plan right. There are always good chances for people who try.

B
(Pres)
The second one said: I don't know whether my children will be better off, worse off, or just the same. Things always go up and down even if one works hard, so we can't really tell.

A
(Past)
The third one said: I expect my children to have just about the same as I have had or bring things back as they once were. It is their job to work hard and find ways to keep things going as they have been in the past.

Which of these people do you think had the best idea?

Which of the other two persons had the better idea?

Which of these three people would most other _____ your age think had the best idea?

6. Facing Conditions

man-nature: Item MN2

There are different ways of thinking about how God (the gods) is (are) related to man and to weather and all other natural conditions which make the crops and animals live or die. Here are three possible ways.

C
(With)
God (the gods) and people all work together all the time; whether the conditions which make the crops and animals grow are good or bad depends upon whether people themselves do all the proper things to keep themselves in harmony with their God (gods) and with the forces of nature.

B
(Over)
God (the gods) does (do) not directly use his (their) power to control all the conditions which affect the growth of crops or animals. It is up to the people themselves to figure out the ways conditions change and to try hard to find the ways of controlling them.

A
(Subj)
Just how God (the gods) will use his (their) power over all the conditions which affect the growth of crops and animals cannot be known by man. But it is useless for people to think they can change conditions very much for very long. The best way is to take conditions as they come and do as well as one can.

Which of these ways of looking at things do you think is best?

Which of the other two ways do you think is better?

Which of the three ways of looking at things would most other people in _____ think is best?

7. Help in Misfortune   relational: Item R2

A man had a crop failure, or, let us say, had lost most of his sheep or cattle. He and his family had to have help from someone if they were going to get through the winter. There are different ways of getting help. Which of these three ways would be best?

B
(Coll)
Would it be best if he depended mostly on his brothers and sisters or other relatives all to help him out as much as each one could?

C
(Ind)
Would it be best for him to try to raise the money on his own outside the community (his own people) from people who are neither relatives nor employers?

A
(Lin)
Would it be best for him to go to a boss or to an older important relative who is used to managing things in his group, and ask him to help out until things get better?

Which way of getting the help do you think would usually be best?

Which way of getting the help do you think is next best?

Which way do you think you yourself would really follow?

Which way do you think most other people in _____ would think best?

8. Family Work Relations   relational: Item R3

I'm going to tell you about three different ways families can arrange work. These families are related and they live close together.

C
(Ind)
In some groups (or communities) it is usually expected that each of the separate families (by which we mean just husband, wife, and children) will look after its own business separate from all others and not be responsible for the others.

B
(Coll)

In some groups (or communities) it is usually expected that the close relatives in the families will work together and talk over among themselves the way to take care of whatever problems come up. When a boss is needed they usually choose (get) one person, not necessarily the oldest able person, to manage things.

A
(Lin)

In some groups (or communities) it is usually expected that the families which are closely related to each other will work together and have the oldest able person (hermano mayor or father) be responsible for and take charge of most important things.

Which of these ways do you think is usually best in most cases?

Which of the other two ways do you think is better?

Which of all the ways do you think most other persons in _____ would think is usually best?

9. Choice of Delegate   relational: Item R4

A group like yours (community like yours) is to send a delegate--a representative--to a meeting away from here (this can be any sort of meeting). How will this delegate be chosen?

B
(Coll)

Is it best that a meeting be called and everyone discuss things until almost everyone agrees so that when a vote is taken almost all people would be agreed on the same person?

A
(Lin)

Is it best that the older, important, leaders take the main responsibility for deciding who should represent the people since they are the ones who have had the long experience in such matters?

C
(Ind)

Is it best that a meeting be called, names be put up, a vote be taken, then send the man who gets the majority of votes even if there are many people who are still against this man?

Which of these ways of choosing is usually best in cases like this?

Which of the other two ways is usually better?

Which would most other persons in _____ say is usually best?

10. Use of Fields   man-nature: Item MN3

There were three men who had fields with crops (were farmers). The three men had quite different ways of planting and taking care of crops.

C
(With)
One man put in his crops, worked hard, and also set himself to living in right and proper ways. He felt that it is the way a man works and tries to keep himself in harmony with the forces of nature that has the most effect on conditions and the way crops turn out.

A
(Subj)
One man put in his crops. Afterwards he worked on them sufficiently but did not do more than was necessary to keep them going along. He felt that it mainly depended on weather conditions how they would turn out, and that nothing extra that people do could change things much.

B
(Over)
One man put in his crops and then worked on them a lot of time and made use of all the new scientific ideas he could find out about. He felt that by doing this he would in most years prevent many of the effects of bad conditions.

Which of these ways do you believe is usually best?

Which of the other two ways do you believe is better?

Which of the three ways would most other persons in _____ think is best?

11. Philosophy of Life   time: Item T3

People often have very different ideas about what has gone before and what we can expect in life. Here are three ways of thinking about these things.

B
(Pres)
Some people believe it best to give most attention to what is happening now in the present. They say that the past has gone and the future is much too uncertain to count on. Things do change, but it is sometimes for the better and sometimes for the worse, so in the long run it is about the same. These people believe the best way to live is to keep those of the old ways that one can--or that one likes--but to be ready to accept the new ways which will help to make life easier and better as we live from year to year.

A
(Past)
Some people think that the ways of the past (ways of the old people or traditional ways) were the most right and the best, and as changes come things get worse. These people think the best way to live is to work hard to keep up the old ways and try to bring them back when they are lost.

C
(Fut)
Some people believe that it is almost always the ways of the future--the ways which are still to come--which will be best, and they say that even though there are sometimes small setbacks, change brings improvements in the long run. These people think the best way to live is to look a long time ahead, work hard, and give up many things now so that the future will be better.

Which of these ways of looking at life do you think is best?

Which of the other two ways do you think is better?

Which of the three ways of looking at life do you think most other persons in _____ would think is best?

12. Wage Work   relational: Item R5

There are three ways in which men who do not themselves hire others may work.

C
(Ind)
One way is working on one's own as an individual. In this case a man is pretty much his own boss. He decides most things himself, and how he gets along is his own business. He only has to take care of himself and he doesn't expect others to look out for him.

B
(Coll)
One way is working in a group of men where all the men work together without there being one main boss. Every man has something to say in the decisions that are made, and all the men can count on each other.

A
(Lin)
One way is working for an owner, a big boss, or a man who has been running things for a long time (a patrón). In this case, the men do not take part in deciding how the business will be run, but they know they can depend on the boss to help them out in many ways.

Which of these ways is usually best for a man who does not hire others?

Which of the other two ways is better for a man who does not hire others?

Which of the three ways do you think most other persons in _____ would think is best?

13. Belief in Control   man-nature: Item MN4

Three men from different areas were talking about the things that control the weather and other conditions. Here is what they each said.

A
(Subj)
One man said: My people have never controlled the rain, wind, and other natural conditions and probably never will. There have always been good years and bad years. That is the way it is, and if you are wise you will take it as it comes and do the best you can.

B
(Over)
The second man said: My people believe that it is man's job to find ways to overcome weather and other conditions

just as they have overcome so many things. They believe they will one day succeed in doing this and may even over-come drought and floods.

C
(With)
The third man said: My people help conditions and keep things going by working to keep in close touch with all the forces which make the rain, the snow, and other conditions. It is when we do the right things--live in the proper way--and keep all that we have--the land, the stock, and the water--in good condition, that all goes along well.

Which of these men do you think had the best idea?

Which of the other two men do you think had the better idea?

Which of the three men do you think most other persons in _____ would think had the best idea?

14. Ceremonial Innovation   time: Item T4

Some people in a community like your own saw that the religious cere-monies (the church services) were changing from what they used to be.

C
(Fut)
Some people were really pleased because of the changes in religious ceremonies. They felt that new ways are usually better than old ones, and they like to keep everything--even ceremonies--moving ahead.

A
(Past)
Some people were unhappy because of the change. They felt that religious ceremonies should be kept exactly--in every way--as they had been in the past.

B
(Pres)
Some people felt that the old ways for religious ceremonies were best but you just can't hang on to them. It makes life easier just to accept some changes as they come along.

Which of these three said most nearly what you would believe is right?

Which of the other two do you think is more right?

Which of the three would most other _____ say was most right?

15. Ways of Living   activity: Item A3

There were two people talking about how they liked to live. They had different ideas.

A
(Doing)
One said: What I care about most is accomplishing things--getting things done just as well or better than other people do them. I like to see results and think they are worth working for.

B
(Being)

The other said: What I care most about is to be left alone to think and act in the ways that best suit the way I really am. If I don't always get much done but can enjoy life as I go along, that is the best way.

Which of these two persons do you think has the better way of thinking?

Which of the two do you think you are more like?

Which do you think most other _____ would say had the better way of living?

16. Livestock Inheritance   relational: Item R6

Some sons and daughters have been left some livestock (sheep or cattle) by a father or mother who has died. All these sons and daughters are grown up, and they live near each other. There are three different ways they can run the livestock.

A
(Lin)

In some groups of people it is usually expected that the oldest able person (son or daughter, hermano mayor) will take charge of, or manage, all the stock held by himself and the other sons and daughters.

C
(Ind)

In some groups of people it is usually expected that each of the sons and daughters will prefer to take his or her own share of the stock and run his or her own business completely separate from all the others.

B
(Coll)

In some groups of people it is usually expected that all the sons and daughters will keep all their cattle and sheep together and work together and decide among themselves who is best able to take charge of things, not necessarily the oldest, when a boss is needed.

Which way do you think is usually best in most cases?

Which of the other two ways do you think is better?

Which of all three ways do you think most other persons in _____ would think is usually best?

17. Land Inheritance   relational: Item R7

Now I want to ask a similar question concerning farm and grazing land instead of livestock.

Some sons and daughters have been left some farm and grazing land by a father or mother who has died. All these sons and daughters are grown and live near each other. There are three ways they can handle the property.

A (Lin)	In some groups of people it is usually expected that the oldest able person (<u>hermano mayor</u>) will take charge of or manage the land for himself and all the other sons and daughters, even if they all share it.
C (Ind)	In some groups of people it is usually expected that each son and daughter will take his own share of the land and do with it what he wants--separate from all the others.
B (Coll)	In some groups of people it is usually expected that all the sons and daughters will make use of the land together. When a boss is needed, they all get together and agree to choose someone of the group, not necessarily the oldest, to take charge of things.

Which of these ways do you think is usually best in most cases?

Which of the other two ways do you think is better?

Which of all three ways do you think most other persons in _____ would think is usually best?

18. Care of Fields   activity: Item A4

There were two men, both farmers (men with fields). They lived differently.

B (Being)	One man kept the crops growing all right but didn't work on them more than he had to. He wanted to have extra time to visit with friends, go on trips, and enjoy life. This was the way he liked best.
A (Doing)	One man liked to work with his fields and was always putting in extra time keeping them clean of weeds and in fine condition. Because he did this extra work, he did not have much time left to be with friends, to go on trips, or to enjoy himself in other ways. But this was the way he really liked best.

Which kind of man do you believe it is better to be?

(<u>For men only</u>): Which kind of man are you really most like?

Which kind of man would most other _____ think it better to be?

19. Length of Life   man-nature: Item MN5

Three men were talking about whether people themselves can do anything to make the lives of men and women longer. Here is what each said.

B (Over)	One said: It is already true that people like doctors and others are finding the way to add many years to the lives of most men by discovering (finding) new medicines, by studying foods, and doing other such things as vaccinations. If people will pay attention to all these new things they will almost always live longer.
A (Subj)	The second one said: I really do not believe that there is much human beings themselves can do to make the lives of men and women longer. It is my belief that every person has a set time to live, and when that time comes it just comes.
C (With)	The third one said: I believe that there is a plan to life which works to keep all living things moving together, and if a man will learn to live his whole life in accord with that plan, he will live longer than other men.

Which of these three said most nearly what you would think is right?

Which of the other two ways is more right?

Which of the three would most other persons in _____ say was most right?

20. Water Allocation   time: Item T5

   The government is going to help a community like yours to get more water by redrilling and cleaning out a community well. The government officials suggest that the community should have a plan for dividing the extra water, but don't say what kind of plan. Since the amount of extra water that may come in is not known, people feel differently about planning.

A (Past)	Some say that whatever water comes in should be divided just about like water in the past was always divided.
C (Fut)	Others want to work out a really good plan ahead of time for dividing whatever water comes in.
B (Pres)	Still others want to just wait until the water comes in before deciding on how it will be divided.

Which of these ways do you think is usually best in cases like this?

Which of the other two ways do you think is better?

Which of the three ways do you think most other persons in _____ would think best?

21. Housework

There were two women talking about the way they liked to live.

B
(Being)
One said that she was willing to work as hard as the average, but that she didn't like to spend a lot of time doing the kind of extra things in her house or taking up extra things outside like _____. Instead she liked to have time free to enjoy visiting with people--to go on trips--or to just talk with whoever was around.

A
(Doing)
The other woman said she liked best of all to find extra things to work on which would interest her--for example, _____. She said she was happiest when kept busy and was getting lots done.

Which of these ways do you think it is usually better for women to live?

(For women only): Which woman are you really more like?

Which way of life would most other _____ think is best?

22. Nonworking Time

Two men spend their time in different ways when they have no work to do. (This means when they are not actually on the job.)

A
(Doing)
One man spends most of this time learning or trying out things which will help him in his work.

B
(Being)
One man spends most of this time talking, telling stories, singing, and so on with his friends.

Which of these men has the better way of living?

Which of these men do you think you are more like?

Which of these men would most other _____ think had the better way of living?

SOCIAL VALUES QUESTIONNAIRE (Perloe 1967)

Variable   Perloe designed the SVQ to study the impact of varying kinds of
college environments on students' orientations relevant to participation in a democratic society. Two orientations were
of major interest: social responsibility and participation in
secondary groups.

Description   Several steps were involved in developing the SVQ. First, a large
number of Likert-type items were devised and administered to male
college freshmen (N = 120) at the beginning and end of their first
year in college. A factor analysis was performed using pooled ratings
from the two administrations. Ambiguous items and items with low
communalities were then eliminated. Separate factor analyses were
performed using the remaining item pool and several other college
samples (listed under "Sample" below). In these analyses considerable redundancy appeared; this was overcome by moving from factor
analysis of individual items to analysis of parcels of items.

To avoid capitalizing on chance, parcels were assembled on the basis
of only one sample and were cross-validated on the other samples.
Intra-parcel correlations ranged from .11 to .67, with 88% falling
between .20 and .55. The median was .38. Parcel scores were obtained by summing individual item scores within the parcel. After
several separate factor analyses of parcel scores, it was found that
a consistent four-factor structure could be obtained by omitting
two parcels. The four factors accounted for 58% of the total variance and seemed to Perloe "to provide a fairly concise description
of the major dimensions of variation present in response to the
SVQ."

The parcels yielding loadings of .30 or greater on each of the four
oblique factors comprise the final questionnaire, and these are presented below. Each item is rated on a six step scale running from
"strongly agree" to "strongly disagree." A table of regression
weights for computing factor scores is also presented. Although Perloe recommends its use, he says that scores computed in this way are
well approximated by simply summing item ratings.

Short descriptions given by Perloe of the four factor dimensions are
as follows:

> 1) The first runs from the acceptance of a moral obligation
> to protect and promote the welfare of others outside one's
> primary groups to the denial of this obligation. The in-
> dividualist pole of this factor does not devalue being con-
> cerned with the welfare of others as much as it emphasizes
> that this concern is a matter of individual choice or pref-
> erence rather than moral obligation. (Accounts for 24.8%
> of total variance.)

2) The second is concerned with cooperation and conformity in secondary groups. One pole expresses a positive evaluation of group norms and sanctions as mechanisms to help groups accomplish their purposes. The other rejects the creation and application of group norms. (Accounts for 13.7% of variance.)

3) One end of the third factor stresses the value and necessity, for proper personal development, of becoming deeply involved and identified with some group. The other end expresses man's natural separateness and devalues participation in groups. (Accounts for 16.4% of variance.)

4) The fourth factor taps the extent to which an individual should be concerned with another person's morals (as defined in the introduction to the questionnaire given below). One end values activity designed to increase the conformity of others to general moral standards. The other rejects this view and advocates minding one's business as far as others' morals are concerned. (Accounts for 9.2% of variance.)

In Perloe's samples the first three factors intercorrelated in the low or middle twenties, while the fourth correlated with the other three from .11 to .16.

Sample

Eight separate administrations of the SVQ provided the data for the studies just described.

1) Freshmen class of 1968 from a small, highly selective men's college--tested approximately three weeks before the start of classes (N = 120).

2) Same population as 1), tested approximately six weeks before the end of the second semester of their freshman year (N = 111).

3) Same as 1) and 2), tested at the start of the first semester of their junior year (N = 71).

4) Freshmen from the class of 1969, about three weeks before the start of classes (N = 117).

5) Same as 4) tested four to six weeks before the end of the second semester of their freshman year (N = 124).

6) Undergraduates at all levels in a small men's university which places strong emphasis on engineering and science. The sample was taken from an introductory social relations course required of all students (N = 58).

7) and 8) Two groups of Peace Corps Volunteers of both sexes tested during their initial training periods (N = 56; 58).

Reliability/ Homogeneity — Since the author grouped items into parcels before proceeding with his correlational and factor analyses, it is difficult to assess the homogeneity figures of these scales (given above) against the usual standards. The factor loadings do indicate fairly high homogeneity however. No concrete figures are given, but the author indicates considerable stability in factor scores over a nine month period.

Validity — Two sources of evidence were reported. A sample of 50 students from the class of 1969 was given a two hour interview by a female psychiatric social worker. Responses were coded into categories based on questionnaire items, and these were then used to estimate factor scores. (Inter-observer correlations ranged from .87 to .90.) Correlations were computed between scores on the SVQ and on the interviews; these were .46, .25, .47, and .49 for the respective factors. All were significant at the .05 level.

As a measure of discriminant validity the sample of Peace Corps Volunteers was compared to the students from the science and engineering college. These groups differed on all four factors, the Volunteers being more social welfare oriented, less conforming and cooperative, more affiliative, and more moral support oriented.

Several interesting relationships were found between SVQ factor scores and MMPI, F scale, and other questionnaire item scores in a longitudinal study of the men's college samples, thus lending further support to the validity of the SVQ.

Location — So far the SVQ has not been published, but the following documents are available:

Perloe, S.I. The factorial structure of the social values questionnaire. Dittoed manuscript dated October, 1967.

_____. Final report to the Office of Education on Project S-308, Bureau No. 5-8210, 1967.

_____. Social responsibility and individualism in college students: a preliminary report. Dittoed manuscript dated April, 1968.

Administration — The SVQ is self-administered and the total instrument would take an estimated 40 to 60 minutes to complete.

Results and Comments — The SVQ seems to tap at least two important value orientations related to political beliefs and actions. Because it has received relatively little use since its recent construction, more study is required to map out its relation to other measures of values, personality, political attitudes, etc. In the process it will probably undergo revision.

Researchers interested in longitudinal studies of value change in college students would be interested in the results of Perloe's research employing the SVQ with several other standard measures. These required too much space to be discussed here.

SOCIAL VALUES QUESTIONNAIRE SCALE

The following questionnaire asks you to rate your agreement or disagreement with a number of general statements about individuals, groups, and their interrelationships. In order to make the meanings clear, the definitions assigned to some of the terms used in the statements are given below. Please read the definitions carefully because they may be slightly different than the ones you would spontaneously give. In all cases please respond to the words in terms of the definitions given here.

> Group - An association or organization such as the P.T.A., a local civic or political club, a student government organization, a professional association, a committee functioning within such an organization.
>
> Community - The town, city, or neighborhood in which a person resides. Although a community does not always have exact boundaries, it is generally thought of as a relatively coherent unit by those who live in and near it.
>
> Inconvenient - Annoying, awkward, causing mild to moderate displeasure or discomfort, usually of a temporary nature.
>
> Preference - The state of desiring some alternative more than others. As used in the questionnaire, the term connotes a small to medium difference between the desired and rejected alternatives.
>
> Moral - Just, good, ethical. Although the synonyms listed here vary somewhat in strength, all refer to judgments of right and wrong with respect to some important principles commanding a moderately high degree of agreement by the members of our society, although there is disagreement on the source of the principles and on the range of situations to which they apply. There are moral principles for most areas of human conduct, particularly ones involving interactions among people. When you are asked to judge whether something is moral, right, etc. in the following questionnaire, you should respond in terms of what you personally believe the relevant moral principles are, even if you think that some other people would disagree.

Some of the following statements contain combinations of assertions which might evoke different reactions from you if they were responded to separately. Such combinations are often necessary in order to present complex ideas. In such cases your response to the total statement should be based on some combination of your reactions to each part, with the part which is more important to you being given greater weight. It is important that you assign only a single rating to the combined statement, and that you rate all the statements. Think of the six steps in the rating scale as being evenly spaced.

Reprinted with permission of Perloe, S. I. Social Values Questionnaire. Final report to Office of Education on Project S-308, Bureau No. 5-8210; 1967.

Social Values Questionnaire *

First Factor - Social Welfare

+ Individuals should be ready to inhibit their own pleasures if these inconvenience others.

+ People who try but are unable to provide for their own welfare have a right to expect help from others.

+ People should give up activities which bring them pleasure if these activities cause serious discomfort to others.

- Whether an individual acts to protect the welfare of persons beyond his circle of friends and relatives is a matter of personal preference, not moral obligation.

- The mere fact that one group or nation is prosperous and another is not places no moral obligation on the "have" group to improve the lot of the "have not" group.

+ Not only does everyone have an inalienable right to life, liberty and the pursuit of happiness, he also has an equally inalienable moral obligation to protect others from having these rights taken from them.

- An individual who has not caused another person's misfortune has no moral obligation to help the other person.

+ It is wrong for a person to choose to pay little or no attention to the welfare of persons with whom he has no personal connection.

+ Acting to protect the rights and interests of other members of one's community is a major obligation for all persons.

- An individual's responsibility for the welfare of others extends no further than the boundaries of his immediate circle of friends and relatives.

+ A man should not be respected for his achievements if they were obtained by interfering with the welfare and development of others.

+ Although others may equal it in importance, there is no value more important than compassion for others.

+ It is sympathetic love among persons which alone gives significance to life.

- Although altruism and feelings of responsibility for the welfare of others are generally thought to be admirable qualities, a person should not be required to have them in order to be respected by himself or others.

---

*The various "parcels" within each factor are separated by horizontal lines.

- Except for one's immediate family and closest friends, people have a perfect right to pursue their own goals without regard to the convenience or comfort of others.

- People cannot be considered moral if they are indifferent to the welfare of the members of the community in which they live and work.

+ All men have an obligation to promote not only the welfare of their immediate circle of relatives but also to work for the well being of all the members of the community in which they live.

- Things work best when people concern themselves with their own welfare and let others take care of themselves.

- One's major obligation to other men is to let them alone so that they may sink or swim by their own efforts.

+ Minor conflicts between one's own comfort and convenience and that of a neighbor should be resolved in favor of the neighbor more often than not.

+ An individual most deserves the feeling of satisfaction with himself after he has done something to help someone else.

+ The typical law abiding person who avoids situations in which transgressions occur rather than acting in such situations to protect those who are being injured, does not deserve the respect of his fellow citizens.

+ A person who witnesses an unlawful or immoral act, such as physical assault or sadistic taunting and teasing, and who does not try to do what he can to stop its occurrence shares part of the guilt with the transgressor.

- The only people guilty of immoral acts are those who commit them or directly cause them to be committed; others who might have prevented the acts, but did not, should bear no blame.

+ Individuals should feel responsible for fostering the improvement of moral as well as the physical well being of others.

+ Every person should be his brother's keeper in the physical and moral sense.

- People should leave the prevention of immoral acts up to those whose jobs are specifically concerned with such prevention.

- One should avoid trying to make people more moral and considerate than they generally are.

- It is better for a person to ignore the larger social concerns of the community in which he lives than to force himself to take part in these concerns merely from a sense of moral obligation.

- It is better to ignore a person in need when one feels no personal compassion for him than to act compassionately out of a sense of obligation or guilt.

+ People cannot rely solely upon ministers, policemen and judges to insure moral behavior among the citizens of a community; they must each
  act to dissuade others from anti-social acts.

- When one individual behaves unjustly toward another, it is wrong for
  a third person to intervene to correct the injustice unless he has
  been asked to do so.

- We intrude unjustifiably into the privacy of other persons when we try
  to get them to abide more closely to a moral code which they accept as
  a vague ideal, but which they do not follow in their behavior.

Second Factor - Cooperation toward Group Goals

+ There is nothing wrong in the members of a group trying to persuade
  indifferent or mildly dissenting members to go along with the group.

+ A person should be willing to cooperate with democratically selected
  group leaders, even though they are not the ones he personally preferred.

- Conformity to the policies of your group when you are not whole-
  heartedly in agreement with them is wrong, even when the policies are
  the result of a democratic process in which you were free to participate.

- A person should not feel bound to follow the decisions of the groups
  to which he belongs if these decisions are not in accord with his private preferences.

+ Groups and communities which refuse to regulate the behaviors of their
  members encourage the exploitation of the weak by the powerful.

+ It is proper for a group to decide to mete out some kind of punishment
  to group members who act without regard to the goals and rules of the
  group.

+ A person is right in feeling annoyed or angry when other members of
  his group ignore justifiable group demands.

+ A democratically organized group has the right to determine what should
  be considered proper behavior in areas relevant to the group.

- Group members should not be criticized when they refuse to do something
  in which they have no interest even when the action in question is
  necessary for their group to reach its goals.

- People damage themselves as individuals when they inhibit or in some other way modify their behaviors as a result of the rules of the groups to which they belong.

- Regardless of how democratically a group sets up its rules, it ceases to be a democratic group once it begins to pressure its members to conform to these rules.

- When democratically organized groups begin to influence and regulate the behaviors of their members, they either disintegrate or become transformed into undemocratic, autocratic groups.

- In the long run, people are best off if left to regulate their own behavior rather than setting up group norms and sanctions.

+ It is often better for a group to agree upon specific rules to regulate behaviors of importance to the group than to leave the regulation to the individual judgments of the group members.

+ Individual consciences need the support of laws and social codes in order to function effectively in producing moral behavior.

Third Factor - <u>Identification with Groups</u>

+ It is important for an individual to be closely identified with at least one group.

+ Individuals do not really fulfill their human potentials unless they involve themselves deeply in some group.

- In life an individual should for the most part "go it alone" assuring himself of privacy, having much time to himself, attempting to resist being influenced by others.

- People who identify strongly with some group usually do so at the expense of their development and individual self-fulfillment.

+ Man is a social animal; he cannot flourish and grow without identifying himself with some group.

- Men are first and foremost individual beings; the identifications they may have with groups never really alters their essential separateness from one another.

- Man's natural state is as an independent, unattached individual; he acts in conflict with his essential qualities when he acts with others as a member of a highly unified group.

+ Individuals and groups exist in a symbiotic relationship; neither can flourish without satisfying the needs of the other.

+ An individual truly finds himself when he merges with a social group and joins with others in resolute and determined activity for the realization of social goals.

- Only a person who remains aloof from social organizations and group allegiances can fully develop his potential as an individual.

+ Man's natural state is as a member of a group; the individual who holds himself aloof from active participation in a community is acting against his natural inclinations.

+ It is wrong if an individual refuses to participate actively in at least some of the group activities of the community in which he lives.

- A man's self-fulfillment through his work and his life with family and friends should almost always transcend his obligation to participate in the civic activities of his community, e.g., being active in a local civic, political, cultural or charitable organization.

- Individuals should feel no obligation to participate in the group activities of the communities in which they happen to live or work.

+ Some of life's greatest satisfactions are found in working cooperatively with others.

+ It is often more gratifying to work for the accomplishment of a goal held by a group to which one belongs than to work for the attainment of a purely personal goal.

+ It is just as important to work toward group goals and adhere to the established rules of the group as it is to gratify one's individual desires.

Fourth Factor - Moral Pressure

+ Everyone has an obligation to criticize other members of his community when they act in an immoral, antisocial manner.

+ A person should be willing to openly criticize individuals who break the rules agreed upon by the group.

+ Encouraging others to behave in accord with generally accepted moral standards is as important as one's own living up to these standards.

- A community in which people were very concerned with each others' morality as well as their own would be an intolerable one in which to live.

- It is wrong for a man to point out other people's moral shortcomings.

+ People cannot rely solely upon ministers, policemen and judges to insure moral behavior among the citizens of a community; they must act to dissuade others from antisocial acts.

- When one individual behaves unjustly toward another it is wrong for a third person to intervene to correct the injustice unless he has been asked to do so.

- We intrude unjustifiably into the privacy of other persons when we try to get them to abide more closely to a moral code which they accept as a vague ideal, but which they do not follow in their behavior.

+ Individuals should feel responsible for fostering the improvement of morals as well as the physical well being of others.

+ Every person should be his brother's keeper in the physical and moral sense.

- People should leave the prevention of immoral acts up to those whose jobs are specifically concerned with such prevention.

- One should avoid trying to make people more moral and considerate than they generally are.

+ Minor conflicts between one's own comfort and convenience and that of a neighbor should be resolved in favor of the neighbor more often than not.

+ An individual most deserves the feeling of satisfaction with himself after he has done something to help someone else.

CHAPTER 9 - GENERAL ATTITUDES TOWARD PEOPLE

The measures in this chapter show considerable underuse in relation to the number of phenomena that can be related to them. Orientations toward other people (or human nature) appear to be one attitude area in which people have well-structured and concrete attitudes that are built up and used in everyday experience. In one of the most comprehensive studies of racial attitudes in the literature, Wrightsman and Cook (1965) found that two of the scales in this chapter were practically the only ones (out of 78 examined) to predict a change toward more favorable attitudes toward Negroes. A total of seven scales are reviewed in this section:

1. Machiavellianism (Christie and others 1969)
2. Philosophy of Human Nature (Wrightsman 1964)
3. Faith in People Scale (Rosenberg 1957)
4. Trust in People (Survey Research Center 1969)
5. People in General (Banta 1961)
6. Misanthropy (Sullivan and Adelson 1954)
7. Acceptance of Others (Fey 1955)

Christie's Machiavellianism (or Mach) scale has the most interesting theoretical rationale and has been used in the widest variety of research settings. The strongest component of the scale taps a respondent's feelings about whether other people can be manipulated so as to achieve (usually the respondent's) desired ends. The scale has relatively high internal consistency, although factor analyses reveal that there are at least three dimensions of item content. While not all experiments using the scale have yielded positive results, most of the studies with negative results failed to optimize the conditions under which high "Machs" can operate. Very interesting results have been obtained in field studies using the Mach scale. The scale is available in three different formats in order to control for response sets, although Mach responses are still judged as quite socially undesirable so that to score as a "high Mach" one must be relatively insensitive to social desirability.

Wrightsman's philosophy of human nature instrument is also well-conceived and has been applied in a variety of research settings. Although there are six subscales of human nature, the instrument appears to be two dimensional in nature--the major dimension being favorability toward human nature. The instruments evidence quite satisfactory internal consistency and test-retest stability, and are worded in both positive and negative format to control for agreement response set. The author also presents considerable evidence of the scale's essential validity, although more extensive validity checks might be desirable.

Rosenberg's faith in people scale was one of the earliest scales to focus on this attitudinal area. The scale contains only five items and evidence for reliability is not impressive for the data that Rosenberg collected. However, validity of the scale was well reflected by predictable differences in respondents' occupational choice and a wide variety of related political attitudes. However, all of this research was conducted with college students.

The Survey Research Center has more recently applied three of Rosenberg's items to nationwide samples of adults. Here inter-item correlations are very impressive and hold when controlled for educational level. The scale in national samples is associated as expected with optimistic and efficacious political attitudes, with feelings of personal efficacy, and with feelings of life satisfaction. Interesting differences in trust in people are also found by religious affiliation and for those with varying political views (e.g., supporters of George Wallace, respondents who want to pull out of Vietnam).

The items in Banta's scale are drawn from Christie's early work into Machiavellianism and hence represent little new in the way of item content. Furthermore, they have been applied to a very small sample of college students. The scale is included because it is one of the few attitude scales to employ the unfolding technique. It is interesting to see that scale values derived via this technique are practically identical to those obtained using Thurstone's more detailed procedure.

The misanthropy scale of Sullivan and Adelson is derived directly from an ethnocentrism scale, by replacing references to ethnic minorities with terms such as "most people" in the scale items. The main value of the scale is the significant relation it shows to the original ethnocentrism scale indicating (but not completely demonstrating) that misanthropy is a strong component in ethnocentrism. The items need further refinement (and at least some items need to be written in the reversed direction to counter response set) and tests for validity need to be carried out.

Fey's acceptance of others scale is also mainly distinguished by the interesting results generated from its application--the findings that acceptance of others is associated with acceptance of self and estimated acceptance by others. The scale shows relatively high reliability but needs to be applied in a more comprehensive study than the one on which it was developed. Readers may find some interest in the short "estimated acceptance by others" scale which we have appended to this scale.

References   Wrightsman, L. and Cook, S.   Factor analysis and attitude change, Peabody Papers in Human Development, Vol. III, No. 2, 1965 (Nashville, Tenn.: George Peabody College for Teachers).

MACHIAVELLIANISM (Christie and others 1969)

Variable   This measure attempts to tap a person's general strategy for dealing
                  with people, especially the degree to which he feels other people are
                  manipulable in interpersonal situations.

Description   Seventy-one items were drawn from the writings of Machiavelli (The
                  Prince and The Discourses). These were conceived as falling into three
                  substantive areas: 1) the nature of interpersonal tactics (32 items),
                  2) views of human nature (28 items), and 3) abstract or generalized
                  morality (11 items). An item analysis revealed that about 60 of these
                  correlated at the .05 level with a total "Mach" score based on the sum
                  of all items (the items about human nature being most highly related,
                  the ones about morality least highly related). The ten highest related
                  items of those worded in the Machiavellian direction were selected
                  into the final scale (Mach IV) along with the ten highest related
                  items worded in the opposite direction. An attempt was made to intro-
                  duce as much content variety as possible. The counterbalancing was
                  designed to minimize the effects of indiscriminant agreement or dis-
                  agreement.

                  Items are given in standard 6-category Likert format (agree strongly
                  being scored 7, no answer 4, and disagree strongly 1). A constant
                  score of 20 was added to make the neutral score 100, the lowest possible
                  Machiavellian score 40, and the highest 160.

                  A forced-choice version of this scale (Mach V) was developed to off-
                  set a significant negative correlation (r's around -.40) observed
                  between Mach IV scores and Edward's social desirability scale. Scores
                  on Mach V also range between 40 and 160.

                  A "Kiddie Mach" scale (20 Likert format items) was also developed for
                  use with children or low education adults.

Sample   The items in the initial Mach scale were given to samples of 1,196
                  college students in Iowa, North Carolina, and New York. A total of
                  1,700 college students gave responses to the Mach scale, F-scale,
                  and anomie scale which formed the basis for the factor analysis
                  reported below. The items have also been used to select students for
                  34 separate experiments to test hypotheses about the Mach scale.
                  The items have also been applied to a national cross-section sample of
                  Americans, but no results on this sample have been published. The
                  scale has also been applied in a number of other research settings.

Reliability/   The average item-test correlation for the items in Mach IV was .38,
   Homogeneity   with little difference in this value across the three content cate-
                  gories of items or positive vs. negative item wording. Split-half
                  reliabilities determined on subsequent samples averaged .79. (The
                  values for comparable F-scale items were .33 and .68 respectively.)

Reliabilities for the forced-choice Mach V scale were somewhat lower (in the .60's) but this might be expected to occur with most sets of items in which social desirability is as strictly controlled as it was in this scale.

A factor analysis of Mach items, F-scale items, and anomie items resulted in four factors: one Mach factor, one F-factor, one factor combining F and Mach and one factor combining Mach and anomie. In terms of the items from Mach IV which loaded over .25 on each factor with Mach items, we have the following:

Factor:	Duplicity	Negativism	Distrust of People
	7	8	4
	6	5	14
	9	12	11
	10	13	16
	15	1	(plus 4 anomie items)
	2	18	
	3	20	
		(plus 8 F items)	

Validity

It would be impossible to summarize here the results of all relevant experiments. In some experiments, hypotheses were not confirmed but

> "...in 12 or 13 instances in which face-to-face contact, latitude for improvisation, and irrelevant affect were all judged present, the high Machs won more, were persuaded less, persuaded others more, or behaved as predicted significantly compared to low Machs. ...in seven of the nine cases in which two of the variables were present, high Machs did better."

Some field study results bearing indirectly on validity are reported below (see Results and Comments)

Location

Christie, R. and others. Unpublished manuscript, Department of Social Psychology, Columbia University, 1968.

Administration

Each of the three forms of the scale contains 20 items, and each has been normed so that the score 100 is the neutral point. The Kiddie Mach would seem to be the most rapidly administered, with Mach IV taking slightly more time to complete. Mach V would undoubtedly take the most time to complete. Moreover it would appear that attempts to control social desirability (the raison-d'etre for Mach V) were not successful, as scores on Mach V still correlated -.40 with social desirability.[1] The author notes that he has used Mach IV and Mach V in conjunction in experimental work, selecting for high Machs only people who score high on both scales.

The author has also had the scales translated into a number of foreign languages (e.g., Chinese, Swedish).

---

[1] This correlation is based on an internal measure of social desirability. Subsequent research has shown that Mach V does not correlate significantly with either the Crowne-Marlowe or Edwards social desirability scales (described in Chapter 10).

Results and   The author cautions against the usual perjorative implications
  Comments   that surround the term "Machiavellian." None of his research evidence
                substantiates the view that high Mach's are more hostile, vicious, or
                vindictive than low Machs. Rather it appears that they have a "cool
                detachment," which makes them less emotionally involved with other
                people, with sensitive issues, or with saving face in embarrassing
                situations.

                Generational differences in Mach scores indicate that Americans
                are becoming more manipulative and impersonal in the Machiavellian
                sense. No differences have been found by intelligence, social
                status, or even social mobility. It is hypothesized that high Machs
                are less likely to arise from traditional societies because they
                operate most effectively in unstructured situations.

                Field studies at medical schools have revealed the counter-intuitive
                but plausible finding that psychiatrists score highest on the Mach
                scale and surgeons lowest (it is argued that the psychiatrists'
                role involves manipulation per se vs. the surgeon who has as little
                personal contact with patients as possible). In two further separate
                studies, the Mach scale predicted aspects of lobbyist behavior in
                Washington and differences in acculturation of certain Hungarian
                immigrants into American life.

MACH IV

Listed below are a number of statements. Each represents a commonly
held opinion and there are no right or wrong answers. You will probably
disagree with some items and agree with others. We are interested in
the extent to which you agree or disagree with such matters of opinion.

Read each statement carefully. Then indicate the extent to which you
agree or disagree by circling the number in front of each statement.
The numbers and their meaning are indicated below:

(Score)

(Original Reversed)

If you <u>agree strongly</u>, circle +3	7	1
If you <u>agree somewhat</u>, circle +2	6	2
If you <u>agree slightly</u>, circle +1	5	3
If you <u>disagree slightly</u>, circle -1	3	5
If you <u>disagree somewhat</u>, circle -2	2	6
If you <u>disagree strongly</u>, circle -3	1	7

First impressions are usually best in such matters. Read each statement,
decide if you agree or disagree and the strength of your opinion, and
then circle the appropriate number in front of the statement. <u>Give your
opinion</u> on <u>every statement</u>.

If you find that the numbers to be used in answering do not adequately
indicate your own opinion, use the one which is closest to the way you
feel.

Item-test
Phi coeff.

1. Never tell anyone the real reason you did something unless it
is useful to do so. .41
       +3   +2   +1   -1   -2   -3

2. The best way to handle people is to tell them what they want
to hear. .47

*3. One should take action only when sure it is morally right. .41

*4. Most people are basically good and kind. .35

5. It is safest to assume that all people have a vicious streak and
it will come out when they are given a chance. .41

---

* Reversed item.

Reprinted with permission of Christie, R. Machiavellianism scale in unpublished manuscript,
Department of Social Psychology, Columbia University, 1968.

	Item-test Phi coeff.

*6. Honesty is the best policy in all cases.   .42

*7. There is no excuse for lying to someone else.   .35

8. Generally speaking, men won't work hard unless they're forced to do so.   .31

*9. All in all, it is better to be humble and honest than to be important and dishonest.   .38

*10. When you ask someone to do something for you, it is best to give the real reasons for wanting it rather than giving reasons which carry more weight.   .45

*11. Most people who get ahead in the world lead clean, moral lives.   .33

12. Anyone who completely trusts anyone else is asking for trouble.   .42

13. The biggest difference between most criminals and other people is that the criminals are stupid enough to get caught.   .31

*14. Most men are brave.   .29

15. It is wise to flatter important people.   .40

*16. It is possible to be good in all respects.   .37

*17. Barnum was wrong when he said that there's a sucker born every minute.   .37

18. It is hard to get ahead without cutting corners here and there.   .42

19. People suffering from incurable diseases should have the choice of being put painlessly to death.   .37

20. Most men forget more easily the death of their father than the loss of their property.   .35

Mach V Attitude Inventory

You will find 20 groups of statements listed below. Each group is composed of three statements. Each statement refers to a way of thinking about people or things in general. They reflect opinions and not matters of fact -- there are no "right" or "wrong" answers and different people have been found to agree with different statements.

Please read each of the three statements in each group. Then decide first which of the statements is most true or comes the closest to describing your own beliefs. Circle a plus (+) in the space provided on the answer sheet.

Just decide which of the remaining two statements is most false or is the farthest from your own beliefs. Circle the minus (-) in the space provided on the answer sheet.

Here is an example:

		Most True	Most False
A.	It is easy to persuade people but hard to keep them persuaded.	+	-
B.	Theories that run counter to common sense are a waste of time.	(+)	-
C.	It is only common sense to go along with what other people are doing and not be too different.	+	(-)

In this case, statement B would be the one you believe in most strongly and A and C would be ones that are not as characteristic of your opinion. Statement C would be the one you believe in least strongly and is least characteristic of your beliefs.

You will find some of the choices easy to make; others will be quite difficult. Do not fail to make a choice no matter how hard it

596

may be. You will mark <u>two</u> statements in each group of three -- the
one that comes the closest to your own beliefs with a + and the one
farthest from your beliefs with a -. The remaining statement should
be left unmarked.

<u>Do</u> <u>not</u> <u>omit</u> <u>any</u> <u>groups</u> <u>of</u> <u>statements</u>.

SCORING KEY FOR MACH V (1968)

Points per Item by Response Patterns

Item #	1		3		5		7
1	A+		B+	A+	B+	C+	C+
	C−		C−	B−	A−	B−	A−
2	A+		B+	A+	B+	C+	C+
	C−		C−	B−	A−	B−	A−
3	C+		B+	C+	B+	A+	A+
	A−		A−	B−	C−	B−	C−
4	A+		C+	A+	C+	B+	B+
	B−		B−	C−	A−	C−	A−
5	A+		C+	A+	C+	B+	B+
	B−		B−	C−	A−	C−	A−
6	A+		B+	A+	B+	C+	C+
	C−		C−	B−	A−	B−	A−
7	B+		C+	B+	C+	A+	A+
	A−		A−	C−	B−	C−	B−
8	C+		A+	C+	A+	B+	B+
	B−		B−	A−	C−	A−	C−
9	C+		A+	C+	A+	B+	B+
	B−		B−	A−	C−	A−	C−
10	A+		C+	A+	C+	B+	B+
	B−		B−	C−	A−	C−	A−
11	A+		C+	A+	C+	B+	B+
	B−		B−	C−	A−	C−	A−
12	C+		A+	C+	A+	B+	B+
	B−		B−	A−	C−	A−	C−
13	C+		B+	C+	B+	A+	A+
	A−		A−	B−	C−	B−	C−
14	B+		A+	B+	A+	C+	C+
	C−		C−	A−	B−	A−	B−
15	C+		A+	C+	A+	B+	B+
	B−		B−	A−	C−	A−	C−
16	C+		A+	C+	A+	B+	B+
	B−		B−	A−	C−	A−	C−
17	A+		B+	A+	B+	C+	C+
	C−		C−	B−	A−	B−	A−
18	C+		B+	C+	B+	A+	A+
	A−		A−	B−	C−	B−	C−
19	B+		A+	B+	A+	C+	C+
	C−		C−	A−	B−	A−	B−
20	A+		C+	A+	C+	B+	B+
	B−		B−	C−	A−	C−	A−

Sum for all 20 items and add constant of 20. Range: 40 − 160.

MACH V

1. A. It takes more imagination to be a successful criminal than a successful business man.
   B. The phrase "the road to hell is paved with good intentions" contains a lot of truth.
   C. Most men forget more easily the death of their father than the loss of their property.

2. A. Men are more concerned with the car they drive than with the clothes their wives wear.
   B. It is very important that imagination and creativity in children be cultivated.
   C. People suffering from incurable diseases should have the choice of being put painlessly to death.

3. A. Never tell anyone the real reason you did something unless it is useful to do so.
   B. The well-being of the individual is the goal that should be worked for before anything else.
   C. Once a truly intelligent person makes up his mind about the answer to a problem he rarely continues to think about it.

4. A. People are getting so lazy and self-indulgent that it is bad for our country.
   B. The best way to handle people is to tell them what they want to hear.
   C. It would be a good thing if people were kinder to others less fortunate than themselves.

5. A. Most people are basically good and kind.
   B. The best criteria for a wife or husband is compatibility--other characteristics are nice but not essential.
   C. Only after a man has gotten what he wants from life should he concern himself with the injustices in the world.

6. A. Most people who get ahead in the world lead clean, moral lives.
   B. Any man worth his salt shouldn't be blamed for putting his career above his family.
   C. People would be better off if they were concerned less with how to do things and more with what to do.

7. A. A good teacher is one who points out unanswered questions rather than gives explicit answers.
   B. When you ask someone to do something for you, it is best to give the real reasons for wanting it rather than giving reasons which might carry more weight.
   C. A person's job is the best single guide as to the sort of person he is.

8. A. The construction of such monumental works as the Egyptian pyramids was worth the enslavement of the workers who built them.
   B. Once a way of handling problems has been worked out it is best to stick to it.
   C. One should take action only when sure that it is morally right.

9. A. The world would be a much better place to live in if people would
      let the future take care of itself and concern themselves only with
      enjoying the present.
   B. It is wise to flatter important people.
   C. Once a decision has been made, it is best to keep changing it as
      new circumstances arise.

10. A. It is a good policy to act as if you are doing the things you do
       because you have no other choice.
    B. The biggest difference between most criminals and other people is
       that criminals are stupid enough to get caught.
    C. Even the most hardened and vicious criminal has a spark of decency
       somewhere within him.

11. A. All in all, it is better to be humble and honest than to be important
       and dishonest.
    B. A man who is able and willing to work hard has a good chance of
       succeeding in whatever he wants to do.
    C. If a thing does not help us in our daily lives, it isn't very im-
       portant.

12. A. A person shouldn't be punished for breaking a law which he thinks
       is unreasonable.
    B. Too many criminals are not punished for their crime.
    C. There is no excuse for lying to someone else.

13. A. Generally speaking, men won't work hard unless they're forced to do
       so.
    B. Every person is entitled to a second chance, even after he commits
       a serious mistake.
    C. People who can't make up their minds aren't worth bothering about.

14. A. A man's first responsibility is to his wife, not his mother.
    B. Most men are brave.
    C. It's best to pick friends that are intellectually stimulating rather
       than ones it is comfortable to be around.

15. A. There are very few people in the world worth concerning oneself about.
    B. It is hard to get ahead without cutting corners here and there.
    C. A capable person motivated for his own gain is more useful to society
       than a well-meaning but ineffective one.

16. A. It is best to give others the impression that you can change your
       mind easily.
    B. It is a good working policy to keep on good terms with everyone.
    C. Honesty is the best policy in all cases.

17. A. It is possible to be good in all respects.
    B. To help oneself is good; to help others even better.
    C. War and threats of war are unchangeable facts of human life.

18. A. Barnum was probably right when he said that there's at least one
       sucker born every minute.
    B. Life is pretty dull unless one deliberately stirs up some excitement.
    C. Most people would be better off if they controlled their emotions.

19. A. Sensitivity to the feelings of others is worth more than poise in
       social situations.
    B. The ideal society is one where everybody knows his place and accepts
       it.
    C. It is safest to assume that all people have a vicious streak and it
       will come out when they are given a chance.

20. A. People who talk about abstract problems usually don't know what
       they are talking about.
    B. Anyone who completely trusts anyone else is asking for trouble.
    C. It is essential for the functioning of a democracy that everyone
       votes.

KIDDIE MACH

On the next two pages are some sentences. Each sentence says something about the world or about people. There are no right or wrong answers. You will probably agree with some of the sentences and disagree with others. We want to know how much you agree or disagree. You can show how much you agree or disagree with each sentence by circling one of the answers next to each sentence.

	Score	
	+ item	- item
If you agree very much with the sentence, put a circle around: Agree very much	5	1
If you agree a little with the sentence, put a circle around: Agree a little	4	2
If you disagree a little with the sentence, put a circle around: Disagree a little	2	4
If you disagree very much with the sentence, put a circle around: Disagree very much	1	5

Read each sentence, decide whether you agree or disagree and how much. Then you will put a circle around the answer that best tells how you feel about the sentence.

+ 1. Never tell anyone why you did something unless it will help you.

   Agree very much   Agree a little   Disagree a little   Disagree very much

- 2. Most people are good and kind.

+ 3. The best way to get along with people is to tell them things that make them happy.

- 4. You should do something only when you are sure it is right.

+ 5. It is smartest to believe that all people will be mean if they have a chance.

- 6. You should always be honest, no matter what.

+ 7. Sometimes you have to hurt other people to get what you want.

+ 8. Most people won't work hard unless you make them do it.

  - 9. It is better to be ordinary and honest than famous and dishonest.

- 10. It's better to tell someone why you want him to help you than to make up a good story to get him to do it.

- 11. Successful people are mostly honest and good.

+ 12. Anyone who completely trusts anyone else is asking for trouble.

+ 13. A criminal is just like other people except that he is stupid enough to get caught.

- 14. Most people are brave.

+ 15. It is smart to be nice to important people even if you don't really like them.

- 16. It is possible to be good in every way.

- 17. Most people can not be easily fooled.

+ 18. Sometimes you have to cheat a little to get what you want.

- 19. It is never right to tell a lie.

+ 20. It hurts more to lose money than to lose a friend.

PHILOSOPHY OF HUMAN NATURE (Wrightsman 1964)

Variable   The instrument attempts to assess philosophy of human nature, con-
            ceived of as the expectancies that people have about the ways in
            which other people generally behave.

Description Unlike other investigations into how people perceive human nature,
            Wrightsman's attempts to break the construct into six different
            components:

            1) Trustworthiness - the extent to which people are seen as moral,
               honest, and reliable

            2) Altruism - the extent of unselfishness, sincere sympathy,
               and concern for others

            3) Independence - the extent to which a person can maintain his
               convictions in the face of society's pressures toward con-
               formity

            4) Strength of Will and Rationality - the extent to which people
               understand the motives behind their behavior and the extent
               to which they have control over their outcomes

            5) Complexity of Human Nature - the extent to which people are
               complex and hard to understand vs. simple and easy to under-
               stand

            6) Variability in Human Nature - the extent of individual dif-
               ferences in basic nature and the basic changeability in human
               nature

            The first four dimensions are conceived of as essentially independent
            of the last two, a presupposition borne out empirically (see Reli-
            ability below). An overall favorability toward human nature score
            was therefore calculated from these first four subscales. A total
            of 120 items (20 for each of the six components--10 stated positively,
            10 negatively) were constructed and given to 177 undergraduate stu-
            dents. After an item analysis, the 24 least discriminating items
            were discarded. A further item analysis resulted in the discarding
            of an additional 12 items. The final form of the scale consists of
            six subscales of 14 items each, 7 worded positively and 7 negatively.

Samples   In addition to the samples used for item analyses and ascertaining
            reliability, the scale was administered to 530 undergraduates (253
            males and 377 females) at six colleges in the South, East, and Mid-
            west. Data on self-concepts was obtained from 100 of these females.

Reliability/   The following split-half reliabilities (corrected by the Spearman-
   Homogeneity   Brown formula), test-retest reliabilities, and inter-subscale cor-
              relations were obtained:

	Trust	Altruism	Indep.	Strength	Complex.	Variable
Split-half (average)	.74	.74	.68	.58	.58	.70
Test-retest (3 month)	.74	.83	.75	.75	.52	.84
Trustworthiness	X					
Altruism	.69	X				
Independence	.64	.61	X			
Strength	.35	.39	.30	X		
Complexity	-.20	-.21	-.16	-.26	X	
Variability	-.04	-.10	-.04	-.12	.40	X

The test-retest correlation for the total favorability toward human
nature scale (i.e., the 56 items from the first four subscales) was
.90.

Validity   A number of predictions about hypothesized differences in favorable-
              ness in human nature were confirmed.

1) Females had more favorable views toward human nature than men
at each school tested.

2) Students at a Fundamentalist college revealed themselves as
feeling quite negative about human nature.

3) In two classroom studies, favorably oriented students rated
their instructors more favorably than negatively oriented
students.

4) A strong correlation (r = .65) was found between negative
views and dissatisfaction with one's self-concept.

5) Substantial correlations were found between favorableness towards human nature and other attitudes in the same conceptual
area: Agger et al.'s political cynicism scale (r = -.61),
Rosenberg's faith-in-people scale (r = .77), and Christie's
Machiavellianism scale (r = -.68).

Location   Wrightsman, L. Measurement of philosophies of human nature.
              Psychological Reports. 1964, 14,743-751.

Administration   Each item is presented in standard 6-point Likert format from +3 (agree strongly) through -3 (disagree strongly). Scores on each subscale can vary between -42 (extremely negative view of human nature) to +42 (positive view). Average scores on the six-subscales for 500 college students were as follows:

Trustworthiness	+2.5
Altruism	-3.7
Independence	-2.2
Strength of will	+7.2
Complexity	+13.0
Variability	+17.2

Total scores for the favorableness toward human nature scale can vary between -118 and +118. Although no average scores for this total scale are given, the above information would work out to a value of +3.8.

Results and Comments   Despite the impressive and interesting set of correlations that Wrightsman has presented (under Validity), only one--the finding about differences in colleges with varying religious views--can really be said to bear directly on validity (if one insists on some sort of behavioral criterion, such as contributing money to a charity, to establish validity). The differences in ratings of college instructors, while statistically significant, results from differences of less than one point in overall favorableness.

Although the author dismisses as insignificant the correlations between the first four subscales vs. complexity and variability, the fact that they are consistently negative leads to the interesting conclusion that there is a tendency for people having a positive view of human nature to see human nature as simple and unchangeable. However, as the average scores above indicate, there is much higher agreement among the college students tested that human nature is more complex and variable than it is trustworthy or altruistic.

Philosophy of Human Nature

Here is a series of attitude statements. Each represents a commonly held opinion and there are no right or wrong answers. You will probably disagree with some items and agree with others. We are interested in the extent to which you agree or disagree with such matters of opinion.

Read each statement carefully. Then indicate the extent to which you agree or disagree by circling the number in front of each statement. The numbers and their meaning are indicated below:

        If you agree strongly   -   circle +3

        If you agree somewhat   -   circle +2

        If you agree slightly   -   circle +1

        If you disagree slightly   -   circle -1

        If you disagree somewhat   -   circle -2

        If you disagree strongly   -   circle -3

First impressions are usually best in such matters. Read each statement, decide if you agree or disagree and the strength of your opinion, and then circle the appropriate number in front of the statement. Give your opinion on every statement.

If you find that the numbers to be used in answering do not adequately indicate your own opinion use the one which is closest to the way you feel.

Trustworthiness (Positive items)

2. Most students will tell the instructor when he has made a mistake in adding up their score, even if he had given them more points than they deserved.
    +3   +2   +1   -1   -2   -3

8. If you give the average person a job to do and leave him to do it, he will finish it successfully.

14. People usually tell the truth, even when they know they would be better off by lying.

Scale reprinted with permission of author and publisher: Wrightsman, L. Measurement of Philosophies of Human Nature. *Psychological Reports*, **14 (1964)** pp 743-751.

20. Most students do not cheat when taking an exam.

26. Most people are basically honest.

62. If you act in good faith with people, almost all of them will reciprocate with fairness toward you.

86. Most people lead clean, decent lives.

Trustworthiness (Negative items)

32. People claim they have ethical standards regarding honesty and morality, but few people stick to them when the chips are down.

38. If you want people to do a job right, you should explain things to them in great detail and supervise them closely.

44. If most people could get into a movie without paying and be sure they were not seen, they would do it.

50. Most people are not really honest for a desirable reason; they're afraid of getting caught.

56. Most people would tell a lie if they could gain by it.

74. Most people would cheat on their income tax, if they had a chance.

92. Nowadays people commit a lot of crimes and sins that no one else ever hears about.

Altruism (Positive items)

 4. Most people try to apply the Golden Rule even in today's complex society.

10. Most people do not hesitate to go out of their way to help someone in trouble.

16. Most people will act as "Good Samaritans" if given the opportunity.

22. "Do unto others as you would have them do unto you" is a motto most people follow.

64. The typical person is sincerely concerned about the problems of others.

70. Most people with a fallout shelter would let their neighbors stay in it during a nuclear attack.

88. Most people would stop and help a person whose car is disabled.

Altruism (Negative items)

34. The average person is conceited.

40. It's only a rare person who would risk his own life and limb to help someone else.

46. It's pathetic to see an unselfish person in today's world because so many people take advantage of him.

52. People pretend to care more about one another than they really do.

58. Most people inwardly dislike putting themselves out to help other people.

76. Most people exaggerate their troubles in order to get sympathy.

94. People are usually out for their own good.

Independence (Positive items)

33. Most people have the courage of their convictions.

39. Most people can make their own decisions, uninfluenced by public opinion.

45. It is achievement, rather than popularity with others, that gets you ahead nowadays.

51. The average person will stick to his opinion if he thinks he's right, even if others disagree.

57. If a student does not believe in cheating, he will avoid it even if he sees many others doing it.

75. The person with novel ideas is respected in our society.

93. Most people will speak out for what they believe in.

Independence (Negative items)

3. Most people will change the opinion they express as a result of an on-slaught of criticism, even though they really don't change the way they feel.

9. Nowadays many people won't make a move until they find out what other people think.

15. The important thing in being successful nowadays is not how hard you work, but how well you fit in with the crowd.

27. The typical student will cheat on a test when everybody else does, even though he has a set of ethical standards.

63. It's a rare person who will go against the crowd.

69. Most people have to rely on someone else to make their important decisions for them.

87. The average person will rarely express his opinion in a group when he sees the others disagree with him.

Strength of Will and Rationality (Positive items)

31. If a person tries hard enough, he will usually reach his goals in life.

37. The average person has an accurate understanding of the reasons for his behavior.

43. If people try hard enough, wars can be prevented in the future.

49. The average person is largely the master of his own fate.

55. In a local or national election, most people select a candidate rationally and logically.

73. Most persons have a lot of control over what happens to them in life.

79. Most people have a good idea of what their strengths and weaknesses are.

Strength of Will and Rationality (Negative items)

1. Great successes in life, like great artists and inventors, are usually motivated by forces they are unaware of.

7. Our success in life is pretty much determined by forces outside our own control.

19. Attempts to understand ourselves are usually futile.

25. There's little one can do to alter his fate in life.

61. Most people have little influence over the things that happen to them.

67. Most people have an unrealistically favorable view of their own capabilities.

85. Most people vote for a political candidate on the basis of unimportant characteristics such as his appearance or name, rather than because of his stand on the issues.

Complexity of Human Nature (Positive items)

36. I find that my first impressions of people are frequently wrong.

42. Some people are too complicated for me to figure out.

48. I think you can never really understand the feeling of other people.

54. You can't accurately describe a person in just a few words.

60. You can't classify everyone as good or bad.

78. People are too complex to ever be understood fully.

90. People are so complex it is hard to know what "makes them tick."

Complexity of Human Nature (Negative items)

6. I find that my first impression of a person is usually correct.

12. People can be described accurately by one term, such as "introverted," or "moral," or "sociable."

18. It's not hard to understand what really is important to a person.

24. I think I get a good idea of a person's basic nature after a brief conversation with him.

30. If I could ask a person three questions about himself (and assuming he would answer them honestly), I would know a great deal about him.

72. When I meet a person, I look for one basic characteristic through which I try to understand him.

96. Give me a few facts about a person and I'll have a good idea of whether I'll like him or not.

Variability in Human Nature (Positive items)

11. A person's reaction to things differs from one situation to another.

17. Different people react to the same situation in different ways.

23. Each person's personality is different from the personality of every other person.

29. People are quite different in their basic interests.

65. People are pretty different from one another in what "makes them tick."

83. Often a person's basic personality is altered by such things as a religious conversion, psycho-therapy, or a charm course.

89. People are unpredictable in how they'll act from one situation to another.

Variability in Human Nature (Negative items)

35. People are pretty much alike in their basic interests.

41. People are basically similar in their personalities.

47. If you have a good idea about how several people will react to a certain situation, you can expect most other people to react the same way.

53. Most people are consistent from situation to situation in the way they react to things.

59. A child who is popular will be popular as an adult, too.

77. If I can see how a person reacts to one situation, I have a good idea of how he will react to other situations.

95. When you get right down to it, people are quite alike in their emotional makeup.

FAITH IN PEOPLE SCALE (Rosenberg 1957)

Variable

This scale attempts to assess one's degree of confidence in the trustworthiness, honesty, goodness, generosity, and brotherliness of people in general. It is alternately called the "misanthropy scale."

Description

The instrument consists of a Guttman-type scale of two forced-choice and three agree-disagree statements, which was formed from nine related items culled by judges (five sociologists at Cornell) from an original group of 36 items. Positive responses are those indicating absence of faith in people. Range of scores is 1 (high faith on all 5 items) to 6 (low faith on all 5 items).

Rosenberg intended the dimension covered by this scale to be relevant to occupational choice, under the assumption that inter-personal attitudes could influence the individual's perception of his career.

The following distribution along the scale was found for Cornell students:

High	1	15
	2	28
	3	24
	4	17
	5	11
Low	6	5
		—
		100%

Sample

The sample used was a nationwide sample of 4,585 college students in 1952. The instrument was first administered to a sample of 2,758 Cornell students in 1950, and to 1,571 Cornell students in 1952.

Reliability/ Homogeneity

The coefficient of reproducibility for the five item scale was .92. The author notes that while the fifth item did not meet the Guttman 80-20 positive-negative marginal standard, it was included because the other four items produced a coefficient of over .90.

Validity

Evidence of validity may be found in the fact that the group of respondents whose occupational choices were social work, personnel work, and teaching had the largest proportion of high scores on the scale, while the group choosing sales-promotion, business-finance, and advertising had the greatest proportion of low scores. This relationship remained even when sex differences were controlled. Consistent with these findings, students with a high faith-in-people were more likely to select people-oriented occupational values while those with low faith-in-people were more likely to choose extrinsic values. (The value statements are presented in Robinson et al., 1969.)

Location   Rosenberg, M. <u>Occupations</u> <u>and</u> <u>values</u>. Glencoe, Illinois: The Free Press, 1957, pp. 25-35.

Administration   Estimated administration time is under five minutes. Scoring requires simple summation of item codes.

Results and Comments   In correlating scores on the scale with single-question indices, it was found that high scorers were less willing to use unscrupulous means to get ahead, less likely to believe in the superior efficiency of "contacts" over ability, and less likely to believe it very important to get ahead in life.

In a separate analysis of data from the Cornell University students, Rosenberg (1956) found that students scoring low in faith-in-people were far more likely (than those showing high faith) to profess political attitudes that would be congruent with these general attitudes toward other people. These misanthropic students were more likely to agree with the statements: the general public was "not qualified to vote on today's complex issues" (68% of those scoring 6 on the scale agreed vs. 32% of those scoring 1); "There's little use writing to public officials..." (45% vs. 12%); "political candidates are run by machines" (92% vs. 66%); "people who talk politics without knowing what they are talking about should be kept quiet" (40% vs. 21%); "unrestricted freedom of speech leads to mass hysteria" (32% vs. 16%); "people should be kept from spreading dangerous ideas because they might influence others to adopt them" (51% vs. 32%); "religions which preach unwholesome ideas should be suppressed" (32% vs. 16%); and "it's unwise to give people with dangerous social and economic viewpoints a chance to be elected" (46% vs. 25%). These results held up when controlled for political party affiliation.

References   Robinson, J. <u>et</u> <u>al</u>. <u>Measures of occupational attitudes and occupational characteristics</u>. Ann Arbor, Michigan: Survey Research Center, 1969.

Rosenberg, M. Misanthropy and political ideology , <u>American Sociological Review</u>, 1956, <u>21</u>, 690-695.

614

Faith in People Scale

(one point scored for each response noted with an *)

1. Some people say that most people can be trusted. Others say you can't be too careful in your dealings with people. How do you feel about it?

    _____ Most people can be trusted.

    ___*___ You can't be too careful.

2. Would you say that most people are more inclined to help others, or more inclined to look out for themselves?

    _____ To help others.

    ___*___ To look out for themselves.

3. If you don't watch yourself, people will take advantage of you.

    Agree*   Disagree   ?

4. No one is going to care much what happens to you, when you get right down to it.

    Agree*   Disagree   ?

5. Human nature is fundamentally cooperative.

    Agree   Disagree*   ?

TRUST IN PEOPLE (Survey Research Center   1969)

Variable
This scale consists of slight rephrasings of the first three items in Rosenberg's faith in people scale (see previous scale).

Description
The three items are presented in forced-choice format, a person being given a score of 1 for each trustworthy response. Scores therefore range from 0 (low trust) to 3 (high trust).

The distributions along this scale for a cross-section of Americans in 1964 and 1968 were:

			1964	1968
(low)	0	--	27%	21%
	1	--	9%	15%
	2	--	23%	20%
(high)	3	--	41%	44%
			100%	100%
	Average score		1.78	1.87

Sample
The items were included in the 1964 post-election study of electoral behavior by the Survey Research Center. A national cross-section of 1,450 people answered these questions. The items were similarly applied to a cross-section of 1,330 post-election respondents in the 1968 election study.

Reliability/
  Homogeneity
The following inter-item correlations were obtained in the two studies:

	1964			1968		
	PT	PH	TA	PT	PH	TA
People trusted	X			X		
People helpful	.48	X		.52	X	
Take advantage	.50	.54	X	.48	.54	X

These impressive inter-item correlations held at about the same magnitude for people with just a grade school education.

No test-retest data are currently available.

Validity
Data collected in this study do not bear directly on validity. Validity is directly assessed in the previous scale description.

Location
1964 Election Study. Ann Arbor, Michigan: Inter-University Consortium for Political Research, University of Michigan, (in press).

When formed into a scale in the 1964 election study, the trust in
people items correlated .24 with a short scale measuring trust in
government, .23 with a scale tapping respondents feelings that the
government paid attention to the will of the people, and .25 with
the SRC political efficacy scale. (These items and correlations
appear in Robinson, et al., 1968.) Thus there seems to be a reasonable degree of carry-over from trust of other people onto feelings
toward government and the likelihood that one can influence the
government.

The correlation of .28 between trust in people and the SRC measure
of personal competence (see Chapter 3) indicates that feelings of
self-worth are accompanied by an active trust of people. As noted in
Chapter 2 of this volume, in 1968 trust in people correlated moderately
with life satisfaction.

Trust of people in 1964 was higher among the better-educated (r = .28),
among whites (in 1968 the average score for Negroes was 1.12), and
among residents of rural (vs. urban) areas. The relation with age
was unusual in that highest trust was found in the 30-49 age group
(average score = 1.97) and the lowest in the 20-29 age group (1.64).
Differences in 1968 however were in the same direction but nowhere
near as dramatic (1.82 for those under 30 vs. 1.88 for those aged
30-59). Women were only slightly more (about .10 points) trusting
than men in both studies.

Differences by religion were definitely in the expected direction,
but were not as dramatic as one might anticipate in view of the
general finding (see Wrightsman's scale results) that people belonging to Fundamentalist religions share a pessimistic credo about their
fellow man.

Religion	Average score	
	1964	1968
Protestant	1.74	1.80
Reformation (e.g., Lutheran, Presbyterian)	1.98	2.25
Pietistic (e.g., Baptist, Methodist)	1.64	1.69
Neo-Fundamentalist (e.g., Church of Christ)	1.46	1.38
Non-Traditional (e.g., Quakers)	2.03	1.47
No denominational preference	2.08	1.75
Catholic	1.75	1.94
Jewish	2.34	2.14
No religious preference	1.44	1.60
TOTAL SAMPLE	1.78	1.87

There are of course further differences within the gross categories
of Protestants in the above tabulation. For example, in 1968 Episcopalians (2.52) scored higher than Lutherans and Presbyterians
within the category "Reformation" and Baptists (1.47 for both South
and non-South) scored lowest in the Pietistic category. Whether
any of the differences within Protestant religions

cannot largely be attributed to differences in educational attainment (since members of religions whose members are better-educated, e.g., Episcopalians have highest faith in people) has not been thoroughly investigated in these data. However, the most interesting differences are between the high faith in people of Jewish persons vs. the low trust in people demonstrated by Neo-Fundamentalists and persons with no religious preference.

The following differences by region, observed in the 1964 data, show surprisingly low trust in people for respondents living in the West This did not hold true in the 1968 data, however, the lowest ratings being noted in the South (as would be expected on the basis of lower education and higher prevalence of people with Fundamentalist religion).

	1964	1968
Northeast	1.97	⎱1.93
Midwest	1.77	⎰
South	1.73	1.64
West	1.63	2.03

The trust in people scale related in the following ways to various political orientations in the 1968 data:

i) People who voted for Wallace showed slightly less trust in people
ii) People who wanted to pull our troops out of Vietnam (vs. those who wanted to stay there and those who wanted to invade North Vietnam) showed less trust in people.
iii) People who thought the police used too much force with demonstrators in Chicago were no more trusting of people than people who thought the police used the right amount of force or not enough force.

Reference

Robinson, J.; Rusk, G., and Head, K. Measures of political attitudes. Ann Arbor, Michigan: Survey Research Center, University of Michigan, 1968.

TRUST IN PEOPLE

(* indicates trusting response)

1. Generally speaking, would you say that most people can be trusted or
   that you can't be too careful in dealing with people?

	1964	1968	(low education)
*Most people can be trusted	54%	56%	(40%)
Can't be too careful	46%	44%	(60%)

2. Would you say that most of the time, people try to be helpful, or
   that they are mostly just looking out for themselves?

*Try to be helpful	57%	60%	(48%)
Look out for themselves	43%	40%	(52%)

3. Do you think that most people would try to take advantage of you if they
   got the chance or would they try to be fair?

Take advantage	30%	31%	(42%)
*Try to be fair	70%	69%	(58%)

Trust in People (Survey Research Center 1969) from the *1964 Election Study* (Ann Arbor, Michigan: Inter-University Consortium for Political Research, The University of Michigan, 1971); reprinted here with permission.

PEOPLE IN GENERAL (Banta 1961)

Variable   This scale attempts to measure the extent to which people are disposed to act in an exploitative or manipulative manner toward other
people.

Description   The scale consists of 20 items in five-category Likert format (but
not employing the usual strongly agree-agree, etc. response categories). The items were selected from a pool of 72 items constructed
by Christie (see his scales reviewed earlier in this chapter).

The individual's score can be determined in any one of three ways,
the simplest (and apparently most reliable) being his average score
for those items which the respondent checks as expressing his own
feelings on the issue (i.e., if he answers "0" only to items 1 and
2, his score is 3.0). Total scores apparently vary between 1.0
(very exploitative) and 5.0 (very non-exploitative), with 3.0 marking the neutral point.

Sample   The sample consisted of 28 students in introductory psychology
classes at Columbia University in summer, 1958.

Reliability/   The students responded to the same items on three different occa-
Homogeneity   sions using three different formats: standard Likert format, Thurstone
format, and the format as presented here. The score for the scale as
presented here correlated .71 with the items in Likert and .72 with
the items in Thurstone format (these test-retest correlations are
undoubtedly low considering the change in response format).

Validity   No data bearing on validity are reported.

Location   Banta, T. Social attitudes and response styles. Educational and
Psychological Measurement, 1961, 21, 543-557.

Results and   The intent of this study was mainly methodological, so that substan-
Comments   tive results were minimal.

This is one of the few extant examples of the application of the
unfolding technique to attitude measurement. It is interesting to
see that the scale values for items derived by Banta's technique
correlated .96 with scores derived from Thurstone's more cumbersome
methods.

People in General

Some of the following statements may reflect your own views, while others may not. Of these statements that do not reflect your own views, there are likely to be some that are too favorable toward the issue; on the other hand, there are also likely to be some that are too unfavorable toward the issue to represent your own views.

Please read each statement carefully and indicate your reaction to it in accordance with the following rules:

Circle:

-- - (0) + ++ ?   If the statement expresses your own feelings regarding the issue.

-- - 0 (+) ++ ?   If the statement is somewhat too favorable toward the issue in question to represent your own views.

-- - 0 + (++) ?   If the statement is much too favorable to represent your own views.

-- (-) 0 + ++ ?   If the statement is too unfavorable to represent your own views.

(--) - 0 + ++ ?   If the statement is very definitely too unfavorable to represent your own views.

-- - 0 + ++ (?)   If the statement is not one that expresses your own feelings but you can't determine whether it is too favorable or too unfavorable toward the issue in question.

	UPRO Scale Value
1. Most men will fight back when insulted.	3.2
2. Generally speaking, most people do not truly believe in anything new until they have experienced it.	2.8
3. Anyone who completely trusts anyone else is asking for trouble.	2.2

Reprinted with permission of Banta, T. People in General, in *Educational and Psychological Measurement*, 21 (1961), pp 543-557. Copyright 1961 by G. Frederick Kuder, Box 6907, College Station, Durham, N.C. 27708.

4. Generally speaking, men won't work hard unless they're forced to do so.　　　1.8

5. Even the most hardened and vicious criminal has a spark of decency somewhere within him.　　　3.3

6. Any normal person will stand up for what he thinks is right even if it costs him his job.　　　4.0

7. Most people really don't know what is best for them.　　　2.7

8. Some of the best people have some of the worst vices.　　　2.7

9. Most men forget more easily the death of their father than the loss of their property.　　　2.1

10. Men are quicker to praise than they are to blame.　　　3.4

11. Most men like to tackle new and difficult problems.　　　3.8

12. Most men are brave.　　　3.8

13. Nature has so created men that they desire everything but are unable to attain it.　　　2.4

14. The biggest difference between most criminals and other people is that criminals are stupid enough to get caught.　　　2.0

15. The best way to handle people is to tell them what they want to hear.　　　2.8

16. It is safest to assume that all people have a vicious streak and it will come out when they are given the chance.　　　2.1

17. Most people are basically good and kind.　　　3.5

18. Barnum was very wrong when he said that there's a sucker born every minute.　　　2.6

19. When you come right down to it, it's human nature never to do anything without an eye to one's own advantage.　　　2.3

20. The great majority of men are more satisfied with what seems true than with the truth.　　　2.9

MISANTHROPY (Sullivan and Adelson 1954)

Variable   This instrument attempts to measure misanthropy as a variant
                  of ethnocentrism.

Description   A total of 29 items taken from the ethnocentrism scale (used by
                  the University of California Public Opinion Study) were modified
                  by replacing references to minorities with more general terms
                  such as "most people", etc. Six response categories are provided
                  from complete agreement (+3) to complete disagreement (-3). In
                  scoring, four was added to all the scores to produce a range from
                  1 to 7. Omitted responses were given the score of four.

Sample   The sample consisted of 221 students enrolled in an elementary
                  psychology course at a midwestern university.

Reliability   Odd-even reliability for the scale was found to be .79. The
                  authors maintain that although the instrument is fairly adequate
                  it could easily be refined through item analysis and other means.

Validity   No validity data are reported.

Location   Sullivan, P. and Adelson. J. Ethnocentrism and misanthropy, _Journal_
                  of Abnormal and Social Psychology, 1954, 49 (2), 246-250.

Results and   The product-moment correlation between the original ethnocentrism
Comments   scale and misanthropy was determined to be .43 which is highly
                  significant statistically. The authors concluded that although
                  misanthropy and ethnocentrism are not interchangeable they are
                  definitely related. Ethnocentrism may be partly a manifestation
                  of an ingroup-outgroup situation in which the only ingroup is the
                  self.

Misanthropy

1. People seem to prefer the most luxurious, extravagant, and sensual way of living.

    Completely agree +3 +2 +1 0 -1 -2 -3 Completely disagree

2. In order to maintain a nice residential neighborhood it is best to prevent most people from living in it.

3. A major fault of most people is their conceit.

4. Colleges should adopt a quota system by which they may limit the number of people in fields which have too many now.

5. A step toward solving social problems would be to prevent people from getting into superior, profitable positions in society, for a while at least.

6. One trouble with most people is that they stick together and connive, so that others don't have a fair chance in competition.

7. Our social problems are so general and deep that one often doubts that democratic methods can ever solve them.

8. Most people tend to lower the general standard of living by their willingness to do the most menial work and to live under standards that are far below average.

9. Most people should not pry so much into others' activities and organizations nor seek so much recognition and prestige.

10. Much resentment against most people stems from their tending to keep apart and to exclude others from their social life.

11. One big trouble with people is that they are never contented, but always try for the best jobs and the most money.

12. People go too far in hiding their backgrounds, especially such extremes as changing their names and imitating others' manner and customs.

13. People should make sincere efforts to rid themselves of their conspicuous and irritating faults, if they really want to prevent themselves from being condemned.

14. War shows up the fact that most people are not patriotic or willing to make sacrifices for their country.

15. There is something different and strange about most people; one never knows what they are thinking or planning, nor what makes them tick.

16. People may have moral standards that they apply in their dealings with their friends, but with others most of them are unscrupulous, ruthless, and undependable.

17. Most peoples' first loyalty is to themselves rather than to their country.

18. In order to handle social problems, one must meet fire with fire and use the same ruthless tactics with others that they use.

19. Most people seem to have an aversion to plain hard work; they tend to be parasites on society by finding easy, nonproductive jobs.

20. One general fault of people is their overaggressiveness, a strange tendency always to display their looks, manner, and breeding.

21. There seems to be some revolutionary streak in the human makeup as shown by the fact that there are so many communists and agitators.

22. People should be more concerned with their personal appearance, and not be so dirty and smelly and unkempt.

23. There is little hope of correcting human defects, since these defects are simply in the blood.

24. People keep too much to themselves, instead of taking the proper interest in community problems and good government.

25. When people create large funds for educational or scientific research it is mainly due to a desire for fame and public notice rather than a really sincere scientific interest.

26. People would solve many of their social problems by not being so irresponsible, lazy, and ignorant.

27. It would be best to limit most people to grammar and trade school education since more schooling just gives them ambition and desires which they are unable to fulfill in competition.

28. There is something inherently primitive and uncivilized in most people, as shown in their musical tastes and extreme aggressiveness.

29. There will always be wars because, for one thing, there will always be people who ruthlessly try to grab for more than their share.

ACCEPTANCE OF OTHERS (Fey 1955)

Variable

This scale was devised to test the relationship between three separate variables: feelings of self acceptance, acceptance of others, and feelings of acceptability to others.

Description

The acceptance of others scale consists of 20 attitude statements, possible responses running from almost always (scored as 1) to very rarely (scored as 5). Scale scores thus run from 20 (low acceptance of others) to 100 (high acceptance).

Sample

The sample consisted of 58 third year medical students.

Reliability

Split-half reliability for the acceptance of others scale was .90 (and for estimated acceptability to others .89).

Validity

No validity data are reported.

Location

Fey, W.F. Acceptance by others and its relation to acceptance of self and others: a revaluation. Journal of Abnormal and Social Psychology, 1955, 50 (2), 274-276.

Results and Comments

The author summarizes his results as follows: "Analysis of the data indicated that individuals with high self-acceptance scores tend also to accept others, to feel accepted by others, but actually to be neither more nor less accepted by others than those with low self-acceptance scores. Individuals with high acceptance-of-others scores tend in turn to feel accepted by others, and tend toward being accepted by them. Persons who think relatively much better of themselves than they do of others tend to feel accepted by others, whereas actually they are significantly less well liked by them; this group significantly overestimates its acceptability to others. Estimated acceptability, in this study, is independent of actual acceptability. Comparison of most and least accepted groups shows only that the latter have a significantly larger gap between self acceptance and their acceptance of others."

The five items in the "estimated acceptance by others" scale are also reproduced below.

Acceptance of Others

1. People are too easily led.

   Almost always   1   2   3   4   5   Very rarely

*2. I like people I get to know.

3. People these days have pretty low moral standards.

4. Most people are pretty smug about themselves, never really facing their bad points.

*5. I can be comfortable with nearly all kinds of people.

6. All people can talk about these days, it seems, is movies, TV, and foolishness like that.

7. People get ahead by using 'pull,' and not because of what they know.

8. If you once start doing favors for people, they'll just walk all over you.

9. People are too self-centered.

10. People are always dissatisfied and hunting for something new.

11. With many people you don't know how you stand.

12. You've probably got to hurt someone if you're going to make something out of yourself.

13. People really need a strong, smart leader.

14. I enjoy myself most when I am alone, away from people.

15. I wish people would be more honest with you.

*16. I enjoy going with a crowd.

17. In my experience, people are pretty stubborn and unreasonable.

*18. I can enjoy being with people whose values are very different from mine.

*19. Everybody tries to be nice.

20. The average person is not very well satisfied with himself.

(* Reversed item)

Acceptability to Others

1. People are quite critical of me.

2. I feel 'left out,' as if people don't want me around.

*3. People seem to respect my opinion about things.

*4. People seem to like me.

*5. Most people seem to understand how I feel about things.

(* Reversed item)

CHAPTER 10 - RELIGIOUS ATTITUDES

For many years the sociology and psychology of religion barely overlapped (Swanborn, 1968). Sociologists were interested either in large-scale historical developments, as in Weber's classic study of Protestantism and the Spirit of Capitalism, or in empirical studies of church attendance and related facets of organizational membership. Psychologists were much more concerned with the religious experiences of individuals--their feelings, attitudes, and beliefs about the supernatural. Naturally, then, sociologists tended to employ attendance statistics or interviews with people regarding participation in church activities, while psychologists most often used attitude scales or depth interviews, and sometimes even introspection. As the research tools of each discipline developed--most notably attitude scaling in psychology--the newer techniques were applied to the study of religion, but little theory and little joining of sociological and psychological approaches emerged.

Fortunately, this pattern has changed considerably during the last several years. New journals have arisen to report developing theory and research--e.g., Journal for the Scientific Study of Religion, Review of Religious Research, and the International Yearbook for the Sociology of Religion. These have encouraged joint contributions from social scientists of varying persuasions. Most investigators are now aware that the organizational character of the church as well as the beliefs, attitudes, and behavior of its members must somehow be combined in order to obtain a coherent and complete scientific account of religion.

Perhaps the most outstanding example of this "total approach" can be seen in the work of Glock, Stark, and their colleagues in the Program for the Study of Religion and Society--a subdivision of the Survey Research Center at the University of California, Berkeley. They have contributed substantially to the development of sound theory in the area of religious research (e.g., Glock and Stark, 1965) and to the empirical literature as well (e.g., Glock and Stark, 1966).

Although there already exists a vast amount of information about religious attitudes and beliefs, and too many measuring instruments to be exhaustively covered in this volume, it is fairly easy to reduce the topics commonly investigated to a few central themes. One of these is the problem of representing religious phenomena on some reasonably limited set of theoretical dimensions. Everyone now admits that religious experience is complex, usually involving at least an ideology, ritual practices, organizational maintenance activities, and feelings of transcendence or contact with the supernatural. A serious attempt to study religion empirically, then, must eventually face the difficulty of specifying and measuring the important dimensions of religiosity (Brown, 1966; Fukuyama, 1961; Glock and Stark, 1965).

Another central task for the scientific study of religion is to characterize important dimensions of organizational variation among churches. This is, of course, primarily a sociological issue, but we shall see that it has implications also for the particular way in which members of various religious bodies feel and behave.

Specifying the relationships between religious attitudes and the multitude of potentially associated social attitudes and personality characteristics has been the focus of a third area of religious research.

One of the most intensively studied relationships--still a source of heated controversy--is that between religiosity and racial bigotry.

Measuring instruments employed in all three areas of research are presented in this chapter, along with a few scales devoted to attitudes concerning more specific religious objects, such as the Bible, the Church, and one's "image of God." A brief account of the rationale for the development of these measures will be presented for each research area.

Dimensions of Religiosity

Several attempts have been made to explore the multi-dimensionality of religious commitment; these are represented in the present chapter by the following instruments:

1. Dimensions of Religious Commitment (Glock and Stark 1966)
2. Religiosity Scales (Faulkner and DeJong 1965)
3. Dimensions of Religiosity (King 1967)
4. Dimensions of Religious Ideology (Putney and Middleton 1961)
5. Religious Orientation and Involvement (Lenski 1963)
6. Religious Attitude Inventory (Broen 1956)

For complete coverage of the religious attitude domain the first two scales are probably the most sophisticated developed to date. They are based on a careful theoretical analysis by Glock and Stark of all the conceivable ways in which an individual can be religious. This is of fundamental importance because in the past it has been quite common for religious apologists, and social scientists as well, to criticize empirical research on the grounds that what was being studied was not "really" religion. By attempting seriously to give exhaustive coverage to the various components of religiosity, Glock and Stark hope to avoid criticism on these grounds.

They propose five basic dimensions: the experiential, which refers to the basic assumption in all religions that a religious person will at one time or another experience special feelings or direct knowledge of ultimate reality (e.g., the "presence" or "nearness of God"); the ideological dimension, which reflects the assumption in all formal religions that adherence to a core of beliefs is essential to the religious life; the ritualistic, encompassing the specifically religious activities prescribed by all formal religions, such as prayer and fasting; the intellectual, reflecting the expectation that a religious person will be knowledgeable about the tenets of his faith; and the consequential dimension, different from the other four in that it refers to the effects of religiosity in an individual's life--e.g., doing of "good works" and displaying "love of neighbor." Within each of these categories one can make many other distinctions--kinds of belief, types of consequences, etc.--but according to Glock and Stark these five dimensions are basic.

The scales designed by Glock and Stark and by Faulkner and DeJong represent independent attempts to measure these basic dimensions of religiosity. Glock and Stark have omitted a measure of the consequential dimension for the moment, while Faulkner and De Jong have built indices for all five. Independently both teams of researchers have found the dimensions to be nearly uncorrelated; both agree that ideology (or belief) is the most important.

Whereas Glock and Stark built their indices in correspondence with a prior analytic scheme, King explored the multi-dimensionality of religiosity empirically using factor analytic techniques. Following an unusually comprehensive literature review, King reduced a large battery of items to a relatively small number of factors which, to his mind, represent the entire range of religious beliefs and attitudes. This approach is quite helpful, but because it depends to such a large extent on item selection and sample biases (all of King's respondents were Methodists), much further work is needed before King's dimensions can be well understood or accepted as basic.

The Putney and Middleton instrument appears to be a good, intensive measure of what we have been calling the belief component of religiosity. Similarly, a factor analysis of the Broen Inventory revealed two dimensions, one of which (fundamentalism) seems to be based primarily on differences in belief. The other factor, "nearness to God," can be considered one element of the Glock-Stark experiential component.

Finally, this list contains measures of two dimensions found to be important in Lenski's classic study, The Religious Factor. One of these, "involvement," was classified either as associational--having the characteristics of staid formal organizations--or as communal, with emphasis on emotional primary group ties among members and heavy time and resource commitments to group activities. The second dimension, "religious orientation," was characterized either by doctrinal orthodoxy (strict adherence to dogma and ritual prescriptions) or devotionalism (emphasis on private acts of worship). The significance of these categories for other attitudes and actions is discussed more fully in the following section.

The reader will find additional aspects of religious attitudes in the questionnaire listed in the appendix of Glock and Stark (1966). A further heterogeneous listing of interesting attitude questions on religion appears in the appendix to Thomas (1963), whose questionnaire was applied to a national sample of American adults.

Orthodoxy, Fundamentalism, and Sectness

Most of the religious literature on ideal church organization contains an image of the church as a primary group: the believers know and love each other as they live a life of worship together. However, anyone with a bit of experience in modern American Sunday society has seen blatant contradictions of this image--large masses, many of whom know only a small minority of the others present and who have been absent from services for weeks, listening to a sermon delivered over a public address system. Some Americans even fulfill what they feel is a "Sunday obligation" by listening to services broadcast on the radio or television.

Yet there are also in America some intensely emotional congregations whose members devote extensive time and energy to the group effort. These people sometimes limit social contacts exclusively to fellows within their own religious community.

The church-sect typology proposed by sociologists, beginning with Weber and Troeltsch (Weber, 1946) and continuing down to the present (Dynes, 1957; Johnson, 1963), is an attempt to describe and analyze the deviation and development of churches away from the sect form. What is now called "church-sect theory" has developed to explain a rather general form of evolution: emotional, evangelical, communal, and spiritualistic sects gradually become (or lose members to) more formal, quiet, and less "other-worldly" churches. As Glock and Stark put it, religious communities become religious audiences. Very often the sects attract lower status, somewhat alienated members, while the churches tend to be filled with the more comfortable, better established members of an area or society. (For further discussion see Johnson, 1963; Glock and Stark, 1965; Gustafson, 1967; Goode, 1967; Demerath, 1967; Eister, 1967; and the articles

by Dynes discussed later in the present chapter.) The scales listed below measure attitudes that seem to accompany membership in a sectarian,
as opposed to a church-like, religious organization:

   7. Church-Sect Scale (Dynes 1957)
   8. Religious Fundamentalism (Martin and Westie 1959)
   9. Certainty in Religious Belief Scale (Thouless 1935)
  10. Religiosity Questionnaire (Brown 1962)
  11. Inventory of Religious Belief (Brown and Lowe 1951)
  12. Religious Attitude Scale (Poppleton and Pilkington 1963)

For the most part these instruments tap what to Glock and Stark
is the belief dimension of religiosity, but they do so in a special way.
Usually scores run from orthodox, conservative, superstitious, and emotional, on one hand, to skeptical, liberal, and scientific on the other.
A number of studies (not necessarily using these particular scales) have
discovered reliable correlates of this orthodoxy dimension: lower class
status, relatively low educational level, ethnic prejudice, hostility to
other nations, and the like.   Many of these correlates are discussed in
Chapter 5 (on authoritarianism) in this volume.

Such findings reveal an intriguing paradox.   Whereas religious
doctrine nearly always emphasizes universal love and brotherhood, social
psychological research consistently discloses a _negative_ relationship between religiosity (when defined as orthodoxy) and tolerance.   Beginning in
1946, for example, Allport and Kramer demonstrated that churchgoers were
more intolerant than non-churchgoers.   Kirkpatrick (1949) found religious
people to be less humanitarian than non-religious people (attitudinally
more punitive toward criminals, homosexuals, and other deviants).   Stouffer
(1955) obtained similar findings even after controlling for education,
which might have been thought to account for both intolerance and religiosity.   Rokeach (1960) found non-believers to be less dogmatic and less

ethnocentric than believers. The list could be greatly extended. The paradox led to the development of the scales discussed in the next section.

Intrinsic versus Extrinsic Religiosity

Gordon Allport (1954) offered an explanation for the association between religiosity and prejudice. He reasoned that people who come to church for social support and for relief from personal problems might also be insecure enough to blame outgroups for their troubles, to feel threatened by social change, and so on. If so, they would not be the most frequent attenders, the ones who seek most seriously to expend all their energies on a truly religious life. There should be, he thought, a subset of churchgoers who attend very frequently, attempt to "apply" religion in all their social dealings, and thus exhibit great tolerance for others.

Allport reviewed several studies that indeed found a U-shaped curve relating prejudice scores to frequency of church attendance. In general, people who attend only a few times a month express the most prejudice, while non-attenders and persons who attend two or more times a week are about equally low (summarized in Allport and Ross, 1967).

Following theoretical discussions inspired by Allport's analysis, these two scales were constructed:

13. Extrinsic Religious Values Scale (Wilson 1960)
14. Intrinsic-Extrinsic Religious Orientation (Feagin 1964; Allport and Ross 1967)

The first tapped only the extrinsic end of the proposed dimension; yet using this scale Wilson obtained a median correlation of .65 in 10 religious groups between extrinsic orientation and anti-Semitism. The second instrument was developed to measure both intrinsic and extrinsic ends of the theoretical continuum. In at least two studies (Feagin 1964; Allport and Ross 1967) results indicated that the intrinsic and extrinsic subscales were nearly independent, although each was related to bigotry in the expected way. People with an extrinsic orientation were significantly more prejudiced than people with an intrinsic orientation.

However, there were also a number of people who agreed with both sets of items, and they were the most prejudiced of all! Allport and Ross labelled them "indiscriminately proreligious." Since their sample was drawn from church-attenders, they did not have a chance to observe the fourth possible type of person, the "indiscriminately anti-religious (or non-religious)." Recent unpublished research with college students, however (Robert Brannon, personal communication), indicates that in liberal environments such people abound. It remains to be seen how they would actually score on prejudice measures, however.

To summarize, then, Allport agrees that the majority of religious people are intolerant--and this accounts for the usual correlation. Nevertheless, there is a minority of people who express religiosity of a different, intrinsic sort, and they are generally as tolerant as their beliefs would indicate they should be.

Attitudes Concerning the Church, the Bible, and God

The remaining scales are fairly straightforward. Each was developed to measure attitudes or beliefs about a specific religious "object."

15. Attitude toward the Church Scale (Thurstone and Chave 1929)
16. Attitudes about the Bible (Survey Research Center 1969)
17. Adjective Ratings of God (Gorsuch 1968)

The Thurstone-Chave scale has been used in countless studies as a measure of religiosity and religious change (say, over several years in college). It contains some items that could be considered indices of orthodox beliefs, but primarily it taps attitudes about the church as a social institution.

The Survey Research Center's Bible attitudes measure is simply one item that indicates belief or relative skepticism about the truth of the Bible taken literally. It is probably a good measure of fundamentalism for use in studies requiring a very short index.

Gorsuch's instrument assesses one's conception of God. Though it had not been used in relational studies at the time he published his factor-analytic results, this measure may reveal interesting inter-denominational and cross-cultural differences.

Problems in the Scientific Study of Religion

Considering that empirical research on religion is a relatively recent phenomenon, and that religious people maintain that the most significant component of religious experience--namely direct contact with God--is not subject to scientific scrutiny, it is not surprising that immense difficulties await the social scientist, expert or novice, who decides to measure religiosity.

Even when this obstacle is assumed away--the most common tack being to admit that one's investigations are limited to whatever is potentially measurable--there are still great problems. Religious experiences are not confined to participants in formal organizations; yet social scientists almost always study churches and church members rather than isolated individual mystics. If these were guaranteed to occupy no significant social positions, or were only a tiny minority of the whole society, then little would be missed by ignoring them. But if, as much contemporary research indicates, there is a continuing movement of individuals from the lower classes into and through sects, then into and through churches, finally to emerge non-members, we ought to be concerned with where these people end up. Of course, the process just grossly summarized and oversimplified often requires several generations; and even granting its existence; it is too early to tell what the results will be. But if the rising interest in mysticism, astrology, and related endeavors among students (who rarely attend church) is a portent of the future, religious research will have to take a new direction.

Even in the event this particular trend does not materialize (recent Gallup poll data show the United States to be the only Western country _not_ to show a significant decline in the acceptance of traditional Christian credos over the last 20 years), there are still limitations on the existing approaches. Most studies employ measures of _traditional Christian_ ideologies. Little appears to be known about non-Christian religious beliefs and prejudices, for example. Surely more comparative research is needed. How would Glock and Stark's dimensions be operationalized for Buddhists, for example?

In spite of these and other problems, the scientific study of religion has advanced tremendously in recent years (Argyle, 1958; Knudten, 1967; Swanborn, 1968; see also the recent issues of the journals mentioned earlier), and it will continue to do so. The simultaneous development of theory and research methods indicated of late is quite promising.

References:

Allport, G. The nature of prejudice, Reading, Massachusetts: Addison-Wesley, 1954.

Allport, G. and Kramer, B. Some roots of prejudice, Journal of Psychology, 1946, 22, 9-39.

Allport, G. and Ross, J. Personal orientation and prejudice, Journal of Personality and Social Psychology, 1967, 5, 432-443.

Argyle, M. Religious behaviour, Glencoe, Illinois: Free Press, 1958.

Brown, L. The structure of religious belief, Journal for the Scientific Study of Religion, 1966, 5, 259-272.

Demerath, N., III. Comment: in a sow's ear, Journal for the Scientific Study of Religion, 1967, 6, 77-84.

Dynes, R. The consequences of sectarianism for social participation, Social Forces, 1957, 35, 331-334.

Eister, A. Comment: toward a radical critique of church-sect typologizing, Journal for the Scientific Study of Religion, 1967, 6, 85-90.

Feagin, J. Prejudice and religious types: a focused study of southern fundamentalists, Journal for the Scientific Study of Religion, 1964, 4, 3-13.

Fukuyama, Y. The major dimensions of church membership, Review of Religious Research, 1961, 2, 154-161.

Glock, C. and Stark, R. Christian beliefs and anti-Semitism, New York: Harper and Row, 1966.

Glock, C. and Stark, R. Religion and society in tension, Chicago: Rand McNally, 1965.

Goode, E. Some critical observations on the church-sect dimension, Journal for the Scientific Study of Religion, 1967, 6, 69-77.

Gustafson, P. A restatement of Troeltsch's church-sect typology, Journal for the Scientific Study of Religion, 1967, 6, 64-68.

Johnson, B. On church and sect, American Sociological Review, 1963, 28, 539-549.

Kirkpatrick, C. Religion and humanitarianism: a study of institutional implications, Psychological Monographs, 1949, 63, Whole No. 304.

Knudten, R. (ed.). The sociology of religion: an anthology, New York: Appleton-Century-Crofts, 1967.

Rokeach, M. The open and closed mind, New York: Basic Books, 1960.

Stouffer, S.A. Communism, civil liberties, and conformity, Garden
      City, New Jersey: Doubleday, 1955.

Swanborn, P. Religious research: objects and methods, International
      Yearbook for the Sociology of Religion, 1968, 4, 7-32.

Thomas, J. Religion and the American people, Westminster, Maryland:
      Newman Press, 1963.

Weber, M. Essays in sociology, translated by H. Gerth and C. Mills,
      New York: Oxford University Press, 1946.

DIMENSIONS OF RELIGIOUS COMMITMENT (Glock and Stark 1966)

Variable

As discussed in the introduction to this chapter, Glock and Stark (1965) on theoretical grounds proposed five dimensions of religiosity: Belief, Ritual, Experience, Knowledge, and Consequences. They went on to design measures for four of these -- all but "Consequences" -- for a study of Christian beliefs which will eventually be completely reported in several volumes. The first of these appeared in 1966; the others are still being prepared.

Description

Two survey studies, one involving northern California church members and another national in scope, were conducted. From item analysis and hypotheses based on the theoretical viewpoint elaborated in Glock and Stark (1965), the authors constructed indices of four general dimensions of religious commitment. Most of these indices were built simply by summing points assigned to each item which was answered in a certain direction. The authors state in an appendix (1966, Appendix B) that more elaborate attempts at scale construction were not considered appropriate in this early phase of their research.

Scoring procedures for each index are reported with the items listed below. The rationale for each of the indices is indicated by their labels in the following table.

General Dimensions of Religious Commitment	Primary Measures	Secondary Measures	
1. Belief	Orthodoxy Index (central religious beliefs)	Particularism Index	(beliefs about what
		Ethicalism Index	leads to salvation)
2. Practice	Ritual involvement Index (public worship)		
	Devotionalism Index (private worship)		
3. Experience	Religious Experience Index (contact with the supernatural)		
4. Knowledge	Religious Knowledge Index (knowledge of the Bible)		

Sample

The most detailed indices were developed from a questionnaire study of 3000 persons randomly selected from membership lists of 97 Protestant congregations and 21 Roman Catholic parishes. These particular churches had earlier been drawn randomly from all churches in four northern California counties. Of these people, 72% of the Protestants and 53% of the Catholics completed and returned the questionnaire by mail. Phone calls to 300 Protestant and 200 Catholic nonresponders indicated no substantial bias created by selective responding.

Eighteen months later (October, 1964) some of the most important items from the questionnaire were included in an NORC survey of the nation, in which 1,976 people were intensively interviewed. Findings from this survey, in most every case, replicated the results from the California study.

Reliability No direct evidence reported.

Validity Each index was correlated with the answers to other items designed to measure the same dimension, and invariably substantial associations were found. Also, patterns of denominational differences were checked to see whether they "made sense." For example, the orthodoxy score was expected to increase from a low for Unitarians and Congregationalists to a high for Southern Baptists and small sects, and this pattern was indeed observed.

Location Glock, C. and Stark, R., Christian beliefs and anti-Semitism. New York: Harper and Row, 1965. (This book contains the full questionnaire and several of the indices. However, some of our information also came from an as yet unpublished manuscript: R. Stark and C. Glock, American piety: The nature of religious commitment.)

Administration Something less than a minute can be estimated for each item. Using this as a guide, the reader can compute approximate completion times for each of the indices listed.

Results and Comments The analysis presented in Glock and Stark's 1965 book was an important contribution because it represented a careful attempt to specify, in advance of empirical efforts, what the significant dimensions of religious thought and behavior might be. Results in the 1966 book (and in more recent unpublished reports) indicate that the four measured dimensions are in fact essentially uncorrelated, and that other attitudes and behavior can be predicted from positions on these dimensions. In an independent operationization of this analytic scheme, Faulkner and DeJong (1966; see also the following scale in this chapter) got very similar results with different items and college student rather than nonstudent adult respondents.

In both investigations orthodoxy was found to be the best predictor of all other aspects of religiosity. This is quite important because, as Glock and Stark point out, it implies that belief is the most significant component of religiosity. When belief wanes, as it is currently among members of the more liberal churches, other indications of religiosity will eventually decline -- e.g., church contributions and attendance. Moreover, much of the research reviewed in this chapter suggests that orthodoxy is associated with bigotry, so we must conclude that the most central component of religious commitment (orthodox belief) is somehow linked with intolerance (a finding borne out in Glock and Stark's research on anti-Semitism).

The entire Glock and Stark questionnaire contained over 500 items. The interested reader will want to consult the published analyses of these for details on denominational differences and patterns of inter-item correlation.

References Faulkner, J. and DeJong, G., Religiosity in 5-D: an empirical analysis. Social Forces, 1966, 45, 246-254.

Glock, C. and Stark, R., Religion and society in tension. Chicago: Rand McNally, 1965.

Dimensions of Religious Commitment

I. Belief Dimension
A. Orthodoxy Index

1. Which of the following statements comes closest to expressing what you believe about God? (Please check only one answer.)
   a) I know God really exists and I have no doubts about it.
   b) While I have doubts, I feel that I do believe in God.
   c) I find myself believing in God some of the time, but not at other times.
   d) I don't believe in a personal God, but I do believe in a higher power of some kind.
   e) I don't know whether there is a God and I don't believe there is any way to find out.
   f) I don't believe in God.
   g) None of the above represents what I believe. What I believe about God is _____.
   (please specify)

2. Which of the following statements comes closest to expressing what you believe about Jesus? (Check only one answer.)
   a) Jesus is the Divine Son of God and I have no doubts about it.
   b) While I have some doubts, I feel basically that Jesus is Divine.
   c) I feel that Jesus was a great man and very holy, but I don't feel Him to be the Son of God any more than all of us are children of God.
   d) I think that Jesus was only a man although an extraordinary one.
   e) Frankly, I'm not entirely sure there was such a person as Jesus.
   f) None of the above represents what I believe. What I believe about Jesus is _____.
   (please specify)

3. The Bible tells of many miracles, some credited to Christ and some to other prophets and apostles. Generally speaking, which of the following statements comes closest to what you believe about Biblical miracles? (Check only one answer.)
   a) I'm not sure whether these miracles really happened or not.
   b) I believe miracles are stories and never really happened.
   c) I believe the miracles happened, but can be explained by natural causes.
   d) I believe the miracles actually happened just as the Bible says they did.

4. The Devil actually exists. (Check how certain you are this is true.)
   a) Completely true
   b) Probably true
   c) Probably not true
   d) Definitely not true

Scoring: Glock and Stark gave one point for each of these four questions on which a respondent expressed his certainty of the truth of the orthodox Christian position (1a, 2a, 3d, and 4a); other answers were scored zero. Scores thus ranged from 0 to 4.

Reprinted with permission of Glock, C. and Stark, R. Dimensions of Religious Commitment in *Christian Beliefs and Anti-Semitism* (New York: Harper and Row, 1965). Copyright 1966 by Harper and Row.

B. **Particularism Index** (measuring the importance of holding one's own particular beliefs.)

1. Do you think belief in Jesus Christ as Saviour is ...
    a) absolutely necessary for salvation
    b) would probably help
    c) probably has no influence

2. Do you think being a member of your particular religious faith is ...
    a) absolutely necessary for salvation
    b) would probably help
    c) probably has no influence

3. Do you think being completely ignorant of Jesus, as might be the case for people living in other countries, will ...
    a) definitely prevent salvation
    b) may possibly prevent salvation
    c) probably has no influence on salvation

Scoring: For each item score a = 2, b = 1, and c = 0. Thus the index ranges from 6 (highest particularism) to 0 (lowest).

C. **Ethicalism** (concern for others)

1. Do you think doing good for others is ...
    a) absolutely necessary for salvation
    b) would probably help
    c) probably has no influence

2. Do you think loving thy neighbor is ...
    a) absolutely necessary for salvation
    b) would probably help
    c) probably has no influence

Scoring: For each item score a = 2, b = 1, and c = 0. Thus the index ranges from 4 (holding both to be absolutely necessary) to 0 (rejecting both).

II. Ritual Dimension
A. **Ritual Involvement Index**

1. How often do you attend Sunday worship services? (Check the answer which comes closest to describing what you do.)
    a) Every week
    b) Nearly every week
    c) About three times a month
    d) About twice a month
    e) About once a month
    f) About every six weeks
    g) About every three months
    h) About once or twice a year
    i) Less than once a year
    j) Never

2. How often, if at all, are table prayers or grace said before or after
   meals in your home?
   a) We say grace at all meals
   b) We say grace at least once a day
   c) We say grace at least once a week
   d) We say grace, but only on special occasions
   e) We never, or hardly ever, say grace

Scoring: Persons who both attended church every, or nearly every, week and
   said grace at least once a week were classified as high on the index.
   Those who reported performing either of these ritual obligations this
   often were scored medium. And persons who fell short of these levels
   on both were classified as low.

B. Devotionalism Index

1. How often do you pray privately? (Check the answer which comes closest
   to what you do.)
   a) I never pray, or only do so at church services.
   b) I pray only on very special occasions.
   c) I pray once in a while, but not at regular intervals.
   d) I pray quite often, but not at regular times.
   e) I pray regularly once a day or more.
   f) I pray regularly several times a week.
   g) I pray regularly once a week.

2. How important is prayer in your life?
   a) Extremely important
   b) Fairly important
   c) Not too important
   d) Not important

Scoring: Respondents were classified as high if they felt prayer was
   "extremely" important and they prayed privately once a week or oftener;
   medium if they were devotional in either sense; low if they met
   neither of these standards.

III. Experiential Dimension: Religious Experience Index

Listed below are a number of experiences of a religious nature which
people have reported having. Since you have been an adult have you
ever had any of these experiences, and how sure are you that you had it?

	Yes, I'm sure I have	Yes, I think I have	No
*A feeling that you were somehow in the presence of God...	____	____	____
*A sense of being saved in Christ...	____	____	____

A feeling of being
afraid of God...   _____   _____   _____

*A feeling of being
punished by God for
something you had
done...   _____   _____   _____

A feeling of being
tempted by the
Devil...   _____   _____   _____

> Scoring: Only the starred (*) items were used in the final index. Respondents
> were labelled <u>high</u> if they <u>at least</u> answered "Yes, I think that I have"
> to all three questions; <u>medium</u> if they thought they might have had
> one or two of these experiences; <u>low</u> if they reported having <u>no</u> such
> experience. (It may be worth noting that Protestants more than Catho-
> lics tend to feel saved, while the reverse holds for "being punished.")

IV. Religious Knowledge: <u>Religious Knowledge Index</u>

A. <u>Scripture Quotations</u>. Please read each of the following statements and
do <u>two</u> things: <u>first</u>, decide whether the statement is from the Bible
or <u>not</u>; and <u>second</u>, indicate whether or not you agree with the statement. (Please do this even if you think the statement is not from
the Bible.)

1. For it is easier for a camel to go through a needle's eye than for
a rich man to enter into the kingdom of God.
    From the Bible?   Yes <u>(x)</u>   No _____
    Do you agree?   Yes _____   No _____

2. Blessed are the strong: for they shall be the sword of God.
    From the Bible?   Yes _____   No <u>(x)</u>
    Do you agree?   Yes _____   No _____

3. Thou shalt not suffer a witch to live.
    From the Bible?   Yes <u>(x)</u>   No _____
    Do you agree?   Yes _____   No _____

4. Let your women keep silence in the churches: for it is not permitted
unto them to speak.
    From the Bible?   Yes <u>(x)</u>   No _____
    Do you agree?   Yes _____   No _____

5. For I the Lord thy God am a jealous God, visiting the iniquity of the
fathers upon the children unto the third and fourth generation of
them that hate me.
    From the Bible?   Yes <u>(x)</u>   No _____
    Do you agree?   Yes _____   No _____

Scoring: Persons who got 4 of 5 correct were called _high_; 3, _medium_; and 2 or less, _low_. (Each answer is marked with a parenthesized x.)

B. Prophets

Which of the following were Old Testament prophets? (Check as many answers as you think are correct.)

   (x) Elijah
   _____ Deuteronomy
   (x) Jeremiah
   _____ Paul
   _____ Levitius
   (x) Ezekiel
   _____ None of these

Scoring: _High_ was assigned to persons with all 6 correct; _medium_ for 4 or 5; _low_ for 3 or less.

A combined _Religious Knowledge Index_ was formed by assigning points as follows and then adding:

   Identification of Bible Quotations --
      High = 2
      Medium = 1
      Low = 0

   Identification of Old Testament Prophets --
      High = 2
      Medium = 1
      Low = 0

RELIGIOSITY SCALES (Faulkner and DeJong 1965)

Variable — This scale is the result of an attempt to measure the five dimensions of religiosity proposed by Glock and Stark (1965) using the Guttman technique.

Description — Using items from previous attitude measures and some devised especially for this scale, the authors sought to measure several dimensions of traditional Judeo-Christian beliefs. A random sample of 89 Pennsylvania State University students pretested the instrument; items found to be ambiguous were reworded or eliminated. Items not meeting the Guttman criterion of unidimensionality were also eliminated. The final version contains the following; a five-item ideological subscale; a four-item intellectual subscale; a five-item ritualistic subscale; a five-item experential subscale; and a four-item consequential subscale. Each subscale was scored separately; the exact procedure has not been reported, but apparently one point was given for each item endorsed. After analysis of the total twenty-three item instrument, an eight-item composite scale of religiosity was constructed.

Sample — The sample contained 372 students in introductory sociology at Pennsylvania State University. Twenty-five percent were Freshmen, 38% Sophomores, 25% Juniors, and 12% Seniors. One hundred ninety-six were male and 166 female.

Reliability/ Homogeneity — The coefficient of reproducibility for the eight-item composite scale was .92. For the various subscales the following reproducibility coefficients were reported: ideological .94, intellectual .93, ritualistic .92, experiential .92, and consequential .90. No test-retest data are reported.

Validity — No evidence for validity was cited, except for the construct validity claimed for the Guttman procedure.

Location — Faulkner, J. E. and DeJong, G. F. Religiosity in 5-D: an empirical analysis. Paper presented at American Sociological Association Convention, September, 1965, in Chicago.

Administration — This scale is self administered. It should take approximately fifteen minutes to complete the longer form and five to ten minutes for the short form.

Results and Comments — This scale appears to be a relatively good measure of general religiosity. Since it was based on Glock and Stark's (1965) dimensional analysis, it covers several components of religious commitment commonly ignored by other researchers. The subscales designed to measure each of the five dimensions might be used separately in research concerned with a more detailed view of religious commitment.

Although the dimensions were all moderately correlated with each other (to a statistically significant degree), there was evidence that no two dimensions are the same. Also, it was clear that the belief or ideological dimension was the most highly correlated with the others, suggesting that belief is the central component of religiosity. The least central component was "consequences" of religion, indicating that ethical views are fairly independent of religious beliefs.

Information about the test-retest reliability and construct validity of this scale is now needed. One would like to know how the various subscales differentiate between denominations and between people of different personality types within denominations, and so on.

In short, these dimensional subscales seem to offer a promising approach to the study of religion, but additional work is required before we can have great confidence in this particular set of items as the best representatives of the Glock and Stark dimensions.

Reference   Glock, C. and Stark, R. Religion and society in tension. Chicago: Rand McNally, 1965.

RELIGIOSITY SCALES

The exact wording of items included in the religiosity scales are listed below with an asterisk (*) marking the response defined as indicating a traditional religious response. Items which were included in the total religiosity scale are marked with a plus sign (+).

Ideological Scale

+1. Do you believe that the world will come to an end according to the will of God?

        *1. Yes, I believe this.
         2. I am uncertain about this.
         3. No, I do not believe this.

+2. Which of the following statements most clearly describes your idea about the Deity?

        *1. I believe in a Divine God, Creator of the Universe, Who knows my innermost thoughts and feelings, and to Whom one day I shall be accountable.
         2. I believe in a power greater than myself, which some people call God and some people call Nature.
         3. I believe in the worth of humanity but not in a God or a Supreme Being.
         4. The so-called universal mysteries are ultimately knowable according to the scientific method based on natural laws.
         5. I am not quite sure what I believe.
         6. I am an atheist.

  3. Do you believe that it is necessary for a person to repent before God will forgive his sins?

        *1. Yes, God's forgiveness comes only after repentance.
         2. No, God does not demand repentance.
         3. I am not in need of repentance.

  4. Which one of the following best expresses your opinion of God acting in history?

        *1. God has and continues to act in the history of mankind.
         2. God acted in previous periods but is not active at the present time.
         3. God does not act in human history.

+5. Which of the following best expresses your view of the Bible?

        *1. The Bible is God's word and all it says is true.
        *2. The Bible was written by men inspired by God, and its basic moral and religious teachings are true, but because writers were men, it contains some human errors.
         3. The Bible is a valuable book because it was written by wise and good men, but God had nothing to do with it.
         4. The Bible was written by men who lived so long ago that it is of little value today.

Reprinted with permission of Faulkner, J. E. and DeJong, G. F. Religiosity Scales in "Religiosity in 5-D: An Empirical Analysis;" paper presented at American Sociological Association Convention, September 1965, in Chicago.

Intellectual Scale

 1. How do you personally view the story of creation as recorded
    in Genesis?
             *1. Literally true history.
              2. A symbolic account which is no better or worse than
                 any other account of the beginning.
              3. Not a valid account of creation.

+2. Which of the following best expresses your opinion concerning
    miracles?
             *1. I believe the report of the miracles in the Bible;
                 that is, they occurred through a setting aside of
                 natural laws by a higher power.
              2. I do not believe in the so-called miracles of the Bible.
                 Either such events did not occur at all, or if they
                 did, the report is inaccurate, and they could be ex-
                 plained upon scientific grounds if we had the actual
                 facts.
              3. I neither believe nor disbelieve the so-called miracles
                 of the Bible. No evidence which I have considered
                 seems to prove conclusively that they did or did not
                 happen as recorded.

+3. What is your view of the following statement: Religious truth
    is higher than any other form of truth.
             *1. Strongly agree
             *2. Agree
              3. Disagree
              4. Strongly disagree

 4. Would you write the names of the four Gospels?
    (What are the first five books of the Old Testament?--used for
    Jewish respondents.)
              *   Three or more books correctly identified.

Ritualistic Scale

+1. Do you feel it is possible for an individual to develop a well-
    rounded religious life apart from the instititional church?
             *1. No
              2. Uncertain
              3. Yes

 2. How much time during a week would you say you spend reading the
    Bible and other religious literature?
             *1. One hour or more
             *2. One-half hour
              3. None

3. How many of the past four Sabbath worship services have you
   attended?
       *1. Three or more
       *2. Two
       3. One
       4. None

4. Which of the following best describes your participation in
   the act of prayer?
       *1. Prayer is a regular part of my behavior.
       *2. I pray primarily in times of stress and/or need, but
           not much otherwise.
       3. Prayer is restricted pretty much to formal worship
          services.
       4. Prayer is only incidental to my life.
       5. I never pray.

5. Do you believe that for your marriage the ceremony should be
   performed by:
       *1. A religious official.
       2. Either a religious official or a civil authority.
       3. A civil authority.

Experiential Scale

1. Would you say that one's religious commitment gives life a
   certain purpose which it could not otherwise have?
       *1. Strongly agree
       2. Agree
       3. Disagree

2. All religions stress that belief normally includes some experience of "union" with the divine. Are there particular moments
   when you feel "close" to the divine?
       *1. Frequently
       *2. Occasionally
       3. Rarely
       4. Never

3. Would you say that religion offers a sense of security in the
   face of death which is not otherwise possible?
       *1. Agree
       2. Uncertain
       3. Disagree

+4. How would you respond to the statement: "Religion provides the
   individual with an interpretation of his existence which could
   not be discovered by reason alone."
       *1. Strongly agree
       *2. Agree
       3. Disagree

5. Faith, meaning putting full confidence in the things we hope for and being certain of things we cannot see, is essential to one's religious life.
   - *1. Agree
   - 2. Uncertain
   - 3. Disagree

Consequential Scale

+1. What is your feeling about the operation of non-essential businesses on the Sabbath?
   - *1. They should not be open.
   - 2. I am uncertain about this.
   - 3. They have a legitimate right to be open.

2. A boy and a girl, both of whom attend church frequently, regularly date one another and have entered into sexual relations with each other. Do you feel that people who give at least partial support to the church by attending its worship services should behave in this manner? Which of the following statements expresses your opinion concerning this matter?
   - *1. People who identify themselves with the church to the extent that they participate in its worship services should uphold its moral teachings as well.
   - 2. Sexual intercourse prior to marriage is a matter of individual responsibility.

3. Two candidates are seeking the same political office. One is a member and a strong participant in a church. The other candidate is indifferent, but not hostile, to religious organizations. Other factors being equal, do you think the candidate identified with the church would be a better public servant than the one who has no interest in religion?
   - *1. He definitely would.
   - *2. He probably would.
   - 3. Uncertain.
   - 4. He probably would not.
   - 5. He definitely would not.

4. Suppose you are living next door to a person who confides in you that each year he puts down on his income tax a $50.00 contribution to the church in "loose change," even though he knows that while he does contribute some money to the church in "loose change" each year, the total sum is far below that amount. Do you feel that a person's religious orientation should be reflected in all phases of his life so that such behavior is morally wrong-- that it is a form of lying?
   - *1. Yes
   - 2. Uncertain
   - 3. No

DIMENSIONS OF RELIGIOSITY (King 1967; King and Hunt 1969)

Variable

King's purpose was to consider a wide variety of items in a factor analytic study to test the null hypothesis that the "religious variable" is unidimensional. On the basis of successive factor and cluster analyses (King, 1967) he rejected the hypothesis of unidimensionality and proposed nine dimensions for further study. A subsequent, more rigorous item-scale analysis of the same data (King and Hunt, 1968; 1969) yielded eleven dimensions and generally shorter scales. The eleven-scale instrument is presented here.

Description

Items were chosen from the literature (following an extensive review) or devised to cover eleven potentially important areas of religious life: 1) assent to credal propositions; 2) religious knowledge; 3) theological perspective (e.g., on self, society, church); 4) dogmatism vs. openness to growth and change; 5) extrinsic orientation; 6) participation in and understanding of public and private worship; 7) involvement with friends in the social activities of the congregation; 8) participation in organizational activities; 9) financial support and attitudes toward it; 10) loyalty to the institutional church; 11) attitudes toward ethical questions. Seven to seventeen items were included for each of the eleven dimensions, yielding 121 in all. Each had four response alternatives arranged in Likert fashion along a continuum. About 25 other questions, mostly demographic except for a measure of ethnic tolerance, were added.

Questionnaires were returned by 575 Methodists in Dallas, from which a 131 X 131 matrix was obtained (121 religion items plus 10 ethnic tolerance items). On the basis of a preliminary factor analysis, irrelevant items (31 in all) were eliminated, and a second factor analysis was run on the new 100 X 100 matrix. Finally a cluster analysis was performed.

Following these analyses, King (1967) proposed nine scales for further study. Later, using a computerized item-scale analysis procedure designed by Richard Hunt (1969), these nine sets of items plus 19 of the parent factors and clusters were reanalyzed. The computer technique, which maximizes scale homogeneity, was independently applied to randomly-determined halves of the sample, and the two sets of results were virtually identical. Eleven sets of items emerged from this procedure -- eight of them similar to eight of the original nine.

Sample
: All subjects were members of Methodist congregations in Dallas, Texas, or its suburbs. The congregations were purposely chosen to vary widely in size, demographic characteristics of members, and religious emphasis (e.g., pietistic, liturgical, "liberal"). Questionnaires were mailed to 50 percent of each congregation chosen "over the signature of its pastor." Even after follow-up letters and phone calls, only 48 percent were returned, amounting to 575 persons. Undoubtedly these include a disproportionate number of active and literate members. Still, King reports that the respondents were "heterogeneous on such relevant indices as age, self-rating of activity, education, and income."

Reliability/
Homogeneity
: Values of Cronbach's coefficient alpha for these scales vary between .68 for the religious knowledge dimension and .91 for the credal assent dimension (these values are noted for each dimension below). No test-retest data are reported.

Validity
: King and Hunt (1969) have reported correlates of several scales based on the sample described above. For example, persons reporting that they joined the church "merely to please others" were least religious on nine of the 11 scales, and people who reported having a conversion experience after being raised in the church were most religious on 10 of the 11 -- more religious on all scales than people who said they had "just naturally joined" after having been raised in the church.

Scale scores also related as expected to several demographic variables. In general, women are more religious than men; the old more religious than the young; those raised in rural communities more religious than those from cities; and those with less education and income more religious than those of higher status.

Location
: King, M. Measuring the religious variable: nine proposed dimensions, Journal for the Scientific Study of Religion, 1967, 6, 173-190.

King, M. and Hunt, R. Correlates of eleven religious dimensions. Paper presented to the 1968 convention of the American Sociological Association.

King, M. and Hunt, R. Measuring the religious variable: amended findings, Journal for the Scientific Study of Religion, 1969, 8, (in press).

Administration
: The items are all self-administered; the total instrument would take approximately half an hour to complete.

Results and
Comments
: These scales provide a good foundation for future research. As King points out, several of his dimensions correspond

well with those proposed by other investigators (e.g., Glock, Fukuyama, Lenski), and the thorough literature review which proceeded his analyses guarantees inclusion of most items previously considered relevant to assessing religiosity. (Researchers interested in obtaining a large item pool may want to consult the 1967 article, even though in King's reanalysis many of the items were later discarded).

King's sample was quite limited in representativeness -- composed entirely of Methodists -- yet this is an adequate group for preliminary explorations. And the items were deliberately chosen to apply to a wider population than has so far been sampled. King is still actively pursuing this research and preliminary results do indicate that these dimensions are replicated for members of other religious denominations.

The items primarily tap church-related religious beliefs and activities. King himself has remarked that the social rather than the more private aspects of religiosity are emphasized.

Reference   Hunt, R. A computer procedure for item-scale analysis. (Publication pending, 1969).

SCALES FOR ELEVEN RELIGIOUS DIMENSIONS

I. Credal Assent (.906)[1]
1. I believe in eternal life.[2]
2. I believe in God as a Heavenly Father who watches over me and to whom I am accountable.
3. I believe that Christ is a living reality.
4. I know that I need God's continual love and care.
5. I believe in salvation as release from sin and freedom for new life.
6. I believe that God revealed himself to man in Jesus Christ.
7. I believe that the Word of God is revealed through the Scriptures.

II. Personal Religious Experience (.865)
1. How often do you pray privately in places other than a church? (Regularly -- Never)
2. How often do you ask God to forgive your sins? (Regularly -- Never)
3. When you have decisions to make in your everyday life, how often do you try to find out what God wants you to do? (Regularly -- Never)
4. Private prayer is one of the most important and satisfying aspects of my religious experience.
5. I frequently feel very close to God in prayer, during public worship, or at important moments in my daily life.
6. I know that God answers my prayers.
7. To what extent has God influenced your life? (Very much -- Not at all)

III. Church Attendance (.859)

1. How would you rate your activity in this congregation? (Very active -- Inactive)
2. During the last year, how many Sundays per month on the average have you gone to a worship service? (None -- Three or more)
3. How many Sundays out of the last four have you attended worship services? (None -- Three or more)
4. How often have you taken Communion during the past year? (Regularly -- Never)

---

1. The coefficient of homogeneity shown for each scale is the ratio of the scale covariance among items to the total scale variance.

2. All items had four response alternatives: "very accurate" to "very inaccurate" or "strongly agree" to "strongly disagree" unless otherwise indicated.

Reprinted with permission of King, M. and Hunt, R. Dimensions of Religiosity in "Measuring the Religious Variable," *Journal for the Scientific Study of Religion*, 6 (1967), pp 173-190; in "Correlates of Eleven Religious Dimensions," paper presented to the 1968 convention of the American Sociological Association; and in "Measuring the Religious Variable: Amended Findings," *Journal for the Scientific Study of Religion*, 8 (1969).

IV. Organizational Activities (.792)

1. How often do you spend evenings at church meetings or in church work? (Regularly -- Never)
2. Church activities (meetings, committee work, etc.) are a major source of satisfaction in my life.
3. How many times during the last month have you attended Sunday School or some equivalent educational activity? (None -- Three or more)
4. I keep pretty well informed about my congregation and have some influence on its decisions.
5. I enjoy working in the activities of the Church.
6. List the offices, special jobs, committees, etc., of either the congregation or denomination in which you served during the past church year.

V. Church Work with Friends (.831)

1. Of all your closest friends, how many are also members of your local congregation? (None -- Many)
2. How would you rate your activity in the congregation? (Very active -- Inactive)
3. Think of your five closest friends. How many of them are members of your local congregation? (None -- Three or more)
4. How often do you spend evenings at church meetings or in church work? (Regularly -- Never)
5. How often do you get together with other members of your congregation other than at church or church-sponsored meetings? (Regularly -- Never)
6. How many times during the last month have you attended Sunday School or some equivalent educational activity? (None -- Three or more)

VI. Talking & Reading about Religion (.811)

1. How often do you talk about religion with your friends, neighbors, or fellow workers? (Regularly -- Never)
2. In talking with members of your family how often do you yourself mention religion or religious activities? (Regularly -- Never)
3. How often in the last year have you shared with another church member the problems and joys of trying to live a life of faith in God? (Regularly -- Never)
4. How often do you read the Bible? (Regularly -- Never)
5. How often have you personally tried to convert someone to faith in God? (Regularly -- Never)
6. When faced by decisions regarding social problems and issues, how often do you seek guidance for statements and publication by the Church? (Regularly -- Never)

VII. Financial Support (.801)

1. In proportion to your income, do you consider that your contributions to the Church are: (Generous; Substantial; Modest; Small)?
2. Last year, approximately what percent of your total family income was contributed to the Church? (1% or less; 2% to 4%; 5% to 9%; 10% or more)

3. During the last year, what was the average monthly contribution of your family to your local congregation? (Under $5; $5 - $19; $20 - $49; $50 and up)
4. During the last year, how often have you made contributions to the Church in addition to the general budget and Sunday School? (Regularly; Occasionally; Seldom; Never)
5. Are your financial contributions to the Church: (A planned amount per week, month, etc.; Irregular, but fairly often; Irregular, several times a year; Seldom or Never)

VIII. Religious Knowledge (.681)

1. Which of the following were Old Testament prophets? (Deuteronomy; Elijah; Isaiah; Jeremiah; Leviticus; Paul)
2. Which of the following principles are supported by most Protestant denominations? (Bible as the word of God; Power of Clergy to forgive sin; Separation of Church and State; Final Authority of Church; Justification by Faith; Justification by good works)
3. Which of the following books are in the Old Testament? (Acts; Amos; Galatians; Hebrews; Hosea; Psalms)
4. Which of the following denominations have bishops? (Baptists; Episcopal; Lutherans in USA; Methodist; Presbyterian; Roman Catholic)
5. Which of the following books are included in the Four Gospels? (James; John; Mark; Matthew; Peter; Thomas)
6. A "knowledge score constructed from the above five and four other knowledge items." (not explained further - eds.)

IX. Orientation to Religious Growth & Striving (.763)

1. The truly religious person steadily strives to grow in knowledge and understanding of what it means to live as a child of God.
2. The truly religious person feels compelled to continue growing in understanding of his faith.
3. The truly religious person strives to be moral in all aspects of everyday life.
4. I believe that the Bible provides basic moral principles to guide every decision of my daily life: with family and neighbors, in business and financial transactions, and as a citizen of nation and the world.
5. The main purpose of the Church is to reconcile men to God and each other, thus establishing the conditions for "newness of life."

X. Orientation to Religious Security or Dogmatism (.695)

1. The truly religious person is sure that his beliefs are correct.
2. The truly religious person is sure that he is living in right relationship to God and men.
3. The truly religious person has the joy and peace which comes from recognizing that he is a forgiven sinner.

XI. <u>Extrinsic Orientation</u> (.697)

1. Church membership has helped me to meet the right kind of people.
2. Church is important as a place to go for comfort and refuge from the trials and problems of life.
3. The more liberally I support the Church financially, the closer I feel to it and to God.
4. The Church is important to me as a place where I get the understanding and courage for dealing with the trials and problems of life.
5. It is part of one's patriotic duty to worship in the church of his choice.
6. The Church is most important as a place to formulate good social relationships.

DIMENSIONS OF RELIGIOUS IDEOLOGY

(Putney and Middleton 1961)

Variable   This scale is based on the assumption that religious ideology is composed of four dimensions: orthodoxy, fanaticism, importance, and ambivalence. Each is measured by a subscale of the Ideology instrument.

Description   The combined scales comprise 19 statements--six each for orthodoxy, fanaticism, and importance; one for ambivalence. These 19 were culled from a larger group on the basis of a pretest. Respondents rate each statement on the following Likert-type response scale: 7, strong agreement; 6, moderate agreement; 5, slight agreement; 4, no answer or don't know; 3, slight disagreement; 2, moderate disagreement; 1, strong disagreement. (Asterisks in front of items below indicate reverse scoring.) Scores on each subscale are obtained by summing item scores. In the study reported by the authors no total score was computed.

A check list was also administered, which allowed classification of the respondents as "skeptics," "modernists," or "conservatives," along with measures of authoritarianism, status concern, anomia, and conservatism.

Sample   Questionnaires were distributed to 1200 students in social science courses at 13 colleges and universities in the following states: New York, New Jersey, Pennsylvania, Florida, Georgia, and Alabama. About half were in the Northeastern universities, and half in the Southeastern. Non-Christians were eliminated from the sample, leaving 1,126 questionnaires for analysis.

Reliability   No measure reported.

Validity   There was a close correspondence between responses on the check list and the orthodoxy subscale. "Only 7.7 percent of the skeptics as compared with 91.9 percent of the conservatives scored relatively high on the orthodoxy scale." No evidence for the validity of the other subscales was reported.

Location   Putney, S. and Middleton, R. Dimensions and correlates of religious ideologies, Social Forces, 1961, 39, 285-290.

Administration   The total instrument should take about fifteen minutes to self-administer.

Results and   The findings of the study are difficult to present briefly; the
Comments   authors' summary may suffice.

Four potentially independent dimensions of religious ideology are investigated: the orthodoxy of the belief,

the fanaticism which it inspires, its importance to
the self-conception, and the consciousness of ambivalence concerning the belief. Measured independently
of each other, the first three are found to be directly
related to each other, and the fourth inversely related to the other three. These dimensions are found
to be related--but in different degree--to personality
characteristics such as authoritarianism, status concern, and conservatism, and social characteristics such
as region of residence, size of community, and sex.

The orthodoxy subscale has since been used successfully by several
investigators. All the subscales appear to be potentially useful, although perhaps the ambivalence scale should be lengthened
to increase reliability. Further information must be gathered
before either validity or reliability of this instrument is assured.
Investigators looking for a general measure of "religiosity"
should recall that the Putney-Middleton scale is designed to
measure only the ideological (as distinct from, for example, the
ritualistic) dimension of religious attitudes; nevertheless, as
indicated in the introduction to this chapter, the belief or
ideological dimension does appear to be the best single index of
religiosity.

DIMENSIONS OF RELIGIOUS IDEOLOGY

Each question was scored according to the following response scale: 7, strong agreement; 6, moderate agreement; 5, slight agreement; 4, no answer or don't know; 3, slight disagreement; 2, moderate disagreement; 1, strong disagreement. Reverse scoring items are indicated by an asterisk.

Orthodoxy Scale

1. I believe that there is a physical Hell where men are punished after death for the sins of their lives.

2. I believe there is a supernatural being, the Devil, who continually tries to lead men into sin.

3. To me the most important work of the church is the saving of souls.

4. I believe that there is a life after death.

5. I believe there is a Divine plan and purpose for every living person and thing.

*6. The only benefit one receives from prayer is psychological.

Fanaticism Scale

1. I have a duty to help those who are confused about religion.

2. Even though it may create some unpleasant situations, it is important to help people become enlightened about religion.

*3. There is no point in arguing about religion, because there is little chance of changing other people's minds.

*4. It doesn't really matter what an individual believes about religion as long as he is happy with it.

5. I believe the world would really be a better place if more people held the views about religion which I hold.

6. I believe the world's problems are seriously aggravated by the fact that so many people are misguided about religion.

Importance Scale

1. My ideas about religion are one of the most important parts of my philosophy of life.

2. I find that my ideas on religion have a considerable influence on my views in other areas.

3. Believing as I do about religion is very important to being the kind of person I want to be.

4. If my ideas about religion were different, I believe that my way of life would be very different.

*5. Religion is a subject in which I am not particularly interested.

6. I very often think about matters relating to religion.

Ambivalence Scale

The fourth dimension, ambivalence, called for a Likert-type rating of the statement: "Although one is stronger than the other, there is part of me which believes in religion and part of me which does not."

RELIGIOUS ORIENTATION AND INVOLVEMENT (Lenski 1963)

Variable   Two variables from Lenski's classic The Religious Factor are
            considered: 1) involvement as "associational" or "communal" and
            2) orientation as one of "doctinal orthodoxy" or "devotionalism."
            Associational involvement refers to participation in corporate
            worship, whereas communal involvement refers to the degree to
            which a person's primary group is restricted to members of his own
            religion. Doctrinal orthodoxy involves adherence to church dogma;
            devotionalism involves emphasis on private, or personal, communion
            with God.

Description Under the auspices of the Detroit Area Study, Lenski and his co-
            workers interviewed 656 lay Detroiters in 1958. Also interviewed
            were 127 clergymen. The interview schedule was quite long (see
            Appendix II in Lenski, 1963), and all we shall consider here are
            questions included in the various indices named above. Most of
            the questions called for simple "yes-no" responses, or the choice
            of some alternative, such as frequency of prayer. Other investi-
            gators could, however, use Likert-type agree-disagree answer scales
            if this seemed desirable. Scoring for each index is described with
            the lists of questions below.

Sample   Of 750 Detroiters representatively sampled for the study, 656 (87%)
            completed the interview. They were categorized by social grouping
            and religion as follows: White Protestants (41%), White Catholics
            (35%), Negro Protestants (15%), Jews (4%). The remaining 5% had
            no religious preference or were Eastern Orthodox, Negro Catholics,
            Moslems, or Buddists. In terms of the usual SES variables, the
            group was representative of the population of Detroit (by compari-
            son with Census data and earlier Detroit Area Studies).

Reliability No information given.

Validity   Only face validity is claimed, and since the indices are generally
            quite simple the reader will find it fairly easy to assess this
            for himself. Also, the findings reported by Lenski suggest some
            construct validity, although many of his interpretations are post
            hoc and thus require further study.

Location   Lenski, G., The religious factor. Garden City, New York: Doubleday
            (Anchor), 1963. (Originally published in 1961 by Doubleday.)

Administration The items would each require something less than a minute to com-
            plete if presented in a "self-administered" format. Thus each
            measure would take less than five minutes.

Results and Overall, the associational and communal dimensions were essentially
Comments   uncorrelated. The four "socio-religious" groups were characterized
            by the following patterns of religious involvement:

Socio-religious Group	Strength of bonds: Associational	Communal
Jews	Weak	Strong
White Catholics	Strong	Medium
White Protestants	Medium	Medium
Negro Protestants	Medium	Strong

Associational involvement was found to be correlated with upward social mobility among White Protestants; with a capitalist ideology for White and Negro Protestants; with voting Republican for Whites, Democratic for Negroes; with voting rates for all groups. Communal involvement was inversely related to mobility, especially for Catholics, and was related to voting Democratic among Catholics.

Regarding religious orientation, Lenski summarizes as follows:

> Repeatedly throughout this study we found that the orthodox and the devotional orientations are linked with differing and even opposing behavior patterns. In general, the orthodox orientation is associated with a compartmentalized outlook which separates and segregates religion from daily life. By contrast, the devotional orientation is linked with a unified Weltan-schauung, or view of life, with religious beliefs and practices being intergrated with other major aspects of daily life. In particular, the devotional orientation is linked with a humanitarian orientation (1963, p. 323).

(Notice the similarity between this distinction and Allport's extrinsic-intrinsic dichotomy.)

There are several problems with Lenski's scales. For example, they are dichotomous rather than continuous -- often, as in the case of orthodoxy, seeming arbitrarily divided. They are based only on a few questions, and though appropriate for inclusion in long interview schedules, need to be elaborated for intricate psychological studies of religiosity. Nevertheless, through their use Lenski demonstrated the importance of these dimensions of religiosity in explaining social attitudes and behavior; he concluded that religion is as important a variable as class, and thus increased interest in the study of religion within sociology.

These scales could be easily expanded, where appropriate, for use in future research.

Religious Orientation and Involvement

I. Types of Involvement:

A. Associational

    1. About how often, if ever, have you attended religious services in the
       last year?
            a) Once a week or more
            b) Two or three times a month
            c) Once a month
            d) A few times a year or less
            e) Never
    2. Do you take part in any of the activities or organizations of your
       church (synagogue, temple) other than attending services?
             (IF YES)
       How often have you done these things in the last year? (Use same
       responses categories as for #1 above.)

    Scoring: Lenski labelled "actively involved" all those who attended worship
        services every week, plus those who attended services two or three
        times a month and also some church related group at least once a month.
        All the others he called "marginal members."

B. Communal

    1. What is (was) your husband's (wife's) religious preference?

    2. Of those relatives you really feel close to, what proportion are
       (same religion as respondent)?
            a) All of them
            b) Nearly all of them
            c) More than half of them
            d) Less than half of them
            e) None of them
    3. Thinking of your closest friends, what proportion are (same religion
       as respondent)? (Use same response categories as for previous question.)

    Scoring: High communal involvement was inferred for all those who were
        married to someone of the same socio-religious group, and who also
        reported that all or nearly all of their close friends and relatives
        were of the same group. Low communal involvement was attributed to
        all the others.

II. Types of Religious Orientation

A. Doctrinal Orthodoxy

    1. Do you believe there is a God, or not?
    2. Do you think God is like a Heavenly Father who watches over you, or
       do you have some other belief?

3. Do you believe that God answers people's prayers, or not?
4. Do you believe in a life after death, or not? If so, do you also believe that in the next life some people will be punished and others rewarded by God, or not?
5. Do you believe that, when they are able, God expects people to worship Him in their churches and synagogues _every_ week, or not?
6. Do you believe that Jesus was God's only Son sent into the world by God to save sinful men, or do you believe that he was simply a very good man and teacher, or do you have some other belief?

Scoring: (It should be noted that Jews were not classified according to this scale.) Christians were classified as unorthodox unless they held all six beliefs.

B. Devotionalism

1. How often do you pray?

2. When you have decisions to make in your everyday life, do you ask yourself what God would want you to do -- often, sometimes, or never?

Scoring: Respondents were ranked high in devotionalism if (a) they reported praying more than once a day, plus asking what God would have them do either _often_ or _sometimes_ ; or if (b) they reported praying once a day, but _often_ asked what God would have them do.

RELIGIOUS ATTITUDE INVENTORY (Broen 1956)

Variable

Broen was interested in discovering whether there are important factors within the concept "religiosity." He found two such factors: "nearness to God" and "fundamentalism-humanitarianism." The Inventory to be described purportedly measures these two dimensions, as well as "general religiosity" and differential religious emphasis.

Description

The Inventory contains 58 agree-disagree statements to be Q-sorted. Thirty-two of the statements are scored for Factor I ("nearness to God") and 34 for Factor II ("fundamentalism-humanitarianism"). The 58 items were obtained from a factor analysis of 133 statements which had been Q-sorted into nine categories along an agree-disagree continuum. Some of these had been taken from earlier attitude scales (Romkin, 1938; Stone, 1933), some were devised by the author, and some were suggested by various religious persons. A pretest of 193 statements was made on six people holding different religious views, and 60 items placed by all six sorters in the same category were eliminated before the factor analysis since these were not expected to discriminate well in larger groups.

The final 58-item inventory was cross-validated on four religious groups having different belief systems. For this study, scores were determined by the number of statements under each factor with which the respondent agreed. The sum of scores for Factors I and II was used as an index of general religiosity and the difference as a measure of differential emphasis.

Sample

For performing the initial Q-sort, prior to factor analysis, Broen hypothesized five religious types and then obtained four persons from each of five religious groups "who were seen as being rather strong and 'pure' representatives of the desired religious orientations." A sixth group of four was made up of two Catholics and two Lutherans. All subjects were Christians. There were 16 females and eight males with an average age of 32.1 and an "above average" amount of education.

For the cross-validation study Broen used four groups: "27 persons from a Unitarian group with a largely humanistic attitudinal base; 17 persons from a more theistically oriented Unitarian church; 22 members of a Disciples of Christ Church choir; and 47 students from a strict, fundamentalistic, Lutheran academy."

Reliability

Ten to fourteen days after initial testing a second Q-sort was performed by a randomly sampled quarter of the original group of sorters. The test-retest correlation coefficient was .81.

Validity	Nothing beyond the procedure for elimination of items is offered as evidence for validity.
Location	Broen, W.E., Jr. A factor-analytic study of religious attitudes. Doctoral dissertation, University of Minnesota, 1956. Ann Arbor: University Microfilms, Inc., Pub. No. 17,839.
Administration	The Q-sort took 70 minutes on the average to complete, so it is estimated that the final inventory would take about 30 minutes. Scoring is accomplished by summing the number of endorsed statements within each factor. The key for Factor I is indicated by the circled answers given below. For Factor II the key is as follows: 2 - A, 4 - D, 6 - A, 8 - D, 10 - A, 12 - D, 14 - A, 16 - D, 18 - A, 20 - D, 22 - A, 24 - D, 26 - A, 28 - D, 30 - A, 32 - D, 34 - A, 36 - D, 38 - A, 39 - D, 41 - A, 42 - D, 44 - A, 45 - D, 47 - A, 49 - A, 51 - A, 52 - A, 53 - A, 54 - A, 55 - A, 56 - D, 57 - D, 58 - D.
Results and Comments	The factor-analysis of the original Q-sorting yielded two major factors, a unipolar "nearness to God" factor and a bipolar "fundamentalism-humanitarianism" factor, which correlated .32 with each other. Using scores on Factors I and II, plus their sum (a measure of general religiosity) and their difference (a measure of "positive"--worship, communion, guidance--versus "negative"--sin and punishment--emphasis of the person's beliefs), Broen tested thirteen hypotheses concerning scores on these measures for his four cross-validation groups. All were statistically significant (using the t-test), thus indicating the discriminatory power of the instrument.
	It remains to be seen how scores on this measure relate to other personality and social variables. Further validation is called for. Nevertheless, the items and factor scores appear to be useful at least for the particular Christian groups studies by Broen.
References	Romkin, F.S. The religious attitudes of college students: a comparative study. Doctoral dissertation, George Peabody Teachers College, 1938.
	Stone, S. A comparative study of religious attitudes of parents and children. Masters thesis, University of Minnesota, 1933.

RELIGIOUS ATTITUDE INVENTORY [a]

Directions: Circle the A if you agree with a statement; circle the D if you disagree with the statement. Make a choice for each statement. (We have found that people are able to answer all the items.) Do not spend too much time on any one statement.

Ⓐ D   1. God is constantly with us.

A D   2. Christ died for sinners.

A Ⓓ   3. The Ten Commandments were good for people of olden times but are really not applicable to modern life.

A D   4. There is really no such a place as Hell.

Ⓐ D   5. Miracles are performed by the power of God even today.

A D   6. It is through the righteousness of Jesus Christ and not because of our own works that we are made righteous before God.

A Ⓓ   7. Dancing is a sin.

A D   8. Christ's simple message of concern for your fellow man has been twisted by the superstitious mysticism of such men as Paul.

Ⓐ D   9. God can be approached directly by all believers.

A D 10. The death of Christ on the cross was necessary to blot out man's sin and make him acceptable in the eyes of God.

A Ⓓ 11. It was too bad that Christ died so young or He could have been a greater power for good.

A D 12. "God" is an abstract concept roughly equivalent to the concept "nature."

Ⓐ D 13. God exists in all of us.

A D 14. Man is born in sin.

A Ⓓ 15. The wearing of fashionable dress and worldly adornment should be discontinued because it tends to gratify and encourage pride.

A D 16. Man's essential nature is good.

Ⓐ D 17. I am sometimes very conscious of the presence of God.

A D 18. Man is by nature sinful and unclean.

A Ⓓ 19. All public places of amusement should be closed on Sunday.

A D 20. The stories of miracles in the Bible are like the parables in that they have some deeper meaning or moral but are not to be taken literally.

Ⓐ D 21. God is very real to me.

A D 22. The Bible is the word of God and must be believed in its entirety.

A Ⓓ 23. I believe in God but I am not sure what I believe about Him.

A D 24. Man has a spark of the divine in him which must be made to blossom more fully.

Ⓐ D 25. When in doubt it's best to stop and ask God what to do.

A D 26. Sin brings forth the wrath of God.

A Ⓓ 27. A person should follow his own conscience in deciding right and wrong.

A D 28. The most important idea in religion is the golden rule.

Ⓐ D 29. God should be asked about all important matters.

A D 30. The wrath of God is a terrible thing.

Reprinted with permission of Broen, W. E., Jr. Religious Attitude Inventory in "A Factor-Analytic Study of Religious Attitudes," doctoral dissertation, University of Minnesota, 1956. Copyright held by University Microfilms, Inc., Pub. No. 17,839.

A (D) 31. It is more important to love your neighbor than to keep the Ten Commandments.

A D 32. The scriptures should be interpreted with the constant exercise of reason.

(A) D 33. Because of His presence we can <u>know</u> that God exists.

A D 34. Everyone will be called before <u>God</u> at the judgment day to answer for his sins.

A (D) 35. Man's idea of God is quite vague.

A D 36. Reason is not depraved and untrustworthy for then the natural foundations of religion which rest upon it, would fall.

(A) D 37. Miracles are sometimes performed by persons in close communion with God.

A D 38. Everyone has sinned and deserves punishment for his sins.

A D 39. The church is important because it is an effective agency for organizing the social life of a community.

(A) D 40. My faith in God is complete for "though He slay me yet will I trust Him."

A D 41. No one should question the authority of the Bible.

A D 42. The content of various doctrines is unimportant. What really matters is that they help those who believe in them to lead better lives.

(A) D 43. When the scriptures are interpreted with reason they will be found to be consistent with themselves and with nature.

A D 44. Because of his terrible sinfulness, man has been eternally damned unless he accepts Christ as his savior.

A D 45. Religion is a search for understanding, truth, love and beauty in human life.

(A) D 46. True love of God is shown in obedience to His moral laws.

A D 47. Every person born into this world deserves God's wrath and damnation.

(A) D 48. If we live as pure lives as we can, God will forgive our sins.

A D 49. The world is full of condemned sinners.

(A) D 50. Persons who are in close contact with the Holy Spirit can, and do at times speak in unknown tongues.

(A) D 51. The Devil can enter a man's body and take control.

A (D) 52. The people of the world must repent before it is too late and they find themselves in Hell.

(A) D 53. No one who has experienced God like I have could doubt His existence.

A (D) 54. The Christian must lead a strict life, away from worldly amusements.

A (D) 55. In his natural state of sin, man is too evil to communicate with God.

A (D) 56. Christ was not divine but his teachings and the example set by his life are invaluable.

A (D) 57. The question of Christ's divinity is unimportant; it is his teachings that matter.

(A) D 58. God is the final judge of our behavior but I do not believe that He is as punishing as some seem to say He is.

[a]Answers for Factor I are circled; answers for Factor II are listed above (see Administration).

CHURCH - SECT SCALE (Dynes 1955)

Variable
This scale was designed to operationalize the distinction, introduced by Max Weber and elaborated by Ernst Troeltsch, between Church and Sect. As defined by Dynes: "The construct of the Church has generally signified a type of religious organization which accepts the social order and integrates existing cultural definitions into its religious ideology. The Sect, as a contrasting type, rejects integration with the social order and develops a separate subculture, stressing rather rigid behavioral requirements for its members".

Description
A pool of 35 Likert-type items was pretested on 55 members of a large Protestant church in Columbus, Ohio. An item analysis was performed in which only items that discriminated significantly between upper and lower quartiles were retained. There were 24 of these, which comprise the final scale. Each is rated on a five-point, agree-disagree scale. A score of 1 is assigned for a Sect response, and a 5 for a Church response. Total score is simply the sum of these numbers over all 24 items; low totals indicate acceptance of the Sect form of religious organization and high totals indicate acceptance of the Church form.

Sample
Two samples were obtained. The pretest sample included 55 members of a large, urban Protestant church (mentioned above). A second sample included 360 Protestants from the same city (Columbus, Ohio)---an estimated 53% of the number contacted by mail after drawing names randomly from the City Directory.

Reliability
A corrected split-half coefficient of .92 was obtained for the first sample, and of .82 for the second sample.

Validity
Ten sociologists of varying religious backgrounds judged the items according to the Church-Sect distinction. There was a mean agreement of 98%.

Dynes also offered evidence for the scale's ability to distinguish validly between groups. Episcopalians and Presbyterians ("Church" organizations) were compared with members of several Sectarian groups: Holiness, Pentecostal, Church of God, Church of the Nazarene and Baptist. Mean scale scores for these two sets of respondents were significantly different in the expected direction:

Criterion Group	N	Mean	S.D.	Critical Ratio	P
"Church" members	62	76.1	10.7	10.6	.001
"Sect" members	53	51.8	13.4		

Location   Dynes, R. Church-Sect typology and socio-economic status. <u>Ameri-can Sociological Review</u>, 1955, <u>20</u>, 555-560.

Administration   This scale is self-administered and would take about 15 minutes to complete.

Results and   Using three different measures of socio-economic status, Dynes
Comments   found that "Churchness" is associated with high status and "Sect-ness" with low status. The relationship was almost perfectly monotonic in all cases. One of the SES indicators was education, so it can also be said that "Churchness" is correlated with level of education. This is not just a matter of denominational doctrine, because the relationship holds even when denomination is held constant.

In a later article, Dynes (1957) reported further results from the same research showing that for Sectarians religious groups supplied their most meaningful associations and sources of friendship. "This was indicated by the fact that he attends church more often, belongs to more subgroups within an undifferentiated organization, states almost unanimously that he derives more satisfaction from these religious associations as contrasted with 'secular' groups, and draws most of his close friends from within his religious groups."

Further discussion of the Church-Sect distinction can be found in several articles (by Gustafson, Goode, Demerath, and Eister, respectively) appearing in the Spring 1967 issue of the <u>Journal for the Scientific Study of Religion</u>; see the section entitled "Reappraisal of the Church-Sect Typology."

References   Dynes, R. The consequences of sectarianism for social participation. <u>Social Forces</u>, 1957, <u>35</u>, 331-334.

"Reappraisal of the Church-Sect Typology":

     Gustafson, P. UO-US-PS-PO: A restatement of Troeltsch's Church-Sect typology. Pp. 64-68.

     Goode, E. Some critical observations on the Church-Sect dimension. Pp. 69-77.

     Demerath, N., III. Comment: In a sow's ear. Pp. 77-84.

     Eister, A. Comment: Toward a radical critique of Church-Sect typologizing. Pp. 85-90.

     All in <u>Journal for the Scientific Study of Religion</u>, 1967, <u>6</u>, 64-90.

CHURCH - SECT SCALE

In the scale, when an item stated a Sectarian trait, Strongly Agree was scored as one. When the item stated a Church trait, the scoring was reversed and Strongly Agree was scored as five. The items representing a Church trait are indicated by an asterisk.

1. I think a minister should preach without expecting to get paid for it.   Strongly agree   Agree   ?   Disagree   Strongly disagree

2. I think it is more important to live a good life now than to bother about life after death.*

3. I think a person who is not willing to follow all the rules of the church should not be allowed to belong.

4. Testifying about one's religious experience should be a part of regular church services.

5. I feel that a congregation should encourage the minister during his sermon by saying amen.

6. I think that we should emphasize education in religion and not conversion.*

7. I think that there is practically no difference between what the different Protestant churches believe.*

8. I think a person should make a testimony about his religion before he joins a church.

9. In church, I would rather sing the hymns myself than hear the choir sing.

10. I think being a success in one's job is one mark of a good Christian.*

11. A minister who is "called" is better than one who is "trained."

12. I like the "old-time" religion.

13. I think churches should have more revivals.

14. I think it would be wrong for a church member to have a job as a bartender.

15. I think a person should feel his religion before he joins a church.

16. I like to sing the old gospel songs rather than the new hymns.

17. I don't believe churches do enough about saving souls.

Reprinted with permission of Dynes, R. Church-Sect Scale in "Church-Sect Typology and Socio-Economic Status," *American Sociological Review*, 20 (1955), pp 555-560. Copyright 1955 by the American Sociological Association, 1001 Connecticut Ave., N.W., Washington, D.C. 20036.

18. Heaven and Hell are very real to me.

19. All the miracles in the Bible are true.

20. Children should not become members of the church until they are old enough to understand about it.*

21. I think it is more important to go to church than to be active in politics.

22. I wish ministers would preach more on the Bible and less on politics.

23. I think it is more serious to break God's law than to break man's law.

24. I think every family should have family prayers or say grace before meals.

RELIGIOUS FUNDAMENTALISM SCALE (Martin and Westie 1959)

Variable
: This scale measures religious fundamentalism among Christians -- a construct similar to "orthodoxy" as conceived by other researchers discussed in this chapter.

Description
: In a study of prejudice toward Negroes, Martin and Westie (1959) attempted to characterize the "tolerant personality" -- one who is neither extremely negative nor extremely positive in his attitudes. Tolerance was assessed with Westie's (1953) Summated Difference Scales; two groups were selected from 429 initial respondents -- 41 who were relatively neutral (tolerant) and 59 who were conspicuously prejudiced against Negroes. These groups were then compared on several other dimensions, including religious fundamentalism.

: The scale used to measure fundamentalism contained nine items, each scored along a five-point agree-disagree continuum of the Likert sort. Scoring was accomplished simply by summing item scores across the nine items.

Sample
: The sampling universe for this study was all "white adults (21 years of age or older) residing within the city limits of Indianapolis in blocks containing no Negro residents." From 429 initial respondents who completed a short prognostic scale (used to avoid detailed interviews of too many prejudiced respondents), 41 qualified as "tolerant" and 59 were chosen who had high prejudice scores.

Reliability
: No information given.

Validity
: Scores on the fundamentalism measure differentiated significantly ($p < .005$) between the tolerant and prejudiced respondents. Moreover, fundamentalism correlated .56 with authoritarianism, .32 with intolerance of ambiguity, and .41 with nationalism (all significant at the .05 level) among the tolerant respondents.

Location
: Martin, J. and Westie, F. The tolerant personality. American Sociological Review, 1959, 24, 521-528.

Administration
: This scale would require only about six minutes to complete.

Results and Comments
: In line with other findings in studies relating orthodoxy with intolerance, Martin and Westie found a strong relationship between Christian fundamentalism and bigotry. It should also be noted, however, that no such relationship was found between intolerance and frequency of church attendance, praying, Bible reading, and percentage of income contributed to one's religious group -- all usually associated with sect membership. This pattern of results suggests a cognitive style interpretation, one

in which cognitive rigidity, intolerance of ambiguity, strict
adherence to church dogma, and separation between in-group and out-
group members are all dynamically related.

The Religious Fundamentalism Scale seems to be a good short measure of religious conservatism, but it warrents careful investigation of content. Some of the items -- e.g., "If more people
in this country would turn to Christ we would have a lot less
crime and corruption" -- may be linked to other conservative
attitudes because of specific content. Items using phrases such
as "crime and punishment," "simply a myth," or "are fictitious
and mythical" may reflect dogmatism.

Reference   Westie, F. A technique for the measurement of race attitudes. *American
Sociological Review*, 1953, 18, 73-78.

FUNDAMENTALISM SCALE

1. SA A U D SD The Bible is the inspired word of God.

2. SA A U D SD The religious idea of heaven is not much more than superstition.

3. SA A U D SD Christ was a mortal, historical person, but not a supernatural or divine being.

4. SA A U D SD Christ is a divine being, the Son of God.

5. SA A U D SD The stories in the Bible about Christ healing sick and lame persons by His touch are fictitious and mythical.

6. SA A U D SD Someday Christ will return.

7. SA A U D SD The idea of life after death is simply a myth.

8. SA A U D SD If more of the people in this country would turn to Christ we would have a lot less crime and corruption.

9. SA A U D SD Since Christ brought the dead to life, He gave eternal life to all who have faith.

NOTE: Items 1, 4, 6, 8 and 9 are "positive" for scoring purposes, whereas 2, 3, 5, and 7 are "negative" items. Suggested scoring procedure: +2, +1, 0, -1, -2.

Reprinted with permission of Martin, J. and Westie, F. Religious Fundamentalism Scale in "The Tolerant Personality," *American Sociological Review,* 24 (1959), pp 521-528. Copyright 1959 by the American Sociological Association, 1001 Connecticut Ave., N.W., Washington, D.C. 20036.

CERTAINTY IN RELIGIOUS BELIEF SCALE (Thouless 1935)

Variable   This scale was designed to determine the certainty with which various religious beliefs are held.

Description   The scale includes forty statements, twenty-five of which are religious, eight are neutral, non-religious factual statements and the remaining are political and vague statements condensed from complex propositional wholes. The respondents were asked to answer on a six point Likert-type scale from "complete certainty" to "complete uncertainty" with scores from +3 to -3. The average degree of certainty was determined by summing the scores on the items (disregarding signs) and dividing by the number of items. The possible range was therefore from 0 to 3.

The respondents were asked to read each statement carefully and to mark the degree of certainty with which they hold the belief (on the continuum: complete certainty, strong conviction of certainty, low degree of conviction of certainty, low degree of conviction of uncertainty, strong conviction of uncertainty, complete uncertainty.)

Sample   The sample was made up of 93 men and 45 women students at the University of Glasgow.

Reliability   No measure of reliability was given.

Validity   No measure of validity was given.

Location   Thouless, R. The tendency to certainty in religious belief, British Journal of Psychology, 1935-36, 26, 16-31.

Administration The scale is self-administered and should take about twenty minutes to complete.

Results and   The absence of reliability and validity information, while not
Comments   of great importance for the author's immediate work, hampers the further use of the scale. Also, the non-religious questions would have to be changed for a non-British population. While the question of certainty of belief is important, it represents only one aspect of religiosity, and other measures would have to be constructed to tap other dimensions. The Brown questionnaire (the next scale in this chapter) contains further information on reliability and for dimensions related to scores on a modified Thouless scale.

THE 'BELIEFS' TEST

1. There is a personal God.
2. Jesus Christ was God the Son.
3. There are spiritual realities of some kind.
4. The world was created by God.
5. There is a personal Devil.
6. Matter is the sole reality.
7. There is a God who is all-powerful.
8. There is a God who is altogether good.
9. There are such spiritual beings as angels.
10. Jonah was swallowed by a great fish and afterwards emerged alive.
11. Man has been evolved from lower forms of life.
12. There is an impersonal God.
13. Evil is a reality.
14. The spirits of human beings continue to exist after the death of their bodies.
15. Religion is the opium of the people.
16. There is no God (personal or impersonal).
17. The universe is expanding.
18. Attendance at church is a better way of spending Sunday than taking a walk in the country.
19. Moses was the author of the first five books of the Bible.
20. Christianity is a better religion than Buddhism.
21. The Bible is literally true in all its parts.
22. Man is, in some degree, responsible for his actions.
23. There is a Hell in which the wicked will be everlastingly punished.
24. The spirits of persons who have died can sometimes communicate with the living.
25. Right will triumph.
26. Belief in evolution is compatible with belief in a Creator.
27. Hardship strengthens character.
28. Mary, Queen of Scots, was beheaded between 1580 and 1590.
29. Everything is relative.
30. Tigers are found in parts of China.
31. Hornets live in nests under the ground.
32. Sex is evil.
33. Light travels to us from the sun in less than one minute.
34. Bacon was the author of the plays attributed to Shakespeare.
35. Green is a primary colour.
36. Sunlight is good for human health.
37. Members of the leisured class are supported by the 'surplus value' created by the workers.
38. Tariffs improve trade.
39. India has, on the whole, benefited from British rule.
40. The total national debt of Great Britain is more than a thousand million pounds.

RELIGIOSITY QUESTIONNAIRE (Brown 1962)

Variable   This questionnaire was designed to study functional relation-
                    ships between religious beliefs and other psychological vari-
                    ables.

Description   The questionnaire comprised several parts. The heart of the
                    religiosity measure was a modified version of the Thouless scale
                    for studying certainty of religious beliefs (the previous scale
                    in the present chapter). Eight new items were added, and the
                    whole set of items was then broken into categories by ten judges.
                    Eighty percent agreement was required. The resulting categories
                    were beliefs about Christ and God, other orthodox Christian
                    beliefs, general religious beliefs, opinions, facts, and mis-
                    cellaneous items. Respondents judged these items on a six-point
                    Likert scale of certainty: from "complete certainty that the
                    belief is true" (scored +3) to "complete certainty that the be-
                    lief is false" (scored -3).

                    The scoring categories were later renumbered 1 to 8 and the
                    score for each subpart of the scale was determined by computing
                    the mean of the score values for that area.

                    Several other attitude and personality measures were also in-
                    cluded in the Brown study, including a scale to measure atti-
                    tudes toward the institutional church (Jeeves, 1959), Eysenck's
                    (1958) neuroticism and extraversion scales, the Taylor (1953)
                    manifest anxiety scale, a ten-item F scale, a modified version
                    of previous humanitarianism scales, and the MMPI Lie Scale.
                    Only the religion items used are reproduced below.

Sample   The sample included 203 first year psychology students from the
                    University of Adelaide, having a mean age of 22 years. Nineteen
                    were Roman Catholics, 56 were members of the Church of England,
                    40 were Methodists; 45 were classed as members of "non-conformist"
                    groups (e.g., Presbyterian and Baptist), 18 as "miscellaneous,"
                    and 25 labelled themselves atheists or "nothing."

Reliability   Test-retest measures of reliability were obtained from 40 sub-
                    jects over an eight month interval. For each of the separate
                    categories these were as follows: orthodox beliefs .85, gen-
                    eral religious beliefs .92, opinions .35, facts .30, mis-
                    cellaneous .50, institutionalization .53, and individualism .60.

Validity   No evidence for validity was reported.

Location   Brown, L.B. A study of religious belief. British Journal of
                    Psychology, 1962, 53, 259-272.

Administration   The questionnaire is self-administered and should take about half
                    an hour to complete.

Results and Comments

A factor analysis was performed on all scores from the personality and religious belief scales, yielding two major factors: a religious belief factor (accounting for 43% of the variance) and a neuroticism or anxiety factor (accounting for 15% of the variance). The principal loadings were as follows:

Religious belief:

Orthodox Christian belief	+ .894
General religious belief	+ .812
Institutionalization	+ .656
Authoritarianism	+ .598
Individualism	- .278
Age	- .365
Denomination	- .581

Neuroticism or anxiety:

Manifest Anxiety	+ .725
Neuroticism	+ .704
Opinion Strength	+ .500
Factual certainty	+ .399
Miscellaneous items	+ .285
Individualism	+ .376
Lie Score	- .312
Age	- .337

The results indicated that religious certainty is independent of certainty about factual and opinionative matters (at least for those included), and that anxiety is associated with certainty only on matters of opinion. It was found that untestable religious statements, e.g., regarding the existence of "such spiritual beings as angels," were held _more_ strongly than factual ones.

It is doubtful whether the religious certainty scale used here is a great improvement over Thouless' original scale. However, because of its promising reliability and interesting association with other variables included in Brown's study, it is considered worth further exploration, especially directed toward ascertaining its validity.

References

Eysenck, H.J. A short questionnaire for the measurement of two dimensions of personality. _Journal of Applied Psychology_, 1958, _42_, 14-17.

Jeeves, M.A. Contribution on prejudice and religion in symposium on problems of religious psychology. _Proceedings of the 15th International Congress of Psychology, Brussels_. Amsterdam: North Holland Publishing Company, 1959, 508-509.

Taylor, J.A. A personality scale of manifest anxiety. _Journal of Abnormal and Social Psychology_, 1953, _48_, 285-290.

Thouless, R.H. The tendency to certainty in religious belief. British Journal of Psychology, 1935, 26, 16-31.

For a later study with similar conclusions, using a wider variety of personality measures, see

Brown, L.B. The structure of religious belief. Journal for the Scientific Study of Religion, 1966, 5, 259-272.

STUDY OF RELIGIOUS BELIEF

Institutionalization

1. The Church is necessary to establish and preserve concepts of right and wrong.
2. Every person needs to have the feeling of security given by a church.
3. For the vast majority of people, in order to live a truly religious life the Church or some such other organized religious body is an essential.
4. The aim of missionaries should be to establish church buildings where religious services and ceremonies can be conducted.

Individualism

1. A man ought to be guided by what his own experience tells him is right rather than by what any institution, such as the Church, tells him to do.
2. It is more important for an individual to understand the principles of his personal faith than to have a detailed knowledge of his own denomination.
3. Private devotions are more important in the religious life of a person than is attendance at public church services.
4. True Christianity is seen in the lives of individual men and women rather than in the activities of the Church.

Beliefs about Christ

1. (2)*Jesus Christ was God the Son.
2. Jesus changed water into wine.
3. Jesus Christ was born of a Virgin.
4. Jesus walked upon the water while his disciples waited for him in their boat.

Beliefs about God

1. (1) There is a personal God.
2. (4) The world was created by God.
3. (7) There is a God who is all-powerful.
4. (8) There is a God who is altogether good.
5. God made man out of dust and breathed life into him.
6. (16) There is no God (personal or impersonal). (with scoring reversed)

Other Orthodox Christian Beliefs

1. (3) There are spiritual realities of some kind.
2. (5) There is a personal Devil.
3. (13) Evil is a reality.
4. (14) The spirits of human beings continue to exist after the death of their bodies.
5. (18) Attendance at church is a better way of spending Sunday than taking a walk in the country.

Reprinted with permission of Brown, L.B. Religiosity Scale in *British Journal of Psychology*, 53 (1962), pp 259-272.

688

General Religious Belief

1. (6) Matter is the sole reality. (with scoring reversed)
2. (9) There are such spiritual beings as angels.
3. (10) Jonah was swallowed by a great fish and afterwards emerged alive.
4. (20) Christianity is a better religion than Buddhism.
5. (21) The Bible is literally true in all its parts.
6. (23) There is a Hell in which the wicked will be everlastingly punished.
7. (25) Right will triumph.
8. There is no life after death. (with scoring reversed)

* Item number in the original Thouless scale.

INVENTORY OF RELIGIOUS BELIEF

(Brown and Lowe 1951)

Variable	This scale was designed to measure the degree of acceptance or rejection of Christian dogma.
Description	The scale is made up of fifteen statements which are answered on a five point Likert scale from strongly agree to strongly disagree. Eight of the statements (2, 3, 6, 7, 9, 11, 12, and 15) were positively scored and seven (1, 4, 5, 8, 10, 13, and 14) had reverse scoring (a high score for disagreement rather than agreement). The total score was obtained by summing the item weights and had a possible range of 15 (strongest non-belief) to 75 (strongest belief). An original list of 25 statements was evaluated by 60 undergraduates at the University of Denver and the dean of a Bible college. Ten items were eliminated because they were ambiguous or overlapping.
Subjects	The questionnaire was administered to 887 male and female students enrolled in lower division liberal arts courses at the University of Denver, spring quarter 1948. There were 622 Protestant, 166 Catholic, 68 Jewish, 9 Moslem, and 22 unclassified respondents. The sample was approximately 21% female and 79% male, representative of that college's population.
Reliability	A split-half measure of reliability obtained from a random sample of 100 of the first three hundred to take the questionnaire yielded a value of $.77 \pm .04$. Applying the Spearman-Brown formula this yielded a value of .87 for the total scale.
Validity	As a measure of concurrent validity the scale was given to 35 Bible college students and 21 students at a liberal theological seminary. As predicted, the Bible college students scored much higher (mean 73.77) than the liberal theological school students (mean 48.60).
Location	Brown, D. and Lowe, W. Religious beliefs and personality characteristics of college students. Journal of Social Psychology, 1951, 33. 103-129.
Administration	The scale is self-administered and would take approximately ten minutes to complete.
Results and Comments	The authors confirmed a number of predicted relationships. Conservatism decreased as years in college increased, etc. They also found that the less conservative students were in general more intelligent than the more conservative group. Correlations with other personality scales were also reported.
	This scale seems to be a fairly valid and reliable measure to determine the attitude of a person toward Christian dogma. The

sample is obviously biased but the questions are worded simply
enough that the scale could be administered to persons with
much less education. The reliability and validity measures
are encouraging, as are its differentiating powers across religious denominations (as reported in the article). All in
all this seems to be a promising scale although limited in its
scope since it does not evaluate attitudes toward the church
as an institution or tap other dimensions of religiosity.

Inventory of Religious Belief

This is a study of religious belief. Below are fifteen items which are to be answered in the following manner:

Place a line under <u>Strongly</u> <u>agree</u> if you agree strongly with the statement.
Place a line under <u>Agree</u> if you agree with the statement.
Place a line under <u>Not</u> <u>sure</u> if you are in doubt as to whether you agree or disagree with the statement.
Place a line under <u>Disagree</u> if you disagree with the statement.
Place a line under <u>Strongly</u> <u>Disagree</u> if you disagree strongly with the statement.
Remember to read each statement carefully, and mark only one answer for each item.
People differ widely in their beliefs: please indicate your own in the manner described.

1. It makes no difference whether one is a Christian or not as long as one has good will for others.
   Strongly agree   Agree   Not sure   Disagree   Strongly disagree

2. I believe the Bible is the inspired Word of God.

3. God created man separate and distinct from animals.

4. The idea of God is unnecessary in our enlightened age.

5. There is no life after death.

6. I believe Jesus was born of a Virgin.

7. God exists as: Father, Son and Holy Spirit.

8. The Bible is full of errors, misconceptions and contradictions.

9. The Gospel of Christ is the only way for mankind to be saved.

10. I think there have been many men in history just as great as Jesus.

11. I believe there is a heaven and a hell.

12. Eternal life is the gift of God only to those who believe in Jesus Christ as Savior and Lord.

Reprinted with permission of Brown, D. and Lowe, W. Inventory of Religious Belief, in "Religious Beliefs and Personality Characteristics of College Students," *Journal of Social Psychology,* 33 (1951), pp 103-129. Copyright 1951 by The Journal Press.

13. I think a person can be happy and enjoy life without believing in God.

14. In many ways the Bible has held back and retarded human progress.

15. I believe in the personal, visible return of Christ to the earth.

RELIGIOUS ATTITUDE SCALE (Poppleton and Pilkington 1963)

Variable — This scale was designed to measure the "religious attitudes" of British college students. The authors were motivated in part by the results of American studies in the 1930's using Thurstone scales.

Description — A sample of 156 statements concerning religious beliefs was collected from students and faculty at the University of Sheffield. Using the Thurstone method, two parallel forms of a scale were developed, each containing 22 statements. These two forms were then administered to a sample of 121 students and staff members of the university; half received form A first, half received B first. Each group received the alternate form three weeks later.

Responses were made according to a five-point Likert scale (strongly agree to strongly disagree). An item analysis suggested by Likert resulted in the elimination of 23 items. Response category weights were determined using a method proposed by Guilford. The final scale therefore contained 21 items, each with appropriate category weights. (These are given with the scale items below.) Scores range from 40 (anti-religious) to 136 (pro-religious).

Sample — For their final study, the authors chose a proportionate, stratified random sample of the entire student body of the University of Sheffield. This yielded a mailing sample of 500; 463 completed questionnaires were returned (92.6%).

Reliability/Homogeneity — The scale was split into three equal parts and intercorrelations were computed. Corrected for length, these were $r_{12} = .95$, $r_{13} = .96$, and $r_{23} = .97$. Using Cronbach's formula for the coefficient alpha, a value of $\alpha = .97$ was obtained.

Validity — In order to determine concurrent validity, the sample was divided into three groups as follows: 1) a low religious group, made up of those claiming to be atheists or agnostics on a background data questionnaire; 2) a highly participative religious group - those people who attended church frequently, prayed at least weekly, and were active church members (again assessed by questionnaire); 3) the remainder of the sample - those who failed to meet either set of criteria. The high and low groups differed significantly, with the pro-religious group (N = 107) obtaining a median score of 116, and the anti-religious group (N = 109) a score of 60. There was no overlap between the two groups.

Location — Poppleton, Pamela and Pilkington, G. The measurement of religious attitudes in a university population, British Journal of Social and Clinical Psychology, 1963, 2, 20-36.

Administration — The scale is self-administered and should require approximately fifteen minutes to complete.

694

Results and
Comments
In general the results are quite similar to those usually found
in the United States. For example, there is a significant decline in religious belief among students in the Arts and Pure
Science during early years at the University, but the decline
continues only for the scientists (especially for those later
engaging in research); women tended to be more religious than
men; Catholics and members of small sects scored higher than
members of other denominations.

The scale appears to be an adequate measure of general religious
beliefs, yielding acceptable reliability indexes and appropriate
discrimination between groups. The items are simply worded and
could probably be understood by everyone beyond the high school
educational level. As with most scales of religiosity, this
one taps only what Glock and Stark call the ideological or
belief dimension; it does not ask about religious experiences
or the consequences of faith in the respondent's everyday life.

RELIGIOUS ATTITUDE SCALE

Below are 21 statements which concern religious beliefs. Please indicate the extent to which you agree or disagree with each of them.
On the right-hand side of the page you will find five alternative answers. Place a cross opposite each statement in the column which best
represents your opinion. For example:

	Strongly Agree	Agree	Uncertain	Disagree	Strongly Disagree
More time in broadcasting should be alloted to agnostic speakers.				X	

Please do not leave out any statements even if you find it difficult to
make up your mind.

	Strongly Agree	Agree	Uncertain	Disagree	Strongly Disagree
1. To lead a good life it is necessary to have some religious belief. (3.15)	6	6	5	4	2
2. Jesus Christ was an important and interesting historical figure, but in no way divine. (9.84)	2	2	2	5	7
3. I genuinely do not know whether or not God exists. (5.59)	2	2	4	6	6
4. People without religious beliefs can lead just as moral and useful lives as people with religious beliefs. (6.90)	2	4	5	6	6
5. Religious faith is merely another name for belief which is contrary to reason. (10.05)	2	2	4	5	7
6. The existence of disease, famine and strife in the world makes one doubt some religious doctrines. (7.43)	?	2	4	6	6
7. The miracles recorded in the Bible really happened.	6	6	4	2	2
8. It makes no difference to me whether religious beliefs are true or false. (6.20)	3	3	3	4	5

Reprinted with permission of Poppleton, P. and Pilkington, G. Religious Attitude Scale in "The
Measurement of Religious Attitudes in a University Population," *British Journal of Social and Clinical
Psychology*, 2 (1963), pp 20-36.

	Strongly Agree	Agree	Uncertain	Disagree	Strongly Disagree
9. Christ atoned for our sins by His sacrifice on the cross. (0.62)	7	6	4	2	1
10. The truth of the Bible diminishes with the advance of science. (9.00)	2	2	3	6	6
11. Without belief in God life is meaningless. (0.73)	7	6	4	2	1
12. The more scientific discoveries are made the more the glory of God is revealed. (1.47)	6	6	3	2	2
13. Religious education is essential to preserve the morals of our society. (2.64)	6	5	4	2	2
14. The proof that Christ was the Son of God lies in the record of the Gospels. (1.53)	6	6	3	2	2
15. The best explanation of miracles is as an exaggeration of ordinary events into myths and legends. (8.71)	2	2	4	6	6
16. International peace depends on the world-wide adoption of religion. (2.06)	6	6	5	3	2
17. If you lead a good and decent life it is not necessary to go to church. (7.33)	2	3	4	6	6
18. Parents have a duty to teach elementary Christian truths to their children. (2.70)	6	5	3	2	2
19. There is no survival of any kind after death. (10.37)	1	1	2	5	7
20. The psychiatrist rather than the theologian can best explain the phenomena of religious experience. (8.88)	2	2	3	6	6
21. On the whole, religious beliefs make for better and happier living. (3.32)	6	5	3	2	2

The numbers in parentheses after each statement refer to the Thurstone scale values of the items. Values range from 0-11. Low values indicate pro-religious and high values antireligious attitudes.

Weights are indicated by the numbers in the ruled columns.

EXTRINSIC RELIGIOUS VALUES SCALE   (Wilson 1960)

Variable   This scale was designed to measure the motivation of an individual for af-
                filiating with a religious institution; in particular, to tap what All-
                port (1954) has called <u>extrinsic</u> motivation. According to Allport, the
                usual finding of a relationship between religiosity and prejudice is at-
                tributable to persons with extrinsic religious values.

Description   The instrument contains a total of 15 dichotomous items which may be
                classified in two groups:

                    a) statements reflecting "an allegiance to, and dependence upon, the
                       external or institutional structure of a church", and

                    b) statements reflecting "a utilitarian orientation toward religion,
                       i.e., acceptance of religion as a means."

                (These two categories come from Allport's conception of extrinsic motiva-
                tion.) For each item one response alternative reflects an "extrinsic"
                religious orientation, the other reflects "absence of extrinsic religious
                value." Total score is simply the sum of extrinsic responses (those with
                asterisks in the listing below).

                Wilson administered his scale (ERV), along with Levinson's Religious Con-
                ventionalsim Scale (RC), a 12-item version of the California Anti-Semitism
                Scale (AS), and several filler items, to the several small, homogeneous
                groups (N=207 in all), described under "sample" below. The results are
                presented in the following table:

Group	N	Scale Re-liability[a]	ERV		RC		AS		Correlations[c]		
			Mean	SD	Mean	SD	Mean	SD	ERV-AS	RC-AS	ERV-RC
1	15	.80	7.0	3.0	68.1	9.6	48.0	21.8	.65**	.39	.51*
2	22	.82	6.3	2.0	--	--[b]	36.0	12.5	.66***	--[b]	--[b]
3	22	.72	7.3	2.0	64.5	10.1	44.3	11.9	.56**	.08	.08
4	35	.85	7.5	2.6	60.5	9.5	47.7	15.9	.68***	.29	.20
5	10	.81	5.2	1.8	--	--[b]	35.0	11.2	.68*	--[b]	--[b]
6	26	.85	5.0	1.9	52.5	17.7	33.2	12.7	.71***	.41*	.17
7	11	.86	7.9	2.3	--	--[b]	51.6	15.1	.72*	--[b]	--[b]
8	15	.82	9.2	2.5	69.0	8.4	41.0	10.8	.64**	.31	.23
9	23	.57	6.6	1.7	78.2	6.3	40.8	10.7	.41*	.30	.40*
10	28	.51	6.1	1.7	75.9	5.5	36.0	9.1	.43*	.42*	.57**

Note: The following abbreviations are used in the column headings: ERV,
        Extrinsic Religious Values Scale; RC, Religious Conventionalism Scale;
        and AS, Anti-Semitism Scale.

[a] Corrected equivalent halves.
[b] The Religious Conventionalism Scale was not administered to this sample.
[c] All correlations are by rank-difference method
* P < .05;   ** P < .01;   *** P < .001

Sample	Numbered to correspond with the above table, the groups were as follows:

1., 2., 3., 4. Adult members of four different Congregational Christian churches in the metropolitan Boston area (N = 15, 22, 22, and 35 respectively);

5. Members of a young adult organization in a Methodist church in the Boston area (N = 10);

6. Harvard-Radcliffe students of various Christian denominations who reported attending services regularly (N = 26);

7. Adult members of a Disciples of Christ church in North Carolina (N = 11);

8. Adult members of the choir of a Negro Baptist church in the Boston area (N = 15);

9. Sophomore students in a Catholic girls college in the Boston area (N = 23);

10. Catholic graduate students in the Boston area (N = 28).

Reliability	Corrected split-half reliability coefficients are given in the table. These are low for Catholics because approximately one-fourth of the items, which refer to matters on which the church has a doctrinal position, did not differentiate among Catholics.
Validity	The face validity of the scale was presumably boosted by the contribution of Allport to its formulation (acknowledged in a footnote). Concurrent validity and an indication of construct validity are reported in the table. Correlations between Wilson's ERV and anti-Semitism (AS) ranged from .41 to .72, adding support to the prediction that extrinsically religious people are more prejudiced. Correlations with Levinson's Religious Conventionalism Scale (RC) were much lower on the average, suggesting that conventionalism and extrinsic motivation--although both correlates of prejudice--are not identical. In Wilson's study, the ERV scale accounted for about twice as much of the variance in prejudice (AS) as did the RC scale for the five Protestant groups that responded to all three scales.
Location	Wilson, W.C. Extrinsic religious values and prejudice. _Journal of Abnormal and Social Psychology_, 1960, _60_, 286-288.
Administration	The ERV scale is self-administered and, since it took about half an hour to complete Wilson's entire 50 item questionnaire in this study, it should require about 10 minutes to complete the ERV.
Results and Comments	The ERV scale is interesting not only because it has promising reliability and validity, but also because it represents an attempt to operationalize part of Allport's frequently cited explanation of the contradictory findings relating religiosity and prejudice. But the scale needs further work, especially before it can be used fruitfully for Catholic samples. See the following scale in this chapter for one attempt to improve Wilson's measure.

References: Allport, G.W. The nature of prejudice. Cambridge: Addison-Wesley, 1954.

Levinson, D.J. The intergroup relations workshop: its psychological aims and effects. Journal of Psychology, 1954, 38, 103-126.

For a more recent validation study employing the Edwards Personal Preference Schedule as a measure of personality, see the following:

Tisdale , J.R. Selected Correlates of Extrinsic Religious Values. Paper presented to the American Psychological Association Annual Convention. Chicago, 1965.

EXTRINSIC RELIGIOUS VALUES SCALE

Below are some statements about religion. Each has two possible endings. Will you please read each of these statements and mark an X beside the ending which <u>best</u> fits <u>your</u> feelings about the statement. It may be hard to decide which ending to choose for some of the statements and you may want to mark both, but <u>please</u> <u>mark</u> <u>only</u> <u>one</u> <u>ending</u> for each statement, selecting the one that you most nearly agree with. There are no "right" or "wrong" choices and there will be many religious people who will select each possible ending to the statements.

1. When saying the Lord's Prayer in unison at church my mind is more likely to be on

   _____*_____ the fact that many of us are saying the same prayer.
   _____ the meaning of the prayer for me personally.

2. Religion helps to keep my life balanced and steady in much the same way as my citizenship, friendships and other memberships do.

   _____*_____ I agree.
   _____ I disagree.

3. A person who does not belong to some church must at heart feel very insecure.

   _____*_____ I think this is almost certainly a true statement.
   _____ I think this statement is not necessarily true.

4. The principal reason I am a member of the church is that it gives me a deep feeling of security in this troubled world.

   _____*_____ Yes, this is true.
   _____ No, I do not agree.

5. Without the church mankind would have no concepts of right and wrong.

   _____*_____ I agree.
   _____ I disagree.

6. While the church serves me in a good many ways, on the whole it seems especially important to me personally because:

   _____ it gives me an opportunity to find myself and express my aspirations.
   _____*_____ it teaches, guides and protects me.

7. The religious concept of "Brotherhood of Man" probably refers to:

   _____ a unity of all people regardless of who they are or what they believe
   _____*_____ a unity of believers in the faith.

8. One reason for my being a church member is that such a membership helps to establish a person firmly in the community.

    ____*____ Yes, this is one reason.
    _____ This reason does not apply to me.

9. Prayer is, above all else, a means of obtaining needed benefits, protection, and safety in a dangerous world.

    ____*____ On the whole, I agree.
    _____ On the whole, I disagree.

10. Some people say that they can be genuinely religious without being a member of any church.

    _____ Yes, I agree that they can.
    ____*____ I do not believe this.

11. When I enter a cathedral or large beautiful church I am more likely to feel:

    ____*____ respect for the majesty and greatness it represents.
    _____ some other personal religious emotions of my own.

12. Imagine yourself in the two following situations. In which would you feel your religious life to be most strengthened?

    _____ As a member of a small struggling church.
    ____*____ As a member of a big and influential church.

13. In one respect my church is like a lodge or fraternity: I feel more comfortable and congenial with fellow-members than I do with non-members.

    ____*____ Yes, I agree with this statement.
    _____ No, I cannot agree with it.

14. I have received specific benefits for myself and my family as a result of prayer.

    ____*____ Yes, I can agree with this statement.
    _____ No, I cannot agree with it.

15. When visiting friends in another city who never go to church, I would nonetheless make a definite effort myself to attend church on Sunday.

    ____*____ Probably yes.
    _____ Probably no.

Note: The asterisk (*) indicates the alternative for each item that is considered to reflect the extrinsic religious value. The total score for the scale is simply the number of items on which the extrinsic religious value alternative is chosen.

INTRINSIC-EXTRINSIC RELIGIOUS ORIENTATION (Feagin 1964;
Allport and Ross 1967)

Variable

Whereas Wilson's (1960) scale measures the extrinsic orientation toward religion, according to Allport's (1954) theory, the scale described here contains separate intrinsic and extrinsic items which
seem to form empirically distinct subscales.

Description

This scale was developed jointly by members of a seminar at Harvard,
apparently under Allport's leadership, and has been reported both
by Feagin (1964) and by Allport and Ross (1967). The Feagin version
has one additional extrinsic item; otherwise the two scales are
identical.

Items are scored from 1 to 5, as shown below, with 4 or 5 indicating
an extrinsic orientation, 1 and 2 indicating an intrinsic orientation, and 3 being assigned to any items omitted by a respondent.
Total score is simply the sum of the 20 or 21 item scores. Although
one can obtain a single total score, it is wise to score the intrinsic and extrinsic subscales separately, because for many respondents
they appear to be independent (as discussed below).

Sample

Feagin. In the spring of 1963 Feagin had friends distribute "about"
420 questionnaires to members of five churches in four cities in
Texas and Oklahoma. He received 286 (68%) by return mail and these
constituted his sample. Ages of respondents ranged from 18 to "over
50;" there were 122 males and 163 females distributed widely across
occupational, educational, and income categories. Each questionnaire
included the Intrinsic-Extrinsic Scale along with measures of fundamentalism, anti-Negro prejudice, conformity, and "jungle ideology."

Allport and Ross. Graduate students in the Harvard seminar distributed questionnaires to six church groups, including Catholics, Lutherans, Nazarenes, Presbyterians, Methodists, and Baptists. In all
there were 309 cases. All respondents were contacted as members of
these groups, so some "proreligious" bias may have been introduced.
The authors caution that no generalizations about denominations
should be drawn from their small, non-random samples. The questionnaires included the Intrinsic-Extrinsic Scale and several direct and
indirect measures of racial prejudice.

Reliability

Feagin. Item-to-scale correlations ranged from .22 to .54 when the
whole scale (21 items) was given one score. Feagin noticed that some
items were intercorrelating well while others were not, and so performed a factor analysis. Two orthogonal factors emerged, representing intrinsic (18% of variance) and extrinsic (11% of variance) dimensions. When these are considered as subscales, the following item-
to-subscale correlations were obtained for the top six items on each
factor (item numbers refer to list below):

Items	1	3	4	5	8	9
With Intrinsic Subscale	.64	.67	.54	.56	.71	.66
Items	1	12	2	3	6	11
With Extrinsic Subscale	.65	.61	.56	.68	.59	.48

<u>Allport</u> <u>and</u> <u>Ross</u>. Item-to-subscale correlations ranged from .18 to .58; these are listed in parentheses after the items in the list below.

Validity

In both studies respondents showing an extrinsic religious orientation were found to be more racially prejudiced than the intrinsically religious respondents. Allport and Ross also discovered that some people, labelled "indiscriminately proreligious," tended to endorse <u>both</u> extrinsic and intrinsic items, <u>and</u> <u>that</u> <u>these</u> <u>were</u> <u>the</u> <u>most</u> <u>prejudiced</u> <u>of</u> <u>all</u>. (The "indiscriminately proreligious" include those who on the intrinsic subscale score at least 12 points less than on the extrinsic subscale.) In more liberal groups, such as university students, one might also expect to find people who are "indiscriminately antireligious or nonreligious," and in fact unpublished research has borne out this expectation.

In the studies by Feagin and by Allport and Ross, as well as in unpublished research available to us, the Intrinsic-Extrinsic Scale appears consistently to demonstrate its construct validity.

Location

Feagin, J. Prejudice and religious types: a focused study of southern fundamentalists. <u>Journal</u> <u>for</u> <u>the</u> <u>Scientific</u> <u>Study</u> <u>of</u> <u>Religion</u>, 1964, <u>4</u>, 3-13.

Allport, G. and Ross, J.M. Personal religious orientation and prejudice. <u>Journal</u> <u>of</u> <u>Personality</u> <u>and</u> <u>Social</u> <u>Psychology</u>, 1967, <u>5</u>, 432-443.

Administration

This scale is self-administered and should take about 10-15 minutes to complete.

Results and Comments

As discussed in the introduction to this chapter, Allport explains the repeatedly demonstrated correlation between church attendance and bigotry by postulating two types of church-goers. The extrinsicly motivated, who make up the majority, are racially prejudiced. But a minority of church members, the intrinsically motivated, are actually less prejudiced than nonreligious persons. Research with the Intrinsic-Extrinsic Scale appears to support Allport's claim. Furthermore, it has uncovered two other types of people, the indiscriminately proreligious and the indiscriminately antireligious. These people appear to contradict themselves by expressing blanket support or condemnation for all religious statements.

The items employed in the research of Feagin and of Allport and Ross are listed separately for the extrinsic subscale and for the intrinsic. In actual use, of course, they are interspersed (to avoid agreement response-set). The twelfth extrinsic item, for some unspecified reason, was used only by Feagin.

In both subscales the items are scored in such a way that scores of 4 or 5 indicate an extrinsic orientation, while scores of 1 and 2 indicate an intrinsic orientation. If an item is omitted it receives a score of 3.

While the scores of the 20 items (or 21 including Feagin's #12) may be summed (with high totals indicating an extrinsic orientation), it is probably well, as the reported research demonstrates, to obtain separate scores for the two subscales in order to distinguish cases that are "indiscriminately pro-religious" from those that are consistently extrinsic or intrinsic.

In parentheses following the statement of each item the reader finds the correlation of the item with the total subscale score in Allport and Ross's study, with the contribution of the item to the scale excluded.

The following "cover-up" title and instructions were used by the authors:

Inquiry Concerning Social and Religious Views

The following items deal with various types of religious ideas and social opinions. We should like to find out how common they are.

Please indicate the response you prefer, or most closely agree with, by writing the letter corresponding to your choice in the right margin.

If none of the choices expresses exactly how you feel, then indicate the one which is closest to your own views. If no choice is possible you may omit the item.

There are no "right" or "wrong" choices. There will be many religious people who will agree with all the possible alternative answers.

Reference   Allport, G. The nature of prejudice. Reading, Mass.: Addison-Wesley, 1954.

Wilson, C. Extrinsic religious values and prejudice. Journal of Abnormal and Social Psychology, 1960, 60, 286-288.

Extrinsic Subscale

1. What religion offers me most is comfort when sorrows and misfortune strike. (.49)

    a. I definitely disagree   1
    b. I tend to disagree   2
    c. I tend to agree   4
    d. I definitely agree   5

2. One reason for my being a church member is that such membership helps to establish a person in the community. (.47)

    a. Definitely not true   1
    b. Tends not to be true   2
    c. Tends to be true   4
    d. Definitely true   5

3. The purpose of prayer is to secure a happy and peaceful life. (.51)

    a. I definitely disagree   1
    b. I tend to disagree   2
    c. I tend to agree   4
    d. I definitely agree   5

4. It doesn't matter so much what I believe so long as I lead a moral life. (.39)

    a. I definitely disagree   1
    b. I tend to disagree   2
    c. I tend to agree   4
    d. I definitely agree   5

5. Although I am a religious person I refuse to let religious considerations influence my everyday affairs. (.31)

    a. Definitely not true of me   1
    b. Tends not to be true   2
    c. Tends to be true   4
    d. Clearly true in my case   5

6. The church is most important as a place to formulate good social relationships. (.44)

    a. I definitely disagree   1
    b. I tend to disagree   2
    c. I tend to agree   4
    d. I definitely agree   5

7. Although I believe in my religion, I feel there are many more important things in my life. (.32)

     a. I definitely disagree   1
     b. I tend to disagree   2
     c. I tend to agree   4
     d. I definitely agree   5

8. I pray chiefly because I have been taught to pray. (.31)

     a. Definitely true of me   5
     b. Tends to be true   4
     c. Tends not to be true   2
     d. Definitely not true of me 1

9. A primary reason for my interest in religion is that my church is a congenial social activity. (.33)

     a. Definitely not true of me 1
     b. Tends not to be true   2
     c. Tends to be true   4
     d. Definitely true of me   5

10. Occasionally I find it necessary to compromise my religious beliefs in order to protect my social and economic well-being. (.18)

     a. Definitely disagree   1
     b. Tend to disagree   2
     c. Tend to agree   4
     d. Definitely agree   5

11. The primary purpose of prayer is to gain relief and protection. (.50)

     a. I definitely agree   5
     b. I tend to agree   4
     c. I tend to disagree   2
     d. I definitely disagree   1

12. Religion helps to keep my life balanced and steady in exactly the same way as my citizenship, friendships, and other memberships do. (This item not used by Allport and Ross.)

     a. I definitely agree   5
     b. I tend to agree   4
     c. I tend to disagree   2
     d. I definitely disagree   1

Intrinsic Subscale

1. I try hard to carry my religion over into all my other dealings in
   life. (.39)

        a. I definitely disagree   5
        b. I tend to disagree   4
        c. I tend to agree   2
        d. I definitely agree   1

2. Quite often I have been keenly aware of the presence of God or the
   Divine Being. (.44)

        a. Definitely not true   5
        b. Tends not to be true   4
        c. Tends to be true   2
        d. Definitely true   1

3. My religious beliefs are what really lie behind my whole approach
   to life. (.50)

        a. This is definitely not so 5
        b. Probably not so   4
        c. Probably so   2
        d. Definitely so   1

4. The prayers I say when I am alone carry as much meaning and personal
   emotion as those said by me during services. (.30)

        a. Almost never   5
        b. Sometimes   4
        c. Usually   2
        d. Almost always   1

5. If not prevented by unavoidable circumstances, I attend church: (.47)

        a. more than once a week   1
        b. about once a week   2
        c. two or three times a month 4
        d. less than once a month   5

6. If I were to join a church group I would prefer to join (1) a Bible
   Study group, or (2) a social fellowship. (.49)

        a. I would prefer to join (1) 1
        b. I probably would prefer (1) 2
        c. I probably would prefer (2) 4
        d. I would prefer to join (2) 5

7. Religion is especially important to me because it answers many questions about the meaning of life.   (.28)

      a. Definitely disagree   5
      b. Tend to disagree   4
      c. Tend to agree   2
      d. Definitely agree   1

8. I read literature about my faith (or church).   (.41)

      a. Frequently   1
      b. Occasionally   2
      c. Rarely   4
      d. Never   5

9. It is important to me to spend periods of time in private religious thought and meditation.   (.58)

      a. Frequently true   1
      b. Occasionally true   2
      c. Rarely true   4
      d. Never true   5

ATTITUDE TOWARD CHURCH SCALE (Thurstone and Chave 1929)

Variable	The scale purportedly measures a respondent's position on a continuum ranging from strong depreciation to strong appreciation of "the" (his) "church."
Description	A list of 130 statements about the church was compiled from various people and from a search of the literature. These statements were then sorted into eleven piles by 300 subjects according to Thurstone's method. By eliminating ambiguous and irrelevant items a final scale of 45 statements was obtained. An individual's score on this scale is obtained by averaging the values associated with items he endorses.
Sample	In the studies initially reported the scale was administered to students at the University of Chicago (548 freshmen, 127 sophomores, 107 juniors, 107 seniors, and 210 graduate students), 103 Divinity students and 181 members of the Chicago Forum.
Reliability	A split-half measure of .848 was obtained. Corrected by the Spearman-Brown formula this became .92. In another study mentioned, using 100 subjects, the split-half measure was .89, corrected to .94.
Validity	As a measure of discriminant validity and a rough indicant of construct validity the subjects were classified by religion and, as expected, the Catholic group obtained the highest mean score. Another classification, according to church attendance rate, showed that frequent attenders were more favorable to the church. Similar results were obtained for a split between active and inactive church members.
Location	Thurstone, L. and Chave, E. The measurement of attitude, Chicago, Ill.: University of Chicago Press, 1929.
Administration	Approximately thirty minutes would be needed for self-administration of the scale.
Results and Comments	This instrument has been fairly widely used even in recent years. It has adequate reliability and has been shown to relate reasonably to other variables. It is general enough to be used with any of the major religious groups. However, it is directed almost entirely toward institutional and ritual concerns and does not top individual religious beliefs or notions about God, doctrine, etc. Perhaps some of its better items could be used in conjunction with scales designed to measure other dimensions of religiosity.

For an interesting study of religious attitude change over more than a decade using the Thurstone-Chave scale, see Nelson (1956).

Reference   Nelson, E. Patterns of religious attitude shifts from college to fourteen years later. Psychological Monographs, 1956, 70, Whole No. 424.

ATTITUDE TOWARD CHURCH SCALE

Check (✓) every statement below that expresses your sentiment toward the church. Interpret the statements in accordance with your own experience with churches.

(8.3)* 1. I think the teaching of the church is altogether too superficial to have much social significance.

(1.7) 2. I feel the church services give me inspiration and help me to live up to my best during the following week.

(2.6) 3. I think the church keeps business and politics up to a higher standard than they would otherwise tend to maintain.

(2.3) 4. I find the services of the church both restful and inspiring.

(4.0) 5. When I go to church I enjoy a fine ritual service with good music.

(4.5) 6. I believe in what the church teaches but with mental reservations.

(5.7) 7. I do not receive any benefit from attending church services but I think it helps some people.

(5.4) 8. I believe in religion but I seldom go to church.

(4.7) 9. I am careless about religion and church relationships but I would not like to see my attitude become general.

(10.5) 10. I regard the church as a static, crystallized institution and as such it is unwholesome and detrimental to society and the individual.

(1.5) 11. I believe church membership is almost essential to living life at its best.

(3.1) 12. I do not understand the dogmas or creeds of the church but I find that the church helps me to be more honest and creditable.

(8.2) 13. The paternal and benevolent attitude of the church is quite distasteful to me.

---

* Scale value

Reprinted with permission of Thurstone, L. and Chave, E. Attitude Toward Church Scale in *The Measurement of Attitude* (Chicago: University of Chicago Press, 1929). Copyright 1929 by the University of Chicago Press.

(2.6)   14. I feel that church attendance is a fair index of the nation's morality.

(5.6)   15. Sometimes I feel that the church and religion are necessary and sometimes I doubt it.

(3.9)   16. I believe the church is fundamentally sound but some of its adherents have given it a bad name.

(11.0)   17. I think the church is a parasite on society.

(6.1)   18. I feel the need for religion but do not find what I want in any one church.

(7.5)   19. I think too much money is being spent on the church for the benefit that is being derived.

(4.0)   20. I believe in the church and its teachings because I have been accustomed to them since I was a child.

(9.5)   21. I think the church is hundreds of years behind the times and cannot make a dent on modern life.

(1.0)   22. I believe the church has grown up with the primary purpose of perpetuating the spirit and teachings of Jesus and deserves loyal support.

(0.8)   23. I feel the church perpetuates the values which man puts highest in his philosophy of life.

(6.9)   24. I feel I can worship God better out of doors than in the church and I get more inspiration there.

(9.1)   25. My experience is that the church is hopelessly out of date.

(8.6)   26. I feel the church is petty, always quarreling over matters that have no interest or importance.

(5.9)   27. I do not believe in any brand of religion or in any particular church but I have never given the subject serious thought.

(8.8)   28. I respect any church-member's beliefs but I think it is all "bunk."

(3.3)   29. I enjoy my church because there is a spirit of friendliness there.

(10.5)   30. I think the country would be better off if the churches were closed and the ministers set to some useful work.

(0.2)   31. I believe the church is the greatest institution in America today.

(6.7)   32. I believe in sincerity and goodness without any church ceremonies.

(0.4) 33. I believe the church is the greatest influence for good government and right living.

(10.7) 34. I think the organized church is an enemy of science and truth.

(7.4) 35. I believe the church is losing ground as education advances.

(5.9) 36. The churches may be doing good and useful work but they do not interest me.

(9.6) 37. I think the church is a hindrance to religion for it still depends upon magic, superstition, and myth.

(1.4) 38. The church is needed to develop religion, which has always been concerned with man's deepest feelings and greatest values.

(7.2) 39. I believe the churches are too much divided by factions and denominations to be a strong force for righteousness.

(10.4) 40. The church represents shallowness, hypocrisy, and prejudice.

(9.2) 41. I think the church seeks to impose a lot of worn-out dogmas and medieval superstitions.

(7.2) 42. I think the church allows denominational differences to appear larger than true religion.

(5.1) 43. I like the ceremonies of my church but do not miss them much when I stay away.

(1.2) 44. I believe the church is a powerful agency for promoting both individual and social righteousness.

(2.2) 45. I like to go to church for I get something worth while to think about and it keeps my mind filled with right thoughts.

ATTITUDES ABOUT THE BIBLE (Survey Research Center 1969)

Variable   This question inquires into whether a person takes a literal view of
              the Bible or takes a less literal view.

Description   The question has four choices and the respondent is asked to make
              but one choice.   (The item is used in the Faulkner and DeJong scale
              described previously in this chapter.)

              The following distributions of response for those who choose one of
              the alternatives (only 3% cannot make a choice) have been obtained
              in the 1964 and 1968 pre-election samples of the Survey Research
              Center:

		1964	1968
1.	Bible is all true.	53%	51%
2.	Bible has human errors.	42%	42%
3.	Bible is just a good book.	4%	6%
4.	Bible is worth little.	1%	1%
		100%	100%

Sample   The samples consisted of a nationwide probability sample of 1,571
              adults interviewed in September and October 1964 and 1,558 adults
              interviewed in the same months in 1968.

Reliability/ No test-retest reliability data are available.
  Homogeneity

Validity   No data bearing directly on validity are available.

Location   1964 Election Study.   Ann Arbor, Michigan: Survey Research Center
              (ICPR) (in press)

Results and   Attitudes about the Bible are strongly related to education (tau-
  Comments   beta = .30) and religion (especially for those of Jewish faith) as
              shown by the following results from the 1968 data:

	All true	Some errors	Good book	Worth little
Grade school or less	76	17	4	3
High school incomplete	66	30	3	1
High school grad	54	42	5	1
Some college	40	53	6	1
College grad	20	69	9	2
Graduate degree	16	69	24	3
Protestant	60	35	4	1
Catholic	47	46	5	2
Jewish	2	63	33	2
No preference	34	31	23	11

There are large variations within the Protestant category that cannot be
detailed here; e.g., from 42% of Reformation Protestants (e.g., Lutheran,
Presbyterian) to 80% of Neo-Fundamentalists choosing the most literal

interpretation. Within the Pietistic religions the percent taking the most literal view varies between 57% for Methodists (72% in the South) and 73% for Baptists (78% in the South).

Any "generation-gap" that exists in views about the Bible is certainly confined to the college graduate segment of those under 30. Percentages saying the Bible is all true according to age and education are as follows for the 1968 data:

	Total sample	People under 30	People over 30
No high school	76	77	76
Some high school	66	65	66
High school grad	53	57	52
Some college	40	35	42
College grad	20	11	22

This college graduate under 30 segment still takes the Bible more seriously than classroom samples at the University of Michigan that the major author of this volume has studied:

	All true	Some errors	Good book	Worth little
University of Michigan undergrads	4	49	42	5

Data collected from a haphazard sample at Adrian College, a small college in southeastern Michigan show quite a different pattern:

Adrian college undergrads	18	72	7	3

These results are consistent with the following differentials in Bible views in the 1964 study among graduates of colleges which have various AAUP ratings of quality:

High (A and B rating)	5	79	16	0
Medium and Low (C through F rating)	26	70	4	0

Finally the major author of this volume has found the following pattern of correlations (tau-beta for total sample = -.16) between liberal views of the Bible and the opinion that the police used too much force with the demonstrators at the 1968 Chicago convention:

Less than high school education	-.05
High school graduate	-.12
Some college	-.22
College graduate	-.22

In all groups then individuals with literal views of the Bible were most likely to feel that the police did not use enough force with the demonstrators. However, the correspondence between the two "hard-line" responses was hardly noticeable for those of less education and became quite pronounced for persons who had been to college.

ATTITUDES ABOUT THE BIBLE

Here are four statements about the Bible (HAND CARD TO R), and I'd like you to tell me which is closest to your own view.

1. The Bible is God's Word and all it says is true.

2. The Bible was written by men inspired by God but it contains some human errors.

3. The Bible is a good book because it was written by wise men but God had nothing to do with it.

4. The Bible was written by men who lived so long ago that it is worth very little today.

8. Don't know

Attitudes about the Bible (Survey Research Center 1969) in the *1964 Election Study* (Ann Arbor, Michigan: Inter-University Consortium for Political Research, The University of Michigan, 1971); reprinted here with permission.

ADJECTIVE RATINGS OF GOD (Gorsuch   1968)

Variable   Previous research had identified several dimensions used in
                    people's conception of God, and Semantic Differential research
                    had revealed three adjectival factors (evaluation, potency, and
                    activity) which apply to numerous concepts. Gorsuch sought to
                    combine these approaches in discovering replicable factors un-
                    derlying conceptions of God.

Description   Sixty-three adjectives were taken from a previous study by
                    Spilka, Armatas, and Nussbaum (1964) and another 28 were selected
                    to represent the three major factors usually found in Semantic
                    Differential studies (Osgood, Suci, and Tannenbaum, 1957). Sub-
                    jects rated each adjective on a three-point scale: 1)"the word
                    does not describe 'God;'" 2) "the word describes 'God;'" 3) "the
                    word describes 'God' particularly well." To these 91 adjectives,
                    eight random variables and sex were added.

                    For 500 respondents the 100 variables were correlated and hier-
                    archically factored. Three orders of factors were obtained. In
                    the list below all "salient" adjectives (those with loadings above
                    .30) are listed for each factor. Gorsuch states: "Each loading
                    can be interpreted as the correlation of the adjective with the
                    factor when the influence of any factor at a higher order than the
                    one under consideration has been removed." The relationship be-
                    tween factors is indicated in the following outline:

                         I. Traditional Christian
                            A. Companionable
                               1. Evaluation
                               2. Kindness
                               3. Relevancy
                            B. Benevolent Deity
                               1. Lack of deisticness
                               2. Sternality
                               3. Kindness
                        II. Wrathfulness
                       III. Omni-ness
                        IV. Potently passive

                    Gorsuch attempted to find at least three salient adjectives to
                    form a scale for each factor. Variables were selected from a
                    Schmidt-Leiman (1957) analysis which met three conditions: 1)
                    each variable loaded at least .40 on the factor, 2) each had
                    no stronger loading on another factor, and 3) each had no loading
                    on another factor within .10 of its major loading. Only five
                    factors met these conditions; the adjectives chosen for these
                    five are asterisked in the list below. For a sample of 85 males
                    alpha coefficients were computed to determine the internal con-
                    sistency reliability of each factor scale.

Sample	A total of 585 undergraduates taking general psychology courses at Vanderbilt completed the adjective ratings; 234 were females. Eighty-five males were randomly selected from the sample for the reliability study, the remaining 500 were included in the factor analyses. Only the composition of the entire group is specified: Methodists (21%), Presbyterians (21%), Episcopalians (14%), Baptists (11%), Catholics (8%), no preference (7%), Jewish (4%), Church of Christ (3%), Lutheran (3%), Congregational (2%), Disciples of Christ (2%), and other bodies (4%). Twenty-nine percent reported attending religious services at least once a week; 27% said "several times a year or less."

Reliability
The alpha coefficients for the five satisfactory scales were as follows:

Traditional Christian (15 adjectives)	.94
Wrathfulness (11 adjectives)	.83
Deisticness (3 adjectives)	.71
Omni-ness (4 adjectives)	.89
Irrelevancy (4 adjectives)	.49

The last reliability coefficient is low in part because 77 of the 85 respondents received the lowest possible score.

Validity
No direct evidence for validity was offered, but the close correspondence between several of the factors and factors obtained earlier by Spilka, et al. (1964) was discussed.

Location
Gorsuch, R. The conceptualization of God as seen in adjective ratings. Journal for the Scientific Study of Religion, 1968, 7, 56-64.

Administration
The adjective scales are self-administered and take approximately 15 minutes to complete.

Results and Comments
This instrument has not as yet been used in published studies, but it is worth consideration because it offers a differentiated approach to the conceptualization of God which has at least some validation in previous work. After further development such an instrument might be useful for comparing the conception of the deity held by various groups (liberal, fundamentalist, etc.) or different cultures. Gorsuch intends to alter and refine the scales and to undertake such comparative studies, and he explicitly suggests that interested researchers contact him for up-to-date information. (Department of Psychology, Vanderbilt University)

References
Osgood, C.E., Suci, G.J., and Tannenbaum, P.H. Measurement of meaning. Urbana, Ill.: University of Illinois Press, 1957.

Schmidt, J. and Leiman, J.M. The development of hierarchical factor solutions. Psychometrika, 1957, 22, 53-61.

Spilka, B., Armatas, P., and Nussbaum, J. The concept of God: a factor analytic approach. Review of Religious Research, 1964, 6, 28-36.

ADJECTIVE RATINGS OF GOD[1]

Third Order Factor

Factor 1: Traditional Christian

Absolute	39	Fatherly	44	Kingly*	46	Real*	48
All-wise	44	Firm*	48	Loving	44	Redeeming	51
Blessed*	40	Forgiving	42	Majestic*	52	Righteous*	51
Charitable	41	Gentle	44	Matchless*	53	Sovereign*	51
Comforting	37	Glorious	57	Meaningful	42	Steadfast*	53
Considerate	38	Gracious*	48	Merciful	45	Stern	38
Controlling	40	Guiding	42	Moving	45	Strong*	55
Creative*	45	Helpful	44	Omnipotent	43	Supporting	41
Divine	46	Holy	44	Omnipresent	38	True*	50
Eternal	43	Important*	51	Omniscient	40	Valuable	43
Everlasting	43	Infinite	35	Patient	43	Vigorous	40
Fair	46	Just	49	Powerful*	50	Warm	42
Faithful	45	Kind	49	Protective	44		

Second Order Factors

Factor 2: Benevolent Deity

All-wise	44	Divine	37	Inaccessible	-36	Passive	-38
Comforting	37	Forgiving	44	Loving	43	Protective	40
Distant	-35	Impersonal	-37	Merciful	38	Redeeming	43

Factor 3: Companionable

Considerate	37	Faithful	38	Kind	35	Warm	40
Fair	39	Helpful	35	Moving	36		

Primary Factors

Factor 4: Kindliness

Charitable	42	Fair	38	Gracious	38	Loving	41
Comforting	40	Forgiving	44	Just	41	Merciful	46
Considerate	40	Gentle	45	Kind	51	Patient	40

Factor 5: Wrathfulness

Avenging*	52	Damning*	54	Punishing*	42	Stern*	46
Blunt*	48	Hard*	57	Severe*	69	Tough	38
Critical*	50	Jealous	36	Sharp*	51	Wrathful*	61
Cruel*	49						

Reprinted with permission of Gorsuch, R. Adjective Ratings of God in "The Conceptualization of God as Seen in Adjective Ratings," *Journal for the Scientific Study of Religion*, 7 (1968), pp 56-64.

Factor 6:   Deisticness

| Distant* | 54 | Inaccessible* | 57 | Mythical | 35 | Passive | 34 |
| Impersonal* | 55 | | | | | | |

Factor 7:   Omni-ness

| Infinite* | 46 | Omnipotent* | 58 | Omnipresent* | 66 | Omniscient* | 64 |

Factor 8:   Evaluation

| Important | 38 | Timely | 40 | Valuable | 51 | Vigorous | 39 |
| Meaningful | 36 | | | | | | |

Factor 9:   Irrelevancy

| False* | 62 | Feeble* | 70 | Weak* | 65 | Worthless* | 60 |

Factor 10:   Eternality

| Divine | 49 | Eternal | 58 | Everlasting | 59 | Holy | 37 |

Factor 11:   Potently Passive

| Slow | 53 | Still | 57 | Tough | 35 |

---

[1]Each adjective was rated on a three point scale:
1. The word does not describe "God."
2. The word describes "God."
3. The word describes "God" particularly well.

The following were omitted from the above listing:
    a. decimal points
    b. non-salient loadings (i.e., less than .30)
    c. loadings less than .35 on factors with 6 or more salient
       loadings
    d. factors without at least 3 salient loadings

CHAPTER 11 - METHODOLOGICAL SCALES

In this final chapter we examine four sets of attitudinal instruments that are primarily of methodological relevance. The four are intended to control for the response set tendencies of social desirability and acquiescence (Wiggins, 1968, p. 308), lists references to four scales which _measure_, as distinct from controlling for, acquiescence). The scales reviewed are:

1. Social Desirability Scale (Crowne and Marlowe 1964)

2. Social Desirability (SD) Scale (Edwards 1957)

3. Various Social Attitude Scales (Campbell 1966)

4. Agreement Response Scale (Couch and Keniston 1960)

The Crowne-Marlowe scale, while initially constructed as a control for response set, gradually developed into a platform for a complex series of studies of individual motivation. Some problems do arise in this connection and the scale itself seems to possess relatively low inter-item homogeneity. Nevertheless there are few scales in the literature that have their validity as well established through experimentation as this one. The amount of normative data (e.g., average scores for various groups) that the authors provide is a further laudable feature of this scale.

The Edwards scale is taken directly from the Minnesota Multiphasic Personality Inventory, a copyrighted instrument which cannot be reproduced here. A main disadvantage of these items, compared to those of Crowne-Marlowe, is that their content is heavily laden with references to psychologically abnormal behavior. In other words, scores on the Edwards scale should be higher relative to the number of items employed because it is so difficult to admit many of the abnormal behaviors employed. This, in fact, is reflected in the average number of items endorsed in the socially desirable direction for the two scales. Crowne and Marlowe generally report their subjects answer in the desirable direction to less than half of their items in comparison to the two-thirds rate for the Edwards items.

The six scales by Campbell have yet to be used in any reported research so that we are unable to evaluate them psychometrically. It is the way in which the items are formatted, however, that draws our attention to these scales. In order to control for acquiescence, each item has two alternatives which define opposite ends of the continuum of interest. After picking one alternative the respondent is then asked to indicate the strength of his preference of one end of the continuum over the other. This item format thus allows all respondents to gauge their attitudes on an item in reference to the same concrete alternatives.

The Couch and Keniston scale is the basic measure of agreeing response set. The scale was developed from a methodologically impressive item analysis that involved a wide range of well-established psychometric instruments. Supplemental evidence on the validity of the scale was provided in an interesting clinical study. The major drawback of the scale is that norms and evidence are only available for college student samples. A good deal of controversy continues to surround the importance of response sets in attitude and personality research. Research up to the mid-1960s generally took the position that response sets were so strong that perhaps that was all most personality inventories were measuring (see the review of Christie and Lindauer, 1963). With the writings of Rorer (1965) and Block (1965), the pendulum swung to the opposite extreme. More recent articles (Campbell et al., 1967; Bock et al., 1969) suggest a modified position in which response sets are seen as seldom obliterating item content but as seriously confounding the

interpretation of scale scores in some content areas. Wiggins (1968) provides
a readable overview of the state-of-the-art through mid-1967. This research,
however, has been conducted with college students and therefore leaves
unanswered the importance of the operation of such response sets among less-
educated persons in sample surveys (Campbell et al., 1960; Lenski and Leggett,
1960).

REFERENCES

Bock, R., Dicken, C., and Van Pelt, J. Methodological implications of content-acquiescence correlations in the MMPI, Psychological Bulletin, 1969, 71, 127-139.

Block, J. The challenge of response sets. New York: Appleton-Century-Crofts, 1965.

Campbell et al. The American voter. New York: Wiley, 1960.

Campbell, D., Seigman, C., and Rees, M. Direction-of-wording effects in the relationship between scales, Psychological Bulletin, 1967, 68, 293-303.

Christie, R. and Lindauer, F. Personality Structure, Annual Review of Psychology, 1963, 14, 201-230.

Couch, A. and Keniston, K. Yeasayers and naysayers: agreeing response set as a personality variable. Journal of Abnormal and Social Psychology, 1960, 60, 151-174.

Lenski, G. and Leggett, J. Caste, class, and deference in the research interview, American Journal of Sociology, 1960, 65, 463-467.

Rorer, L. The great response-style myth, Psychological Bulletin, 1965, 63, 129-156.

Wiggins, J. Personality structure, Annual Review of Psychology, 1968, 19, 293-350.

SOCIAL DESIRABILITY SCALE (Crowne and Marlowe 1964)

Variable   This scale attempts to locate individuals who describe themselves
in favorable, socially desirable terms in order to achieve the
approval of others.

Description   The items in the scale were modelled so as to achieve a balance of
two types of statements: half culturally acceptable but probably
untrue, the other half true but undesirable. Current personality
inventories were consulted to find items of this type which
had minimal abnormal implications. A set of 50 such items were
selected and reduced to 33 by ratings of experienced judges and by
item analyses with psychology students. Of these 18 are keyed in the
true direction, 15 in the false direction. One point is scored for
each response in the socially desirable direction with scores therefore varying between 0 (no social desirability) to 33 (highest social
desirability).   The following data on scale norms were drawn from
1,400 students in introductory psychology students at Ohio State
University.   The mean for males was 15.1 (s.d. = 5.6), for females
16.8 (s.d. = 5.5) with the following distribution of scale scores:

Score Range	Males	Females
0-4	2	1
5-9	14	8
10-14	31	26
15-19	32	33
20-24	16	24
25-29	4	7
30-33	1	1
	100%	100%

Average scores for other samples:

	Males	Females
Northwestern Univ.	11.7 (N = 100)	13.5 (N = 86)
Dartmouth	10.1 (N = 32)	
Univ. of Washington	14.4 (N = 110)	
Univ. of North Dakota	13.9 (N = 49)	16.0 (N = 59)
Lesley College		14.2 (N = 60)
Boston Univ.	13.7 (N = 41)	
Secretarial school		16.3 (N = 60)
Insurance company		15.4 (N = 88) and
		24.6 (N = 285 applicants
		told scores to be con-
		sidered in hiring)
Schizophrenic in-patients	16.5 (N = 60)	
Psychiatric out-patients	12.2 (N = 40)	11.5 (N = 46)
California prisoners	16.7 (N = 80)	
Massachusetts prisoners	21.4 (N = 17 prostitutes)	
	19.1 (N = 26 prostitutes)	
	16.3 (N = 19 non-prostitutes)	

Sample   The various samples are described above. For the most part these appear to be captive samples, with no attempt made at selective or probability sampling procedures.

Reliability/   The items retained in the scale were those that had originally
Homogeneity   correlated at the .05 level with total scale scores. Internal consistency (Kuder-Richardson 20) came out at .88.

A test-retest correlation over a one-month interval with 57 college students also was .88. Less encouraging data on the homogeneity of scale items is reported under "Results and Comments" below.

Validity   The validity of the scale was supported by the confirmation of several hypotheses in experimental settings. These experiments are too complex to detail here except for the authors' conclusion:

> "The greater amenability to social influence of persons who characterize themselves in very desirable terms is seen in (a) the favorability of their attitudes toward an extremely dull and boring task; (b) their greater verbal conditionability, both directly and vicariously; (c) social conformity; (d) a tendency to give popular word associations; (e) the cautious setting of goals in a risk-taking situation; (f) their greater reactivity, depending on their expectancies about the evaluative consequences of their behavior, in a "dirty word" perceptual-defense task; and (g) susceptibility to persuasion."

Location   Crowne, D. and Marlowe, D. The approval motive. New York: Wiley, 1964.

Results and   One essential element in the need for approval that experiments in
Comments   this study brought to light was the way in which this need was dependent on an idealized version of the self that had to be maintained and defended. "Many of the behaviors which are associated with defensive self-evaluation appear to follow from and to support the approval-dependent person's self-esteem......more is involved than a contrived and deliberate presentation of self."

Scores on this scale generally correlate considerably lower with scales of the MMPI that do Edward's (1957) items, as the authors had intended. No correlation between the two social desirability scales is reported however.

Application of these items to a national probability sample of tenth-grade boys (Bachman et al., 1967) produced relatively low interitem correlations .

Out of a total of 465 inter-item correlations, only 15 exceeded .20 (for a random subset of 778 boys), and about half of all inter-item correlations were not significant at the .01 level (.10 being the point at which significance would be attained). Consider the following four items, for example:

	1	2	3	4
1. I am always a good listener.	X			
2. I have doubts about my ability to succeed in life.	-.06	X		
3. I almost never have the urge to tell somebody off.	.06	-.03	X	
4. I am sometimes irritated by people who ask favors of me.	-.10	.08	.02	X

For this sample, Arscott (1968) reports data which calculate out to
an average score of 14.8, with a standard deviation of 5.3. The
percentages giving the socially desirable response to each question
in this study are included with the presentation of items. (Two
inapplicable items were not included in the Bachman et al. study.)

Further research with this scale in the Mental Health in Industry
Program at the Institute for Social Research has raised certain
questions about the theoretical foundations of this scale. Jack
French (personal communication) has noted that motivational theory
and previous research would indicate that the items could be fruit-
fully divided under three headings:

> Approach: Items 2, 3, 5, 7, 8, 13, 16, 17, 18,
>   20, 21
>
> General avoidance: Items 9, 10, 11, 14, 15, 22, 24
>
> Avoid aggression: Items 4, 6, 12, 19, 23, 25, 26, 28, 29,
>   30, 31, 32, 33

The items might also be divided according to whether they refer
to intrinsic or extrinsic content. Factor analyses of the items
in the scale suggest further that the items need to be distinguished
on the grounds of positive vs. negative wording.

John Lillibridge (personal communication) comments:

> "Preliminary analyses support the idea that the basic dimen-
> sion measured by the M-C scale is denial rather than need
> for social approval. That is, culturally undesirable but
> common attributes are true of the self rather than measuring
> the need to conform to social norms about good and bad
> behavior.
>
>   A factor analysis of 778 adolescents in a current study
> (Youth-in-Transition data) indicates that the scale may
> comprise at least two subscales: Deny Bad Qualities and
> Claim Good Qualities. In a second study of men aged 35
> to 60 (Employment Termination data) it appears that the
> Deny Bad Qualities subscale contributes most of the variance
> in correlations between the M-C total score and several
> other variables especially measures of negative affect.
> Work is continuing to assess the role of this denial dimen-
> sion in response set phenomena."

A comprehensive review of mainly positive results using the Crowne-Marlowe Scale through mid-1967 is provided by Wiggins (1968, pp. 305-308). A specific application of the Crowne-Marlowe scale to the control of a response set tendencies in the survey setting is provided by Smith (1967).

References   Arscott, A. <u>Univariate statistics describing a nationwide sample of tenth-grade boys</u>. Working paper 2. Ann Arbor, Michigan: Institute for Social Research, July, 1968.

Bachman, J. <u>et al</u>. <u>Youth in transition: volume I.</u> Ann Arbor, Michigan: Survey Research Center, 1967.

Edwards, A. <u>The social desirability variable in personality assessment</u>. New York: Dryden, 1957.

Smith, D. Correcting for social desirability response sets in opinion-attitude survey research, <u>Public Opinion Quarterly</u>, 1967, <u>31</u>, 87-94.

Wiggins, J. Personality structure, <u>Annual Review of Psychology</u>, 1968, <u>19</u>, 293-350.

SOCIAL DESIRABILITY SCALE

Listed below are a number of statements concerning personal attitudes and traits. Read each item and decide whether the statement is true or false as it pertains to you personally.

Percent*

(T) 1. Before voting I thoroughly investigate the qualifications of all the candidates. Not asked

(T) 2. I never hesitate to go out of my way to help someone in trouble. 61

(F) 3. It is sometimes hard for me to go on with my work if I am not encouraged. 33

(T) 4. I have never intensely disliked anyone. 49

(F) 5. On occasion I have had doubts about my ability to succeed in life. 31

(F) 6. I sometimes feel resentful when I don't get my way. 46

(T) 7. I am always careful about my manner of dress. 83

(T) 8. My table manners at home are as good as when I eat out in a restaurant. 57

(F) 9. If I could get into a movie without paying for it and be sure I was not seen, I would probably do it. 43

(F) 10. On a few occasions, I have given up doing something because I thought too little of my ability. 46

(F) 11. I like to gossip at times. 43

(F) 12. There have been times when I felt like rebelling against people in authority even though I knew they were right. 38

(T) 13. No matter who I'm talking to, I'm always a good listener. 60

(F) 14. I can remember "playing sick" to get out of something. 36

(F) 15. There have been occasions when I took advantage of someone. 25

(T) 16. I'm always willing to admit it when I make a mistake. 55

(T) 17. I always try to practice what I preach. 69

(T) 18. I don't find it particularly difficult to get along with loud mouthed, obnoxious people. 43

---

* Percent of a nationwide sample of tenth grade boys answering the item in the keyed direction.

		Percent
(F) 19.	I sometimes try to get even, rather than forgive and forget.	33
(T) 20.	When I don't know something I don't at all mind admitting it.	71
(T) 21.	I am always courteous, even to people who are disagreeable.	54
(F) 22.	At times I have really insisted on having things my own way.	19
(F) 23.	There have been occasions when I felt like smashing things.	35
(T) 24.	I would never think of letting someone else be punished for my wrongdoings.	75
(T) 25.	I never resent being asked to return a favor.	82
(T) 26.	I have never been irked when people expressed ideas very different from my own.	55
(T) 27.	I never make a long trip without checking the safety of my car.	Not asked
(F) 28.	There have been times when I was quite jealous of the good fortune of others.	34
(T) 29.	I have almost never felt the urge to tell someone off.	24
(F) 30.	I am sometimes irritated by people who ask favors of me.	55
(T) 31.	I have never felt that I was punished without cause.	41
(F) 32.	I sometimes think when people have a misfortune they only got what they deserved.	50
(T) 33.	I have never deliberately said something that hurt someone's feelings.	45

Reprinted with permission of Crowne, D. and Marlow, D. Social Desirability Scale in *The Approval Motive* (New York: John Wiley and Sons, Inc., 1964). Copyright 1964 by John Wiley and Sons, Inc., 605 Third Ave., New York, N.Y. 10016.

SOCIAL DESIRABILITY (SD) SCALE (Edwards 1957)

Variable   The items in this scale are intended to tap a tendency to endorse
              statements on the basis of their implicit social desirability rather
              than their actual explicit content.

Description   All items are drawn from the MMPI. The present 39 item scale consists
              of a subset of an original 79 item scale devised earlier from judg-
              ments about the desirability of MMPI items. The 39 items were those
              that proved to show the greatest differentiation on total SD scores
              from the 79 item scale.

              One point is scored for each item answered in the keyed direction,
              therefore yielding a range from 0 (lowest SD) to 39 (highest desir-
              ability). A sample of 84 male students had a mean of 28.6 (s.d. =
              6.5) on this scale while 108 female students had a mean 27.1 (s.d. =
              6.5).

Sample   A number of college student samples were employed in this research.

Reliability/ A corrected split-half reliability of .83 is reported for 192 students.
Homogeneity   No test-retest data are reported.

Validity   No data bearing directly on validity are reported, except that the
              author presents evidence to suggest that results with his scale
              could not have been obtained as a result of acquiescence.

Location   Edwards, A. The social desirability variable in personality assess-
              ment and research. New York: Dryden, 1957. (The actual items in
              this scale are part of the copyrighted MMPI, which is available from
              the Psychological Corporation in New York City.)

Results and   The following high correlations between SD scores and various per-
Comments   sonality scales led Edwards to hypothesize that these scales were
              measuring little more than social desirability:

Other MMPI Scales		Other Scales	
Dominance	.49	Insecurity	-.85
Responsibility	.52	Cooperativeness	.63
Status	.61	Agreeableness	.53
Social Introversion	-.90	Objectivity	.71
Manifest Anxiety	-.84		
Neuroticism	-.50		
Hostility	-.75		
Dependency	-.73		

SOCIAL DESIRABILITY SCALE

MMPI Booklet Numbers and Scoring Key for the
39-Item SD Scale

No.	Key		No.	Key
7	T		252	F
18	T		257	T
32	F		263	F
40	F		267	F
42	F		269	F
43	F		286	F
54	T		301	F
107	T		321	F
138	F		335	F
148	F		337	F
156	F		352	F
158	F		371	T
163	T		383	F
169	T		424	F
171	F		431	F
186	F		439	F
218	F		528	T
241	F		549	F
245	F		555	F
247	F			

Reprinted with permission of Edwards, A. Social Desirability (SD) Scale in *The Social Desirability Variable in Personality Assessment and Research* (New York: Dryden, 1957). The actual items in this scale are part of the copyrighted MMPI which is available from the Psychological Corporation in New York, N.Y.

VARIOUS SOCIAL ATTITUDE SCALES (Campbell 1966)

Variable	The variables included in these scales cover the following areas: self-esteem (self-assessment), values (individualism, material-ism, trust in people), and political attitudes (local-cosmopolitan, foreign policy).
Description	The items in these scales were derived primarily to illustrate a method of item construction that has advantages over traditional item format, mainly in controlling for acquiescence response set and defining the attitude continuum for respondents. Even though these items have not been used extensively, we feel that they are well-constructed enough to deserve exposure, if for no other reason than to illustrate a promising method of item construction.
Sample	The items have been used in classroom studies at Northwestern University.
Reliability/ Homogeneity	No data on reliability have been published.
Validity	No data on validity have been published.
Location	Campbell, D. Unpublished papers, Department of Psychology, Northwestern University.
Administration	Items would be scored in Likert style, depending on the keying of the items. Thus scores for self-assessment would cover the range 8 (all replies in the non-asterisk direction and use capital letters) through 40 (all asterisk replies and use capital letters).
Results and Comments	These scales represent only a few of the many attitude areas for which the author has constructed scales. An inner-directedness scale using this method has been published (Kassargian 1962).
	Variations on the technique can be found in the Berkowitz-Wolkon and Schuman-Harding scales reviewed in Chapter 5.
References	Kassargian, W. A study of Riesman's theory of social character. Sociometry, 1962, 25, 213-230. (Reproduced in Robinson, J. et al. Measures of occupational attitudes and occupational characteristics. Ann Arbor, Michigan: Survey Research Center, 1969).

VARIOUS SOCIAL ATTITUDE SCALES

This is a survey of attitudes and opinions on a variety of topics.

Each item consists of two alternatives, A and B, between which you are asked to choose by circling one of these indicators:

> A = Statement A is entirely preferred to Statement B as an expression of my opinion.
>
> a = Statement A is somewhat preferred over Statement B.
>
> ? = I cannot choose between A and B.
>
> b = Statement B is somewhat preferred to Statement A.
>
> B = Statement B is entirely preferred to Statement A as an expression of my opinion.

Please show your attitude leanings on each item, even though you do not feel strongly on the topic or do not feel well informed. Please choose between the alternatives, even though both may seem acceptable to you, or both unacceptable.

Items in the Assessment of Self

(* indicates high self-assessment)

A a ? b B 1. A. My progress toward the goals of success I set for my-self has been disappointing.
  *B. I feel that I have made significant progress toward the goals of success I set for myself.

A a ? b B 2.*A. The conception I now have of myself is more compli-mentary than the conception I have had in the past.
  B. I now have a less complimentary conception of myself than I have had in the past.

A a ? b B 3. A. In determining how others feel about me, I am not con-fident in my ability to do so.
  *B. I am confident of my ability to ascertain how others feel about me.

Reprinted with permission of Campbell, D. Various Social Attitude Scales in unpublished papers, Department of Psychology, Northwestern University.

4. A. Knowing the evaluations of myself by others is important for the
        way I see myself.
    *B. The way I see myself does not depend upon my knowing the evalua-
        tions of me by others.

5. A. In a given situation, I am inadequate in telling how others
        perceive me.
    *B. It is my feeling that I am able adequately to tell how others
        perceive me in a given situation.

6. A. I tend to identify myself in terms of the reactions of others
        toward me.
    *B. The way others react toward me does not influence the way I
        tend to react toward those others.

7. *A. The way I play my role in a given social situation is dependent
        upon how I conceive myself.
    B. In a given social situation, the way I play my role is dependent
        upon how others conceive me.

8. *A. My self conception is not shaped by factors external to the
        given social situation in which I am playing a role.
    B. The conception I have of myself is shaped by the way I play my
        role in a given social situation.

Individuality

(* indicates individualistic response)

1. A. Schools and colleges should teach their students to accept their
        morals of society and to adjust themselves to community life.
    *B. The primary purpose of education is to make the student independent
        and to help him develop his own conceptions of life, morals and
        values.

2. A. Since man is basically evil he must be taught to accept society
        and his innate spontaneity must be constrained by regulations.
    *B. Man is fundamentally good and will always develop his good
        faculties under positive environmental conditions.

3. A. Good and evil are values which are determined by society or
        religious concepts.
    *B. Man should consider all moral values in relation to himself; he
        alone is the standard (of judgment) of good and evil.

4. A. The U.S.A. places great emphasis on developing people who are
        well-adjusted to society and who take an active responsible
        role in social life.
    *B. The U.S.A. encourages a self-dependent, and individualistic atti-
        tude towards life.

5. *A. The integrated person is capable of getting along by himself
and avoids unnecessary social contacts.
   B. A well-adjusted and mature person seeks and enjoys social contacts and likes to affiliate with others.

6. *A. Mature persons use their individual aspirations alone as a
standard of self-evaluation.
   B. The only way to attain appropriate self-evaluation is by comparing
one's self with the community in which one lives.

7. *A. Fraternity life is too dominant because it does not give students
a chance to stand entirely on their own feet, to get a real estima-
tion of themselves and to develop their own social relations.
   B. Fraternities and sororities are very positive because they
help students who are away from home for the first time to get
adjusted to the new form of life.

8. *A. There are no basic values worth striving for except those which
come from the individual himself.
   B. Man should strive to meet fundamental values which are pointed
out by society and religion.

Materialism

(* indicates materialist response)

1. A. "A loaf of bread, a jug of wine..." this epitomizes all the
material requirements for personal happiness.
   *B. "A loaf of bread and a jug of wine" may have been alright for
someone who hasn't known anything else, but let's face it; in
twentieth century America we approach happiness as the carpet
gets thicker and the steaks less "rare."

2. *A. My philosophy is: to have or to have not is the question, and
if I'm lucky enough to have, I'm going to enjoy it.
   B. To have wealth and material goods is not more conducive to
happiness than to have debts and cancer.

3. *A. An orderly, uncluttered house and a well-kept lawn will be
important features of my future home.
   B. I'm frankly not really interested in how my physical surroundings
will be disposed in my future home.

4. A. The joys which wealth and material possessions bring are super-ficial and short-term as compared to the <u>real</u> joys in life.
   *B. The only people who can say "money can't buy happiness" are those who never had a chance to try.

5. A. A society that worships such extravagances as "golfmobiles" and all electric kitchens is indeed a "sick" society.
   *B. If things were such that everybody in the world had stereophonic record players and champagne, wars would probably be obsolete.

6. *A. To conjecture upon the size of one's starting salary when leaving college is a natural tendency on the part of a modern college student.
   B. A person with a "healthy" value system rarely if ever reflects on his future salary.

7. A. Neatness and physical appearance of my like-sexed friends are entirely accidental in terms of my associations.
   *B. Important determinants in my choice of like-sexed friends in my living group at college are physical attractiveness and stylish-ness of dress.

8. *A. A place for everything and everything in it's place is a good maxim to abide by.
   B. Although cleanliness is important in material things, order, <u>per se</u>, bores me.

Social Attitudes

(* indicates positive views of others)

1. *A. Confidence in others is seldom misplaced.
   B. If you leave yourself open to being hurt, you probably will be.

2. *A. People would rather help than hurt one another.
   B. In this dog-eat-dog world, you can't trust anyone.

3. A. Working for others is a situation of basic insecurity.
   *B. Friends and co-workers are the best security that a person can have.

4. *A. Faith in others is essential for survival these days.
   B. Having faith in others is just asking for trouble.

5. A. If an acquaintance asks to borrow money, it is better to try to avoid lending it.
   *B. Being able to help those in need is part of the joy of living.

6. *A. The golden rule is still the best rule to live by.
   B. Nice guys finish last.

7. A. You can't beat city hall.
    *B. Where there's a will there's a way.

8. A. There's no place for friendship in business.
    *B. Business' first function is to meet a social need.

Cosmopolitan - Local Measure

(* cosmopolitan response)

1. A. It's a good idea to look around for a place to settle but there's
       nothing like setting one's roots in one spot.
    *B. When it comes to what I do in my spare time I don't pay much
        attention to what people might think.

2. *A. I don't care to know people unless there is something to the person.
    B. I judge a man by who he is more than I do by what kind of person he is.

3. A. It's best to join clubs where there are people most like yourself.
    *B. It's best to know a few selected people than a lot of them.

4. A. News from home seems more meaningful than other news found in
       the newspaper.
    *B. In order to better himself and his family, a man sometimes has
        to give up some of his friends.

5. A. In general, it is preferable reading daily newspapers than magazines.
    *B. If a person gets tired of people he's known for years he should
        stop seeing them.

6. A. Joining such clubs as the Elks and Kiwanis is preferable over such
       clubs as debate and cultural ones.
    *B. One of the best ways to judge a man is by his success in his job
        or career.

7. *A. The findings of science may someday show that many of our most
        deeply-held beliefs are wrong.
    B. If given a choice between an American good or item and a foreign
       one, I would select the American good even if the foreign good
       was slightly cheaper.

8. *A. People ought to pay more attention to new ideas, even if they seem
        to go against the American way of life.
    B. It is best to borrow needed funds from close friends or one's
       family than from a bank or loan firm.

Foreign Policy

(* internationalist response)

1. *A. The important thing for the U.S. foreign aid program is to see to it that poor countries benefit.
   B. The important thing for the U.S. foreign aid program is to see to it that the U.S. gains a political advantage.

2. A. If the U.S. policy of regional blocs of countries protects the member states, it is a good policy.
   *B. If the U.S. policy of regional blocs of countries creates difficult world conditions for small neutral countries, it is a bad policy.

3. A. The laws of the United States should be used as a model for developing international laws.
   *B. International laws should be developed out of the laws of all nations.

4. *A. U.S. foreign trade is desirable if it raises the standard of living of all countries involved in the trades.
   B. U.S. foreign trade is desirable if it raises the U.S. standard of living.

5. A. A U.S. citizen must remember his duty to his country whatever the international issue.
   *B. The position a U.S. citizen takes on an international issue should depend on how much good it does for how many people in the world, regardless of their nation.

6. *A. The United States should abide by United Nations decisions, whether it agrees with them or not.
   B. The United States should abide by United Nations decisions only if it agrees with them.

7. *A. It will be all right if Communism replaces capitalism if it means a better life for most people in the world.
   B. Capitalism must be defended against attack.

8. A. Countries needing our agricultural surpluses should pay for them instead of getting something for nothing.
   *B. Countries needing our agricultural surpluses should get them free if we cannot use them.

AGREEMENT RESPONSE SCALE
(Couch and Keniston 1960)

Variable

This scale attempts to measure agreeing response set as a personality variable, particularly the inner dynamics of this agreeing personality syndrome.

Description

A total of 681 items made up the original instrument. Over 200 of these were new items included in an attempt to develop factor scales of psychological concepts, like orality and super-ego integration; the remainder came from developed tests such as the Davids' Affect Questionnaire and Cattell's 16 P.F. Personality Inventory. Of this total, 360 were selected from 30 heterogeneous scales that had "psychological" opposites (such as Trust vs. Distrust), and these comprise the Overall Agreement Score (OAS).

All items were answered in Likert response format, running from strongly agree (1) to strongly disagree (7). The OAS consists of the average response to the 360 items. For these items, the mean was 3.9 and the standard deviation 0.3.

The 15 items in the ARS described here were those that correlated highest with the overall 360-item scale. These are considered by the authors as "the best short scale measure of the agreeing response tendency."

Sample

The sample consisted of 61 paid volunteer subjects from Harvard College (selected from a larger pool of 200 volunteers enrolled in an undergraduate course in the social sciences). These subjects filled out questionnaires at four different time periods.

Reliability/
Homogeneity

The split-half reliability of the entire scale was .85. For a 20-item scale (apparently including the 15 items reproduced here) the split-half figure was .86 for the original sample and .72 for a separate student sample.

A correlation of .73 was obtained between 120 of the OAS items and 240 of the OAS items taken at one to two week intervals, which provides some evidence for test-retest reliability.

Validity

The measure of response bias exhibited considerable generality across tests, a wide range of which were studied (e.g., all the scales of MMPI, 16 P.F., and the Thurstone Temperament Scale).

The bulk of almost 20 hypotheses about differences between "yeasayers" and "naysayers" was confirmed in a clinical comparative study of the 10 highest yeasayers and 11 highest naysayers of the original sample of 61. Yeasayers were found "to be individuals with weak ego controls, who accept impulses without reservation."

Location

Couch, A. and Keniston, K. Yeasayers and naysayers: agreeing response set as a personality variable, Journal of Abnormal and Social Psychology, 1960, 60, 151-174.

Results and Comments

The agreement response scale was found to correlate with several personality characteristics, but most particularly with impulsivity, dependence, anxiety, mania, anal preoccupation and anal resentment. Moreover it correlated negatively with scales measuring the opposite tendencies (such as impulse control, ego strength) as well as stability, responsibility, and tolerance. A factor analysis indicated that a major factor of stimulus acceptance (vs. stimulus rejection) was central to the agreeing response set.

AGREEMENT RESPONSE SCALE

	Correlation With OAS (N=61)
1. Novelty has a great appeal to me (4.9)*	.54

(1)	(2)	(3)	(4)	(5)	(6)	(7)
Strongly Disagree	Disagree	Slightly Disagree	No Answer	Slightly Agree	Agree	Strongly Agree

2. I crave excitement (4.5)   .54

3. It's a wonderful feeling to sit surrounded by your possessions (3.5)   .51

4. There are few things more satisfying than really to splurge on something--books, clothes, furniture, etc. (3.3)   .48

5. Only the desire to achieve great things will bring a man's mind into full activity (4.2)   .47

6. Nothing is worse than an offensive odor (3.6)   .46

7. In most conversations, I tend to bounce from topic to topic (3.6)   .45

8. I really envy the man who can walk up to anybody and tell him off to his face (2.9)   .44

9. I could really shock people if I said all of the dirty things I think (4.1)   .44

10. There are few more miserable experiences than going to bed night after night knowing you are so upset that worry will not let you sleep (4.3)   .42

11. I tend to make decisions on the spur of the moment (3.8)   .42

12. Little things upset me (3.8)   .41

13. Drop reminders of yourself wherever you go and your life's trail will be well remembered (3.0)   .41

14. I like nothing better than having breakfast in bed (2.1)   .40

15. My mood is easily influenced by the people around me (4.2)   .40

*Mean on the seven-point scale.

INDEX OF NAMES

748

OTHER SOCIAL PSYCHOLOGICAL VOLUMES

Justifying Violence: Attitudes of American Men. Monica D. Blumenthal, Robert L. Kahn, Frank M. Andrews, and Kendra B. Head. 1972. 380 p.

White Attitudes Toward Black People. Angus Campbell. 1971. 117 p.

Drugs and American Youth. Lloyd Johnston. 1973. 287 p.

Youth in Transition, Volume II: The Impact of Family Background and Intelligence on Tenth-Grade Boys. Jerald G. Bachman. 1970. 250 p.

Youth in Transition, Volume III: Dropping Out—Problem or Symptom? Jerald G. Bachman, Swayzer Green, and Ilona Wirtanen. 1972. 250 p.

Studies in Social Power. Edited by Dorwin P. Cartwright. 1959. Reprinted 1971. 225 p.

Information about current prices and available editions may be obtained from the Publications Sales Department, Institute for Social Research, The University of Michigan, Box 1248, Ann Arbor, Michigan 48106. Free catalogs and descriptive brochures are available on request.